THE WORLD WEATHER GUIDE

Now retired, E.A. Pearce spent all his working life in advertising, becoming managing director of a leading agency. As a result of travel in many parts of the world he realized the need for a compilation of weather information for travellers. He has spent some two years working on *The World Weather Guide* with C.G. Smith.

C.G. Smith, MBE, MA, FRGS, FRMetS, is a Fellow of Keble College, Oxford, and University Lecturer in Geography at Oxford University. He has been concerned with the teaching of meteorology and climatology for over thirty years. He is Director of the Radcliffe Meteorological Station, Oxford, which possesses the longest series of continuous meteorological observations in Britain. He has published numerous papers on weather and climate in academic journals and contributed to books and atlases, mostly on climatological and Middle Eastern matters.

THE WORLD WEATHER GUIDE

E.A.Pearce and C.G.Smith

Hutchinson

London Melbourne Sydney Auckland Johannesburg

Hutchinson & Co. (Publishers) Ltd

An imprint of the Hutchinson Publishing Group

17–21 Conway Street, London W1P 6JD

Hutchinson Group (Australia) Pty Ltd
30–32 Cremorne Street, Richmond South, Victoria 3121
PO Box 151, Broadway, New South Wales 2007

Hutchinson Group (NZ) Ltd
32–34 View Road, PO Box 40-086, Glenfield, Auckland 10

Hutchinson Group (SA) Pty Ltd
PO Box 337, Bergvlei 2012, South Africa

First published 1984

Set in Linotron Plantin by Tradespools Ltd,
Frome, Somerset
Printed and bound in Great Britain by
Butler & Tanner Ltd, Frome and London

British Library Cataloguing in Publication Data
Pearce, E.A.
    The world weather guide.
    1. Weather forecasting
    I. Title   II. Smith, C.G.
    551.6'3   QC995

ISBN 0 09 151750 8 cased
ISBN 0 09 151751 6   Hutchinson Paperback

Contents

Acknowledgements

In addition to the sources listed in the bibliography, the climatic data in the vast majority of the tables in this book has been adapted and, where necessary, converted to both Centigrade and Fahrenheit scales or inches and millimetre scales from the following publications of the British Meteorological Office. The data is reproduced in this form by permission of the Controller of Her Majesty's Stationery Office:

Tables of Temperature, Relative Humidity and Precipitation for the World (Met. 0. 617), HMSO, London.

Part I.   North America, Greenland and the North Pacific Ocean (Met. 0. 617a), 1958; reprinted 1975 with additions.

Part II.   Central and South America, the West Indies and Bermuda (Met. 0. 617b), 1959; sixth impression 1977.

Part IV.   Africa, the Atlantic Ocean south of 35° N and the Indian Ocean (Met. 0. 617d), 2nd edition 1967; fourth impression 1978 with updated place names.

Part V.   Asia (Met. 0. 617e), 2nd edition 1966; sixth impression 1978 with updated place names.

Part VI.   Australasia and the South Pacific Ocean, including the corresponding sectors of Antarctica (Met. 0. 617f), 1958.

Tables of Temperature, Relative Humidity, Precipitation and Sunshine for the World (Met. 0. 856), HMSO, London.

Part III.   Europe and the Azores (Met. 0. 856c), 1973.

Bibliography

Additional data and valuable descriptions and explanations of the weather and climate of most countries and all regions of the world can be found in the following books. Unfortunately climatic data is not always given in the standard form used in this book (as described on page 8) and care is therefore needed in its interpretation. These books are written for the specialist and are expensive. They will not be found in many public libraries but may usually be obtained on interlibrary loan through national central lending libraries.

W.G. Kendrew, *The Climates of the Continents*, Oxford University Press, London, 5th edition, 1961 (out of print).

H.E. Landsberg (ed.), *World Survey of Climatology*, Elsevier North Holland, New York, 15 volumes, 1969–84 (volumes 5 to 15 are concerned with regional climatology).

Willy Rudloff, *World-Climates, with tables of climatic data and practical suggestions*, Wissenschaftliche Verlagsgesellschaft, Stuttgart, 1981.

Glenn T. Trewartha, *The Earth's Problem Climates*, University of Wisconsin Press, Madison, Wisconsin, 1981.

Memoranda with tables giving climatic data for numerous places are published by the national weather services of most countries. Such publications are often in a form not readily accessible or even comprehensible to the layman. However, such publications are usually available to the general public on application to the library or archive section of their national meteorological organization which will often be willing to provide both information and advice for which a charge may be made.

Preface

You may be a businessman travelling to Nigeria in November, to Texas in May or to Rumania in February; or perhaps you are planning a family holiday in some unknown country or even thinking of a trip around the world. But, wherever you travel, at whatever time of year, the same question always comes up: What weather can I expect?

Unless you are a meteorologist or a geographer and can discover the answers for yourself, your most convenient source of information has been holiday brochures. These are easy to understand but can be misleading. They may talk about glorious sunshine and not mention the fact that the climate is very humid or that there may be strong winds or night frosts. *The World Weather Guide* aims to answer your questions in a simple and reliable way.

We cannot claim to give exact weather forecasts.

Weather can be unseasonable and freakish and even expert forecasters are often proved wrong. By examining in detail statistics of world weather which have been compiled over a long period of time, however, we can deduce what the weather is *likely* to be, what one can *reasonably* expect.

We have set out to include all the facts which are of practical help to the traveller. It is not only a question of temperature or sunshine – humidity, rainfall and wind are all important and need to be known when packing your suitcase.

We believe that *The World Weather Guide* is the first guide that answers, simply and accurately, the questions people ask about weather throughout the world.

E.A. Pearce
C.G. Smith

How to use this book

Countries are listed in alphabetical order within continents. One exception is the USSR, the whole of which is included in Europe because most visitors to that country will be travelling to European Russia, and it is more convenient to show the whole of one country in one section. The other exception is Turkey which is also included in Europe. Some smaller countries that share similar weather conditions have been grouped together. Reference to the index will explain. For very large countries such as the USA information is shown under regions or groups of states.

For the larger, or more important, countries or groups of countries, there is an outline map showing the main climatic regions and the locations from which weather information has been gathered. Weather details for several representative places within a country are shown. There is also a concise description of the climate and most important seasonal differences. This includes a note of any weather hazards or dangerous features.

The tables for each location show, month by month, temperatures (in both Fahrenheit and Centigrade), relative humidity, and precipitation (rainfall and snow).

Temperature

Average daily maximum and minimum temperatures are given for each month in degrees Fahrenheit and Centigrade (Celsius). These are shade temperatures. Maximum temperatures usually occur in early afternoon and minimum temperatures just before sunrise. The highest and lowest temperatures ever recorded in each month are also listed. These give an idea of the extremes that can occur.

Humidity

Relative humidity is expressed as a percentage. A relative humidity of 100 per cent means the air cannot hold any more water vapour at any given temperature. It is measured as a daily figure at one or more fixed hours during the day. Since relative humidity varies inversely with temperature, it is normally lowest in the early afternoon and highest just before sunrise. High humidity combined with high temperatures increases discomfort. See the Comfort Index on p. 11.

Precipitation

'Precipitation' includes all forms of moisture falling on the earth, mainly rain and snow. The average monthly fall is shown in both inches and millimetres for each month. Also shown is the average number of days in each month on which a significant fall occurs. What is 'significant' varies from country to country so look closely at the heading for this column. By dividing the monthly fall by the number of days with rain you can get an idea of the intensity of rainfall in each place. A large number of days with rain indicates a cloudy, changeable climate.

Other information

The latitude, longitude and altitude of each location is given. The number of years over which temperatures have been taken is also indicated.

Introduction

If you are in a hurry read the short notes 'How to use this book' before looking up the country you intend to visit. They will tell you how the book is put together and what the statistics mean.

Most people – to get the most out of the facts – will probably find it interesting and worthwhile to read on. You will discover more about the meaning of climatic statistics and particularly how these can be interpreted in terms of the weather we experience.

Temperature alone is not enough

Most of us know what temperature suits us best and when we feel most comfortable. We become accustomed to the range of temperatures of the country where we live. For most people a temperature below 64° F (18° C) is too cool for sitting around. A temperature above 86° F (30° C) is too hot, particularly for strenuous exercise. Of course, these figures are only a general guide.

All temperatures in this book are shade temperatures. In the sun temperatures may be as much as 18°–27° F (10°–15° C) higher in calm weather but much less in windy conditions. The same temperatures will not necessarily produce the same feeling of heat or cold indoors as distinct from outdoors, where wind and sun also play a part. This is where two other important factors come in: *humidity* and *wind*.

Comfort – how we feel – can vary enormously between places with much the same temperatures, just as we feel a difference between conditions indoors and outdoors – even without heating or air conditioning. How hot or cold we feel depends upon a precise combination of temperature, humidity and wind.

It's not the heat, it's the humidity

How true this is! We can stand dry heat much better than damp heat which makes us feel listless and takes away energy. By studying the humidity figures for the country you visit, together with the temperatures, you can work out, with a little effort, how you are going to feel. This is where the Comfort Index on p. 11 comes in. But first, take a little time to understand what humidity is.

Humidity is the amount of moisture in the air. It can be measured in various ways, but the most usual is to describe it as 'relative humidity'. Relative humidity is used throughout this book. It is expressed as a percentage.

A relative humidity of 100 per cent means the moisture content of the air is the maximum possible at any particular temperature. The hotter the air the more moisture it can hold. So, at 79° F (26° C) the air holds more moisture at 100 per cent relative humidity than it does at 50° F (10° C) at the same 100 per cent relative humidity. When relative humidity is low, evaporation is rapid. Soil dries out, wet clothes dry quickly and perspiration evaporates from the skin. When relative humidity is high, clothes dry slowly and body sweat cannot evaporate easily.

In high temperatures with high relative humidity we feel sticky and hot; the higher the temperature the more we perspire and, as this perspiration cannot evaporate quickly, the more uncomfortable we feel. This is why in the tropics we can feel very uncomfortable for part of, or even the whole of, the year, while in hot and dry countries we can enjoy high temperatures as body sweat evaporates quickly.

Here are some examples. At a temperature of 70° F (21° C) and a relative humidity of 100 per cent some people will feel slightly uncomfortable in still air. Much the same effect is felt at around 81° F (27° C) with a relative humidity of only 20 per cent. If the humidity rises to 60 per cent we feel very much hotter although the temperature is the same. In a breeze the discomfort associated with humidity is greatly lessened. Even a temperature of 95° F (35° C) and a relative humidity of 20 per cent may not feel very uncomfortable in a strong breeze. In still air the same temperature and the same relative humidity would feel very hot indeed.

The following graph is an example of the Comfort Index for Singapore in January.

Read off the average daily maximum temperature for January. It is 86° F (30° C). From the same graph you will see that the relative humidity in January is 78 per cent (afternoon). The dotted line at 86° F (30° C) intersects with 78 per cent humidity in the band 'Everyone feels discomfort'. You will feel hot and sticky in Singapore in January.

Now look up the temperatures and relative humidity for the place you intend to visit and work out how you will feel on the Comfort Index on p. 11.

At temperatures below freezing point humidity

makes almost no difference to how we feel because at such low temperatures the air can hold very little moisture. The popular belief that damp cold (raw cold) is more unpleasant than dry cold has some truth in it, but this applies mainly at temperatures above freezing point up to about 59° F (15° C). At low temperatures wind becomes much more important than humidity in determining how we feel.

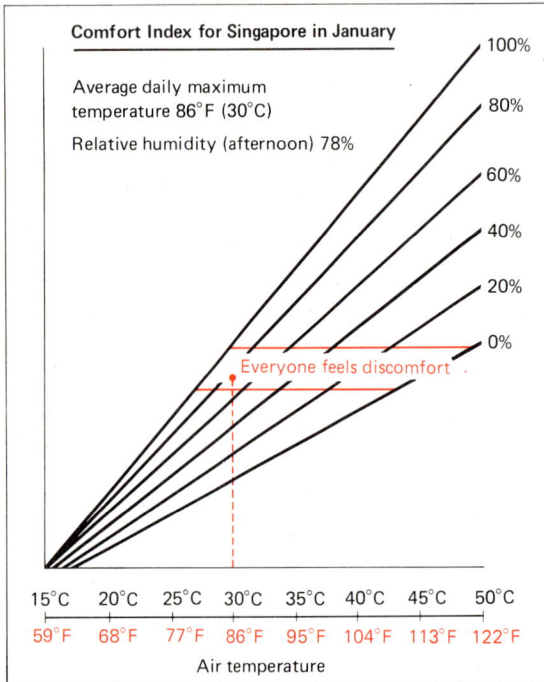

Comfort Index for Singapore in January

Average daily maximum
temperature 86°F (30°C)
Relative humidity (afternoon) 78%

100%
80%
60%
40%
20%
0%

Everyone feels discomfort

| 15°C | 20°C | 25°C | 30°C | 35°C | 40°C | 45°C | 50°C |
| 59°F | 68°F | 77°F | 86°F | 95°F | 104°F | 113°F | 122°F |

Air temperature

How to use the Comfort Index

1. Temperatures are shown along the base line.
2. Relative humidity is shown by the diagonal lines.
3. The bands across the index show how most people will feel in any combination of temperature and humidity *in still air*.
4. To discover temperature/relative humidity conditions look up the average daily temperatures and relative humidity figures. Remember to match *maximum* temperatures with *afternoon* relative humidity figures.
5. Read off temperature from the base line and humidity from the diagonal lines. The band in which humidity and temperature intersect indicates the approximate comfort you can anticipate.

Remember: *this index shows the conditions in still air.* Wind will reduce the effect of high humidity.

Blow, blow, thou winter wind . . .

How hot or cold we feel also depends on the strength of the wind. In hot climates and on hot days a brisk wind

helps to keep us cool. In cold climates, and on days with very low temperatures, a strong wind makes us feel even colder. This is because air moving rapidly past our body causes it to lose heat quickly.

At high temperatures the evaporation of perspiration is one of the principal methods by which body temperature is regulated. When air temperature exceeds normal skin temperature (about 93° F or 34° C), as may happen in very hot dry climates, the cooling power of the wind becomes critical.

In countries such as Canada, the USA and the USSR, where very low temperatures and strong winds are normal in the winter, this cooling power is assessed by the Wind Chill Index (p. 12).

This indicates how any combination of wind speed and temperature can be read off as a particular degree of wind chill. It also shows why a temperature of 32° F (0° C) and a wind speed of 30 m.p.h. (50 k.p.h.) feels colder than a much lower temperature of −4° F (−20° C) in completely calm conditions. This could be the difference between being exposed to the wind or being inside a tent.

Because wind speed varies very much from place to place and even from hour to hour, it is not easy to provide meaningful wind statistics. Averages are of little value if gales occur on a few days and most days have light winds. As a general rule wind usually drops at night and increases by day, particularly on the coast. We find that wind almost always increases in strength as we climb hills and mountains – something amateur mountaineers should remember. Where strong winds are an important aspect of a country's weather they are described in the notes for each country.

In some countries, the USA for example, forecasts of wind speeds are given on television and radio. Newspapers also carry weather forecasts in which estimated wind speed may be given. If you know what the forecast wind speed is, then reference to the Wind Chill Index will give you a good idea of how you are going to feel. It works in much the same way as the Comfort Index.

Local winds are so important to the feel of the country that in some places they are given special names. Such winds may occur regularly at certain times of the day or at certain seasons of the year. A glossary of these major winds throughout the world is given on pp. 20–22.

In most parts of the world during warm, settled weather the daily onshore sea breeze is a regular feature of coasts and beaches. This usually begins about midday and can be useful in having a noticeable cooling effect. In some tropical and subtropical climates the onshore wind occurs at almost the same time each day. When this breeze drops in the late evening the temperature can feel quite oppressive. In the early hours of the morning there may be a return land breeze blowing offshore, but this is usually less strong than the daytime sea breeze.

Comfort Index

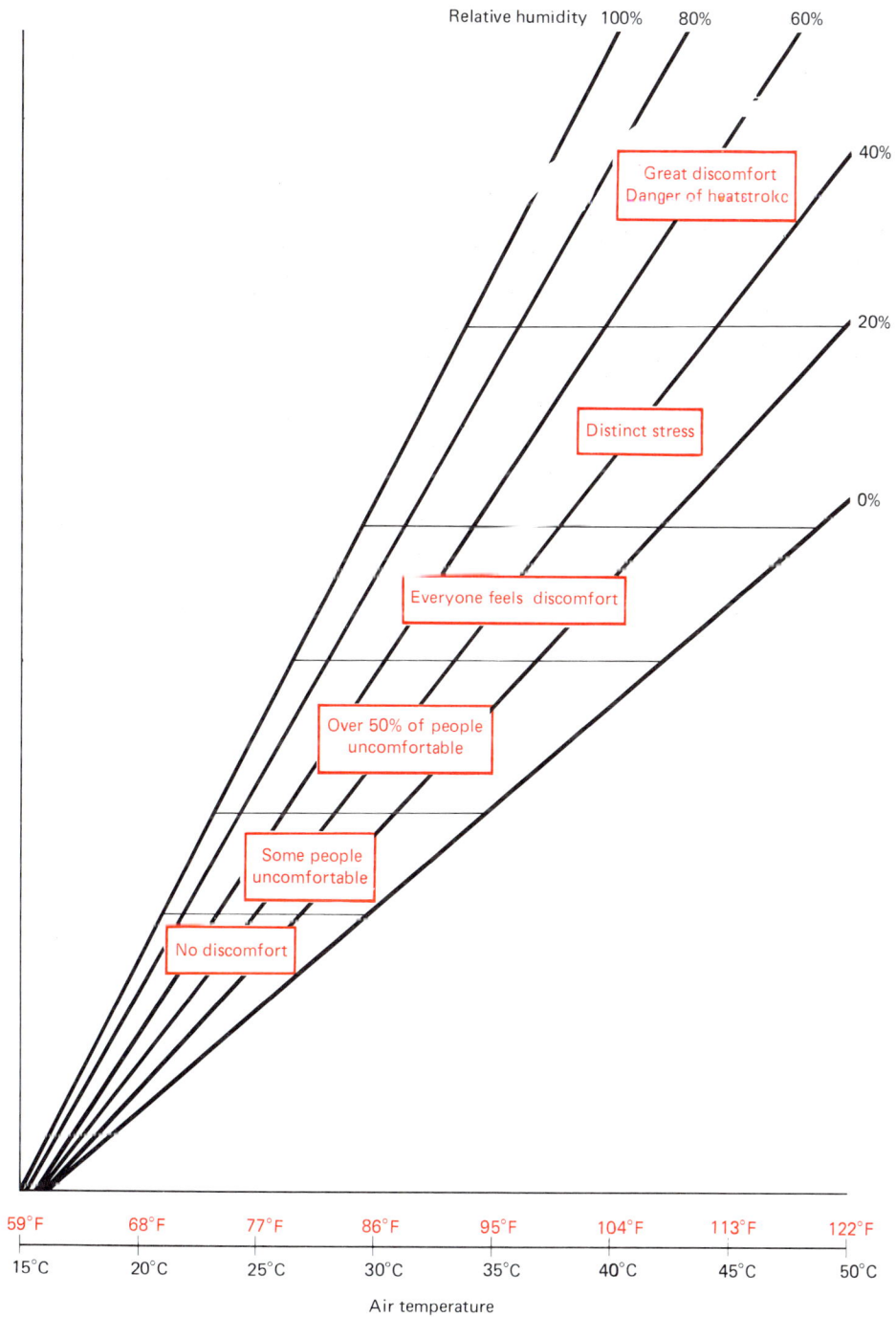

Relative humidity 100% 80% 60%

40%

Great discomfort
Danger of heatstroke

20%

Distinct stress

0%

Everyone feels discomfort

Over 50% of people
uncomfortable

Some people
uncomfortable

No discomfort

59°F	68°F	77°F	86°F	95°F	104°F	113°F	122°F
15°C	20°C	25°C	30°C	35°C	40°C	45°C	50°C

Air temperature

Wind Chill Index

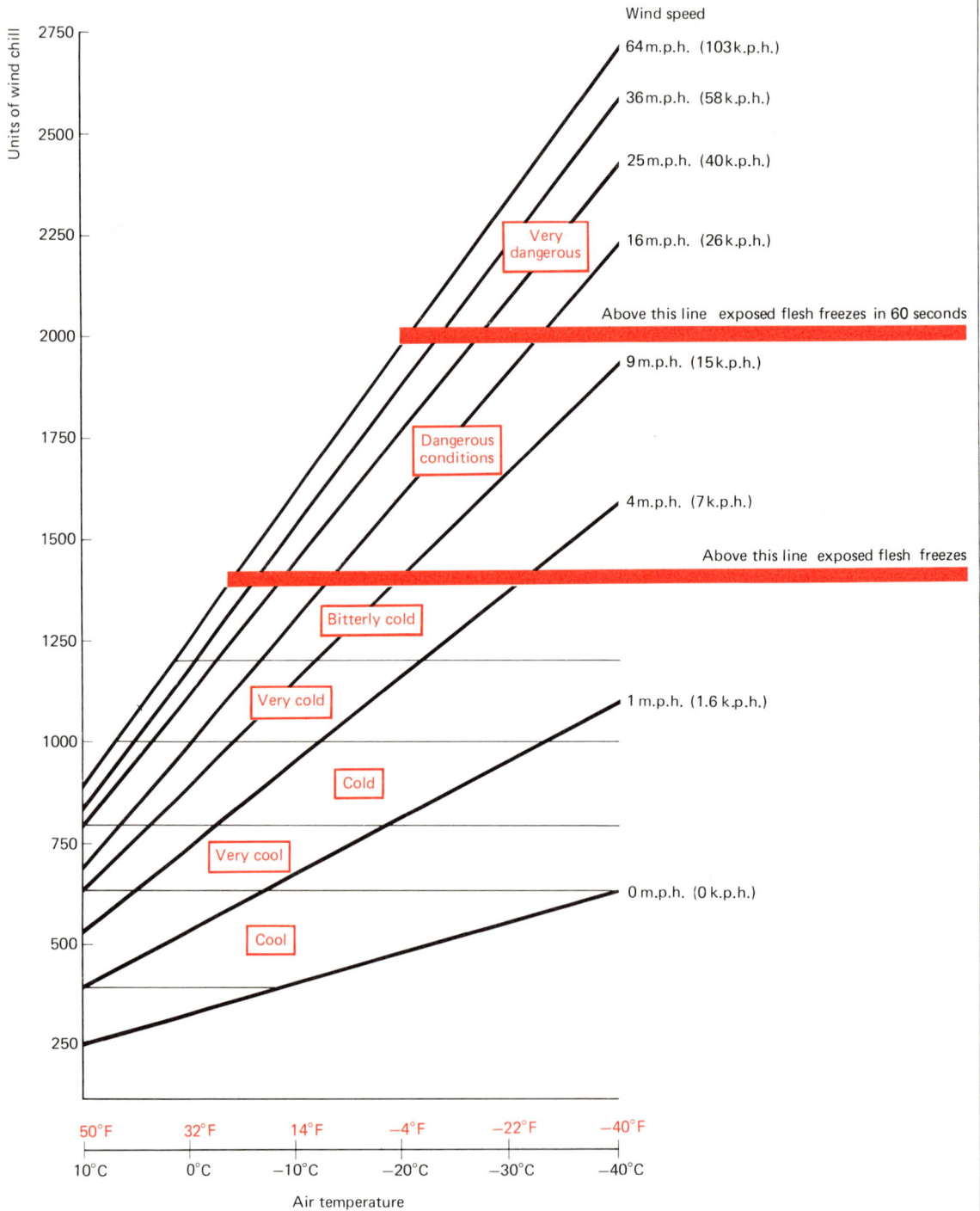

Units of wind chill

Wind speed

64 m.p.h. (103 k.p.h.)

36 m.p.h. (58 k.p.h.)

25 m.p.h. (40 k.p.h.)

16 m.p.h. (26 k.p.h.)

Very dangerous

Above this line exposed flesh freezes in 60 seconds

9 m.p.h. (15 k.p.h.)

Dangerous conditions

4 m.p.h. (7 k.p.h.)

Above this line exposed flesh freezes

Bitterly cold

Very cold

1 m.p.h. (1.6 k.p.h.)

Cold

Very cool

0 m.p.h. (0 k.p.h.)

Cool

2750
2500
2250
2000
1750
1500
1250
1000
750
500
250

50°F   32°F   14°F   −4°F   −22°F   −40°F
10°C   0°C   −10°C   −20°C   −30°C   −40°C

Air temperature

How to use the Wind Chill Index

1. Temperatures are shown along the base line.
2. Wind speeds are shown by the diagonal lines.
3. The bands running across the index show how a suitably clothed person would feel.
4. Where a known temperature intersects with a forecast wind speed, conditions out of doors are shown.

Thus at a temperature of 23° F (−5° C) there is danger of frostbite in a wind of 40 m.p.h. (65 k.p.h.).

A sunny day will, of course, produce extra warmth the body can feel. This would not make much difference in extreme conditions of wind and cold, but it would appreciably affect comfort in calm conditions in temperatures down to about 5° F (−15° C).

For the scientifically minded The Wind Chill Index was first developed, from experiments in the Antarctic, as an indication of safe conditions outside shelter. The units of wind chill on the left of the diagram show the rate of loss of heat from the body in kilogramme calories per square metre of body surface per hour.

Hot days – cold nights

In some countries there is a much greater difference between daytime and night-time temperatures than in other countries. The tables in this book give the average daily *maximum* and *minimum* temperatures for each month at a number of representative places in each country. The maximum temperature usually occurs just after midday and the minimum temperature just before dawn. The difference between these two is the *daily range of temperature* and is an important feature of the climate. It can also affect considerably our comfort.

On cloudy, rainy days the range of temperature may be quite small. In climates which are very sunny and dry, such as desert areas (for example, North Africa and Arizona, USA) there may be a very large daily range with surprisingly cold nights. Be prepared for very chilly nights in desert and mountain areas where daytime temperatures may be either very hot or quite comfortable.

As a general rule the range is greatest inland and least on the coast. For example the average daily range of temperature at New Delhi (India) in May is 27° F (15° C). In August it is only 14° F (8° C). At Bombay the equivalent figures are 11° F (6° C) and 9° F (5° C). At both places May is in the dry season and August in the wet season, but Bombay is on the coast whereas New Delhi is in the middle of India.

By working out the range of temperature you will have a good idea of the clothes you need to take with you.

Rain and snow

As well as temperature, humidity and wind which, together, determine how hot or cold we feel we are likely to be interested in rain and snow. We may wish to know not only the amount that falls but the probability of wet days. In this book the meteorological term 'precipitation' is used. This term includes all forms of moisture falling on the ground whether it be rain, snow, sleet, hail, dew or fog drip.

In most climates precipitation generally falls as rain. On high mountains, or in countries with very cold winters such as Canada, the USSR, parts of the USA, China and Scandinavia much of the precipitation may fall as snow. Snow, sleet and hail are measured as the melted equivalent of rain. (One foot of snow is roughly equivalent to 1 inch of rain.)

As a general rule, at temperatures around 36° F (2° C), snow or sleet are as likely as rain. With temperatures at or below freezing point, precipitation is most likely to be snow. Freezing rain (rain falling with the temperature below freezing point) is a rare occurrence but it is a very serious danger on the roads, not least for those on foot.

In this book the average monthly precipitation is given. The average number of days with measurable precipitation is also given for each month. This may be a better guide to the raininess of a place as some places have a relatively large monthly rainfall which falls for a few hours on one or two days. The two columns should be used in conjunction.

How weather can vary

It is impossible, without giving more figures than there is room for, to take account of the fact that, in many parts of the world, the weather is highly variable for at least part of the year. A month may include hot sunny spells and wet cloudy spells. In one July the weather may be more disturbed than in another. One January may have much more snow than another January.

Some indication of variability is given by the columns giving the highest and lowest temperatures ever recorded in each month. These figures indicate what the temperature *can* be. It is, of course, very unlikely that these extremes will be reached while you are visiting, even for a long stay, but the possibility exists!

A month with an average daily minimum temperature below 28° F (−2° C) is likely to have frequent snow and, if the average daily maximum is 32° F (0° C) or below, then snow may lie on the ground for long periods.

How high will you be?

Everyone knows that the higher we go above sea level the colder it gets. As a general rule this fall in temperature is at the rate of 1° F for every 330 ft (0.6° C for every 100 m). This may not apply locally during the day, particularly if the sun is shining. But you will very soon be aware of it if the sky clouds over or you are in cloud.

Height above sea level can also mean a wide range of day and night-time temperatures. Nairobi (Kenya), nearly 6000 ft (1800 m) has a range of 23° F (13° C) in September. The average daytime temperature is 75° F (24° C) while the night-time temperature is 52° F (11° C). Mexico City, over 7500 ft (2300 m) has almost identical figures for September. The nights in both places can be distinctly cool. Altitude figures are given for every place in this book so you can see how high you are going to be.

Remember also that the atmosphere becomes thinner at altitudes over 6000 ft (1800 m). The sun's rays (especially the ultra-violet light) are more powerful and you will tan – or burn – more quickly than at sea level. In the more rarefied atmosphere above these heights breathing and exertion become progressively more difficult. The body of a healthy person adapts to these conditions fairly quickly, but it may take you longer to climb or to walk than you think. So, do not forget that on mountains temperature drops with height especially in cloud, even more with wind, and much more at night. Always take warm clothing when walking or climbing.

Compare what you know with where you are going

You may find it useful to compare the figures for your home area, where you know what the weather is like the whole year round, with the figures given for your destination. Work out:

Will it be hotter or colder by day and by night?
Is there a wide range of temperature between day and night?
Will humidity make it feel hotter than the temperatures suggest? Refer to the Comfort Index on p. 11.
Is it very wet and how many rainy days are there likely to be?
How much colder is it likely to be if you visit a place 3000 ft (1000 m) higher than the nearest place for which figures are given? (Use the approximate rule given above.)

When weather can be dangerous

Most of us are unlikely to run into conditions of extreme heat or extreme cold, both of which in their different ways can be dangerous. But this can happen through accident, carelessness or misadventure, so here is a brief description of the ways in which weather can be dangerous.

Too hot   In high temperatures the body keeps cool by the evaporation of sweat from the skin. In low humidity evaporation occurs quickly and the movement of air, by wind or fan, also increases evaporation. However, there is an upper limit to the air temperature we can endure with comfort even in low humidity. This is because in very high temperatures we may not be able to sweat fast

enough to match the rate of evaporation. Also, the body can gain heat from very hot air. An increase in wind speed will make conditions even more dangerous because evaporation will be even faster.

Heat exhaustion   When the body cannot lose heat fast enough there is a possibility of heat exhaustion. There is a feeling of lassitude, loss of appetite and general discomfort. Visual hallucinations are possible and also vomiting. The sufferer should be moved to a cool place and drink salt and water to replace the sweat and salts lost through perspiration.

Heatstroke   Heatstroke is a much more dangerous condition and, although rare, is more likely to follow from the less obvious condition of heat exhaustion. It can be fatal. Heatstroke is the result of the body's normal cooling mechanism ceasing to function. The skin becomes dry and body temperature starts to rise. The symptoms are burning sensations, dry skin, followed by feverish feelings. These symptoms can develop into restlessness, headache and confusion. Unless treated at once body temperature will continue to rise until the victim becomes unconscious and death may follow.

For a person suffering from heatstroke, medical attention is necessary. The patient must be put in the coolest possible place and cooled as fast as possible. He or she should be splashed with cold water or, better still, ice water. Wrapping him or her in a wet sheet with a fan directed on the body will help to reduce body temperature quickly. Vigorous massage can also help.

Precautions   There are, of course, precautions that can be taken against both heat exhaustion and heatstroke. When arriving in a very hot country do not overexert the body until you are acclimatized – about a week. Air travel is so fast that, unlike slow sea journeys, the body has no time gradually to acclimatize itself to high temperatures. Also, air conditioning in hotels, offices, etc., delays the process of acclimatization. Drink plenty of liquid, but not too much alcohol. Take more salt with food, or even salt tablets. Wear comfortable light clothing and certainly avoid sunburn.

The Comfort Index shows when a danger of heatstroke can arise, and the descriptions of the climate of hot countries indicate at what time of year the danger exists.

It is always sensible to adopt local customs in hot countries. The inhabitants *know* what it's like.

Too cold   In very cold climates we put on more clothes – in polar regions special clothing – and we can keep relatively warm by generating body heat by walking or other activities. But, if we stop moving, become tired and remain in a strong wind below freezing, we can very soon become very cold indeed. The main dangers of very cold climates and high mountains are hypothermia and frostbite.

Hypothermia   Hypothermia, often called 'exposure', is the failure to maintain body heat. The possibility of hypothermia is greatly increased if clothes become wet; evaporation from wet clothes causes the body to lose heat even more rapidly. Rain and snow with a strong wind increase the danger.

Most cases of hypothermia out of doors occur through lack of proper clothing in mountains or at sea. Climbers and walkers who get lost and are forced to spend all night on a mountainside are risking hypothermia – especially if they are wearing light clothing. Even in a hut, out of the wind, hypothermia can occur if there are no blankets. Old people are particularly susceptible. At a very low level of body temperature – around 77°–82° F (25°–28° C) – the condition becomes critical.

To counteract hypothermia, the body should be warmed by any means available. Rapid rewarming in a water bath of 104°–113° F (40°–45° C) is very important. If breathing has stopped artificial respiration and cardiac massage are required immediately.

Frostbite   Frostbite is the extreme condition when the flesh freezes. It is most likely to affect the face, hands and feet, and a bad case of frostbite may mean the loss of limbs or other permanent injury. The affected parts should be rewarmed as soon as possible. If possible, rewarming in water no hotter than 104°–111° F (40°–44° C) will help a great deal. Water hotter than this increases pain and swelling. There should be no massage, no rubbing and no exercise and the affected part should not be bandaged.

The Wind Chill Index shows the temperatures and wind speeds at which danger of frostbite exists. Most people will never experience these conditions, but hypothermia can occur at low temperatures long before conditions approach the hazard of frostbite.

Fahrenheit and Centigrade (Celsius) temperature scales

The *Fahrenheit* scale was introduced by the German scientist Gabriel Fahrenheit in 1714, and was the scale most widely used by English-speaking countries. 0° F was chosen as the temperature of a mixture of water, ice and sal-ammoniac (the lowest man-made temperature possible before the days of refrigeration), and 32° F as the freezing point of water. 96° F was chosen as the temperature of a healthy human being. From these fixed points the scale was extended below zero and above 96°. Thus the boiling point of water on the Fahrenheit scale is 212° F.

The *Centigrade* scale is the most widely used throughout the world and is recommended by the World Meteorological Organization.

First proposed by the Swedish astronomer Anders Celsius in 1742, it is based on two fixed points – the freezing and boiling points of water. The interval between is divided into 100°. Freezing point is 0° C and boiling point is 100° C. Minus temperatures on the Centigrade scale always indicate temperatures below freezing.

A quick way of converting Centigrade to Fahrenheit For temperatures *above* 0° C double the Centigrade figure and add 30.

$10° C \times 2 = 20 + 30 = 50° F.$

To convert Centigrade to Fahrenheit the reverse applies. Deduct 30 and halve the result.

$70° F - 30 = 40 \div 2 = 20° C.$

The higher the temperature the more inaccurate this easy method becomes. Remember the method does not work below freezing point.

A more accurate method of conversion This method is more accurate and, if you can memorize the following temperatures at 9° F and 5° C intervals, conversion is easy.

Freezing point is 32° on the Fahrenheit scale and 0° on the Centigrade scale. 1° C equals 1.8° F. Therefore 5° C equals 9° F, thus:

$$5° C \times 1.8 = 9° + 32° = 41° F$$

$$
\begin{aligned}
5° C &= 41° F \\
10° C &= 50° F \\
15° C &= 59° F \\
20° C &= 68° F \\
25° C &= 77° F \\
30° C &= 86° F \\
35° C &= 95° F \\
40° C &= 104° F
\end{aligned}
$$

For temperatures below freezing:

$$
\begin{aligned}
-5° C &= 23° F \\
-10° C &= 14° F \\
-15° C &= 5° F \\
-20° C &= -4° F \\
-25° C &= -13° F \\
-30° C &= -22° F \\
-35° C &= -31° F \\
-40° C &= -40° F
\end{aligned}
$$

If you use 2 as a multiplier instead of 1.8, the result is accurate enough for most purposes.

Temperature Conversion

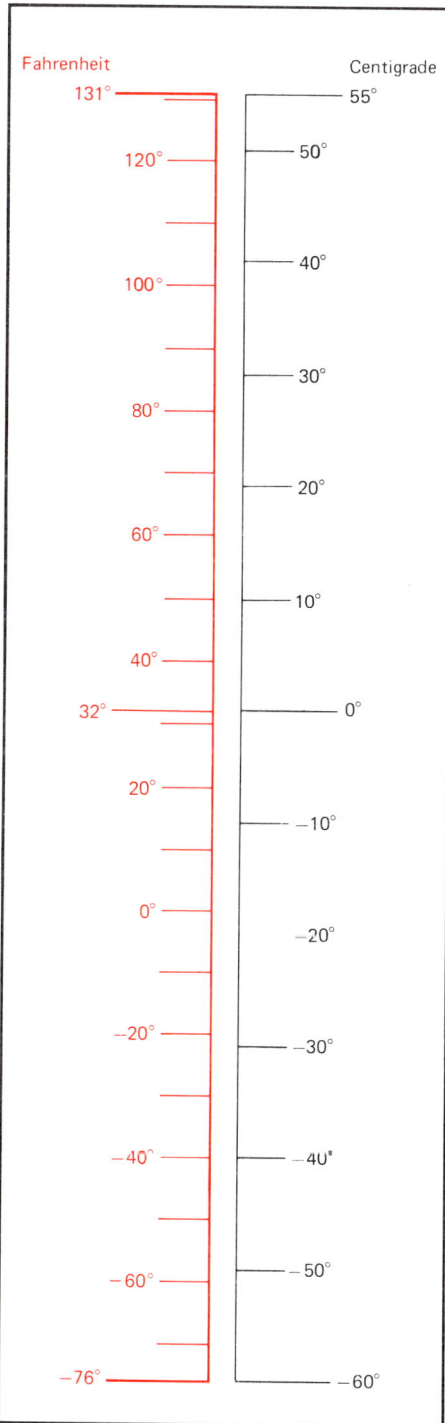

Fahrenheit

Centigrade

Fahrenheit	Centigrade
131°	55°
120°	50°
100°	40°
80°	30°
60°	20°
40°	10°
32°	0°
20°	−10°
0°	−20°
−20°	−30°
−40°	−40°
−60°	−50°
−76°	−60°

Rainfall conversion: inches/millimetres

Inches/Millimetres Conversion

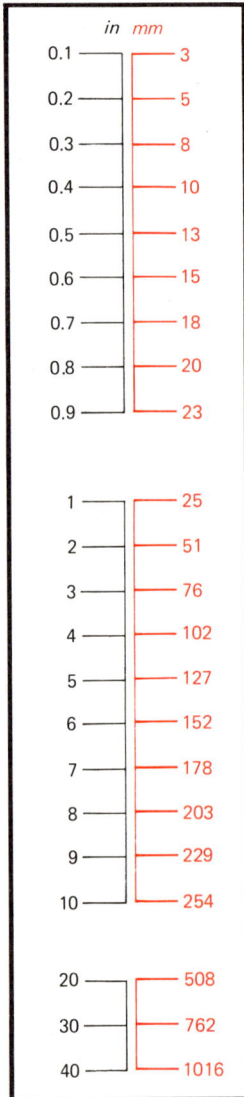

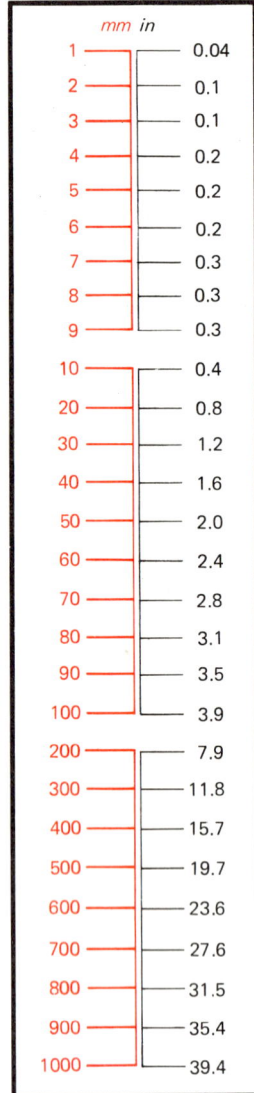

in	mm
0.1	3
0.2	5
0.3	8
0.4	10
0.5	13
0.6	15
0.7	18
0.8	20
0.9	23

in	mm
1	25
2	51
3	76
4	102
5	127
6	152
7	178
8	203
9	229
10	254

in	mm
20	508
30	762
40	1016

mm	in
1	0.04
2	0.1
3	0.1
4	0.2
5	0.2
6	0.2
7	0.3
8	0.3
9	0.3

mm	in
10	0.4
20	0.8
30	1.2
40	1.6
50	2.0
60	2.4
70	2.8
80	3.1
90	3.5
100	3.9

mm	in
200	7.9
300	11.8
400	15.7
500	19.7
600	23.6
700	27.6
800	31.5
900	35.4
1000	39.4

Hours of daylight by latitude

This table shows the varying length of day with latitude. Day length is here understood to be the period between the rising and setting of the sun. It does not include the period of twilight before and after sunrise and sunset. The length of the period of twilight increases from the equator to about 65° N and S where, on the longest day of the year, it lasts all night. On the equator twilight lasts about twenty minutes. At 30° N and S twilight lasts about half an hour before and after sunrise and sunset. At 50° N and S this period increases to about forty minutes. The term twilight here refers to 'civil twilight' which is the period during which the sun is not more than 6° below the horizon. Under clear skies and with good atmospheric conditions normal outdoor activities should be possible during the period of civil twilight. If the length of twilight is doubled and added to figures for day length given in the table below, it will give a good idea of the length of adequate daylight for each latitude.

Read the months on the left of the table for the northern hemisphere and the months on the right of the table for the southern hemisphere.

Length of day in various latitudes (in hours and minutes on the 15th of each month)

Month	Equator	10°	20°	30°	40°	50°	60°	70°	80°	Poles	Month
J	12:07	11:35	11:02	10:24	9:37	8:30	6:38	0:00	0:00	0:00	J
F	12:07	11:49	11:21	11:10	10:42	10:07	9:11	7:20	0:00	0:00	A
M	12:07	12:04	12:00	11:57	11:53	11:48	11:41	11:28	10:52	0:00	S
A	12:07	12:21	12:36	12:53	13:14	13:44	14:31	16:06	24:00	24:00	O
M	12:07	12:34	13:04	13:38	14:22	15:22	17:04	22:13	24:00	24:00	N
J	12:07	12:42	13:20	14:04	15:00	16:21	18:49	24:00	24:00	24:00	D
J	12:07	12:40	13:16	13:56	14:49	15:38	17:31	24:00	24:00	24:00	J
A	12:07	12:28	12:50	13:16	13:48	14:33	15:46	18:26	24:00	24:00	F
S	12:07	12:12	12:17	12:23	12:31	12:42	13:00	13:34	15:16	24:00	M
O	12:07	11:55	11:42	11:28	11:10	10:47	10:11	9:03	5:10	0:00	A
N	12:07	11:40	11:12	10:40	10:01	9:06	7:37	3:06	0:00	0:00	M
D	12:07	11:32	10:56	10:14	9:20	8:05	5:54	0:00	0:00	0:00	J

Glossary: wind names and other meteorological terms

Agulhas current A current of warm ocean water flowing westwards along the south coast of South Africa. It is a local name for the Mozambique current (q.v.).

Air mass An extensive mass of air with broadly similar properties, particularly surface temperature and humidity: e.g. warm and dry, cold and humid, etc. Different types of weather are associated with different air masses.

Anticyclone An area where the atmospheric pressure is high relative to the areas surrounding it and thus forming a distinctive pattern on a weather map. At or near the centre of an anticyclone the weather is usually calm and settled.

Bai-U Japanese name for the early summer rains which mark the transition from the winter monsoon to the rainy season of the summer monsoon.

Benguela current A current of cold ocean water flowing northwards along the west coast of southern Africa. This has the effect of lowering the coastal temperatures from Cape Town northwards to about latitude 10° S as compared with the east coast of southern Africa washed by the Mozambique current (q.v.).

Berg wind A wind in the coastal districts of South Africa and Namibia. It blows from the interior and brings high temperatures and low humidity particularly in the winter season.

Bora A cold, dry and gusty wind which blows from the land along the Adriatic coast of Yugoslavia and also affects the Italian shores of the Adriatic. It is particularly strong in the area of Trieste and most frequent in winter and spring.

Buran A Russian word applied to a bitterly cold wind which is often associated with blizzard conditions, particularly in Siberia.

Californian current A current of cold ocean water flowing southwards along the west coast of Mexico and California. It has the effect of reducing the temperature of the coastal regions and is responsible for the frequent sea fogs on this coast.

Canaries current A current of cold ocean water flowing southwards along the coast of northwest Africa. It has a similar effect to that of the Californian current (q.v.). It particularly affects Morocco, Mauritania and the Canary Islands.

Chinook A warm dry wind of the föhn type (q.v.) which blows from the west immediately to the east of the Rocky Mountains in Canada and the United States. In winter and spring it melts lying snow very rapidly.

Continental climate A term generally used to denote a climate with a large seasonal range of temperature as found in the interior of a large land mass, particularly in temperate latitudes. The opposite of a maritime climate (q.v.).

Crachin A French term for light rain or drizzle occurring on parts of the coast and northern mountain slopes in Vietnam during the cool season.

Cyclone A particularly severe type of tropical storm with very low atmospheric pressure at the centre and strong winds blowing around it. Violent winds and heavy rain may affect an area of some hundreds of square miles. The name applied to such storms in the Indian Ocean. 'Typhoon' and 'hurricane' are other names applied to the same phenomena in the Pacific and Atlantic Ocean respectively.

Depression A region where the surface atmospheric pressure is low. The opposite of an anticyclone (q.v.) and a distinctive feature on a weather map. Usually associated with cloud and rain and sometimes with strong winds. A less severe weather disturbance than a tropical cyclone.

Doldrums The old term used by sailors for the belt of light winds or calms in tropical and equatorial latitudes between the regular and constant trade winds and monsoons (q.v.). The modern meteorological term 'ITCZ' or Inter Tropical Convergence Zone is now used more frequently.

El Niño A Spanish term given to a warm ocean current, and to the unusually warm and rainy weather associated with it, which sometimes occurs for a few weeks off the coast of Peru (which is otherwise an extremely dry and rather cool region of the tropics). Several years may pass without this current appearing.

Etesian wind The very constant northerly to northwesterly winds which blow between June and

September in the Aegean and the eastern Mediterranean. During this season the weather remains fine and sunny but the sea may be rough at times.

Föhn A warm and very dry wind which blows in some valleys in the Alps. It can melt snow very rapidly and during a spell of föhn there is a greatly increased fire risk. Similar winds in other parts of the world are the 'chinook' and the 'berg' wind (q.v.).

Garúa Light coastal drizzle falling frequently on the coast of Peru and northern Chile which are otherwise very dry regions.

Ghibli The Arabic name given in Libya to a hot, dry and often dusty wind blowing from the south which raises coastal temperatures to very high levels for brief periods, particularly between March and early June.

Guinea monsoon The warm and humid southwesterly winds which blow to the south of the ITCZ (q.v.) in West Africa between April and September and which are associated with the rainy season.

Gulf Stream A current of warm surface ocean water in the North Atlantic flowing from the Gulf of Mexico towards northwest Europe. Also called the North Atlantic Drift, it is an important influence in maintaining relatively mild winters in the British Isles and along the coast of Norway to beyond the Arctic Circle.

Haboob An Arabic word used in the Sudan for a wind squall lasting for an hour or so. The strong wind may raise a wall of dust particles as the squall advances, usually from an easterly direction.

Harmattan The name given in West Africa to the northeast trade winds which blow from the Sahara desert towards the ITCZ (q.v.). During the dry season from October to March the harmattan sometimes reaches the coast of the Gulf of Guinea. The wind is associated with the hot, dry and dusty weather of the dry season. The opposite of the Guinea monsoon (q.v.).

High sun A convenient term used in tropical countries for the season when the sun is at its maximum noon altitude. In the tropics there is no real winter in the sense of the word in temperate latitudes. In most parts of the tropics the high-sun period is the wettest period of the year.

Humboldt current A current of cold surface water moving northwards along the Pacific coast of South America almost as far north as the equator. It lowers the temperature of the coastlands of northern Chile and Peru.

Hurricane The name applied in the Caribbean and United States to tropical cyclones (q.v.). West Indian islands and the coasts of Mexico and the southern United States are often struck by severe hurricanes.

ITCZ (Inter Tropical Convergence Zone) The

Doldrums (q.v.). The area of light winds in the tropics between the trade winds and monsoons blowing from opposite directions. Cloud and rain are often frequent and heavy in this zone.

Khamsin The Arabic name given in Egypt, Palestine, Syria and Lebanon to a hot dry southerly or easterly wind blowing from the interior which raises temperature in the coastal regions, particularly between March and early June. Often associated with dust storms or a hazy atmosphere.

Labrador current A current of cold surface water moving southwards along the east coast of Canada as far south as Newfoundland. It carries many icebergs and helps to keep temperatures on the Labrador coast rather cool in summer as compared with inland.

Land and sea breezes A local wind system which occurs during fine calm weather on most coasts in the tropics and on most tropical islands; also around the Mediterranean in the summer months. A light wind or breeze blows from the sea by day and from the land by night. The sea breeze is usually welcomed since it arrives at the hottest time of day and has a distinct cooling effect.

Leveche The name given in the coastal regions of southern Spain to a hot dry wind which blows from North Africa and which is associated with a heat-wave.

Low sun The opposite season to that of high sun (q.v.) in the tropics. Usually the drier period of the year when the sun is at its minimum noonday elevation.

Maritime climate A term used to denote a climate with both a small annual and daily range of temperature such as is found on most coasts, but particularly on west coasts in mid-latitudes, e.g. the British Isles and the states of Washington and Oregon, also New Zealand and oceanic islands.

Mediterranean climate A distinctive seasonal rhythm of weather and climate such as is found in most countries around the Mediterranean. Characterized by warm to hot and dry summers with mild to cool winters with more disturbed weather and rain. Also found in California, Australia, South Africa and Chile.

Mistral A blustery wind which blows in the South of France, particularly in the lower Rhône valley. In winter and spring it brings rather cold air to this region. It may blow strongly at any time of the year and in summer it can greatly increase the risk of forest fires.

Monsoon rains The name given in India and other parts of Asia to the heavy rains of the wet season. Also frequently used to describe the rains in Ethiopia and West Africa.

Monsoon winds A term usually applied in Asia but also used for East and West Africa and Australia. The seasonal reversal of wind direction when the winds are predominantly off the ocean during the wet season and blow outwards from the land during the dry season: e.g. in India the northeast monsoon blows off the land and the southwest monsoon blows from the ocean.

Mountain and valley winds   The daily reversal of wind which occurs in the valleys of mountain regions such as the Alps in fine settled weather. During the day winds tend to blow up the valley and during the night down the valley. The wind direction may be quite different at higher levels on the mountains.

Mozambique current   A current of warm surface water moving south along the coast of Mozambique and Natal which helps to maintain higher temperatures along the coast, particularly during the season of low sun (q.v.) when it may be much cooler inland.

Permafrost   Permanently frozen ground as occurs in north Canada, northern Russia and Alaska. Although the top few feet of soil and rock may thaw out during the short summer, the ground remains permanently frozen below this layer.

Polar front   The boundary zone between cold air of Arctic or polar origin and warm air of tropical origin. The polar front is an important feature in the weather and climate of mid-latitudes because many weather disturbances develop in this region of contrasting air masses, particularly in the North Atlantic and North Pacific.

Rasputitsa   The Russian name for the short period in spring when the snow melts and the ground thaws out.

Shamal   The Arabic name for a persistent northwesterly wind which blows between June and September in Iraq and the Persian Gulf when the weather is very hot and dry.

Sharav   The Hebrew name now given in Israel for the hot dry 'khamsin' (q.v.) blowing from the south and east.

Sirocco (or scirocco)   The name widely applied in the Mediterranean region, particularly in Greece and Italy, to a warm southerly wind. Of the same origin as other hot winds in this region: ghibli, khamsin, leveche and sharav (q.v.). On the northern shores of the Mediterranean the sirocco is warm and humid.

Smog   A combination of atmospheric pollution and fog. When thick or toxic it may cause severe distress through irritation of the eyes, nose, throat and lungs. Sometimes applied to a badly polluted atmosphere in the absence of visible fog as in large cities such as Los Angeles, Tokyo, Athens, etc., under calm and sunny conditions.

Sukhovey   A warm desiccating south or southeast wind in southern Russia. If it blows for a few days at a time it can be harmful to crops.

Tierra caliente   A term used in the Spanish-speaking countries of Central and South America for the lower slopes of the mountains where the climate is tropical all the year round, generally hot and with abundant rain. Below about 3000 ft (900 m).

Tierra fria   A term used in Central and South America for the higher mountain regions where temperatures are much reduced by altitude and frost and even snow may occur. The lower limit of tierra fria is between 6000 and 8000 ft (1800 and 2400 m).

Tierra templada   The intermediate slopes of mountains in Central and South America between the tierra fria and the tierra caliente. Here temperatures are rarely excessively hot and never really cold. A tropical upland climate such as occurs in the Kenya highlands.

Tornado   The name given in the United States to a very strong and damaging whirlwind with a clearly visible dark, snake-like funnel extending from a thunder cloud to the ground. The track of a tornado at ground level is rarely more than a few hundred yards wide but within this area buildings, trees and crops may be totally devastated.

Trade winds   The very constant winds found over most oceans within the tropics. These winds blow towards the equator as the northeast trades in the northern hemisphere and as the southeast trades in the southern hemisphere. Of great importance to shipping in the days of sail; hence the name.

Typhoon   The name given in the western Pacific and particularly in the China Sea to violent tropical storms or 'cyclones' (q.v.).

Willy Willies   A colloquial Australian term for a violent tropical storm or 'cyclone' (q.v.) affecting the coasts of northern Australia.

Africa

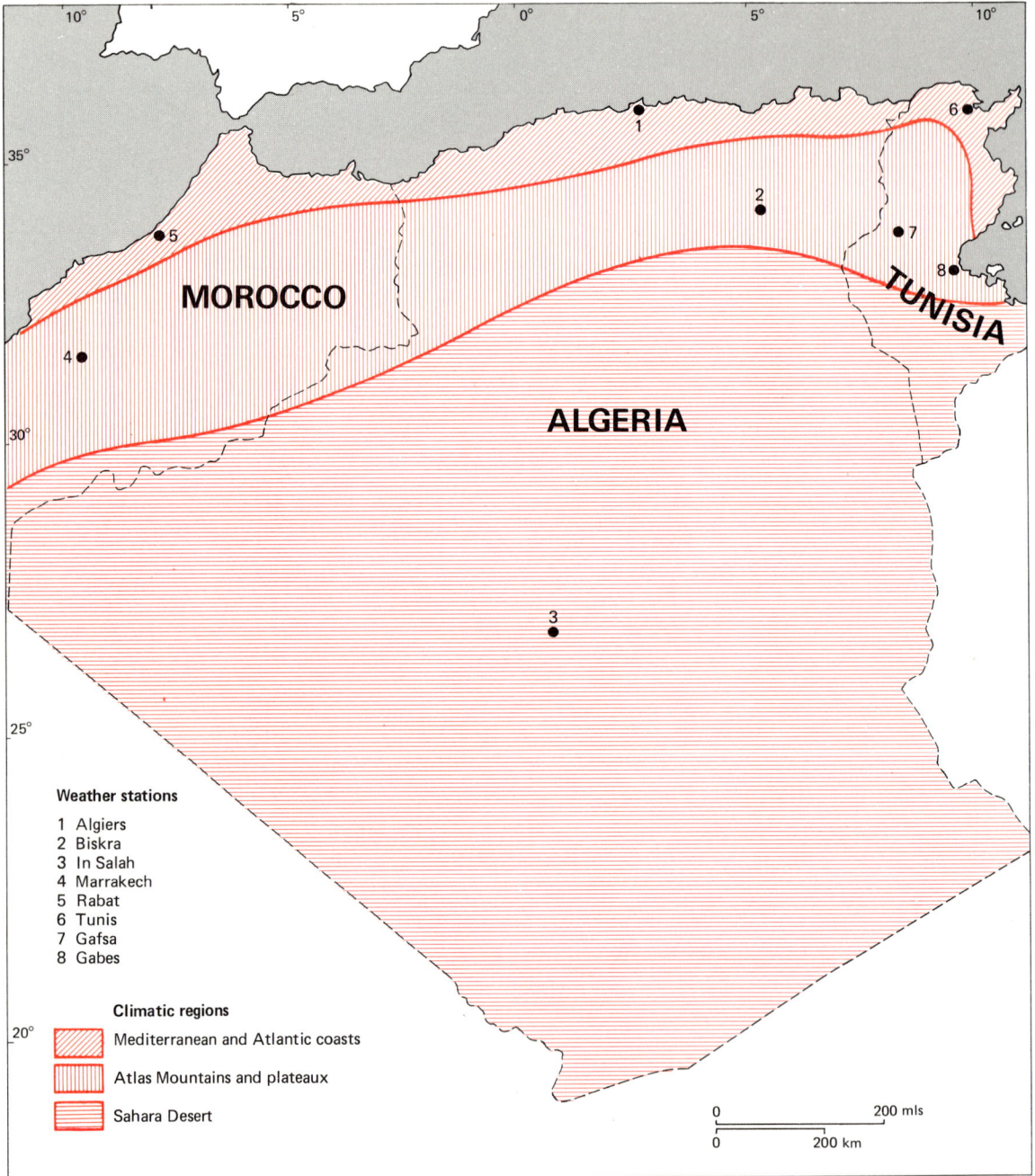

10°   5°   0°   5°   10°

35°

30°

25°

20°

MOROCCO

ALGERIA

TUNISIA

1

2

3

4

5

6

7

8

Weather stations

1 Algiers
2 Biskra
3 In Salah
4 Marrakech
5 Rabat
6 Tunis
7 Gafsa
8 Gabes

Climatic regions

Mediterranean and Atlantic coasts

Atlas Mountains and plateaux

Sahara Desert

0   200 mls

0   200 km

Algeria is a North African country four times as large as France. About one sixth of the country, comprising the Mediterranean coastlands and the northern mountains, has a typical Mediterranean climate with winter rainfall. The rest of the country to the south of the Saharan Atlas mountains is almost rainless and is part of the great Sahara desert.

Northern Algeria has a varied relief with two ranges of moderately high mountains: the Tell Atlas and the Saharan Atlas separated by a region of elevated plains and interior basins, the Plateau of the Chotts. Climate and weather here vary locally depending on altitude. Rainfall is heaviest and most reliable along the Mediterranean coast and in the higher parts of the Tell Atlas where it varies from 16 to 32 in (400 to 800 mm) per year. Most rainfall occurs between September and May with the heaviest and most reliable rains occurring from November to March. Above 3000 ft (900 m) precipitation often falls as snow and at the highest levels this may lie for several weeks. From May to September the weather here is generally settled and hot with almost continuous sunshine. During the rest of the year it is more changeable with an alternation from warm sunny days and cool nights to disturbed periods with rain and cloud. The mildest weather in winter is to be found on the coast and this area also tends to escape the fiercest summer heat, except when hot dry sirocco from the south carries the heat of the Sahara northwards. The table for **Algiers** is representative of the coast.

Inland the plateau of the Chotts and the Saharan Atlas have a rather more extreme continental type of climate with hotter summers and colder winters. Frost and snow occur here in winter and the nights can be very cold after quite warm days. The heat in summer frequently reaches levels typical of the Sahara but is made more tolerable by the low humidity. Over much of the area rainfall is rather low with a tendency to a double maximum, in autumn and spring. Immediately south of the Saharan Atlas there is a narrow belt of steppe country, similar to that in southern Tunisia. There is a definite wet season in winter but rainfall is low and unreliable. The table for **Biskra** is typical of this area on the fringes of the Sahara.

The Saharan desert region of Algeria has a climate that is virtually rainless. Occasional rain may fall in any month but the amounts are so small and unreliable as to make averages meaningless. In the extreme south of Algeria sporadic rainfall is more probable in the period June to September as the inter-tropical rain-belt, which affects West Africa at this time, occasionally spreads this far north. In the southeast of Algeria the great mountain mass of the Hoggar, rising to nearly 9000 ft (2700 m) receives rather more rain which may fall at any season. The table for **In Salah**, in the centre of the Sahara, is representative of this vast desert region. Summer temperatures are consistently high but temperatures at night fall low enough to be quite tolerable. Winter nights in the Sahara can be chilly and frost is by no means unknown but the days are warm and sunny.

Algeria has a very sunny climate. In the north daily sunshine hours average from five to six hours in winter and eleven to twelve in summer. In the Sahara they approach the maximum possible duration: nine to ten in winter and twelve to thirteen in summer.

In the Sahara strong winds occasionally raise dust and sand which can be dangerous as well as most unpleasant. During the hottest weather there is some danger of heat exhaustion, or even heatstroke, unless proper precautions are taken.

Algiers 194 ft (59 m) 36°46′ N 3°03′ E 25 years

	Temperature °F			Temperature °C				Relative humidity		Precipitation		
	Highest recorded	Average daily		Lowest recorded	Highest recorded	Average daily		Lowest recorded	0700 hours	1300 hours	Average monthly		Average no. days with 0.04 in + (1 mm +)
		max.	min.				max.	min.		%	%	in	mm	
J	76	59	49	34	24	15	9	1	75	66	4.4	112	11	J
F	86	61	49	34	30	16	9	1	72	60	3.3	84	9	F
M	84	63	52	37	29	17	11	3	71	59	2.9	74	9	M
A	99	68	55	43	37	20	13	6	67	57	1.6	41	5	A
M	101	73	59	44	38	23	15	7	72	60	1.8	46	5	M
J	101	78	65	55	38	26	18	13	72	60	0.6	15	2	J
J	106	83	70	62	41	28	21	17	73	60	0	0	0.4	J
A	107	85	71	64	42	29	22	18	70	60	0.2	5	0.5	A
S	103	81	69	53	39	27	21	12	74	62	1.6	41	4	S
O	100	74	63	45	38	23	17	7	72	60	3.1	79	7	O
N	88	66	56	40	31	19	13	4	73	63	5.1	130	11	N
D	76	60	51	32	24	16	11	0	72	64	5.4	137	12	D

ALGERIA

Biskra 407 ft (124 m) 34°51′ N 5°44′ E 26 years

	Temperature °F			Temperature °C				Relative humidity		Precipitation		
	Highest recorded	Average daily		Lowest recorded	Highest recorded	Average daily		Lowest recorded	0730 hours	1330 hours	Average monthly		Average no. days with 0.004 in + (0.1 mm +)
		max.	min.				max.	min.		%	%	in	mm	
J	75	61	44	30	24	16	7	−1	69	52	0.7	18	4	J
F	82	65	46	32	28	18	8	0	62	44	0.4	10	3	F
M	88	71	52	34	31	22	11	1	58	40	0.7	18	5	M
A	100	79	58	42	38	26	14	6	47	32	0.4	10	2	A
M	104	87	65	47	40	31	18	8	47	32	0.6	15	3	M
J	115	97	75	62	46	36	24	17	42	27	0.3	8	2	J
J	117	107	80	68	47	42	27	20	36	20	0.1	3	1	J
A	121	105	79	67	49	41	26	19	38	25	0.1	3	1	A
S	110	94	73	54	43	34	23	12	50	34	0.7	18	3	S
O	101	82	63	47	38	28	17	8	57	39	0.6	15	3	O
N	85	70	53	36	29	21	12	2	64	45	0.9	23	4	N
D	80	62	45	30	27	17	7	−1	69	49	0.7	18	3	D

	Temperature °F			Temperature °C				Relative humidity		Precipitation			
	Highest recorded	Average daily		Lowest recorded	Highest recorded	Average daily		Lowest recorded	0700 hours	1300 hours	Average monthly		Average no. days with 0.004 in + (0.1 mm +)	
		max.	min.			max.	min.		%	%	in	mm		
J	88	69	43	26	31	21	6	−3	63	37	0.1	3	0.4	J
F	95	75	47	28	35	24	8	−2	64	34	0.1	3	0.6	F
M	102	83	53	36	39	28	12	2	51	35	0	0	0.4	M
A	107	92	62	48	42	33	17	9	40	27	0	0	0.6	A
M	114	99	69	54	46	37	21	12	37	23	0	0	0.9	M
J	122	110	80	61	50	43	27	16	36	25	0	0	0.6	J
J	122	113	83	73	50	45	28	23	29	16	0	0	0	J
A	122	111	82	72	50	44	28	22	31	19	0.1	3	0.6	A
S	120	105	77	63	49	41	25	17	38	24	0	0	0.7	S
O	111	94	66	48	44	34	19	9	44	28	0	0	0.8	O
N	97	80	53	38	36	27	12	3	61	38	0.2	5	1.0	N
D	88	71	45	32	31	22	7	0	65	38	0.1	3	0.9	D

ANGOLA

Angola is over twice the size of France. It lies between 6° and 18° S in southern Africa with a coastline on the Atlantic Ocean. It is bordered by Zaïre on the north, by Zambia on the east and by Namibia (Southwest Africa) on the south. There is a steep rise inland from a narrow coastal plain to an extensive interior plateau with an average height of between 2000 and 4000 ft (600 and 1200 m). The highest areas of the plateau rise to over 8000 ft (2400 m). To the north and east of these higher areas the land slopes gradually towards the basins of the Congo and Zambesi rivers.

Over most of Angola the weather and climate are typical of a tropical plateau with a single wet season at the time of high sun between October and March and a long dry season. The table for **Huambo** shows this very clearly. Here both daytime and, particularly, night-time temperatures are reduced by altitude to produce a pleasant variety of tropical climate. Above 5000 ft (1500 m) temperatures around the year are temperate rather than tropical and frost is not unknown. The dry season shortens by a month or two in the north of the country, as compared with **Huambo** which has five virtually rainless months. Over most of the interior the mean annual rainfall is between 40 and 60 in (1000 and 1500 mm), being greater at higher levels.

The coastal region of Angola has a most unusual climate for the latitude. Temperature and rainfall are much reduced in a strip about fifty miles wide as a direct consequence of the cold Benguela current which flows from south to north along the shore. This current is responsible for the coast of Namibia to the south being virtually rainless. The same extreme dryness prevails in the southern coastal district of Angola as shown by the table for **Mossamedes**. The coastal region is desert or semi-desert as far north as **Luanda** but there is a gradual increase of rainfall northwards until, in the far north, it is over 24 in (600 mm) per year.

The coast experiences much low cloud and fog as a consequence of warm air moving over the cold ocean surface. Temperatures on the coast only rise to high levels when there is a pronounced offshore wind bringing heated air from the interior. The almost constant daytime sea breezes keep the temperatures on the coast low for a tropical region. Sunshine amounts are rather low on the coast averaging from four to six hours per day. They are much higher inland, ranging from four to five hours a day in the wet season to as much as nine to ten hours in the dry season.

Because of the reduced temperatures inland, and the dry cool nature of the coastal weather, Angola has a healthy and pleasant climate for a tropical country.

ANGOLA — Huambo 5577 ft (1700 m) 12°48′ S 15°45′ E 14 years

	Temperature °F			Temperature °C			Relative humidity		Precipitation		
	Highest recorded	Average daily	Lowest recorded	Highest recorded	Average daily	Lowest recorded	0900 hours	1500 hours	Average monthly		Average no. days with 0.04 in + (1 mm +)
		max.	min.			max.	min.		%	%	in	mm	
J	88	78	58	48	31	26	14	9	74	60	8.7	221	15	J
F	88	78	58	50	31	26	14	10	78	63	7.8	198	15	F
M	86	78	58	50	30	26	14	10	75	65	9.8	249	16	M
A	84	78	57	45	29	26	14	7	68	54	5.7	145	9	A
M	84	78	51	42	29	26	11	6	51	38	0.4	10	1	M
J	83	76	46	36	28	24	8	2	43	31	0	0	0	J
J	83	77	47	36	28	25	8	2	35	24	0	0	0.1	J
A	88	81	51	42	31	27	11	6	34	25	0	0	0.2	A
S	90	84	55	46	32	29	13	8	47	33	0.6	15	3	S
O	90	81	58	51	32	27	14	11	67	54	5.5	140	14	O
N	87	78	58	47	31	26	14	8	73	65	9.6	244	18	N
D	87	78	58	49	31	26	14	9	75	64	8.9	226	18	D

Luanda 194 ft(59 m) 8°49′ S 13°13′ E 27 years

	Temperature °F			Temperature °C			Relative humidity		Precipitation			
	Highest recorded	Average daily		Lowest recorded	Highest recorded	Average daily		Lowest recorded	0900 hours	1500 hours	Average monthly		Average no. days with 0.04 in + (1 mm +)
		max.	min.			max.	min.		%	%	in	mm	
J	91	83	74	69	33	28	23	21	79	76	1.0	25	3	J
F	95	85	75	70	35	29	24	21	77	74	1.4	36	3	F
M	95	86	75	70	35	30	24	21	79	75	3.0	76	6	M
A	94	85	75	70	34	29	24	21	82	77	4.6	117	8	A
M	97	82	73	64	36	28	23	18	81	78	0.5	13	2	M
J	89	77	68	59	32	25	20	15	81	76	0	0	0.1	J
J	85	74	65	58	29	23	18	14	82	77	0	0	0	J
A	83	74	64	58	28	23	18	14	84	78	0	0	0.4	A
S	84	76	67	62	29	24	19	17	82	78	0.1	3	0.9	S
O	89	79	71	65	32	26	22	18	80	78	0.2	5	2	O
N	98	82	73	68	37	28	23	20	79	77	1.1	28	4	N
D	94	83	74	67	34	28	23	19	78	76	0.8	20	3	D

Mossamedes 10 ft(3 m) 15°12′ S 12°09′ E 15 years

ANGOLA

	Temperature °F			Temperature °C			Relative humidity		Precipitation			
	Highest recorded	Average daily		Lowest recorded	Highest recorded	Average daily		Lowest recorded	0900 hours	1500 hours	Average monthly		Average no. days with 0.04 in + (1 mm +)
		max.	min.			max.	min.		%	%	in	mm	
J	91	79	65	57	33	26	18	14	80	74	0.3	8	1	J
F	94	83	68	58	34	28	20	14	79	73	0.4	10	1	F
M	96	84	69	54	36	29	21	12	78	72	0.7	18	2	M
A	102	82	66	53	39	28	19	12	80	73	0.5	13	1	A
M	100	77	59	51	38	25	15	11	81	74	0	0	0	M
J	101	72	57	47	38	22	14	8	85	79	0	0	0	J
J	85	68	56	44	29	20	13	7	85	79	0	0	0	J
A	83	70	57	47	28	21	14	8	86	78	0	0	0	A
S	82	72	59	48	28	22	15	9	83	76	0	0	0	S
O	88	74	61	54	31	23	16	12	82	77	0	0	0.2	O
N	90	78	63	52	32	26	17	11	79	75	0.1	3	0.5	N
D	92	79	64	54	33	26	18	12	79	73	0.1	3	0.5	D

BENIN

Benin is a West African country with a short coastline on the Gulf of Guinea. It is situated between Nigeria to the east and Togo to the west and extends between 6° and 12° N. It is very narrow from east to west. It shares the same climatic belts and sequence of weather around the year as those described on p. 72 for Nigeria and adjacent countries.

The table for **Cotonou**, which is on the coast, is representative of the south of the country. The coast is a little drier round the year than the districts immediately inland for the same reasons as those described for Ghana on p. 48. For the centre and north of the country the climatic conditions round the year are well represented by the tables for **Ibadan** and **Kano** respectively; both these places are in Nigeria. (See map p. 73.)

BOTSWANA

This large but very sparsely populated country lies in the centre of southern Africa and is surrounded by Namibia and Zimbabwe on the north and by South Africa on the east and south. Its weather and climate are described and explained on pp. 81–2 under the heading: 'The western interior'. It is largely desert and scrubland with a low and unreliable rainfall, being a part of the great Kalahari desert. What rain there is tends to come in the summer or warm season. Winters can be quite chilly with occasional frost. Annual rainfall decreases westwards and southwards. The climatic table for **Francistown** is representative of the wetter north and east. Here mean annual rainfall is usually over 16 in (400 mm) but in the west and south it falls below 8 in (200 mm). (See map p. 81.)

Cotonou 23 ft (7 m) 6°12′ N 2°26′ E 5 years   **BENIN**

	Temperature °F			Temperature °C			Relative humidity		Precipitation			
	Highest recorded	Average daily	Lowest recorded	Highest recorded	Average daily	Lowest recorded	0800 hours	1300 hours	Average monthly		Average no. days with 0.04 in + (1 mm +)	
		max.	min.			max.	min.		%	%	in	mm	
J	90	80	74	66	32	27	23	19	90	68	1.3	33	2	J
F	93	82	77	70	34	28	25	21	88	70	1.3	33	2	F
M	94	83	79	70	34	28	26	21	85	69	4.6	117	5	M
A	95	83	78	70	35	28	26	21	83	70	4.9	125	7	A
M	94	81	76	70	34	27	24	21	86	74	10.0	254	11	M
J	91	78	74	65	33	26	23	18	90	78	14.4	366	13	J
J	89	78	74	68	32	26	23	20	88	77	3.5	89	7	J
A	87	77	73	69	31	25	23	21	88	76	1.5	38	3	A
S	89	78	74	68	32	26	23	20	88	76	2.6	66	6	S
O	91	80	75	71	33	27	24	22	87	75	5.3	135	9	O
N	92	82	76	71	33	28	24	22	88	74	2.3	58	6	N
D	91	81	76	67	33	27	24	19	91	71	0.5	13	1	D

Francistown 3294 ft (1004 m) 21°13′ S 27°30′ E 20 years   **BOTSWANA**

	Temperature °F			Temperature °C			Relative humidity	Precipitation			
	Highest recorded	Average daily	Lowest recorded	Highest recorded	Average daily	Lowest recorded	0800 hours	Average monthly		Average no. days with 0.04 in + (1 mm +)	
		max.	min.			max.	min.	%	in	mm	
J	104	88	65	48	40	31	18	9	69	4.2	107	8	J
F	103	86	64	48	39	30	18	9	73	3.1	79	7	F
M	100	85	61	48	38	29	16	9	74	2.8	71	5	M
A	96	83	56	32	36	28	13	0	70	0.7	18	2	A
M	94	79	48	28	34	26	9	−2	68	0.2	5	0.7	M
J	88	74	41	24	31	23	5	−4	70	0.1	3	0.3	J
J	89	75	41	27	32	24	5	−3	63	0	0	0.1	J
A	95	79	45	27	35	26	7	−3	60	0	0	0.1	A
S	100	86	54	31	38	30	12	−1	55	0	0	0.5	S
O	105	90	61	41	41	32	16	5	56	0.9	23	3	O
N	107	89	64	44	42	32	18	7	63	2.2	56	5	N
D	105	88	65	50	41	31	18	10	65	3.4	86	7	D

BURUNDI

This small country in central Africa is about the size of Wales or Israel and is densely populated. It lies between 2° and 4° S and is bordered by Rwanda to the north, Tanzania to the east and Zaïre to the west. It is a hilly and mountainous country with the highest point rising to over 15,000 ft (4600 m). Climate and weather are similar to that found in eastern Zaïre and southwestern Uganda. Rainfall is equatorial but temperatures are much reduced because of the altitude. The months

June to September are predominantly dry but the rest of the year is moderately wet. By equatorial standards the climate is quite healthy and not unpleasant. The climatic table for **Bujumbura** on the northern shores of Lake Tanganyika is representative of the lower regions of the country. That for **Rubona** in Rwanda illustrates conditions in some of the higher areas. The mountains are much wetter with rather more cloud.

CAMEROON

The Cameroon Republic is a central African country about the size of France, situated between 2° and 12° N. It has a short coastline on the Gulf of Guinea but has land borders with Nigeria on the west, with Chad on the north, with the Central African Empire on the east and with Congo and Gabon on the south. (See map p. 73.)

The climate and weather of the northern part of the country are similar to those described for northern Nigeria on p. 72 and for Chad on p. 36. There is a single wet season between April and September at the time of high sun and a pronounced dry season during the rest of the year. Annual rainfall is between 40 and 70 in (1000 and 1750 mm). In the south of the country rainfall occurs in all months with an equatorial pattern

of distribution: two wet seasons and two dry seasons, similar to that described in the more detailed account of this region for Zaïre on p. 98.

The table for **Yaoundé** is typical of the southern part of the country. That for **Douala**, on the coast, shows the much heavier annual rainfall here and the particularly wet period between June and September. This is a consequence of the exposure to the moist southwesterly winds of the Guinea monsoon which are uplifted as they strike the high mountain of the Cameroon Peak. A small area of the Peak is one of the three places in the world experiencing an average annual rainfall in excess of 400 in (10,000 mm)! The other places are in the Hawaiian Islands and Assam in India.

Bujumbura 2640 ft (805 m) 3°23′ S 29°21′ E 10 years   **BURUNDI**

	Temperature °F			Temperature °C			Relative humidity	Precipitation		
	Highest recorded	Average daily	Lowest recorded	Highest recorded	Average daily	Lowest recorded	All hours	Average monthly		Average no. days with 0.004 in + (0.1 mm +)
		max.	min.			max.	min.		%	in	mm	
J	—	82	66	—	—	28	19	—	79	3.7	94	15	J
F	—	82	66	—	—	28	19	—	79	4.3	109	14	F
M	—	82	66	—	—	28	19	—	81	4.8	121	17	M
A	—	82	66	—	—	28	19	—	82	4.9	125	18	A
M	—	82	66	—	—	28	19	—	78	2.2	57	10	M
J	—	84	64	—	—	29	18	—	67	0.4	11	3	J
J	—	84	63	—	—	29	17	—	62	0.2	5	1	J
A	—	86	64	—	—	30	18	—	55	0.4	11	2	A
S	—	88	66	—	—	31	19	—	59	1.5	37	8	S
O	—	86	68	—	—	30	20	—	65	2.5	64	12	O
N	—	82	66	—	—	28	19	—	75	3.9	100	19	N
D	—	82	66	—	—	28	19	—	78	4.5	114	19	D

Douala 26 ft (8 m) 4°03′ N 9°41′ E 17 years   **CAMEROON**

	Temperature °F			Temperature °C			Relative humidity		Precipitation		
	Highest recorded	Average daily	Lowest recorded	Highest recorded	Average daily	Lowest recorded	0700 hours	1400 hours	Average monthly		Average no. days with 0.04 in + (1 mm +)
		max.	min.			max.	min.		%	%	in	mm	
J	93	86	73	68	34	30	23	20	95	74	1.8	46	4	J
F	91	86	74	68	33	30	23	20	96	75	3.7	94	6	F
M	91	86	73	66	33	30	23	19	95	76	8.0	203	12	M
A	92	86	73	66	33	30	23	19	94	76	9.1	231	12	A
M	95	86	73	66	35	30	23	19	95	79	11.8	300	16	M
J	90	83	72	66	32	28	22	19	95	82	21.2	539	19	J
J	89	80	71	66	32	27	22	19	96	86	29.2	742	24	J
A	86	80	71	67	30	27	22	19	96	84	27.3	693	24	A
S	87	81	72	67	31	27	22	19	95	84	20.9	531	21	S
O	88	81	71	65	31	27	22	18	95	83	16.9	429	20	O
N	91	84	73	66	33	29	23	19	95	80	6.1	155	10	N
D	90	85	73	67	32	29	23	19	95	78	2.5	64	6	D

		Temperature °F				Temperature °C			Relative humidity		Precipitation			
	Highest recorded	Average daily		Lowest recorded	Highest recorded	Average daily		Lowest recorded	0700 hours	1300 hours	Average monthly		Average no. days with 0.004 in + (0.1 mm +)	
		max.	min.			max.	min.		%	%	in	mm		
J	91	85	67	57	33	29	19	14	97	62	0.9	23	3	J
F	92	85	67	59	33	29	19	15	97	62	2.6	66	5	F
M	91	85	67	60	33	29	19	16	97	65	5.8	147	13	M
A	96	85	66	59	36	29	19	15	97	67	6.7	170	15	A
M	94	83	67	60	34	28	19	16	98	70	7.7	196	18	M
J	90	81	66	59	32	27	19	15	97	73	6.0	152	17	J
J	87	80	66	60	31	27	19	16	97	74	2.9	74	11	J
A	93	80	65	60	34	27	18	16	97	75	3.1	79	10	A
S	88	81	66	59	31	27	19	15	98	73	8.4	213	20	S
O	91	81	65	59	33	27	18	15	98	72	11.6	295	24	O
N	89	83	66	62	32	28	19	17	98	66	4.6	117	14	N
D	90	83	66	60	32	28	19	16	98	60	0.9	23	4	D

This country was formerly known as the Central African Republic. It is a landlocked state situated between 2° and 10° N. Rather larger than France, it is very sparsely populated. The northern part of the country has weather and climate rather similar to that described for northern Nigeria and illustrated by the table for **Kano** (p. 74). There is a single rainy season and a moderate annual rainfall of between 35 and 40 in (875 and 1000 mm). Daytime temperatures rise quite high in the period preceding the main rainy season between May and September. During the rest of the year rainfall is light and sparse. The southern half of the country has a more equatorial type of climate as described in more detail on p. 98 for Zaïre. The annual rainfall is between 60 and 80 in (1500 and 2000 mm), falling in all months but with a relatively drier period from December to February at the time of low sun. The table for **Bangui** illustrates conditions in the south of the country.

Bangui 1270 ft (387 m) 4°22′ N 18°34′ E 5 years

	Temperature °F			Temperature °C			Relative humidity		Precipitation		
	Highest recorded	Average daily	Lowest recorded	Highest recorded	Average daily	Lowest recorded	0700 hours	1300 hours	Average monthly		Average no. days with 0.004 in + (0.1 mm +)
		max.	min.			max.	min.		%	%	in	mm	
J	98	90	68	57	37	32	20	14	92	49	1.0	25	3	J
F	101	93	70	57	38	34	21	14	90	49	1.7	43	5	F
M	100	91	71	64	38	33	22	18	91	57	5.0	127	11	M
A	99	91	71	65	37	33	22	18	92	59	5.3	135	10	A
M	96	89	70	65	36	32	21	18	94	64	7.4	188	15	M
J	95	87	70	65	35	31	21	18	95	67	4.5	114	12	J
J	94	85	69	64	34	29	21	18	96	71	8.9	226	17	J
A	93	85	69	62	34	29	21	17	96	72	8.1	206	19	A
S	94	87	69	65	34	31	21	18	95	68	5.9	150	16	S
O	94	87	69	64	34	31	21	18	94	66	7.9	201	19	O
N	94	88	68	63	34	31	20	17	94	63	4.9	125	11	N
D	96	90	66	57	36	32	19	14	92	47	0.2	5	2	D

CHAD

Chad is a country slightly larger than Egypt, situated in interior West Africa between 10° and 23° N. It is rather sparsely populated as the northern part of the country includes part of the Sahara desert. The general features of the climate of this part of Africa are described for Mali on p. 62. Chad borders Niger on the west and the Sudan on the east and includes the same climatic belts.

The northern half of the country, the Sahara desert, is virtually rainless. Here the climate is hot around the year with abundant sunshine. The table for **Faya**, which lies beyond the northern limit of the summer rain-belt, is representative of this area. The southern half of the country, roughly south of 15° N is part of the Sahel belt where rain occurs during the period of high sun between May and September. The table for **N'djamena** is representative of this wetter Sahel region. Here sunshine amounts are lower during the rainy ·season from July to September, averaging six to seven hours a day as compared with nine to ten during the dry season.

Faya 837 ft (225 m) 18°00′ N 19°10′ E 5 years — CHAD

		Temperature °F			Temperature °C				Relative humidity		Precipitation			
	Highest recorded	Average daily		Lowest recorded	Highest recorded	Average daily		Lowest recorded	0730 hours	1330 hours	Average monthly		Average no. days with 0.004 in + (0.1 mm +)	
		max.	min.			max.	min.		%	%	in	mm		
J	103	84	54	40	39	29	12	4	47	26	0	0	0	J
F	109	89	57	44	43	32	14	7	44	23	0	0	0	F
M	111	97	65	52	44	36	18	11	35	18	0	0	0	M
A	121	104	69	57	49	40	21	14	35	17	0	0	0	A
M	121	112	76	63	49	44	24	17	39	21	0	0	0.4	M
J	120	110	76	62	49	43	24	17	39	23	0	0	0	J
J	116	109	76	61	47	43	24	16	54	29	0	0	0.2	J
A	114	104	75	60	46	40	24	16	66	36	0.7	18	4	A
S	115	103	76	63	46	39	24	17	46	30	0	0	0.4	S
O	116	103	72	54	47	39	22	12	37	21		0	0	O
N	102	91	65	48	39	33	18	9	45	22	0	0	0	N
D	97	82	55	37	36	28	13	3	50	28	0	0	0	D

N'djamena 968 ft (295 m) 12°07′ N 15°02′ E 5 years — CHAD

		Temperature °F			Temperature °C				Relative humidity		Precipitation			
	Highest recorded	Average daily		Lowest recorded	Highest recorded	Average daily		Lowest recorded	0700 hours	1300 hours	Average monthly		Average no. days with 0.004 in + (0.1 mm +)	
		max.	min.			max.	min.		%	%	in	mm		
J	107	93	57	47	42	34	14	8	51	13	0	0	0	J
F	109	98	61	51	43	37	16	11	39	10	0	0	0	F
M	111	104	70	56	44	40	21	13	32	10	0	0	0	M
A	114	107	74	61	46	42	23	16	37	13	0.1	3	1	A
M	112	104	77	62	44	40	25	17	62	30	1.2	31	6	M
J	109	100	76	65	43	38	24	18	74	40	2.6	66	10	J
J	106	92	72	65	41	33	22	18	85	59	6.7	170	15	J
A	96	87	72	66	36	31	22	19	93	72	12.6	320	22	A
S	98	91	72	66	37	33	22	19	91	63	4.7	119	13	S
O	103	97	70	57	39	36	21	14	83	41	1.4	36	4	O
N	104	97	63	52	40	36	17	11	46	17	0	0	0	N
D	101	92	57	47	38	33	14	8	50	16	0	0	0	D

CONGO

The Congo Republic, formerly a French colony, should not be confused with the larger neighbouring country of Zaïre, formerly known as the Belgian Congo. It lies between 4° N and 5° S in central Africa and has the river Congo and its tributary the Ubangui as its southeastern border with Zaïre. It is a little larger than Great Britain but is sparsely populated. Most of the country is a low plateau between 650 and 3250 ft (200 and 1000 m) above sea level. There is a low coastal plain on the Atlantic coast. The weather and climate of the country are similar to those described in more detail for Zaïre on p. 98.

Annual rainfall is almost everywhere between 50 and 70 in (1250 and 1750 mm) and it is well distributed around the year. Rainfall is least in the south of the country and along the coast. The table for **Brazzaville** is representative of the south of the country. This shows a distinct dry season between June and September when the sun and the inter-tropical rain-belt are farthest north; there is a second but brief drier period in January when the rain-belt is farthest south.

DJIBOUTI

This small country was formerly known as French Somaliland and later as 'Afars and Issas'. It is at the entrance to the Red Sea with a coastline on the southern shores of the Gulf of Aden. It is about as big as Wales or the state of Vermont. It is bordered by Ethiopia on the west and by the Somali Republic on the south.

There is a low-lying coastal plain which is very hot all the year round but with lower temperatures at the period of low sun (see the table for **Djibouti**). Inland there are extensive areas above 2000 ft (600 m) where temperatures and humidity are a little lower than on the coast. Annual rainfall is almost everywhere below 20 in (500 mm) and is much less in many places. The scanty rainfall on the coast is more likely to come in the period November to March, but inland the rains are more probable during the period of high sun from April to October. Hours of sunshine average from eight to nine hours a day around the year.

Brazzaville 1043 ft (318 m) 4°15′ S 15°15′ E 7 years — CONGO

	Temperature °F			Temperature °C			Relative humidity		Precipitation			
	Highest recorded	Average daily	Lowest recorded	Highest recorded	Average daily	Lowest recorded	0800 hours	1600 hours	Average monthly		Average no. days with 0.4 in + (10 mm +)	
		max.	min.			max.	min.		%	%	in	mm	
J	94	88	69	64	34	31	21	18	86	65	6.3	160	2	J
F	95	89	70	63	35	32	21	17	86	66	4.9	125	5	F
M	98	91	70	65	37	33	21	18	86	65	7.4	188	6	M
A	95	91	71	67	35	33	22	19	87	65	7.0	178	6	A
M	96	89	70	63	36	32	21	17	89	69	4.3	109	4	M
J	93	84	65	56	34	29	18	13	88	67	0.6	15	0	J
J	89	82	63	54	32	28	17	12	86	60	0	0	0	J
A	93	85	65	55	34	29	18	13	79	56	0	0	0	A
S	95	88	68	61	35	31	20	16	77	54	2.2	56	1	S
O	97	89	70	63	36	32	21	17	80	61	5.4	137	5	O
N	97	88	70	65	36	31	21	18	87	69	11.5	292	9	N
D	95	87	70	64	35	31	21	18	87	71	8.4	213	5	D

Djibouti 23 ft (7 m) 11°36′ N 43°09′ E 11 years — DJIBOUTI

	Temperature °F			Temperature °C			Relative humidity		Precipitation			
	Highest recorded	Average daily	Lowest recorded	Highest recorded	Average daily	Lowest recorded	0600 hours	1200 hours	Average monthly		Average no. days with 0.04 in + (1 mm +)	
		max.	min.			max.	min.		%	%	in	mm	
J	93	84	73	66	34	29	23	19	82	69	0.4	10	3	J
F	93	84	75	65	34	29	24	18	82	71	0.5	13	2	F
M	98	87	77	69	37	31	25	21	83	73	1.0	25	2	M
A	101	90	79	70	38	32	26	21	84	74	0.5	13	1	A
M	112	93	82	70	44	34	28	21	83	70	0.2	5	1	M
J	117	99	86	73	47	37	30	23	62	53	0	0	0.3	J
J	117	106	87	72	47	41	31	22	57	43	0.1	3	1	J
A	116	103	85	72	47	39	29	22	62	44	0.3	8	1	A
S	112	96	85	73	44	36	29	23	73	60	0.3	8	1	S
O	102	92	80	70	39	33	27	21	77	65	0.4	10	1	O
N	96	88	77	65	36	31	25	18	79	67	0.9	23	2	N
D	94	85	73	63	34	29	23	17	82	71	0.5	13	2	D

Egypt, almost twice the size of France, is situated in the northeast of Africa. It has long coastlines on the Mediterranean and on the Red Sea. A small part of the country, the Sinai desert, lies east of the Suez Canal and is, strictly speaking, in Asia. Egypt has land boundaries with Libya on the west, with the Sudan on the south and a shorter boundary with Israel on the east.

Egypt is one of the hottest and sunniest countries in the world. With the exception of a strip about fifty miles wide along the Mediterranean coast Egypt has a desert climate, being entirely within the Sahara. The legendary fertility of Egypt is a consequence of the fact that about 3 per cent of the country consists of the Nile valley and delta. The river Nile has no tributaries within Egypt but is nourished by the heavy rains falling far to the south in Ethiopia and East Africa. The Nile valley and delta are intensively cultivated by irrigation and contain about 95 per cent of Egypt's population.

The Mediterranean coastal strip has an average annual rainfall of between 4 and 8 ins (100 and 200 mm) which is not sufficient to support crops. Over the rest of Egypt, roughly south of Cairo, the annual rainfall is a mere 1–2 in (25–50 mm). In central and southern Egypt several years may pass without any significant rain. When rain does fall it is usually in the form of a brief and sometimes damaging downpour which may cause a local flood.

The climate of the Mediterranean coastal strip is represented by the table for **Alexandria**. Here the weather in the winter period from November to March may be quite variable with some cloudy days when rain and disturbed weather are brought by depressions moving from west to east in the Mediterranean. For much of the time, however, the winter weather is warm and sunny; but some cold days occur when northerly winds are strong. Summers are sunny and hot, but the daytime temperature is modified by strong sea breezes on the coast.

The most unpleasant weather near the coast occurs between March and early June when a weak depression draws very hot air from the Sahara towards the coast. These hot dry khamsin winds are often dust-laden and may raise sand particles in the desert which obscure visibility and irritate eyes, nose and mouth. A severe khamsin is most unpleasant and even dangerous. Virtually any part of Egypt can experience them. The very high temperatures occasionally experienced at **Alexandria** and **Cairo** almost always occur during the khamsin season. Otherwise the northern part of Egypt does not experience the high temperatures regularly recorded in the south of the country.

Winters are generally warm in the south of Egypt but temperatures fall rather abruptly at night so that desert evenings in winter can be quite chilly (see the table for **Aswan**). Farther north the nights can be distinctly chilly and occasional ground frost is not unknown. In the Nile valley the humidity from the large irrigated areas causes local morning mist and fog, particularly in winter but this quickly clears as the sun becomes powerful. On the higher hills of Sinai behind the Red Sea coast, which rise to between 7000 and 8000 ft (2000 and 2400 m), snow may fall in winter but it rarely lies for more than a day or so.

The heat of southern Egypt in summer is fierce and there is almost no relief from one day to another. The very low humidity, however, makes the heat more bearable and it is rarely dangerous to the acclimatized visitor. The visitor should allow a period of acclimatization before engaging in vigorous activity during the heat of the day and should also take precautions against sunburn. Shade temperatures are misleading in Egypt where the sun is ubiquitous, and there is no shade in the desert! Visitors are more likely to suffer minor sickness and stomach disorders in Egypt from unhygienic food and drink rather than from the direct effect of the climate.

From what has been said above it is clear that Egypt has a very sunny climate; daily sunshine hours average about twelve hours a day in summer to between eight and ten hours a day in winter. There are occasional completely cloudy days in winter in the north, but very few in the south. Places such as Luxor and **Aswan** and the few oases in the Sahara desert have an almost perfect winter climate: dry, sunny and not excessively hot.

Alexandria 105 ft (32 m) 31°12′ N 29°53′ E 45 years

	Temperature °F			Temperature °C			Relative humidity		Precipitation			
	Highest recorded	Average daily	Lowest recorded	Highest recorded	Average daily	Lowest recorded	0800 hours	1400 hours	Average monthly		Average no. days with 0.04 in + (1 mm +)	
		max.	min.			max.	min.		%	%	in	mm	
J	82	65	51	38	28	18	11	3	71	61	1.9	48	7	J
F	91	66	52	37	33	19	11	3	70	59	0.9	23	5	F
M	103	70	55	44	40	21	13	7	67	57	0.4	10	3	M
A	108	74	59	49	42	23	15	9	67	60	0.1	3	1	A
M	111	79	64	54	44	26	18	12	70	64	0	0	0.5	M
J	111	83	69	59	44	28	21	15	72	68	0	0	0	J
J	103	85	73	63	40	29	23	17	76	70	0	0	0	J
A	105	87	74	64	41	31	23	18	72	68	0	0	0	A
S	106	86	73	60	41	30	23	16	68	63	0	0	0.1	S
O	104	83	68	54	40	28	20	12	68	61	0.2	5	1	O
N	95	77	62	46	35	25	17	8	69	60	1.3	33	4	N
D	88	69	55	37	31	21	13	3	72	60	2.2	56	7	D

Aswan 366 ft (112 m) 24°02′ N 32°53′ E 20 years

	Temperature °F			Temperature °C			Relative humidity		Precipitation			
	Highest recorded	Average daily	Lowest recorded	Highest recorded	Average daily	Lowest recorded	0800 hours	1400 hours	Average monthly		Average no. days with 0.04 in + (1 mm +)	
		max.	min.			max.	min.		%	%	in	mm	
J	100	74	50	38	38	23	10	3	52	29	0	0	0	J
F	102	78	52	35	39	26	11	2	46	22	0	0	0	F
M	110	87	58	43	43	31	14	6	36	17	0	0	0	M
A	115	96	66	49	46	36	19	9	29	15	0	0	0.1	A
M	118	103	74	52	48	39	23	11	29	15	0	0	0.5	M
J	123	107	78	68	51	42	26	20	26	16	0	0	0	J
J	124	106	79	70	51	41	26	21	31	16	0	0	0	J
A	120	106	79	67	49	41	26	19	34	18	0	0	0	A
S	117	103	75	63	47	39	24	17	37	19	0	0	0	S
O	112	98	71	57	44	37	22	14	40	21	0	0	0	O
N	107	87	62	43	42	31	17	6	46	26	0	0	0	N
D	99	77	53	40	37	25	12	4	50	31	0	0	0	D

	Temperature °F				Temperature °C				Relative humidity		Precipitation			
	Highest recorded	Average daily		Lowest recorded	Highest recorded	Average daily		Lowest recorded	0800 hours	1400 hours	Average monthly		Average no. days with 0.04 in + (1 mm +)	
		max.	min.			max.	min.		%	%	in	mm		
J	88	65	47	35	31	18	8	2	69	40	0.2	5	1	J
F	92	69	48	35	33	21	9	2	64	33	0.2	5	1	F
M	101	75	52	38	38	24	11	3	63	27	0.2	5	0.8	M
A	113	83	57	42	45	28	14	6	55	21	0.1	3	0.4	A
M	116	91	63	49	47	33	17	9	50	18	0.1	3	0.2	M
J	117	95	68	55	47	35	20	13	55	20	0	0	0	J
J	109	96	70	61	43	36	21	16	65	24	0	0	0	J
A	109	95	71	63	43	35	22	17	69	28	0	0	0	A
S	108	90	68	58	42	32	20	14	68	31	0	0	0	S
O	109	86	65	51	43	30	18	11	67	31	0	0	0.3	O
N	100	78	58	42	38	26	14	6	68	38	0.1	3	0.8	N
D	87	68	50	34	31	20	10	1	70	41	0.2	5	1	D

Formerly the Spanish colony of Rio Muni, Equatorial Guinea is about the size of Wales or Israel. It lies on the coast of the Gulf of Guinea between Cameroon to the north and Gabon to the south. The country includes the offshore island of Fernando Po, which is mountainous and therefore particularly wet, and a number of smaller islands. Both the mainland and the islands have a typical equatorial climate with high temperatures, high humidity, heavy rainfall and much cloud around the year. Annual rainfall is almost everywhere around 80 in (2000 mm). Weather and climate are similar to those described for Zaïre on p. 98. Conditions are represented by the table for **Malabo**.

Malabo (Fernando Po) alt. not known 3°46′ N 8°46′ E 2 years — **EQUATORIAL GUINEA**

	Temperature °F			Temperature °C				Relative humidity	Precipitation			
	Highest recorded	Average daily	Lowest recorded	Highest recorded	Average daily		Lowest recorded	All hours	Average monthly		Average no. days with 0.004 in + (0.1 mm +)	
		max.	min.			max.	min.		%	in	mm		
J	89	87	67	64	32	31	19	18	86	0.2	5	3	J
F	91	89	69	66	33	32	21	19	85	1.2	31	5	F
M	90	88	69	66	32	31	21	19	90	7.6	193	13	M
A	90	89	70	67	32	32	21	19	89	6.4	163	15	A
M	89	87	71	66	32	31	22	19	87	10.3	262	23	M
J	87	85	69	65	31	29	21	18	90	11.9	302	23	J
J	85	84	69	64	29	29	21	18	90	6.3	160	17	J
A	86	85	69	63	30	29	21	17	92	4.5	114	14	A
S	87	86	69	64	31	30	21	18	95	7.9	201	24	S
O	87	86	70	65	31	30	21	18	94	9.1	231	23	O
N	88	86	71	66	31	30	22	19	93	4.6	117	12	N
D	88	87	70	63	31	31	21	17	91	0.8	20	4	D

ETHIOPIA

Ethiopia is a mountainous country about the size of Egypt. Situated between 18° and 4° N in East Africa, it is bordered by the Sudan on the west, by Kenya on the south and by Somalia and Djibouti on the east. Large parts of the country lie between 6000 and 8000 ft (1800 and 2400 m) and the highest mountain rises to over 15,000 ft (4600 m). There are lowland regions in the east of the country. Most of Ethiopia has a tropical climate moderated by altitude with a marked wet season at the time of high sun. The eastern lowlands are much drier with a hot, semi-arid to desert climate.

In the highlands of Ethiopia temperatures are reasonably warm around the year but rarely very hot. Above 6000 ft (1800 m) the daily temperatures are rather similar to those in summer in northern France or New England. Most of the rain comes during the period April to September. In the west there tends to be a single maximum of rainfall in July and August, but towards the east there is often a brief wetter period in April and May then a pause before the heavier rains in July and August. The rainy season is often called the monsoon in Ethiopia because it is associated with a change in the predominant wind direction; northeast winds prevail during the dry season and westerly to southwesterly winds during the rains. Rainfall is above 40 in (1000 mm) a year almost everywhere in the highlands and it rises to as much as 60–80 in (1500–2000 mm) in the wetter western parts.

Night-time temperatures may fall to near or below freezing in the mountains, particularly during the dry season. Occasional snow may fall on the highest peaks but there are no permanent snowfields.

In the northeastern lowlands, the Danakil desert, and in the southeastern lowlands, the Ogaden region, rainfall is low and temperatures are high around the year. The weather and climate are similar to that in the neighbouring countries of Somalia and **Djibouti** (see the table for **Djibouti** on p. 39). The scanty rainfall, usually below 20 in (500 mm) a year is very unreliable and severe droughts often occur.

Over most of Ethiopia sunshine is much reduced during the wet season when there is an average of two to four hours a day in July and August as compared with eight to nine hours during the months November to February. Thunderstorms are very frequent in the wetter parts of the country, occurring almost daily during the wet season; in many places there are over a hundred thunderstorms a year. Except in the hot lowlands the climate of Ethiopia is generally healthy and pleasant although the constant cloud and rain during the height of the wet season can be rather depressing for the visitor. The tables for **Addis Ababa** and **Harrar** are representative of conditions throughout the year in the highlands.

Addis Ababa 8038 ft (2450 m) 9°20′ N 38°45′ E 12 years ETHIOPIA

	Temperature °F			Temperature °C				Relative humidity		Precipitation			
	Highest recorded	Average daily	Lowest recorded	Highest recorded	Average daily	Lowest recorded		0700 hours	1300 hours	Average monthly		Average no. days with 0.004 in + (0.1 mm +)	
		max.	min.			max.	min.		%	%	in	mm		
J	82	75	43	35	28	24	6	2	61	33	0.5	13	2	J
F	86	76	47	36	30	24	8	2	64	39	1.5	38	5	F
M	84	77	49	38	29	25	9	3	58	37	2.6	66	8	M
A	88	77	50	40	31	25	10	4	65	44	3.4	86	10	A
M	91	77	50	39	33	25	10	4	63	43	3.4	86	10	M
J	94	74	49	44	34	23	9	7	76	59	5.4	137	20	J
J	88	69	50	45	31	21	10	7	86	73	11.0	279	28	J
A	84	69	50	43	29	21	10	6	86	72	11.8	300	27	A
S	81	72	49	38	27	22	9	3	79	64	7.5	191	21	S
O	91	75	45	36	33	24	7	2	56	39	0.8	20	3	O
N	81	73	43	33	27	23	6	1	59	37	0.6	15	2	N
D	82	73	41	32	28	23	5	0	62	29	0.2	5	2	D

Harrar 6071 ft (1851 m) 9°42′ N 42°30′ E 10 years ETHIOPIA

	Temperature °F			Temperature °C				Relative humidity	Precipitation			
	Highest recorded	Average daily	Lowest recorded	Highest recorded	Average daily	Lowest recorded		0800 hours	Average monthly		Average no. days with 0.04 in + (1 mm +)	
		max.	min.			max.	min.		%	in	mm		
J	82	77	55	45	28	25	13	7	52	0.3	8	1	J
F	84	78	57	52	29	26	14	11	50	1.3	33	3	F
M	90	80	58	52	32	27	14	11	56	3.0	76	7	M
A	86	80	59	55	30	27	15	13	59	4.7	119	11	A
M	88	80	59	55	31	27	15	13	76	5.0	127	10	M
J	88	78	58	54	31	26	14	12	73	3.5	89	9	J
J	84	75	57	52	29	24	14	11	76	5.1	130	12	J
A	82	74	57	52	28	23	14	11	76	6.3	160	15	A
S	84	76	58	54	29	24	14	12	74	3.7	94	13	S
O	84	78	58	50	29	26	14	10	55	1.4	36	5	O
N	82	78	56	46	28	26	13	8	49	0.6	15	1	N
D	84	78	56	45	29	26	13	7	52	0.4	10	0.9	D

GABON

The Republic of Gabon is one of the four territories which formerly made up the French colony of Equatorial Africa; the others are the Congo Republic, Cameroon and the Central African Empire. Gabon is bordered on the north by Cameroon and on the south by the Congo Republic. It has a coastline on the South Atlantic and lies between 2° N and 4° S. It is part of the same major climatic region described in more detail for Zaïre on p. 98.

The whole country has a typical equatorial type of climate: hot, wet and humid around the year with much cloud. Annual rainfall is almost everywhere between 50 and 80 in (1250 and 2000 mm) and is as much as 120 in (2500 mm) near the coast and in the higher districts. The table for **Libreville** illustrates conditions over most of the country. The driest months are almost everywhere June to August when the inter-tropical rain-belt has moved to its farthest position north.

GAMBIA

This tiny country is situated on the west coast of Africa on 13° N. It is entirely surrounded by Senegal and extends in a narrow strip inland on either side of the Gambia river. It is about the same size as the county of Yorkshire or the state of Connecticut. It has climate and weather similar to that of central Senegal. The table for **Banjul** is representative of the whole country and shows conditions very similar to those in the table for **Dakar** (p. 77).

Libreville 115 ft (35 m) 0°23′ N 9°26′ E 11 years   **GABON**

	Temperature °F			Temperature °C			Relative humidity		Precipitation		
	Highest recorded	Average daily	Lowest recorded	Highest recorded	Average daily	Lowest recorded	0630 hours	1230 hours	Average monthly		Average no. days with 0.004 in + (0.1 mm +)
		max.	min.			max.	min.		%	%	in	mm	
J	94	87	73	63	34	31	23	17	93	76	9.8	249	13	J
F	94	88	72	63	34	31	22	17	94	75	9.3	236	11	F
M	96	89	73	63	36	32	23	17	94	74	13.2	335	15	M
A	95	89	73	64	35	32	23	18	95	75	13.4	340	14	A
M	99	88	72	64	37	31	22	18	93	75	9.6	244	11	M
J	95	85	70	63	35	29	21	17	85	71	0.5	13	1	J
J	92	83	68	62	33	28	20	17	85	69	0.1	3	0.7	J
A	92	84	69	63	33	29	21	17	86	70	0.7	18	3	A
S	92	85	71	66	33	29	22	19	88	74	4.1	104	11	S
O	92	86	71	67	33	30	22	19	92	79	13.6	345	19	O
N	95	86	71	67	35	30	22	19	94	79	14.7	373	19	N
D	92	87	72	66	33	31	22	19	92	76	9.8	249	13	D

Banjul 90 ft (27 m) 13°21′ N 16°40′ W 9 years   **GAMBIA**

	Temperature °F			Temperature °C			Relative humidity		Precipitation		
	Highest recorded	Average daily	Lowest recorded	Highest recorded	Average daily	Lowest recorded	0500 hours	1400 hours	Average monthly		Average no. days with 0.04 in + (1 mm +)
		max.	min.			max.	min.		%	%	in	mm	
J	99	88	59	45	37	31	15	7	67	27	0.1	3	0.1	J
F	102	90	61	50	39	32	16	10	66	26	0.1	3	0.3	F
M	104	94	63	53	40	34	17	12	76	29	0	0	0	M
A	106	91	65	54	41	33	18	12	82	41	0	0	0	A
M	106	89	67	57	41	32	19	14	88	49	0.4	10	0.9	M
J	100	89	73	65	38	32	23	18	91	61	2.3	58	5	J
J	93	86	74	69	34	30	23	21	94	72	11.1	282	16	J
A	92	85	73	68	33	29	23	20	95	78	19.7	500	19	A
S	94	87	73	63	34	31	23	17	95	73	12.2	310	19	S
O	99	89	72	61	37	32	22	16	95	65	4.3	109	8	O
N	96	89	65	54	36	32	18	12	90	47	0.7	18	0.8	N
D	96	88	61	48	36	31	16	9	77	36	0.1	3	0.2	D

GHANA

Ghana is situated in West Africa with a coastline on the Gulf of Guinea. In area it is about the size of Great Britain and it extends between 5° and 11° N. It is bordered on the west by the Ivory Coast, on the north by Upper Volta and on the east by Togo.

Ghana experiences the same sequence of weather and climate around the year as that described for Nigeria (p. 72) and adjacent countries. There is, however, one local peculiarity about the distribution of rainfall in Ghana. Rainfall is lower in the coastal region than is the case a short distance inland. This is thought to be a consequence of two local features which apply to this part of the West African coastline. At the time when rainfall is heaviest in much of West Africa the waters offshore on this part of the coast are unusually cool for near-equatorial latitudes; a cool current appears on the ocean surface. The coast here follows a direction from west-southwest to east-northeast and is parallel with the prevailing winds; this is another factor which reduces coastal rainfall.

The table for **Accra** is representative of this drier coastal strip. Farther inland rainfall increases. In the northern half of the country there is an increasing tendency for a single rainy season and the table for **Tamale** is representative of this region. Annual rainfall is lower here as also in the north of Nigeria. As a consequence of the lower rainfall and less cloud **Accra** is rather sunnier than many other places on this coast; hours of sunshine average about five a day during the rainy season and as much as seven to eight hours during the drier months. Sunshine hours are reduced in the wetter districts inland but increase again in the drier regions of northern Ghana. (See map p. 73.)

Accra 88 ft (27 m) 5°33′ N 0°12′ W 17 years   **GHANA**

	Temperature °F			Temperature °C			Relative humidity		Precipitation			
Highest recorded	Average daily		Lowest recorded	Highest recorded	Average daily		Lowest recorded	0600 hours	1200 hours	Average monthly		Average no. days with 0.01 in + (0.25 mm +)	
	max.	min.			max.	min.		%	%	in	mm		
J	94	87	73	59	34	31	23	15	95	61	0.6	15	1	J
F	100	88	75	62	38	31	24	17	96	61	1.3	33	2	F
M	100	88	76	68	38	31	24	20	95	63	2.2	56	4	M
A	93	88	76	67	34	31	24	19	96	65	3.2	81	6	A
M	95	87	75	69	35	31	24	21	96	68	5.6	142	9	M
J	92	84	74	68	33	29	23	20	97	74	7.0	178	10	J
J	90	81	73	66	32	27	23	19	97	76	1.8	46	4	J
A	89	80	71	64	32	27	22	18	97	77	0.6	15	3	A
S	89	81	73	68	32	27	23	20	96	72	1.4	36	4	S
O	90	85	74	67	32	29	23	19	97	71	2.5	64	6	O
N	91	87	75	69	33	31	24	21	97	66	1.4	36	3	N
D	94	88	75	63	34	31	24	17	97	64	0.9	23	2	D

Tamale 635 ft (194 m) 9°24′ N 0°50′ W 13 years   **GHANA**

	Temperature °F			Temperature °C			Relative humidity		Precipitation			
Highest recorded	Average daily		Lowest recorded	Highest recorded	Average daily		Lowest recorded	0600 hours	1200 hours	Average monthly		Average no. days with 0.01 in + (0.25 mm +)	
	max.	min.			max.	min.		%	%	in	mm		
J	103	96	69	59	39	36	21	15	36	20	0.1	3	0.6	J
F	104	99	73	63	40	37	23	17	56	33	0.1	3	0.4	F
M	105	99	76	66	41	37	24	19	62	37	2.1	53	0.4	M
A	106	97	76	68	41	36	24	20	80	52	2.7	69	6	A
M	102	92	75	66	39	33	24	19	88	62	4.1	104	10	M
J	97	88	72	66	36	31	22	19	92	69	5.6	142	12	J
J	94	85	72	65	34	29	22	18	94	72	5.3	135	14	J
A	92	84	71	67	33	29	22	19	95	74	7.7	196	16	A
S	92	86	71	66	33	30	22	19	95	74	8.9	226	19	S
O	96	90	71	66	36	32	22	19	94	66	3.9	99	13	O
N	99	94	71	61	37	34	22	16	78	42	0.4	10	1	N
D	100	95	68	59	38	35	20	15	54	27	0.2	5	0.8	D

GUINEA

Guinea is a West African country with a coastline on the Atlantic. In area it is about as large as Great Britain. It has an extensive coastal plain and inland the country rises to a plateau which slopes gradually eastwards towards the upper Niger valley. The climate of Guinea is similar to that of Sierra Leone and is described on p. 76. The climate of the coastal region is represented by the table for **Conakry**. Rainfall is particularly heavy at **Conakry** which is situated on a headland. The driest part of Guinea is in the northeast along the border with Mali. Here the climate is better illustrated by the table for **Bamako** in Mali on p. 63. (See map p. 73.)

GUINEA-BISSAU

This small country was, until quite recently, a Portuguese colony. It is situated on the west coast of Africa at about 12° N. In area it is a little larger than Israel. It has a climate similar to that of southern Senegal, which it borders on the north, and northern Guinea, which it borders on the south. The description of the climate and weather of Senegal are equally appropriate for Guinea-Bissau and the climatic tables for **Dakar** (p. 77) and **Banjul** (p. 47) give a good idea of conditions around the year. Being farther south than most of Senegal, annual rainfall in Guinea-Bissau is marginally greater. (See map p. 73.)

IVORY COAST

The Ivory Coast is situated in West Africa with a coastline on the Gulf of Guinea between Liberia on the west and Ghana on the east. It extends between 4° and 10° N. It shares the same climatic belts and sequence of weather around the year as that described on p. 72 for Nigeria.

The climate of the coastal region is represented by the table for **Abidjan** which is wetter than **Accra** in Ghana. **Abidjan** has a climate very similar to that of **Lagos** in Nigeria. Rainfall becomes progressively less inland and the two separate rainy seasons merge into a single wet season; there is a much longer dry season at the time of low sun. Conditions in the north of the country are well represented by the climatic tables for **Tamale** in Ghana or **Kano** in Nigeria. (See map p. 73.)

	Temperature °F				Temperature °C				Relative humidity		Precipitation			
	Highest recorded	Average daily		Lowest recorded	Highest recorded	Average daily		Lowest recorded	0700 hours	1200 hours	Average monthly		Average no. days with 0.04 in + (1 mm +)	
		max.	min.			max.	min.		%	%	in	mm		
J	94	88	72	64	34	31	22	18	89	65	0.1	3	0.1	J
F	94	88	73	63	34	31	23	17	90	65	0.1	3	0.3	F
M	96	89	73	69	36	32	23	21	85	63	0.4	10	0.6	M
A	95	90	73	68	35	32	23	20	83	64	0.9	23	2	A
M	95	89	75	66	35	32	24	19	85	70	6.2	158	11	M
J	92	86	73	65	33	30	23	18	89	77	22.0	559	22	J
J	89	83	72	67	32	28	22	19	93	84	51.1	1298	29	J
A	87	82	72	68	31	28	22	20	94	87	41.5	1054	27	A
S	90	85	73	66	32	29	23	19	94	82	26.9	683	24	S
O	91	87	73	64	33	31	23	18	92	77	14.6	371	19	O
N	91	87	75	69	33	31	24	21	91	74	4.8	122	8	N
D	93	88	74	66	34	31	23	19	88	67	0.4	10	0.5	D

	Temperature °F				Temperature °C				Relative humidity		Precipitation			
	Highest recorded	Average daily		Lowest recorded	Highest recorded	Average daily		Lowest recorded	0530 hours	1130 hours	Average monthly		Average no. days with 0.04 in + (1 mm +)	
		max.	min.			max.	min.		%	%	in	mm		
J	94	88	73	59	34	31	23	15	96	73	1.6	41	3	J
F	95	90	75	64	35	32	24	18	94	71	2.1	53	4	F
M	96	90	75	67	36	32	24	19	94	72	3.9	99	6	M
A	95	90	75	68	35	32	24	20	93	72	4.9	125	9	A
M	94	88	75	68	34	31	24	20	94	76	14.2	361	16	M
J	93	85	73	68	34	29	23	20	95	82	19.5	495	18	J
J	91	83	73	64	33	28	23	18	93	78	8.4	213	8	J
A	88	82	71	63	31	28	22	17	95	79	2.1	53	7	A
S	90	83	73	65	32	28	23	18	95	80	2.8	71	8	S
O	92	85	74	67	33	29	23	19	94	79	6.6	168	13	O
N	94	87	74	67	34	31	23	19	94	73	7.9	201	13	N
D	95	88	74	62	35	31	23	17	96	72	3.1	79	6	D

KENYA

Kenya is a country about as large as France and situated in East Africa between 5° N and 5° S. It has a very diverse relief with a low coastal plain on the Indian Ocean shore, extensive inland plateaux regions between 3000 and 5000 ft (915 and 1500 m) and several mountain ranges and isolated peaks such as Mount Kenya which rises to 17,000 ft (5200 m) and has a permanent snow-cap. It is bordered on the north by Ethiopia and Somaliland, on the south by Tanzania, and on the west by Uganda and the shores of Lake Victoria.

Although Kenya lies athwart the equator annual rainfall over most of the country is surprisingly low and rather variable from year to year. This is because the inter-tropical belt of cloud and rain passes rather quickly across Kenya in April and October and because the predominant seasonal winds, the north and south monsoons as they are called in East Africa, have a track parallel to the coast and have already passed over large areas of land before reaching Kenya. Because of the reduction of temperature with altitude, temperatures over much of Kenya are subtropical or temperate,

similar to those in California, and summer in France or southern Britain rather than those elsewhere in equatorial Africa. Only the coastal lowlands experience the constant high temperatures and humidity associated with equatorial latitudes. Even here they are less oppressive than one might expect because of the regular daytime sea breezes and longer hours of sunshine. It is not surprising that with such a favourable climate – sunny, only moderately wet and not too hot – and a great variety of scenery, wild life, game parks, good communications and a stable government, Kenya has many attractions for the tourist.

The variety of relief and the range of altitude in Kenya produce a considerable number of distinctive local climates and local weather too numerous to be detailed here. The country can be divided broadly into four climatic regions, each with certain features of equatorial climates. There is a double rainy season between March and May and between November and December, with two intervening dry seasons. There is a small difference of temperature from month to month through the year. Both these features can be seen in the three tables for Kenya included here. The four climatic regions are:

The coastal region

The average annual rainfall is over 40 in (1000 mm) except in the north where it is rather less. The wettest season is in April and May as the inter-tropical rain-belt moves north. The second rainy season in October and November, sometimes called the 'little rains' in Kenya, is less conspicuous. Some rain, often in the form of night or early morning showers, occurs in all months. Temperatures remain quite high around the year as does humidity; but the weather is less oppressive than might be thought because of the regular and strong onshore winds in the daytime and the greater number of sunshine hours which average seven to eight a day in all months. The weather, however, can feel sultry, particularly at night. The table for **Mombasa** is representative of this region.

The Northern Frontier districts and the lower inland plateaux

Much of this region has a very low annual rainfall for an equatorial region. Rainfall is generally below 20 in (500 mm) and in the far north is often below 10 in (250 mm). In the lower districts temperatures are high round the year, there is much sunshine, and the region is a typical hot desert like the adjoining southern parts of Somaliland and Ethiopia. Humidity is low and, apart from occasional excessive heat, it is a healthy climate.

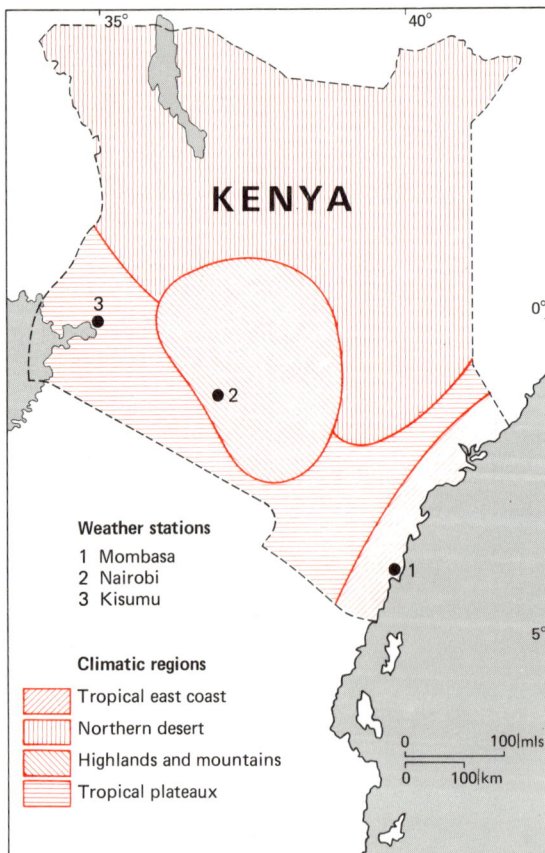

KENYA

Weather stations
1 Mombasa
2 Nairobi
3 Kisumu

Climatic regions
Tropical east coast
Northern desert
Highlands and mountains
Tropical plateaux

The Kenya highlands

Most of this region lies between 4000 and 7000 ft (1220 and 2150 m) and occupies the centre and west of the country on either side of the eastern Rift valley, extending to the Ugandan border. It is the most densely populated part of the country and contains the most productive agricultural land. There is a double rainy season but rainfall is moderate and only exceeds 50 in (1250 mm) a year on the higher parts. Over most of the region the sunniest time of the year is from December to March. The cloudiest period is from June to September when there is much drizzle but little heavy rain. This period is often called 'winter' in the Kenya Highlands and the evenings may feel chilly compared with the sunnier months. The table for **Nairobi** is representative of much of the region. The table for **Kisumu** on the shores of Lake Victoria, which is virtually an inland sea, shows that there is rather more rainfall in each month here. This is a consequence of the greater humidity picked up by winds crossing the lake and a liability for thunderstorms to break out during the night.

The higher mountain regions

These are the small regions above 8000 ft (2500 m) and isolated higher mountains such as Mount Elgon and Mount Kenya. Here temperatures fall low enough for frost to occur and at higher levels some precipitation may be snow. Mount Kenya has permanent snowfields.

Kisumu 3769 ft (1148 m) 0°06′ S 34°45′ E 20 years

	Temperature °F			Temperature °C			Relative humidity		Precipitation			
	Highest recorded	Average daily	Lowest recorded	Highest recorded	Average daily	Lowest recorded	0800 hours	1400 hours	Average monthly		Average no. days with 0.01 in +	
		max.	min.			max.	min.		%	%	in	mm	(0.25 mm +)	
J	97	85	65	57	36	29	18	14	60	41	1.9	48	6	J
F	98	84	66	57	37	29	19	14	62	41	3.2	81	8	F
M	98	83	66	60	37	28	19	16	68	46	5.5	140	12	M
A	98	82	65	60	37	28	18	16	74	52	7.5	191	14	A
M	93	81	65	60	34	27	18	16	77	57	6.1	155	14	M
J	89	80	63	55	32	27	17	13	76	53	3.3	84	9	J
J	91	80	63	56	33	27	17	13	76	52	2.3	58	8	J
A	97	81	63	54	36	27	17	12	73	50	3.0	76	10	A
S	93	83	63	54	34	28	17	12	66	47	2.5	64	8	S
O	94	85	64	55	34	29	18	13	61	41	2.2	56	7	O
N	95	85	65	56	35	29	18	13	62	43	3.4	86	9	N
D	98	84	64	56	37	29	18	13	61	41	4.0	102	8	D

KENYA

Mombasa 52 ft (16 m) 4°03′ S 39°39′ E 45 years

	Temperature °F				Temperature °C				Relative humidity		Precipitation			
	Highest recorded	Average daily		Lowest recorded	Highest recorded	Average daily		Lowest recorded	0800 hours	1400 hours	Average monthly		Average no. days with 0.01 in + (0.25 mm +)	
		max.	min.				max.	min.		%	%	in	mm		
J	95	87	75	69	35	31	24	21	76	66	1.0	25	6	J
F	95	87	76	70	35	31	24	21	75	63	0.7	18	3	F
M	96	88	77	71	36	31	25	22	77	63	2.5	64	7	M
A	96	86	76	69	36	30	24	21	81	71	7.7	196	15	A
M	92	83	74	67	33	28	23	19	85	76	12.6	320	20	M
J	89	82	73	61	32	28	23	16	82	72	4.7	119	15	J
J	92	81	71	64	33	27	22	18	82	72	3.5	89	14	J
A	88	81	71	63	31	27	22	17	76	72	2.5	64	16	A
S	90	82	72	64	32	28	22	18	81	70	2.5	64	14	S
O	90	84	74	64	32	29	23	18	79	69	3.4	86	10	O
N	93	85	75	68	34	29	24	20	78	69	3.8	97	10	N
D	96	86	75	69	36	30	24	21	78	69	2.4	61	9	D

KENYA

Nairobi 5971 ft (1820 m) 1°16′ S 36°48′ E 15 years

	Temperature °F				Temperature °C				Relative humidity		Precipitation			
	Highest recorded	Average daily		Lowest recorded	Highest recorded	Average daily		Lowest recorded	0800 hours	1400 hours	Average monthly		Average no. days with 0.01 in + (0.25 mm +)	
		max.	min.				max.	min.		%	%	in	mm		
J	84	77	54	47	29	25	12	8	74	44	1.5	38	5	J
F	87	79	55	48	31	26	13	9	74	40	2.5	64	6	F
M	86	77	57	49	30	25	14	9	81	45	4.9	125	11	M
A	82	75	58	52	28	24	14	11	88	56	8.3	211	16	A
M	82	72	56	48	28	22	13	9	88	62	6.2	158	17	M
J	80	70	53	45	27	21	12	7	89	60	1.8	46	9	J
J	79	69	51	43	26	21	11	6	86	58	0.6	15	6	J
A	80	70	52	44	27	21	11	7	86	56	0.9	23	7	A
S	82	75	52	41	28	24	11	5	82	45	1.2	31	6	S
O	86	76	55	45	30	24	13	7	82	43	2.1	53	8	O
N	82	74	56	43	28	23	13	6	86	53	4.3	109	15	N
D	82	74	55	47	28	23	13	8	81	53	3.4	86	11	D

This small country lies entirely surrounded by the Republic of South Africa. It is about as large as Wales or Israel and lies in the eastern part of the High Veld between the Orange Free State and Natal. Most of the country is above 6000 ft (1800 m) and includes the highest land in southern Africa which rises to 11,000 ft (3300 m). Lesotho's weather and climate are similar to that described for the eastern interior or high veld of South Africa on p. 80. Temperatures, however, are significantly lower at higher levels and snow is quite frequent in winter. The table for **Bloemfontein** (South Africa) on p. 82 is representative of the rather warmer temperatures at lower levels. (See map p. 81.)

LIBERIA

Liberia is about as large as England and is situated on the west coast of Africa between 4° and 10° N. It has an extensive coastal plain and inland rises to a plateau with a maximum altitude of about 3300 ft (1000 m). The climate of the country is similar to that of Sierra Leone (p. 76). The climatic table for **Monrovia**, on the coast of Liberia, illustrates conditions in most of the country. In parts of Liberia the rainy season is a little longer than in Sierra Leone with a brief drier season in August so that the summer rains may have a double maximum. (See map p. 73.)

Monrovia 75 ft (23 m) 6°18′ N 10°48′ W 3 years **LIBERIA**

	Temperature °F			Temperature °C			Relative humidity		Precipitation		
	Highest recorded	Average daily	Lowest recorded	Highest recorded	Average daily	Lowest recorded	0730 hours	1130 hours	Average monthly		Average no. days with 0.01 in + (0.25 mm +)
		max.	min.			max.	min.		%	%	in	mm	
J	90	86	73	55	32	30	23	13	95	78	1.2	31	5	J
F	91	85	73	68	33	29	23	20	94	76	2.2	56	5	F
M	90	87	74	67	32	31	23	19	92	77	3.8	97	10	M
A	91	87	73	60	33	31	23	16	91	80	8.5	216	17	A
M	93	86	72	60	34	30	22	16	89	79	20.3	516	21	M
J	87	81	73	65	31	27	23	18	89	82	38.3	973	26	J
J	85	80	72	61	29	27	22	16	88	83	39.2	996	24	J
A	86	80	73	65	30	27	23	18	87	84	14.7	373	20	A
S	85	81	72	65	29	27	22	18	92	86	29.3	744	26	S
O	86	83	72	66	30	28	22	19	92	84	30.4	772	22	O
N	89	85	73	61	32	29	23	16	91	80	9.3	236	19	N
D	89	86	73	57	32	30	23	14	93	79	5.1	130	12	D

LIBYA

Libya is a large country in North Africa. It has a long coastline on the Mediterranean but the greater part consists of the central Saharan desert. The Mediterranean coastal fringes have a Mediterranean climate with some rain between October and March, but the vast area of desert inland has very little rain at all and here some of the highest temperatures in the world have been recorded.

The general climatic and weather conditions over Libya are similar to those described for coastal and interior Egypt (p. 40) and Algeria (p. 25). The climatic tables for **Tripoli** in western Libya (Tripolitania) and **Benghazi** in eastern Libya (Cyrenaica) are representative of conditions around the year in the coastal regions. The scanty winter rainfall is brought by Mediterranean depressions but the amounts are rather variable from year to year. Along the coast of the Gulf of Sidra, between Misurata and **Benghazi**, rainfall is rather less so that the desert reaches the coast. The wettest area of the country is in the hill and plateau region of the Jebel Akhdar (the Green Mountain) between **Benghazi** and Derna, where the land rises to over 1600 ft (500 m) and rainfall is as much as 24 in (600 mm) a year.

Beyond a distance of 100 miles (160 km) or less from the coast annual rainfall drops below 4 in (100 mm) and is often very much less. Indeed, over much of the Sahara, rainfall is so slight and irregular as to make any average figure almost meaningless.

As elsewhere on the coasts of the southern Mediterranean the winter weather can be changeable from day to day with cool, cloudy rainy spells interrupting the generally warm, sunny and settled weather. Inland, in the desert, conditions are almost uniformly settled and sunny with very high temperatures in summer and warm days in winter. The climate here is similar to that shown by the tables for **Aswan** in Egypt on p. 41 or **Biskra** and **In Salah** in Algeria on pp. 26–7.

The coastal districts of Libya are affected in the period March to June by very hot, dusty winds from the desert which bring very high temperatures, often exceeding 122° F (50° C) for a day or two. They are similar in origin to the khamsin winds of Egypt. They go under the local name of ghibli.

Benghazi 82 ft (25 m) 32°06′ N 20°04′ E 40 years — LIBYA

	Temperature °F				Temperature °C				Relative humidity		Precipitation			
	Highest recorded	Average daily		Lowest recorded	Highest recorded	Average daily		Lowest recorded	0930 hours	1530 hours	Average monthly		Average no. days with 0.004 in + (1 mm +)	
		max.	min.			max.	min.		%	%	in	mm		
J	76	63	50	38	24	17	10	3	69	60	2.6	66	13	J
F	82	64	51	38	28	18	11	3	63	58	1.6	41	9	F
M	101	69	54	37	38	21	12	3	51	49	0.8	20	6	M
A	105	74	58	41	41	23	14	5	49	50	0.2	5	2	A
M	108	79	63	48	42	26	17	9	49	51	0.1	3	1	M
J	109	83	68	55	43	28	20	13	53	56	0	0	0.2	J
J	105	84	71	57	41	29	22	14	59	61	0	0	0.1	J
A	105	85	72	60	41	29	22	16	61	61	0	0	0.1	A
S	106	83	69	52	41	28	21	11	55	56	0.1	3	1	S
O	100	80	66	51	38	27	19	11	49	51	0.7	18	4	O
N	95	74	60	45	35	23	16	7	57	54	1.8	46	8	N
D	78	66	53	40	26	19	12	4	65	59	2.6	66	12	D

Tripoli 72 ft (22 m) 32°54′ N 13°11′ E 47 years — LIBYA

	Temperature °F				Temperature °C				Relative humidity		Precipitation			
	Highest recorded	Average daily		Lowest recorded	Highest recorded	Average daily		Lowest recorded	0700 hours	1200 hours	Average monthly		Average no. days with 0.004 in + (0.1 mm +)	
		max.	min.			max.	min.		%	%	in	mm		
J	83	61	47	34	28	16	8	1	68	59	3.2	81	11	J
F	91	63	49	37	33	17	9	3	71	60	1.8	46	7	F
M	101	67	52	39	38	19	11	4	65	57	1.1	28	5	M
A	105	72	57	43	41	22	14	6	62	57	0.4	10	2	A
M	109	76	61	43	43	24	16	6	58	62	0.2	5	3	M
J	112	81	67	50	44	27	19	10	57	70	0.1	3	1	J
J	114	85	71	60	46	29	22	16	54	72	0	0	0.2	J
A	112	86	72	62	44	30	22	17	72	69	0	0	0.3	A
S	113	85	71	59	45	29	22	15	67	67	0.4	10	2	S
O	106	80	65	50	41	27	18	10	65	59	1.6	41	5	O
N	96	73	57	42	36	23	14	6	66	53	2.6	66	7	N
D	86	64	49	33	30	18	9	1	65	55	3.7	94	11	D

MADAGASCAR

This large island, the size of France, is situated in the Indian Ocean between 12° and 26° S at an average distance of 400 miles (640 km) from the African coast. The eastern side of the island is exposed to the moisture-laden southeast trade winds for much of the year. Between November and February, at the time of high sun, the island is affected by the belt of cloud and rain associated with the inter-tropical convergence. Madagascar is a mountainous island with a steep escarpment rising to 4000–6000 ft (1200–1800 m) behind the east coast. Much of the interior is a plateau above which some isolated, extinct volcanoes rise to heights of 7000–9500 ft (2100–2900 m). The island slopes down more gradually to the south and west where there are wider coastal plains.

The whole island has a tropical climate, but above 3000 ft (900 m) temperatures are sufficiently reduced by altitude as to be rarely oppressive or uncomfortable. The lowlands are hot and rather humid, particularly during the rainy season. The east coast is wet for much of the year as it is exposed to the trade winds which are forced to rise as they meet the steep eastward-facing escarpment; see the table for **Tamatave** which has an annual rainfall of 140 in (3500 mm) falling on 240 days a year. Most of the east coast receives over 80 in (2000 mm) annual rainfall as does another small area in the northwest around Diego Suarez. Rainfall is lower on the interior plateau and decreases to the west and south.

The lowlands in the southwest of the island only receive between 16 and 32 in (400 and 800 mm) of rain a year, mostly falling between December and March. The central plateau areas receive an annual rainfall, intermediate between these extremes, varying between 40 and 60 in (1000 and 1500 mm). Most rain here falls between November and March, much of it in heavy downpours associated with hail and thunder. The rainfall during the rest of the year is mostly very light and sporadic (see the table for **Antananarivo**). On the plateau temperatures fall to moderate levels during the dry season and the nights may be chilly, but frost only occurs on the highest mountains.

Hours of sunshine are quite high around the year even on the wetter east coast. At **Tamatave** average daily sunshine hours range from six during the cloudier wet months to eight during the drier months. In the drier parts of the island sunshine hours range from eight to ten hours a day. Apart from the combination of heat and humidity which affects the lower districts of the island during the wet season, the weather and climate of much of the island is sunny, warm and pleasant for much of the year and this is particularly the case on the plateau.

Two or three times a year some part of Madagascar is affected by torrential rain and high winds associated with tropical cyclones which develop in the Indian Ocean north of the island. These may move southwards either on the western or eastern side of the island and the most damaging effects of their strong winds are felt in the coastal districts.

	Temperature °F			Temperature °C			Relative humidity		Precipitation			
	Highest recorded	Average daily	Lowest recorded	Highest recorded	Average daily	Lowest recorded	0700 hours	1300 hours	Average monthly		Average no. days with 0.04 in + (1 mm +)	
		max.	min.			max.	min.		%	%	in	mm	
J	91	79	61	53	33	26	16	12	91	70	11.8	300	21	J
F	90	78	61	52	32	26	16	11	92	71	11.0	279	20	F
M	87	79	60	51	31	26	16	11	93	68	7.0	178	17	M
A	87	76	58	45	31	24	14	7	93	66	2.1	53	11	A
M	85	73	54	40	29	23	12	4	94	63	0.7	18	9	M
J	80	69	50	34	27	21	10	1	93	62	0.3	8	9	J
J	80	68	48	37	27	20	9	3	93	61	0.3	8	10	J
A	85	70	48	35	29	21	9	2	92	57	0.4	10	9	A
S	92	74	51	38	33	23	11	3	88	53	0.7	18	7	S
O	95	80	54	42	35	27	12	6	85	49	2.4	61	9	O
N	94	81	58	42	34	27	14	6	86	54	5.3	135	13	N
D	91	80	60	52	33	27	16	11	89	64	11.3	287	20	D

	Temperature °F			Temperature °C			Relative humidity		Precipitation			
	Highest recorded	Average daily	Lowest recorded	Highest recorded	Average daily	Lowest recorded	0730 hours	1330 hours	Average monthly		Average no. days with 0.04 in + (1 mm +)	
		max.	min.			max.	min.		%	%	in	mm	
J	98	86	74	69	37	30	23	21	89	75	14.4	366	20	J
F	95	86	74	70	35	30	23	21	90	75	14.8	376	19	F
M	96	85	73	68	36	29	23	20	92	77	17.8	452	20	M
A	91	83	72	67	33	28	22	19	93	79	15.7	399	19	A
M	86	80	69	63	30	27	21	17	94	78	10.4	264	18	M
J	83	77	66	57	28	25	19	14	92	79	11.1	282	20	J
J	83	75	65	59	28	24	18	15	92	80	11.9	302	20	J
A	81	76	64	56	27	24	18	13	92	78	8.0	203	19	A
S	84	78	65	59	29	26	18	15	89	73	5.2	132	15	S
O	86	81	67	60	30	27	19	16	85	68	3.9	99	12	O
N	89	84	70	62	32	29	21	17	87	70	4.6	117	12	N
D	92	85	73	66	35	29	23	19	87	72	10.3	262	18	D

MALAWI

Malawi is about as large as England, situated in south-central Africa. It is bordered on the north by Tanzania, on the east and south by Mozambique and on the west by Zambia. The general features of the weather and climate of Malawi are similar to those of Zambia and Zimbabwe and are described on p. 101 for Zambia.

Malawi is a long narrow country extending from north to south and containing within its borders the large Lake Malawi (formerly Lake Nyasa). It also has a rather diverse relief with mountains rising above 10,000 ft (3000 m) and land in the lower Shire valley below 600 ft (180 m). It thus has a greater range of weather and climate than either Zambia or Zimbabwe.

Conditions in the Shire valley are typically tropical, with high temperatures around the year and a most unpleasant combination of high temperature and humidity during the rainy season. Frost is unknown here. The table for **Zumbo**, actually in Mozambique, is representative of conditions in these tropical lowlands. **Lilongwe** has a range of weather and climate throughout the year similar to that of the uplands of much of Zambia and Zimbabwe. Daytime temperatures here rarely rise to very high or uncomfortable levels and there is abundant sunshine during the dry season when occasional frosts occur.

The mountainous regions of southern Malawi, and in the north overlooking Lake Malawi, are amongst the wettest districts in this part of Africa with an annual rainfall of between 60 and 80 in (1500 and 2000 mm). Unusually for this area the heaviest rains are delayed until March or April and some rain may fall in all months. Over most of the country an annual rainfall of between 35 and 50 in (875 and 1250 mm) is more usual.

Apart from the lowlands in the south which are unhealthy, sultry and oppressive, the weather and climate over the rest of the country are generally healthy and pleasant. At times the weather can be surprisingly cold during the dry season, particularly above 5000 ft (1500 m).

Lilongwe 3610 ft (1100 m) 13°59′ S 33°45′ E 8 years   **MALAWI**

| | Temperature °F | | | Temperature °C | | | Relative humidity | | Precipitation | | |
| | Highest recorded | Average daily | Lowest recorded | Highest recorded | Average daily | Lowest recorded | 0800 hours | 1400 hours | Average monthly | | Average no. days with 0.01 in + (0.25 mm +) |
		max.	min.			max.	min.		%	%	in	mm	
J	90	80	63	55	32	27	17	13	85	64	8.2	208	19	J
F	88	80	63	54	31	27	17	12	89	66	8.6	218	18	F
M	89	80	61	52	32	27	16	11	86	60	4.9	125	13	M
A	86	80	57	50	30	27	14	10	84	50	1.7	43	5	A
M	86	77	51	39	30	25	11	4	82	41	0.1	3	1	M
J	82	74	47	36	28	23	8	2	79	38	0	0	0.1	J
J	82	74	45	31	28	23	7	−1	77	33	0	0	0.1	J
A	88	77	47	31	31	25	8	−1	68	31	0	0	1	A
S	89	81	53	39	32	27	12	4	55	30	0	0	0.6	S
O	93	86	59	48	34	30	15	9	50	28	0	0	1	O
N	91	85	63	54	34	29	17	12	60	42	2.1	53	7	N
D	92	82	64	56	33	28	18	13	76	58	4.9	125	15	D

Zumbo (Mozambique) 1125 ft (343 m) 15°37′ S 30°27′ E 15 years   **MALAWI**

| | Temperature °F | | | Temperature °C | | | Relative humidity | | Precipitation | | |
| | Highest recorded | Average daily | Lowest recorded | Highest recorded | Average daily | Lowest recorded | 0900 hours | 1500 hours | Average monthly | | Average no. days with 0.04 in + (1 mm +) |
		max.	min.			max.	min.		%	%	in	mm	
J	107	90	71	63	42	32	22	17	79	60	8.2	208	13	J
F	104	90	71	62	40	32	22	17	78	58	6.7	170	9	F
M	104	91	70	54	40	33	21	12	76	51	4.1	104	6	M
A	106	91	67	52	41	33	19	11	69	45	0.1	3	0.9	A
M	101	89	59	44	38	32	15	7	65	42	0	0	0.3	M
J	96	83	55	42	36	28	13	6	65	42	0	0	0	J
J	95	83	55	38	35	28	13	3	64	37	0	0	0	J
A	102	87	58	47	39	31	14	8	60	32	0.1	3	0.3	A
S	110	94	66	51	43	34	19	11	53	28	0	0	0	S
O	111	100	73	62	44	38	23	17	48	27	0.2	5	0.6	O
N	120	98	73	63	49	37	23	17	57	38	3.3	84	5	N
D	110	94	72	54	43	34	22	12	71	50	6.5	165	11	D

MALI

(Including a description of the climate and weather of Upper Volta, Niger and Chad in the Sahel belt of interior West Africa)

Mali has a climate which is very similar to that found in three other countries of interior West Africa: Upper Volta, Niger and Chad. These four countries all lie on the southern side of the Sahara desert, in what is called the Sahel belt or the Soudan region. Only Upper Volta does not extend far enough north to include part of the Sahara desert within its borders. The general features of the weather and climate of all four countries are described here.

These countries are landlocked and lie in a belt between 25° and 10° N. In the south of this belt annual rainfall is about 40 in (1000 mm) a year and this decreases northwards to virtually nil in the Sahara. Effectively the desert border is at about 15° N where annual rainfall is about 16 in (400 mm). The length of the rainy season, and the reliability of the rain, also decrease from south to north. The rainy season here is the period of high sun from May until September, with the heaviest and most reliable rains coming in July and August. The period from November until March is virtually rainless everywhere. This is the dry season with warm to hot, sunny days with persistent northeasterly winds (the harmattan). The arrival of the rains is heralded by light to variable winds and then, when the rains arrive, the winds become persistently west to southwest. These winds bring cloudy and more humid air from the equatorial regions of the South Atlantic.

Temperatures are highest from March to May before the change of wind direction. Much of the rain occurs in heavy downpours associated with thunder squalls which are more likely to occur in the afternoon or evening and to die out at night. Some longer spells of light rain or drizzle occur, however. Humidity is low during the very hot period before the arrival of the rains. Although the heat can be fierce and impose some stress at this time, it is no more unpleasant than the slightly cooler but more humid conditions during the rainy season.

The weather and climate of the northern part of this region are typical of the Sahara desert: very hot and dry during the period of high sun from May until September; rather cooler but still very warm and persistently sunny during the period of low sun. Any rare and sporadic rainfall is likely to occur during the hottest season as occasional thunderstorms break out when the rain-belt is at its most northerly position.

Mali is the most westerly of these four countries. It has an area rather larger than Egypt and is sparsely populated except in the south. About half of Mali lies in the southern Sahara and is virtually rainless. Climate and weather here are represented by the table for **Faya** in Chad (see p. 37). The table for **Timbuktu** shows conditions in central Mali at the northern limit of the summer rain-belt. This table shows the reduction in temperature and the increase of humidity in July after the arrival of the rains. The table for **Bamako** shows the heavier rainfall and longer rainy season experienced in the south of the country. When the harmattan is strong it is often dust-laden and this, combined with high temperatures and very low humidity, can be unpleasant. (See map p. 73.)

Bamako 1116 ft (340 m) 12°39′ N 7°58′ W 11 years   **MALI**

	Temperature °F			Temperature °C			Relative humidity		Precipitation			
	Highest recorded	Average daily	Lowest recorded	Highest recorded	Average daily	Lowest recorded	0530 hours	1130 hours	Average monthly		Average no. days with 0.04 in + (1 mm +)	
		max.	min.			max.	min.		%	%	in	mm	
J	107	91	61	48	42	33	16	9	38	19	0	0	0.1	J
F	117	97	66	51	47	36	19	11	33	18	0	0	0	F
M	109	102	71	58	43	39	22	14	41	23	0.1	3	0.7	M
A	111	103	76	65	44	39	24	18	63	36	0.6	15	2	A
M	115	102	76	66	46	39	24	19	70	40	2.9	74	5	M
J	105	94	73	64	41	34	23	18	74	49	5.4	137	10	J
J	102	89	71	64	39	32	22	18	91	70	11.0	279	16	J
A	96	87	71	63	36	31	22	17	94	73	13.7	348	17	A
S	97	89	71	63	36	32	22	17	93	68	8.1	206	12	S
O	104	93	71	59	40	34	22	15	73	41	1.7	43	6	O
N	110	94	65	53	43	34	18	12	70	34	0.6	15	1	N
D	104	92	62	47	40	33	17	8	69	40	0	0	0.1	D

Timbuktu 988 ft (301 m) 16°46′ N 3°01′ W 13 years   **MALI**

	Temperature °F			Temperature °C			Relative humidity		Precipitation			
	Highest recorded	Average daily	Lowest recorded	Highest recorded	Average daily	Lowest recorded	0600 hours	1200 hours	Average monthly		Average no. days with 0.04 in + (1 mm +)	
		max.	min.			max.	min.		%	%	in	mm	
J	102	87	55	41	39	31	13	5	39	22	0	0	0.1	J
F	107	93	58	42	42	34	14	6	33	19	0	0	0.2	F
M	115	100	66	48	46	38	19	9	34	18	0.1	3	1	M
A	118	107	72	57	48	42	22	14	27	15	0	0	0.3	A
M	118	110	78	66	48	43	26	19	34	18	0.2	5	2	M
J	119	109	80	68	48	43	27	20	55	31	0.9	23	5	J
J	119	103	77	66	48	39	25	19	74	45	3.1	79	9	J
A	111	97	75	67	44	36	24	19	83	57	3.2	81	9	A
S	115	103	76	68	46	39	24	20	76	45	1.5	38	5	S
O	113	104	73	63	45	40	23	17	50	23	0.1	3	2	O
N	109	98	65	47	43	37	18	8	36	17	0	0	0	N
D	102	89	56	42	39	32	13	6	35	19	0	0	0	D

MAURITANIA

A large but very sparsely populated country of West Africa, Mauritania occupies the western part of the Sahara desert with a coastline on the Atlantic Ocean and landborders with the former Spanish Sahara (West Sahara) territory on the north, with Algeria and Mali on the east, and with Senegal on the south.

Situated between 15° and 27° N it has a very hot, dry climate for most of the year. The southern half of the country has some unreliable and sparse rainfall between June and October, when southwesterly winds (the West African monsoon) bring moisture-laden air from the South Atlantic. At this time of year there is more cloud and the air is rather humid. During the rest of the year the prevailing winds are from the northeast, bringing very dry and sometimes dusty, hazy air from the northern Sahara. This is the harmattan of West Africa which has a very low humidity.

The north of the country is virtually rainless but occasional rare downpours can occur at any season. As the table for **Nouakchott** shows, there is some rain between July and October; this table is representative of the Atlantic coast of Mauritania. In the extreme south of the country annual rainfall averages between 12 and 15 in (300 and 375 mm) but is very variable from year to year. This is insufficient for cultivation as it comes at the hottest time of the year. Sunshine amounts are high throughout the year, averaging from eight to ten hours a day. They are least in midwinter when the days are shorter, but are also reduced in midsummer since this is the season when there is more cloud in the humid southwesterly winds.

For much of the year the climate is too hot and dry by day to be pleasant. The slightly cooler conditions on the coast are a result of daily sea breezes, but this is partly offset by the higher humidity.

MAURITANIA — Nouakchott 69 ft (21 m) 18°07′ N 15°36′ W 5 years

	Temperature °F			Temperature °C				Relative humidity		Precipitation		
	Highest recorded	Average daily	Lowest recorded	Highest recorded	Average daily	Lowest recorded		0500 hours	1100 hours	Average monthly		Average no. days with 0.04 in + (1 mm +)
		max.	min.			max.	min.		%	%	in	mm	
J	96	85	57	45	36	29	14	7	51	31	0	0	0.1	J
F	103	87	59	49	39	31	15	9	54	30	0.1	3	0.2	F
M	106	89	63	51	41	32	17	11	65	30	0	0	0.1	M
A	109	90	64	54	43	32	18	12	68	32	0	0	0.1	A
M	115	93	69	58	46	34	21	14	73	35	0	0	0.1	M
J	114	92	73	64	46	33	23	18	79	48	0.1	3	0.3	J
J	109	89	74	70	43	32	23	21	85	63	0.5	13	1	J
A	108	90	75	68	42	32	24	20	88	69	4.1	104	3	A
S	111	93	75	71	44	34	24	22	85	59	0.9	23	3	S
O	109	91	71	63	43	33	22	17	73	41	0.4	10	1	O
N	107	89	65	56	42	32	18	13	64	35	0.1	3	0.2	N
D	98	83	56	44	37	28	13	7	58	34	0	0	0.3	D

Morocco, a country a little smaller than France, occupies the northwestern corner of Africa. With a coastline both on the Atlantic and the Mediterranean it commands the southern shores of the narrow Straits of Gibraltar. It includes parts of the same three relief areas shown for Algeria on p. 24. There is a narrow coastal belt with a typical Mediterranean climate; an interior region of high mountains and plateaux; and a southern fringe on the margin of the Sahara desert. Morocco has a long eastern border with Algeria and a short southern border with the disputed territory of West Sahara (formerly Spanish Sahara).

The northern coast of Morocco and the interior mountains, the Rif, have a Mediterranean climate similar to that described for Algeria. Northwestern Morocco, especially the Rif mountains, is exposed to Atlantic depressions in winter and rainfall is moderately heavy. The Atlantic coast as far south as Agadir receives over 8 in (200 mm) of rain in winter but farther south the climate becomes progressively drier and the Sahara desert extends to the coast. Rainfall increases to over 16 in (400 mm) north of Casablanca.

Sea and air temperatures on the Atlantic coast are kept lower than along the Mediterranean coast by the cool waters of the Canaries current. Along this coast summer temperatures are significantly cooler than inland and the cold offshore water causes some cloud and fog in summer. Winters on the Atlantic coast are very mild and snow is unknown. The table for **Rabat** illustrates conditions on this coast.

Inland in the high Atlas mountains the weather and climate are much influenced by height. The Atlas mountains here are at their grandest with the highest point rising to 13,655 ft (4163 m). Winter snowfall can be heavy and the highest areas are snow-covered well into the summer. Inland at lower levels the summers are very hot while in winter and spring, winds blowing off the mountains can cause some very chilly days. At medium altitudes the climate of Morocco is healthy and very pleasant around the year. Summers are hot but the humidity is quite low while the winters are generally mild and sunny despite some spells of changeable weather (see the table for **Marrakech**).

The climate of the Saharan region of Morocco is similar to that described for Algeria on p. 25 except that, in the south where the desert reaches the coast, summer temperatures are moderated by the cool ocean waters and persistent daytime sea breezes. Here winter temperatures are also milder than inland.

Daily hours of sunshine on the Atlantic coast average nine to ten hours as compared with up to twelve inland in the desert. Cloud in the Atlas mountains also reduces summer sunshine to some extent. In winter, sunshine hours range from five to six a day in the north to as many as eight south of Agadir. (See map p. 24.)

Marrakech 1509 ft (460 m) 31°36′ N 8°01′ W 34 years

	Temperature °F			Temperature °C			Relative humidity		Precipitation			
	Highest recorded	Average daily	Lowest recorded	Highest recorded	Average daily	Lowest recorded	0530 hours	1130 hours	Average monthly		Average no. days with 0.004 in + (0.1 mm +)	
		max.	min.			max.	min.		%	%	in	mm	
J	83	65	40	28	28	18	4	−2	90	63	1.0	25	7	J
F	87	68	43	27	31	20	6	−3	88	58	1.1	28	5	F
M	100	74	48	33	38	23	9	1	87	53	1.3	33	6	M
A	102	79	52	36	39	26	11	2	83	47	1.2	31	6	A
M	112	84	57	44	44	29	14	7	77	42	0.6	15	2	M
J	114	92	62	48	46	33	17	9	74	41	0.3	8	1	J
J	120	101	67	54	49	38	19	12	69	36	0.1	3	1	J
A	117	100	68	57	47	38	20	14	69	37	0.1	3	1	A
S	113	92	63	51	45	33	17	11	74	40	0.4	10	3	S
O	101	83	57	40	38	28	14	4	77	45	0.9	23	4	O
N	95	73	49	33	35	23	9	1	80	49	1.2	31	3	N
D	81	66	42	29	27	19	6	−2	84	57	1.2	31	7	D

Rabat 213 ft (65 m) 34°00′ N 6°50′ W 35 years

	Temperature °F			Temperature °C			Relative humidity		Precipitation			
	Highest recorded	Average daily	Lowest recorded	Highest recorded	Average daily	Lowest recorded	0530 hours	1130 hours	Average monthly		Average no. days with 0.004 in + (0.1 mm +)	
		max.	min.			max.	min.		%	%	in	mm	
J	81	63	46	33	27	17	8	1	89	72	2.6	66	9	J
F	87	65	47	34	31	18	8	1	90	67	2.5	64	8	F
M	95	68	49	34	35	20	9	1	88	65	2.6	66	10	M
A	100	71	52	40	38	22	11	4	89	60	1.7	43	7	A
M	106	74	55	43	41	23	13	6	89	61	1.1	28	6	M
J	105	78	60	45	41	26	16	7	87	60	0.3	8	2	J
J	118	82	63	53	48	28	17	12	88	59	0	0	0.3	J
A	113	83	64	50	45	28	18	10	91	61	0	0	0.3	A
S	111	81	62	47	44	27	17	8	92	62	0.4	10	2	S
O	102	77	58	44	39	25	14	7	89	65	1.9	48	6	O
N	99	70	53	38	37	21	12	3	89	67	3.3	84	9	N
D	83	65	48	32	28	18	9	0	87	68	3.4	86	10	D

Mozambique is three times the size of Great Britain. It is situated on the east coast of southern Africa between 11° and 27° S with a coastline of over 1200 miles (1900 km). It is bordered on the west by Malawi, Zimbabwe and South Africa. Although it extends outside the tropics, in the extreme south the whole country has a typically tropical climate. The extensive coastal lowlands are warm to hot most of the year, while the interior plateau and the hills along the border with Malawi and Zimbabwe are mild to warm even in the cooler dry season from April to September. The warm Mozambique current which flows southwards along the coast is an important influence on the climate of the country. The whole country experiences a single rainy season at the time of high sun when the inter-tropical belt of cloud and rain is farthest south.

The wettest regions are the highlands on the Malawi and Zimbabwe borders and the southeast coast between Beira and Maputo which are more exposed to the southeast trade winds throughout the year. Here annual rainfall is between 40 and 60 in (1000 and 1500 mm). The driest areas are the lowlands inland, particularly the Zambesi valley, with between 20 and 30 in (500 and 750 mm). In some places the annual rainfall is as low as 15 in (375 mm).

In the south most of the rain falls between December and March but farther north this period lengthens by a few weeks. The coast of northern Mozambique is occasionally affected by tropical cyclones in the Indian Ocean. These move south between Madagascar and the mainland but the majority pass east of Madagascar and hardly affect Mozambique. These cyclones bring heavy rain and strong winds which can cause extensive damage. One reason for the comparatively low rainfall over much of the coastal lowlands is the shelter provided by the large mountainous island of Madagascar which is fully exposed to the moist southeast trades. The eastern side of Madagascar is particularly wet as compared with Mozambique.

Temperatures on the coast and in some lowland regions can be rather sultry and oppressive and this is made worse by the high humidity during the rainy season. Although the days may be hot inland at higher levels, there is a welcome drop of temperature at night and humidity is lower. Over most of the country the weather is fairly sunny for much of the year with daily sunshine hours averaging from seven to nine hours. The tables for **Maputo** and **Sofala** are representative of conditions on the coast in the drier south and in the wetter centre respectively. That for **Tete** shows the higher temperatures and lower humidity found inland; also the low rainfall typical of some inland areas. (See map p. 81.)

Maputo 194 ft (59 m) 25°58′ S 32°36′ E 42 years   MOZAMBIQUE

	Temperature °F			Temperature °C			Relative humidity		Precipitation		
	Highest recorded	Average daily	Lowest recorded	Highest recorded	Average daily	Lowest recorded	0900 hours	1500 hours	Average monthly		Average no. days with 0.04 in +
		max.	min.			max.	min.		%	%	in	mm	(1 mm +)
J	110	86	71	61	43	30	22	16	72	66	5.1	130	9	J
F	103	87	71	62	39	31	22	17	73	65	4.9	125	8	F
M	104	85	69	60	40	29	21	16	75	67	4.9	125	9	M
A	102	83	66	52	39	28	19	11	72	63	2.1	53	5	A
M	101	80	60	46	38	27	16	8	71	61	1.1	28	3	M
J	94	77	56	46	34	25	13	8	70	57	0.8	20	2	J
J	96	76	55	45	36	24	13	7	71	59	0.5	13	2	J
A	100	78	57	47	38	26	14	8	68	60	0.5	13	2	A
S	114	80	61	49	46	27	16	9	65	63	1.1	28	3	S
O	113	82	64	53	45	28	18	12	65	66	1.9	48	5	O
N	112	83	67	52	44	28	19	11	67	67	3.2	81	7	N
D	112	85	69	59	44	29	21	15	69	66	3.8	97	9	D

MOZAMBIQUE

Sofala 28 ft (9 m) 19°50′ S 34°51′ E 39 years

		Temperature °F				Temperature °C			Relative humidity		Precipitation			
	Highest recorded	Average daily		Lowest recorded	Highest recorded	Average daily		Lowest recorded	0930 hours	1530 hours	Average monthly		Average no. days with 0.04 in + (1 mm +)	
		max.	min.			max.	min.		%	%	in	mm		
J	108	89	75	63	42	32	24	17	73	66	10.9	277	12	J
F	100	89	75	61	38	32	24	16	75	65	8.4	213	11	F
M	100	87	74	64	38	31	23	18	77	65	10.1	257	13	M
A	99	86	71	61	37	30	22	16	77	64	4.2	107	8	A
M	97	82	65	55	36	28	18	13	78	63	2.2	56	6	M
J	92	79	61	48	33	26	16	9	80	63	1.3	33	5	J
J	95	77	61	49	35	25	16	9	81	65	1.2	31	4	J
A	96	78	62	50	36	26	17	10	78	66	1.1	28	3	A
S	103	82	65	55	39	28	18	13	73	66	0.8	20	3	S
O	107	87	71	56	42	31	22	13	68	66	5.2	132	3	O
N	109	87	72	61	43	31	22	16	68	67	5.3	135	7	N
D	106	88	73	63	41	31	23	17	70	66	9.2	234	10	D

MOZAMBIQUE

Tete 456 ft (139 m) 16°11′ S 33°35′ E 12 years

		Temperature °F				Temperature °C			Relative humidity		Precipitation			
	Highest recorded	Average daily		Lowest recorded	Highest recorded	Average daily		Lowest recorded	0900 hours	2100 hours	Average monthly		Average no. days with 0.04 in + (1 mm +)	
		max.	min.			max.	min.		%	%	in	mm		
J	110	95	69	45	43	35	21	7	70	58	6.0	152	8	J
F	109	94	71	46	43	34	22	8	73	59	6.4	163	9	F
M	109	91	69	48	43	33	21	9	72	62	4.6	117	6	M
A	110	93	68	52	43	34	20	11	71	54	0.5	13	1	A
M	104	91	63	50	40	33	17	10	72	64	0.1	3	0.9	M
J	102	86	59	45	39	30	15	7	71	66	0.1	3	0.4	J
J	97	84	57	46	36	29	14	8	69	65	0.1	3	0.4	J
A	104	88	60	49	40	31	16	9	68	61	0.1	3	0.2	A
S	111	95	64	50	44	35	18	10	63	50	0	0	0.4	S
O	113	101	69	50	45	38	21	10	60	45	0.3	8	0.7	O
N	115	99	71	50	46	37	22	10	64	50	1.1	28	2	N
D	111	98	70	52	44	37	21	11	68	53	3.9	99	6	D

Namibia, formerly called Southwest Africa, is a large territory almost two thirds the size of the Republic of South Africa. It is bordered by Angola on the north, by Botswana on the east and by South Africa on the south. It is very sparsely populated and most of it is desert or semi-desert. It includes a large part of the Kalahari desert. The general features of weather and climate are described on p. 81 for South Africa. Namibia includes part of the climatic regions named as 'The western interior' and 'The Namib'.

The table for **Walvis Bay** is representative of the very arid coastal strip where temperatures are kept quite low all round the year by the cold Benguela current. That for **Windhoek** is representative of the higher parts of the interior where much land is above 3000 ft (900 m). The interior receives some scanty but unreliable summer rain which increases eastwards and northwards. Like most interior deserts Namibia's has a very sunny climate but, on the coast, cloud and fog reduce the sunshine. (See map p. 81.)

Walvis Bay 24 ft (7 m) 22°56′ S 14°30′ E 20 years   **NAMIBIA**

	Temperature °F			Temperature °C			Relative humidity		Precipitation			
	Highest recorded	Average daily	Lowest recorded	Highest recorded	Average daily	Lowest recorded	0730 hours	1400 hours	Average monthly		Average no. days with 0.01 in + (0.25 mm +)	
		max.	min.			max.	min.		%	%	in	mm	
J	100	73	59	45	38	23	15	7	91	73	0	0	1	J
F	97	74	60	45	36	23	16	7	92	73	0.2	5	1	F
M	97	74	59	45	36	23	15	7	95	74	0.3	8	2	M
A	103	75	55	43	39	24	13	6	89	66	0.1	3	1	A
M	104	74	52	35	40	23	11	2	88	68	0.1	3	1	M
J	97	74	48	35	36	23	9	2	78	64	0	0	0.8	J
J	98	70	47	25	37	21	8	−4	83	65	0	0	1	J
A	99	68	46	34	37	20	8	1	89	73	0.1	3	3	A
S	100	66	48	32	38	19	9	0	90	69	0	0	2	S
O	97	67	51	32	36	19	11	0	91	72	0	0	1	O
N	95	71	54	43	35	22	12	6	90	71	0	0	1	N
D	91	72	57	45	33	22	14	7	90	72	0	0	1	D

		Temperature °F			Temperature °C				Relative humidity		Precipitation			
	Highest recorded	Average daily		Lowest recorded	Highest recorded	Average daily		Lowest recorded	0800 hours	1400 hours	Average monthly		Average no. days with 0.04 in + (1 mm +)	
		max.	min.			max.	min.		%	%	in	mm		
J	97	85	63	49	36	29	17	9	50	27	3.0	76	8	J
F	94	83	61	44	34	28	16	7	62	35	2.9	74	8	F
M	94	80	59	39	34	27	15	4	59	33	3.1	79	8	M
A	87	77	55	36	31	25	13	2	55	30	1.6	41	4	A
M	89	72	48	29	32	22	9	−2	51	24	0.3	8	0.9	M
J	79	68	44	27	26	20	7	−3	50	24	0	0	0.3	J
J	77	68	43	27	25	20	6	−3	42	18	0	0	0.1	J
A	85	73	47	25	29	23	8	−4	34	14	0	0	0.1	A
S	91	77	53	31	33	25	12	−1	28	11	0.1	3	0.3	S
O	93	84	59	35	34	29	15	2	27	13	0.4	10	2	O
N	96	84	59	33	36	29	15	1	34	18	0.9	23	3	N
D	97	86	62	38	36	30	17	3	41	23	1.9	48	6	D

Niger is a relatively large country, about the size of Egypt, but with a small and sparse population. Situated in the middle of North Africa it has landborders with seven countries and includes a large part of the Sahara desert. The southern part of the country is in the Sahel belt of interior West Africa and has a sparse to moderate, but rather unreliable, rainfall. (See map p. 81.)

The general features of the weather and climate of this part of Africa are described for Mali on p. 62. The table for **Niamey** is representative of the southern part of Niger and here the climate is very similar to that of northern Nigeria. There is a marked rainy season at the period of high sun. Average rainfall is moderate but rather unreliable. Between this southern region and the northern border rainfall progressively decreases both in amount and reliability. The northern districts are virtually rainless. Weather and climate here are well represented by the tables for **Faya** in Chad (p. 37) and **In Salah** in Algeria (p. 27). In the centre of the country where rainfall is sparse and unreliable, conditions are represented by the table for **Timbuktu** in Mali (p. 63).

Niamey 709 ft (216 m) 13°31′ N 2°06′ E 10 years

	Temperature °F			Temperature °C			Relative humidity		Precipitation			
	Highest recorded	Average daily	Lowest recorded	Highest recorded	Average daily	Lowest recorded	0600 hours	1200 hours	Average monthly		Average no. days with 0.04 in + (1 mm +)	
		max.	min.			max.	min.		%	%	in	mm	
J	102	93	58	47	39	34	14	8	32	12	0	0	0	J
F	109	98	65	50	43	37	18	10	28	12	0	0	0.1	F
M	112	105	71	51	44	41	22	11	26	11	0.2	5	0.2	M
A	114	108	77	62	46	42	25	17	37	18	0.3	8	0.6	A
M	114	106	80	67	46	41	27	19	61	35	1.3	33	4	M
J	114	101	77	67	46	38	25	19	74	44	3.2	81	6	J
J	104	94	74	64	40	34	23	18	83	56	5.2	132	9	J
A	100	89	73	63	38	32	23	17	91	68	7.4	188	12	A
S	105	93	73	67	41	34	23	19	89	60	3.7	94	7	S
O	109	101	74	61	43	38	23	16	78	40	0.5	13	1	O
N	109	101	65	53	43	38	18	12	52	17	0	0	0	N
D	104	94	59	48	40	34	15	9	39	14	0	0	0	D

NIGERIA

(Including a description of the climate and weather of the Ivory Coast, Ghana, Togo and Benin)

Nigeria is the largest of five West African countries, all of which have a south coast on the Gulf of Guinea at about 5° N and extend inland to between 10° and 14° N. All five countries have a broadly similar geography: an extensive, low, coastal plain which rises gradually inland to hill and plateaux country with an average height of between 1500 and 3000 ft (460 and 920 m). Only in the southeast of Nigeria are there mountains significantly higher than this.

This whole area, three times the size of France and over twice as large as the state of Texas, has a similar sequence of weather around the year. The same broad climatic belts extend from west to east through all five countries. The following general description and explanation of these climates can be taken as applying to all these countries. Where there are significant local variations or exceptions they are mentioned in the entry for each country.

The key to an understanding of the weather and climate of this region is the annual migration of the inter-tropical belt of cloud and associated heavy rain, high humidity and lower temperature; drier and sunnier weather, with higher temperatures, prevails on the northern side of this belt of cloud and rain. The belt of cloud and rain lies on the southern side of the discontinuity between the southwesterly to westerly winds of the Guinea monsoon and the northeast trade winds, or harmattan, which are dry and bring higher temperatures. This discontinuity, often called the inter-tropical convergence, lies over or near the coast in December and January and moves north to about 20° N by July and August. It then returns southwards rather more rapidly between September and December. Thus much of this region experiences two rainy periods as the inter-tropical convergence moves north or south; but in the north of these countries the two rainy seasons merge to give a single wet season between July and September. This can be seen by looking at the tables for **Kano** in northern Nigeria and **Tamale** in northern Ghana. Both these places have a single rainy season just after the time of high sun.

On the other hand, places on or near the coast have two rainy seasons with maximum falls in May or June and again in October. Although in the south near the coast no months are completely dry, there are two relatively drier periods between December and February and between July and September. In the north of the region there is a single long dry season between October and April. At this time there is very little rain in the north and temperatures are warm to hot with a very low relative humidity. During this season the harmattan, which is often dust-laden, blows from the northeast day after day. During the period December to February the harmattan penetrates south so that the whole region, except a strip along the coast, is affected by it. For most of the year the coast has southwesterly winds; but on a few days these are overcome by the harmattan which brings its higher temperatures, lower humidity and dusty air right to the coast. This brings some relief from the heat and humidity which prevails here for most of the year.

On the coast the period from December to February is least likely to experience rainy days and this dry period is more clearly recognizable than the 'little dry season' between July and September. Inland, and particularly towards the north of these countries, the time of arrival of the rains and the amount of rain may vary from year to year. The wettest areas of this region are usually those on or just inland of the coast. The driest regions are those farthest north and inland but there are some exceptions which are mentioned under the individual country headings.

Nigeria is the largest of the countries in the region described above. It is about one and a half times as large as the state of Texas and extends northwards to 14° N. It is bordered by Benin on the west, by Niger on the north and by Cameroon on the east.

The wettest parts of Nigeria are the coastal region of the Niger delta and the mountainous border with Cameroon in the southeast. Here the annual rainfall exceeds 100 in (2500 mm), as compared with 50–60 in (1250–1500 mm) in much of the west and centre of Nigeria. In the far north annual rainfall is below 40 in (1000 mm) almost everywhere and in places it is as low as 24 in (600 mm). Here the rainy season is rather short and the dry period is prolonged.

The table for **Lagos** is representative of the southern coast of Nigeria, that for **Ibadan** of the inland districts of the centre and west and that for **Kano** of the dry northern region. Temperatures rise very high in the north during the period March to May before the arrival of the rains, but the rainy season may be equally unpleasant because of the higher humidity brought by the moist southwesterly winds. On the coast high humidity and constant high temperatures with very little relief make the weather rather uncomfortable throughout the year.

Hours of sunshine average from six hours a day during the rainy season to as many as ten in the dry season in the north of the country. Near the coast they average about three hours a day in the wettest months to six or seven hours during the driest period of the year.

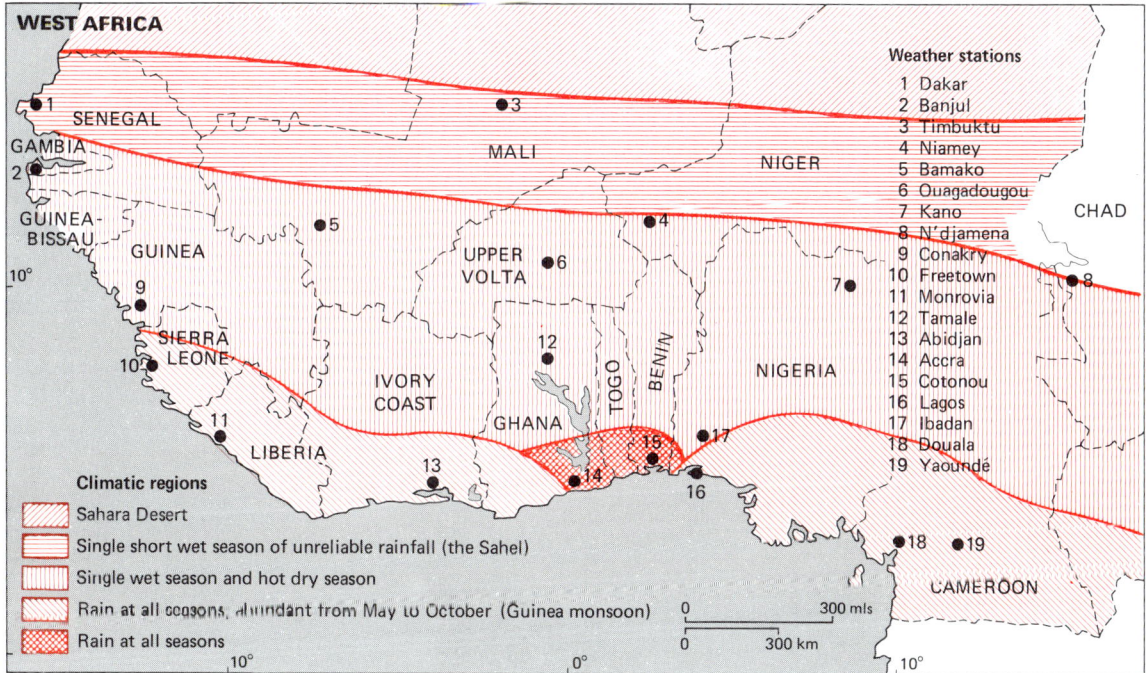

WEST AFRICA

Weather stations
1 Dakar
2 Banjul
3 Timbuktu
4 Niamey
5 Bamako
6 Ouagadougou
7 Kano
8 N'djamena
9 Conakry
10 Freetown
11 Monrovia
12 Tamale
13 Abidjan
14 Accra
15 Cotonou
16 Lagos
17 Ibadan
18 Douala
19 Yaoundé

SENEGAL
GAMBIA
GUINEA-BISSAU
GUINEA
SIERRA LEONE
LIBERIA
IVORY COAST
MALI
UPPER VOLTA
GHANA
TOGO
BENIN
NIGER
NIGERIA
CHAD
CAMEROON

Climatic regions
Sahara Desert
Single short wet season of unreliable rainfall (the Sahel)
Single wet season and hot dry season
Rain at all seasons, abundant from May to October (Guinea monsoon)
Rain at all seasons

0   300 mls
0   300 km

Ibadan 656 ft (200 m) 7°26′ N 3°54′ E 14 years

	Temperature °F			Temperature °C			Relative humidity		Precipitation		
	Highest recorded	Average daily	Lowest recorded	Highest recorded	Average daily	Lowest recorded	0630 hours	1230 hours	Average monthly		Average no. days with 0.04 in + (1 mm +)
		max.	min.			max.	min.		%	%	in	mm	
J	99	91	70	50	37	33	21	10	94	51	0.3	8	1	J
F	102	93	71	54	39	34	22	12	92	49	0.9	23	2	F
M	101	93	73	64	38	34	23	18	95	54	3.0	76	5	M
A	100	91	73	65	38	33	23	18	95	60	4.9	125	9	A
M	95	89	72	64	35	32	22	18	96	67	5.7	145	11	M
J	91	85	71	64	33	29	22	18	97	74	6.4	163	12	J
J	89	82	70	61	31	28	21	16	97	78	5.2	132	12	J
A	89	81	69	60	31	27	21	16	97	78	2.9	74	10	A
S	96	84	71	63	36	29	22	17	97	75	6.7	170	15	S
O	92	86	72	65	33	30	22	18	98	70	6.0	152	12	O
N	94	89	71	58	34	32	22	14	97	63	1.7	43	4	N
D	95	91	69	57	35	33	21	14	96	56	0.4	10	1	D

	Temperature °F			Temperature °C				Relative humidity		Precipitation			
	Highest recorded	Average daily	Lowest recorded	Highest recorded	Average daily		Lowest recorded	0630 hours	1530 hours	Average monthly		Average no. days with 0.01 in + (0.25 mm +)	
		max.	min.			max.	min.		%	%	in	mm		
J	106	86	55	43	41	30	13	6	40	13	0	0	0	J
F	110	91	59	48	43	33	15	9	36	13	0	0	0	F
M	112	98	67	50	44	37	19	10	33	11	0.1	3	0	M
A	114	101	75	57	46	38	24	14	47	14	0.4	10	1	A
M	111	99	75	62	44	37	24	17	72	33	2.7	69	8	M
J	105	94	73	62	41	34	23	17	81	43	4.6	117	8	J
J	98	88	71	62	37	31	22	17	90	59	8.1	206	14	J
A	97	85	70	61	36	29	21	16	94	68	12.2	310	19	A
S	100	88	70	62	38	31	21	17	93	57	5.6	142	12	S
O	106	94	67	56	41	34	19	13	82	32	0.5	13	1	O
N	108	92	61	51	42	33	16	11	52	16	0	0	0	N
D	110	87	56	45	43	31	13	7	45	14	0	0	0	D

	Temperature °F			Temperature °C				Relative humidity		Precipitation			
	Highest recorded	Average daily	Lowest recorded	Highest recorded	Average daily		Lowest recorded	0800 hours	1400 hours	Average monthly		Average no. days with 0.01 in + (0.25 mm +)	
		max.	min.			max.	min.		%	%	in	mm		
J	95	88	74	63	35	31	23	17	84	65	1.1	28	2	J
F	96	89	77	66	36	32	25	19	83	69	1.8	46	3	F
M	99	89	78	60	37	32	26	16	82	72	4.0	102	7	M
A	99	89	77	69	37	32	25	21	81	72	5.9	150	10	A
M	104	87	76	69	40	31	24	21	83	76	10.6	269	16	M
J	93	85	74	69	34	29	23	21	87	80	18.1	460	20	J
J	93	83	74	68	34	28	23	20	87	80	11.0	279	16	J
A	96	82	73	67	36	28	23	19	85	76	2.5	64	10	A
S	94	83	74	68	34	28	23	20	86	77	5.5	140	14	S
O	96	85	74	69	36	29	23	21	86	76	8.1	206	16	O
N	99	88	75	70	37	31	24	21	85	72	2.7	69	7	N
D	99	88	75	66	37	31	24	19	86	68	1.0	25	2	D

This small Central African country situated at about 2° S is similar in size to its neighbour Burundi (or Israel). Like Burundi it is hilly and mountainous and has a very similar climate. Its climate and weather throughout the year are illustrated by the table for **Rubona** and also by that for **Kabale** in Uganda (p. 95).

Rubona 5592 ft (1706 m) 2°29′ S 29°46′ E 10 years   **RWANDA**

	Temperature °F			Temperature °C			Relative humidity	Precipitation			
	Highest recorded	Average daily		Lowest recorded	Highest recorded	Average daily		Lowest recorded	All hours	Average monthly		Average no. days with 0.004 in + (0.1 mm +)
		max.	min.			max.	min.		%	in	mm	
J	—	77	57	—	—	25	14	—	79	4.4	111	15	J
F	—	77	55	—	—	25	13	—	78	6.1	156	15	F
M	—	77	57	—	—	25	14	—	78	5.5	140	18	M
A	—	77	57	—	—	25	14	—	83	7.2	183	22	A
M	—	75	57	—	—	24	14	—	72	6.5	164	18	M
J		75	55	—	—	24	13	—	70	0.9	23	4	J
J	—	79	54	—	—	26	12	—	59	0.3	7	2	J
A	—	81	55	—	—	27	13	—	60	1.1	27	5	A
S	—	81	57	—	—	27	14	—	60	2.5	63	11	S
O	—	79	57	—	—	26	14	—	71	4.0	102	16	O
N	—	77	57	—	—	25	14	—	76	4.3	110	20	N
D	—	77	57	—	—	25	14	—	80	3.7	93	17	D

SENEGAL

(Including a description of the climate and weather of Gambia and Guinea-Bissau)

Senegal is on the west coast of Africa between 12° and 16° N. Its northern border with Mauritania is along the Senegal river. It has an eastern border with Mali and a southern border with Guinea and Guinea-Bissau.

Senegal has a tropical climate with a single short rainy season between June and September at the time of high sun. Temperatures are high throughout the year but there is a relatively cooler period from December to April during which rain is very rare. The following description of the climate and weather of Senegal is also applicable to Gambia and Guinea-Bissau. All three countries are low-lying with very little land higher than 650 ft (200 m) above sea level.

The chief controls over the climate of these countries are latitude and distance from the sea. Rainfall increases from north to south in Senegal. The north of the country is affected by the inter-tropical belt of cloud and rain between June and September; during these months rain only falls on twenty to thirty days and the average annual rainfall is about 12–14 in (300–350 mm). In the south annual rainfall increases to between 40 and 60 in (1000 and 1500 mm) and falls on between sixty and ninety days. Here the rainy season

extends into October. The table for **Dakar** shows that, in the centre of the country, rainfall amounts are between these two extremes. Northern Senegal, on the edge of the Sahara, experiences conditions similar to the Saharan districts of Mali and Mauritania.

There is a marked seasonal contrast between the wet season, when winds are from the southwest and west, blowing from the South Atlantic, and the dry season, when they blow from the northeast out of the Sahara. The southwesterlies are warm and humid while the northeasterly harmattan wind is hot and dry and frequently dust-laden. This contrast can be seen in the values for the relative humidity at **Dakar** and also those for **Banjul** in Gambia (p. 47); both these stations are on the coast and the humidity is increased by the frequent sea breezes. Inland the humidity is much lower during the time of the harmattan. Temperatures are also considerably higher inland than on the coast during the dry season, but they fall lower at night.

The climate of Senegal is most oppressive during the wet season, particularly on the coast where there is a combination of high humidity and high night-time temperatures. Hours of sunshine average nine to ten a day throughout the year; sunshine hours are lower on the coast where there is more cloud and higher during the dry season. (See map p. 73.)

SIERRA LEONE

(Including a description of the climate and weather of Guinea and Liberia)

The three countries of Sierra Leone, Guinea and Liberia lie on the west coast of Africa between 4° and 12° N. All have a coastline facing southwest towards the Atlantic Ocean and include an extensive coastal plain rising inland to a plateau area where heights exceed 3300 ft (1000 m). This similarity of situation and relief gives them a broadly similar climate.

In this part of Africa the inter-tropical belt of cloud and rain migrates northwards and southwards with the apparent movement of the overhead sun but lagging behind by some four to six weeks. From October to March, during the period of low sun, the weather is generally dry with many fine, hot, sunny days. The season of high sun, from April to September, is the rainy season. The rainfall increases to a peak in July and August and then decreases until rain has almost ceased by November. In the north of Guinea the rainy season is a little shorter than in Liberia to the south. Along the coast of these three countries, however, there is not much difference in the total annual rainfall which is everywhere heavy, between 160 and 180 in (3500 and 4000 mm). This can be seen by comparing the table for **Freetown**, in Sierra Leone, with those for **Conakry** in Guinea, and **Monrovia** in Liberia. Annual rainfall only

falls below 80 in (2000 m) inland in the extreme east of Guinea, near the border with Mali.

Temperatures are consistently high around the year on the coast and, during the dry season, rise even higher inland. During the rainy season the coastal region is most uncomfortable because of the high relative humidity which rarely drops below 80 per cent during the daytime. The climate of this part of Africa has for long had an unenviable reputation; Sierra Leone was known as 'the white man's grave'. The high death rate among Europeans living there was more attributable to tropical diseases than to the direct effects of the climate. There is no doubt, however, that the combination of constant high temperature and humidity makes this an uncomfortable climate. The higher temperatures inland are to some extent mitigated by the lower humidity. The harmattan, a persistent northeast wind, which blows during the dry season, is often dust-laden.

Sunshine amounts are rather low on the coast, particularly during the wet season when they average two to three hours a day. These figures rise inland, particularly in eastern Guinea. During the dry season they rise to eight to nine hours a day inland but in some places on the coast they may be as low as five to six.

The table for **Freetown** illustrates conditions around the year in the coastal districts of Sierra Leone. (See map p. 73.)

Dakar 131 ft (40 m) 14°42′ N 17°29′ W 16 years **SENEGAL**

		Temperature °F				Temperature °C				Relative humidity		Precipitation			
	Highest recorded	Average daily		Lowest recorded	Highest recorded	Average daily		Lowest recorded	0600 hours	1300 hours	Average monthly		Average no. days with 0.04 in + (1 mm +)		
		max.	min.			max.	min.		%	%	in	mm		
J	102	79	64	56	39	26	18	13	71	45	0	0	0	J
F	100	80	63	58	38	27	17	14	80	45	0	0	0.1	F
M	109	80	64	59	43	27	18	15	87	51	0	0	0.1	M
A	101	81	65	61	38	27	18	16	86	55	0	0	0	A
M	100	84	68	61	38	29	20	16	86	59	0	0	0	M
J	100	88	73	65	38	31	23	18	85	62	0.7	18	2	J
J	99	88	76	69	37	31	24	21	84	66	3.5	89	7	J
A	99	87	76	69	37	31	24	21	87	74	10.0	254	13	A
S	100	89	76	69	38	32	24	21	88	72	5.2	132	11	S
O	101	89	76	70	38	32	24	21	86	65	1.5	38	3	O
N	99	86	73	64	37	30	23	18	80	50	0.1	3	1	N
D	95	81	67	53	35	27	19	12	70	46	0.3	8	0.1	D

Freetown 37 ft (11 m) 8°30′ N 13°14′ W 14 years **SIERRA LEONE**

		Temperature °F				Temperature °C				Relative humidity		Precipitation			
	Highest recorded	Average daily		Lowest recorded	Highest recorded	Average daily		Lowest recorded	0800 hours	1400 hours	Average monthly		Average no. days with 0.01 in + (0.25 mm +)		
		max.	min.			max.	min.		%	%	in	mm		
J	91	85	75	68	33	29	24	20	82	67	0.5	13	0.8	J
F	93	86	76	70	34	30	24	21	80	67	0.1	3	0.7	F
M	95	86	77	70	35	30	25	21	81	69	0.5	13	2	M
A	95	87	77	70	35	31	25	21	81	71	2.2	56	6	A
M	94	86	77	69	34	30	25	21	83	74	6.3	160	15	M
J	92	86	75	68	33	30	24	20	86	76	11.9	302	23	J
J	90	83	74	69	32	28	23	21	89	81	35.2	894	27	J
A	88	82	73	68	31	28	23	20	91	82	35.5	902	28	A
S	90	83	74	69	32	28	23	21	90	81	24.0	610	25	S
O	91	85	74	67	33	29	23	19	87	77	12.2	310	23	O
N	94	85	75	68	34	29	24	20	85	75	5.2	132	12	N
D	89	85	76	67	32	29	24	19	82	71	1.6	41	4	D

SOMALI

The Somali Republic occupies the northeastern corner of Africa, often called the Horn of Africa. It is bordered on the west by Ethiopia and on the south by Kenya. It extends from 2° S to 12° N and has a long coastline on the Indian Ocean and Gulf of Aden.

For a country on or near the equator it has a surprisingly dry climate. Much of the country is desert or desert scrub. Almost no part has an annual rainfall exceeding 25 in (625 mm) and much of it receives less than 10 in (250 mm). In the north some rain occurs during the season of low sun when temperatures are a little lower, but this area is very dry for the rest of the year (see the table for **Berbera**). Elsewhere the rainy season is the period of high sun from April to September as in most of Ethiopia. The rains are very variable from year to year and drought is a constant problem for the nomadic pastoralists.

Temperatures along the east coast from Cape Guardafui southwards are prevented from rising too high by a cold offshore current which makes the sea surface temperature in this part of the Indian Ocean surprisingly low for tropical waters. This cold water may be one of the reasons for the very low rainfall in much of the country. The table for **Mogadishu** shows that temperatures vary little from month to month and relative humidity remains high.

By contrast, along the north coast very high temperatures are experienced between April and September as the offshore waters here are very warm. This part of Somali and the adjoining areas around the Gulf of Aden have a most uncomfortable climate at this time, being very hot and also humid on the coast. Inland it is even hotter but with lower humidity. Some places here have the highest mean annual temperatures in the world and there is a serious risk of heat exhaustion or even heatstroke during the hottest period.

Sunshine amounts are high in most of the country, averaging eight to ten hours a day around the year. They are lowest on the east coast during the rainy season when there is more cloud and some coastal fog as warm air passes over the cold sea surface.

Berbera 45 ft (14 m) 10°26′ N 45°02′ E 30 years   **SOMALI**

	Temperature °F			Temperature °C				Relative humidity		Precipitation			
	Highest recorded	Average daily		Lowest recorded	Highest recorded	Average daily		Lowest recorded	0600 hours	1500 hours	Average monthly		Average no. days with 0.04 in + (1 mm +)	
		max.	min.			max.	min.		%	%	in	mm		
J	94	84	68	58	34	29	20	14	87	69	0.3	8	0.6	J
F	92	84	71	60	33	29	22	16	87	70	0.1	3	0.6	F
M	95	86	73	62	35	30	23	17	86	71	0.2	5	0.5	M
A	108	89	77	66	42	32	25	19	89	73	0.5	13	0.7	A
M	112	96	80	69	44	36	27	21	80	66	0.3	8	0.8	M
J	117	107	86	72	47	42	30	22	51	46	0	0	0.1	J
J	116	107	88	69	47	42	31	21	45	43	0	0	0.3	J
A	116	106	87	68	47	41	31	20	44	46	0.1	3	0.5	A
S	114	103	84	64	46	39	29	18	52	50	0	0	0.4	S
O	107	92	76	62	42	33	24	17	78	65	0.1	3	0.2	O
N	98	88	71	61	37	31	22	16	81	66	0.2	5	0.3	N
D	96	85	68	59	36	29	20	15	84	68	0.2	5	0.4	D

Mogadishu 39 ft (12 m) 2°02′ N 45°21′ E 10 years   **SOMALI**

	Temperature °F			Temperature °C				Relative humidity		Precipitation			
	Highest recorded	Average daily		Lowest recorded	Highest recorded	Average daily		Lowest recorded	0800 hours	1400 hours	Average monthly		Average no. days with 0.004 in + (0.1 mm +)	
		max.	min.			max.	min.		%	%	in	mm		
J	94	86	73	68	34	30	23	20	80	78	0	0	0.3	J
F	89	86	74	65	32	30	23	18	78	75	0	0	0.3	F
M	91	88	76	68	33	31	24	20	78	75	0	0	1	M
A	97	90	78	68	36	32	26	20	78	75	2.3	58	5	A
M	94	89	77	65	34	32	25	18	82	77	2.3	58	7	M
J	90	85	74	68	32	29	23	20	83	79	3.8	97	14	J
J	89	83	73	59	32	28	23	15	84	80	2.5	64	20	J
A	86	83	73	60	30	28	23	16	85	80	1.9	48	11	A
S	89	84	74	64	32	29	23	18	84	80	1.0	25	7	S
O	90	86	76	65	32	30	24	18	82	78	0.9	23	5	O
N	90	87	75	69	32	31	24	21	81	78	1.6	41	5	N
D	93	86	75	68	34	30	24	20	81	78	0.5	13	2	D

SOUTH AFRICA

(Including a description of the weather and climate of Namibia, Botswana, Lesotho and Swaziland)

These countries occupy the southern portion of the African continent, approximately south of 18° S. The Republic of South Africa extends from 22° S to 35° S at Cape Agulhas, the most southerly point of the African continent. Most of this area and almost the whole of South Africa are thus extra-tropical. Much of the interior consists of extensive high plains, known in South Africa as 'veld', with an altitude between 3000 and 6000 ft (900 and 1800 m). The interior is divided from the narrow coastal plain by a steep escarpment (the Great Escarpment) forming lofty mountains in the east and south. The eastern shores of southern Africa are warmed by the Agulhas current which flows southwards from tropical latitudes; while the western shores are cooled by the Benguela current, flowing northwards from the cold southern ocean surrounding Antarctica. These influences of relief and ocean currents produce a distinctive pattern of climatic regions which cut across the political boundaries separating the Republic from its neighbours. The whole region has an area of just over 1 million square miles (2.6 million sq. km) of which the Republic comprises almost half.

The general features of the weather and climate of the whole area are described below together with an account of the influences which produce a pattern of very different climatic regions. Parts of all these climatic regions are found in the Republic. Brief notes on the distinctive features of the remaining countries are given for their own entries.

Both the southerly latitude and the altitude of the interior regions produce a temperate climate such that only the lowlying districts in the north, along the border with Zimbabwe and Mozambique, have a climate that is tropical. The southern part of South Africa is sufficiently far south to be influenced in winter by weather disturbances associated with the belt of westerly winds in the southern ocean. For this reason a small portion of the southwestern Cape Province, below the Great Escarpment, has a Mediterranean type of climate with mild, changeable winters, during which most of the annual rainfall occurs, and a warm to hot, sunny summer. Eastwards of **Cape Town** this merges into a region where some rain occurs in all months but where temperature conditions are similar. In the coastlands of Natal and the lowlands below the Great Escarpment up to the border with Mozambique, and including Swaziland, the climate becomes almost tropical; winters are warmer and summer is the wetter season, although rain falls throughout the year. This coast is exposed both to warm water offshore and the southeast trade winds for most of the year.

By contrast the west coast from about 32° S to the border of Namibia with Angola is a desert region with a remarkably small annual temperature range. This is because the cold Benguela current chills the air and produces atmospheric conditions unfavourable to rainfall; fog and low cloud are frequent along this coast.

In the interior of southern Africa there is a broad contrast between east and west. Total rainfall is greatest in the east and gradually decreases westwards so that much of the western Transvaal, Cape Province, Botswana and the whole of interior Namibia is semi-desert with a low and unreliable rainfall. The wettest regions are the eastern parts of the Transvaal, Orange Free State, Swaziland and Lesotho, where both altitude and exposure to the moist air coming off the Indian Ocean produce the heaviest and most reliable rainfall. Over the whole of this interior region rainfall comes mainly in the summer season, much of it in thundery downpours. Because of the altitude and the 'continental' influence there is a large daily and seasonal range of temperature so that frost is a frequent occurrence in winter and snow is by no means unknown above 5000 ft (1500 m). Winters are predominantly dry and sunny and the summers warm to hot.

The greater part of southern Africa has a very sunny climate with much fine, settled weather. The southern coastal regions have their most disturbed and changeable weather in winter and the eastern coastlands and the interior their most disturbed and rainy weather in summer. In few parts of southern Africa are the weather and climate unhealthy or likely to cause great discomfort or stress. Daily sunshine hours are high over most of South Africa, averaging eight to ten hours a day around the year. The cloudiest regions are the coast of Namibia and the coast of Natal, particularly in the summer months.

The eastern interior or high veld

Most of this area is above 4000 ft (1200 m) and comprises the greater part of the Transvaal, Orange Free State and the lower parts of Lesotho. This is the most developed part of South Africa. As the tables for **Pretoria**, **Johannesburg** and **Bloemfontein** show, the winters are dry and mild but with frequent cold nights. Summers are warm with more frequent rain, but temperatures are rarely excessively high. The low humidity and large number of sunshine hours make for a pleasant and healthy climate for most of the year.

The western interior

The chief feature of this large region is its low rainfall; much of it is semi-desert or even desert. It includes much of interior Cape Province; Botswana, except the extreme north; the western fringe of the Transvaal and the whole of interior Namibia. Apart from the low rainfall the general features of weather and climate are similar to those of the eastern interior. The tables for

Francistown in northern Botswana (p. 31) and **Windhoek** in the higher districts of Namibia (p. 70) are representative of much of the region.

The Namib or coastal desert

Weather and climate here are unusual and quite distinctive. The region receives very little rain and is a complete desert, but temperatures are kept low most of the time by the cold Benguela current. On a few days each month, particularly in winter, midday temperatures rise quite high when the berg wind blows from the interior. This is a föhn-type wind bringing very dry air which is heated as it descends to the coast. Apart from the rare shower of rain and the frequent coastal fog, the berg is almost the only weather feature of this arid region (see the table for **Walvis Bay** in Namibia, p. 69).

The Cape Mediterranean region

The coastal lowlands and southern slopes of the mountains around Cape Town have mild and generally wet winters with much changeable weather and dry, settled summers similar to the climate of much of the Mediterranean or California. Summers are not completely dry and occasional rainstorms occur. The table for **Cape Town** is representative of this region, but inland some sheltered areas are warmer and drier. This was the area first settled by Europeans in the seventeenth century; French Huguenot settlers introduced the grape vine which grows well in this climate.

The lowlands of the eastern Cape

Between **Cape Town** and the border with Natal the lowlands and hilly region below the Great Escarpment have weather and climate that is intermediate between that of the Cape Mediterranean and the eastern coastlands regions. The main difference is that rainfall is well distributed around the year and disturbed weather can occur in both winter and summer (see the table for **Port Elizabeth**).

The eastern coastlands and the low veld of Natal and Swaziland

This is the part of southern Africa where the climate comes nearest to being tropical. The summers are warm and humid on the coast, particularly towards the north in Zululand and Swaziland where conditions are similar to those found in southern Mozambique (see the table for **Maputo** on p. 67). Summer is the wettest season but some rain falls in all months. The table for **Durban** is representative of the coastal lowlands. The heat and humidity are here moderated by daily sea breezes but conditions are often sultry in summer. Winters are mild to warm. Inland, and at medium altitudes below the Great Escarpment, temperatures are lower, particularly in winter, but rainfall is greater (see the table for **Mbabane** in Swaziland, p. 88).

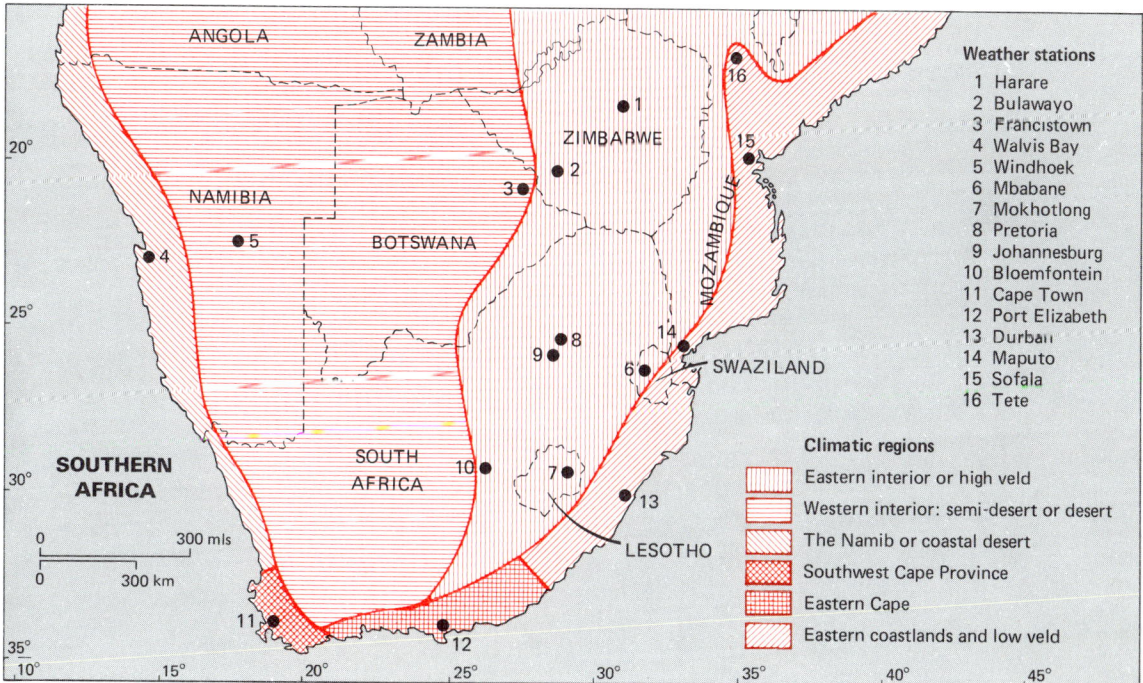

Weather stations

1 Harare
2 Bulawayo
3 Francistown
4 Walvis Bay
5 Windhoek
6 Mbabane
7 Mokhotlong
8 Pretoria
9 Johannesburg
10 Bloemfontein
11 Cape Town
12 Port Elizabeth
13 Durban
14 Maputo
15 Sofala
16 Tete

Climatic regions

Eastern interior or high veld
Western interior: semi-desert or desert
The Namib or coastal desert
Southwest Cape Province
Eastern Cape
Eastern coastlands and low veld

SOUTH AFRICA — Bloemfontein 4665 ft (1419 m) 29°07′ S 26°11′ E 14 years

		Temperature °F			Temperature °C			Relative humidity		Precipitation			
	Highest recorded	Average daily		Lowest recorded	Highest recorded	Average daily		Lowest recorded	0730 hours	1330 hours	Average monthly		Average no. days with 0.04 in + (1 mm +)	
		max.	min.			max.	min.		%	%	in	mm		
J	100	86	60	42	38	30	16	6	62	33	3.6	91	8	J
F	95	83	59	39	35	28	15	4	71	42	3.1	79	9	F
M	93	79	55	37	34	26	13	3	73	42	3.0	76	8	M
A	88	73	47	28	31	23	8	−2	72	38	2.2	56	6	A
M	81	66	39	22	27	19	4	−6	75	36	1.0	25	4	M
J	78	62	33	16	26	17	1	−9	74	33	0.3	8	1	J
J	73	61	33	17	23	16	1	−8	71	32	0.4	10	2	J
A	80	67	38	16	27	19	3	−9	60	29	0.8	20	2	A
S	90	73	43	21	32	23	6	−6	51	25	0.8	20	2	S
O	95	78	50	28	35	26	10	−2	55	28	2.0	51	5	O
N	94	81	54	35	34	27	12	2	53	27	2.6	66	5	N
D	97	85	58	37	36	29	14	3	56	29	2.4	61	7	D

SOUTH AFRICA — Cape Town 56 ft (17 m) 33°54′ S 18°32′ E 19 years

		Temperature °F			Temperature °C			Relative humidity		Precipitation			
	Highest recorded	Average daily		Lowest recorded	Highest recorded	Average daily		Lowest recorded	0700 hours	1300 hours	Average monthly		Average no. days with 0.04 in + (1 mm +)	
		max.	min.			max.	min.		%	%	in	mm		
J	99	78	60	44	37	26	16	7	72	54	0.6	15	3	J
F	100	79	60	41	38	26	16	5	77	54	0.3	8	2	F
M	103	77	58	42	39	25	14	6	85	57	0.7	18	3	M
A	102	72	53	38	39	22	12	3	90	60	1.9	48	6	A
M	95	67	49	31	35	19	9	−1	91	65	3.1	79	9	M
J	85	65	46	29	29	18	8	−2	91	64	3.3	84	9	J
J	84	63	45	28	29	17	7	−2	91	67	3.5	89	10	J
A	89	64	46	31	32	18	8	−1	90	65	2.6	66	9	A
S	93	65	49	33	34	18	9	1	87	62	1.7	43	7	S
O	90	70	52	34	32	21	11	1	79	58	1.2	31	5	O
N	93	73	55	40	34	23	13	4	74	56	0.7	18	3	N
D	100	76	58	41	38	24	14	5	71	54	0.4	10	3	D

Durban 16 ft (5 m) 29°50′ S 31°02′ E 15 years

	Temperature °F			Temperature °C			Relative humidity		Precipitation			
	Highest recorded	Average daily		Lowest recorded	Highest recorded	Average daily		Lowest recorded	0800 hours	1400 hours	Average monthly		Average no. days with 0.04 in + (1 mm +)
		max.	min.			max.	min.		%	%	in	mm	
J	92	81	69	57	33	27	21	14	77	72	4.3	109	10	J
F	89	81	69	59	32	27	21	15	79	73	4.8	122	9	F
M	90	80	68	58	32	27	20	14	80	74	5.1	130	9	M
A	99	78	64	51	37	26	18	11	78	71	3.0	76	7	A
M	95	75	57	44	35	24	14	7	72	66	2.0	51	4	M
J	90	73	53	41	32	23	12	5	69	61	1.3	33	3	J
J	92	72	52	39	33	22	11	4	71	61	1.1	28	3	J
A	89	72	55	41	32	22	13	5	75	68	1.5	38	4	A
S	107	73	59	46	42	23	15	8	74	71	2.8	71	4	S
O	87	75	62	50	31	24	17	10	75	73	4.3	109	10	O
N	102	77	65	51	39	25	18	11	76	74	4.8	122	11	N
D	90	79	67	56	32	26	19	13	75	73	4.7	119	10	D

Johannesburg 5463 ft (1665 m) 26°14′ S 28°09′ E 18 years

	Temperature °F			Temperature °C			Relative humidity		Precipitation			
	Highest recorded	Average daily		Lowest recorded	Highest recorded	Average daily		Lowest recorded	0800 hours	1400 hours	Average monthly		Average no. days with 0.04 in + (1 mm +)
		max.	min.			max.	min.		%	%	in	mm	
J	91	78	58	42	33	26	14	6	75	50	4.5	114	12	J
F	91	77	58	45	33	25	14	7	78	53	4.3	109	9	F
M	88	75	55	41	31	24	13	5	79	50	3.5	89	9	M
A	85	72	50	30	29	22	10	−1	74	44	1.5	38	4	A
M	78	66	43	22	26	19	6	−6	70	36	1.0	25	3	M
J	76	62	39	19	24	17	4	−7	70	33	0.3	8	1	J
J	74	63	39	19	23	17	4	−7	69	32	0.3	8	0.9	J
A	79	68	43	20	26	20	6	−7	64	29	0.3	8	0.9	A
S	86	73	48	27	30	23	9	−3	59	30	0.9	23	2	S
O	90	77	53	32	32	25	12	0	64	37	2.2	56	7	O
N	93	77	55	35	34	25	13	2	67	45	4.2	107	10	N
D	92	78	57	42	33	26	14	6	70	47	4.9	125	11	D

Port Elizabeth 190 ft (58 m) 33°59′ S 25°36′ E 14 years

	Temperature °F			Temperature °C				Relative humidity		Precipitation			
	Highest recorded	Average daily		Lowest recorded	Highest recorded	Average daily		Lowest recorded	0730 hours	1330 hours	Average monthly		Average no. days with 0.04 in + (1 mm +)	
		max.	min.			max.	min.		%	%	in	mm		
J	94	78	61	45	34	26	16	7	77	64	1.2	31	11	J
F	104	78	62	46	40	26	17	8	82	67	1.3	33	10	F
M	104	76	60	45	40	24	16	7	86	67	1.9	48	10	M
A	101	73	55	42	38	23	13	6	83	64	1.8	46	7	A
M	95	71	50	31	35	22	10	−1	83	58	2.4	61	4	M
J	86	68	45	33	30	20	7	1	83	56	1.8	46	3	J
J	90	67	45	32	32	19	7	0	82	57	1.9	48	4	J
A	98	68	47	32	37	20	8	0	83	59	2.0	51	5	A
S	103	68	50	35	39	20	10	2	81	65	2.3	58	7	S
O	97	70	54	39	36	21	12	4	78	68	2.2	56	11	O
N	104	72	57	42	40	22	14	6	76	66	2.2	56	12	N
D	96	75	59	44	36	24	15	7	74	65	1.7	43	13	D

Pretoria 4491 ft (1369 m) 25°45′ S 28°14′ E 13 years

	Temperature °F			Temperature °C				Relative humidity		Precipitation			
	Highest recorded	Average daily		Lowest recorded	Highest recorded	Average daily		Lowest recorded	0800 hours	1400 hours	Average monthly		Average no. days with 0.04 in + (1 mm +)	
		max.	min.			max.	min.		%	%	in	mm		
J	95	81	60	49	35	27	16	9	71	47	5.0	127	12	J
F	91	81	60	49	33	27	16	9	73	49	4.3	109	9	F
M	91	78	57	43	33	26	14	6	75	48	4.5	114	8	M
A	83	75	50	33	28	24	10	1	74	42	1.7	43	5	A
M	79	70	42	26	26	21	6	−3	74	36	0.9	23	3	M
J	77	66	37	24	25	19	3	−4	74	32	0.6	15	1	J
J	75	66	37	24	24	19	3	−4	72	31	0.3	8	1	J
A	83	71	42	28	28	22	6	−2	65	29	0.2	5	0.8	A
S	89	77	49	30	32	25	9	−1	57	29	0.8	20	2	S
O	92	80	55	37	33	27	13	3	60	34	2.2	56	7	O
N	96	80	57	41	36	27	14	5	65	40	5.2	132	11	N
D	95	82	59	43	35	28	15	6	68	45	5.2	132	10	D

The Sudan is the largest country in Africa with an area of nearly 1 million square miles (2.5 million sq. km). It lies entirely within the tropics between 22° and 4° N. The northern part of the country is desert and has a climate similar to that of the Egyptian, Libyan and Algerian Sahara. From **Khartoum** southwards to the southern border there is a progressive increase in the annual rainfall from 6 in to over 40 in (150 to over 1000 mm). Rainfall in the north is rare and very sporadic in time and place. The southern margin of the Sahara effectively is where annual rainfall is about 16 in (400 mm), since evaporation is high during the very hot summer.

The rainy season in the Sudan is almost everywhere the period between April and October although, in the extreme south, some rain may occur in any month. The length of the rainy season decreases from six to eight months in the south to as little as two months on the southern margins of the desert. The northern part of the Sudan experiences almost constant northeasterly winds throughout the year. In this dry air-mass humidity is low during the day and this makes the very high daytime temperatures more tolerable. During the cooler winter months temperatures may occasionally fall quite low and early morning frost is not unknown in the desert. There is a progressive increase of temperature to the maximum levels reached in July and August when, even at night, the thermometer rarely falls below 75° F (24° C).

During the rainy season in the south and centre of the Sudan southerly and southwesterly winds replace the northeasterlies. They bring slightly lower temperatures, higher humidity and more cloud. In the far south monthly temperatures vary little around the year and are highest just before the arrival of the rains. This moist southerly air has its origins in the South Atlantic or Congo basin and is the source of the Sudan's summer rain. During the rainy season there are spells of dry and sunny weather and even in the wettest areas rain only falls on about one day in three. The higher humidity during the rainy season does not make the lower temperatures any more comfortable. From April to September some heat stress can be experienced in all parts of the country.

An unpleasant and, on occasions, dangerous feature of the weather is the haboob, a local Arabic name for a violent but brief squall of wind which can raise a thick pall of dust or sand. Haboobs are most likely to occur in the afternoon and evening before, or at the beginning of, the rainy season. They often precede a thunderstorm which brings rain and lays the dust and sand.

The tables for **Khartoum** and **Port Sudan** are representative of the northern desert regions of the Sudan. On the coast of the Red Sea and in the hills behind there is some sporadic rainfall during the months October to December. The table for **Juba** shows conditions throughout the year in the extreme south. In the north annual sunshine amounts are almost the maximum possible, ranging from eleven to thirteen hours a day. Sunshine is least in the far south where, during the rainy season, it averages six to seven hours a day. During the dry season in the south sunshine averages nine to ten hours a day.

Temperature °F				Temperature °C				Relative humidity		Precipitation		
Highest recorded	Average daily		Lowest recorded	Highest recorded	Average daily		Lowest recorded	0800 hours	1400 hours	Average monthly		Average no. days with 0.04 in + (1 mm +)
	max.	min.			max.	min.		%	%	in	mm	
J 108	99	68	60	42	37	20	16	54	26	0.2	5	1 J
F 109	100	71	60	43	38	22	16	56	28	0.6	15	2 F
M 108	99	72	61	42	37	22	16	65	34	1.3	33	6 M
A 108	96	72	64	42	36	22	18	75	44	4.8	122	9 A
M 111	92	71	63	44	33	22	17	82	54	5.9	150	10 M
J 101	91	69	61	38	33	21	16	83	56	5.3	135	9 J
J 98	88	68	62	37	31	20	17	87	60	4.8	122	10 J
A 97	88	68	61	36	31	20	16	88	59	5.2	132	9 A
S 100	91	68	61	38	33	20	16	83	53	4.2	107	8 S
O 103	94	68	57	39	34	20	14	80	48	3.7	94	8 O
N 105	96	68	56	41	36	20	13	75	40	1.4	36	4 N
D 105	98	68	59	41	37	20	15	64	33	0.7	18	1 D

Temperature °F				Temperature °C				Relative humidity		Precipitation		
Highest recorded	Average daily		Lowest recorded	Highest recorded	Average daily		Lowest recorded	0800 hours	1400 hours	Average monthly		Average no. days with 0.04 in + (1 mm +)
	max.	min.			max.	min.		%	%	in	mm	
J 104	90	59	41	40	32	15	5	37	20	0	0	0 J
F 111	93	61	44	44	34	16	7	28	15	0	0	0 F
M 113	100	66	49	45	38	19	9	21	11	0	0	0 M
A 117	105	72	53	47	41	22	12	18	10	0	0	0 A
M 117	107	77	61	47	42	25	16	24	13	0.1	2.5	1 M
J 118	106	79	67	48	41	26	19	38	18	0.3	7	1 J
J 117	101	77	65	47	38	25	18	57	33	2.1	53	5 J
A 109	98	76	64	43	37	24	18	67	41	2.8	71	6 A
S 113	102	77	61	45	39	25	16	55	30	0.7	18	2 S
O 113	104	75	62	45	40	24	17	38	21	0.2	5	1 O
N 107	97	68	55	42	36	20	13	34	19	0	0	0 N
D 104	92	62	45	40	33	17	7	38	21	0	0	0 D

	Temperature °F				Temperature °C				Relative humidity		Precipitation			
	Highest recorded	Average daily		Lowest recorded	Highest recorded	Average daily		Lowest recorded	0830 hours	1430 hours	Average monthly		Average no. days with 0.04 in + (1 mm +)	
		max.	min.			max.	min.		%	%	in	mm		
J	89	81	68	50	32	27	20	10	66	65	0.2	5	0.9	J
F	90	81	66	52	32	27	19	11	65	66	0.1	3	0.3	F
M	95	84	67	53	35	29	19	12	64	63	0	0	0.1	M
A	101	89	71	58	38	32	22	14	56	59	0	0	0.2	A
M	111	95	75	59	44	35	24	15	45	51	0	0	0.2	M
J	117	102	78	68	47	39	26	20	37	45	0	0	0.1	J
J	117	106	83	68	47	41	28	20	39	44	0.3	8	0.8	J
A	117	105	84	67	47	41	29	19	41	47	0.1	3	0.6	A
S	113	100	79	57	45	38	26	14	47	51	0	0	0	S
O	107	93	76	61	42	34	24	16	66	64	0.4	10	1	O
N	96	88	74	52	36	31	23	11	68	64	1.7	43	4	N
D	93	83	71	53	34	28	22	12	69	66	0.9	23	2	D

SWAZILAND

This small landlocked country lies in 27° S between the Transvaal and Natal provinces of South Africa and Mozambique. It is rather smaller than Wales or Israel. The western part includes some of the high veld of the Transvaal region of South Africa and the country slopes eastwards until, along the Mozambique border, it is lowlying and almost tropical in climate. The table for Mbabane illustrates conditions throughout the year in the higher parts of the country, similar to those described on pp. 80–81 for South Africa. In the lower parts the climatic tables for **Durban** in South Africa (p. 83) and **Maputo** in Mozambique (p. 67) are more representative. (See map p. 81.)

SWAZILAND

Mbabane 3816 ft (1163 m) 26°19′ S 31°08′ E 20 years

	Temperature °F				Temperature °C				Relative humidity	Precipitation			
	Highest recorded	Average daily		Lowest recorded	Highest recorded	Average daily		Lowest recorded	0800 hours	Average monthly		Average no. days with 0.04 in + (1 mm +)	
		max.	min.			max.	min.		%	in	mm		
J	92	77	59	49	33	25	15	9	78	10.0	254	15	J
F	95	77	59	47	35	25	15	8	79	8.4	213	14	F
M	92	75	57	45	33	24	14	7	81	7.6	193	13	M
A	92	74	53	38	33	23	12	3	76	2.8	71	8	A
M	85	70	47	31	29	21	8	−1	71	1.3	33	4	M
J	85	66	42	25	29	19	6	−4	64	0.8	20	3	J
J	81	67	42	28	27	19	6	−2	64	0.9	23	3	J
A	89	70	45	23	32	21	7	−5	67	1.1	28	4	A
S	99	73	49	28	37	23	9	−2	59	2.4	61	7	S
O	96	75	54	38	36	24	12	3	68	5.0	127	12	O
N	96	76	56	40	36	24	13	4	73	6.7	170	14	N
D	97	77	58	46	36	25	14	8	76	8.2	208	16	D

Tanzania is the largest country in East Africa. It is situated south of the equator between 1° and 12° S. It has a long coastline on the Indian Ocean. It is bordered by Kenya and Uganda on the north, by Mozambique, Malawi and Zambia on the south and by Zaïre on the west. There is a fairly narrow coastal plain in the east but most of the interior consists of a plateau between 3000 and 5000 ft (900 and 1500 m) above sea level. There are a number of mountain ranges which rise to between 7000 and 10,000 ft (2100 and 3000 m). In the north of the country the isolated peak of Mount Kilimanjaro, the highest mountain in Africa, rises to nearly 20,000 ft (6000 m). It has a permanent snow-cap and small glaciers.

The whole country, except the higher mountains, has a tropical climate but above 3000 ft this is modified by a significant reduction of temperature, particularly at night. Compare the higher temperatures recorded on the coast at **Dar es Salaam** with those for **Dodoma** in the central plateau. Minimum temperatures and day-time humidity are much lower at **Dodoma** and cause the climate to be less enervating.

The coastal regions, including the large offshore islands of Pemba and Zanzibar, have a heavier and more reliable rainfall than most of the areas inland. Average annual rainfall is almost everywhere above 40 in (1000 mm) on the coast and up to 60 in (1500 mm) in the wetter places. This compares with an annual fall of between 20 and 40 in (500 and 1000 mm) over most of the interior. Only the higher mountain areas receive more rain than the coastal region. The annual rainfall inland is notoriously unreliable and much of it is very sporadic in both time and place. Rainfall increases a little, and also becomes more reliable, towards the west and around the shores of the three great lakes which are partly included within the boundaries of Tanzania: lakes Victoria, Tanganyika and Malawi (see the table for **Kigoma** on Lake Tanganyika).

Over most of the country there is a single rainy season with the heaviest falls between November and April; the period May to October is dry and sunny. The coastal region is rather an exception in that it gets some rain in all months with the main rains falling between March and May. The southern coastal district is occasionally affected by heavy rain and strong winds associated with tropical cyclones in the south Indian Ocean.

Although weather on the coast is often rather oppressive because of the higher temperatures, particularly at night, and the high humidity, conditions here are not persistently uncomfortable thanks to regular daily sea breezes. Inland, the lower humidity and cooler night temperatures mean that heat stress is rare although daytime temperatures are quite high and sunshine abundant. Much of Tanzania has a very sunny climate with many places averaging from seven to ten hours of sunshine a day with fewer hours during the rainy season. As in most other tropical countries the year is usually divided into the rainy and dry seasons, since the terms winter and summer have little meaning in respect of temperature.

TANZANIA — Dar es Salaam 47 ft (14 m) 6°50′ S 39°18′ E 44 years

	Temperature °F				Temperature °C				Relative humidity		Precipitation			
	Highest recorded	Average daily		Lowest recorded	Highest recorded	Average daily		Lowest recorded	0800 hours	1400 hours	Average monthly		Average no. days with 0.01 in + (0.25mm +)	
		max.	min.			max.	min.		%	%	in	mm		
J	95	87	77	69	35	31	25	21	81	74	2.6	66	8	J
F	95	88	77	68	35	31	25	20	81	74	2.6	66	6	F
M	96	88	75	69	36	31	24	21	85	76	5.1	130	12	M
A	95	86	73	66	35	30	23	19	88	77	11.4	290	19	A
M	91	85	71	64	33	29	22	18	87	72	7.4	188	15	M
J	90	84	68	60	32	29	20	16	84	64	1.3	33	6	J
J	90	83	66	60	32	28	19	16	85	62	1.2	31	6	J
A	89	83	66	59	32	28	19	15	84	64	1.0	25	7	A
S	91	83	67	61	33	28	19	16	81	67	1.2	31	7	S
O	92	85	69	62	33	29	21	17	78	70	1.6	41	7	O
N	94	86	72	66	34	30	22	19	79	73	2.9	74	9	N
D	95	87	75	69	35	31	24	21	80	75	3.6	91	11	D

TANZANIA — Dodoma 3675 ft (1120 m) 6°10′ S 35°46′ E 14 years

	Temperature °F				Temperature °C				Relative humidity		Precipitation			
	Highest recorded	Average daily		Lowest recorded	Highest recorded	Average daily		Lowest recorded	0800 hours	1400 hours	Average monthly		Average no. days with 0.01 in + (0.25 mm +)	
		max.	min.			max.	min.		%	%	in	mm		
J	95	85	65	61	35	29	18	16	80	52	6.0	152	12	J
F	96	84	65	55	36	29	18	13	83	53	4.3	109	9	F
M	94	83	64	59	34	28	18	15	84	56	5.4	137	11	M
A	91	83	64	59	33	28	18	15	82	54	1.9	48	7	A
M	91	82	61	51	33	28	16	11	76	49	0.2	5	2	M
J	89	81	57	48	32	27	14	9	75	45	0	0	0.2	J
J	88	79	55	46	31	26	13	8	74	43	0	0	0	J
A	93	80	57	49	34	27	14	9	74	42	0	0	0	A
S	92	84	59	52	33	29	15	11	71	38	0	0	0	S
O	97	87	62	55	36	31	17	13	70	36	0.2	5	1	O
N	97	88	64	58	36	31	18	14	71	39	0.9	23	4	N
D	97	87	65	58	36	31	18	14	77	48	3.6	91	9	D

	Temperature °F			Temperature °C			Relative humidity		Precipitation		
	Highest recorded	Average daily	Lowest recorded	Highest recorded	Average daily	Lowest recorded	0730 hours	1330 hours	Average monthly		Average no. days with 0.01 in + (0.25 mm +)
		max.	min.			max.	min.		%	%	in	mm	
J	89	80	67	61	32	27	19	16	85	73	4.8	122	14	J
F	92	81	68	61	33	27	20	16	84	74	5.0	127	12	F
M	89	81	68	60	32	27	20	16	85	74	5.9	150	17	M
A	89	81	67	63	32	27	19	17	84	74	5.1	130	17	A
M	89	83	67	61	32	28	19	16	79	66	1.7	43	8	M
J	88	82	65	58	31	28	18	14	76	59	0.2	5	1	J
J	89	83	63	53	32	28	17	12	69	55	0.1	3	1	J
A	91	84	65	58	33	29	18	14	64	56	0.2	5	1	A
S	92	85	67	59	33	29	19	15	62	61	0.7	18	3	S
O	96	84	69	60	36	29	21	16	67	64	1.9	48	8	O
N	90	80	68	60	32	27	20	16	81	74	5.6	142	17	N
D	89	79	67	60	32	26	19	16	85	75	5.3	135	19	D

TOGO

This small country is situated in West Africa between Ghana to the west and Benin to the east. It has a very short coastline on the Gulf of Guinea and extends between 6° and 11° N. It shares the same climatic belts and sequence of weather around the year as that described on p. 72 for Nigeria and adjacent countries. The coastal region is rather drier than the districts immediately inland for the same reasons described for Ghana (p. 48). The tables for **Accra** in Ghana (p. 49) and **Cotonou** in Benin (p. 31) are equally well representative of conditions on the coast of Togo. The north of the country is drier with a single rainy season and here the table for **Tamale** in Ghana (p. 49) is representative. (See map p. 73.)

TUNISIA

Tunisia is a small country on the southern shores of the Mediterranean; most of the coastline faces eastwards on the Gulf of Gabes. It has a western boundary with Algeria and a southern border with Libya. Although only about the same size as England, it is geographically diverse. Tunisia includes parts of the three major regions described for Algeria (pp. 24–5); in the north a narrow coastal strip backed by mountains; a central and western district of mountain and plateau or 'tell' country; and a lowlying region in the south which is either steppe or desert, the fringe of the Sahara.

In recent years Tunisia has developed a large tourist trade, taking advantage of a Mediterranean climate with mild to warm, sunny winters and hot summers which are almost completely dry. Most of the major tourist centres and hotels are situated on the coast and near the main towns: **Tunis**, Bizerta, Sfax and Sousse.

The coastal regions, particularly in the north, and the northern mountains have a typically Mediterranean climate with moderate winter rainfall. Occasional rain may occur in the early summer and autumn and this can take the form of heavy but rare downpours. Summers are fine and hot. In the wettest parts of the hills annual rainfall ranges between 24 and 32 in (600 and 900 mm). Snow may occur on about ten days a year in the higher parts but is very rare on the coast. The table for **Tunis** is representative of these regions.

Rainfall in central Tunisia and the southern hills on the Algerian border is lower. Inland winter temperatures may drop quite low with occasional frosts. Summer temperatures are higher than near the coast. The table for **Gafsa** illustrates inland conditions.

The climate becomes progressively drier towards the south of Tunisia and summer temperatures can rise very high inland since this area has a virtual Saharan climate. Rainfall can occasionally be heavy in spring and autumn although days with rain are rare.

Daily sunshine amounts are everywhere large, ranging from between seven and eight in winter to as much as twelve hours in summer. The occasional very hot, dry and dusty wind bringing air from the Sahara can affect any part of the country, particularly in spring, when a depression, moving into the Gulf of **Gabes** from the west, induces southerly winds on its eastern flank. This wind and associated weather is similar to the khamsin of Egypt but goes under the local name of chili. When this occurs temperatures may rise as high as 122° F (50° C), bringing a risk of heat exhaustion or even heatstroke; but such extreme conditions are rare and for most of the year the climate of Tunisia is healthy and pleasant. Temperatures on the coast are moderated by daily sea breezes, while the higher temperatures inland are rendered less enervating by low humidity.

TUNISIA

Gabes 7 ft (2 m) 33°53′ N 10°07′ E 50 years

		Temperature °F				Temperature °C			Relative humidity		Precipitation			
	Highest recorded	Average daily		Lowest recorded	Highest recorded	Average daily		Lowest recorded	0530 hours	1130 hours	Average monthly		Average no. days with 0.004 in + (0.1 mm +)	
		max.	min.			max.	min.		%	%	in	mm		
J	81	61	43	27	27	16	6	−3	76	54	0.9	23	4	J
F	88	64	44	28	31	18	7	−2	74	52	0.7	18	3	F
M	99	69	49	36	37	21	9	2	73	52	0.8	20	4	M
A	108	74	54	39	42	23	12	4	79	62	0.4	10	3	A
M	109	79	61	39	43	26	16	4	78	64	0.3	8	2	M
J	115	83	66	43	46	28	19	6	76	64	0	0	2	J
J	122	89	71	48	50	32	22	9	77	60	0	0	0	J
A	117	91	72	57	47	33	22	14	76	60	0.1	3	1	A
S	120	87	69	54	49	31	21	12	79	62	0.5	13	3	S
O	111	81	62	43	44	27	17	6	82	61	1.2	31	4	O
N	97	72	52	34	36	22	11	1	77	51	1.2	31	4	N
D	81	63	45	32	27	17	7	0	75	55	0.6	15	4	D

Gafsa 1030 ft (314 m) 34°25′ N 8°49′ E 50 years **TUNISIA**

	Temperature °F			Temperature °C				Relative humidity		Precipitation			
	Highest recorded	Average daily		Lowest recorded	Highest recorded	Average daily		Lowest recorded	0530 hours	1130 hours	Average monthly		Average no. days with 0.004 in + (0.1 mm +)	
		max.	min.			max.	min.		%	%	in	mm		
J	77	58	39	21	25	14	4	−6	79	52	0.7	18	3	J
F	90	62	40	25	32	17	4	−4	71	42	0.5	13	3	F
M	95	69	45	27	35	21	7	−3	70	42	0.9	23	3	M
A	99	77	51	36	37	25	11	2	74	41	0.6	15	3	A
M	109	85	59	43	43	29	15	6	67	36	0.4	10	3	M
J	121	94	66	48	49	34	19	9	62	33	0.3	8	1	J
J	127	101	70	50	53	38	21	10	59	30	0.1	3	1	J
A	118	100	70	54	48	38	21	12	62	31	0.2	5	1	A
S	113	92	65	50	45	33	18	10	73	40	0.5	13	3	S
O	102	81	58	37	39	27	14	3	75	45	0.5	13	3	O
N	91	69	48	27	33	21	9	−3	75	46	0.7	18	3	N
D	84	59	40	25	29	15	4	−4	82	55	0.5	13	3	D

Tunis 217 ft (66 m) 36°47′ N 10°12′ E 50 years **TUNISIA**

	Temperature °F			Temperature °C				Relative humidity		Precipitation			
	Highest recorded	Average daily		Lowest recorded	Highest recorded	Average daily		Lowest recorded	0530 hours	1330 hours	Average monthly		Average no. days with 0.004 in + (0.1 mm +)	
		max.	min.			max.	min.		%	%	in	mm		
J	77	58	43	30	25	14	6	−1	83	64	2.5	64	13	J
F	84	61	44	32	29	16	7	0	83	61	2.0	51	12	F
M	91	65	47	34	33	18	8	1	85	57	1.6	41	11	M
A	104	70	51	37	40	21	11	3	84	53	1.4	36	9	A
M	104	76	56	43	40	24	13	6	79	51	0.7	18	6	M
J	109	84	63	48	43	29	17	9	74	45	0.3	8	5	J
J	118	90	68	50	48	32	20	10	75	40	0.1	3	2	J
A	117	91	69	52	47	33	21	11	72	47	0.3	8	3	A
S	111	87	66	52	44	31	19	11	80	51	1.3	33	7	S
O	104	77	59	45	40	25	15	7	86	55	2.0	51	9	O
N	90	68	51	34	32	20	11	1	85	59	1.9	48	11	N
D	81	60	44	30	27	16	7	−1	85	63	2.4	61	14	D

UGANDA

Uganda is an East African country about the same size as Great Britain; it is situated between 4° N and 1° S. It is a landlocked country but includes within its borders about half Lake Victoria, the largest lake in Africa, about half Lake Albert and the whole of the smaller Lake Kioga. These lakes form part of the source region of the White Nile fed by the equatorial rains of Uganda and adjacent countries. The country is bordered on the north by the Sudan, on the east by Kenya, on the south by Tanzania and Rwanda and on the west by Zaïre. Uganda shares with Kenya and Zaïre the same features of equatorial climate; this is modified by the elevation of the country, most of which is a plateau between 3500 and 4500 ft (1000 and 1400 m) above sea level. In the west and southwest there are high mountains, including the Ruwenzori Range, which rise well over 10,000 ft (3000 m).

The sequence of weather and climate around the year is similar to that described for Kenya on pp. 52–3. Much of Uganda, however, is rather wetter than Kenya. This is because of the influence of Lake Victoria, an important local source of atmospheric moisture, and thunderstorms; in addition, the west of the country is often influenced by moist southwesterly winds bringing rains from Zaïre. The wettest areas are along the shores of Lake Victoria and in the western mountain districts; these receive over 60 in (1500 mm) of rain a year. Parts of central and northeast Uganda receive less than 40 in (1000 mm) of rain per year; this is often much less since rainfall is unreliable from year to year.

Most of Uganda has the typical double rainy season found in the Kenya Highlands but towards the north these two rainy seasons tend to merge into a single long wet period with a single dry period. Over most of Uganda the weather is pleasant and not uncomfortable for much of the year. There is much sunny weather with daily hours of sunshine averaging from six to eight and only much less than this in the wetter mountain districts. Temperatures are never excessively high and humidity does not reach the consistently high levels found in equatorial lowlands. Wet spells lasting a day or two are not unusual but much of the rain comes in heavy thundery showers. There is no real cool season but the daily range of temperature is enough to make the nights cool rather than chilly.

The table for **Entebbe** shows the influence of Lake Victoria on rainfall and humidity as compared with that for **Kampala** which is a few miles from the lakeshore. These are representative of much of Uganda except the drier north and centre. The table for **Kabale**, which is situated in the hillier southwest and is sheltered from heavy rains on the mountains, shows the greater reduction of temperature during all months as a result of higher altitude.

UGANDA

Entebbe 3878 ft (1182 m) 0°04′ N 32°29′ E 15 years

	Temperature °F			Temperature °C			Relative humidity		Precipitation		
	Highest recorded	Average daily	Lowest recorded	Highest recorded	Average daily	Lowest recorded	0730 hours	1330 hours	Average monthly		Average no. days with 0.01 in + (0.25 mm +)
		max.	min.			max.	min.		%	%	in	mm	
J	89	80	64	57	32	27	18	14	85	63	2.6	66	9	J
F	90	80	64	57	32	27	18	14	85	65	3.6	91	11	F
M	91	79	65	57	33	26	18	14	86	69	6.3	160	16	M
A	83	78	65	59	28	26	18	15	86	72	10.1	257	22	A
M	82	77	65	59	28	25	18	15	87	74	9.6	244	23	M
J	84	77	63	58	29	25	17	14	86	72	4.8	122	14	J
J	82	76	62	54	28	24	17	12	86	70	3.0	76	10	J
A	84	77	62	56	29	25	17	13	87	70	2.9	74	12	A
S	87	78	62	57	31	26	17	14	85	68	2.9	74	11	S
O	85	79	63	57	29	26	17	14	82	66	3.7	94	13	O
N	89	79	64	58	32	26	18	14	84	67	5.2	132	17	N
D	85	79	63	57	29	26	17	14	85	66	4.6	117	12	D

Kabale 6138 ft (1871 m) 1°17′ S 29°59′ E 14 years   **UGANDA**

	Temperature °F			Temperature °C			Relative humidity		Precipitation			
	Highest recorded	Average daily	Lowest recorded	Highest recorded	Average daily	Lowest recorded	0730 hours	1330 hours	Average monthly		Average no. days with 0.01 in + (0.25 mm +)	
		max.	min.			max.	min.		%	%	in	mm	
J	85	75	49	40	29	24	9	4	94	55	2.3	58	11	J
F	85	75	51	43	29	24	11	6	94	57	3.8	97	13	F
M	83	74	51	44	28	23	11	7	95	61	5.1	130	16	M
A	81	73	52	44	27	23	11	7	96	66	4.9	125	20	A
M	79	72	52	43	26	22	11	6	96	68	3.6	91	16	M
J	81	72	49	40	27	22	9	4	94	62	1.1	28	5	J
J	82	74	47	38	28	23	8	3	90	53	0.8	20	3	J
A	85	74	49	37	29	23	9	3	91	49	2.3	58	8	A
S	83	75	50	42	28	24	10	6	92	55	3.8	97	15	S
O	81	74	51	43	27	23	11	6	93	60	3.9	99	18	O
N	82	73	51	43	28	23	11	6	94	64	4.3	109	19	N
D	79	73	50	41	26	23	10	5	95	61	3.4	86	15	D

Kampala 4304 ft (1312 m) 0°02′ N 32°36′ E 15 years   **UGANDA**

	Temperature °F			Temperature °C			Relative humidity		Precipitation			
	Highest recorded	Average daily	Lowest recorded	Highest recorded	Average daily	Lowest recorded	0730 hours	1330 hours	Average monthly		Average no. days with 0.01 in + (0.25 mm +)	
		max.	min.			max.	min.		%	%	in	mm	
J	92	83	65	54	33	28	18	12	78	54	1.8	46	9	J
F	97	82	65	57	36	28	18	14	81	56	2.4	61	9	F
M	92	81	64	56	33	27	18	13	84	62	5.1	130	14	M
A	91	79	64	57	33	26	18	14	88	69	6.9	175	19	A
M	84	78	63	59	29	25	17	15	89	72	5.8	147	19	M
J	85	77	63	53	29	25	17	12	88	69	2.9	74	11	J
J	85	77	62	53	29	25	17	12	89	66	1.8	46	10	J
A	85	78	61	53	29	25	16	12	89	66	3.4	86	14	A
S	88	80	62	56	31	27	17	13	86	65	3.6	91	12	S
O	90	81	63	56	32	27	17	13	83	64	3.8	97	14	O
N	89	80	63	58	32	27	17	14	83	63	4.8	122	16	N
D	90	80	63	53	32	27	17	12	81	62	3.9	99	12	D

UPPER VOLTA

This is a small landlocked country about the size of Great Britain. It is situated in interior West Africa and is bordered by Mali and Niger on the north and by the Ivory Coast and Ghana on the south. It has a typical tropical climate with a single rainy season and a long dry season. The general features of the weather and climate of this part of Africa are described for Mali on p. 62.

Upper Volta has a climate similar to that of southern Mali. The table for **Ouagadougou** is representative of the country and if this is compared with the table for **Bamako** in Mali on p. 63 it can be seen that there is little difference. The climate is hot around the year and the heat is most uncomfortable during the period May to October when humidity and cloud are greatest. During the low-sun period from November to March, drier air is brought by the northeasterly harmattan, although on occasions this also brings unpleasant conditions with dust-laden air. Hours of sunshine are greatest during the dry season when they average eight to nine hours a day as compared with six to seven hours during the rainy season. (See map p. 73.)

WEST SAHARA

This territory on the coast of northwest Africa between Morocco and Mauritania was formerly the Spanish colony of West Sahara. In 1975 it was partitioned between Morocco and Mauritania after an agreement with Spain. In 1979, however, it was united with Morocco. Since then it has been disputed between Morocco and the local population who are in rebellion. It has an area about as large as Great Britain but a very small population.

The whole territory is part of the Sahara desert and it has a similar climate to the adjacent parts of southern Morocco (p. 65) and northern Mauritania (p. 64).

Ouagadougou 991 ft (302 m) 12°22′ N 1°31′ W 10 years   **UPPER VOLTA**

	Temperature °F				Temperature °C				Relative humidity		Precipitation			
	Highest recorded	Average daily		Lowest recorded	Highest recorded	Average daily		Lowest recorded	0700 hours	1400 hours	Average monthly		Average no. days with 0.04 in + (1 mm +)	
		max.	min.			max.	min.		%	%	in	mm		
J	113	92	60		45	33	16	9	42	19	0	0	0.1	J
F	113	98	68		45	37	20	12	38	19	0.1	3	0.3	F
M	113	104	73		45	40	23	15	39	20	0.5	13	0.7	M
A	116	103	79		47	39	26	15	51	28	0.6	15	2	A
M	118	101	78		48	38	26	19	65	40	3.3	84	6	M
J	111	96	76		44	36	24	17	73	49	4.8	122	9	J
J	106	91	74		41	33	23	18	78	62	8.0	203	12	J
A	101	87	72		38	31	22	14	81	67	10.9	277	14	A
S	102	89	73		39	32	23	19	79	60	5.7	145	11	S
O	106	95	74		41	35	23	18	72	44	1.3	33	3	O
N	107	96	71		42	36	22	16	58	30	0	0	0.2	N
D	113	95	62		45	35	17	11	46	23	0	0	0	D

ZAÏRE

(Including a description of the climate and weather of central Africa: Cameroon, Central African Empire, Congo, Gabon and Equatorial Guinea)

These six countries occupy an area of about a million and a half square miles (3.9 million sq. km); this is almost half the area of Brazil or the United States. The countries extend almost equal distances on either side of the equator from 13° N to 13° S. A large part of the region consists of the basin of the Congo (Zaïre) river and its numerous tributaries, and lies between 1000 and 3000 ft (300 and 600 m) above sea level. The land rises on the southern border of Zaïre with Angola; along the northeastern border with Uganda, Rwanda and Burundi there is a mountain range with peaks such as Ruwenzori rising to between 14,500 and 16,500 ft (4500 and 5100 m). There are also some high isolated mountain peaks in the Cameroon. Only in these high mountain regions are temperatures significantly below tropical levels; snow may fall on the summits of the mountains.

With the exception of the high mountains the region has an equatorial or tropical climate. The central part of the region, roughly between 4° N and the equator, has rain around the year with two periods when rain is heaviest and most probable. On either side of this typical equatorial rainfall area there are districts where rainfall is concentrated into a single rainy season at the time of high sun; there is a marked dry season at the time of low sun.

The double wet season with some rain in all months is well illustrated by the table for **Kisangani** in Zaïre, which is almost on the equator; the single wet season with a pronounced dry season is illustrated by the table for **Lubumbashi** in 12° S in southern Zaïre. In the northern parts of Cameroon and the Central African Empire there is also a single rainy season as found in northern Nigeria and Chad when the sun is north of the equator between March and September.

The annual rainfall is moderately high over the whole of this large area, ranging from 48 to 80 in (1200 to 2000 mm). The only districts where rainfall falls below this amount are on the coast near the mouth of the Congo river and in the extreme northern and southern fringes of the region. In small parts of the region, on the western side of the Cameroon mountains and on the mountains near the eastern border of Zaïre, annual rainfall is significantly greater.

This is a region where temperatures remain high throughout the year. At lower levels near the equator they rarely fall below 64° F (18° C) even at night. Daytime maximum temperatures, however, rarely rise above 95° F (35° C). Humidity remains high throughout the year and rarely falls very low during the hottest part of the day so that, for most of the time, the weather feels sultry and oppressive. Except during occasional thunder squalls winds are light so that the temperature feels higher than the thermometer might suggest. Temperatures rise rather higher during the daytime in those areas where there is a pronounced dry season; at this time humidity is also lower and these higher temperatures may not feel so oppressive as the lower temperatures during the wet season when there is higher humidity, much cloud and little sunshine.

Temperatures are reduced by the effect of altitude in the mountain areas of Cameroon and eastern Zaïre but these areas have much cloud, high humidity, less sun and frequent heavy rain so that the climate is rather monotonous and unpleasant except during the brief spells of dry, clear and sunny weather. Over much of this region of central Africa the very monotony of the weather and the absence of any great seasonal contrast have an enervating and depressing effect. It has been said that 'night is the winter of the Tropics' and that in these areas 'there is no weather only climate'. While these are perhaps overstatements, there is certainly truth in them.

Zaïre is the largest country in the region and amounts to over half the total area. It is almost entirely landlocked with only a very short coastal strip on the Atlantic around the mouth of the Congo, between the Congo Republic and Angola. This small area is affected by the same relative dryness that is typical of coastal Angola. Rainfall increases inland. The weather and climate of much of central Zaïre are represented by the table for **Kisangani**. The table for **Kinshasa** at 4° S shows a distribution of rainfall around the year more typical of the districts south of the equator; there is a single, long wet season with a short dry season from June to September when the sun is north of the equator. The table for **Lubumbashi** situated at 12° S and at an altitude of 4260 ft (1300 m) shows a prolonged dry season between May and October during which the night-time temperatures fall much lower than elsewhere. There is rather more sunshine here, particularly during the dry season. Rainfall is lower during the rainy season so that the climate is more like that found in the neighbouring regions of Zambia and Angola. Here the average number of sunshine hours a day ranges from four to five in the wet season to as many as nine to ten in the dry season. This is a greater variation and a larger number of hours of sunshine a year than occurs almost anywhere else in Zaïre, and much more than in the consistently wet regions.

Kinshasa 1066 ft (322 m) 4°20′ S 15°18′ E 8 years **ZAÏRE**

	Temperature °F			Temperature °C			Relative humidity		Precipitation			
Highest recorded	Average daily		Lowest recorded	Highest recorded	Average daily		Lowest recorded	0600 hours	1200 hours	Average monthly		Average no. days with 0.004 in + (0.1 mm +)	
	max.	min.			max.	min.		%	%	in	mm		
J	96	87	70	64	36	31	21	18	94	72	5.3	135	11	J
F	97	88	71	64	36	31	22	18	94	71	5.7	145	11	F
M	97	89	71	64	36	32	22	18	94	71	7.7	196	12	M
A	97	89	71	67	36	32	22	19	95	70	7.7	196	16	A
M	95	88	71	64	35	31	22	18	95	73	6.2	159	12	M
J	93	84	67	59	34	29	19	15	94	71	0.3	8	1	J
J	90	81	64	58	32	27	18	14	93	67	0.1	3	0.1	J
A	95	84	65	58	35	29	18	14	89	61	0.1	3	0.6	A
S	96	87	68	61	36	31	20	16	88	61	1.2	30	5	S
O	97	88	70	59	36	31	21	15	92	66	4.7	119	11	O
N	94	87	71	62	34	31	22	17	94	71	8.7	222	16	N
D	97	86	70	63	36	30	21	17	94	73	5.6	142	15	D

Kisangani 1370 ft (418 m) 0°26′ N 25°14′ E 9 years **ZAÏRE**

	Temperature °F			Temperature °C			Relative humidity		Precipitation			
Highest recorded	Average daily		Lowest recorded	Highest recorded	Average daily		Lowest recorded	0530 hours	1130 hours	Average monthly		Average no. days with 0.004 in + (0.1 mm +)	
	max.	min.			max.	min.		%	%	in	mm		
J	97	88	69	63	36	31	21	17	97	66	2.1	53	6	J
F	97	88	69	65	36	31	21	18	97	63	3.3	84	9	F
M	96	88	69	62	36	31	21	17	96	64	7.0	178	11	M
A	95	88	70	64	35	31	21	18	97	68	6.2	158	10	A
M	94	87	69	65	34	31	21	18	97	69	5.4	137	10	M
J	93	86	69	64	34	30	21	18	97	71	4.5	114	9	J
J	92	84	67	63	33	29	19	17	97	72	5.2	132	10	J
A	92	83	68	63	33	28	20	17	97	75	6.5	165	11	A
S	93	85	68	62	34	29	20	17	97	69	7.2	183	13	S
O	93	86	68	64	34	30	20	18	97	70	8.6	218	14	O
N	95	85	68	64	35	29	20	18	97	67	7.8	198	15	N
D	95	86	68	61	35	30	20	16	95	60	3.3	84	10	D

	Temperature °F			Temperature °C			Relative humidity		Precipitation		
	Highest recorded	Average daily	Lowest recorded	Highest recorded	Average daily	Lowest recorded	0800 hours	1200 hours	Average monthly		Average no. days with 0.004 in + (0.1 mm +)
		max.	min.			max.	min.		%	%	in	mm	
J	91	82	61	50	33	28	16	10	91	50	10.5	267	25	J
F	90	82	62	54	32	28	17	12	90	54	9.6	244	24	F
M	93	82	61	46	34	28	16	8	93	46	8.4	213	22	M
A	90	82	57	41	32	28	14	5	90	41	2.2	56	12	A
M	89	81	50	38	32	27	10	3	89	38	0.2	5	2	M
J	86	79	44	34	30	26	7	1	86	34	0	0	0	J
J	89	79	43	33	32	26	6	1	89	33	0	0	0	J
A	94	83	46	33	34	28	8	1	94	33	0	0	0.3	A
S	99	89	52	37	37	32	11	3	99	37	0.1	3	1.0	S
O	98	91	58	45	37	33	14	7	98	45	1.2	31	6	O
N	97	87	61	50	36	31	16	10	97	50	5.9	150	18	N
D	93	82	62	54	34	28	17	12	93	54	10.6	269	25	D

(Including a description of the weather and climate of Zimbabwe and Malawi)

Zambia, Zimbabwe and Malawi are three landlocked countries in south-central Africa between 8° and 22° S. These countries have a broad similarity of weather and climate and any significant differences from place to place are a consequence of the range of altitude found in each country. All three countries include extensive areas between 3000 and 5000 ft (900 and 1500 m) above sea level. Only in the valleys of the major rivers: the Zambesi, which forms the border between Zambia and Zimbabwe; the Limpopo, which is the border between Zimbabwe and South Africa; and their tributaries, such as the Shire in Malawi, are there areas of land below 2000 ft (600 m). In these lowland areas the climate is typically tropical with no real cool season and high temperatures during the period of overhead sun between October and February. This period of high sun is also the rainy season in all these countries. The climate of these lowlands is oppressive and sultry, particularly during the rainy season, and has a bad reputation for the health of man and beast because of the prevalence of both malaria and sleeping sickness.

By contrast the lower temperatures on the upland plateaux which make up the greater part of these countries are much more healthy and pleasant so that white settlers have been attracted in some numbers. Above 4000 ft (1200 m) temperatures around the year are typical of warm-temperate rather than tropical climates. During the long dry season there is abundant sunshine and the sun's rays are more powerful as a consequence of the altitude. The air temperature however, is rarely so high as to cause stress or discomfort and it is mitigated by the generally low humidity. The most uncomfortable season is the period November to February when both temperature and humidity are greatest and there is a smaller daily temperature range so that nights are not so cool. At altitudes above 4000–5000 ft (1200–1500 m) frost is not uncommon at night during the dry season from April to August. This is the period of low sun and some days may be chilly if there is much cloud.

Over the whole area rainfall is largely confined to the period October to March with a maximum in the months December to February when the inter-tropical belt of cloud and rain is farthest south. It then lies across southern Zambia and Malawi. Much of the rain is heavy and showery and accompanied by thunder, but periods of almost continuous rain lasting two or three days are by no means unusual. Except in the higher mountainous areas of Malawi rainfall is very rare during the period April to September.

Zambia is the largest of the three countries. It has the greatest extent both from east to west and north to south. It is bordered on the north by Zaïre and Tanzania, on the east by Malawi, on the south by Zimbabwe and on the west by Angola. In northern Zambia the rainy season is a few weeks longer than elsewhere since it is nearest to the equator.

The tables for **Ndola**, near the border with Zaïre, and for **Kasama**, in the northeast, are representative of the wetter parts of the country. That for **Lusaka**, farther south, is typical of the drier parts. All three places, however, show very little difference in temperature since they are at similar altitudes. The higher temperatures in the lowlands can be represented by the table for **Zumbo**, which is in the Zambesi valley in Mozambique, but which is shown for Malawi on p. 61. The southwestern parts of Zambia, and the valleys of the Zambesi and its tributary, the Luangwa, are the driest regions.

	Temperature °F			Temperature °C				Relative humidity		Precipitation			
	Highest recorded	Average daily		Lowest recorded	Highest recorded	Average daily		Lowest recorded	0830 hours	1400 hours	Average monthly		Average no. days with 0.01 in + (0.25 mm +)	
		max.	min.			max.	min.		%	%	in	mm		
J	86	79	61	57	30	26	16	14	83	59	10.7	272	24	J
F	86	79	62	56	30	26	17	13	84	59	9.9	252	19	F
M	84	78	62	58	29	26	17	14	85	56	10.9	277	21	M
A	84	79	60	51	29	26	16	11	77	51	2.8	71	7	A
M	85	78	56	44	29	26	13	7	71	40	0.5	13	1	M
J	82	76	51	39	28	24	11	4	61	33	0	0	0	J
J	83	76	50	40	28	24	10	4	61	29	0	0	0.1	J
A	87	79	52	42	31	26	11	6	57	22	0	0	0.1	A
S	93	85	58	47	34	29	14	8	47	20	0	0	0.2	S
O	95	87	62	53	35	31	17	12	44	19	0.8	20	3	O
N	93	83	62	55	34	28	17	13	63	38	6.4	163	16	N
D	87	80	62	58	31	27	17	14	79	55	9.5	241	22	D

	Temperature °F			Temperature °C				Relative humidity		Precipitation			
	Highest recorded	Average daily		Lowest recorded	Highest recorded	Average daily		Lowest recorded	0830 hours	1400 hours	Average monthly		Average no. days with 0.01 in + (0.25 mm +)	
		max.	min.			max.	min.		%	%	in	mm		
J	88	78	63	58	31	26	17	14	84	71	9.1	231	21	J
F	87	79	63	56	31	26	17	13	85	70	7.5	191	17	F
M	86	78	62	55	30	26	17	13	83	56	5.6	142	15	M
A	87	79	59	50	31	26	15	10	71	47	0.7	18	3	A
M	85	77	54	47	29	25	12	8	59	37	0.1	3	0.9	M
J	83	73	50	39	28	23	10	4	56	32	0	0	0.4	J
J	83	73	49	40	28	23	9	4	54	28	0	0	0.1	J
A	87	77	53	43	31	25	12	6	46	26	0	0	0	A
S	95	84	59	46	35	29	15	8	41	19	0	0	0.4	S
O	100	88	64	54	38	31	18	12	39	23	0.4	10	3	O
N	98	84	64	55	37	29	18	13	57	46	3.6	91	11	N
D	93	80	63	57	34	27	17	14	76	61	5.9	150	17	D

	Temperature °F			Temperature °C			Relative humidity		Precipitation			
	Highest recorded	Average daily		Lowest recorded	Highest recorded	Average daily		Lowest recorded	0830 hours	1400 hours	Average monthly		Average no. days with 0.01 in + (0.25 mm +)
		max.	min.			max.	min.		%	%	in	mm	
J	86	79	62	54	30	26	17	12	87	63	13.8	351	22	J
F	86	79	62	54	30	26	17	12	88	61	10.4	264	19	F
M	86	79	61	52	30	26	16	11	87	51	9.2	234	17	M
A	87	81	56	45	31	27	13	7	78	43	1.3	33	4	A
M	86	79	49	34	30	26	9	1	71	32	0.1	3	0.5	M
J	83	76	41	32	28	24	5	0	65	29	0	0	0	J
J	84	77	41	28	29	25	5	−2	62	24	0	0	0	J
A	89	80	45	35	32	27	7	2	50	21	0	0	0	A
S	93	86	53	41	34	30	12	5	43	17	0	0	0 1	S
O	97	89	59	49	36	32	15	9	45	20	0.7	18	3	O
N	94	84	62	55	34	29	17	13	66	42	5.5	140	13	N
D	89	80	62	53	32	27	17	12	81	61	9.9	252	19	D

ZIMBABWE

Zimbabwe was until recently known as Rhodesia. It is the most southerly of the three countries of south-central Africa which share a similar climate and which are described in more detail for Zambia on p. 101. In area Zimbabwe is almost twice as large as Great Britain. It is bordered on the north by Zambia, on the east by Mozambique, on the south by South Africa and on the west by Botswana.

Most of the country consists of a plateau with an average height of over 4000 ft (1200 m). Along the eastern border with Mozambique there are hills rising to over 8000 ft (2400 ft) while in the north and south of the country, in the valleys of the Zambesi and Limpopo respectively, altitude falls below 1500 ft (450 m). The lowlying parts of the country have a rather dry climate with an unreliable rainfall of between 16 and 24 in (400 and 600 mm). In the eastern highlands annual rainfall is as much as 60–80 in (1500–2000 mm). Over most of the country annual rainfall is between 30 and 40 in (750 and 1000 mm). Most of the rain falls during the period November to March at the time of high sun. Except in the lower regions temperatures are warm but rarely hot around the year. Hours of sunshine average eight to nine hours a day during the dry season and as much as six to seven hours during the rainy season.

Most of Zimbabwe has a healthy and generally pleasant climate around the year. The tables for **Harare** (formerly Salisbury) and **Bulawayo** are typical of the upland regions between 4000 and 5000 ft (1200 and 1500 m). The table for **Zumbo**, in the Zambesi valley but actually in Mozambique (p. 61), is typical of conditions in the lower parts of northern Zimbabwe. (See map p. 81.)

Bulawayo 4405 ft (1341 m) 20°09′ S 28°37′ E 15 years   **ZIMBABWE**

		Temperature °F			Temperature °C			Relative humidity		Precipitation			
	Highest recorded	Average daily		Lowest recorded	Highest recorded	Average daily		Lowest recorded	0830 hours	1500 hours	Average monthly		Average no. days with 0.01 in + (0.25 mm +)	
		max.	min.			max.	min.		%	%	in	mm		
J	96	81	61	49	36	27	16	9	70	51	5.6	142	14	J
F	94	80	61	46	34	27	16	8	74	52	4.3	109	11	F
M	93	79	59	48	34	26	15	9	72	48	3.3	84	9	M
A	91	79	56	38	33	26	13	3	63	39	0.7	18	4	A
M	87	74	49	33	31	23	9	1	56	33	0.4	10	2	M
J	82	69	45	28	28	21	7	−2	56	33	0.1	3	0.9	J
J	83	70	45	32	28	21	7	0	52	29	0	0	0.5	J
A	89	74	48	32	32	23	9	0	46	26	0	0	0.4	A
S	96	81	54	37	36	27	12	3	42	24	0.2	5	1	S
O	97	85	59	44	36	29	15	7	41	26	0.8	20	4	O
N	99	84	61	49	37	29	16	9	53	41	3.2	81	10	N
D	95	82	61	51	35	28	16	11	62	49	4.8	122	12	D

Harare 4831 ft (1473 m) 17°50′ S 31°08′ E 15 years   **ZIMBABWE**

		Temperature °F			Temperature °C			Relative humidity		Precipitation			
	Highest recorded	Average daily		Lowest recorded	Highest recorded	Average daily		Lowest recorded	0830 hours	1400 hours	Average monthly		Average no. days with 0.01 in + (0.25 mm +)	
		max.	min.			max.	min.		%	%	in	mm		
J	90	78	60	47	32	26	16	8	74	57	7.7	196	18	J
F	88	78	60	49	31	26	16	9	77	53	7.0	178	15	F
M	86	78	58	46	30	26	14	8	75	52	4.6	117	13	M
A	89	78	55	43	32	26	13	6	68	44	1.1	28	5	A
M	83	74	49	36	28	23	9	2	60	37	0.5	13	2	M
J	79	70	44	32	26	21	7	0	58	36	0.1	3	1	J
J	82	70	44	32	28	21	7	0	56	33	0	0	0.7	J
A	88	74	47	34	31	23	8	1	50	28	0.1	3	0.6	A
S	92	79	53	37	33	26	12	3	43	26	0.2	5	1	S
O	93	83	58	44	34	28	14	7	43	26	1.1	28	4	O
N	95	81	60	46	35	27	16	8	56	43	3.8	97	11	N
D	92	79	60	49	33	26	16	9	67	57	6.4	163	16	D

North America

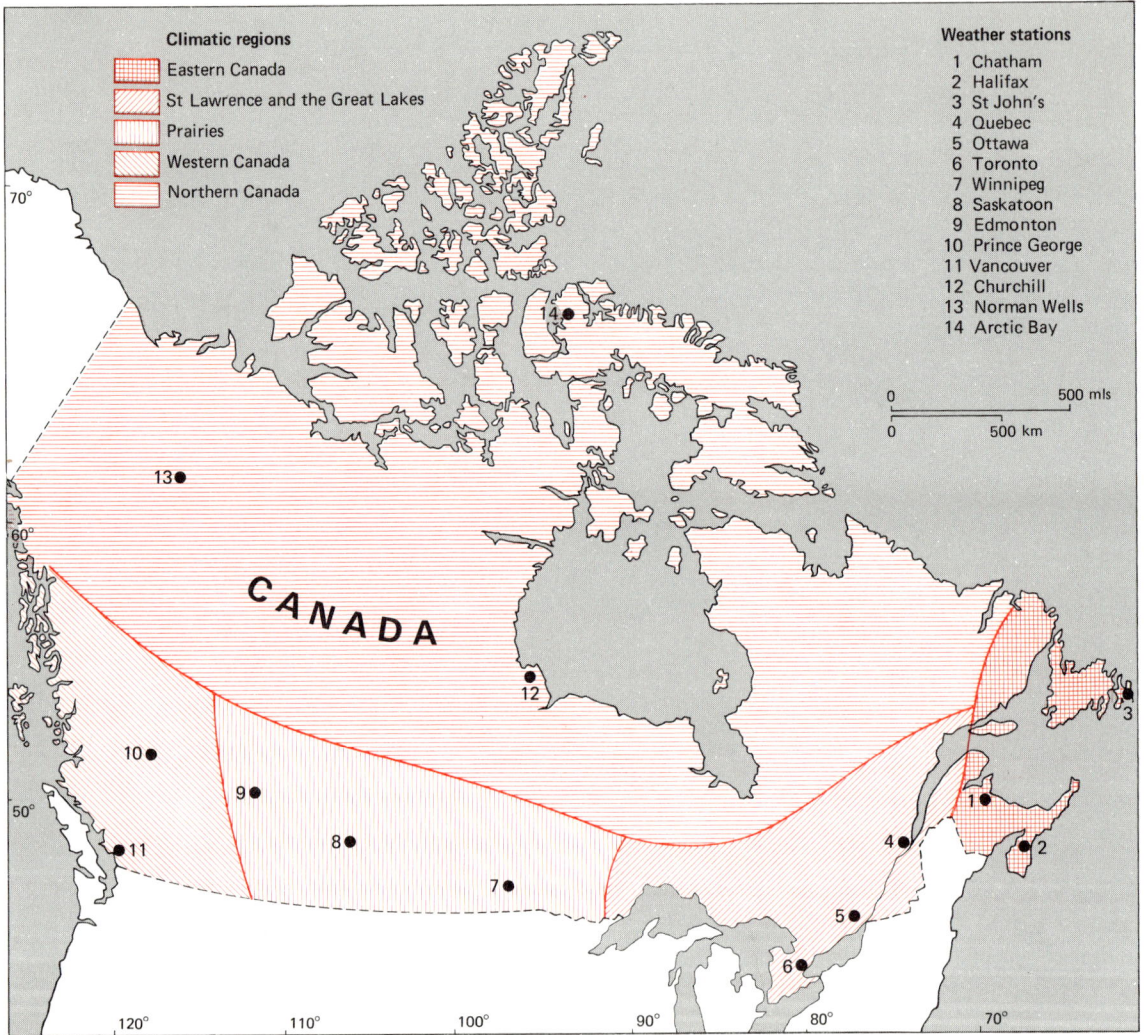

CANADA

Climatic regions
- Eastern Canada
- St Lawrence and the Great Lakes
- Prairies
- Western Canada
- Northern Canada

Weather stations
1 Chatham
2 Halifax
3 St John's
4 Quebec
5 Ottawa
6 Toronto
7 Winnipeg
8 Saskatoon
9 Edmonton
10 Prince George
11 Vancouver
12 Churchill
13 Norman Wells
14 Arctic Bay

CANADA

0   500 mls
0   500 km

Canada is a vast country about half the size of the USSR and about as large as China. Situated between 42° and 83° N, a larger proportion of Canada lies within the Arctic Circle than is the case with the Soviet Union, with which the climate of Canada can be rightly compared. Only a narrow strip of Canada close to the southern border with the United States has a temperate climate and much of this more favoured area has a severe winter with prolonged frost and snow. With the exception of Hudson Bay, which is frozen over for about nine months of the year, the northern coast of Canada on the Arctic Ocean is permanently ice-bound or severely obstructed for most of the year by ice floes. Only the Pacific coast of British Columbia and the Atlantic coasts of Newfoundland and the maritime provinces south of the Gulf of St Lawrence have harbours that do not regularly freeze in winter.

The reasons for the very cold winters over most of Canada are the high latitude of much of the country and the generally flat and lowlying land east of the Rocky Mountains. Cold air from the Canadian Arctic has virtually no obstruction as it sweeps south and east in winter and spring, thus importing very cold conditions to most of the country. Southern Canada also lies in one of the most frequented tracks of cyclonic depressions in North America; many of these cross the region of the Great Lakes and the St Lawrence valley before moving out into the Atlantic. The cold air involved in the circulation of these depressions frequently has its origin far to the north.

The influence of warmer maritime air of Pacific Ocean origin is mainly confined to the small area of Canada west of the Rockies in British Columbia. The coast and some inland valleys in this province have a very different climate to the rest of the country, resembling that of the British Isles and other parts of northwest Europe. Here winters are mild and summers warm, with rain falling all through the year but with a winter maximum fall.

Winter temperatures on the Atlantic shores of Canada are somewhat warmer than those in the interior of the continent, particularly where the sea does not freeze, but the summer temperatures are kept lower than in the interior because of the cold Labrador current which flows southwards close to the coast.

Much of the southern interior of Canada has a very continental climate with surprisingly high summer temperatures, in spite of the shortness of the summer, and a long, very cold winter. Even the barren north-lands of Canada have quite warm summers and in this there is a close parallel with much of Siberia.

For a more detailed description of the weather and climate of Canada it is most convenient to divide the country into the following climatic regions: eastern Canada, the St Lawrence and Great Lakes region, the Prairies, western Canada including the Rockies, and northern Canada.

This region includes those areas where the influence of the Atlantic Ocean modifies the harshness of winter to some extent and makes the summers rather more cool and changeable than farther inland. It consists of the island of Newfoundland, the Labrador coast and the maritime provinces: Nova Scotia, New Brunswick and Prince Edward Island. This region has the most changeable weather around the year because of the large number of cyclonic depressions which follow a track from the Great Lakes to Newfoundland. Frequent changes of weather from day to day are the rule in all months, and cloud and rain are well distributed around the year. Much of the winter precipitation is in the form of snow which, except on the coast, may lie for long periods. The tables for **St John's** and **Halifax** show the influence of the open sea in keeping winter temperatures a little higher and summer temperatures slightly lower than at places farther inland. The table

for **Chatham**, which is only a little way inland from the Gulf of St Lawrence, shows how the annual range of temperature increases away from the sea.

This area is very liable to sea fog, and this can be persistent offshore during the summer months. The Grand Banks area south of Newfoundland and the Gulf of St Lawrence are among the foggiest sea areas in the world and lies across an important shipping route. Another navigational hazard in this sea area is the frequent occurrence of icebergs in summer; they drift south in the cold waters of the Labrador current. The temperature contrast between the warm waters of the Gulf Stream and the cold Labrador current is the principal cause of the fogs. This is one of the least sunny regions of Canada. Hours of sunshine a day range from two to three in winter to seven or eight in summer.

CANADA — Chatham (New Brunswick) 98 ft (30 m) 47°02′ N 65°27′ W 50 years

	Temperature °F				Temperature °C				Relative humidity		Precipitation			
	Highest recorded	Average daily		Lowest recorded	Highest recorded	Average daily		Lowest recorded	0800 hours	2000 hours	Average monthly		Average no. days with 0.01 in + (0.25 mm +)	
		max.	min.			max.	min.		%	%	in	mm		
J	52	23	2	−43	11	−5	−17	−42	89	83	3.4	86	11	J
F	55	25	2	−39	13	−4	−17	−39	89	83	2.7	69	13	F
M	67	35	15	−25	19	2	−9	−32	80	73	3.3	84	13	M
A	85	47	28	−4	29	8	−2	−20	76	73	3.0	76	12	A
M	92	60	39	20	33	16	4	−7	72	69	3.2	81	13	M
J	96	71	49	30	36	22	9	−1	75	72	3.6	91	13	J
J	98	77	56	38	37	25	13	3	79	73	3.9	99	12	J
A	102	75	54	33	39	24	12	1	81	76	4.0	102	13	A
S	92	66	46	23	33	19	8	−5	84	83	3.1	79	13	S
O	84	55	37	12	29	13	3	−11	87	80	4.0	102	12	O
N	70	40	25	−12	21	4	−4	−24	90	87	3.4	86	14	N
D	58	27	10	−30	14	−3	−12	−34	87	82	3.2	81	12	D

Halifax (Nova Scotia) 99 ft (30 m) 44°39′ N 63°36′ W 72 years — CANADA

	Temperature °F				Temperature °C				Relative humidity		Precipitation			
	Highest recorded	Average daily		Lowest recorded	Highest recorded	Average daily		Lowest recorded	0830 hours	1430 hours	Average monthly		Average no. days with 0.01 in + (0.25 mm +)	
		max.	min.			max.	min.		%	%	in	mm		
J	58	32	15	−17	14	0	−9	−27	82	69	5.4	137	17	J
F	52	31	15	−21	11	−1	−9	−29	81	63	4.3	109	14	F
M	70	38	23	−10	21	3	−5	−23	77	60	4.9	125	15	M
A	83	47	31	7	28	8	−1	−14	76	60	4.5	114	14	A
M	90	59	40	24	32	15	4	−4	76	62	4.1	104	14	M
J	94	68	48	32	34	20	9	0	77	63	4.0	102	14	J
J	99	74	55	39	37	23	13	4	81	64	3.8	97	13	J
A	94	74	56	39	34	23	13	4	82	65	4.4	112	12	A
S	94	67	50	29	34	19	10	−2	82	65	4.1	104	12	S
O	88	57	41	21	31	14	5	−6	82	63	5.4	137	13	O
N	69	46	32	4	21	8	0	−16	84	71	5.3	135	14	N
D	62	35	21	−14	17	2	−6	−26	80	68	5.4	137	15	D

St John's (Newfoundland) 243 ft (74 m) 47°34′ N 52°42′ W 68 years — CANADA

	Temperature °F				Temperature °C				Relative humidity	Precipitation			
	Highest recorded	Average daily		Lowest recorded	Highest recorded	Average daily		Lowest recorded	All hours	Average monthly		Average no. days with 0.01 in + (0.25 mm +)	
		max.	min.			max.	min.		%	in	mm		
J	59	29	18	−19	15	−2	−8	−28	76	5.3	135	15	J
F	56	28	16	−21	13	−2	−9	−29	77	4.9	125	15	F
M	67	33	22	−14	19	1	−6	−26	79	4.6	117	15	M
A	72	41	30	−1	22	5	−1	−18	81	4.2	107	15	A
M	81	50	35	20	27	10	2	−7	79	3.6	91	15	M
J	87	61	44	27	31	16	7	−3	77	3.5	89	13	J
J	90	68	51	33	32	20	11	1	79	3.5	89	13	J
A	93	69	53	32	34	21	12	0	80	3.7	94	13	A
S	84	62	47	29	29	17	8	−2	80	3.8	97	14	S
O	87	53	40	22	31	12	4	−6	78	5.3	135	16	O
N	68	42	32	6	20	6	0	−14	80	5.9	150	17	N
D	60	34	24	−4	16	1	−4	−20	79	5.5	140	17	D

THE ST LAWRENCE AND GREAT LAKES REGION

This region consists of the southern portions of the provinces of Quebec and Ontario. It is bordered by the Great Lakes and the United States on the south and is the most southerly part of Canada. It is the most densely settled and developed part of the country. The southerly latitude and the warmth of the waters of the lakes, which do not usually freeze over completely until December, help to make this one of the warmest parts of Canada.

As the tables for **Ottawa**, **Quebec** and **Toronto** show, however, winters here are severe. **Toronto**, on the shore of Lake Ontario, has appreciably higher winter temperatures than **Ottawa** and **Quebec**. Summers are quite warm with considerable amounts of sunshine, averaging eight to nine hours a day. Most of

the winter precipitation is snow and the ground is usually snow-covered from mid-December to mid-March. This is one of the snowiest regions of North America, except for parts of the western Rockies. In an average winter between 8 and 10 ft (2.5 and 3 m) of snow may fall, but it does not necessarily accumulate to this depth because of periodic thaws and evaporation.

Like eastern Canada, the weather here can be very variable at all times of the year so that in some years there may be early or late cold spells and midwinter thaws. This variability of weather and the relatively large precipitation around the year are a consequence of this region's position in the track of numerous cyclonic storms.

CANADA — Ottawa (Ontario) 339 ft (103 m) 45°20′ N 75°41′ W 65 years

	Temperature °F				Temperature °C				Relative humidity		Precipitation		
	Highest recorded	Average daily		Lowest recorded	Highest recorded	Average daily		Lowest recorded	0730 hours	1330 hours	Average monthly		Average no. days with 0.01 in + (0.25 mm +)	
		max.	min.			max.	min.		%	%	in	mm		
J	54	21	3	−32	12	−6	−16	−36	83	76	2.9	74	13	J
F	54	22	3	−35	12	−6	−16	−37	88	73	2.2	56	12	F
M	78	33	16	−34	26	1	−9	−37	84	66	2.8	71	12	M
A	86	51	31	−2	30	11	−1	−19	76	58	2.7	69	11	A
M	94	66	44	21	34	19	7	−6	77	55	2.5	64	11	M
J	97	76	54	33	36	24	12	1	80	56	3.5	89	10	J
J	101	81	58	38	38	27	14	3	80	53	3.4	86	11	J
A	100	77	55	35	38	25	13	2	84	54	2.6	66	10	A
S	102	68	48	24	39	20	9	−4	90	59	3.2	81	11	S
O	87	54	37	14	31	12	3	−10	86	63	2.9	74	12	O
N	71	39	26	−10	22	4	−3	−23	84	68	3.0	76	12	N
D	55	24	9	−34	13	−4	−13	−37	83	75	2.6	66	14	D

Quebec (Quebec) 296 ft (90 m) 46°48′ N 71°13′ W 68 years   **CANADA**

	Temperature °F			Temperature °C			Relative humidity		Precipitation		
	Highest recorded	Average daily	Lowest recorded	Highest recorded	Average daily	Lowest recorded	0800 hours	2000 hours	Average monthly		Average no. days with 0.01 in + (0.25 mm +)
		max.	min.			max.	min.		%	%	in	mm	
J	52	18	2	−34	11	−8	−17	−37	80	78	3.5	89	14	J
F	49	20	4	−32	9	−7	−16	−36	80	64	2.7	69	14	F
M	64	31	15	−22	18	−1	−9	−30	79	75	3.0	76	14	M
A	80	45	29	−1	27	7	−2	−18	75	67	2.3	58	12	A
M	91	61	41	20	33	16	5	−7	73	63	3.1	79	13	M
J	94	72	52	31	34	22	11	−1	79	68	3.7	94	14	J
J	96	76	57	39	36	24	14	4	79	70	4.0	102	13	J
A	97	73	54	37	36	23	12	3	83	73	4.0	102	12	A
S	88	64	47	27	31	18	8	−3	85	77	3.6	91	13	S
O	77	51	37	14	25	11	3	−10	81	75	3.4	86	13	O
N	71	36	24	−20	22	2	−4	−29	81	79	3.2	81	14	N
D	54	22	9	−32	12	−6	−13	−36	81	80	3.2	81	17	D

Toronto (Ontario) 379 ft (116 m) 43°40′ N 79°24′ W 105 years   **CANADA**

	Temperature °F			Temperature °C			Relative humidity		Precipitation		
	Highest recorded	Average daily	Lowest recorded	Highest recorded	Average daily	Lowest recorded	0630 hours	1230 hours	Average monthly		Average no. days with 0.01 in + (0.25 mm +)
		max.	min.			max.	min.		%	%	in	mm	
J	58	30	16	−26	14	−1	−9	−32	78	70	2.7	69	16	J
F	55	30	15	−25	13	−1	−9	−32	78	67	2.4	61	12	F
M	80	37	23	−16	27	3	−5	−27	76	62	2.6	66	13	M
A	90	50	34	5	32	10	1	−15	74	56	2.5	64	12	A
M	93	63	44	25	34	17	7	−4	73	55	2.9	74	13	M
J	97	73	54	28	36	23	12	−2	78	58	2.7	69	11	J
J	105	79	59	39	41	26	15	4	79	56	2.9	74	10	J
A	102	77	58	40	39	25	14	4	83	58	2.7	69	9	A
S	96	69	51	28	36	21	11	−2	87	60	2.9	74	12	S
O	85	56	40	16	29	13	4	−9	87	62	2.4	61	11	O
N	70	43	31	−5	21	6	−1	−21	82	68	2.8	71	13	N
D	61	33	21	−22	16	1	−6	−30	80	71	2.6	66	13	D

THE CANADIAN PRAIRIES

This region consists of the southern parts of the three prairie provinces: Manitoba, Saskatchewan and Alberta. Lying between the western shores of Lake Superior and the Rocky Mountains, it has the most continental climate of any part of Canada. Winters are long and severe, with minimum temperatures not much higher than those recorded farther north in the Canadian Arctic. The relatively short summers are rather warm with a moderate rainfall, much of which falls in heavy showers. The summers are warm enough, and just long enough, to make this an important wheat-growing region. Like the Midwest region of the United States, which borders it on the south, there is much fine, sunny weather. Sunshine hours a day average three to four in winter and nine to ten in summer. Winter snowfall is comparatively light and the ground is often swept bare of snow by strong winds before the next fall occurs. The transition from summer to winter and from winter to summer often occurs very quickly, so that the concept of spring and autumn as understood in more temperate or maritime climates is misleading.

The tables for **Winnipeg**, **Saskatoon** and **Edmonton** are representative of this region. **Edmonton** has experienced rather higher temperatures in the midwinter months of January and February than the other two places. This shows the effect of the chinook which can suddenly raise winter temperatures for a day or two at the foot of the Rockies. It is a föhn-type wind and occurs when air is drawn from the west across the mountains and is warmed as it descends on the eastern side. It can be very effective in melting snow quickly.

CANADA Edmonton (Alberta) 2199 ft (677 m) 53°35′ N 113°30′ W 56 years

		Temperature °F				Temperature °C			Relative humidity		Precipitation			
	Highest recorded	Average daily		Lowest recorded	Highest recorded	Average daily		Lowest recorded	0500 hours	1100 hours	Average monthly		Average no. days with 0.01 in + (0.25 mm +)	
		max.	min.			max.	min.		%	%	in	mm		
J	57	15	−4	−57	14	−9	−20	−50	86	78	0.9	23	12	J
F	62	22	1	−57	17	−6	−17	−50	86	75	0.6	15	9	F
M	72	34	12	−40	22	1	−11	−40	85	68	0.8	20	10	M
A	88	52	28	−15	31	11	−2	−26	79	50	0.9	23	8	A
M	94	64	38	10	34	18	3	−23	81	47	1.9	48	12	M
J	99	70	45	25	37	21	7	−4	88	65	3.1	79	15	J
J	98	74	49	29	37	23	9	−2	89	58	3.3	84	14	J
A	96	72	47	26	36	22	8	−3	91	58	2.3	58	12	A
S	90	62	38	12	32	17	3	−11	90	61	1.3	33	9	S
O	83	52	30	−15	28	11	−1	−27	84	62	0.7	18	9	O
N	74	34	16	−44	23	1	−9	−42	88	74	0.7	18	11	N
D	61	21	5	−46	16	−6	−15	−43	87	78	0.8	20	12	D

Saskatoon (Saskatchewan) 1690 ft (515 m) 52°08′ N 106°38′ W 38 years　　　　　**CANADA**

	Temperature °F				Temperature °C				Relative humidity		Precipitation			
	Highest recorded	Average daily		Lowest recorded	Highest recorded	Average daily		Lowest recorded	0530 hours	1730 hours	Average monthly		Average no. days with 0.01 in + (0.25 mm +)	
		max.	min.			max.	min.		%	%	in	mm		
J	50	9	−11	−55	10	−13	−24	−49	98	86	0.9	23	9	J
F	55	13	−8	−49	13	−11	−22	−45	94	89	0.5	13	10	F
M	73	27	6	−34	23	−3	−14	−37	93	75	0.7	18	6	M
A	91	49	26	−9	33	9	−3	−23	84	52	0.7	18	7	A
M	99	64	38	9	37	18	3	−13	83	47	1.4	36	10	M
J	104	71	48	26	40	22	9	−3	85	50	2.6	66	12	J
J	104	77	52	31	40	25	11	−1	87	47	2.4	61	9	J
A	100	75	48	28	38	24	9	−2	89	46	1.9	48	9	A
S	92	63	38	12	33	17	3	−11	86	53	1.5	38	8	S
O	90	51	27	−14	32	11	−3	−26	86	62	0.9	23	7	O
N	68	31	12	−31	20	−1	−11	−35	90	83	0.5	13	9	N
D	58	16	−2	−41	14	−9	−19	−41	92	88	0.6	15	7	D

Winnipeg (Manitoba) 786 ft (240 m) 49°54′ N 97°14′ W 66 years　　　　　**CANADA**

	Temperature °F				Temperature °C				Relative humidity		Precipitation			
	Highest recorded	Average daily		Lowest recorded	Highest recorded	Average daily		Lowest recorded	0600 hours	1200 hours	Average monthly		Average no. days with 0.01 in + (0.25 mm +)	
		max.	min.			max.	min.		%	%	in	mm		
J	46	7	−13	−48	8	−14	−25	−44	89	83	0.9	23	12	J
F	47	12	−9	−47	8	−11	−23	−44	92	83	0.9	23	11	F
M	74	27	5	−38	23	−3	−15	−39	89	78	1.2	31	9	M
A	90	48	27	−18	32	9	−3	−28	82	57	1.4	36	9	A
M	100	65	39	11	38	18	4	−12	80	52	2.3	58	10	M
J	101	74	50	21	38	23	10	−6	85	60	3.1	79	12	J
J	108	79	55	35	42	26	13	2	85	53	3.1	79	10	J
A	103	76	51	30	39	24	11	−1	88	53	2.5	64	10	A
S	99	65	43	17	37	18	6	−8	90	61	2.3	58	9	S
O	86	51	31	−5	30	11	−1	−21	86	62	1.5	38	6	O
N	71	30	13	−34	22	−1	−11	−37	89	79	1.1	28	9	N
D	53	15	−3	−54	12	−9	−19	−48	92	85	0.9	23	11	D

WESTERN CANADA INCLUDING THE ROCKIES

This is a mountainous region with a very indented coastline on the Pacific Ocean. It includes the southern part of the province of British Columbia and the western part of Alberta within the Rocky Mountains. The highest mountains rise to between 10,000 and 13,000 ft (3000 and 4000 m) and are found in two chains: the western or Coast Mountains and the eastern or main chain of the Rockies. The area between consists of deep valleys and high plateaux. Because of this varied relief and wide range of altitude there are many local differences of weather and climate.

The Coast Mountains have a very heavy precipitation and above 4000 ft (1200 m) much of this is snow. Some of the valleys have a very low annual precipitation; as little as 15 in (375 mm). The coastal region, which includes numerous islands, has a very mild winter climate with much rainfall at this season. It has the warmest winters of any part of Canada. Weather and climate around the year are very similar to that found in the British Isles, but the summers are a little warmer and sunnier. These mild winters quickly give way to severe conditions inland with frequent snowfalls in the mountains and quite low temperatures in the valleys where winter frosts are hard and frequent. This difference is well illustrated by the two tables for **Vancouver**, on the coast, and **Prince George** which is well inland in the valley of the Fraser river. The winter minimum temperatures at **Prince George** are almost as low as those experienced in the Prairies. The winter precipitation at **Prince George** is very much less than that on the coast.

This region is less sunny than much of central Canada. Winter sunshine is reduced by the more frequent cloudy days, and on the coast fog is a frequent occurrence. The summers are fairly sunny with an average eight to nine hours a day as compared with only two to three in winter. Although the weather is often changeable this is perhaps the most climatically favourable region of Canada; the coastal districts escape the harsh Canadian winter and the summers are warm and rarely too hot or oppressive.

Prince George (British Columbia) 2218 ft (677 m) 53°53′ N 122°40′ W 27 years — CANADA

	Temperature °F				Temperature °C				Relative humidity		Precipitation			
	Highest recorded	Average daily		Lowest recorded	Highest recorded	Average daily		Lowest recorded	0430 hours	1630 hours	Average monthly		Average no. days with 0.01 in + (0.25 mm +)	
		max.	min.			max.	min.		%	%	in	mm		
J	54	23	3	−57	12	−5	−16	−49	89	86	1.8	46	14	J
F	58	31	6	−52	14	−1	−14	−47	92	77	1.2	31	12	F
M	68	42	18	−35	20	6	−8	−37	82	59	1.4	36	13	M
A	86	54	27	−13	30	12	−3	−25	84	49	0.8	20	12	A
M	95	64	34	12	35	18	1	−11	83	41	1.3	33	11	M
J	93	70	42	24	34	21	6	−4	88	55	2.1	53	15	J
J	102	75	44	28	39	24	7	−2	93	52	1.6	41	15	J
A	96	74	43	25	36	23	6	−4	92	48	1.9	48	14	A
S	92	65	36	6	33	18	2	−14	92	58	2.0	51	13	S
O	84	52	30	−4	29	11	−1	−20	91	68	2.0	51	16	O
N	62	38	21	−28	17	3	−6	−33	93	86	1.9	48	14	N
D	55	25	8	−56	13	−4	−13	−48	93	89	1.9	48	13	D

Vancouver (British Columbia) 45 ft (14 m) 49°17′ N 123°05′ W 43 years — CANADA

	Temperature °F				Temperature °C				Relative humidity		Precipitation			
	Highest recorded	Average daily		Lowest recorded	Highest recorded	Average daily		Lowest recorded	0430 hours	1630 hours	Average monthly		Average no. days with 0.01 in + (0.25 mm +)	
		max.	min.			max.	min.		%	%	in	mm		
J	59	41	32	2	15	5	0	−17	93	85	8.6	218	20	J
F	61	44	34	8	16	7	1	−13	91	78	5.8	147	17	F
M	68	50	37	15	20	10	3	−9	91	70	5.0	127	17	M
A	79	58	40	27	26	14	4	−3	89	67	3.3	84	14	A
M	83	64	46	33	28	18	8	1	88	63	2.8	71	12	M
J	92	69	52	35	33	21	11	2	87	65	2.5	64	11	J
J	91	74	54	40	33	23	12	4	89	62	1.2	31	7	J
A	92	73	54	39	33	23	12	4	90	62	1.7	43	8	A
S	85	65	49	30	29	18	9	−1	92	72	3.6	91	9	S
O	77	57	44	21	25	14	7	−6	92	80	5.8	147	16	O
N	74	48	39	10	23	9	4	−12	91	84	8.3	211	19	N
D	60	43	35	8	16	6	2	−13	91	88	8.8	224	22	D

This region comprises at least two thirds of Canada but it is very sparsely populated because it has such a harsh climate which is quite unsuitable for any form of agriculture. It resembles the climate of northern European Russia and Siberia. In the south it consists of a vast area of coniferous forest, to the north of which lies the Arctic tundra region, covered with snow for eight to nine months of the year. In the far north the islands of the Arctic archipelago to the west of Greenland are covered with snow and ice throughout the year. This vast region includes the Yukon and Northwest Territories and the northern parts of the provinces of British Columbia, Alberta, Saskatchewan, Manitoba, Ontario and Quebec.

The harsh conditions during the long winter are well illustrated by the temperatures in the tables for **Churchill**, on the shores of Hudson Bay, for **Norman Wells**, on the Mackenzie river just south of the Arctic Circle, and for **Arctic Bay**, on the northern shore of Baffin Island. The tables show that at **Churchill** and **Norman Wells** temperatures can rise to quite high levels during the short summer. For much of the summer, however, the weather can be changeable and disturbed. Snow and frost may occur in any month when cold air is drawn down from the polar regions.

In the north of this region the phenomenon of permafrost is widespread. The top two or three feet of ground thaw during the summer but below this the earth is frozen for tens or even hundreds of feet. This poses particular problems for building and construction works which involve any foundations, whether housing, roads or oil and gas pipelines. The line marking the approximate southern limit of permafrost runs from northwest to southeast from the Yukon and Great Slave Lake to the southern shore of Hudson Bay and then eastwards to the coast of Labrador.

Wind chill (see pp. 10–11) is a frequent, and probably the most dangerous, weather hazard in northern Canada. During severe weather in winter it can be a serious problem in almost any part of the country, except on the west coast. A combination of low temperature and high wind is much more dangerous than very low temperature in still air or a very light wind.

CANADA — Arctic Bay (Northwest Territories) 36 ft (11 m) 73°16′ N 84°17′ W 12 years

	Temperature °F				Temperature °C				Relative humidity		Precipitation			
	Highest recorded	Average daily		Lowest recorded	Highest recorded	Average daily		Lowest recorded	0700 hours	1900 hours	Average monthly		Average no. days with 0.01 in + (0.25 mm +)	
		max.	min.			max.	min.		%	%	in	mm		
J	28	−14	−28	−51	−2	−26	−33	−46	—	—	0.3	8	6	J
F	36	−19	−33	−57	2	−28	−36	−50	—	—	0.2	5	3	F
M	27	−7	−25	−49	−3	−22	−32	−45	—	—	0.3	8	6	M
A	34	6	−14	−37	1	−14	−26	−38	—	—	0.2	5	6	A
M	51	27	12	−14	11	−3	−11	−26	86	80	0.3	8	6	M
J	63	42	30	11	17	6	−1	−12	81	75	0.5	13	6	J
J	75	51	36	22	24	11	2	−6	82	75	0.7	18	7	J
A	64	47	35	24	18	8	2	−4	87	81	1.3	33	10	A
S	56	34	26	9	13	1	−3	−13	85	82	0.9	23	8	S
O	44	20	10	−12	7	−7	−12	−24	83	82	0.7	18	8	O
N	34	2	−10	−42	1	−17	−23	−41	—	—	0.3	8	6	N
D	34	−10	−22	−41	1	−23	−30	−41	—	—	0.2	5	5	D

Churchill (Manitoba) 43 ft (13 m) 58°47′ N 94°11′ W 30 years — CANADA

		Temperature °F				Temperature °C			Relative humidity		Precipitation		
	Highest recorded	Average daily		Lowest recorded	Highest recorded	Average daily		Lowest recorded	0600 hours	1200 hours	Average monthly		Average no. days with 0.01 in + (0.25 mm +)
		max.	min.			max.	min.		%	%	in	mm	
J	39	−11	−27	−57	4	−24	−33	−49	—	—	0.5	13	5	J
F	31	−8	−25	−52	−1	−22	−32	−48	—	—	0.6	15	6	F
M	41	4	−16	−52	5	−16	−27	−48	—	—	0.9	23	6	M
A	62	24	4	−26	17	−4	−16	−32	93	88	0.9	23	6	A
M	87	38	22	−14	31	3	−6	−26	92	86	0.9	23	7	M
J	88	52	34	13	31	11	1	−11	88	73	1.9	48	9	J
J	96	64	43	22	36	18	6	−6	88	71	2.2	56	10	J
A	90	62	43	25	32	17	6	−4	93	74	2.7	69	12	A
S	84	49	34	15	29	9	1	−9	94	84	2.3	58	11	S
O	65	34	20	−17	18	1	−7	−27	95	89	1.4	36	12	O
N	45	13	−2	−53	7	−11	−19	−47	94	91	1.0	25	9	N
D	34	−3	−19	−47	1	−19	−28	−44	97	93	0.7	18	8	D

Norman Wells (Northwest Territories) 290 ft (88 m) 65°15′ N 126°38′ W 7 years — CANADA

		Temperature °F				Temperature °C			Relative humidity		Precipitation		
	Highest recorded	Average daily		Lowest recorded	Highest recorded	Average daily		Lowest recorded	0400 hours	1000 hours	Average monthly		Average no. days with 0.01 in + (0.25 mm +)
		max.	min.			max.	min.		%	%	in	mm	
J	27	−11	−26	−63	−3	−24	−32	−53	90	88	0.7	18	14	J
F	22	−7	−23	−66	−6	−22	−31	−54	85	81	0.6	15	11	F
M	52	10	−12	−51	11	−12	−24	−46	85	84	0.3	8	8	M
A	58	31	7	−25	14	−1	−14	−32	85	71	0.5	13	8	A
M	88	53	32	8	31	12	0	13	81	65	0.7	18	6	M
J	88	68	46	30	31	20	8	−1	77	59	1.4	36	10	J
J	89	72	50	30	32	22	10	−1	81	63	2.0	51	10	J
A	89	65	45	21	32	18	7	−6	88	71	2.7	69	13	A
S	78	50	35	7	26	10	2	−14	89	81	1.7	43	13	S
O	59	32	20	−17	15	0	−7	−27	90	87	0.8	20	11	O
N	35	9	−4	−45	2	−13	−20	−43	94	94	0.8	20	14	N
D	35	−6	−21	−53	2	−21	−29	−47	90	89	0.7	18	12	D

119

Greenland has an area four times as large as France or the state of Texas and is situated between 60° and 83° N so that threequarters of the country lies within the Arctic Circle. Only about 16 per cent of its area is free from permanent snow and ice. These ice-free areas consist of high mountains around the coast through which great glaciers descend to deposit masses of ice in the surrounding seas. They are the main source of icebergs in the North Atlantic. The northern shores are permanently blocked by sea ice. Baffin Bay on the west of Greenland has more open water in winter than the Greenland Sea to the east.

The table for **Godthaab** on the west coast is representative of the coasts of Greenland. Winters are long and severe and summers very short and cool. Precipitation, mostly snow, is moderately heavy around the coasts so that the ice-cap is continuously replenished.

The interior of the country consists of a great ice-cap up to 10,000 ft (3000 m) thick; it is the largest accumulation of snow and ice in the northern hemisphere. The table for **Thule** in the north of Greenland is representative of most of the interior ice-cap. This has a true Arctic climate with temperatures only above freezing for brief periods in the summer. There are occasional relatively warm summer days when the weather may feel quite pleasant if the wind is light or calm and the sun is shining. The low precipitation at **Thule** is probably typical of much of the interior ice-cap.

Conditions are most hazardous when there is a combination of low temperature and strong wind and, consequently, a high wind chill (see pp. 10–11). Strong winds are often a feature of the winter weather on the coast as very cold air from the interior is funnelled down the glaciated valleys when a North Atlantic depression passes near the coast. The Greenland ice-cap is the source of some of the coldest air to affect northwest Europe.

	Temperature °F				Temperature °C				Relative humidity	Precipitation			
	Highest recorded	Average daily		Lowest recorded	Highest recorded	Average daily		Lowest recorded	All hours	Average monthly		Average no. days with 0.004 in + (0.01 mm +)	
		max.	min.			max.	min.		%	in	mm		
J	52	19	10	−20	11	−7	−12	−29	85	1.4	36	13	J
F	51	20	9	−17	11	−7	−13	−27	86	1.7	43	12	F
M	53	24	13	−19	12	−4	−11	−28	87	1.6	41	13	M
A	56	31	20	−6	13	−1	−7	−21	85	1.2	31	11	A
M	61	40	29	11	16	4	−2	−12	83	1.7	43	10	M
J	74	47	34	22	23	8	1	−6	92	1.4	36	10	J
J	76	52	38	29	24	11	3	−2	85	2.2	56	10	J
A	71	51	38	27	22	11	3	−3	86	3.1	79	12	A
S	62	43	34	18	17	6	1	−8	85	3.3	84	13	S
O	65	35	26	6	18	2	−3	−14	84	2.5	64	13	O
N	58	28	19	−1	14	−2	−7	−18	85	1.9	48	13	N
D	59	23	14	−14	15	−5	−10	−26	85	1.5	38	12	D

	Temperature °F				Temperature °C				Relative humidity		Precipitation			
	Highest recorded	Average daily		Lowest recorded	Highest recorded	Average daily		Lowest recorded	0330 hours	1530 hours	Average monthly		Average no. days with 0.1 in + (0.25 mm +)	
		max.	min.			max.	min.		%	%	in	mm		
J	36	1	−16	−37	2	−17	−27	−38	76	76	0.1	3	0	J
F	36	−4	−21	−41	2	−20	−29	−41	76	76	0.1	3	0	F
M	34	−2	−19	−38	1	−19	−28	−39	75	73	0.1	3	0	M
A	37	9	−10	−26	3	−13	−23	−32	88	71	0.1	3	0	A
M	44	28	16	−8	7	−2	−9	−22	77	74	0.1	3	0	M
J	59	41	30	22	15	5	−1	−6	81	78	0.2	5	1	J
J	59	46	36	28	15	8	2	−2	84	80	0.5	13	2	J
A	57	43	33	24	14	6	1	−4	77	71	0.5	13	2	A
S	45	33	21	6	7	1	−6	−14	80	76	0.4	10	1	S
O	50	23	8	−11	10	−5	−13	−24	80	78	0.1	3	0	O
N	38	13	−3	−28	3	−11	−19	−33	79	81	0.1	3	0	N
D	35	−1	−17	−37	2	−18	−27	−38	75	76	0.2	5	0	D

Mexico, the largest country of Central America, is bordered on the north by the United States and on the south by Guatemala and Belize. About three times as large as Texas, it is shaped roughly like a wedge, widest in the north and tapering to the narrow Isthmus of Tehuantepec in the south. It is situated between 14° and 32° N, the northern half of the country lying outside the tropics. Almost two thirds of the country consists of plateaux and high mountains with a climate that is warm-temperate; other parts have a tropical climate with temperature reduced by altitude.

There are three important climatic influences which help to determine the character of the climate of different parts of Mexico. The cold Californian current which sweeps southwards on the Pacific coast has the effect of lowering temperatures and reducing rainfall on the west coast as far south as the tip of the peninsula of Lower California. This and the influence of the North Pacific anticyclone help to make much of the northwest of the country desert or semi-desert; this is a continuation of the dry zone of the United States in southern California, New Mexico and Arizona.

The warm waters of the Caribbean Sea, and the influence of the constant northeast trade winds, make the eastern coastal region a typical tropical coast with a marked single wet season in summer. The weather and climate of this region, particularly south of Tampico, have much in common with that of the Caribbean Islands described on pp. 316–29.

An important influence is the presence to the north of the great continental landmass of the United States and Canada. This area becomes very cold in winter, particularly when cold air sweeps down from the Canadian Arctic, and very warm in summer. The northern part of Mexico shares in these extreme temperature conditions. In winter cold waves, or 'northers', can bring near-freezing conditions for a few days to the east coast as far south as Tampico or Vera Cruz. Snow has fallen as far south as Tampico which is within the tropics. The west coast is protected from such cold waves by the mountains and plateaux of central Mexico.

As in other mountainous South and Central American countries, the climatic zones are described on the basis of altitude, using the Spanish terms: tierra caliente, the area below about 2000 ft (600 m); tierra templada, the land between 2000 and 6000 ft (600 and 1800 m); and tierra fria, the mountain and plateaux above this level. Only a very narrow coastal belt on the Pacific shore falls into the tierra caliente category but there is a more extensive area on the Caribbean shore, including the whole Yucatan peninsula. The largest part of Mexico falls into tierra templada and tierra fria. This division takes little account of rainfall and is mainly on the basis of temperature. In most of the tierra fria, frost is frequent at night in winter and snow can occur anywhere, but only lies above 10,000–12,000 ft (3000–3600 m).

The rainy season over the whole country is the period

of high sun from May to October. The rest of the year is not completely rainless but the amount and frequency of rain in the winter season is low. The wettest part of the country is the lowland on the Caribbean coast; the north coast of the Yucatan peninsula is relatively much drier than the east coast or the interior. Annual rainfall here is between 40 and 60 in (1000 and 1500 m), but some places in northern Yucatan get less than 20 in (500 mm). The shores of the Pacific and Gulf of California, north of the Tropic of Cancer, get less than 10 in (250 mm) of rain a year, but this increases southwards to between 40 and 60 in (1000 and 1500 mm). Where the coast is backed by high mountains rainfall is heaviest. On the plateaux, where some of the winter precipitation may fall as snow, the annual rainfall is rather less than on the coast. Much of the plateaux is sheltered from maritime influences by the high mountains of the eastern and western Sierra Madre so that it has a reduced rainfall. Annual amounts of from 20 in (500 mm) or less in the extreme north to 35 in (875 mm) in the centre and south are typical of the central highland region.

Most of Mexico has sunny weather for a large part of the year. The cloudiest regions are the wetter parts of the east coast and the northern part of the Pacific coast where low cloud and fog are formed over the cold ocean current. The drier regions of the interior and much of the tierra templada have high amounts of sunshine: as much as seven to eight hours a day in the drier months to five or six during the wetter season.

The table for **Guaymas** is representative of the drier northwest of the country. Conditions in the interior are represented by the tables for **Monterrey** and **Mexico City**; these show a larger daily range of temperature. **Monterrey** is at the upper limit of the tierra caliente, while **Mexico City** is typical of the tierra fria.

The tables for **Merida**, in northern Yucatan, **Acapulco** and **Salina Cruz**, on the Pacific coast in the south, show the higher and typically tropical temperatures of the southern lowlands. **Merida** is wetter than some parts of Yucatan. The combination of heat and humidity can be rather uncomfortable during the wet season. Otherwise most of Mexico has a healthy and reasonably pleasant climate for most of the year.

At the altitude of Mexico City and above, visitors may take a few days to adjust to the lower atmospheric pressure as sudden exertion can lead to breathlessness. On the higher parts of the plateau the sun may at times feel very powerful by day and the rapid drop of temperature at night may strike very chilly.

Both the east and west coasts of Mexico are occasionally affected by tropical storms which develop in the Caribbean or the Pacific and bring two or three days of heavy rain. These are most likely to occur in the months August to October. Very few of these reach the strength of fully developed hurricanes and if they do the east-coast districts are more liable to severe damage.

Acapulco 10 ft (3 m) 16°50′ N 96°56′ W 30 years   **MEXICO**

	Temperature °F			Temperature °C			Relative humidity	Precipitation			
	Highest recorded	Average daily	Lowest recorded	Highest recorded	Average daily	Lowest recorded	All hours	Average monthly		Average no. days with 0.01 in + (0.25 mm +)	
		max.	min.		max.	min.		%	in	mm		
J	97	88	72	52	36	31	22	11	74	0.2	6	1	J
F	97	88	72	64	36	31	22	18	75	0	1	0	F
M	100	88	72	64	38	31	22	18	75	0	0	0	M
A	99	90	73	64	37	32	23	18	73	0	1	0	A
M	106	90	77	68	41	32	25	20	74	1.4	36	3	M
J	99	91	77	70	37	33	25	21	76	11.1	281	13	J
J	100	90	77	70	38	32	25	21	77	10.1	256	14	J
A	99	91	77	77	37	33	25	25	75	9.9	252	13	A
S	99	90	75	68	37	32	24	20	79	13.8	349	16	S
O	99	90	75	70	37	32	24	21	79	6.3	159	9	O
N	99	90	73	66	37	32	23	19	77	1.1	28	2	N
D	106	88	72	52	41	31	22	11	77	0.3	8	1	D

Guaymas 26 ft (8 m) 27°55′ N 110°53′ W 6 years   **MEXICO**

	Temperature °F			Temperature °C			Relative humidity	Precipitation			
	Highest recorded	Average daily	Lowest recorded	Highest recorded	Average daily	Lowest recorded	All hours	Average monthly		Average no. days with trace or more	
		max.	min.		max.	min.		%	in	mm		
J	86	73	55	45	30	23	13	7	52	0.2	5	2	J
F	102	75	57	43	39	24	14	6	53	0	0	1	F
M	95	79	60	49	35	26	16	9	50	0.3	8	2	M
A	104	84	64	53	40	29	18	12	48	0.2	5	1	A
M	111	88	69	56	44	31	21	13	50	0.2	5	1	M
J	109	93	76	64	43	34	24	18	57	0.1	3	1	J
J	111	94	80	69	44	34	27	21	63	1.7	43	7	J
A	117	95	80	69	47	35	27	21	64	3.6	91	8	A
S	109	95	78	64	43	35	26	18	66	2.4	61	6	S
O	109	70	72	55	43	21	22	13	67	0.4	10	2	O
N	99	82	64	48	37	28	18	9	70	0.6	15	3	N
D	100	74	56	46	38	23	13	8	72	1.5	38	5	D

	Temperature °F			Temperature °C			Relative humidity		Precipitation		
	Highest recorded	Average daily	Lowest recorded	Highest recorded	Average daily	Lowest recorded	0700 hours	1400 hours	Average monthly		Average no. days with trace or more
		max.	min.			max.	min.	%	%	in	mm	
J	92	83	62	53	33	28	17	12	87	53	1.0	25	8	J
F	95	85	63	51	35	29	17	11	84	48	0.7	18	6	F
M	98	89	66	52	37	37	19	11	84	46	1.1	28	6	M
A	106	92	69	58	41	41	21	14	80	41	1.1	28	5	A
M	104	94	72	63	40	40	22	17	81	45	3.1	79	10	M
J	103	92	73	69	39	33	23	21	87	58	6.8	173	19	J
J	97	92	73	64	36	33	23	18	88	56	4.8	122	20	J
A	100	91	73	67	38	33	23	19	89	58	5.3	135	19	A
S	96	90	73	68	36	32	23	20	90	62	6.1	155	20	S
O	94	87	71	63	34	31	22	17	87	62	4.0	102	17	O
N	91	85	67	56	33	29	19	13	86	55	1.3	33	12	N
D	92	82	64	55	33	28	18	13	87	53	1.2	31	9	D

	Temperature °F			Temperature °C			Relative humidity		Precipitation		
	Highest recorded	Average daily	Lowest recorded	Highest recorded	Average daily	Lowest recorded	0630 hours	1330 hours	Average monthly		Average no. days with trace or more
		max.	min.			max.	min.	%	%	in	mm	
J	74	66	42	27	23	19	6	−3	79	34	0.5	13	4	J
F	81	69	43	29	27	21	6	−2	72	28	0.2	5	5	F
M	84	75	47	34	29	24	8	1	68	26	0.4	10	9	M
A	90	77	51	33	32	25	11	1	66	29	0.8	20	14	A
M	89	78	54	43	32	26	12	6	69	29	2.1	53	17	M
J	87	76	55	49	31	24	13	9	82	48	4.7	119	21	J
J	83	73	53	47	28	23	12	8	84	50	6.7	170	27	J
A	81	73	54	49	27	23	12	9	85	50	6.0	152	27	A
S	78	74	53	34	26	23	12	1	86	54	5.1	130	23	S
O	78	70	50	35	26	21	10	2	83	47	2.0	51	13	O
N	77	68	46	36	25	20	8	2	82	41	0.7	18	6	N
D	73	66	43	32	23	19	6	0	81	37	0.3	8	4	D

Monterrey 1732 ft (528 m) 25°40′ N 100°18′ W 11 years — MEXICO

	Temperature °F			Temperature °C				Relative humidity		Precipitation			
	Highest recorded	Average daily	Lowest recorded	Highest recorded	Average daily		Lowest recorded	0730 hours	1430 hours	Average monthly		Average no. days with trace or more	
		max.	min.			max.	min.	%	%	in	mm		
J	94	68	48	25	34	20	9	−4	77	60	0.6	15	.6	J
F	99	72	52	26	37	22	11	−3	78	59	0.7	18	5	F
M	100	76	57	30	38	24	14	−1	68	45	0.8	20	7	M
A	105	84	62	42	41	29	17	6	77	53	1.3	33	7	A
M	107	87	68	51	42	31	20	11	76	51	1.3	33	9	M
J	105	91	71	55	41	33	22	13	83	57	3.0	76	8	J
J	102	90	71	60	39	32	22	16	75	49	2.3	58	8	J
A	102	92	72	60	39	33	22	16	79	57	2.4	61	7	A
S	101	86	70	51	38	30	21	11	76	66	5.2	132	10	S
O	95	80	64	45	35	27	18	7	73	67	3.0	76	9	O
N	94	71	55	30	34	22	13	−1	65	60	1.5	38	8	N
D	94	65	50	30	34	18	10	−1	66	55	0.8	20	6	D

Salina Cruz 184 ft (56 m) 16°12′ N 95°12′ W 10 years — MEXICO

	Temperature °F			Temperature °C				Relative humidity	Precipitation			
	Highest recorded	Average daily	Lowest recorded	Highest recorded	Average daily		Lowest recorded	All hours	Average monthly		Average no. days with trace or more	
		max.	min.			max.	min.	%	in	mm		
J	91	85	72	62	33	29	22	17	60	0.1	3	0.3	J
F	92	85	72	63	33	29	22	17	62	0.2	5	0.5	F
M	95	86	74	63	35	30	23	17	63	0	0	0.6	M
A	97	88	76	65	36	31	24	18	64	0	0	0.5	A
M	98	91	78	70	37	33	26	21	64	2.0	51	3	M
J	97	88	77	66	36	31	25	19	72	9.5	241	12	J
J	95	89	76	68	35	32	24	20	70	6.5	165	11	J
A	97	89	77	68	36	32	25	20	69	7.4	188	9	A
S	95	87	75	68	35	31	24	20	74	11.7	297	12	S
O	93	87	75	66	34	31	24	19	65	2.4	61	4	O
N	94	86	74	62	34	30	23	17	58	0.5	13	1	N
D	93	85	72	63	34	29	22	17	59	0.1	3	0.6	D

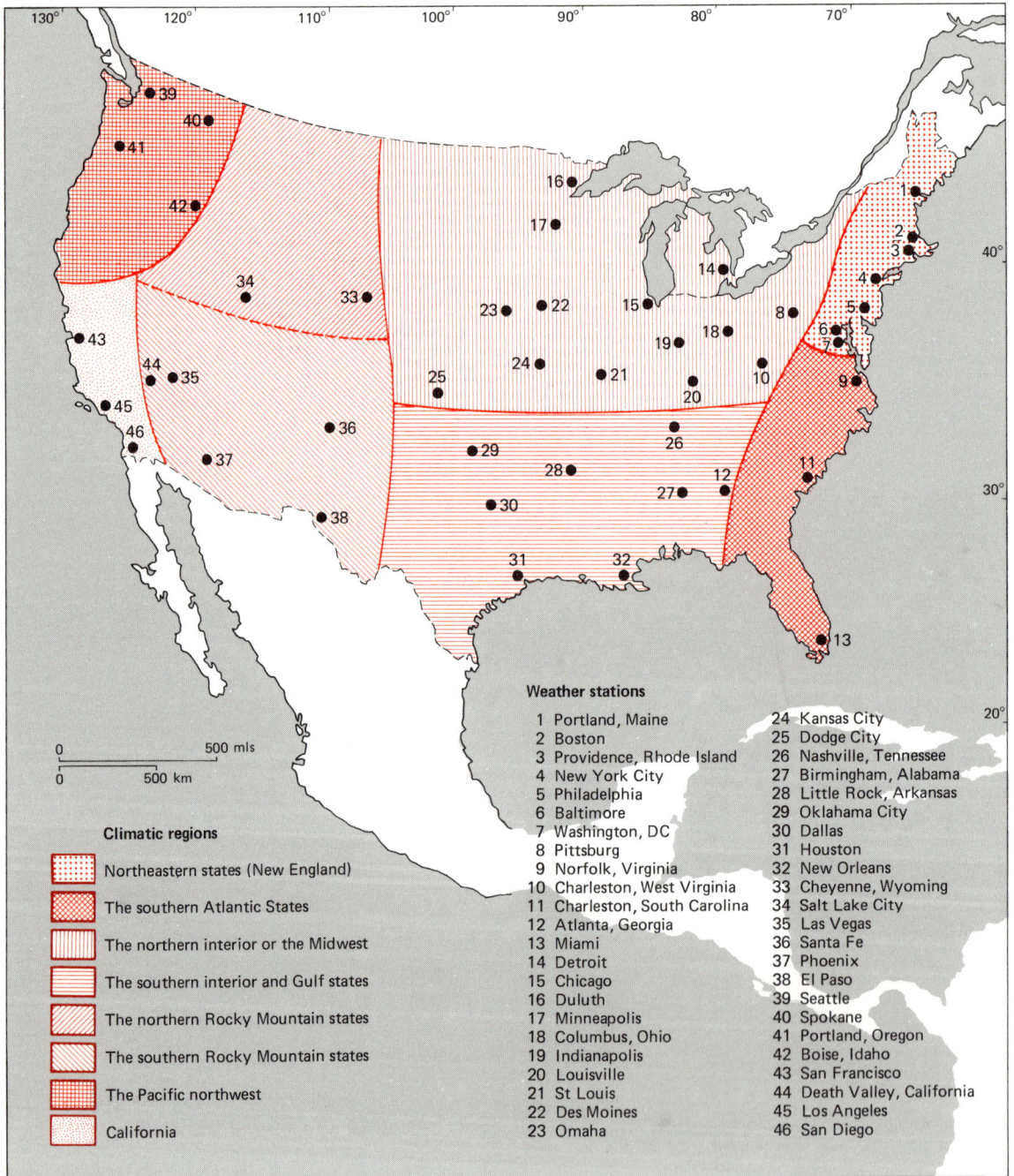

Weather stations

1	Portland, Maine	24	Kansas City
2	Boston	25	Dodge City
3	Providence, Rhode Island	26	Nashville, Tennessee
4	New York City	27	Birmingham, Alabama
5	Philadelphia	28	Little Rock, Arkansas
6	Baltimore	29	Oklahoma City
7	Washington, DC	30	Dallas
8	Pittsburg	31	Houston
9	Norfolk, Virginia	32	New Orleans
10	Charleston, West Virginia	33	Cheyenne, Wyoming
11	Charleston, South Carolina	34	Salt Lake City
12	Atlanta, Georgia	35	Las Vegas
13	Miami	36	Santa Fe
14	Detroit	37	Phoenix
15	Chicago	38	El Paso
16	Duluth	39	Seattle
17	Minneapolis	40	Spokane
18	Columbus, Ohio	41	Portland, Oregon
19	Indianapolis	42	Boise, Idaho
20	Louisville	43	San Francisco
21	St Louis	44	Death Valley, California
22	Des Moines	45	Los Angeles
23	Omaha	46	San Diego

Climatic regions

- Northeastern states (New England)
- The southern Atlantic States
- The northern interior or the Midwest
- The southern interior and Gulf states
- The northern Rocky Mountain states
- The southern Rocky Mountain states
- The Pacific northwest
- California

The United States is the fourth largest country in the world with an area of over three million square miles (7.8 million sq. km). It is bordered on the north by Canada and on the south by Mexico. Alaska and the Hawaiian Islands are both states of the Union but, because of their geographical detachment from the United States, they are described under separate headings on pp. 157 and 456 respectively. The area described here is situated between 25° and 49° N and lies entirely outside the tropics. It includes areas with a very great range of weather and climatic conditions around the year. On occasions parts of the USA experience extremes of heat and cold characteristic of hot tropical deserts or cold Arctic continental regions. Another feature of the weather and climate of the United States is the variation of weather over quite short periods at all seasons of the year.

The reason for this variation of weather is the position of the country in the belt of disturbed westerly winds so that, for much of the year, most regions of the USA are affected by cyclonic storms, or depressions, with their associated warm and cold fronts. Most of these depressions move across the country from west or southwest to east or northeast, bringing cloud, precipitation and disturbed, changeable weather. The central and northeastern parts of the USA are particularly liable to sudden changes of temperature during such periods of disturbed weather.

The central part of the USA – the Great Plains – which extend from the Rockies in the west to the Appalachian Mountains in the east, is mainly flat and mostly below 2000 ft (600 m) in height. This area is wide open to the influence of two very contrasting types of air-masses. Cold polar and Arctic air can sweep southwards from the Canadian Arctic regions, and warm, humid tropical air can move north from the Caribbean and the Gulf of Mexico. Each imports its own properties of temperature and humidity. When one air-mass is replaced by another, particularly during winter and spring, the temperature may change by as much as 40°–50° F (22°–28° C) within a few hours. Such sudden changes may also occur in the northeast of the country as far south as Virginia; farther south on the Atlantic and Gulf coasts the temperature changes are less dramatic but still produce a significant weather change. On the Pacific coast and west of the main chain of the Rocky Mountains the influence of the Pacific Ocean makes for a more equable climate with a much smaller range of temperature from winter to summer or from day to day. These maritime influences are to a large extent excluded from the centre of the country by the great mass of mountains and plateaux country which comprises the Rockies – the Western Cordillera.

The large size, particularly from west to east, of the North American continent also makes for seasonal extremes of temperature: winter cold and summer heat. Only the Pacific shores and, to a lesser extent, the coasts on the Gulf of Mexico and the Atlantic south of Virginia, benefit from the moderating effect of the sea in keeping temperatures more equable around the year. Compared with countries of western Europe in the same latitude, the United States has greater extremes of temperature, and daily or weekly changes are more noticeable. Much of the Midwest has a more extreme or continental climate than central or eastern Europe. Only Canada or the USSR east of the Urals is more extreme in terms of its annual range of temperature.

Some parts of the USA are liable to experience two particularly violent and destructive weather phenomena: hurricanes and tornados. Hurricanes affect the southeastern states bordering the Gulf of Mexico and the Atlantic once or twice in most years. These tropical storms, which bring very strong winds and torrential rainfall, move northeastwards from the Caribbean region before dying out in mid-Atlantic. They are described in more detail for the Caribbean islands on p. 316. Tornados are a very much more local and destructive storm of wind, often described as a 'whirlwind' or, in the USA, as a 'twister'. They can cause almost complete destruction of buildings on a narrow path not more than a few hundred yards wide. They mainly occur in spring and summer on days when there are violent thunderstorms associated with rapid changes of temperature along, or near, a cold front.

Much of the western third of the United States consists of a series of high mountain chains and interior plateaux and basins which are collectively termed the Rockies or the Western Cordillera. Weather and climate are here very variable from place to place depending on altitude and the degree of exposure or shelter. There are many lofty mountain ranges with peaks above 14,000 ft (4250 m), extensive high plateaux between 4000 and 7000 ft (1200 and 2000 m) and some small areas, such as Death Valley and the Salton Sink in southern California, which are below sea level. This makes for a great variety of climatic conditions with some very wet and snowy mountain regions and some semi-arid or even desert lowlands with great extremes of temperature. By contrast, in the central plains of the USA and, to a lesser extent, on the Atlantic coast, changes of weather and climate are much more gradual, and almost imperceptible, over great distances.

For a more detailed account of the weather and climate of this large country it is convenient to divide the USA into the following climatic regions, broadly coinciding with particular groups of states: the northeastern states, the southern Atlantic states, the Midwest or northern interior, the southern interior and the Gulf states, the states of the Rocky Mountains region, the states of the Pacific northwest, California, and Alaska. Climatic tables for the more important and representative places are included with the description of the appropriate region.

THE NORTHEASTERN STATES

This region consists of the small states which are often called New England: Maine, New Hampshire, Vermont, Massachusetts, Rhode Island, Connecticut, together with Delaware, New Jersey, Maryland and the eastern parts of the larger states of New York and Pennsylvania. The District of Columbia with the federal capital, **Washington**, is also included.

This region can experience changeable weather around the year with moderate amounts of precipitation in all months. Towards the north the winters are wet and usually snowy but south of New York summer tends to be slightly wetter. Summer heat-waves can produce temperatures over 100° F (38° C) for a few days and such hot spells are usually made the more uncomfortable because the humidity on or near the coast is high. In the great cities of this densely populated area heat-waves are even more uncomfortable for the temperatures in the city streets are often a few degrees higher than those recorded at meteorological stations, usually in large parks or rural districts.

Very cold spells can affect the whole region from time to time in winter or even spring; very severe snowfalls are likely in the north. The region includes the northern Appalachian Mountains whose heights rise to between 4000 and 6000 ft (1200 and 1800 m). At these higher levels winters can be prolonged and severe and there are many opportunities for winter sports. In summer the mountains provide resorts where relief can be obtained from the heat and humidity of the extensive coastal plains which contain the largest cities. This region has a more extreme or continental climate than the British Isles; summers are warmer and winters colder. It is also more extreme in other respects: day to day changes of temperature can be much greater and individual falls of rain and snow are often heavier than in most parts of Britain.

Although this is one of the less sunny parts of the United States it receives more sunshine round the year than most of northwest Europe. Daily sunshine hours on the coast, and at lower levels inland, average from four to five in winter and as much as nine or ten in summer. Locally, sunshine may be reduced on the coast by fog both in summer and winter; inland, or in the larger cities, winter fog may reduce the sunshine. Some valleys in the Appalachians are particularly foggy through a combination of industrial pollution and valley mists in winter.

Baltimore (Maryland) 14 ft (4 m) 39°17′ N 76°37′ W 48 years   USA

| | Temperature °F | | | Temperature °C | | | | Relative humidity | | Precipitation | | |
| | Highest recorded | Average daily | Lowest recorded | Highest recorded | Average daily | Lowest recorded | | 0800 hours | 1200 hours | Average monthly | | Average no. days with 0.01 in + (0.25 mm +) |
		max.	min.		max.	min.		%	%	in	mm	
J	79	42	28	−6	26	6	−2	−21	72	58	3.4	86	11	J
F	83	43	28	−7	28	6	−2	−22	70	56	3.2	81	10	F
M	90	51	35	5	32	11	2	−15	69	53	3.7	94	12	M
A	94	63	45	15	34	17	7	−9	65	50	3.5	89	11	A
M	98	74	56	34	37	23	13	1	67	51	3.6	91	11	M
J	105	82	65	46	41	28	18	8	70	53	3.8	97	11	J
J	107	86	69	54	42	30	21	12	71	52	4.4	112	11	J
A	105	84	67	51	41	29	19	11	74	55	4.5	114	11	A
S	101	78	61	39	38	26	16	4	75	56	3.5	89	8	S
O	97	67	50	30	36	19	10	1	74	53	3.0	76	8	O
N	82	54	40	12	28	12	4	−11	72	55	2.8	71	9	N
D	74	44	31	−3	23	7	−1	−19	71	58	3.1	79	10	D

Boston (Massachusetts) 124 ft (38 m) 42°22′ N 71°04′ W 59 years   USA

| | Temperature °F | | | Temperature °C | | | | Relative humidity | | Precipitation | | |
| | Highest recorded | Average daily | Lowest recorded | Highest recorded | Average daily | Lowest recorded | | 0800 hours | 1200 hours | Average monthly | | Average no. days with 0.01 in + (0.25 mm +) |
		max.	min.		max.	min.		%	%	in	mm	
J	70	36	20	−13	21	2	−7	−25	72	63	3.6	91	12	J
F	68	37	21	−18	20	3	−6	−28	71	61	3.3	84	10	F
M	86	43	28	−8	30	6	−2	−22	70	58	3.8	97	12	M
A	89	54	38	11	32	12	3	−12	69	57	3.5	89	11	A
M	97	66	49	31	36	19	9	−1	70	61	3.1	79	11	M
J	100	75	58	41	38	24	14	5	72	59	3.2	81	10	J
J	104	80	63	50	40	27	17	10	71	66	3.3	84	10	J
A	101	78	62	46	38	26	17	8	76	61	3.6	91	10	A
S	102	71	55	34	39	22	13	1	77	62	3.2	81	9	S
O	90	62	46	25	32	17	8	−4	75	58	3.3	84	9	O
N	78	49	35	−2	26	9	2	−19	73	65	3.6	91	10	N
D	69	40	25	−17	21	4	−4	−27	74	62	3.4	86	11	D

New York City (New York) 314 ft (96 m) 40°43′ N 74°00′ W 46 years

	Temperature °F			Temperature °C				Relative humidity		Precipitation			
	Highest recorded	Average daily	Lowest recorded	Highest recorded	Average daily		Lowest recorded	0730 hours	1200 hours	Average monthly		Average no. days with 0.01 in + (0.25 mm +)	
		max.	min.			max.	min.		%	%	in	mm		
J	68	37	24	−6	20	3	−4	−21	72	60	3.7	94	12	J
F	73	38	24	−14	23	3	−4	−26	70	58	3.8	97	10	F
M	84	45	30	3	29	7	−1	−16	70	55	3.6	91	12	M
A	91	57	42	12	33	14	6	−11	68	53	3.2	81	11	A
M	95	68	53	34	35	20	12	1	70	54	3.2	81	11	M
J	97	77	60	44	36	25	16	7	74	58	3.3	84	10	J
J	102	82	66	54	39	28	19	12	77	58	4.2	107	12	J
A	102	80	66	51	39	27	19	11	79	60	4.3	109	10	A
S	100	79	60	39	38	26	16	4	79	61	3.4	86	9	S
O	90	69	49	27	32	21	9	−3	76	57	3.5	89	9	O
N	75	51	37	7	24	11	3	−14	75	60	3.0	76	9	N
D	69	41	29	−13	21	5	−2	−25	73	61	3.6	91	10	D

Philadelphia (Pennsylvania) 26 ft (8 m) 39°57′ N 75°09′ W 58 years

	Temperature °F			Temperature °C				Relative humidity		Precipitation			
	Highest recorded	Average daily	Lowest recorded	Highest recorded	Average daily		Lowest recorded	0800 hours	1330 hours	Average monthly		Average no. days with 0.01 in + (0.25 mm +)	
		max.	min.			max.	min.		%	%	in	mm		
J	73	40	26	−5	23	4	−3	−21	75	65	3.3	84	12	J
F	79	41	27	−11	26	5	−3	−24	74	62	3.3	84	11	F
M	86	49	33	5	30	9	1	−15	73	60	3.4	86	12	M
A	93	61	43	14	34	16	6	−10	69	56	3.1	79	11	A
M	96	72	54	35	36	22	12	2	70	55	3.3	84	11	M
J	102	80	62	46	39	27	17	8	72	56	3.2	81	10	J
J	104	85	68	52	40	29	20	11	73	56	4.1	104	11	J
A	106	83	67	51	41	28	19	11	76	58	4.6	117	11	A
S	102	76	60	40	39	24	16	4	77	59	3.1	79	8	S
O	94	66	50	29	34	19	10	−2	75	56	2.8	71	8	O
N	78	53	39	8	26	12	4	−13	74	62	2.7	69	9	N
D	70	43	30	−5	21	6	−1	−21	74	63	3.4	86	10	D

Pittsburg (Pennsylvania) 749 ft (228 m) 40°26′ N 80°00′ W 73 years — USA

	Temperature °F			Temperature °C			Relative humidity		Precipitation		
	Highest recorded	Average daily	Lowest recorded	Highest recorded	Average daily	Lowest recorded	0730 hours	1200 hours	Average monthly		Average no. days with 0.01 in + (0.25 mm +)
		max. / min.			max. / min.		%	%	in	mm	
J	75	38 / 24	−16	24	3 / −4	−27	80	69	3.0	76	16	J
F	77	39 / 23	−20	25	4 / −5	−29	79	68	2.6	66	14	F
M	84	49 / 31	−1	29	9 / −1	−18	76	61	3.0	76	15	M
A	90	61 / 41	11	32	16 / 5	−12	72	57	3.0	76	13	A
M	95	72 / 52	27	35	22 / 11	−3	72	55	3.1	79	13	M
J	98	80 / 60	38	37	27 / 16	4	74	56	3.7	94	12	J
J	103	84 / 64	46	39	29 / 18	8	75	54	4.2	107	12	J
A	103	82 / 63	45	39	28 / 17	7	78	57	3.2	81	10	A
S	102	76 / 57	34	39	24 / 14	1	80	57	2.5	64	9	S
O	91	64 / 46	20	33	18 / 8	−7	80	60	2.6	66	10	O
N	79	51 / 36	1	26	11 / 2	−17	77	67	2.3	58	12	N
D	73	41 / 27	−9	23	5 / −3	−23	78	71	2.8	71	14	D

Portland (Maine) 103 ft (31 m) 43°39′ N 70°15′ W 67 years — USA

	Temperature °F			Temperature °C			Relative humidity		Precipitation		
	Highest recorded	Average daily	Lowest recorded	Highest recorded	Average daily	Lowest recorded	0800 hours	1200 hours	Average monthly		Average no. days with 0.01 in + (0.25 mm +)
		max. / min.			max. / min.		%	%	in	mm	
J	65	31 / 15	−18	18	−1 / −9	−28	75	62	4.0	102	12	J
F	58	32 / 16	−18	14	0 / −9	−28	74	61	3.9	99	11	F
M	79	40 / 26	−7	26	4 / −3	−22	71	60	4.0	102	13	M
A	89	50 / 35	9	32	10 / 2	−13	68	57	3.5	89	11	A
M	96	61 / 46	27	36	16 / 8	−3	70	58	3.3	84	12	M
J	96	71 / 54	38	36	22 / 12	3	73	60	3.3	84	12	J
J	103	76 / 60	48	39	24 / 16	9	75	63	3.3	84	12	J
A	98	74 / 59	44	37	23 / 15	7	78	62	3.2	81	11	A
S	96	68 / 52	32	36	20 / 11	0	79	63	3.2	81	10	S
O	85	57 / 42	22	29	14 / 6	−6	77	60	3.2	81	10	O
N	74	45 / 32	−6	23	7 / 0	−21	76	63	3.5	89	11	N
D	65	34 / 21	−21	18	1 / −6	−29	75	64	3.9	99	12	D

Providence (Rhode Island) 159 ft (49 m) 41°50′ N 71°25′ W 43 years

	Temperature °F				Temperature °C				Relative humidity		Precipitation			
	Highest recorded	Average daily		Lowest recorded	Highest recorded	Average daily		Lowest recorded	0730 hours	1330 hours	Average monthly		Average no. days with 0.01 in + (0.25 mm +)	
		max.	min.			max.	min.		%	%	in	mm		
J	68	37	22	−9	20	3	−6	−23	72	60	3.5	89	12	J
F	69	37	21	−17	21	3	−6	−27	72	59	2.9	74	10	F
M	90	46	29	4	32	8	−2	−16	69	55	3.5	89	12	M
A	91	56	38	11	33	13	3	−12	66	51	3.3	84	11	A
M	95	68	48	32	35	20	9	0	67	52	2.8	71	11	M
J	98	76	57	39	37	24	14	4	71	57	3.1	79	11	J
J	100	82	63	50	38	28	17	10	74	58	3.2	81	10	J
A	100	80	62	44	38	27	17	7	76	57	3.3	84	9	A
S	95	73	55	33	35	23	13	1	78	59	3.3	84	9	S
O	88	63	45	25	31	17	7	−4	76	55	2.8	71	9	O
N	75	51	35	9	24	11	2	−13	76	60	3.2	81	10	N
D	68	40	25	−12	20	4	−4	−24	72	60	3.5	89	10	D

Washington (District of Columbia) 72 ft (22 m) 38°54′ N 77°03′ W 78 years

	Temperature °F				Temperature °C				Relative humidity		Precipitation			
	Highest recorded	Average daily		Lowest recorded	Highest recorded	Average daily		Lowest recorded	0730 hours	1330 hours	Average monthly		Average no. days with 0.01 in + (0.25 mm +)	
		max.	min.			max.	min.		%	%	in	mm		
J	77	42	27	−14	25	6	−3	−26	73	56	3.4	86	11	J
F	84	44	28	−15	29	7	−2	−26	71	53	3.0	76	10	F
M	93	53	35	4	34	12	2	−16	72	48	3.6	91	12	M
A	95	64	44	15	35	18	7	−9	68	45	3.3	84	11	A
M	97	75	54	33	36	24	12	1	72	48	3.7	94	12	M
J	102	83	63	43	39	28	17	6	75	52	3.9	99	11	J
J	106	87	68	52	41	31	20	11	79	53	4.4	112	11	J
A	106	84	66	49	41	29	19	9	80	53	4.3	109	11	A
S	104	78	59	36	40	26	15	2	81	53	3.7	94	8	S
O	96	67	48	26	36	19	9	−3	81	50	2.9	74	8	O
N	83	55	38	11	28	13	3	−12	77	51	2.6	66	9	N
D	74	45	29	−13	23	7	−2	−25	74	55	3.1	79	10	D

This region includes the states of Florida, Georgia, North and South Carolina, Virginia and West Virginia. There is a gradual increase in the warmth of winter southwards along the Atlantic coast so that Florida has an almost tropical climate with only very rare and short cold spells when frost and snow occur. The northern part of Virginia and much of West Virginia in the Appalachian Mountains have winter conditions more typical of the northeastern region (see p. 128). On the other hand there is much less difference between the north and south of this region in terms of summer temperatures. The contrast is rather in the length of the summer season and the warmth of spring and autumn. Florida has a very oceanic climate, being much influenced by the surrounding warm Atlantic waters, so that summer temperatures do not reach the heights sometimes recorded as far north as New York. On the other hand Florida and the coastal lowlands of Georgia and the Carolinas have mild winters and frost and snow are much less frequent than in **Washington, DC**, or North Virginia. In northern Florida and southern Georgia snow only falls every ten or fifteen years but in southern Virginia it falls in at least two years out of three.

The proportion of the annual rainfall coming in the summer months increases southwards and a significant amount of this is associated with thunderstorms. Florida has more thunderstorms than any other state in the USA; over a hundred a year in parts of the state. This region is also affected by hurricanes, or less severe tropical storms, at least once or twice a year and they account for some of the heavier falls of rain in the months July to October. This is the sunniest part of the eastern United States with sunshine hours averaging from about six in winter to as much as nine or ten in summer. Florida is particularly sunny in winter which, combined with its much warmer temperature at this time, makes it a popular winter resort. The summer months in Florida are slightly less sunny than in areas farther north because of the regular afternoon build-up of cloud leading to thunderstorms.

Atlanta (Georgia) 1054 ft (321 m) 33°45′ N 84°23′ W 68 years — USA

	Temperature °F				Temperature °C				Relative humidity		Precipitation			
	Highest recorded	Average daily		Lowest recorded	Highest recorded	Average daily		Lowest recorded	0730 hours	1200 hours	Average monthly		Average no. days with 0.01 in (0.25 mm +)	
		max.	min.			max.	min.		%	%	in	mm		
J	76	51	35	−2	24	11	2	−19	80	67	4.9	125	12	J
F	78	54	37	−8	26	12	3	−22	78	66	4.8	122	11	F
M	87	62	43	8	31	17	6	−13	76	57	5.5	140	11	M
A	93	71	51	25	34	22	11	−4	73	54	3.7	94	10	A
M	97	79	60	38	36	26	16	3	74	55	3.6	91	10	M
J	102	86	67	39	39	30	19	4	77	55	3.7	94	11	J
J	103	87	70	58	39	31	21	14	82	57	4.7	119	13	J
A	101	86	69	55	38	30	21	13	84	59	4.3	109	12	A
S	102	82	64	43	39	28	18	6	81	57	3.2	81	8	S
O	94	72	54	28	34	22	12	−2	78	56	2.6	66	7	O
N	82	61	43	14	28	16	6	−10	77	60	3.1	79	8	N
D	75	52	37	1	24	11	3	−17	79	66	4.5	114	11	D

	Temperature °F			Temperature °C			Relative humidity	Precipitation		
	Highest recorded	Average daily	Lowest recorded	Highest recorded	Average daily	Lowest recorded		Average monthly		Average no. days with 0.01 in + (0.25 mm +)
		max.	min.			max.	min.			in	mm	
J	79	50	26	−9	26	10	−3	−23	—	3.8	97	13	J
F	80	51	27	−11	27	11	−3	−24	—	3.5	89	11	F
M	92	61	35	10	33	16	2	−12	—	4.3	109	12	M
A	96	70	42	18	36	21	6	−8	—	3.7	94	12	A
M	98	79	52	31	37	26	11	−1	—	4.0	102	11	M
J	103	85	61	41	39	29	16	5	—	4.4	112	11	J
J	106	89	64	48	41	32	18	9	—	4.2	107	10	J
A	108	87	63	48	42	31	18	9	—	4.5	114	10	A
S	101	84	58	33	38	29	14	1	—	3.0	76	7	S
O	96	72	45	20	36	22	7	−7	—	2.9	74	8	O
N	85	61	35	6	29	16	2	−14	—	3.1	79	9	N
D	77	51	28	−17	25	11	−2	−27	—	3.4	86	11	D

	Temperature °F			Temperature °C			Relative humidity		Precipitation		
	Highest recorded	Average daily	Lowest recorded	Highest recorded	Average daily	Lowest recorded	0730 hours	1200 hours	Average monthly		Average no. days with 0.01 in + (0.25 mm +)
		max.	min.			max.	min.	%	%	in	mm	
J	82	58	43	10	28	14	6	−12	81	64	2.9	74	10	J
F	82	59	44	7	28	15	7	−14	80	63	3.3	84	9	F
M	94	66	50	24	34	19	10	−4	79	62	3.4	86	9	M
A	93	73	57	32	34	23	14	0	75	61	2.8	71	8	A
M	99	80	66	45	37	27	19	7	75	63	3.2	81	8	M
J	104	86	73	49	40	30	23	9	77	65	4.7	119	11	J
J	104	88	75	61	40	31	24	16	79	67	7.3	185	13	J
A	102	87	75	62	39	31	24	17	82	68	6.6	168	13	A
S	100	83	71	49	38	28	22	9	83	68	5.1	130	10	S
O	95	75	61	37	35	24	16	3	80	62	3.2	81	6	O
N	83	66	51	23	28	19	11	−5	79	61	2.3	58	7	N
D	81	59	44	12	27	15	7	−11	81	65	2.8	71	9	D

Miami (Florida) 25 ft (8 m) 25°48′ N 80°12′ W 51 years USA

	Temperature °F			Temperature °C			Relative humidity		Precipitation			
	Highest recorded	Average daily	Lowest recorded	Highest recorded	Average daily	Lowest recorded	0730 hours	1200 hours	Average monthly		Average no. days with 0.01 in + (0.25 mm +)	
		max.	min.			max.	min.		%	%	in	mm	
J	85	74	61	29	29	23	16	−2	81	66	2.8	71	9	J
F	88	75	61	27	31	24	16	−3	82	63	2.1	53	6	F
M	92	78	64	34	33	26	18	1	77	62	2.5	64	7	M
A	93	80	67	45	34	27	19	7	73	64	3.2	81	7	A
M	94	84	71	50	34	29	22	10	75	67	6.8	173	12	M
J	94	86	74	61	34	30	23	16	75	69	7.0	178	13	J
J	96	88	76	66	36	31	24	19	75	68	6.1	155	15	J
A	96	88	76	60	36	31	24	16	76	68	6.3	160	15	A
S	95	87	75	62	35	31	24	17	79	70	8.0	203	18	S
O	93	83	72	52	34	28	22	11	80	69	9.2	234	16	O
N	88	78	66	36	31	26	19	2	77	64	2.8	71	10	N
D	91	76	62	30	33	24	17	−1	82	65	2.0	51	7	D

Norfolk (Virginia) 11 ft (3 m) 36°51′ N 76°17′ W 74 years USA

	Temperature °F			Temperature °C			Relative humidity		Precipitation			
	Highest recorded	Average daily	Lowest recorded	Highest recorded	Average daily	Lowest recorded	0730 hours	1330 hours	Average monthly		Average no. days with 0.01 in + (0.25 mm +)	
		max.	min.			max.	min.		%	%	in	mm	
J	80	49	34	5	27	9	1	−15	79	62	3.2	81	11	J
F	82	50	34	2	28	10	1	−17	77	56	3.4	86	11	F
M	92	58	40	14	33	14	4	−10	77	56	3.8	97	11	M
A	95	66	48	23	35	19	9	−5	74	53	3.3	84	10	A
M	98	76	58	33	37	24	14	1	76	54	3.7	94	11	M
J	102	83	66	49	39	28	19	9	79	58	4.2	107	11	J
J	104	87	71	57	40	31	22	14	81	61	5.8	147	13	J
A	105	85	70	56	41	29	21	13	82	62	5.2	132	11	A
S	100	80	65	40	38	27	18	4	82	63	3.8	97	8	S
O	94	70	55	31	34	21	13	−1	81	59	3.0	76	8	O
N	82	60	45	17	28	16	7	−8	80	58	2.5	64	8	N
D	76	51	36	5	24	11	2	−15	79	60	3.2	56	10	D

THE MIDWEST OR NORTHERN INTERIOR

This is a large region which includes all those states between the western Appalachians and the foothills of the Rocky Mountains approximately to the north of 37° N: North and South Dakota, Minnesota, Wisconsin, Michigan, Nebraska, Iowa, Illinois, Ohio, Kansas, Missouri, Indiana and Kentucky.

There are extensive plains in the valleys of the Ohio, Missouri and northern Mississippi. Most of the region is below 2000 ft (600 m) and much of it is below 1000 ft (300 m). It has the most continental climate of any part of the United States. Winters are cold, summers warm with quite frequent heat-waves and drought. There is a gradual increase in summer warmth southwards, but a more noticeable increase in the severity and length of winter northwards. Precipitation in winter is light, particularly in the west of this region, and much winter precipitation is snow. In the north, along the Canadian border and around the Great Lakes, winter conditions occasionally can be very severe with blizzards, as very cold air sweeps south from the Canadian Arctic.

There is a gradual decrease in the amount of annual precipitation westwards, and the western plains suffer most frequently from drought. The eastern states of Michigan, Indiana, Illinois and Kentucky have a heavier annual precipitation with much wetter winters than those farther west. An unpleasant feature of the weather in the north of this region is the frequent occurrence of freezing rain in winter as rain falls from a warm air-mass on to ground previously frozen hard. This is a serious danger to road traffic and it may occur on as many as five to ten days a year.

Almost the whole of the region has at least one winter month with an average temperature below freezing but, since the weather is frequently changeable, unseasonally mild conditions may occur for a few days even in midwinter. Clear skies and abundant sunshine are a feature of the weather for much of the time, even in winter. Sunshine hours a day average from four to five in winter and as much as ten or eleven in summer.

A feature of the western part of this region at the foot of the Rockies is the occasional warm dry wind, the chinook, which raises temperature and quickly melts snow in winter and spring. This is a föhn-type wind, warmed as the air descends to the east of the mountains.

Chicago (Illinois) 823 ft (251 m) 41°53′ N 87°38′ W 75 years USA

	Temperature °F			Temperature °C			Relative humidity		Precipitation		
	Highest recorded	Average daily	Lowest recorded	Highest recorded	Average daily	Lowest recorded	0700 hours	1200 hours	Average monthly		Average no. days with 0.01 in + (0.25 mm +)
		max.	min.		max.	min.		%	%	in	mm	
J	65	32	18	−20	18	0	−8	−29	80	70	2.0	51	11	J
F	68	34	20	−21	20	1	−7	−29	79	69	2.0	51	10	F
M	62	43	29	−12	17	6	−2	−24	77	64	2.6	66	12	M
A	91	55	40	17	33	13	4	−8	74	61	2.8	71	11	A
M	98	65	50	27	37	18	10	−3	73	59	3.4	86	12	M
J	102	75	60	35	39	24	16	2	76	61	3.5	89	11	J
J	105	81	66	49	41	27	19	9	75	58	3.3	84	9	J
A	102	79	65	47	39	26	18	8	79	61	3.2	81	9	A
S	100	73	58	29	38	23	14	−2	80	59	3.1	79	9	S
O	88	61	47	14	31	16	8	−10	78	59	2.6	66	9	O
N	78	47	34	−2	26	8	1	−19	79	65	2.4	61	10	N
D	68	36	23	−23	20	2	−5	−31	80	72	2.0	51	11	D

Columbus (Ohio) 724 ft (221 m) 39°58′ N 83°00′ W 68 years USA

	Temperature °F			Temperature °C			Relative humidity		Precipitation		
	Highest recorded	Average daily	Lowest recorded	Highest recorded	Average daily	Lowest recorded	0730 hours	1200 hours	Average monthly		Average no. days with 0.01 in + (0.25 mm +)
		max.	min.		max.	min.		%	%	in	mm	
J	72	37	22	−20	22	3	−6	−29	83	72	3.1	79	14	J
F	72	39	23	−20	22	4	−5	−29	82	72	2.7	69	12	F
M	84	49	32	0	29	9	0	−18	79	64	3.4	86	14	M
A	90	61	42	15	32	16	6	−9	74	61	2.9	74	12	A
M	96	72	52	31	36	22	11	−1	75	59	3.5	89	12	M
J	102	81	61	39	39	27	16	4	77	58	3.4	86	12	J
J	106	85	65	49	41	29	18	9	77	53	3.6	91	11	J
A	103	83	63	42	39	28	17	6	79	57	3.2	81	10	A
S	99	77	57	32	37	25	14	0	80	58	2.5	64	9	S
O	90	65	46	20	32	18	8	−7	81	60	2.5	64	9	O
N	78	50	35	−5	26	10	2	−21	82	68	2.8	71	11	N
D	67	39	26	−12	19	4	−3	−24	83	74	2.7	69	13	D

Des Moines (Iowa) 800 ft (244 m) 41°35′ N 93°37′ W 52 years

	Temperature °F			Temperature °C			Relative humidity		Precipitation			
	Highest recorded	Average daily	Lowest recorded	Highest recorded	Average daily	Lowest recorded	0700 hours	1200 hours	Average monthly		Average no. days with 0.01 in + (0.25 mm +)	
		max.	min.			max.	min.		%	%	in	mm	
J	65	30	12	−30	18	−1	−11	−34	83	68	1.1	28	8	J
F	78	33	15	−26	26	1	−9	−32	82	66	1.1	28	8	F
M	88	46	27	−10	31	8	−3	−23	79	56	1.8	46	9	M
A	92	61	40	11	33	16	4	−12	76	53	2.9	74	10	A
M	98	71	51	26	37	22	11	−3	76	49	4.4	112	12	M
J	102	80	61	37	39	27	16	3	79	55	4.8	122	11	J
J	109	86	65	48	43	30	18	9	78	51	3.4	86	9	J
A	110	84	63	40	43	29	17	4	82	54	3.6	91	9	A
S	99	76	55	26	37	24	13	−3	83	55	3.6	91	9	S
O	91	64	43	7	33	18	6	−14	80	52	2.5	64	8	O
N	79	48	30	−10	26	9	−1	−23	80	63	1.5	38	7	N
D	69	34	18	−21	21	1	−8	−29	82	69	1.2	31	8	D

Detroit (Michigan) 619 ft (189 m) 42°24′ N 83°00′ W 73 years

	Temperature °F			Temperature °C			Relative humidity		Precipitation			
	Highest recorded	Average daily	Lowest recorded	Highest recorded	Average daily	Lowest recorded	0730 hours	1200 hours	Average monthly		Average no. days with 0.01 in + (0.25 mm +)	
		max.	min.			max.	min.		%	%	in	mm	
J	66	31	19	−16	19	−1	−7	−27	85	76	2.1	53	13	J
F	65	32	18	−20	18	0	−8	−29	84	74	2.1	53	12	F
M	81	42	27	−7	27	6	−3	−22	80	67	2.5	64	13	M
A	88	55	37	8	31	13	3	−13	75	62	2.5	64	11	A
M	95	67	48	28	35	19	9	−2	73	59	3.3	84	13	M
J	104	77	58	38	40	25	14	3	74	58	3.6	91	11	J
J	105	82	63	48	41	28	17	9	73	53	3.3	84	9	J
A	104	80	62	43	40	27	17	6	77	53	2.7	69	9	A
S	100	73	55	30	38	23	13	−1	80	59	2.8	71	10	S
O	89	60	44	22	32	16	7	−6	81	62	2.4	61	10	O
N	75	46	33	0	24	8	1	−18	82	71	2.4	61	12	N
D	65	35	24	−24	18	2	−4	−31	84	78	2.3	58	14	D

Dodge City (Kansas) 2594 ft (791 m) 37°46′ N 99°58′ W 56 years — USA

	Temperature °F			Temperature °C				Relative humidity		Precipitation			
	Highest recorded	Average daily	Lowest recorded	Highest recorded	Average daily	Lowest recorded		0630 hours	1200 hours	Average monthly		Average no. days with 0.01 in + (0.25 mm +)	
		max.	min.			max.	min.		%	%	in	mm		
J	79	41	17	−20	26	5	−8	−29	80	54	0.4	10	4	J
F	84	46	21	−26	29	8	−6	−32	80	50	0.7	18	5	F
M	98	56	29	−10	37	13	−2	−23	76	46	0.9	23	6	M
A	95	67	41	13	35	19	5	−11	77	48	1.9	48	7	A
M	101	75	51	19	38	24	11	−7	80	51	2.9	74	11	M
J	107	85	61	36	42	29	16	2	80	48	3.2	81	9	J
J	108	90	66	46	42	32	19	8	78	43	3.1	79	8	J
A	105	89	64	43	41	32	18	6	80	43	2.6	66	7	A
S	102	82	56	30	39	28	13	−1	81	45	1.9	48	5	S
O	94	69	43	10	34	21	6	−12	79	47	1.4	36	5	O
N	85	56	30	−13	29	13	−1	−25	79	49	0.8	20	4	N
D	79	44	21	−15	26	7	−6	−26	80	56	0.6	15	4	D

Duluth (Minnesota) 1128 ft (344 m) 46°47′ N 92°06′ W 72 years — USA

	Temperature °F			Temperature °C				Relative humidity		Precipitation			
	Highest recorded	Average daily	Lowest recorded	Highest recorded	Average daily	Lowest recorded		0700 hours	1200 hours	Average monthly		Average no. days with 0.01 in + (0.25 mm +)	
		max.	min.			max.	min.		%	%	in	mm		
J	55	16	−1	−41	13	−9	−18	−41	88	80	1.0	25	10	J
F	58	20	3	−36	14	−7	−16	−38	87	78	1.0	25	9	F
M	81	32	16	−26	27	0	−9	−32	83	69	1.5	38	10	M
A	85	45	29	1	29	7	−2	−17	87	62	2.0	51	9	A
M	95	56	38	16	35	13	3	−9	75	60	3.2	81	12	M
J	97	67	48	31	36	19	9	−1	80	66	4.1	104	13	J
J	106	73	54	42	41	23	12	6	81	65	3.8	97	12	J
A	97	71	54	38	36	22	12	3	83	65	3.2	81	11	A
S	94	63	47	25	34	17	8	−4	84	69	3.5	89	11	S
O	85	51	37	8	29	11	3	−13	83	68	2.4	61	10	O
N	73	37	23	−29	23	3	−5	−34	85	74	1.5	38	9	N
D	56	23	8	−35	13	−5	−13	−37	88	82	1.1	28	11	D

Indianapolis (Indiana) 718 ft (216 m) 39°46′ N 86°10′ W 76 years

	Temperature °F				Temperature °C				Relative humidity		Precipitation			
	Highest recorded	Average daily		Lowest recorded	Highest recorded	Average daily		Lowest recorded	0730 hours	1200 hours	Average monthly		Average no. days with 0.01 in + (0.25 mm +)	
		max.	min.			max.	min.		%	%	in	mm		
J	70	36	22	−25	21	2	−6	−32	83	69	3.0	76	13	J
F	73	39	23	−18	23	4	−5	−28	81	67	2.7	69	11	F
M	84	49	32	−5	29	9	0	−21	78	60	4.0	102	13	M
A	90	61	43	19	32	16	6	−7	73	55	3.6	91	12	A
M	96	72	54	31	36	22	12	−1	72	51	3.9	99	13	M
J	101	82	63	39	38	28	17	4	74	53	4.0	102	11	J
J	106	86	67	48	41	30	19	9	72	49	3.9	99	10	J
A	103	84	65	44	39	29	18	7	77	53	3.3	84	9	A
S	100	77	58	30	38	25	14	−1	79	54	3.2	81	9	S
O	89	65	47	22	32	18	8	−6	79	55	2.8	71	9	O
N	78	50	35	−5	26	10	2	−21	79	64	3.3	84	11	N
D	59	39	26	−15	15	4	−3	−26	82	71	3.0	76	12	D

Kansas City (Missouri) 741 ft (226 m) 39°07′ N 94°35′ W 58 years

	Temperature °F				Temperature °C				Relative humidity		Precipitation			
	Highest recorded	Average daily		Lowest recorded	Highest recorded	Average daily		Lowest recorded	0630 hours	1200 hours	Average monthly		Average no. days with 0.01 in + (0.25 mm +)	
		max.	min.			max.	min.		%	%	in	mm		
J	70	38	22	−20	21	3	−6	−29	78	64	1.3	33	7	J
F	81	41	24	−22	27	5	−4	−30	78	59	1.7	43	8	F
M	91	53	34	−3	33	12	1	−19	75	53	2.6	66	9	M
A	95	65	46	16	35	18	8	−9	74	51	3.2	81	11	A
M	103	74	56	27	39	23	13	−3	75	54	4.9	125	12	M
J	108	83	65	44	42	28	18	7	78	56	4.8	122	11	J
J	110	89	70	53	43	32	21	12	76	51	4.1	104	9	J
A	113	87	68	46	45	31	20	8	78	52	4.1	104	9	A
S	107	80	60	34	42	27	16	1	79	54	4.6	117	10	S
O	98	68	49	17	37	20	9	−8	76	53	2.8	71	7	O
N	83	53	36	4	28	12	2	−16	74	57	1.9	48	6	N
D	74	41	26	−13	23	5	−3	−25	78	64	1.3	33	7	D

Louisville (Kentucky) 525 ft (160 m) 38°15′ N 85°45′ W 75 years — USA

	Temperature °F			Temperature °C				Relative humidity		Precipitation			
	Highest recorded	Average daily		Lowest recorded	Highest recorded	Average daily		Lowest recorded	0730 hours	1200 hours	Average monthly		Average no. days with 0.01 in + (0.25 mm +)	
		max.	min.			max.	min.		%	%	in	mm		
J	77	43	27	−20	25	6	−3	−29	78	67	4.1	104	12	J
F	78	45	29	−14	26	7	−2	−26	77	64	3.5	89	10	F
M	88	55	37	3	31	13	3	−16	75	56	4.3	109	12	M
A	91	66	47	21	33	19	8	−6	71	52	4.0	102	12	A
M	98	76	56	33	37	24	13	1	72	53	3.8	97	11	M
J	102	84	65	43	39	29	18	6	74	54	4.0	102	11	J
J	107	88	69	49	42	31	21	9	74	51	3.7	94	10	J
A	105	86	67	45	41	30	19	7	78	53	3.2	81	9	A
S	102	80	61	36	39	27	16	2	79	55	2.7	69	8	S
O	91	69	49	23	33	21	9	−5	79	54	2.8	71	8	O
N	82	55	38	1	28	13	3	−17	76	61	3.6	91	10	N
D	74	45	29	−7	23	7	−2	−22	78	67	3.7	94	11	D

Minneapolis (Minnesota) 830 ft (253 m) 44°53′ N 93°13′ W 57 years — USA

	Temperature °F			Temperature °C				Relative humidity	Precipitation			
	Highest recorded	Average daily		Lowest recorded	Highest recorded	Average daily		Lowest recorded	1200 hours	Average monthly		Average no. days with 0.01 in + (0.25 mm +)	
		max.	min.			max.	min.		%	in	mm		
J	58	22	6	−34	14	−6	−14	−37	71	1.0	25	8	J
F	64	25	8	−32	18	−4	−13	−36	72	1.0	25	7	F
M	83	38	22	−27	28	3	−6	−33	59	1.6	41	8	M
A	91	56	36	6	33	13	2	−14	51	2.3	58	10	A
M	106	68	48	22	41	20	9	−6	49	3.4	86	12	M
J	104	77	58	34	40	25	14	1	56	4.4	112	12	J
J	108	83	63	44	42	28	17	7	52	3.4	86	9	J
A	103	80	61	42	39	27	16	6	51	3.4	86	9	A
S	104	72	52	26	40	22	11	−3	56	3.4	86	9	S
O	90	59	41	10	32	15	5	−12	56	2.1	53	9	O
N	77	40	26	−13	25	4	−3	−25	65	1.4	36	7	N
D	63	27	12	−27	17	−3	−11	−33	73	1.2	31	8	D

	Temperature °F			Temperature °C				Relative humidity		Precipitation			
	Highest recorded	Average daily	Lowest recorded	Highest recorded	Average daily		Lowest recorded	0630 hours	1200 hours	Average monthly		Average no. days with 0.01 in + (0.25 mm +)	
		max.	min.			max.	min.		%	%	in	mm		
J	67	30	13	−32	19	−1	−11	−36	81	66	0.7	18	7	J
F	78	35	17	−26	26	2	−8	−32	80	63	0.9	23	6	F
M	91	47	28	−8	33	8	−2	−22	76	54	1.3	33	7	M
A	94	61	42	6	34	16	6	−14	74	54	2.7	69	10	A
M	99	72	53	25	37	22	12	−4	74	53	3.7	94	12	M
J	105	81	62	42	41	27	17	6	77	56	4.6	117	11	J
J	109	86	67	50	43	30	19	10	75	52	4.0	102	9	J
A	111	84	65	44	44	29	18	7	78	54	3.4	86	9	A
S	102	76	57	30	39	24	14	−1	80	54	3.3	84	9	S
O	92	64	45	8	33	18	7	−13	76	52	2.3	58	7	O
N	80	48	30	−14	27	9	−1	−26	77	62	1.2	31	5	N
D	71	35	19	−20	22	2	−7	−29	81	68	0.9	23	7	D

	Temperature °F			Temperature °C				Relative humidity		Precipitation			
	Highest recorded	Average daily	Lowest recorded	Highest recorded	Average daily		Lowest recorded	0700 hours	1200 hours	Average monthly		Average no. days with 0.01 in + (0.25 mm +)	
		max.	min.			max.	min.		%	%	in	mm		
J	74	40	24	−22	23	4	−4	−30	79	64	2.3	58	9	J
F	84	43	26	−18	29	6	−3	−28	78	62	2.5	64	9	F
M	92	54	36	3	33	12	2	−16	76	56	3.5	89	11	M
A	93	65	47	0	34	18	8	−18	72	55	3.8	97	11	A
M	96	75	57	32	36	24	14	0	74	56	4.5	114	11	M
J	104	84	66	44	40	29	19	7	75	55	4.5	114	11	J
J	110	88	71	55	43	31	22	13	74	50	3.5	89	9	J
A	108	87	69	52	42	31	21	11	77	53	3.4	86	8	A
S	103	80	62	36	39	27	17	2	79	56	3.2	81	8	S
O	93	68	50	21	34	20	10	−6	77	54	2.9	74	8	O
N	83	54	38	3	28	12	3	−16	75	61	2.8	71	8	N
D	75	43	28	−15	24	6	−2	−26	78	65	2.5	64	9	D

This large region includes the states roughly south of 37° N between the Rockies and the Appalachians and those with a coastline on the Gulf of Mexico: Oklahoma, Arkansas, Tennessee, Texas, Louisiana, Mississippi and Alabama. The general sequence of weather and climate around the year is rather similar to that in the Midwest; but, being in a more southerly latitude and more open to the flow of warm tropical air from the Atlantic and the Gulf of Mexico, the winters are both warmer and shorter than those farther north. It is rare for a winter month here to have an average temperature below freezing point, but occasional very cold spells may last for a few days when Arctic air penetrates this region from the north. Occasional snow and frost can occur as far south as the shores of the Gulf of Mexico, and in western Texas such cold spells are more frequent and more severe. Summers are a little warmer than farther north, but the increasing length of the summer period and the warmth of spring and autumn are more noticeable.

The eastern part of this region is much wetter than the west. Annual precipitation is almost everywhere between 40 and 50 in (1000 and 1250 mm) in the east, but it falls as low as 15–20 in (350–500 mm) in the west. Summer is the wettest season and thunderstorms are very frequent in the east of this region. Parts of the states of Tennessee and Alabama include the southern Appalachian Mountains; here winter precipitation is heavier and the weather and climate are more like those of the eastern Atlantic states.

Most of the region has a sunny climate, particularly the western parts of Texas and Oklahoma. Sunshine hours a day average from five to seven in winter to ten or eleven in summer. The summer heat is rarely unpleasant, except along the coast of the Gulf of Mexico where the combination of heat and humidity can be trying. Compare the afternoon relative humidity at **New Orleans** with that at **Dallas** or **Oklahoma City** in the tables.

This region is the one most affected by weather hazards: hurricanes and tornados, mentioned in the general account of the United States (p. 127).

Birmingham (Alabama) 610 ft (186 m) 33°34′ N 86°45′ W 35 years   USA

	Temperature °F			Temperature °C			Relative humidity		Precipitation			
	Highest recorded	Average daily		Lowest recorded	Highest recorded	Average daily		Lowest recorded	0700 hours	1200 hours	Average monthly		Average no. days with 0.01 in + (0.25 mm +)
		max.	min.			max.	min.		%	%	in	mm	
J	77	55	37	1	25	13	3	−17	79	59	5.4	137	11	J
F	82	57	38	−10	28	14	3	−23	76	57	4.8	122	10	F
M	90	66	46	12	32	19	8	−11	75	51	5.9	150	11	M
A	90	73	53	28	32	23	12	−2	74	50	5.0	127	9	A
M	99	81	61	38	37	27	16	3	77	54	4.3	109	10	M
J	101	88	68	47	38	31	20	8	78	54	4.4	112	10	J
J	107	90	70	57	42	32	21	14	83	55	5.2	132	12	J
A	103	90	70	55	39	32	21	13	85	55	4.2	107	11	A
S	106	86	66	41	41	30	19	5	82	51	3.1	79	7	S
O	94	76	55	27	34	24	13	−3	79	49	2.4	61	6	O
N	84	64	44	14	29	18	7	−10	77	54	3.5	89	8	N
D	77	55	38	5	25	13	3	−15	79	61	4.8	122	10	D

Dallas (Texas) 512 ft (156 m) 32°46′ N 96°47′ W 34 years

	Temperature °F				Temperature °C				Relative humidity		Precipitation			
	Highest recorded	Average daily		Lowest recorded	Highest recorded	Average daily		Lowest recorded	0630 hours	1200 hours	Average monthly		Average no. days with 0.01 in + (0.25 mm +)	
		max.	min.			max.	min.		%	%	in	mm		
J	88	55	36	−3	31	13	2	−19	79	60	2.5	64	9	J
F	93	60	40	2	34	16	4	−17	78	56	2.4	61	7	F
M	96	67	46	11	36	19	8	−12	74	50	3.3	84	7	M
A	96	75	55	30	36	24	13	−1	77	51	4.2	107	9	A
M	103	82	63	44	39	28	17	7	82	55	4.5	114	9	M
J	105	90	71	53	41	32	22	12	81	53	3.8	97	7	J
J	105	94	75	56	41	34	24	13	76	48	2.8	71	5	J
A	110	94	74	57	43	34	23	14	77	46	3.0	76	6	A
S	106	88	68	36	41	31	20	2	80	49	2.7	69	6	S
O	100	78	57	26	38	26	14	−3	81	51	2.8	71	7	O
N	87	66	47	19	31	19	8	−7	78	52	2.7	69	6	N
D	81	57	38	10	27	14	3	−12	78	55	2.5	64	7	D

Houston (Texas) 41 ft (13 m) 29°46′ N 95°22′ W 34 years

	Temperature °F				Temperature °C				Relative humidity		Precipitation			
	Highest recorded	Average daily		Lowest recorded	Highest recorded	Average daily		Lowest recorded	0630 hours	1200 hours	Average monthly		Average no. days with 0.01 in + (0.25 mm +)	
		max.	min.			max.	min.		%	%	in	mm		
J	84	62	44	5	29	17	7	−15	85	66	3.5	89	9	J
F	87	65	46	6	31	18	8	−14	85	61	3.0	76	8	F
M	94	72	54	23	34	22	12	−5	84	59	3.3	84	8	M
A	92	78	60	34	33	26	16	1	86	59	3.6	91	7	A
M	98	84	66	45	37	29	19	7	87	60	4.7	119	7	M
J	103	90	72	55	39	32	22	13	87	60	4.6	117	8	J
J	104	92	74	55	40	33	23	13	88	57	3.9	99	10	J
A	108	93	74	54	42	34	23	12	88	54	3.9	99	10	A
S	101	88	70	47	38	31	21	8	88	58	4.1	104	8	S
O	99	81	61	33	37	27	16	1	86	54	3.7	94	5	O
N	89	71	52	23	32	22	11	−5	84	58	3.5	89	8	N
D	83	63	45	15	28	17	7	−9	84	64	4.3	109	10	D

Little Rock (Arkansas) 357 ft (109 m) 34°45′ N 92°16′ W 67 years   USA

	Temperature °F			Temperature °C			Relative humidity		Precipitation			
	Highest recorded	Average daily	Lowest recorded	Highest recorded	Average daily	Lowest recorded	0700 hours	1200 hours	Average monthly		Average no. days with 0.01 in + (0.25 mm +)	
		max.	min.			max.	min.		%	%	in	mm	
J	81	50	34	−8	27	10	1	−22	79	65	4.8	122	10	J
F	87	54	36	−12	31	12	2	−24	78	61	3.8	97	9	F
M	90	63	44	11	32	17	7	−12	76	55	4.5	114	10	M
A	94	72	53	28	34	22	12	−2	77	54	5.1	130	10	A
M	97	79	61	39	36	26	16	4	80	57	4.9	125	10	M
J	105	87	69	51	41	31	21	11	81	57	3.8	97	10	J
J	108	90	72	58	42	32	22	14	82	53	3.4	86	9	J
A	110	90	71	52	43	32	22	11	84	53	3.7	94	9	A
S	104	84	65	37	40	29	18	3	84	54	3.1	79	7	S
O	93	74	54	27	34	23	12	−3	82	55	2.8	71	7	O
N	84	61	43	10	29	16	6	−12	80	59	4.1	104	8	N
D	78	52	36	5	26	11	2	−15	80	63	4.1	104	9	D

Nashville (Tennessee) 546 ft (166 m) 36°10′ N 87°47′ W 75 years   USA

	Temperature °F			Temperature °C			Relative humidity		Precipitation			
	Highest recorded	Average daily	Lowest recorded	Highest recorded	Average daily	Lowest recorded	0700 hours	1200 hours	Average monthly		Average no. days with 0.01 in + (0.25 mm +)	
		max.	min.			max.	min.		%	%	in	mm	
J	78	47	31	−10	26	8	−1	−23	81	65	4.6	117	12	J
F	79	50	33	−13	26	10	1	−25	80	62	4.1	104	11	F
M	89	59	40	3	32	15	4	−16	77	55	5.1	130	12	M
A	90	69	49	25	32	21	9	−4	74	50	4.3	109	11	A
M	96	78	58	36	36	26	14	2	77	54	3.8	97	11	M
J	101	86	67	42	38	30	19	6	78	54	4.1	104	11	J
J	106	89	70	54	41	32	21	12	79	51	4.0	102	11	J
A	105	88	68	51	41	31	20	11	83	54	3.6	91	9	A
S	104	82	62	38	40	28	17	3	84	53	3.4	84	8	S
O	92	72	50	26	33	22	10	−3	83	53	2.6	66	7	O
N	85	58	40	8	29	14	4	−13	80	60	3.5	89	9	N
D	75	49	33	−2	24	9	1	−19	81	64	4.0	102	11	D

New Orleans (Louisiana) 8 ft (2 m) 29°57′ N 90°04′ W 73 years

	Temperature °F				Temperature °C				Relative humidity		Precipitation		
	Highest recorded	Average daily		Lowest recorded	Highest recorded	Average daily		Lowest recorded	0700 hours	1200 hours	Average monthly		Average no. days with 0.01 in + (0.25 mm +)
		max.	min.			max.	min.		%	%	in	mm	
J	83	62	47	15	28	17	8	−9	85	69	4.6	117	10	J
F	84	65	50	7	29	18	10	−14	85	66	4.2	107	12	F
M	90	71	55	28	32	22	13	−2	85	64	4.7	119	9	M
A	90	77	61	38	32	25	16	3	83	62	4.8	122	7	A
M	96	83	68	52	36	28	20	11	82	61	4.5	114	8	M
J	102	88	74	58	39	31	23	14	81	62	5.5	140	13	J
J	102	90	76	66	39	32	24	19	83	63	6.6	168	15	J
A	100	90	76	63	38	32	24	17	84	63	5.8	147	14	A
S	99	86	73	54	37	30	23	12	84	62	4.8	122	10	S
O	94	79	64	40	34	26	18	4	82	60	3.5	89	7	O
N	89	70	55	29	32	21	13	−2	83	63	3.8	97	7	N
D	84	64	48	19	29	18	9	−7	84	68	4.6	117	10	D

Oklahoma City (Oklahoma) 1254 ft (382 m) 35°29′ N 97°32′ W 56 years

	Temperature °F				Temperature °C				Relative humidity		Precipitation		
	Highest recorded	Average daily		Lowest recorded	Highest recorded	Average daily		Lowest recorded	0630 hours	1200 hours	Average monthly		Average no. days with 0.01 in + (0.25 mm +)
		max.	min.			max.	min.		%	%	in	mm	
J	83	47	28	−11	28	8	−2	−24	81	62	1.3	33	6	J
F	90	51	30	−17	32	11	−1	−27	79	54	1.0	25	5	F
M	97	62	39	1	36	17	4	−17	76	48	2.2	56	7	M
A	96	71	49	20	36	22	9	−7	77	51	3.3	84	8	A
M	99	78	58	33	37	26	14	1	82	57	5.1	130	10	M
J	107	87	67	46	42	31	19	8	82	55	3.5	89	8	J
J	109	92	71	55	43	33	22	13	80	48	2.9	74	7	J
A	113	92	70	49	45	33	21	9	80	46	2.7	69	7	A
S	105	85	63	35	41	29	17	2	82	51	3.0	76	7	S
O	97	73	52	16	36	23	11	−9	79	55	3.0	76	6	O
N	86	60	39	9	30	16	4	−13	79	58	2.0	51	5	N
D	79	49	30	−2	26	9	−1	−19	80	59	1.6	41	6	D

All, or a large part, of each of the following states are situated in the mountainous country of the great Western Cordillera: Montana, Idaho, Wyoming, Nevada, Utah, Colorado, Arizona and New Mexico.

It is possible to make a broad distinction between the three northern states of Idaho, Montana and Wyoming and the rest. In general these northern states are cooler in both winter and summer, have a much longer cold season and are generally wetter than those farther south. Within this whole region, however, there are so many local variations of temperature and precipitation, because of the range of altitude, that one can find cold spots in the southern parts of the region and some dry areas in the north. The tables for this region give a good indication of the range of altitude and the effect this has on temperature in each month. For example, there is no great difference between precipitation and temperatures for **Cheyenne** in Wyoming and **Santa Fé** in New Mexico, both of which are above 6000 ft (1800 m). On the other hand, temperatures are very much higher in all months at **Phoenix** (Arizona) at 1083 ft (330 m) than at **Santa Fé**.

Much of this region has a low yearly precipitation, particularly in the south where large areas of Arizona, New Mexico, Utah and Colorado are desert or semi-desert with annual precipitation below 12 or even 8 in (300 or 200 mm). This is partly a consequence of the rain shadow of the western mountains in California which extract much of the moisture from air which comes in from the Pacific. It is also a result of the frequent and persistent anticyclonic weather which prevails in this region.

The table for **El Paso**, in Texas, has been included with those for this region, for this part of western Texas is mountainous.

The highest recorded and lowest recorded temperatures in the tables show that some extremely high and also extremely low temperatures have been recorded at different places in this mountain region: very low temperatures in the north and very high temperatures in the south. The southern part has the sunniest climate in the United States; both **Phoenix** and **Las Vegas** have about eight hours sunshine a day in winter and between twelve and thirteen hours in the summer months. The high summer temperatures in this area are made more bearable by the low humidity and the climate of this whole region is generally healthy. Under extreme conditions, however, both heat stress and cold stress can be experienced.

Cheyenne (Wyoming) 6139 ft (1871 m) 41°09′ N 104°49′ W 74 years

		Temperature °F				Temperature °C			Relative humidity		Precipitation		
	Highest recorded	Average daily		Lowest recorded	Highest recorded	Average daily		Lowest recorded	0600 hours	1200 hours	Average monthly		Average no. days with 0.01 in + (0.25 mm +)
		max.	min.			max.	min.		%	%	in	mm	
J	64	36	15	−38	18	2	−9	−39	61	49	0.4	10	6	J
F	66	38	16	−34	19	3	−9	−37	65	49	0.6	15	6	F
M	77	44	22	−21	25	7	−6	−29	67	49	1.0	25	8	M
A	82	53	29	−6	28	12	−2	−21	71	49	1.9	48	10	A
M	88	62	38	8	31	17	3	−13	73	46	2.4	61	12	M
J	97	74	47	28	36	23	8	−2	70	42	1.6	41	9	J
J	100	80	53	33	38	27	12	1	69	40	2.1	53	11	J
A	96	79	52	25	36	26	11	−4	70	39	1.6	41	10	A
S	91	71	43	16	33	22	6	−9	66	40	1.2	31	6	S
O	85	58	32	−5	29	14	0	−21	64	46	1.0	25	6	O
N	75	46	23	−21	24	8	−5	−29	60	48	0.5	13	5	N
D	69	39	18	−28	21	4	−8	−33	61	51	0.5	13	5	D

El Paso (Texas) 3920 ft (1194 m) 31°48′ N 106°24′ W 60 years

		Temperature °F				Temperature °C			Relative humidity		Precipitation		
	Highest recorded	Average daily		Lowest recorded	Highest recorded	Average daily		Lowest recorded	0600 hours	1200 hours	Average monthly		Average no. days with 0.01 in + (0.25 mm +)
		max.	min.			max.	min.		%	%	in	mm	
J	77	57	32	−6	25	14	0	−21	60	37	0.4	10	3	J
F	86	62	37	5	30	17	3	−15	54	32	0.5	13	3	F
M	93	69	42	14	34	21	6	−10	46	26	0.3	8	3	M
A	95	77	50	26	35	25	10	−3	40	21	0.2	5	2	A
M	102	86	58	36	39	30	14	2	38	20	0.3	8	2	M
J	106	94	67	46	41	34	19	8	43	22	0.6	15	3	J
J	105	93	70	56	41	34	21	13	60	33	1.8	46	9	J
A	103	91	68	52	39	33	20	11	65	36	1.6	41	9	A
S	100	86	63	41	38	30	17	5	63	35	1.3	33	6	S
O	94	77	52	26	34	25	11	−3	60	36	0.7	18	4	O
N	85	66	40	11	29	19	4	−12	60	36	0.5	13	3	N
D	77	57	33	−5	25	14	1	−21	62	42	0.5	13	4	D

Las Vegas (Nevada) 2006 ft (612 m) 36°10′ N 115°09′ W 20 years   USA

	Temperature °F			Temperature °C			Relative humidity		Precipitation			
	Highest recorded	Average daily	Lowest recorded	Highest recorded	Average daily	Lowest recorded	0500 hours	1700 hours	Average monthly		Average no. days with 0.01 in + (0.25 mm +)	
		max.	min.			max.	min.		%	%	in	mm	
J	80	60	29	8	27	16	−2	−13	59	33	0.7	18	2	J
F	89	67	34	10	32	19	1	−12	56	25	0.5	13	2	F
M	96	72	39	16	36	22	4	−9	47	21	0.3	8	2	M
A	102	81	45	26	39	27	7	−3	41	16	0.3	8	1	A
M	114	89	52	28	46	32	11	−2	31	12	0.2	5	1	M
J	113	99	61	35	45	37	16	2	26	10	0.2	5	1	J
J	115	103	68	40	46	39	20	4	30	14	0.5	13	2	J
A	114	102	66	47	46	39	19	8	32	15	0.5	13	2	A
S	108	95	57	38	42	35	14	3	30	13	0.3	8	1	S
O	101	84	47	29	38	29	8	−2	39	18	0.3	8	1	O
N	89	71	36	14	32	22	2	−10	49	25	0.2	5	1	N
D	91	61	30	12	33	16	−1	−11	61	35	0.4	10	2	D

Phoenix (Arizona) 1083 ft (330 m) 33°28′ N 112°04′ W 52 years   USA

	Temperature °F			Temperature °C			Relative humidity		Precipitation			
	Highest recorded	Average daily	Lowest recorded	Highest recorded	Average daily	Lowest recorded	0530 hours	1730 hours	Average monthly		Average no. days with 0.01 in + (0.25 mm +)	
		max.	min.			max.	min.		%	%	in	mm	
J	84	65	39	16	29	18	4	−9	69	39	0.8	20	4	J
F	92	69	43	24	33	21	6	−4	67	34	0.8	20	4	F
M	95	75	47	30	35	24	8	−1	61	28	0.7	18	4	M
A	103	82	53	35	39	28	12	2	51	21	0.4	10	2	A
M	114	91	60	39	46	33	16	4	42	16	0.1	3	1	M
J	118	101	69	49	48	38	21	9	37	14	0.1	3	1	J
J	118	104	77	63	48	40	25	17	53	24	1.0	25	5	J
A	115	101	76	58	46	38	24	14	60	27	1.0	25	6	A
S	113	97	69	49	45	36	21	9	56	27	0.7	18	3	S
O	105	86	56	36	41	30	13	2	56	30	0.4	10	2	O
N	96	75	45	27	36	24	7	−3	64	38	0.6	15	3	N
D	84	66	40	22	29	19	4	−6	67	40	0.9	23	4	D

Salt Lake City (Utah) 4260 ft (689 m) 40°46′ N 111°54′ W 19 years

	Temperature °F				Temperature °C				Relative humidity		Precipitation			
	Highest recorded	Average daily		Lowest recorded	Highest recorded	Average daily		Lowest recorded	0530 hours	1200 hours	Average monthly		Average no. days with 0.01 in + (0.25 mm +)	
		max.	min.			max.	min.		%	%	in	mm		
J	62	35	17	−20	17	2	−8	−29	75	64	1.3	33	10	J
F	68	41	24	−13	20	5	−4	−25	73	59	1.5	38	9	F
M	78	51	31	0	26	11	−1	−18	65	49	2.0	51	10	M
A	85	62	38	18	29	17	3	−8	60	44	2.0	51	9	A
M	93	73	45	25	34	23	7	−4	57	36	2.0	51	8	M
J	103	82	52	32	39	28	11	0	49	28	0.8	20	5	J
J	105	92	61	43	41	33	16	6	46	29	0.6	15	4	J
A	102	90	60	42	39	32	16	6	47	30	0.8	20	6	A
S	97	79	49	29	36	26	9	−2	50	34	1.0	25	5	S
O	88	66	40	22	31	19	4	−6	59	42	1.5	38	7	O
N	74	49	28	−2	23	9	−2	−19	65	53	1.4	36	7	N
D	68	40	22	−10	20	4	−6	−23	74	62	1.4	36	10	D

Santa Fé (New Mexico) 7000 ft (2134 m) 35°41′ N 105°57′ W 54 years

	Temperature °F				Temperature °C				Relative humidity		Precipitation			
	Highest recorded	Average daily		Lowest recorded	Highest recorded	Average daily		Lowest recorded	0600 hours	1200 hours	Average monthly		Average no. days with 0.01 in + (0.25 mm +)	
		max.	min.			max.	min.		%	%	in	mm		
J	76	40	19	−13	24	4	−7	−25	64	51	0.7	18	6	J
F	75	43	23	−11	24	6	−5	−24	66	49	0.8	20	6	F
M	82	51	29	−2	28	11	−2	−19	60	45	0.8	20	7	M
A	84	59	35	11	29	15	2	−12	54	37	1.0	25	6	A
M	89	68	43	20	32	20	6	−7	49	31	1.3	33	7	M
J	92	78	52	33	33	26	11	1	47	31	1.1	28	6	J
J	96	80	57	43	36	27	14	6	61	38	2.4	61	13	J
A	97	79	56	40	36	26	13	4	65	39	2.3	58	12	A
S	90	73	49	21	32	23	9	−6	62	39	1.4	36	8	S
O	85	62	38	13	29	17	3	−11	59	38	1.2	31	5	O
N	77	50	28	−11	25	10	−2	−24	59	42	0.7	18	4	N
D	65	40	20	−13	18	4	−7	−25	65	54	0.7	18	6	D

This climatic region has weather and climate very similar to that of northwest Europe and Britain in particular. It consists of the states of Washington and Oregon; but some parts of the state of Idaho in the Rocky Mountain region have similarities with it. These states include a number of high mountains, part of the Western Cordillera, which rise to over 14,000 ft (4250 m) and are snow-covered throughout the year. Thus the higher parts of these two states have some similarity with the weather and climate of the northern part of the Rocky Mountains.

The coastal districts have the smallest annual range of temperature anywhere in the United States; winters are mild and summers only moderately warm. It is a cloudy region and the least sunny part of the USA, with a large number of rainy days. Some of the mountain areas are very wet with as much as 100–120 in (2500–3000 mm) of precipitation a year. By contrast, in the sheltered valleys and in some of the extensive high plateaux districts, annual precipitation is as low as 12 in (300 mm). This is also the one region of the country where winter is the wettest season, although some rain and changeable weather can occur in all months. There is no real summer drought such as occurs farther south in California.

The tables for **Seattle** and **Portland** are representative of the coastal districts, while those for **Spokane** and **Boise** are typical of areas farther inland at moderate height. Sea fog in summer can affect some of the coastal regions and reduce sunshine and lower temperature.

The region owes its wetness and mildness to the influence of the Pacific Ocean and the frequent passage of cyclonic depressions which originate on the North Pacific polar front. The air-masses involved in these depressions do not have the extreme conditions of temperature which give so much of the interior of the United States a continental type of climate with frequent alternations of warm and very cold weather as well as a great contrast between summer heat and winter cold.

The average number of hours of sunshine a day ranges from two to three in winter and nine to ten in summer on the coast. Inland and at higher levels the winters are sunnier with as much as five to six hours a day.

	Temperature °F			Temperature °C			Relative humidity		Precipitation			
	Highest recorded	Average daily	Lowest recorded	Highest recorded	Average daily	Lowest recorded	0530 hours	1730 hours	Average monthly		Average no. days with 0.01 in + (0.25 mm +)	
		max.	min.			max.	min.		%	%	in	mm	
J	62	38	22	−28	17	3	−6	−33	82	70	1.9	48	11	J
F	69	43	27	−13	21	6	−3	−25	79	59	1.4	36	9	F
M	83	53	33	−5	28	12	1	−21	74	46	1.6	41	9	M
A	92	62	38	11	33	17	3	−12	70	37	1.2	31	7	A
M	100	71	45	25	38	22	7	−4	70	34	1.4	36	7	M
J	109	80	51	30	43	27	11	−1	67	30	0.8	20	5	J
J	113	90	58	40	45	32	14	4	54	21	0.2	5	2	J
A	112	88	56	32	44	31	13	0	52	22	0.2	5	2	A
S	103	76	47	23	39	24	8	−5	61	31	0.5	13	3	S
O	95	64	39	14	35	18	4	−10	70	42	1.1	28	5	O
N	85	50	31	−10	29	10	−1	−23	74	57	1.4	36	8	N
D	70	40	24	−18	21	4	−4	−28	84	74	1.7	43	10	D

	Temperature °F			Temperature °C			Relative humidity		Precipitation			
	Highest recorded	Average daily	Lowest recorded	Highest recorded	Average daily	Lowest recorded	0430 hours	1630 hours	Average monthly		Average no. days with 0.01 in + (0.25 mm +)	
		max.	min.			max.	min.		%	%	in	mm	
J	65	44	34	−2	18	7	1	−19	86	78	6.1	155	19	J
F	68	48	36	7	20	9	2	−14	85	71	5.2	132	17	F
M	83	54	39	20	28	12	4	−7	85	61	4.6	117	17	M
A	93	61	43	28	34	16	6	−2	84	54	2.8	71	14	A
M	99	66	47	32	37	19	8	0	84	51	2.1	53	13	M
J	102	72	53	39	39	22	12	4	83	51	1.6	41	10	J
J	107	77	56	43	42	25	13	6	82	45	0.5	13	3	J
A	102	77	56	43	39	25	13	6	84	46	0.6	15	4	A
S	102	71	52	35	39	22	11	2	86	53	1.8	46	8	S
O	88	62	47	29	31	17	8	−2	89	66	3.3	84	12	O
N	73	53	41	11	23	12	5	−12	88	77	6.2	158	17	N
D	65	46	37	3	18	8	3	−16	86	80	7.0	178	19	D

Seattle (Washington) 125 ft (38 m) 47°36′ N 122°20′ W 57 years — USA

| | Temperature °F | | | Temperature °C | | | | Relative humidity | | Precipitation | | |
	Highest recorded	Average daily	Lowest recorded	Highest recorded	Average daily	Lowest recorded		0430 hours	1630 hours	Average monthly		Average no. days with 0.01 in + (0.25 mm +)
		max.	min.		max.	min.		%	%	in	mm	
J	67	45	36	3	19	7	2	−16	86	79	4.8	122	18	J
F	70	48	37	4	21	9	3	−16	85	73	3.7	94	16	F
M	81	52	39	20	27	11	4	−7	85	65	3.1	79	16	M
A	87	58	43	30	31	14	6	−1	85	58	2.3	58	13	A
M	92	64	47	36	33	18	8	2	85	56	1.8	46	12	M
J	98	69	52	40	37	21	11	4	84	54	1.4	36	9	J
J	100	72	54	46	38	22	12	8	85	51	0.6	15	4	J
A	96	73	55	46	36	23	13	8	87	54	0.7	18	5	A
S	92	67	52	36	33	19	11	2	89	61	1.7	43	8	S
O	82	59	47	29	28	15	8	−2	90	73	2.9	74	13	O
N	68	51	41	15	20	11	5	−9	88	80	4.8	122	17	N
D	65	47	38	12	18	8	3	−11	87	81	5.6	142	19	D

Spokane (Washington) 2357 ft (719 m) 43°37′ N 117°31′ W 66 years — USA

| | Temperature °F | | | Temperature °C | | | | Relative humidity | | Precipitation | | |
	Highest recorded	Average daily	Lowest recorded	Highest recorded	Average daily	Lowest recorded		0500 hours	1700 hours	Average monthly		Average no. days with 0.01 in + (0.25 mm +)
		max.	min.		max.	min.		%	%	in	mm	
J	62	33	22	−30	17	1	−6	−34	86	78	2.1	53	14	J
F	60	39	24	−23	16	4	−4	−31	85	68	1.7	43	12	F
M	74	49	31	−10	23	9	−1	−23	79	51	1.2	31	11	M
A	90	60	38	14	32	15	3	−10	75	39	1.1	28	9	A
M	97	68	45	29	36	20	7	−2	74	37	1.3	33	9	M
J	100	75	51	34	38	24	11	1	70	33	1.3	33	8	J
J	108	84	56	41	42	29	13	5	63	24	0.6	15	4	J
A	104	83	54	37	40	28	12	3	63	25	0.6	15	4	A
S	98	72	47	22	37	22	8	−6	73	35	0.9	23	7	S
O	87	60	38	9	31	16	3	−13	81	49	1.1	28	8	O
N	70	44	31	−13	21	7	−1	−25	86	73	2.1	53	13	N
D	60	36	26	−18	16	2	−3	−28	86	81	2.1	53	14	D

CALIFORNIA

California enjoys a very distinctive climate of the Mediterranean type and this climatic region is almost coincident with the state boundary. The northern coast of California has a climate similar to the coastal districts of the northwest but there is a gradual increase in summer temperature southwards and a decrease of rainfall until the summers become completely dry in central and southern California. In the southeast of the state precipitation decreases until conditions become similar to those of the desert regions of neighbouring Arizona and northern Mexico. Most of California enjoys mild and moderately wet winters and warm to hot and very dry summers. There are some large mountain regions within the state: the coast ranges and the Sierra Nevada, which rise to over 12,000 ft (3700 m). These mountains have a heavy precipitation and, at higher levels, much of this is snow so there are many opportunities for winter sports within a state which is often associated with sea, sun and warmth.

The tables for **San Francisco, Los Angeles** and **San Diego** are representative of the coastal region. **San Francisco** is unusual in having cool to mild summers. This is a very local feature caused by the frequent sea fog which sweeps into the bay through the Golden Gate gap in the coast range. Elsewhere this sea fog rarely affects the land but the cool waters of the California current help to maintain much lower summer temperatures on the coast than inland. In the Great Valley of California and in the desert areas in the southeast, summer temperatures are much higher. Frost and snow are very rare occurrences on the coast but occur more frequently inland in winter. The table for **Death Valley** shows the extremely high temperatures here in summer. This place has not only

experienced the highest temperatures in the United States but some of the highest recorded anywhere in the world.

The winter precipitation of California is caused by the same sequence of cyclonic depressions as bring rain to the states of the northwest. In summer such disturbances are pushed farther north by the almost permanent presence of the North Pacific subtropical anticyclone which brings calm, settled and sunny weather. This anticyclone is also responsible, however, for the most unpleasant and dangerous weather phenomenon which particularly affects the great urban area of **Los Angeles**: urban smog. This is a combination of fog and pollution from automobiles and industry. The pollution is trapped beneath a layer of warm air which overlies the coast; the light winds are unable to disperse it beyond the encircling hills and mountains.

Apart from this particular hazard most of California has a very agreeable and healthy climate throughout the year: sunny and dry with only short periods of relatively cold weather in winter. The visitor should obviously avoid going to such 'hot spots' as **Death Valley** without taking sensible precautions, or ignoring the fact that very heavy snowstorms can occur in the mountains of California. California is one of the sunniest states in the country. Sunshine hours a day average from seven to eight in winter to as many as twelve to fourteen in summer in the driest regions inland. On the coast they are rather less: from six to seven in winter and nine to ten in summer. The reduction in summer sunshine on the coast is because of sea fog.

Death Valley (California) −178 ft (−54 m) 36°28′ N 116°51′ W 37 years **USA**

	Temperature °F			Temperature °C			Relative humidity	Precipitation		
	Highest recorded	Average daily	Lowest recorded	Highest recorded	Average daily	Lowest recorded		Average monthly		Average no. days with 0.01 in + (0.25 mm +)
		max.	min.			max.	min.			in	mm	
J	85	66	38	15	29	19	3	−9	—	0.1	3	1	J
F	92	72	44	21	33	22	7	−6	—	0	0	1	F
M	100	81	51	30	38	27	11	−1	—	0.1	3	2	M
A	109	90	60	35	43	32	16	2	—	0.1	3	1	A
M	120	99	69	42	49	37	21	6	—	0.2	5	0.5	M
J	124	109	78	49	51	43	26	9	—	0.1	3	0.1	J
J	134	116	87	62	57	47	31	17	—	0.3	8	0.3	J
A	127	114	84	65	53	46	29	18	—	0.3	8	0.7	A
S	121	106	73	41	49	41	23	5	—	0.2	5	0.3	S
O	110	91	59	32	43	33	15	0	—	0	0	1	O
N	93	76	46	24	34	24	8	−4	—	0.1	3	1	N
D	86	66	39	19	30	19	4	−7	—	0	0	2	D

Los Angeles (California) 312 ft (95 m) 34°03′ N 118°15′ W 70 years **USA**

	Temperature °F			Temperature °C			Relative humidity		Precipitation		
	Highest recorded	Average daily	Lowest recorded	Highest recorded	Average daily	Lowest recorded	0500 hours	1200 hours	Average monthly		Average no. days with 0.01 in + (0.25 mm +)
		max.	min.			max.	min.	%	%	in	mm	
J	90	65	46	28	32	18	8	−2	67	47	3.1	79	6	J
F	92	66	47	28	33	19	8	−2	74	53	3.0	76	6	F
M	99	67	48	31	37	19	9	−1	77	51	2.8	71	6	M
A	100	70	50	36	38	21	10	2	82	55	1.0	25	4	A
M	103	72	53	40	39	22	12	4	86	59	0.4	10	2	M
J	105	76	56	46	41	24	13	8	87	58	0.1	3	1	J
J	109	81	60	49	43	27	16	9	88	55	0	0	0	J
A	106	82	60	49	41	28	16	9	87	54	0	0	0	A
S	108	81	58	44	42	27	14	7	82	52	0.2	5	1	S
O	102	76	54	40	39	24	12	4	75	49	0.6	15	2	O
N	96	73	50	34	36	23	10	1	62	38	1.2	31	3	N
D	92	67	47	30	33	19	8	−1	60	44	2.6	66	6	D

San Diego (California) 19 ft (6 m) 32°44′ N 117°10′ W 72 years

	Temperature °F			Temperature °C				Relative humidity		Precipitation			
	Highest recorded	Average daily	Lowest recorded	Highest recorded	Average daily	Lowest recorded		0430 hours	1630 hours	Average monthly		Average no. days with 0.01 in + (0.25 mm +)	
		max.	min.			max.	min.		%	%	in	mm		
J	85	63	47	25	29	17	8	−4	73	67	1.9	48	6	J
F	89	63	48	34	32	17	9	1	79	68	2.1	53	7	F
M	99	64	50	36	37	18	10	2	80	66	1.5	38	7	M
A	96	66	53	39	36	19	12	4	82	68	0.7	18	4	A
M	98	67	56	45	37	19	13	7	83	71	0.3	8	3	M
J	96	69	59	50	36	21	15	10	86	72	0.1	3	1	J
J	100	73	63	54	38	23	17	12	87	73	0.1	3	1	J
A	94	74	64	54	34	23	18	12	87	73	0.1	3	1	A
S	110	73	62	50	43	23	17	10	86	72	0.1	3	1	S
O	96	71	57	44	36	22	14	7	81	71	0.4	10	3	O
N	93	69	52	36	34	21	11	2	71	67	0.9	23	4	N
D	84	65	48	32	29	18	9	0	70	67	2.0	51	6	D

San Francisco (California) 52 ft (16 m) 37°47′ N 122°25′ W 73 years

	Temperature °F			Temperature °C				Relative humidity		Precipitation			
	Highest recorded	Average daily	Lowest recorded	Highest recorded	Average daily	Lowest recorded		0500 hours	1200 hours	Average monthly		Average no. days with 0.01 in + (0.25 mm +)	
		max.	min.			max.	min.		%	%	in	mm		
J	78	55	45	29	26	13	7	−2	85	69	4.7	119	11	J
F	80	59	47	33	27	15	8	1	84	66	3.8	97	11	F
M	86	61	48	33	30	16	9	1	83	61	3.1	79	10	M
A	89	62	49	40	32	17	9	4	83	61	1.5	38	6	A
M	97	63	51	42	36	17	11	6	85	62	0.7	18	4	M
J	100	66	52	46	38	19	11	8	88	64	0.1	3	2	J
J	99	65	53	47	37	18	12	8	91	69	0	0	0	J
A	92	65	53	46	33	18	12	8	92	70	0	0	0	A
S	101	69	55	47	38	21	13	8	88	63	0.3	8	2	S
O	96	68	54	43	36	20	12	6	85	58	1.0	25	4	O
N	83	63	51	38	28	17	11	3	83	60	2.5	64	7	N
D	74	57	47	27	23	14	8	−3	83	68	4.4	112	10	D

Alaska is one of the states of the USA but is separately described here because of its geographical separation from the rest of the continental United States. Twice as large as Texas, it is the largest state of the Union. It comprises the northwestern lands of the North American continent, between 60° and 72° N, and two separate and distinct appendages. There is a narrow mountainous coastal strip with numerous offshore islands extending south to 55° N to give Alaska a long landborder with Canada. The Aleutian Islands extend westwards into the North Pacific between 50° and 55° N towards the coast of Siberia.

Much of Alaska is mountainous as it includes the northern ranges of the Rocky Mountains with some of the highest mountains in North America. Large and impressive glaciers descend from these mountains almost to sea level. Inland there are extensive lowlands including the valleys of the Yukon and Porcupine rivers.

The interior and north coast of Alaska have a cold Arctic or sub-Arctic climate similar to that described on p. 118 for northern Canada. The mountains have permanent snow and ice and the lowlands suffer from permafrost. The rivers remain frozen from September until late May. The table for **Fairbanks** is representative of much of interior Alaska. The short summer can be surprisingly warm for the latitude and this is helped by the long hours of daylight and, in fine weather, the prolonged sunshine. The winters are long and very severe. Wind chill is a serious hazard when low temperatures are accompanied by strong winds (see pp. 10–11). The low annual precipitation is largely snow, but summer is the wettest season and some rain occurs then.

The table for **Barrow** on the shores of the Arctic Ocean shows that summer here is colder and shorter. The sea is frozen for most of the year or partially blocked by drift ice in summer.

On the Pacific coast the weather and climate are rather different. This is a region of much heavier precipitation with more changeable and disturbed weather throughout the year. Summer temperatures are cool and may be less warm than inland. Winters are cool but mild compared with the very low temperatures inland. Weather and climate here are very much influenced by the frequent frontal depressions which develop in the North Pacific between Japan and the Aleutian Islands. Cloud and fog are frequent at all seasons. The table for **Anchorage**, in a deep-sheltered bay on the west coast, shows warmer winter temperatures than inland. **Anchorage**, however, is much colder than the offshore islands and the Aleutians, which benefit from the relatively warm sea temperatures of the Pacific. The coastal region and the islands have weather and climate very similar to that experienced on the coasts of Norway. The climatic table for **Atka** is representative of the weather and climate of the Aleutian Islands.

	Temperature °F			Temperature °C				Relative humidity		Precipitation			
	Highest recorded	Average daily		Lowest recorded	Highest recorded	Average daily		Lowest recorded	0630 hours	1230 hours	Average monthly		Average no. days with 0.01 in + (0.25 mm +)	
		max.	min.			max.	min.		%	%	in	mm		
J	56	19	5	−33	13	−7	−15	−36	75	73	0.8	20	7	J
F	55	27	9	−32	13	−3	−13	−36	73	62	0.7	18	6	F
M	56	33	13	−19	13	1	−11	−28	73	59	0.6	15	5	M
A	63	44	27	−15	17	7	−3	−26	66	51	0.4	10	4	A
M	71	54	36	20	22	12	2	−7	64	49	0.5	13	5	M
J	92	62	44	29	33	17	7	−2	68	57	0.7	18	6	J
J	81	65	49	34	27	18	9	1	75	63	1.6	41	10	J
A	82	64	47	31	28	18	8	−1	78	65	2.6	66	15	A
S	73	57	39	19	23	14	4	−7	84	66	2.6	66	14	S
O	63	43	29	−6	17	6	−2	−21	83	69	2.2	56	12	O
N	62	30	15	−18	17	−1	−9	−28	78	74	1.0	25	7	N
D	53	20	6	−36	12	−7	−14	−38	77	76	0.9	23	6	D

	Temperature °F			Temperature °C				Relative humidity		Precipitation			
	Highest recorded	Average daily		Lowest recorded	Highest recorded	Average daily		Lowest recorded	0800 hours	1400 hours	Average monthly		Average no. days with 0.01 in + (0.25 mm +)	
		max.	min.			max.	min.		%	%	in	mm		
J	33	−9	−22	−53	1	−23	−30	−47	68	67	0.2	5	3	J
F	31	−12	−25	−56	−1	−24	−32	−50	66	66	0.1	3	3	F
M	30	−8	−22	−52	−1	−22	−30	−47	67	69	0.1	3	3	M
A	42	7	−8	−42	6	−14	−22	−41	76	75	0.1	3	3	A
M	45	24	13	−18	7	−4	−11	−28	88	86	0.1	3	3	M
J	70	39	29	8	21	4	−2	−13	93	92	0.3	8	4	J
J	78	46	33	22	26	8	1	−6	91	88	0.9	23	8	J
A	73	44	33	20	23	7	1	−7	93	89	0.8	20	10	A
S	59	34	27	4	15	1	−3	−16	92	90	0.5	13	8	S
O	40	22	12	−19	4	−6	−11	−28	87	87	0.5	13	9	O
N	39	7	−5	−40	4	−14	−21	−40	77	77	0.3	8	5	N
D	34	−4	−17	−55	1	−20	−27	−48	69	70	0.2	5	4	D

Fairbanks (Alaska) 440 ft (134 m) 64°51′ N 147°43′ W 43 years — USA

	Temperature °F			Temperature °C				Relative humidity		Precipitation			
	Highest recorded	Average daily		Lowest recorded	Highest recorded	Average daily		Lowest recorded	0200 hours	1400 hours	Average monthly		Average no. days with 0.01 in + (0.25 mm +)	
		max.	min.			max.	min.		%	%	in	mm		
J	42	−2	−20	−66	6	−19	−29	−54	81	81	0.9	23	10	J
F	50	11	−10	−58	10	−12	−23	−50	80	72	0.5	13	6	F
M	56	23	−4	−56	13	−5	−20	−49	79	50	0.7	18	6	M
A	69	42	17	−32	21	6	−8	−36	76	41	0.3	8	4	A
M	86	59	35	0	30	15	2	−18	77	39	0.6	15	9	M
J	95	71	46	28	35	22	8	−2	83	41	1.3	33	10	J
J	99	72	48	30	37	22	9	−1	88	48	1.9	48	13	J
A	90	66	44	19	32	19	7	−7	90	55	2.1	53	15	A
S	80	54	33	11	27	12	1	−12	86	55	1.3	33	10	S
O	67	35	18	−28	19	2	−8	−33	84	67	0.8	20	11	O
N	54	12	−5	−54	12	−11	−21	−47	82	79	0.7	18	10	N
D	58	1	−16	−59	14	−17	−27	−51	82	83	0.6	15	7	D

Atka (Aleutian Islands) 26 ft (8 m) 52°10′ N 174°12′ W 13 years — USA

	Temperature °F			Temperature °C				Relative humidity	Precipitation			
	Highest recorded	Average daily		Lowest recorded	Highest recorded	Average daily		Lowest recorded		Average monthly		Average no. days with 0.01 in + (0.25 mm +)	
		max.	min.			max.	min.			in	mm		
J	50	37	30	14	10	3	−1	−10	—	6.4	163	21	J
F	47	37	29	12	8	3	−2	−11	—	4.7	119	17	F
M	51	38	29	15	11	3	−2	−9	—	5.0	127	19	M
A	59	42	32	21	15	6	0	−6	—	4.9	125	18	A
M	65	45	36	24	18	7	2	−4	—	4.8	122	17	M
J	72	51	40	28	22	11	4	−2	—	3.9	99	14	J
J	76	55	44	35	24	13	7	2	—	5.3	135	16	J
A	76	57	46	38	24	14	8	3	—	5.4	137	16	A
S	66	57	43	29	19	14	6	−2	—	7.1	180	21	S
O	57	47	37	24	14	8	3	−4	—	7.4	188	23	O
N	57	41	33	13	14	5	1	−11	—	8.3	211	23	N
D	48	37	29	12	9	3	−2	−11	—	6.1	155	21	D

Central and South America

Climatic regions: *Argentina*

- Pampas
- Northeast
- West
- Patagonia

Climatic regions: *Chile*

- North
- Centre
- South

Weather stations

1 Santiago del Estero
2 Buenos Aires
3 Mendoza
4 Victorica
5 Bahia Blanca
6 Sarmiento
7 Asunción (Paraguay)
8 Antofagasta
9 Santiago
10 Valdivia
11 Punta Arenas

CHILE

ARGENTINA

0   400 mls

0   400 km

The Argentine Republic is a large country with an area exceeding one million square miles (2.6 million sq. km), about one third the size of the United States and almost as large as India. It extends between 22° and 55° S and occupies the southern portion of South America east of the crest-line of the Andes which form its border with Chile. On the north it is bordered by Bolivia and Paraguay and on the east by Brazil and Uruguay. From the estuary of the river Plate to the southern tip of Tierra del Fuego its coastline is on the Atlantic Ocean.

The centre and east of the country are mostly flat and not very high; but the west has much mountainous country rising to the higher peaks of the Andes. These include the highest mountain in South America, Aconcagua at 22,800 ft (7000 m); north of here the range rarely falls below 10,000 ft (3000 m). The northern Andes in Argentina have surprisingly low precipitation so that the snowline may be as high as 20,000 ft (6000 m).

The southern Andes have much more precipitation, similar to that on the western slopes in southern Chile, so that here there are glaciers and permanent snowfields. The high Andean region of Argentina is very sparsely peopled.

Because of these great differences of latitude and altitude there are many differences of weather and climate within Argentina. The effect of the southern Andes is to produce a sharp contrast between the very cloudy and wet climate of southern Chile and the dry, almost desert, conditions of Argentine Patagonia in the south which is sheltered from the persistent westerly winds which blow in these latitudes. Argentina can be divided into four broad climatic regions: east central Argentina or the Pampas, the northeastern interior, western Argentina, and Patagonia or southern Argentina, to which should be added the distinctive mountain climate of the high Andes.

EAST CENTRAL ARGENTINA OR THE PAMPAS

This area has a climate similar to that of Uruguay. It is well outside the tropics and has an adequate rainfall of between 20 and 40 in (500 and 1000 mm) per year. Winters are mild and summers warm with more rainfall during the summer months. The rain falls on a few days so that wet, changeable weather is not very frequent and rain is often heavy. The annual rainfall decreases westwards and southwards and this is illustrated by the tables for **Buenos Aires** and **Bahia Blanca** in the south of the Pampas, and **Victorica** in the west. The weather here is moderately sunny with an average of four to five hours sunshine a day in winter and eight to nine hours in summer. The region does not often experience extremes of heat or cold. Frost may occur in most winter months but is not prolonged or severe. The climate is generally healthy and pleasant. This is the most important agricultural region of the country and occasional drought is the main economic hazard.

ARGENTINA Bahia Blanca 95 ft (29 m) 38°43′ S 62°16′ W 31 years

	Temperature °F				Temperature °C				Relative humidity		Precipitation			
	Highest recorded	Average daily		Lowest recorded	Highest recorded	Average daily		Lowest recorded	0700 hours	1400 hours	Average monthly		Average no. days with 0.01 in + (0.25 mm +)	
		max.	min.			max.	min.		%	%	in	mm		
J	107	88	62	42	42	31	17	6	63	41	1.7	43	5	J
F	109	84	60	36	43	29	16	2	70	41	2.2	56	5	F
M	100	79	57	39	38	26	14	4	77	46	2.5	64	6	M
A	90	71	51	30	32	22	11	−1	80	50	2.3	58	5	A
M	85	63	45	25	29	17	7	−4	82	56	1.2	31	4	M
J	76	57	39	18	24	14	4	−8	86	64	0.9	23	3	J
J	79	57	39	19	26	14	4	−7	79	56	1.0	25	4	J
A	85	60	40	18	29	16	4	−8	80	54	1.0	25	4	A
S	91	65	44	23	33	18	7	−5	76	45	1.6	41	5	S
O	96	71	48	25	36	22	9	−4	68	40	2.2	56	6	O
N	101	78	54	30	38	26	12	−1	63	38	2.1	53	6	N
D	105	85	59	37	41	29	15	3	58	35	1.9	48	5	D

Buenos Aires 89 ft (27 m) 34°35′ S 58°29′ W 23 years   ARGENTINA

	Temperature °F			Temperature °C			Relative humidity		Precipitation			
	Highest recorded	Average daily	Lowest recorded	Highest recorded	Average daily	Lowest recorded	0700 hours	1400 hours	Average monthly		Average no. days with 0.01 in + (0.25 mm +)	
		max.	min.			max.	min.		%	%	in	mm	
J	104	85	63	43	40	29	17	6	81	61	3.1	79	7	J
F	103	83	63	40	39	28	17	4	83	63	2.8	71	6	F
M	99	79	60	39	37	26	16	4	87	69	4.3	109	7	M
A	97	72	53	28	36	22	12	−2	88	71	3.5	89	8	A
M	84	64	47	25	29	18	8	−4	90	74	3.0	76	7	M
J	77	57	41	23	25	14	5	−5	91	78	2.4	61	7	J
J	84	57	42	22	29	14	6	−6	92	79	2.2	56	8	J
A	87	60	43	27	31	16	6	−3	90	74	2.4	61	9	A
S	86	64	46	28	30	18	8	−2	86	68	3.1	79	8	S
O	91	69	50	28	33	21	10	−2	83	65	3.4	86	9	O
N	95	76	56	36	35	24	13	2	79	60	3.3	84	9	N
D	102	82	61	39	39	28	16	4	79	62	3.9	99	8	D

Victorica 1024 ft (312 m) 36°13′ S 65°26′ W 24 years   ARGENTINA

	Temperature °F			Temperature °C			Relative humidity		Precipitation			
	Highest recorded	Average daily	Lowest recorded	Highest recorded	Average daily	Lowest recorded	0730 hours	1330 hours	Average monthly		Average no. days with 0.04 in + (1 mm +)	
		max.	min.			max.	min.		%	%	in	mm	
J	112	93	59	36	44	34	15	2	53	33	2.8	71	6	J
F	109	90	58	36	43	32	14	2	65	35	2.8	71	5	F
M	102	83	54	30	39	28	12	−1	73	44	2.8	71	5	M
A	98	75	46	21	37	24	8	−6	79	41	1.2	31	4	A
M	89	66	38	16	32	19	3	−9	88	47	1.0	25	3	M
J	78	59	32	0	26	15	0	−18	91	55	0.7	18	2	J
J	82	59	37	12	28	15	3	−11	88	52	0.6	15	2	J
A	85	64	34	13	29	18	1	−11	80	47	0.7	18	2	A
S	97	68	40	20	36	20	4	−7	62	33	1.1	28	4	S
O	106	75	46	26	41	24	8	−3	62	35	3.0	76	7	O
N	105	83	51	28	41	28	11	−2	53	29	2.5	64	5	N
D	110	89	57	36	43	32	14	2	51	26	3.0	76	7	D

THE NORTHEASTERN INTERIOR

This region has a warmer climate than the Pampas and towards the north, where it includes part of the Chaco region described on p. 197 for Paraguay, has a tropical or near-tropical climate (see the table for **Asunción** on p. 197). Rainfall decreases westwards and the table for **Santiago del Estero** is representative of the drier western part. Temperatures remain quite high around the year. The combination of heat and humidity may at times be uncomfortable in the summer months as this is the cloudier, wetter season. For much of the time, however, conditions are sunny and dry. Occasional cold spells in winter may bring temperatures near or below freezing for a few hours but the winters are generally mild or even warm.

WESTERN ARGENTINA

Western Argentina, including the northern Andes, is a dry region. Even on the higher mountains snowfall is light and the dryness matches that of northern Chile on the western side of the Andes. The eastern slopes and foothills of the Andes as far south as 35° S is a semi-arid region and the lowlands are a virtual desert. In many places the annual rainfall is below 10 in (250 mm) and very unreliable. Droughts in this area are frequent and often prolonged. Rainfall is more frequent during the summer months which are generally hot and very sunny. Sunshine hours average as much as ten hours a day in summer and between seven and eight hours in winter. The table for **Mendoza** is representative of this region.

Santiago del Estero 653 ft (199 m) 27°46′ S 64°18′ W 23 years — ARGENTINA

	Temperature °F			Temperature °C			Relative humidity		Precipitation		
	Highest recorded	Average daily	Lowest recorded	Highest recorded	Average daily	Lowest recorded	0630 hours	1330 hours	Average monthly		Average no. days with 0.01 in+ (0.25 mm +)
		max.	min.			max.	min.		%	%	in	mm	
J	115	97	69	52	46	36	21	11	72	47	3.4	86	6	J
F	113	94	68	50	45	34	20	10	74	49	3.0	76	6	F
M	112	89	65	43	44	32	18	6	80	58	3.0	76	6	M
A	104	82	59	33	40	28	15	1	82	66	1.3	33	4	A
M	94	75	51	27	34	24	11	−3	82	55	0.6	15	2	M
J	87	69	44	20	31	21	7	−7	80	56	0.3	8	2	J
J	96	70	44	19	36	21	7	−7	76	48	0.2	5	1	J
A	102	75	46	19	39	24	8	−7	70	39	0.2	5	1	A
S	108	82	53	27	42	28	12	−3	66	41	0.5	13	2	S
O	109	87	59	32	43	31	15	0	69	42	1.4	36	4	O
N	114	92	64	34	46	33	18	1	67	43	2.5	64	5	N
D	116	94	67	48	47	34	19	9	67	42	4.1	104	5	D

Mendoza 2625 ft (801 m) 32°53′ S 68°49′ W 23 years — ARGENTINA

	Temperature °F			Temperature °C			Relative humidity		Precipitation		
	Highest recorded	Average daily	Lowest recorded	Highest recorded	Average daily	Lowest recorded	0630 hours	1330 hours	Average monthly		Average no. days with 0.01 in+ (0.25 mm +)
		max.	min.			max.	min.		%	%	in	mm	
J	109	90	60	41	43	32	16	5	59	42	0.9	23	5	J
F	105	87	59	41	41	31	15	5	63	44	1.2	31	5	F
M	99	82	55	29	37	28	13	−2	68	47	1.1	28	4	M
A	91	73	47	30	33	23	8	−1	73	50	0.5	13	3	A
M	86	65	41	23	30	18	5	−5	74	52	0.4	10	2	M
J	86	59	36	15	30	15	2	−9	73	50	0.3	8	2	J
J	83	59	35	16	28	15	2	−9	72	48	0.2	5	2	J
A	92	63	38	23	33	17	3	−5	67	42	0.3	8	2	A
S	93	69	44	25	34	21	7	−4	55	33	0.5	13	2	S
O	97	76	50	32	36	24	10	0	51	34	0.7	18	4	O
N	106	83	54	36	41	28	12	2	52	34	0.7	18	4	N
D	108	88	58	36	42	31	14	2	54	37	0.7	18	5	D

PATAGONIA OR SOUTHERN ARGENTINA

The southern third of Argentina, south of **Bahia Blanca**, is a rather dry region compared with the very wet region of southern Chile on the other side of the Andes. In terms of temperature and changeable weather the region has a typical cool, temperate climate, rather similar to that of the British Isles; but the dryness is unusual for such a high altitude. The table for **Sarmiento** is representative of the coast and much of the interior. Towards the west, in the foothills of the Andes, rainfall is greater as cloud spills over from the western side of the range. The dryness of the eastern side continues to the cooler southern districts around the Strait of Magellan. The table for **Punta Arenas**, in southern Chile (p. 182), is representative of the extreme south where summers are distinctly cool. Winters are long with frequent frost and snow but, because of the influence of the ocean, the cold is never very severe or prolonged.

ARGENTINA   Sarmiento 879 ft (268 m) 45°36′ S 69°05′ W 8 years

		Temperature °F				Temperature °C				Relative humidity		Precipitation			
	Highest recorded	Average daily		Lowest recorded	Highest recorded	Average daily		Lowest recorded	0730 hours	1330 hours	Average monthly		Average no. days with 0.04 in + (1 mm +)		
		max.	min.			max.	min.		%	%	in	mm		
J	99	78	52	34	37	26	11	1	52	29	0.2	5	1	J
F	96	77	51	34	36	25	11	1	59	32	0.3	8	1	F
M	93	70	47	27	34	21	8	−3	64	34	0.3	8	2	M
A	83	62	42	18	28	17	6	−8	72	45	0.4	10	3	A
M	71	54	36	11	22	12	2	−12	74	51	0.8	20	4	M
J	64	46	31	8	18	8	−1	−13	77	58	0.8	20	4	J
J	68	45	29	7	20	7	−2	−14	77	59	0.6	15	3	J
A	67	51	33	3	19	11	1	−16	76	49	0.5	13	3	A
S	76	57	36	14	24	14	2	−10	67	40	0.4	10	3	S
O	86	66	41	19	30	19	5	−7	56	31	0.3	8	2	O
N	92	70	46	29	33	21	8	−2	51	32	0.2	5	2	N
D	99	74	49	32	37	23	9	0	54	30	0.3	8	2	D

Belize is one of the smaller countries of Central America whose weather and climate are described in more detail for Panama (p. 195). It is situated between 16° and 18° N and is bordered by Guatemala on the south and west and by Mexico on the north. It has a long coastline on the Caribbean Sea. A large part of the country is low-lying so that it has weather and climate typical of the tierra caliente (p. 195), except in the southwest where some hills rise to over 3800 ft (1200 m).

Annual rainfall is rather heavy on the coast and, although there is a wetter season between May and November, some rain occurs all through the year. The country is occasionally affected by very heavy rains brought by tropical storms or hurricanes which can wreak havoc to both dwellings and crops. The weather is rather hot and humid throughout the year.

Belize City 17 ft (5 m) 17°31′ N 88°11′ W 27 years

	Temperature °F			Temperature °C			Relative humidity		Precipitation			
	Highest recorded	Average daily	Lowest recorded	Highest recorded	Average daily	Lowest recorded	0700 hours	1900 hours	Average monthly		Average no. days with 0.04 in + (1 mm +)	
		max.	min.			max.	min.		%	%	in	mm	
J	90	81	67	49	32	27	19	9	92	89	5.4	137	12	J
F	93	82	69	49	34	28	21	9	91	87	2.4	61	6	F
M	95	84	71	54	35	29	22	12	90	87	1.5	38	4	M
A	97	86	74	59	36	30	23	15	91	87	2.2	56	5	A
M	96	87	75	60	36	31	24	16	91	87	4.3	109	7	M
J	97	87	75	64	36	31	24	18	93	87	7.7	196	13	J
J	95	87	75	62	35	31	24	17	93	86	6.4	163	15	J
A	96	88	75	60	36	31	24	16	92	87	6.7	170	14	A
S	97	87	74	60	36	31	23	16	94	87	9.6	244	15	S
O	96	86	72	58	36	30	22	14	94	88	12.0	305	16	O
N	95	83	68	52	35	28	20	11	94	91	8.9	226	12	N
D	92	81	68	49	33	27	20	9	93	90	7.3	185	14	D

BOLIVIA

Bolivia lies between 10° and 23° S. It is a landlocked country twice the size of France or the state of Texas. It is bordered on the north by Brazil, on the east by Paraguay, on the south by Argentina and on the west by Chile and Peru.

The country is divided into two very contrasting physical regions which have very different weather and climate. In the west the great mountain range of the Andes, here at its broadest, rises to peaks of over 20,000 ft (6100 m). Between the western and eastern ranges of the Andes there is an extensive highland plateau, called *páramos* or *altiplano*, at an altitude of between 10,000 and 13,000 ft (3000 and 4000 m). East of the Andes the land drops sharply to the forested lowlands of the Amazon basin on the Brazilian border and the lowland of the Chaco region on the border with Paraguay.

The climate of the Andean plateau is represented by the table for **La Paz**. Here there is an extreme type of tropical highland climate. Annual precipitation is low and most of it falls between December and March during the high sun period when there are many rainy days. Temperatures are much reduced by altitude with only small differences from month to month. The daily range of temperature is large so that the nights are quite cold, particularly during the dry winter or low sun period when frost is almost a nightly occurrence.

In some parts of this region annual precipitation is as low as 10 in (250 mm). This is particularly so in the western mountains and valleys; consequently the permanent snowline may be as high as 20,000 ft (6100 m). The high altitude of this region means that at 10,000 ft (3050 m) the atmospheric pressure is only about two thirds that at sea level and at 17,000 ft (5200 m) it is only about half. This reduced pressure causes problems for visitors who may suffer from mountain sickness, called here the *soroche*, on arrival. For a fit person acclimatization takes a few days to a week or so; but the area is not recommended for those who suffer from weak hearts or lung complaints.

Sunshine ranges from about six hours a day in the rainy season, when there is usually cloud in the afternoon, to as much as eight hours a day in the dry season. The sun's rays are particularly powerful because of the thin atmosphere at this height and sunburn can be a hazard.

Temperature drops very rapidly after sunset and the nights feel distinctly chilly. The greatest differences of weather and climate in this high mountain region are those experienced during the course of the day and those arising from sudden changes of altitude.

The lowlands east of the Andes, comprising rather more than half the country, have a very different climate. Most of this region lies between 750 and 3000 ft (230 and 900 m) and its weather and climate are similar to those found in the equatorial regions of the Amazon basin in Brazil or the Chaco region of Paraguay. Temperatures are warm to hot around the year with a single rainy season at the time of high sun.

This region is much wetter than the Andean plateau with the annual precipitation being everywhere more than 40 in (1000 mm), rising to 60 in (1500 mm) towards the north. Here the combination of heat and humidity can cause discomfort and heat stress during the months October to March (see the table for **Conceptión**). During the dry period of low sun occasional bursts of colder air reach these lowlands as a result of outbreaks of polar air from Antarctica. Temperatures may fall to a few degrees above freezing for a night or so. Such extreme events are rare, however.

In the Andean region of Bolivia, as elsewhere in Central and northern South America, the inhabitants distinguish three or four climatic zones depending on altitude: tierra caliente, from sea level to about 3000 ft (900 m); tierra templada, between 3000 and 6000 ft (900 and 1800 m); and tierra fria, from 6000 to 10,000 ft (1800 to 3000 m), above which is the *páramos* or *altiplano*.

Conceptión 1607 ft (490 m) 16°15′ S 62°03′ W 5 years **BOLIVIA**

		Temperature °F				Temperature °C			Relative humidity		Precipitation			
	Highest recorded	Average daily		Lowest recorded	Highest recorded	Average daily		Lowest recorded	0800 hours	1400 hours	Average monthly		Average no. days with 0.04 in + (1 mm +)	
		max.	min.			max.	min.		%	%	in	mm		
J	96	85	66	55	36	29	19	13	93	63	7.6	193	15	J
F	93	86	66	49	34	30	19	9	93	74	6.1	155	13	F
M	93	85	65	54	34	29	18	12	91	71	4.6	117	12	M
A	93	86	62	48	34	30	17	9	91	65	2.4	61	5	A
M	93	83	59	43	34	28	15	6	88	61	3.1	79	6	M
J	90	80	56	45	32	27	13	7	93	61	0.9	23	4	J
J	94	81	54	36	34	27	12	2	87	55	1 1	28	2	J
A	97	87	56	39	36	31	13	4	81	47	0.6	15	4	A
S	100	91	61	40	38	33	16	4	80	49	2.3	58	4	S
O	98	88	62	45	37	31	17	7	77	58	3.0	76	8	O
N	101	88	66	52	38	31	19	11	81	61	8.1	206	11	N
D	94	86	65	47	34	30	18	8	87	69	5.2	132	15	D

La Paz 12,001 ft (3658 m) 16°30′ S 68°08′ W 31 years **BOLIVIA**

		Temperature °F				Temperature °C			Relative humidity	Precipitation			
	Highest recorded	Average daily		Lowest recorded	Highest recorded	Average daily		Lowest recorded		Average monthly		Average no. days with 0.04 in + (1 mm +)	
		max.	min.			max.	min.			in	mm		
J	77	63	43	33	25	17	6	1	—	4.5	114	21	J
F	76	63	43	36	24	17	6	2	—	4.2	107	18	F
M	76	64	42	36	24	18	6	2	—	2.6	66	16	M
A	75	65	40	30	24	18	4	−1	—	1.3	33	9	A
M	72	64	37	30	22	18	3	−1	—	0.5	13	5	M
J	70	62	34	27	21	17	1	−3	—	0.3	8	2	J
J	71	62	33	26	22	17	1	−3	—	0.4	10	2	J
A	72	63	35	27	22	17	2	−3	—	0.5	13	4	A
S	80	64	38	30	27	18	3	−1	—	1.1	28	9	S
O	76	66	40	30	24	19	4	−1	—	1.6	41	9	O
N	77	67	42	30	25	19	6	−1	—	1.9	48	11	N
D	76	65	42	35	24	18	6	2	—	3.7	94	18	D

Climatic regions

Amazon basin
Brazilian plateau
Tropical east coast
Southern states

0°

B R A Z I L

10°

20°

30°

Weather stations

1 Belem
2 Manaus
3 Sena Madureira
4 Iguatú
5 Goiás
6 Parana
7 Recife
8 Rio de Janeiro
9 Porto Alegre

0   500 mls
0   500 km

Brazil is a little larger than the United States. Almost half South America falls within its borders. Extending from 5° N to 34° S, it is broadest at about 7° S, the greater part of the country lying within the tropics. Unlike most other South American countries it does not include any part of the Andes mountains so no area of the country has permanent snowfields. The highest areas within Brazil just fail to reach 10,000 ft (3000 m) and there are no large areas above 6000 ft (1800 m).

The two largest physical regions of the country are the Amazon basin and the Brazilian plateau. The Amazon basin occupies the whole north and centre of the country and is everywhere below 1000 ft (300 m); it has the climate of an equatorial lowland with few differences from place to place. The Brazilian plateau lies to the south and east of the Amazon basin and is highest near the Atlantic coast. Most of the plateau has an average height of between 2000 and 3000 ft (600 and 900 m) and it decreases in height northwards and westwards towards the basins of the Amazon and Paraguay rivers. From **Recife** in the north to **Porto Alegre** in the south, the Atlantic coastlands of Brazil are narrow and are overlooked by the hills forming the high edge of the plateau. Only around the mouth of the Amazon in the north are there extensive lowlands on the Atlantic coast.

This geography makes for a simple division of the country into four climatic regions: the Amazon basin, the Brazilian plateau, the coastlands within the tropics and the southern states of Parana, Rio Grande do Sul and Santa Catarina. This last division is distinctive because it is outside the tropics and has a temperate climate similar to that of Uruguay, but modified by the greater height of the interior.

THE AMAZON BASIN

This is the largest area in the world with a typical equatorial climate. Rainfall is everywhere above 60 in (1500 mm) a year and in much of the region over 80 in (2000 mm). There is no real dry season but there are some variations in the period of the year when most rain falls. Temperatures are typically tropical in all months with average midday temperatures in the range 80°–90° F (27°–32° C). Frost is unknown although in the southern parts of the region occasional cold spells, lasting a day or two and going under the name *friagem*, cause night temperatures to fall below 50° F (10° C). These spells are most uncomfortable for the local inhabitants who then stay indoors and light fires. They are most likely to occur at the time of low sun between May and September. They are caused by invasions of cold air, originating from Antarctica and the southern oceans, which track northwards across Argentina and Paraguay into central Brazil.

Excessively high temperatures are almost unknown in the Amazon basin; daytime temperatures of 100° F (38° C) are very rare. The high humidity and the monotony of the temperature from day to day make this area unpleasant for those unfamiliar with, or un-acclimatized to, the hot, wet tropics but conditions are not physically dangerous.

The tables for **Belem**, **Manaus** and **Sena Madureira** are representative of this vast region. These tables show that there is little difference in terms of temperatures and humidity from place to place. **Belem** at the mouth of the Amazon is the wettest place and the heaviest rainfall comes in the months January to May, but all months have many days with rain. **Manaus** in the central part of the region is not quite so wet and the period June to September is drier than at **Belem**. **Sena Madureira** in the extreme southwest of the region is nearer the Andes and so wetter. Being farther south, it has a greater concentration of rain in the period of high sun from December to March and a distinct, drier season at the time of low sun. Hours of sunshine a day range from three to four in the wetter months to seven to eight in the drier season.

BRAZIL — Belem 42 ft (13 m) 1°27′ S 48°29′ W 16 years

	Temperature °F			Temperature °C			Relative humidity		Precipitation		
	Highest recorded	Average daily	Lowest recorded	Highest recorded	Average daily	Lowest recorded	0700 hours	1200 hours	Average monthly		Average no. days with 0.01 in + (0.25 mm +)
		max. / min.			max. / min.		%	%	in	mm	
J	95	87 / 72	66	35	31 / 22	19	96	88	12.5	318	27	J
F	94	86 / 72	68	34	30 / 22	20	98	91	14.1	358	26	F
M	95	87 / 73	66	35	31 / 23	19	98	90	14.1	358	28	M
A	95	87 / 73	69	35	31 / 23	21	98	89	12.6	320	27	A
M	94	88 / 73	68	34	31 / 23	20	98	87	10.2	259	24	M
J	93	88 / 72	68	34	31 / 22	20	98	85	6.7	170	22	J
J	94	88 / 71	64	34	31 / 22	18	97	86	5.9	150	19	J
A	95	88 / 71	67	35	31 / 22	19	97	85	4.4	112	16	A
S	96	89 / 71	65	36	32 / 22	18	97	83	3.5	89	16	S
O	98	89 / 71	67	37	32 / 22	19	97	80	3.3	84	15	O
N	97	90 / 71	67	36	32 / 22	19	97	81	2.6	66	12	N
D	97	89 / 72	66	36	32 / 22	19	98	84	6.1	155	19	D

Manaus 144 ft (44 m) 3°08′ S 60°01′ W 11 years

	Temperature °F				Temperature °C				Relative humidity		Precipitation			
	Highest recorded	Average daily		Lowest recorded	Highest recorded	Average daily		Lowest recorded	0600 hours	1300 hours	Average monthly		Average no. days with 0.01 in + (0.25 mm +)	
		max.	min.			max.	min.		%	%	in	mm		
J	99	88	75	65	37	31	24	18	89	70	9.8	249	20	J
F	100	88	75	68	38	31	24	20	89	71	9.1	231	19	F
M	97	88	75	67	36	31	24	19	89	72	10.3	262	20	M
A	94	87	75	68	34	31	24	20	90	73	8.7	221	19	A
M	95	88	75	68	35	31	24	20	89	72	6.7	170	18	M
J	95	88	75	65	35	31	24	18	87	68	3.3	84	11	J
J	95	89	75	64	35	32	24	18	87	64	2.3	58	8	J
A	98	91	75	67	37	33	24	19	85	59	1.5	38	6	A
S	99	92	75	68	37	33	24	20	84	57	1.8	46	7	S
O	100	92	76	68	38	33	24	20	85	59	4.2	107	11	O
N	99	91	76	68	37	33	24	20	86	63	5.6	142	12	N
D	101	90	75	67	38	32	24	19	88	68	8.0	203	16	D

Sena Madureira 443 ft (135 m) 9°04′ S 68°39′ W 12 years

BRAZIL

	Temperature °F				Temperature °C				Relative humidity		Precipitation			
	Highest recorded	Average daily		Lowest recorded	Highest recorded	Average daily		Lowest recorded	0530 hours	1930 hours	Average monthly		Average no. days with 0.01 in + (0.25 mm +)	
		max.	min.			max.	min.		%	%	in	mm		
J	99	92	69	61	37	33	21	16	98	98	11.2	285	18	J
F	99	92	69	59	37	33	21	15	98	98	11.3	287	16	F
M	99	91	69	60	37	33	21	16	98	98	10.2	259	17	M
A	99	91	68	57	37	33	20	14	98	99	9.4	239	15	A
M	98	90	67	54	37	32	19	12	98	99	4.1	104	8	M
J	98	90	65	45	37	33	18	7	98	98	2.2	56	7	J
J	99	91	63	47	37	33	17	8	97	98	1.1	28	5	J
A	99	93	65	41	37	34	18	5	97	99	1.5	38	5	A
S	99	93	68	46	37	34	20	8	98	98	4.0	102	8	S
O	99	93	69	57	37	34	21	14	98	98	7.0	178	11	O
N	100	93	69	57	38	34	21	14	98	98	7.5	191	12	N
D	99	93	70	63	37	34	21	17	98	98	11.7	297	16	D

THE BRAZILIAN PLATEAU

(*Including the states of Parana, Santa Catarina and Rio Grande do Sul*)

This region is as large and extensive as the Amazon basin but, lying farther south and being at a moderate altitude, it has a very different climate. There is a much more distinct wet and dry season and both the daily and annual temperature ranges are quite marked. With the exception of the northeast of this region, in the valley of the river São Francisco and the province of Ceará, annual rainfall is about 50–60 in (1250–1500 mm). There is a very distinct wet season at the time of high sun with almost all the rain falling between October and April. The remaining months are almost dry.

The dry region in the northeast not only has a much lower average rainfall, with many places receiving less than 30 in (750 mm), but the rainfall is most unreliable from year to year. This district suffers many prolonged droughts which cause great distress and damage to both agriculture and cattle rearing. Average conditions in this dry region are represented by the table for **Iguatú**.

The table for **Goiás** is representative of conditions in the area of the new capital of the country, Brasilia, which has not been established long enough for reliable weather statistics to be collected. The tables for **Goiás** and for **Parana** both show conditions over the wetter parts of this region. There is not a great variation in average monthly temperatures around the year but during the drier months of low sun the daily range of temperature is greater because the nights are generally clear and the days sunnier. These months are the most comfortable because midday humidity is lower. The wet season has more cloud, higher humidity and higher night temperatures.

Average daily sunshine hours in this region range from five to six during the wetter months to as much as nine to ten during the dry season. Frost is virtually unknown except in some valleys in the extreme south or on the higher parts near the east coast.

BRAZIL   Goiás 1706 ft (520 m) 15°58′ S 50°04′ W 8 years

	Temperature °F				Temperature °C				Relative humidity		Precipitation			
	Highest recorded	Average daily		Lowest recorded	Highest recorded	Average daily		Lowest recorded	0630 hours	1330 hours	Average monthly		Average no. days with 0.01 in + (0.25 mm +)	
		max.	min.			max.	min.		%	%	in	mm		
J	99	86	63	55	37	30	17	13	88	73	12.5	317	16	J
F	100	89	63	55	38	32	17	13	87	69	9.9	251	14	F
M	98	89	63	56	37	32	17	13	85	65	10.2	259	15	M
A	99	91	63	55	37	33	17	13	82	60	4.6	117	7	A
M	96	91	60	52	36	33	16	11	77	51	0.4	10	1	M
J	95	90	55	43	35	32	13	6	74	50	0.3	8	0	J
J	96	89	56	41	36	32	13	5	67	48	0	0	0	J
A	101	93	59	49	38	34	15	9	64	40	0.3	8	1	A
S	104	94	64	53	40	34	18	12	66	42	2.3	58	4	S
O	104	94	63	50	40	34	17	10	77	51	5.3	135	8	O
N	102	90	63	54	39	32	17	12	86	65	9.4	239	13	N
D	101	87	62	52	38	31	17	11	90	73	9.5	241	13	D

Iguatú 685 ft (209 m) 6°24′ S 39°35′ W 12 years   **BRAZIL**

	Temperature °F			Temperature °C			Relative humidity		Precipitation		
	Highest recorded	Average daily	Lowest recorded	Highest recorded	Average daily	Lowest recorded	0730 hours	1430 hours	Average monthly		Average no. days with 0.01 in + (0.25 mm +)
		max.	min.		max.	min.		%	%	in	mm	
J	101	94	74	63	38	34	23	17	83	44	3.5	89	7	J
F	102	91	73	63	39	33	23	17	89	52	6.8	173	12	F
M	99	90	73	63	37	32	23	17	93	60	7.3	185	13	M
A	99	88	73	63	37	31	23	17	93	62	6.3	160	13	A
M	97	88	71	59	36	31	22	15	91	61	2.4	61	7	M
J	95	89	70	50	35	32	21	10	87	59	1.4	36	3	J
J	96	90	69	49	36	32	21	9	81	44	0.2	5	2	J
A	99	93	69	51	37	34	21	11	77	35	0.1	3	0	A
S	101	95	72	61	38	35	22	16	78	32	0.7	18	2	S
O	101	96	73	59	38	36	23	15	75	31	0.7	18	2	O
N	101	96	74	61	38	36	23	16	77	36	0.4	10	1	N
D	101	96	74	61	38	36	23	16	82	38	1.3	33	3	D

Parana 853 ft (260 m) 12°26′ S 48°06′ W 19 years   **BRAZIL**

	Temperature °F			Temperature °C			Relative humidity		Precipitation		
	Highest recorded	Average daily	Lowest recorded	Highest recorded	Average daily	Lowest recorded	0700 hours	1400 hours	Average monthly		Average no. days with 0.01 in + (0.25 mm +)
		max.	min.		max.	min.		%	%	in	mm	
J	101	90	58	49	38	32	14	9	93	69	11.3	287	14	J
F	97	89	59	49	36	32	15	9	94	69	9.3	236	13	F
M	98	89	59	49	37	32	15	9	94	69	9.4	239	13	M
A	99	90	58	49	37	32	14	9	93	64	4.0	102	7	A
M	98	91	54	43	37	33	12	6	92	58	0.5	13	1	M
J	97	91	49	41	36	33	9	5	89	50	0	0	0	J
J	97	91	48	37	36	33	9	3	89	51	0.1	3	0	J
A	100	93	50	37	38	34	10	3	81	48	0.2	5	1	A
S	105	95	55	42	41	35	13	6	87	51	1.1	28	3	S
O	104	94	58	45	40	34	14	7	88	53	5.0	127	8	O
N	100	91	58	50	38	33	14	10	93	67	9.1	231	13	N
D	103	90	58	50	39	32	14	10	93	66	12.2	310	15	D

THE EAST COAST WITHIN THE TROPICS

This long, narrow region extends from south of the mouth of the Amazon to Santos, and has a typically hot, tropical climate. There are, however, some important differences in the season of greatest rainfall from north to south. Near the mouth of the Amazon all months are wet but rainfall is greater in the months December to May as shown by the table for **Belem**. From about 3° S to Bahia at 14° S the wettest months are from May to August and the rest of the year is comparatively dry (see the table for **Recife**). This unusual regime of rainfall only applies to the coastal lowlands; inland on the plateau the rainfall is less and the wet season is the period of high sun.

South of Bahia the distribution of rainfall changes and the table for **Rio de Janeiro** shows that the wettest period is from November to April. Here some appreci-able rainfall occurs in all months. Nowhere on this coast do maximum temperatures rise so high as to be uncomfortable but the combination of warmth and humidity can be uncomfortable at night.

Daytime heat is often tempered by the sea breeze. Along this coast, from **Recife** southwards, cloudy and cool weather with some rain or drizzle may last for a few days at the period of low sun. As the tables show, temperatures never drop very low and frost is unknown on the coast but in the hills, behind Santos, occasional frosts may damage the valuable coffee crop. Hours of sunshine on the coast are less round the year than at similar latitudes inland on the plateau. They average from five to six in the wetter season to six to seven in the drier months.

Recife 97 ft (30 m) 8°04′ S 34°53′ W 26 years   **BRAZIL**

	Temperature °F			Temperature °C			Relative humidity		Precipitation		
Highest recorded	Average daily		Lowest recorded	Highest recorded	Average daily		Lowest recorded	0730 hours	1430 hours	Average monthly		Average no. days with 0.01 in + (0.25 mm +)
	max.	min.			max.	min.		%	%	in	mm	
J	94	86	77	71	34	30	25	22	77	69	2.1	53	10	J
F	93	86	77	69	34	30	25	21	81	70	3.3	84	12	F
M	94	86	76	69	34	30	24	21	81	71	6.3	160	14	M
A	93	85	75	69	34	29	24	21	83	73	8.7	221	17	A
M	90	83	74	69	32	28	23	21	84	74	10.5	267	21	M
J	89	82	73	66	32	28	23	19	84	75	10.9	277	21	J
J	87	80	71	64	31	27	22	18	83	75	10.0	254	22	J
A	88	81	71	64	31	27	22	18	82	73	6.0	152	19	A
S	90	82	73	66	32	28	23	19	78	70	2.5	64	11	S
O	91	84	75	68	33	29	24	20	75	67	1.0	25	8	O
N	91	85	76	69	33	29	24	21	74	68	1.0	25	7	N
D	92	85	77	70	33	29	25	21	76	67	1.1	28	6	D

Rio de Janeiro 201 ft (61 m) 22°55′ S 43°12′ W 38 years   **BRAZIL**

	Temperature °F			Temperature °C			Relative humidity		Precipitation		
Highest recorded	Average daily		Lowest recorded	Highest recorded	Average daily		Lowest recorded	0700 hours	1400 hours	Average monthly		Average no. days with 0.01 in + (0.25 mm +)
	max.	min.			max.	min.		%	%	in	mm	
J	102	84	73	60	39	29	23	16	82	70	4.9	125	13	J
F	98	85	73	63	37	29	23	17	84	71	4.8	122	11	F
M	97	83	72	64	36	28	22	18	87	74	5.1	130	12	M
A	94	80	69	60	34	27	21	16	87	73	4.2	107	10	A
M	95	77	66	56	35	25	19	13	87	70	3.1	79	10	M
J	90	76	64	52	32	24	18	11	87	69	2.1	53	7	J
J	91	75	63	52	33	24	17	11	86	68	1.6	41	7	J
A	93	76	64	53	34	24	18	12	84	66	1.7	43	7	A
S	100	75	65	50	38	24	18	10	84	72	2.6	66	11	S
O	102	77	66	57	39	25	19	14	83	72	3.1	79	13	O
N	100	79	68	59	38	26	20	15	82	72	4.1	104	13	N
D	102	82	71	56	39	28	22	13	82	72	5.4	137	14	D

THE SOUTHERN STATES OF BRAZIL OUTSIDE THE TROPICS

This region consists of the southern states of Parana, Santa Catarina and Rio Grande do Sul. Both along the coast and in the plateaux districts inland the climate is warm-temperate rather than tropical and is similar to that found in Uruguay and northern Argentina. As the table for **Porto Alegre** shows, even on the coast there is a distinct cooler season when frost can be expected in the winter months. Here winter has a real significance and the difference between the seasons is determined by temperature rather than rainfall.

On the coast rainfall is well distributed throughout the year but the cooler months are also slightly wetter.

This area is affected by travelling depressions which form in the disturbed region of the westerlies farther south and by more frequent invasions of colder air from the Antarctic. During the warmer summer months temperatures reach similar levels to those found farther north in the tropical regions of Brazil. This region has a generally healthy and pleasant climate with an average of eight to nine hours' sunshine a day in the summer months.

Inland where the land is higher frosts are quite common in winter but snow is very rare. Inland the wettest months are during the summer, in contrast to the coastal district.

BRAZIL Porto Alegre 33 ft (10 m) 30°02′ S 51°13′ W 22 years

	Temperature °F			Temperature °C				Relative humidity		Precipitation			
	Highest recorded	Average daily	Lowest recorded	Highest recorded	Average daily	Lowest recorded		0630 hours	1330 hours	Average monthly		Average no. days with 0.01 in + (0.25 mm +)	
		max.	min.			max.	min.		%	%	in	mm		
J	103	87	67	51	39	31	19	11	79	55	3.5	89	8	J
F	105	87	68	52	41	31	20	11	84	56	3.2	81	9	F
M	102	83	65	48	39	28	18	9	87	57	3.9	99	8	M
A	97	78	60	41	36	26	16	5	91	61	4.1	104	9	A
M	91	71	54	30	33	22	12	−1	92	64	4.5	114	9	M
J	89	66	49	28	32	19	9	−2	92	66	5.1	130	10	J
J	89	66	49	25	32	19	9	−4	92	66	4.5	114	9	J
A	92	68	50	30	33	20	10	−1	92	65	5.0	127	11	A
S	97	70	54	32	36	21	12	0	89	63	5.2	132	10	S
O	100	74	57	39	38	23	14	4	84	60	3.4	86	10	O
N	100	80	60	43	38	27	16	6	79	55	3.1	79	8	N
D	103	85	64	46	39	29	18	8	77	54	3.5	89	7	D

Chile has a remarkable shape. It extends over 2600 miles (4200 km), between 22° and 55° S, on the Pacific coast of South America, yet has an average breadth of only 100–200 miles (160–320 km). Its eastern border with Bolivia and Argentina follows the crest-line of the main Andes mountain chain, so that the eastern part of this narrow country is very mountainous with the higher parts rising to over 16,000 ft (5000 km). South of **Santiago** the mountains are lower and more broken, but the country is rugged with hundreds of small islands offshore from Puerto Montt to Tierra del Fuego.

Much of Chile, therefore, has a mountain climate with perpetual snow and glaciers in the higher parts. The height of the snowline gradually decreases from north to south as temperature decreases and precipitation increases. Precipitation is light on the mountains in northern Chile so the snowline is high.

Most people live in the lowlands of central Chile between Valparaiso and **Valdivia**. The north of the country is a desert and the southern third is rugged, densely forested, and with a changeable, cool, wet climate.

The lowlands of northern Chile, from the border with Peru southwards to about Coquimbo at 30° S, is one of the driest regions in the world. This is a typical 'cold-water-coast desert' where, in spite of being virtually rainless, the weather is often cloudy and relatively cool for the latitude. The coastal strip has much fog and frequent light drizzle with rather low amounts of sunshine. The cloud usually breaks up by day inland in summer and temperatures here are a little higher.

There is a small difference of temperature from summer to winter and the weather is remarkably constant from one day to another. The table for **Antofagasta** illustrates conditions in this coastal desert.

Central Chile, between about 32° and 38° S, has a Mediterranean type of climate. Summers are virtually rainless and quite warm while the winter months from April to September are mild and moderately wet with changeable weather. Frost and snow occasionally occur inland but are rare on the coast. Daily hours of sunshine on the coast average from two to three in winter to eight or nine in summer. Inland, where there is less cloud, this increases to three to four in winter and nine to ten in summer. The table for **Santiago** is typical of this central portion of Chile.

Southern Chile, from about 38° S, is the third climatic region. The table for **Valdivia** is representative of the north of this area while that for **Punta Arenas**, on the Strait of Magellan, is representative of the extreme south of the country. Much of this area is very wet all the year round with much cloud and frequent disturbed, changeable weather. Annual precipitation is between 100 and 200 in (2500 and 5000 mm) and much of this falls as snow on the higher mountains and farther south.

Winters are rarely very cold on the coast but the summers are cool and cloudy. The weather and climate here are very similar to that on the coasts of British Columbia, Alaska or Norway. **Punta Arenas** is exceptional in having a very low annual rainfall because it is sheltered from the wet, westerly winds by the southern Andes. The weather and climate here are similar to that of southern Argentina. (See map p. 162.)

CHILE   **Antofagasta** 308 ft (94 m) 23°42′ S 70°24′ W 22 years

	Temperature °F				Temperature °C				Relative humidity		Precipitation			
	Highest recorded	Average daily		Lowest recorded	Highest recorded	Average daily		Lowest recorded	0730 hours	1330 hours	Average monthly		Average no. days with 0.04 in + (1 mm +)	
		max.	min.			max.	min.		%	%	in	mm		
J	83	76	63	52	28	24	17	11	77	71	0	0	0	J
F	85	76	63	57	29	24	17	14	78	70	0	0	0	F
M	83	74	61	55	28	28	16	13	80	71	0	0	0	M
A	80	70	58	50	27	21	14	10	78	72	0	0	0.1	A
M	75	67	55	47	24	19	13	8	79	73	0	0	0.1	M
J	78	65	52	43	26	18	11	6	78	71	0.1	3	0.2	J
J	79	63	51	43	26	17	11	6	80	73	0.2	5	0.5	J
A	75	62	52	41	24	17	11	5	79	73	0.1	3	0.4	A
S	72	64	53	45	22	18	12	7	77	71	0	0	0.5	S
O	73	66	55	47	23	19	13	8	75	71	0.1	3	0.2	O
N	76	69	58	51	24	21	14	11	74	71	0	0	0.3	N
D	80	72	60	51	27	22	16	11	75	70	0	0	0	D

CHILE   **Punta Arenas** 26 ft (8 m) 53°10′ S 70°54′ W 15 years

	Temperature °F				Temperature °C				Relative humidity		Precipitation			
	Highest recorded	Average daily		Lowest recorded	Highest recorded	Average daily		Lowest recorded	0730 hours	1330 hours	Average monthly		Average no. days with 0.04 in + (1 mm +)	
		max.	min.			max.	min.		%	%	in	mm		
J	86	58	45	26	30	14	7	−3	74	68	1.5	38	6	J
F	79	58	44	28	26	14	7	−2	74	64	0.9	23	5	F
M	75	54	41	24	24	12	5	−4	78	69	1.3	33	7	M
A	69	50	39	23	21	10	4	−5	82	73	1.4	36	9	A
M	63	45	35	16	17	7	2	−9	83	76	1.3	33	6	M
J	52	41	33	11	11	5	1	−12	84	80	1.6	41	8	J
J	53	40	31	12	12	4	−1	−11	83	79	1.1	28	6	J
A	55	42	33	15	13	6	1	−9	83	77	1.2	31	5	A
S	61	46	35	19	16	8	2	−7	81	71	0.9	23	5	S
O	67	51	38	25	19	11	3	−4	75	65	1.1	28	5	O
N	76	54	40	23	24	12	4	−5	73	65	0.7	18	5	N
D	75	57	43	23	24	14	6	−5	74	67	1.4	36	8	D

Santiago 1706 ft (520 m) 33°27' S 70°42' W 14 years   **CHILE**

	Temperature °F			Temperature °C				Relative humidity		Precipitation			
	Highest recorded	Average daily		Lowest recorded	Highest recorded	Average daily		Lowest recorded	0730 hours	1430 hours	Average monthly		Average no. days with 0.04 in + (1 mm +)	
		max.	min.			max.	min.		%	%	in	mm		
J	96	85	53	43	36	29	12	6	70	38	0.1	3	0	J
F	98	84	52	43	37	29	11	6	78	40	0.1	3	0	F
M	94	80	49	38	34	27	9	3	86	41	0.2	5	1	M
A	88	74	45	33	31	23	7	1	89	46	0.5	13	1	A
M	87	65	41	27	31	18	5	−3	92	58	2.5	64	5	M
J	80	58	37	26	27	14	3	−3	93	64	3.3	84	6	J
J	81	59	37	24	27	15	3	−4	91	60	3.0	76	6	J
A	85	62	39	26	29	17	4	−3	91	58	2.2	56	5	A
S	88	66	42	31	31	19	6	−1	89	55	1.2	31	3	S
O	92	72	45	32	33	22	7	0	83	50	0.6	15	3	O
N	97	78	48	37	36	26	9	3	73	41	0.3	8	1	N
D	99	83	51	36	37	28	11	2	69	38	0.2	5	0	D

Valdivia 16 ft (5 m) 39°48' S 73°14' W 29 years   **CHILE**

	Temperature °F			Temperature °C				Relative humidity		Precipitation			
	Highest recorded	Average daily		Lowest recorded	Highest recorded	Average daily		Lowest recorded	0700 hours	1300 hours	Average monthly		Average no. days with 0.04 in + (1 mm +)	
		max.	min.			max.	min.		%	%	in	mm		
J	97	73	52	37	36	23	11	3	87	64	2.6	66	7	J
F	95	73	51	35	35	23	11	2	90	67	2.9	74	7	F
M	91	69	49	36	33	21	9	2	93	70	5.2	132	11	M
A	82	62	46	29	28	17	8	−2	94	77	9.2	234	12	A
M	71	56	43	26	22	13	6	−3	95	87	14.2	361	21	M
J	63	52	42	25	17	11	6	−4	95	89	17.7	550	21	J
J	66	52	41	24	19	11	5	−4	95	89	15.5	394	20	J
A	68	54	40	25	20	12	4	−4	95	83	12.9	328	18	A
S	79	58	41	27	26	14	5	−3	94	74	8.2	208	13	S
O	84	63	44	31	29	17	7	−1	93	71	5.0	127	13	O
N	90	65	46	32	32	18	8	0	89	68	4.9	125	10	N
D	92	69	50	37	33	21	10	3	89	67	4.1	104	10	D

Colombia has a coastline both on the Pacific Ocean and on the Caribbean Sea. It borders Panama on the northwest, Venezuela and Brazil on the east, and Peru and Ecuador on the south. It is about twice as large as France or the state of Texas.

Extending between 12° N and 4° S, it experiences a tropical climate but in the higher parts of the country this is much modified by altitude. There are narrow plains along the coast but inland altitude rises sharply to the high ranges of the Andes. In the east of the country there are extensive lowlands in the forested Amazon basin.

On the Pacific coast, and on the lower slopes of the western Andes, rainfall is almost everywhere over 100 in (2500 mm) and in many places it is more than 200 in (5000 mm). All months are wet. Temperatures and humidity remain high throughout the year and the climate is generally sultry and oppressive. An unusual feature of this area is the fact that the heaviest rainfall occurs during the night, which is rare for equatorial regions, although there are frequent afternoon thunderstorms. The table for **Andagoya** is typical of this area.

The coastlands on the Caribbean are not so wet and there is a drier period from December to March. The area is also hot and humid. In the east of this coast, near the Venezuelan border, annual rainfall is low for a tropical coastland.

Most of central Colombia is mountainous; the higher Andean peaks rise to over 18,000 ft (5500 m). The Andes are here made up of a series of mountain ranges between which the large rivers, the Magdalena and the Cauca, flow northwards in wide valleys. There are considerable differences of temperature depending on altitude. The mountains above 15,000 ft (4500 m) receive most of their precipitation as snow. The whole region receives abundant precipitation of between 40 and 100 in (1000 and 2500 mm) a year and this is well distributed throughout the year with no real dry season. The western ranges are wetter than those to the east. The threefold division into tierra caliente, tierra templada and tierra fria, as decribed for Bolivia on p. 170, is equally true for Colombia. The table for **Bogota** is typical of conditions in the higher tierra fria zone. Here the weather and climate are truly those of 'perpetual spring', as understood in temperate latitudes.

Nights are cool but never really cold and at this height frost is unknown. The days feel warm in the sun but are never really hot. Rain and afternoon cloud are frequent. Sunshine averages from three to five hours a day throughout the year. At lower levels, and in the drier valleys, sunshine is rather more, from six to seven hours a day.

The lowland in the east of the country is sparsely populated and as yet largely undeveloped. Climate here is hot throughout the year and wet weather is frequent, with an annual rainfall of between 80 and 100 in (2000 and 2500 mm). As in other parts of the northern Amazon basin there are two relatively wetter periods: December to January and April to May. The table for **Manaus** in Brazil (p. 175) is representative of this wet equatorial lowland.

Andagoya 197 ft (60 m) 5°06′ N 74°40′ W 8 years   **COLOMBIA**

	Temperature °F			Temperature °C			Relative humidity	Precipitation		
	Highest recorded	Average daily		Lowest recorded	Highest recorded	Average daily		Lowest recorded		Average monthly	Average no. days with 0.01 in + (0.25 mm +)
		max.	min.			max.	min.			in	mm	
J	95	90	75	68	35	32	24	20	—	25.0	635	26	J
F	96	89	75	69	36	32	24	21	—	21.4	544	21	F
M	96	90	75	69	36	32	24	21	—	19.5	495	23	M
A	96	90	75	69	36	32	24	21	—	26.1	663	25	A
M	96	89	75	70	36	32	24	21	—	25.5	647	26	M
J	94	89	74	68	34	32	23	20	—	25.8	655	25	J
J	96	89	74	69	36	32	23	21	—	23.3	592	27	J
A	95	89	74	70	35	32	23	21	—	23.3	592	27	A
S	95	90	74	70	35	32	23	21	—	24.6	625	27	S
O	97	90	74	62	36	32	23	17	—	22.7	577	25	O
N	95	88	74	66	35	31	23	19	—	22.4	569	27	N
D	95	88	74	70	35	31	23	21	—	19.5	495	27	D

Bogota 8678 ft (2645 m) 4°36′ N 74°05′ W 10 years   **COLOMBIA**

	Temperature °F			Temperature °C			Relative humidity		Precipitation		
	Highest recorded	Average daily		Lowest recorded	Highest recorded	Average daily		Lowest recorded	0600 hours	1400 hours	Average monthly	Average no. days with 0.01 in + (0.25 mm +)
		max.	min.			max.	min.		%	%	in	mm	
J	74	67	48	40	23	19	9	4	84	51	2.3	58	6	J
F	75	68	49	42	24	20	9	6	83	53	2.6	66	7	F
M	75	67	50	42	24	19	10	6	83	54	4.0	102	13	M
A	75	67	51	45	24	19	11	7	84	57	5.8	147	20	A
M	74	66	51	45	23	19	11	7	85	58	4.5	114	17	M
J	72	65	51	44	22	18	11	7	85	56	2.4	61	16	J
J	72	64	50	44	22	18	10	7	83	56	2.0	51	18	J
A	72	65	50	44	22	18	10	7	83	54	2.2	56	16	A
S	73	66	49	44	23	19	9	7	82	54	2.4	61	13	S
O	73	66	50	43	23	19	10	6	86	61	6.3	160	20	O
N	73	66	50	44	23	19	10	7	88	64	4.7	119	16	N
D	73	66	49	40	23	19	9	4	85	56	2.6	66	15	D

COSTA RICA

This small Central American country is situated between 8° and 11° N and has a border with Panama on the south and with Nicaragua on the north. It is about twice the size of Wales or the state of Massachusetts. The general conditions of weather and climate in this region are described in detail for Panama (pp. 195–6). Like other countries of Central America, Costa Rica is mountainous with the highest peaks exceeding 12,000 ft (3700 m). It has a coastline on both the Pacific and the Caribbean.

The table for the capital, **San José**, illustrates conditions in the tierra templada, where the nights are much cooler than at sea level and the days less hot and humid. Conditions at sea level on the Pacific shore are similar to those shown in the table for **Balboa Heights** in Panama (p. 196). The Caribbean shore to the east is equally hot and rather wetter.

COSTA RICA **San José** 3760 ft (1146 m) 9°56′ N 84°08′ W 8 years

	Temperature °F			Temperature °C				Relative humidity		Precipitation			
	Highest recorded	Average daily	Lowest recorded	Highest recorded	Average daily	Lowest recorded		0630 hours	1330 hours	Average monthly		Average no. days with 0.004 in + (0.1 mm +)	
		max.	min.			max.	min.		%	%	in	mm		
J	87	75	58	49	31	24	14	9	83	63	0.6	15	3	J
F	88	76	58	51	31	24	14	11	82	57	0.2	5	1	F
M	91	79	59	50	33	26	15	10	81	55	0.8	20	2	M
A	89	79	62	53	32	26	17	12	80	60	1.8	46	7	A
M	88	80	62	54	31	27	17	12	85	70	9.0	229	19	M
J	92	79	62	57	33	26	17	14	91	74	9.5	241	22	J
J	84	77	62	54	29	25	17	12	89	74	8.3	211	23	J
A	85	78	61	56	29	26	16	13	89	73	9.5	241	24	A
S	86	79	61	56	30	26	16	13	91	76	12.0	305	24	S
O	85	77	60	55	29	25	16	13	92	78	11.8	300	25	O
N	84	77	60	52	29	25	16	11	87	71	5.7	145	14	N
D	87	75	58	49	31	24	14	9	85	67	1.6	41	6	D

Ecuador, as its name implies, lies athwart the equator between 1° N and 5° S on the west coast of South America. It is a small country, a little larger than Great Britain and about the size of the state of Arizona. It includes three types of country which form three different and distinctive climatic regions: a narrow coastal plain, a high mountainous central region including the main Andean mountain ranges, and a forested lowland region in the east which is part of the Amazon basin.

The climate of the coastlands is indicated by the table for **Guayaquil**. Temperature and humidity are high here throughout the year. **Guayaquil** has a single main rainy season from December to April. Towards the north the total annual rainfall increases to as much as 80 in (2000 mm) or more and some rain falls in all months; this is a typical equatorial pattern of rainfall. In the extreme south of the coastal district rainfall decreases sharply and is as low as 8 in (200 mm) a year as the dry coastal belt of Peru is approached.

In the central Andean mountain region temperatures are much reduced by altitude and the division into

tierra caliente, tierra templada and tierra fria described on p. 170 for Bolivia is appropriate. Because of the heavier precipitation in Ecuador as compared with Peru and Bolivia the snowline is at an altitude of about 16,000 ft (5000 m). The effect of altitude at heights above 10,000 ft (3000 m) is something that the visitor should take into account.

Quito (see table) has a climate that is often described as one of 'perpetual spring' with warm days and chilly nights and little variation of temperature around the year. Much of the rainfall in this mountainous region comes in the afternoon and evening as clouds build up over the mountains and thunderstorms develop. Sunshine hours are least at **Quito** in the rainy season when they average four to five a day and greatest in the dry season when they are as much as seven to eight.

The eastern part of the country at the foot of the Andes is low-lying and has a typical hot, wet, equatorial type of climate with rainfall well distributed throughout the year. It is similar to that described on p. 174 for the extensive Amazon forest region of Brazil.

Guayaquil 20 ft (6 m) 2°10′ S 79°53′ W 3 years

	Temperature °F			Temperature °C			Relative humidity	Precipitation			
	Highest recorded	Average daily	Lowest recorded	Highest recorded	Average daily	Lowest recorded			Average monthly	Average no. days with trace or more	
		max.	min.			max.	min.			in	mm	
J	96	88	70	67	36	31	21	19	—	9.4	239	20	J
F	93	87	71	66	34	31	22	19	—	9.8	249	25	F
M	92	88	72	64	33	31	22	18	—	10.9	277	24	M
A	93	89	71	69	34	32	22	21	—	4.6	117	14	A
M	95	88	68	65	35	31	20	18	—	1.1	28	9	M
J	94	87	68	64	34	31	20	18	—	0.3	8	4	J
J	91	84	67	62	33	29	19	17	—	0.2	5	2	J
A	92	86	65	62	33	30	18	17	—	0	0	0	A
S	93	87	66	57	34	31	19	14	—	0.1	3	2	S
O	94	86	68	62	34	30	20	17	—	0.3	8	3	O
N	94	88	68	61	34	31	20	16	—	0.1	3	4	N
D	98	88	70	66	37	31	21	19	—	2.0	51	10	D

	Temperature °F			Temperature °C				Relative humidity		Precipitation			
	Highest recorded	Average daily		Lowest recorded	Highest recorded	Average daily		Lowest recorded	0500 hours	1300 hours	Average monthly		Average no. days with 0.4 in + (10 mm +)	
		max.	min.			max.	min.		%	%	in	mm		
J	79	72	46	37	26	22	8	3	93	54	3.9	99	16	J
F	80	71	47	34	27	22	8	1	93	59	4.4	112	17	F
M	80	71	47	40	27	22	8	4	93	59	5.6	142	20	M
A	78	70	47	40	26	21	8	4	93	60	6.9	175	22	A
M	79	70	47	35	26	21	8	2	93	60	5.4	137	21	M
J	78	71	45	36	26	22	7	2	88	51	1.7	43	12	J
J	79	72	44	33	26	22	7	1	81	43	0.8	20	7	J
A	82	73	45	36	28	23	7	2	80	40	1.2	31	9	A
S	83	73	45	35	28	23	7	2	85	44	2.7	69	14	S
O	86	72	46	32	30	22	8	0	92	53	4.4	112	18	O
N	80	72	45	33	27	22	7	1	92	53	3.8	97	14	N
D	81	72	46	34	27	22	8	1	94	54	3.1	79	16	D

This is one of the smallest countries of Central America whose weather and climate are described in more detail on pp. 195–6 for Panama. It is about as large as Wales or the state of Massachusetts and is situated between 13° and 14° N. It is a mountainous country with the highest points reaching over 6000 ft (1800 m). It is the only country in this region with no coastline on the Caribbean Sea.

There is a narrow coastal plain on the Pacific shore and this forms the most extensive region of tierra caliente, with a typical hot, tropical climate and a single rainy season between May and October. Annual rainfall in this lowland is similar to that shown in the table for **San Salvador** which is in the lower part of the hill country; here daytime temperatures are similar but with much cooler nights than in the lowlands. In the higher areas of the tierra templada climatic conditions are similar to those shown for **Guatemala City** on p. 191.

San Salvador 2238 ft (682 m) 13°42′ N 89°13′ W 33 years   **EL SALVADOR**

	Temperature °F			Temperature °C			Relative humidity		Precipitation			
	Highest recorded	Average daily	Lowest recorded	Highest recorded	Average daily	Lowest recorded	0700 hours	1400 hours	Average monthly		Average no. days with tracc or more	
		max.	min.			max.	min.		%	%	in	mm	
J	101	90	60	45	38	32	16	7	81	45	0.3	8	1	J
F	103	92	60	49	39	33	16	9	80	43	0.2	5	1	F
M	105	94	62	45	41	34	17	7	79	44	0.4	10	1	M
A	104	93	65	54	40	34	18	12	79	50	1.7	43	4	A
M	103	91	67	58	39	33	19	14	86	60	7.7	196	13	M
J	98	87	66	56	37	31	19	13	89	66	12.9	328	19	J
J	98	89	65	58	37	32	18	14	88	61	11.5	292	19	J
A	98	89	66	60	37	32	19	16	89	62	11.7	297	19	A
S	99	87	66	53	37	31	19	12	91	69	12.1	307	20	S
O	101	87	65	54	38	31	18	12	88	66	9.5	241	16	O
N	102	87	63	49	39	31	17	9	80	56	1.6	41	4	N
D	101	89	61	47	38	32	16	8	81	50	0.4	10	2	D

FRENCH GUIANA

This is a small country on the north coast of South America, bordered on the west by Surinam and on the south and east by Brazil. Situated between 2° and 6° N it has an equatorial type of climate which is described in more detail on p. 192 for Guyana. French Guiana has a large area of lowland; the table for **Cayenne** on the coast is representative of a large part of the country. Here the main rainy season is from December to June and the months August to October are almost dry. This is the principal climatic difference between French Guiana and Surinam and Guyana. Otherwise temperature and humidity remain high throughout the year and there is little difference between the lowlands in all these countries. **Cayenne** is rather wetter, taking the year as a whole, than Georgetown in Guyana and Paramaribo in Surinam. Only a small area in the south of the country consists of upland plateau where climatic conditions are better represented by the table for **Santa Elena** (p. 205) in Venezuela.

GUATEMALA

Guatemala is one of the larger countries of Central America whose weather and climate are described in more detail on pp. 195–6 for Panama. Lying between 14° and 18° N, Guatemala is bordered on the north by Mexico, on the east by Belize and on the south by Honduras and El Salvador. It has a very short coastline on the Caribbean Sea and a longer west coast on the Pacific. In area it is about the size of the state of Pennsylvania and a little smaller than England.

The northern part of the country is a low plain and forms part of the tierra caliente, an area of typical hot, tropical climate with some rain all the year round and a maximum fall between May and September. The west and south of the country are very mountainous with some volcanic peaks rising to over 13,000 ft (4000 m). A large part of the hilly country is typical tierra templada and the climatic conditions are well represented by the table for **Guatemala City** which has a very pleasant climate. Rainfall here is moderate with a distinct dry season from November to April. Conditions on the Pacific coast, where there is a narrow strip of tierra caliente, are similar in terms of the dry and wet seasons, but rainfall is rather heavier and there is little relief from the high temperatures at night.

Cayenne 20 ft (6 m) 4°56′ N 52°27′ W 23 years — FRENCH GUIANA

	Temperature °F				Temperature °C				Relative humidity		Precipitation			
	Highest recorded	Average daily		Lowest recorded	Highest recorded	Average daily		Lowest recorded	0900 hours	1500 hours	Average monthly		Average no. days with 0.04 in + (1 mm +)	
		max.	min.			max.	min.		%	%	in	mm		
J	91	84	74	67	33	29	23	19	83	80	14.4	366	20	J
F	93	85	74	68	34	29	23	20	81	78	12.3	312	16	F
M	92	85	74	66	33	29	23	19	83	80	15.8	401	22	M
A	92	86	75	65	33	30	24	18	84	81	18.9	480	21	A
M	92	85	74	68	33	29	23	20	86	83	21.7	551	26	M
J	93	87	73	69	34	31	23	21	85	79	15.5	394	23	J
J	93	88	73	68	34	31	23	20	82	75	6.9	175	18	J
A	96	90	73	68	36	32	23	20	77	71	2.8	71	9	A
S	97	91	74	70	36	33	23	21	73	69	1.2	31	4	S
O	97	91	74	68	36	33	23	20	73	69	1.3	33	4	O
N	95	89	74	68	35	32	23	20	78	74	4.6	117	11	N
D	93	86	74	68	34	30	23	20	83	79	10.7	272	18	D

Guatemala City 4855 ft (1480 m) 14°37′ N 90°31′ W 6 years — GUATEMALA

	Temperature °F				Temperature °C				Relative humidity		Precipitation			
	Highest recorded	Average daily		Lowest recorded	Highest recorded	Average daily		Lowest recorded	0700 hours	1400 hours	Average monthly		Average no. days with 0.01 in + (0.25 mm +)	
		max.	min.			max.	min.		%	%	in	mm		
J	86	73	53	41	30	23	12	5	91	69	0.3	8	4	J
F	85	77	54	43	29	25	12	6	89	62	0.1	3	2	F
M	86	81	57	41	30	27	14	5	86	51	0.5	13	3	M
A	90	82	58	47	32	28	14	8	81	51	1.2	31	5	A
M	89	84	60	52	32	29	16	11	83	55	6.0	152	15	M
J	86	81	61	52	30	27	16	11	89	70	10.8	274	23	J
J	84	78	60	51	29	26	16	11	91	67	8.0	203	21	J
A	83	79	60	52	28	26	16	11	90	72	7.8	198	21	A
S	82	79	60	54	28	26	16	12	92	71	9.1	231	22	S
O	82	76	60	50	28	24	16	10	92	72	6.8	173	18	O
N	83	74	57	44	28	23	14	7	89	71	0.9	23	7	N
D	83	72	55	41	28	22	13	5	89	70	0.3	8	4	D

GUYANA

(Including a description of the weather and climate of Surinam and French Guiana)

Guyana – a former British colony – is situated on the Atlantic coast of South America between 1° and 8° N. It is about as large as Britain. It is bordered by Venezuela on the west, by Brazil on the south and by Surinam on the east.

The weather and climate of Guyana are similar to those of the neighbouring countries of Surinam (formerly Dutch Guiana) and French Guiana to the east. All these countries have coastlines on the Atlantic, open for most of the year to the influence of the moist northeast trade winds. Inland the country rises, towards the Venezuelan and Brazilian borders, to a plateau which is surmounted by isolated hills. The whole area comes under the influence of the inter-tropical belt of cloud and rain, called by meteorologists the inter-tropical convergence, twice a year.

The lowlands have a typical hot, wet, equatorial type of climate with constant, high humidity. This area is often very sultry and oppressive as well as having a very monotonous weather regime for there is little change from day to day. Wet days alternate almost equally with dry days. The nights are particularly oppressive but during the day the regular sea breeze brings some relief on the coast. Temperatures never rise to very high levels and so are not dangerous; but the heat and humidity are enervating to the unacclimatized visitor. Sunshine amounts are moderately large; from four to five hours a day in the wetter months and as much as eight hours a day during the drier seasons.

Inland in the higher plateaux areas rainfall may be slightly less and there is a tendency for a single rainy season from April to September, although all months get some rain. Daytime temperatures are here a little lower than on the coast and night temperatures are much cooler so that the climate is less uncomfortable. Humidity is also lower during the drier months. Climatic conditions here are well represented by the table for **Santa Elena** (p. 205) which is just across the border in western Venezuela.

Guyana is the most northerly and the largest of the three countries. It has the largest area of upland plateau with the highest mountain rising to over 9000 ft (2750 m).

The table for **Georgetown** is representative of the coastal area and the lowlands. The rainiest months are May to July and November to January as the inter-tropical convergence brings the heaviest and most reliable rains. These are the months with most cloud and least sun. Note the constant high humidity and the remarkably constant temperature around the year.

HONDURAS

Honduras is one of the larger countries of Central America whose weather and climate are described in more detail on pp. 195–6 for Panama. It is situated between 13° and 16° N between Nicaragua to the south and Guatemala to the north. It has a western border with El Salvador and a very short coastline on the Pacific. In size it is similar to Pennsylvania and a little smaller than England. Much of the country is mountainous and the only extensive lowland is in the extreme east.

Reliable climatic data for Honduras is sparse. The table for **Tegucigalpa** is representative of the hilly country of the tierra templada, where there is a larger daily temperature range and cooler nights than is found in the low-lying tierra caliente. The Caribbean coast of Honduras mostly faces north and it has a much lower annual rainfall than Nicaragua to the south or Belize to the north. It appears that annual rainfall here is no more than on the Pacific shore and, unusual for this region, most rain falls in the winter period of low sun. At this time the northeast trade winds are blowing more directly onshore.

Georgetown 6 ft (2 m) 6°50′ N 58°12′ W 45 years　　　　　　　　**GUYANA**

	Temperature °F			Temperature °C			Relative humidity		Precipitation			
	Highest recorded	Average daily	Lowest recorded	Highest recorded	Average daily	Lowest recorded	0700 hours	1300 hours	Average monthly		Average no. days with 0.04 in + (1 mm +)	
		max.	min.			max.	min.		%	%	in	mm	
J	88	84	74	68	31	29	23	20	87	75	8.0	203	17	J
F	89	84	74	69	32	29	23	21	85	72	4.5	114	13	F
M	89	84	75	69	32	29	24	21	83	71	6.9	175	12	M
A	90	85	76	71	32	29	24	22	84	71	5.5	140	12	A
M	90	85	75	70	32	29	24	21	88	75	11.4	290	20	M
J	89	85	75	69	32	29	24	21	92	77	11.9	302	24	J
J	90	85	75	70	32	29	24	21	93	74	10.0	254	21	J
A	90	86	75	71	32	30	24	22	92	73	6.9	175	16	A
S	93	87	76	69	34	31	24	21	90	69	3.2	81	7	S
O	93	87	76	70	34	31	24	21	88	69	3.0	76	9	O
N	91	86	76	69	33	30	24	21	88	69	6.1	155	10	N
D	90	84	75	70	32	29	24	21	89	75	11.3	287	20	D

Tegucigalpa 3304 ft (1007 m) 14°04′ N 87°13′ W 10 years　　　　　　　　**HONDURAS**

	Temperature °F			Temperature °C			Relative humidity	Precipitation			
	Highest recorded	Average daily	Lowest recorded	Highest recorded	Average daily	Lowest recorded		Average monthly		Average no. days with 0.01 in + (0.25 mm +)	
		max.	min.			max.	min.		in	mm		
J	—	77	57	—	—	25	14	—	0.5	12	5	J
F	—	80	57	—	—	27	14	—	0.1	2	3	F
M	—	84	59	—	—	29	15	—	0	1	2	M
A	—	86	62	—	—	30	17	—	1.0	26	2	A
M	—	85	64	—	—	30	18	—	7.1	180	9	M
J	—	82	65	—	—	28	18	—	7.0	177	13	J
J	—	81	64	—	—	27	18	—	2.8	70	11	J
A	—	83	63	—	—	28	17	—	2.9	74	11	A
S	—	83	63	—	—	28	17	—	5.9	151	16	S
O	—	80	63	—	—	27	17	—	3.4	87	13	O
N	—	78	60	—	—	26	16	—	1.5	38	8	N
D	—	77	59	—	—	25	15	—	0.5	14	7	D

NICARAGUA

Nicaragua is the largest of the seven countries of Central America whose weather and climate are described in more detail for Panama on pp. 195–6. Nicaragua is about as large as England or the state of Michigan and is situated between 11° and 15° N. It is not quite so mountainous as some countries of this region, but there are mountains rising to between 5000 and 7000 ft (1500 and 2100 m). Most of the country is thus included in the two zones of the tierra caliente, the hot tropical lowland, and the tierra templada, the cooler hill region with a larger daily range of temperature. The table for **Managua**, the capital, is representative of conditions at low levels on the Pacific side of the country.

There are very few reliable climatic statistics for the whole country; but, as a general guide, it can be assumed that the table for **San José** in Costa Rica (p. 186) is representative of the cooler tierra templada in Nicaragua. Conditions on the Caribbean coast would be similar to those shown by the table for **Belize City** in Belize (p. 169) as regards temperature. The east coast of Nicaragua, however, is one of the wettest parts of Central America with an annual rainfall of between 100 and 150 in (2500 and 3750 mm).

NICARAGUA — Managua 184 ft (56 m) 12°08′ N 86°11′ W 10 years

	Temperature °F			Temperature °C			Relative humidity	Precipitation		
	Highest recorded	Average daily	Lowest recorded	Highest recorded	Average daily	Lowest recorded		Average monthly		Average no. days with 0.04 in + (1 mm +)
		max.	min.			max.	min.			in	mm	
J	—	88	68	—	—	31	20	—	—	0.2	5	3	J
F	—	90	70	—	—	32	21	—	—	0	1	1	F
M	—	93	72	—	—	34	22	—	—	0.2	5	1	M
A	—	93	73	—	—	34	23	—	—	0.2	5	1	A
M	—	93	73	—	—	34	23	—	—	3.0	76	6	M
J	—	88	73	—	—	31	23	—	—	11.7	296	21	J
J	—	88	72	—	—	31	22	—	—	5.3	134	20	J
A	—	88	72	—	—	31	22	—	—	5.1	130	17	A
S	—	88	72	—	—	31	22	—	—	7.2	182	20	S
O	—	88	72	—	—	31	22	—	—	9.6	243	19	O
N	—	88	70	—	—	31	21	—	—	2.3	59	10	N
D	—	88	68	—	—	31	20	—	—	0.2	5	2	D

(Including a description of the weather and climate of Belize, Guatemala, Honduras, El Salvador, Nicaragua and Costa Rica.)

There are seven small countries in the narrow isthmus of Central America between the southern border of Mexico and the northern border of Colombia. From north to south these countries are: Belize, Guatemala, Honduras, El Salvador, Nicaragua, Costa Rica and Panama. Together these countries have an area of 180,000 square miles (470,000 sq. km), a little larger than the state of California and about twice the size of Great Britain. The area lies between 18° and 7° N and between 85° and 95° W. The whole area is within the tropics and, because of the narrowness of the isthmus, is strongly influenced by the ocean with the result that almost everywhere the climate is tropical with abundant rainfall. At its narrowest point the isthmus is only about fifty miles (80 km) in width but, in Nicaragua and Honduras, it widens to about 350 miles (560 km). A chain of mountains, ranging in height from 4000 to 13,000 ft (1200 to 4000 m), runs approximately through the centre of the isthmus.

Climate and weather in all these countries are broadly similar and are described here. Only brief notes amplifying this description, with a note of any local peculiarities, are given for individual entries.

Situated well within the tropics, but north of the equator, all these countries have a typically tropical climate with high temperatures around the year at low altitudes. Temperatures are significantly modified by altitude and a simple and useful threefold division into climatic zones can be made using the local terms: tierra caliente, tierra templada and tierra fria.

In the tierra caliente, from sea level up to about 3000 ft (900 m), temperatures are hot throughout the year. The tierra templada from 3000 to 6000 ft (900 to 1800 m) has cooler temperatures, but many tropical or subtropical crops such as coffee are grown. Here there are many local differences in the amount of rainfall depending on altitude and the aspect of the mountains in relation to the prevailing winds. The tierra fria, from 6000 to 10,000 ft (800 to 3000 m) is limited in extent, but here conditions are quite cool and typical of temperate latitudes. Frost and snow may occasionally occur but the mountains are not high enough to carry permanent snow.

Over most of this region the season of maximum rainfall is between May and September, the period of high sun in the northern hemisphere. Places on the eastern coast, or the Caribbean shore, tend to be rather wetter, and to have a longer rainy season, than those on the Pacific coast to the west. In some places on the Caribbean shore there is a tendency for a double rainy season and all months have significant rainfall; this is well illustrated by the table for **Belize City** (p. 169). Even in the narrow isthmus of Panama annual rainfall

at Cristobal on the Caribbean coast is double that at **Balboa Heights** on the Pacific. Some of the wettest places in this region are where mountains face the persistent northeast to easterly trade winds which blow onshore for most of the year.

Another significant feature of the weather and climate of Central America is the liability of most of the area to suffer hurricanes between June and November. These severe tropical storms develop well to the east of the Caribbean in the central Atlantic at about 5° to 10° N. The most usual track of these disturbances is across the West Indian islands, after which they curve north or northeastwards. The coastlands of Central America are affected less frequently and less severely than the islands farther east but those hurricanes which reach the mainland can produce very heavy rainfall and their strong winds can cause extensive damage. Costa Rica and Panama are rarely affected by them but the remaining countries can experience hurricanes which, even when weakening and losing the more violent winds, can add appreciably to the rainfall in the months August to October. The Pacific coastlands of Central America are also occasionally affected by less violent tropical storms which develop in the eastern Pacific Ocean.

In the lowlands of the tierra caliente temperatures remain high in all months with a very small daily range of temperature. Near the coast humidity is also high and the principal relief from this perpetually warm, humid climate is the daily sea breeze. Extremely high temperatures are never recorded on the coast and midday temperatures may even be higher inland than in the tierra templada. Inland and at higher levels there is a much larger daily range of temperature and the nights are pleasantly cool. This can be seen by comparing the average and extreme temperatures for **Guatemala City** or **San Salvador** with those for **Belize City** in the tables for the respective countries.

Sunshine amounts are quite high throughout the year in most of Central America. Average daily sunshine hours range from six to eight in the wetter months to as many as ten hours during the dry months, even though this is the time of low sun. Costa Rica and Panama have a rather more cloudy climate with more frequent rain so that here the sunshine hours range from four or five in the wettest months to eight or nine in the driest season.

Many areas in Central America had a bad reputation in the past for fever and tropical diseases. The climatic conditions of the lowlands encouraged malaria and yellow fever, but these have largely been eradicated and were only indirect effects of the climate. The climate itself, although sultry and oppressive for much of the year in the wetter lowlands, is not particularly unhealthy. Indeed, in the drier areas and in the hills it is pleasant and sunny for much of the year.

Panama itself occupies the narrowest part of the Central American isthmus. It lies between 7° and 9° N and owes its existence as an independent state to the cutting of the Panama Canal by the United States; previously it was part of Colombia. Although there are areas of lowland on both the Caribbean and Pacific coasts, much of the interior is hilly with some mountains rising above 11,000 ft (3300 m). Within this small area, therefore, are examples of the three climatic zones described above. The table for **Balboa Heights** is representative of the Pacific coast. The lowlands on the northern or Caribbean coast are almost twice as wet but temperatures are almost the same. Panama is about the same size as the state of Maine.

PANAMA   **Balboa Heights** 118 ft (33 m) 8°57′ N 79°33′ W 34 years

	Temperature °F			Temperature °C			Relative humidity		Precipitation		
	Highest recorded	Average daily	Lowest recorded	Highest recorded	Average daily	Lowest recorded	0730 hours	1930 hours	Average monthly		Average no. days with 0.04 in + (1 mm +)
		max.	min.			max.	min.		%	%	in	mm	
J	93	88	71	63	34	31	22	17	88	84	1.0	25	4	J
F	95	89	71	64	35	32	22	18	85	81	0.4	10	2	F
M	96	90	72	65	36	32	22	18	81	78	0.7	18	1	M
A	97	87	74	64	36	31	23	18	81	81	2.9	74	6	A
M	96	86	74	69	36	30	23	21	87	88	8.0	203	15	M
J	95	87	74	70	35	31	23	21	90	90	8.4	213	16	J
J	95	87	74	67	35	31	23	19	90	91	7.1	180	15	J
A	94	86	74	68	34	30	23	20	90	91	7.9	201	15	A
S	94	85	74	68	34	29	23	20	91	91	8.2	208	16	S
O	95	85	73	68	35	29	23	20	90	92	10.1	257	18	O
N	94	85	73	67	34	29	23	19	91	92	10.2	259	18	N
D	94	87	73	66	34	31	23	19	90	89	4.8	122	12	D

Paraguay is entirely landlocked and is situated between 18° and 28° S. It is as large as the state of California. It is bordered on the north by Bolivia and Brazil and on the south by Argentina. Most of the country lies below 1500 ft (450 m). The northwestern part of the country lies entirely within the tropics and has a typical tropical climate with hot summers, warm winters and most of its rainfall in the hottest months between October and March. The southeastern half of the country has temperatures a little lower in all months but the summers are sufficiently hot and wet to be typically tropical.

The northwest of Paraguay is part of the Chaco region which extends into the adjoining regions of Bolivia and Argentina. Here annual rainfall ranges between 30 and 50 in (750 and 1250 mm), increasing northwards. Occasionally in winter the region is affected by outbreaks of colder polar air from Antarctica; this cold air lowers the temperature for a day or so but frost is very rare. This is a rather desolate and sparsely populated region. It is very flat and level; the elevation of the land rises very gradually towards the Bolivian

border. Differences of climate and weather are small within the Chaco.

The southeastern half of the country contains some land which is a little higher and the more southerly latitude means that the winter here is somewhat cooler; however, cold days with frost are very rare. Summer temperatures are hot to warm so that conditions are then quite tropical. Rainfall is between 50 and 70 in (1250 and 1750 mm) a year and it increases eastwards. Rain can be expected on about one day in five in winter and on about one day in three in summer. The table for **Asunción** illustrates conditions in the centre of the country. To the northwest, in the Chaco, conditions are a little hotter in all months and there is less rainfall. In the southeast of the country it is rather wetter with slightly lower temperatures in all months. The southeast is the most developed and densely populated part of Paraguay.

The weather can often be distinctly sultry and oppressive during the wet summer months and this is particularly the case in the Chaco region.

Asunción 456 ft (139 m) 25°17′ S 57°30′ W 15 years **PARAGUAY**

	Temperature °F				Temperature °C				Relative humidity		Precipitation		
	Highest recorded	Average daily		Lowest recorded	Highest recorded	Average daily		Lowest recorded	0700 hours	1400 hours	Average monthly		Average no. days with 0.004 in + (0.1 mm +)
		max.	min.			max.	min.		%	%	in	mm	
J	109	95	71	54	43	35	22	12	81	56	5.5	140	8	J
F	109	94	71	52	43	34	22	11	82	55	5.1	130	6	F
M	106	92	69	49	41	33	21	9	84	55	4.3	109	6	M
A	104	84	65	42	40	29	18	6	86	59	5.2	132	7	A
M	99	77	58	34	37	25	14	1	89	62	4.6	117	6	M
J	98	72	53	29	37	22	12	-2	88	61	2.7	69	6	J
J	103	74	53	29	39	23	12	-2	84	56	2.2	56	5	J
A	101	78	57	30	38	26	14	-1	79	53	1.5	38	4	A
S	105	83	60	37	41	28	16	3	76	48	3.1	79	7	S
O	106	86	62	38	41	30	17	3	73	50	5.5	140	8	O
N	108	90	65	45	42	32	18	7	74	53	5.9	150	8	N
D	110	94	70	47	43	34	21	8	73	50	6.2	158	7	D

PERU

Peru is twice the size of France or the state of Texas, extending between the equator and 18° S. It has a long coastline on the Pacific Ocean and is bordered by Ecuador on the north, by Brazil and Bolivia on the east and by Chile on the south. The central portion of Peru includes the great mountain and plateaux region of the Andes with numerous peaks rising to over 20,000 ft (6000 m) and with extensive plateaux districts between 10,000 and 14,000 ft (3000 and 4300 m). There is a very narrow coastal plain on the Pacific shore while, to the east of the Andes, the land drops steeply to the forested lowlands of the Amazon basin.

The Pacific coastal district has a most unusual type of dry desert climate. This is caused by the cold waters of the Humboldt current which flows northwards. This area is a continuation of the coastal desert of northern Chile. The cold ocean water maintains low temperatures for a tropical latitude almost up to the equator and there are very small differences from month to month. The dryness is so marked that in some places several years have passed without appreciable rain. In the northern coastal districts, however, there is a remarkable change of weather for a few weeks every ten or fifteen years. Temperature rises, clouds build up and torrential rain may fall for many days. It is as if the equatorial belt of cloud and rain, which normally lies to the north on the coasts of Ecuador and Colombia, had moved south. Such unusual and unexpected heavy rain may cause widespread damage. At the same time the sea temperature offshore rises and the cold current retreats southwards. The phenomenon is called El Niño and is most likely to occur in December and January.

This otherwise arid coastal strip experiences frequent low cloud and fog from which a light drizzle, called locally *garúa*, may fall. This is another unusual feature for such a dry climate. The climatic table for **Lima** is representative of the climate of the coastal district although the city is a short distance inland. Midday temperatures are here a little higher than on the coast. **Lima** has an average of only one to two hours of sunshine a day in the low sun period, but this rises to between five and seven hours a day during the warmer months of December to April.

The Andean mountain and plateaux region of Peru has similar weather and climate to that described on p. 170 for the Andean region of Bolivia. Here the main differences are a consequence of the altitude. The tables for **Cajamarca** in the north of the country and **Cuzco** in the south illustrate the marked reduction of temperature in all months and the single rainy season at the time of high sun between November and March. The greater cloudiness during the rainy season prevents the temperature from rising higher at this time. As another consequence of the high altitude there is a large daily range of temperature which falls quite low at night. During the dry season frosts may be a nightly occurrence at these heights. Above about 10,000 ft (3000 m) visitors may suffer from mountain sickness as described on p. 170 for Bolivia.

The climate and weather of the eastern lowlands in the Peruvian portion of the Amazon basin are similar to those described for Brazil and Bolivia; they are illustrated by the tables for **Conceptión** in Bolivia (p. 171) and **Sena Madureira** in Brazil (p. 175).

Cajamarca 8662 ft (2640 m) 7°09′ S 78°30′ W 9 years   PERU

	Temperature °F				Temperature °C			Relative humidity		Precipitation			
	Highest recorded	Average daily		Lowest recorded	Highest recorded	Average daily		Lowest recorded	0700 hours	1300 hours	Average monthly		Average no. days with 0.04 in + (1 mm +)	
		max.	min.			max.	min.		%	%	in	mm		
J	77	71	48	38	25	22	9	4	85	38	3.6	91	13	J
F	77	70	48	32	25	21	9	0	88	45	4.2	107	17	F
M	79	70	48	37	26	21	9	3	92	46	4.6	117	17	M
A	77	70	47	32	25	21	8	0	90	42	3.4	86	14	A
M	77	71	44	30	25	22	7	−1	86	41	1.7	43	9	M
J	77	70	42	30	25	21	6	−1	81	37	0.5	13	4	J
J	77	70	41	28	25	21	5	−2	86	33	0.2	5	2	J
A	78	71	42	30	26	22	6	−1	81	29	0.3	8	2	A
S	77	71	45	32	25	22	7	0	85	38	2.3	58	9	S
O	79	71	47	33	26	22	8	1	81	34	2.3	58	9	O
N	79	72	46	31	26	22	8	−1	79	33	1.9	48	8	N
D	79	71	47	25	26	22	8	−4	86	37	3.2	81	11	D

Cuzco 10,581 ft (3225 m) 13°33′ S 71°55′ W 13 years   PERU

	Temperature °F				Temperature °C			Relative humidity		Precipitation			
	Highest recorded	Average daily		Lowest recorded	Highest recorded	Average daily		Lowest recorded	0700 hours	1300 hours	Average monthly		Average no. days with 0.04 in + (1 mm +)	
		max.	min.			max.	min.		%	%	in	mm		
J	82	68	45	37	28	20	7	3	79	40	6.4	163	18	J
F	81	69	45	36	27	21	7	2	85	37	5.9	150	13	F
M	79	70	44	35	26	21	7	2	84	31	4.3	109	11	M
A	79	71	40	25	26	22	4	−4	87	33	2.0	51	8	A
M	78	70	35	24	26	21	2	−4	89	29	0.6	15	3	M
J	77	69	33	23	25	21	1	−5	91	23	0.2	5	2	J
J	77	70	31	16	25	21	−1	−9	95	23	0.2	5	2	J
A	77	70	34	23	25	21	1	−5	90	24	0.4	10	2	A
S	81	71	40	30	27	22	4	−1	80	26	1.0	25	7	S
O	84	72	43	30	29	22	6	−1	73	27	2.6	66	8	O
N	82	73	43	33	28	23	6	1	71	26	3.0	76	12	N
D	81	71	44	34	27	22	7	1	75	33	5.4	137	16	D

	Temperature °F				Temperature °C				Relative humidity		Precipitation			
	Highest recorded	Average daily		Lowest recorded	Highest recorded	Average daily		Lowest recorded	0700 hours	1300 hours	Average monthly		Average no. days with 0.04 in + (1 mm +)	
		max.	min.			max.	min.		%	%	in	mm		
J	89	82	66	59	32	28	19	15	93	69	0.1	3	0.5	J
F	92	83	67	59	33	28	19	15	92	66	0	0	0.1	F
M	91	83	66	61	33	28	19	16	92	64	0	0	0.1	M
A	93	80	63	56	34	27	17	13	93	66	0	0	0.2	A
M	84	74	60	52	29	23	16	11	95	76	0.2	5	0.8	M
J	81	68	58	49	27	20	14	9	95	80	0.2	5	1	J
J	81	67	57	49	27	19	14	9	94	77	0.3	8	1	J
A	81	66	56	50	27	19	13	10	95	78	0.3	8	2	A
S	78	68	57	51	26	20	14	11	94	76	0.3	8	1	S
O	79	71	58	53	26	22	14	12	94	72	0.1	3	0.2	O
N	85	74	60	51	29	23	16	11	93	71	0.1	3	0.2	N
D	87	78	62	56	31	26	17	13	93	70	0	0	0.1	D

Surinam, formerly Dutch Guiana, is situated between 2° and 6° N on the Atlantic coast of South America between Guyana to the west and French Guiana to the east. In area it is smaller than Guyana and about as large as England and Wales together. The general nature of the climate and weather of this whole area is described on p. 192 for Guyana. The table for **Paramaribo** is representative of the lowland coastal area of the country. It shows conditions almost identical with those for **Georgetown** in Guyana. The southern half of the country is part of the plateau region which extends eastwards from Venezuela through Guyana. Here the climatic conditions are well represented by the table for **Santa Elena** in Venezuela (p. 205).

Paramaribo 12 ft (4 m) 5°49′ N 55°09′ W 35 years   **SURINAM**

	Temperature °F			Temperature °C			Relative humidity		Precipitation		
	Highest recorded	Average daily		Lowest recorded	Highest recorded	Average daily		Lowest recorded	0830 hours	1430 hours	Average monthly		Average no. days with 0.04 in + (1 mm +)
		max.	min.			max.	min.		%	%	in	mm	
J	95	85	72	62	35	29	22	17	92	77	8.4	213	18	J
F	92	85	71	63	33	29	22	17	90	74	6.5	165	13	F
M	94	85	72	62	34	29	22	17	89	75	7.9	201	14	M
A	93	86	73	62	34	30	23	17	89	75	9.0	229	16	A
M	94	86	73	64	34	30	23	18	90	79	12.2	310	23	M
J	94	86	73	66	34	30	23	19	91	80	11.9	302	23	J
J	94	87	73	62	34	31	23	17	90	76	9.1	231	20	J
A	94	89	73	65	34	32	23	18	88	70	6.2	158	14	A
S	95	91	73	65	35	33	23	18	87	66	3.1	79	9	S
O	98	91	73	67	37	33	23	19	87	67	3.0	76	9	O
N	99	89	73	66	37	32	23	19	88	71	4.9	125	12	N
D	94	86	72	63	34	30	22	17	91	77	8.8	224	18	D

URUGUAY

Uruguay is a little smaller than Great Britain and about the same size as the state of Washington. It lies on the east coast of South America between 30° and 35° S. It is bordered on the north by Brazil and on the west by the river Uruguay which forms the border with Argentina. Most of the country is lowlying and rather flat with the highest hills rising to about 1500 ft (450 m).

The climate of Uruguay is similar to that of the Pampas region of Argentina and because of the level nature of the country there is little variation of weather and climate within Uruguay. The table for **Montevideo** is representative of the coastal districts and there are only slight differences between these and the areas farther inland.

Most of Uruguay has a moderate annual rainfall of about 40 in (1000 mm) which is well distributed throughout the year but with a tendency for the autumn months to be slightly wetter. Rain falls on a comparatively small number of days; about one day in five at all seasons. Thus the rainfall when it occurs is often moderate to heavy.

The summers are warm but not as hot as in some other countries in similar latitudes such as the southern Atlantic coastlands of the USA or parts of southeast Australia. Winters are mild and frost and snow are very rare. Southerly winds can bring occasional spells of colder weather, which may be associated with squally winds or gales in the estuary of the river Plate. However, such outbreaks of colder polar air from Antarctica are much modified after they have crossed some thousands of miles of warmer water in the South Atlantic.

Inland the summer temperatures are a little higher than those found on the coast. Sunshine hours are high in Uruguay, ranging from five to six hours a day in winter to as much as nine to ten in summer. The climate of Uruguay is rarely uncomfortable or unpleasant and can be described as healthy for most of the year.

URUGUAY — Montevideo 72 ft (22 m) 34°52′ S 56°12′ W 56 years

	Temperature °F			Temperature °C			Relative humidity		Precipitation		
	Highest recorded	Average daily	Lowest recorded	Highest recorded	Average daily	Lowest recorded	0700 hours	1400 hours	Average monthly		Average no. days with 0.04 in + (1 mm +)
		max. / min.			max. / min.		%	%	in	mm	
J	109	83 / 62	46	43	28 / 17	8	76	53	2.9	74	6	J
F	105	82 / 61	46	41	28 / 16	8	81	55	2.6	66	5	F
M	101	78 / 59	40	38	26 / 15	4	85	57	3.9	99	5	M
A	98	71 / 53	36	37	22 / 12	2	87	61	3.9	99	6	A
M	87	64 / 48	29	31	18 / 9	−2	89	66	3.3	84	6	M
J	81	59 / 43	25	27	15 / 6	−4	89	69	3.2	81	5	J
J	83	58 / 43	26	28	14 / 6	−3	89	69	2.9	74	6	J
A	79	59 / 43	25	26	15 / 6	−4	88	67	3.1	79	7	A
S	86	63 / 46	29	30	17 / 8	−2	87	65	3.0	76	6	S
O	94	68 / 49	29	34	20 / 9	−2	82	62	2.6	66	6	O
N	98	74 / 54	38	37	23 / 12	3	77	56	2.9	74	6	N
D	102	79 / 59	41	39	26 / 15	5	73	52	3.1	79	7	D

Venezuela is the most northerly country in South America, situated between 1° and 12° N. It is rather more than twice the size of France or the state of Texas. It has a long coastline on the Caribbean Sea and is bordered on the west by Colombia, on the east by Guyana and on the south by Brazil.

In Venezuela the main chain of the Andes mountains runs from west to east, thus leaving a narrow coastal plain on the Caribbean shore. In the west there is a more extensive marshy lowland around Lake Maracaibo. To the south of the Andes there is a large lowland area in the valley of the river Orinoco, known as the Llanos; this has a typical tropical climate with a single rainy season. In the southeast of the country the land rises to a plateau, extending into Guyana, with an average height of some 2000 ft (600 m); from this plateau numerous hills rise to more than 6000 ft (1800 m).

Venezuela is unusual amongst South American countries in that almost everywhere the main rainy season is from April to October at the time of high sun. Towards the west of the country there is a tendency for a double rainy season, as in Colombia. The northern lowland, particularly in the west, has a surprisingly dry climate for a tropical coast. This is thought to be a consequence of the direction of the coastline in relation to the frequent northeast trade winds.

The Andes in Venezuela are lower and narrower than in Colombia, Peru and Bolivia, but there are a number of individual peaks rising above 15,000 ft (4600 m) which carry snow throughout the year. There are many local variations of weather and climate as a result of altitude; the threefold division into tierra

caliente, tierra templada and tierra fria, described on p. 170 for Bolivia, applies to this region.

The northern slopes of the Andes tend to have less rainfall than the southern side. **Caracas**, at an altitude of 3400 ft (1040 m), has a climate typical of the tierra templada but shows traces of the relative dryness which affects the whole north coast. Over most of this area sunshine amounts are moderately high as a consequence of the lack of cloud and rain; ranging from six hours a day in the wetter months to as much as eight hours in the drier months. Annual rainfall in the mountains is usually over 40 in (1000 mm) but is less in some sheltered valleys and on the northern slopes. On the coast the rainfall increases from the very low annual totals around Lake Maracaibo (see the table for **Maracaibo**) to as much as 40 in (1000 mm) in the east. The lowlands around Lake Maracaibo are particularly hot in all months.

In the Llanos region of the Orinoco valley there is a typical hot, tropical climate with a single wetter season between April and October. Over most of this region annual rainfall is between 40 and 60 in (1000 and 1500 mm). Temperature varies little from month to month and there is never any really cool weather. The wet months are the most uncomfortable because of the combination of heat and high humidity.

In the southeast on the Guyana plateau rainfall is rather heavier, generally above 60 in (1500 mm) per year but with a definite dry season at the time of low sun. Temperatures are moderated by the higher altitude and humidity is rather lower than in the Llanos. The table for **Santa Elena** is representative of this plateau region.

VENEZUELA — Caracas 3418 ft (1042 m) 10°30′ N 66°56′ W 21 years

	Temperature °F				Temperature °C				Relative humidity	Precipitation			
	Highest recorded	Average daily		Lowest recorded	Highest recorded	Average daily		Lowest recorded		Average monthly		Average no. days with 0.01 in + (0.25 mm +)	
		max.	min.			max.	min.			in	mm		
J	83	75	56	47	28	24	13	8	—	0.9	23	6	J
F	88	77	56	46	31	25	13	8	—	0.4	10	2	F
M	91	79	58	45	33	26	14	7	—	0.6	15	3	M
A	89	81	60	51	32	27	16	11	—	1.3	33	4	A
M	89	80	62	52	32	27	17	11	—	3.1	79	9	M
J	86	78	62	53	30	26	17	12	—	4.0	102	14	J
J	84	78	61	52	29	26	16	11	—	4.3	109	15	J
A	86	79	61	53	30	26	16	12	—	4.3	109	15	A
S	85	80	61	53	29	27	16	12	—	4.2	107	13	S
O	86	79	61	54	30	26	16	12	—	4.3	109	12	O
N	84	77	60	51	29	25	16	11	—	3.7	94	13	N
D	83	78	58	47	28	26	14	8	—	1.8	46	10	D

VENEZUELA — Maracaibo 20 ft (6 m) 10°39′ N 71°36′ W 12 years

	Temperature °F				Temperature °C				Relative humidity		Precipitation			
	Highest recorded	Average daily		Lowest recorded	Highest recorded	Average daily		Lowest recorded	0700 hours	1300 hours	Average monthly		Average no. days with 0.01 in + (0.25 mm +)	
		max.	min.			max.	min.		%	%	in	mm		
J	98	90	73	66	37	32	23	19	80	61	0.1	3	0.5	J
F	97	90	73	68	36	32	23	20	80	61	0	0	0.3	F
M	98	91	74	67	37	33	23	19	78	61	0.3	8	1	M
A	102	92	76	68	39	33	24	20	78	61	0.8	20	1	A
M	100	92	77	68	38	33	25	20	82	63	2.7	69	6	M
J	100	93	77	69	38	34	25	21	80	60	2.2	56	6	J
J	101	94	76	70	38	34	24	21	81	62	1.8	46	5	J
A	102	94	77	69	39	34	25	21	82	62	2.2	56	7	A
S	102	94	77	68	39	34	25	20	84	62	2.8	71	6	S
O	99	92	76	68	37	33	24	20	84	62	5.9	150	9	O
N	98	91	76	70	37	33	24	21	83	63	3.3	84	8	N
D	96	91	75	68	36	33	24	20	82	62	0.6	15	2	D

	Temperature °F			Temperature °C			Relative humidity		Precipitation			
	Highest recorded	Average daily		Lowest recorded	Highest recorded	Average daily		Lowest recorded	0800 hours	1400 hours	Average monthly		Average no. days with 0.01 in + (0.25 mm +)
		max.	min.			max.	min.		%	%	in	mm	
J	91	86	61	55	33	30	16	13	89	63	2.0	51	13	J
F	91	87	62	55	33	31	17	13	89	62	2.4	61	11	F
M	95	88	64	53	35	31	18	12	83	57	3.7	94	15	M
A	93	86	64	57	34	30	18	14	86	61	5.4	137	18	A
M	89	84	65	57	32	29	18	14	90	69	8.4	213	28	M
J	88	82	64	59	31	28	18	15	93	73	9.9	252	28	J
J	86	82	62	57	30	28	17	14	95	73	8.5	216	27	J
A	88	83	63	54	31	28	17	12	95	74	6.8	173	26	A
S	92	84	63	56	33	29	17	13	90	59	3.7	94	19	S
O	93	85	63	55	34	29	17	13	90	55	3.5	89	15	O
N	93	86	62	55	34	30	17	13	86	57	5.1	130	18	N
D	90	84	63	57	32	29	17	14	88	61	4.7	119	17	D

Asia

AFGHANISTAN

This landlocked country, a little larger than France, is bordered by the USSR on the north, by Pakistan on the east and south and by Iran on the west. In the extreme east it has a very short boundary with China in the high Pamir Mountains. Much of the country is mountainous; the highest peaks in the Pamirs and Hindu Kush rise to over 20,000 ft (6600 m). The lowest parts of the country are in the southwest along the Iranian border and in the north along the border with the USSR.

Afghanistan has a harsh climate of the continental type and the severity of winter is accentuated by the altitude of much of the country. Summers are everywhere warm, except in the highest areas, and at lower levels temperatures sometimes rise very high indeed. Winter and spring are the seasons of most changeable weather and most of the annual precipitation occurs at this time. Afghanistan is the most easterly country to experience the influence of the Mediterranean sea where most of the depressions which bring the winter precipitation originate. The high mountains to the south shield Afghanistan from the summer rains brought to India and parts of Pakistan by the southwest monsoon. Almost no rain falls from June to October. The lower parts of the country have a semi-arid or desert climate. In Seistan along the Iranian border hot, dry, dusty winds are among the most unpleasant features of the summer weather.

The table for **Kabul** represents the climatic conditions over most of the country, particularly those in the mountainous centre and east. The table for **Kandahar** is representative of the lower and drier parts of the country. Here winters are milder but there may be spells of very cold weather for a few days at a time. Summers are sunny and generally hot, except in the higher mountains. Sunshine amounts range from six to seven hours a day in winter to as much as twelve to thirteen in summer. Because of the large range of temperature conditions found in Afghanistan there is both a danger of heat exhaustion or even heatstroke in the lower regions in summer and of exposure, wind chill and frostbite in the mountains in winter.

Kabul 5955 ft (1827 m) 34°30′ N 69°13′ E 9 years **AFGHANISTAN**

	Temperature °F			Temperature °C				Relative humidity		Precipitation			
	Highest recorded	Average daily		Lowest recorded	Highest recorded	Average daily		Lowest recorded	0800 hours	1600 hours	Average monthly		Average no. days with 0.1 in + (2.5 mm +)
		max.	min.			max.	min.		%	%	in	mm		
J	58	36	18	−6	14	2	−8	−21	80	70	1.2	31	2	J
F	74	40	22	−5	23	4	−6	−21	79	62	1.4	36	3	F
M	77	53	34	6	25	12	1	−14	76	44	3.7	94	7	M
A	83	66	43	27	28	19	6	−3	69	35	4.0	102	6	A
M	95	78	51	34	35	26	11	1	61	32	0.8	20	2	M
J	99	87	56	42	37	31	13	6	52	24	0.2	5	0.6	J
J	101	92	61	51	38	33	16	11	51	22	0.1	3	0.4	J
A	104	91	59	47	40	33	15	8	54	23	0.1	3	0.4	A
S	97	85	51	36	36	29	11	2	58	18	0	0	0.1	S
O	89	73	42	27	32	23	6	−3	59	22	0.6	15	0.9	O
N	77	62	33	5	25	17	1	−15	67	31	0.8	20	2	N
D	67	47	27	5	19	8	−3	−15	76	53	0.4	10	1	D

Kandahar 3462 ft (1055 m) 31°36′ N 65°40′ E 7 years **AFGHANISTAN**

	Temperature °F			Temperature °C				Relative humidity		Precipitation			
	Highest recorded	Average daily		Lowest recorded	Highest recorded	Average daily		Lowest recorded	0700 hours	1600 hours	Average monthly		Average no. days with 0.1 in + (2.5 mm +)
		max.	min.			max.	min.		%	%	in	mm		
J	70	56	31	14	21	13	−1	−10	83	51	3.1	79	5	J
F	80	62	36	21	27	17	2	−6	75	38	1.7	43	4	F
M	88	72	42	21	31	22	6	−6	74	31	0.8	20	2	M
A	97	83	50	33	36	28	10	1	64	28	0.3	8	1	A
M	107	92	57	39	42	33	14	4	57	28	0.2	5	0.4	M
J	111	99	62	49	44	37	17	9	52	23	0	0	0	J
J	108	102	66	53	42	39	19	12	57	27	0.1	3	0.4	J
A	109	99	63	52	43	37	17	11	53	23	0	0	0	A
S	100	93	51	39	38	34	11	4	56	21	0	0	0	S
O	100	85	44	30	38	29	7	−1	65	23	0	0	0	O
N	89	73	36	16	32	23	2	−9	76	29	0	0	0.4	N
D	77	59	31	15	25	15	−1	−9	81	43	0.8	20	2	D

BAHRAIN

Tiny Bahrain consists of one large island and a number of smaller ones lying off the coast of Saudi Arabia and west of the Qatar peninsula. Its weather and climate are similar to that of the Gulf coast of Arabia but are somewhat modified by Bahrain's insular nature. Humidity is high throughout the year except when hot, dry winds blow off the mainland. The high temperatures between April and October are rendered particularly uncomfortable by the humidity.

Annual rainfall is low and this mainly falls between November and March. Winter temperatures are mild and only rarely, when cold northerly winds blow from Iran, chilly. During the hottest weather in summer there is some danger of heat exhaustion or heatstroke, particularly for visitors not yet acclimatized. For more detail see the description for Saudi Arabia on p. 276.

BAHRAIN

Bahrain 18 ft (6 m) 26°12′ N 50°30′ E 16 years

	Temperature °F			Temperature °C				Relative humidity		Precipitation			
	Highest recorded	Average daily		Lowest recorded	Highest recorded	Average daily		Lowest recorded	0730 hours	1530 hours	Average monthly		Average no. days with 0.1 in + (2.5 mm +)	
		max.	min.			max.	min.		%	%	in	mm		
J	85	68	57	41	29	20	14	5	85	71	0.3	8	1	J
F	94	70	59	45	34	21	15	7	83	70	0.7	18	2	F
M	95	75	63	51	35	24	17	11	80	70	0.5	13	1	M
A	105	84	70	56	41	29	21	13	75	66	0.3	8	1	A
M	108	92	78	66	42	33	26	19	71	63	0	0	0	M
J	111	96	82	70	44	36	28	21	69	64	0	0	0	J
J	112	99	85	75	44	37	29	24	69	67	0	0	0	J
A	113	100	85	75	45	38	29	24	74	65	0	0	0	A
S	112	96	81	71	44	36	27	22	75	64	0	0	0	S
O	103	90	75	66	39	32	24	19	80	66	0	0	0	O
N	97	82	69	58	36	28	21	14	80	70	0.7	18	1	N
D	88	71	60	48	31	22	16	9	85	77	0.7	18	2	D

Bangladesh, formerly East Pakistan, is a very low-lying country at the head of the Bay of Bengal. Apart from the Chittagong hill district in the extreme southeast on the border with Burma the whole country lies below 600 ft (180 m). Most of the country consists of the swampy plains of the great delta of the rivers Ganga (Ganges) and Brahmaputra. Most of the land boundary is with India.

Bangladesh has a tropical monsoon climate with the same threefold division of the year as occurs in India (see p. 229). The cool season from November to February is here warmer than in much of India. During the hot season from March until early June some rainstorms occur and these are often thundery. During the main rainy season of the southwest monsoon from June to September the rainfall is heavy and frequent. Most of the country receives between 60 and 100 in (1500 and 2500 mm) of rain a year and near the eastern border this rises to as much as 150 in (3750 mm) or more. The rainfall is most reliable and frequent during the season of the southwest monsoon and is brought by shallow depressions in the northern Bay of Bengal.

Rainfall in the period September to November is less reliable but is occasionally very heavy and is usually associated with violent tropical cyclones. These severe storms, which bring very strong winds and torrential rain, develop at this time in the Bay of Bengal and are the most dangerous feature of the climate of Bangladesh. The storm waves and sea surges raise the water level along the coast and in the numerous branching water courses of the delta so that widespread flooding of the low-lying areas occurs, adding to the devastation produced by the strong wind. Such storms have caused great loss of life and destruction of crops several times this century.

Although temperatures during the hot season are somewhat lower in Bangladesh than in some parts of India, the heat is made uncomfortable by the high humidity. This muggy, damp heat persists throughout the main rainy season. The heat is rarely dangerous but is certainly unpleasant to the unacclimatized visitor. There is no great difference in temperature conditions around the year from one part of the country to another. During the hot season temperatures are a little higher inland (see the table for **Dacca**) than on the coast (see the table for **Chittagong**). Because of the greater cloudiness during the rainy season, average daily hours of sunshine are least between June and September, about four hours a day. During the rest of the year they average from six to eight hours.

Chittagong 87 ft (27 m) 22°21′ N 91°50′ E 60 years

	Temperature °F			Temperature °C			Relative humidity		Precipitation		
	Highest recorded	Average daily	Lowest recorded	Highest recorded	Average daily	Lowest recorded	0800 hours	1730 hours	Average monthly		Average no. days with 0.1 in + (2.5 mm +)
		max.	min.			max.	min.		%	%	in	mm	
J	89	79	55	45	32	26	13	7	81	58	0.2	5	0.4	J
F	93	82	59	46	34	28	15	8	76	58	1.1	28	1	F
M	99	87	67	51	37	31	19	11	76	65	2.5	64	2	M
A	102	89	73	59	39	32	23	15	78	71	5.9	150	6	A
M	98	89	75	65	37	32	24	18	79	77	10.4	264	11	M
J	98	87	77	68	37	31	25	20	84	83	21.0	533	17	J
J	94	86	77	67	34	30	25	19	87	85	23.5	597	19	J
A	93	86	76	72	34	30	24	22	87	86	20.4	518	17	A
S	95	87	76	71	35	31	24	22	86	84	12.6	320	13	S
O	94	87	73	62	34	31	23	17	85	78	7.1	180	7	O
N	93	84	65	52	34	29	18	11	84	71	2.2	56	2	N
D	88	79	57	47	31	26	14	8	85	68	0.6	15	0.7	D

	Temperature °F			Temperature °C				Relative humidity	Precipitation			
	Highest recorded	Average daily		Lowest recorded	Highest recorded	Average daily		Lowest recorded	1200 hours	Average monthly		Average no. days with 0.1 in + (2.5 mm +)	
		max.	min.			max.	min.		%	in	mm		
J	88	77	54	45	31	25	12	7	46	0.7	18	1	J
F	93	82	55	46	34	28	13	8	37	1.2	31	1	F
M	102	91	61	55	39	33	16	13	38	2.3	58	3	M
A	108	95	73	64	42	35	23	18	42	4.1	103	6	A
M	108	93	77	66	42	34	25	19	59	7.6	194	11	M
J	97	90	79	72	36	32	26	22	72	12.6	321	16	J
J	93	88	79	75	34	31	26	24	72	17.2	437	12	J
A	97	88	79	73	36	31	26	23	74	12.0	305	16	A
S	95	88	79	73	35	31	26	23	71	10.0	254	12	S
O	93	88	75	63	34	31	24	17	65	6.7	169	7	O
N	88	84	64	54	31	29	18	12	53	1.1	28	1	N
D	84	79	55	45	29	26	13	7	50	0.1	2	0	D

BHUTAN

Bhutan is a small, independent state in treaty relationship with its larger neighbour India, to the south. It is bordered by Sikkim on the west and China on the north. It is a mountainous country extending from the highest parts of the Himalayas to the foothill region on the Indian border. The climate and weather of Bhutan are similar to those described for Nepal on p. 264. The table for **Darjeeling** in India (p. 230) is representative of conditions in the lower parts of the state.

Burma is rather larger than France. It has a long mountain-backed coastline on the Bay of Bengal and a long eastern border with Thailand. In the north it borders India and China; this is a very mountainous region which includes part of the eastern Himalayas and the edge of the mountain plateau of Yunnan in South China.

Much of Burma is mountainous with the main mountain and hill ranges running from north to south. The highest regions in the north rise to over 18,000 ft (5500 m), but the average height of the mountains elsewhere is between 8000 and 4000 ft (2400 and 1200 m). The centre of the country north of **Mandalay** to the coast at **Rangoon** is a lowland area in which flow the great rivers Irawaddy and Salween. They rise in the high mountain region of the north where rainfall is heavy. Most of the eastern border with Thailand runs through a high plateaux region where rainfall is also heavy.

Burma has a tropical monsoon type of climate with a marked difference between a cooler, dry season from November to April and a hotter, wet season from May until September or October. This seasonal contrast is a result of the great reversal of winds which occurs over south Asia. As in India the dry season is dominated by the northeast monsoon and the wet season by the southwest monsoon blowing off the Indian Ocean. Differences of altitude within Burma, and the degree of exposure to the rainy southwest monsoon, are responsible for the main differences of climate within the country.

The coastal mountains and the higher mountains of the north and east have abundant or heavy rainfall which ranges from 100 to 200 in (2500 to 5000 mm) a year. The interior lowlands, sheltered from the direct effect of the southwest monsoon, receive as little as 40 in (1000 mm) or even less (see the table for **Mandalay**). Over most of the country at least threequarters of the annual rainfall occurs during the season of the southwest monsoon.

In the lowlands, and particularly on the coast, temperatures are hot throughout the year. The highest temperatures occur during the period March to May before the onset of the heaviest rains. Temperatures are lower in the hills, but for most of the year the weather at places below 4000 ft (1200 m) can be described as hot and tropical. The table for **Lashio** is representative of places inland at medium heights. On the coast the high temperatures are rendered more unpleasant because of high humidity. Even inland the heat is oppressive during the rainy season for the same reason (see the table for **Mandalay**).

The dry season is distinctly cooler and more pleasant in the interior and particularly in the north of the country where increasing altitude lowers the temperature. The period from November to April is distinctly dry over the whole country. At this time, when the country is dominated by the dry northeast monsoon, sunshine amounts are high, averaging from seven to ten hours a day. During the rainy season the weather is much more cloudy and from June to September daily sunshine amounts average only three to four hours a day.

Climatic conditions on the wettest parts of the coast are illustrated by the table for **Akyab**. The table for **Rangoon** shows that here, on the delta of the Irawaddy where the coast runs from west to east and is low-lying, rainfall is less but temperatures and humidities remain high throughout the year.

	Temperature °F				Temperature °C				Relative humidity		Precipitation			
	Highest recorded	Average daily		Lowest recorded	Highest recorded	Average daily		Lowest recorded	0830 hours	1730 hours	Average monthly		Average no. days with 0.1 in + (2.5 mm +)	
		max.	min.			max.	min.		%	%	in	mm		
J	94	81	59	47	34	27	15	8	80	65	0.1	3	0.1	J
F	95	84	61	49	35	29	16	9	75	65	0.2	5	0.4	F
M	100	88	68	54	38	31	20	12	77	70	0.4	10	0.7	M
A	99	90	75	62	37	32	24	17	75	73	2.0	51	2	A
M	99	90	78	66	37	32	26	19	79	77	15.4	391	11	M
J	98	86	77	68	37	30	25	20	90	87	45.3	1151	24	J
J	93	84	77	71	34	29	25	22	92	89	55.1	1400	28	J
A	91	84	77	71	33	29	25	22	90	88	44.6	1133	27	A
S	94	86	77	70	34	30	25	21	88	86	22.7	577	19	S
O	93	87	76	65	34	31	24	18	86	82	11.3	287	9	O
N	91	85	71	60	33	29	22	16	84	79	5.1	130	4	N
D	89	81	63	51	32	27	17	11	84	73	0.7	18	0.7	D

	Temperature °F				Temperature °C				Relative humidity		Precipitation			
	Highest recorded	Average daily		Lowest recorded	Highest recorded	Average daily		Lowest recorded	0900 hours	1800 hours	Average monthly		Average no. days with 0.1 in + (2.5 mm +)	
		max.	min.			max.	min.		%	%	in	mm		
J	79	74	46	35	26	23	8	2	92	63	0.3	8	1	J
F	86	78	49	39	30	26	9	4	82	51	0.3	8	1	F
M	93	86	56	47	34	30	13	8	70	37	0.6	15	1	M
A	99	89	62	54	37	32	17	12	69	44	2.2	56	5	A
M	98	87	67	57	37	31	19	14	80	62	6.9	175	12	M
J	95	84	70	62	35	29	21	17	86	79	9.8	249	15	J
J	92	83	70	64	33	28	21	18	88	81	12.0	305	27	J
A	88	83	70	62	31	28	21	17	90	84	12.7	323	19	A
S	89	84	68	58	32	29	20	14	91	82	7.8	198	14	S
O	88	82	64	51	31	28	18	11	93	82	5.7	145	10	O
N	85	77	56	47	29	25	13	8	93	83	2.7	69	5	N
D	79	73	49	38	26	23	9	3	94	78	0.9	23	1	D

Mandalay 252 ft (77 m) 21°59′ N 96°06′ E 20 years **BURMA**

	Temperature °F			Temperature °C			Relative humidity		Precipitation		
	Highest recorded	Average daily	Lowest recorded	Highest recorded	Average daily	Lowest recorded	0800 hours	1800 hours	Average monthly		Average no. days with 0.1 in + (2.5 mm +)
		max.	min.			max.	min.		%	%	in	mm	
J	91	82	55	45	33	28	13	7	79	52	0.1	3	0.1	J
F	99	88	59	47	37	31	15	8	66	41	0.1	3	0.3	F
M	108	97	66	54	42	36	19	12	53	31	0.2	5	0.5	M
A	110	101	77	64	43	38	25	18	55	33	1.2	31	2	A
M	111	98	79	69	44	37	26	21	68	52	5.8	147	8	M
J	107	93	78	68	42	34	26	20	78	64	6.3	160	7	J
J	106	93	78	72	41	34	26	22	78	66	2.7	69	6	J
A	101	92	77	71	38	33	25	22	83	72	4.1	104	8	A
S	103	91	76	69	39	33	24	21	84	74	5.4	137	9	S
O	102	89	73	62	39	32	23	17	83	78	4.3	109	7	O
N	98	85	66	56	37	29	19	13	83	74	2.0	51	3	N
D	90	80	57	44	32	27	14	7	82	66	0.4	10	0.8	D

Rangoon 18 ft (6 m) 16°46′ N 96°11′ E 60 years **BURMA**

	Temperature °F			Temperature °C			Relative humidity		Precipitation		
	Highest recorded	Average daily	Lowest recorded	Highest recorded	Average daily	Lowest recorded	0900 hours	1800 hours	Average monthly		Average no. days with 0.1 in + (2.5 mm +)
		max.	min.			max.	min.		%	%	in	mm	
J	100	89	65	55	38	32	18	13	71	52	0.1	3	0.3	J
F	101	92	67	56	38	33	19	13	72	52	0.2	5	0.3	F
M	103	96	71	61	39	36	22	16	74	54	0.3	8	0.6	M
A	106	97	76	68	41	36	24	20	71	64	2.0	51	2	A
M	105	92	77	69	41	33	25	21	80	76	12.1	307	14	M
J	98	86	76	71	37	30	24	22	87	85	18.9	480	23	J
J	93	85	76	70	34	29	24	21	89	88	22.9	582	26	J
A	93	85	76	68	34	29	24	20	89	88	20.8	528	25	A
S	94	86	76	72	34	30	24	22	87	86	15.5	394	20	S
O	95	88	76	71	35	31	24	22	83	77	7.1	180	10	O
N	95	88	73	61	35	31	23	16	79	72	2.7	69	3	N
D	96	88	67	55	36	31	19	13	75	61	0.4	10	0.6	D

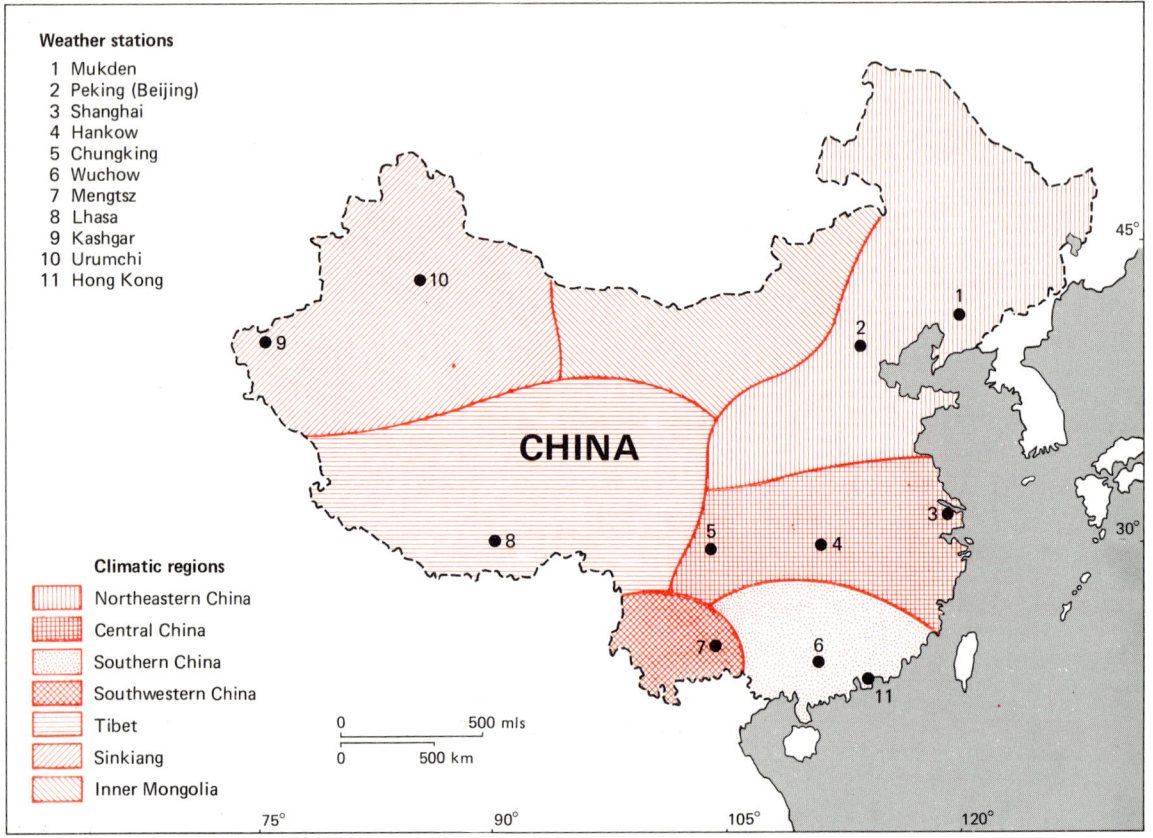

Weather stations

1 Mukden
2 Peking (Beijing)
3 Shanghai
4 Hankow
5 Chungking
6 Wuchow
7 Mengtsz
8 Lhasa
9 Kashgar
10 Urumchi
11 Hong Kong

CHINA

Climatic regions

Northeastern China
Central China
Southern China
Southwestern China
Tibet
Sinkiang
Inner Mongolia

0   500 mls

0   500 km

75°   90°   105°   120°

45°

30°

The People's Republic of China is the second largest country in the world after the USSR. Its vast area extends from 53° to 18° N and from 73° to 134° E in central and eastern Asia. It has a range of climates varying from tropical to cold temperate, and from high mountain to desert.

The country is often divided into China proper and the outer territories. China proper consists of the coastal regions fronting the Pacific and the valleys of the three great rivers: Hwang Ho, Yangtze Kiang and Sikiang. This is the most productive and populated part of the country. The outer territories consist of Manchuria in the northeast, Inner Mongolia in the north, Sinkiang in the west and Tibet in the southwest. China has a long landborder with the USSR in the north and west, and on the south is bordered by Pakistan, India, Nepal, Burma, Laos and Vietnam. Except in Inner Mongolia and Manchuria, these land-borders traverse some of the most mountainous country in the world. This helps to make the climate of most parts of China very distinctive and throughout history has also tended to isolate China from outside influences of other kinds.

The climate of China proper and Manchuria is dominated by the great seasonal wind reversal called the Asiatic monsoon. From October until April winds tend to blow out from China and the heart of Asia under the influence of the great high-pressure system which develops in Siberia and central Asia at this time. From May until September or October, as the continent of Asia heats up, this area becomes one of low atmospheric pressure and winds are drawn into much of China, both from the Indian Ocean and the Pacific. These warm, moist winds bring most of the annual rainfall to Manchuria and China proper at this time. Tibet, Sinkiang and Inner Mongolia, furthest removed from the influence of the sea, receive much less rain.

The second important control over the climate of China is latitude. While most of the country has warm to hot summers there is a great difference in winter temperature both from north to south and from the western provinces to the coastal regions. North China, including Manchuria, has extremely cold winters of almost Siberian severity, while Inner Mongolia and Sinkiang share in this winter cold. Tibet, being a great upland plateau rimmed by some of the highest mountains in the world, has cool summers and very cold winters.

This monsoonal climate regime is so characteristic and dominant over most of the country that some climatologists have referred to the 'Chinese type of climate' to indicate a large seasonal range of temperature, a wet summer and a dry winter. It has certainly been a factor in bringing about the cultural unity of China proper. Except in the far north of China, and in the outer territories, this warm, wet summer results in rice being the dominant food crop of the country.

This similarity of both cause and effect, however, should not be allowed to hide the fact that there are important differences of weather and climate, both from north to south and from the lowlands and river valleys of China proper to the desert and mountainous regions of the outer provinces. South and central China have a tropical or subtropical climate with no real winter cold, while north China, Manchuria and the western provinces have a severe winter. Eastern China has abundant summer rain while the northern and western regions contain much desert and semi-desert.

For a more detailed description of the weather and climate the country is divided into the following major climatic regions: northeast China including Manchuria, central China, south China, southwest China, Tibet, Sinkiang and the western interior, and Inner Mongolia.

NORTHEAST CHINA, INCLUDING MANCHURIA

The tables for **Mukden** in Manchuria and for **Peking** (**Beijing**) are representative of conditions here. This region broadly consists of the great lowland area of the Hwang Ho valley, part of Inner Mongolia and the whole of Manchuria. Winters are very cold with frequent light snow and much frost. The strong outblowing winds often raise clouds of dust which are a troublesome feature of the weather. There is a rapid decrease in both winter and summer temperatures northwards so that in northern Manchuria rivers are frozen for four to six months. The extreme north of Manchuria has a significantly colder summer than **Mukden** or **Peking** and snow lies for between 100 and 150 days.

Summers are warm and humid over much of north China and may be rather uncomfortable. Summer rainfall is almost everywhere sufficient for cultivation but tends to be unreliable; in some years drought may be a problem. The most unpleasant features of the climate are the summer humidity and the cold, increased by wind chill in winter so that warm winter clothing is very necessary.

	Temperature °F			Temperature °C				Relative humidity		Precipitation			
	Highest recorded	Average daily		Lowest recorded	Highest recorded	Average daily		Lowest recorded	0600 hours	1400 hours	Average monthly		Average no. days with 0.04 in + (1 mm +)	
		max.	min.			max.	min.		%	%	in	mm		
J	45	22	−1	−24	7	−6	−18	−31	75	48	0.3	8	2	J
F	51	28	6	−27	11	−2	−14	−33	74	44	0.3	8	2	F
M	66	43	21	−4	19	6	−6	−20	69	37	0.7	18	3	M
A	86	61	37	18	30	16	3	−8	64	34	1.1	28	5	A
M	91	74	50	33	33	23	10	1	71	40	2.7	69	7	M
J	103	84	61	46	39	29	16	8	75	41	3.3	84	8	J
J	102	87	69	58	39	31	21	14	87	59	7.2	183	11	J
A	96	85	67	49	36	29	19	9	91	57	6.7	170	8	A
S	93	75	52	32	34	24	11	0	88	47	2.5	64	7	S
O	80	61	38	18	27	16	3	−8	81	44	1.4	36	5	O
N	78	41	22	−15	26	5	−6	−26	75	46	1.1	28	4	N
D	52	25	5	−20	11	−4	−15	−29	76	51	0.6	15	3	D

	Temperature °F			Temperature °C				Relative humidity	Precipitation			
	Highest recorded	Average daily		Lowest recorded	Highest recorded	Average daily		Lowest recorded	All hours	Average monthly		Average no. days with 0.004 in + (0.1 mm +)	
		max.	min.			max.	min.		%	in	mm		
J	57	34	14	−9	14	1	−10	−23	50	0.2	4	3	J
F	66	39	18	0	19	4	−8	−18	50	0.2	5	3	F
M	82	52	30	7	28	11	−1	−14	48	0.3	8	3	M
A	97	70	45	27	36	21	7	−3	46	0.7	17	4	A
M	100	81	55	37	38	27	13	3	49	1.4	35	6	M
J	109	88	64	50	43	31	18	10	56	3.1	78	8	J
J	106	88	70	59	41	31	21	15	72	9.6	243	13	J
A	100	86	68	52	38	30	20	11	74	5.6	141	11	A
S	93	79	57	36	34	26	14	2	67	2.3	58	7	S
O	88	68	43	23	31	20	6	−5	59	0.6	16	3	O
N	75	48	28	9	24	9	−2	−13	56	0.4	11	3	N
D	55	37	18	−4	13	3	−8	−20	51	0.1	3	2	D

CENTRAL CHINA

The tables for **Shanghai** on the coast and for **Hankow**, about 400 miles inland in the valley of the Yangtze Kiang, are representative of this region, which has warmer summers than north China and milder winters.

Although the main rainy season is summer there is some rain throughout the year and the winter weather is more changeable than in north China. There are periods of wet weather, alternating with cold spells during which frost and snow occur; snow falls on about five to ten days a year. This variable winter weather is not unlike that experienced in parts of western Europe and the mid-Atlantic states of the USA. It is a consequence of frontal systems and depressions moving from west to east along a zone of convergence between cold Siberian air and warm air from the Pacific.

Summer weather is warm and usually humid as warm, damp air moves in from the Pacific; the heat and humidity are occasionally rather uncomfortable. The coastal regions occasionally receive very heavy rainfall from typhoons, or tropical cyclones, which intensify in the South China Sea and move northeastwards along the coast. The very strong winds associated with these disturbances are most severe in the coastal belt.

Farther inland in central China there is a region in the middle and upper Yangtze valley, the basin of Szechwan, where winters are distinctly milder and the summers receive rather less rain. This area has a more pleasant climate as winter snow and frost are less frequent and summer humidity is less uncomfortable (see the table for **Chungking**).

CHINA   Chungking 755 ft (230 m) 29°33′ N 106°33′ E 8 years

	Temperature °F			Temperature °C			Relative humidity	Precipitation		
	Highest recorded	Average daily	Lowest recorded	Highest recorded	Average daily	Lowest recorded	All hours	Average monthly		Average no. days with 0.04 in + (1 mm +)
		max.	min.		max.	min.		%	in	mm	
J	68	49	41	29	20	9	5	−2	87	0.6	15	4	J
F	79	55	45	30	26	13	7	−1	88	0.8	20	4	F
M	104	65	52	37	40	18	11	3	87	1.5	38	7	M
A	104	73	60	44	40	23	16	7	86	3.9	99	9	A
M	104	80	67	54	40	27	19	12	87	5.6	142	13	M
J	103	85	72	58	39	29	22	14	86	7.1	180	11	J
J	110	93	76	59	43	34	24	15	80	5.6	142	6	J
A	111	95	77	62	44	35	25	17	76	4.8	122	6	A
S	104	82	71	57	40	28	22	14	84	5.9	150	11	S
O	94	71	61	46	34	22	16	8	88	4.4	112	13	O
N	83	61	53	41	28	16	12	5	91	1.9	48	9	N
D	72	55	46	31	22	13	8	−1	91	0.8	20	6	D

Hankow 121 ft (37 m) 30°35′ N 114°17′ E 28 years — CHINA

	Temperature °F			Temperature °C				Relative humidity		Precipitation			
	Highest recorded	Average daily		Lowest recorded	Highest recorded	Average daily		Lowest recorded	0430 hours	1230 hours	Average monthly		Average no. days with 0.04 in + (1 mm +)	
		max.	min.			max.	min.		%	%	in	mm		
J	76	46	34	13	24	8	1	−11	83	64	1.8	46	6	J
F	71	49	36	13	22	9	2	−11	85	65	1.9	48	6	F
M	90	57	43	24	32	14	6	−4	86	65	3.8	97	10	M
A	97	69	55	32	36	21	13	0	87	61	6.0	152	7	A
M	96	79	64	40	36	26	18	4	88	61	6.5	165	11	M
J	100	87	73	58	38	31	23	14	88	62	9.6	244	10	J
J	106	93	79	61	41	34	26	16	88	62	7.1	180	9	J
A	106	93	79	60	41	34	26	16	86	60	3.8	97	6	A
S	101	84	69	54	38	29	21	12	84	57	2.8	71	5	S
O	90	73	60	35	32	23	16	2	84	55	3.2	81	5	O
N	79	62	48	28	26	17	9	−2	83	57	1.9	48	5	N
D	72	51	38	20	22	11	3	−7	82	61	1.1	28	5	D

Shanghai 23 ft (7 m) 31°12′ N 121°26′ E 38 years — CHINA

	Temperature °F			Temperature °C				Relative humidity		Precipitation			
	Highest recorded	Average daily		Lowest recorded	Highest recorded	Average daily		Lowest recorded	0600 hours	1400 hours	Average monthly		Average no. days with 0.04 in + (1 mm +)	
		max.	min.			max.	min.		%	%	in	mm		
J	74	46	33	10	23	8	1	−12	87	58	1.9	48	6	J
F	83	47	34	17	28	8	1	−8	89	60	2.3	58	9	F
M	86	55	40	21	30	13	4	−6	89	53	3.3	84	9	M
A	93	66	50	30	34	19	10	−1	91	58	3.7	94	9	A
M	96	77	59	37	36	25	15	3	92	56	3.7	94	9	M
J	103	82	67	51	39	28	19	11	94	66	7.1	180	11	J
J	104	90	74	61	40	32	23	16	93	66	5.8	147	9	J
A	104	90	74	61	40	32	23	16	94	65	5.6	142	9	A
S	100	82	66	44	38	28	19	7	94	64	5.1	130	11	S
O	92	74	57	34	33	23	14	1	92	53	2.8	71	4	O
N	86	63	45	23	30	17	7	−5	90	55	2.0	51	6	N
D	75	53	36	14	24	12	2	−10	89	62	1.4	36	6	D

SOUTH CHINA

This region is partly within the tropics and is the warmest and wettest part of the country in summer. Rainfall is very heavy between May and September along the coast and abundant inland. Winters are mild and frost almost unknown. The summer heat and humidity can be rather uncomfortable. Conditions are represented by the table for **Hong Kong** (see p. 227) and **Wuchow** inland. Conditions at Canton and Macao are very similar. Typhoons are more frequent here and at their most violent and may bring very heavy rain and strong winds for a few days at a time to the coastal regions. Typhoons are most frequent from July to October.

SOUTHWEST CHINA

This inland region along the border with Burma, Vietnam and Laos is hilly and mountainous. Summer temperatures are somewhat moderated by altitude. Winters are generally warm to mild with much sunshine and very little rain. Only occasionally does cold air penetrate here from the north, bringing occasional frost at higher levels. Summers are wet at higher levels but in sheltered valleys the rainfall is not excessive. This region has the most pleasant weather and climate in China around the year (see the table for **Mengtsz**).

	Temperature °F			Temperature °C			Relative humidity		Precipitation		
	Highest recorded	Average daily	Lowest recorded	Highest recorded	Average daily	Lowest recorded	0530 hours	1330 hours	Average monthly		Average no. days with 0.04 in + (1 mm +)
		max.	min.			max.	min.		%	%	in	mm	
J	83	60	47	33	28	16	8	1	79	65	1.3	33	7	J
F	87	62	50	32	31	17	10	0	83	65	2.2	56	10	F
M	89	68	57	39	32	20	14	4	85	69	3.8	97	13	M
A	92	77	67	48	33	25	19	9	87	77	6.3	160	14	A
M	96	84	74	59	36	29	23	15	87	70	8.1	206	16	M
J	96	87	77	67	36	31	25	19	89	73	7.6	193	17	J
J	100	89	78	72	38	32	26	22	87	69	6.3	160	15	J
A	101	89	79	72	38	32	26	22	88	66	7.0	178	15	A
S	96	87	76	62	36	31	24	17	83	61	3.3	84	10	S
O	94	80	67	50	34	27	19	10	83	62	1.7	43	5	O
N	91	74	59	43	33	23	15	6	81	68	1.5	38	6	N
D	83	66	54	35	28	19	12	2	78	59	1.5	38	7	D

	Temperature °F			Temperature °C			Relative humidity	Precipitation		
	Highest recorded	Average daily	Lowest recorded	Highest recorded	Average daily	Lowest recorded	All hours	Average monthly		Average no. days with 0.01 in + (0.25 mm +)
		max.	min.			max.	min.	%	in	mm	
J	84	68	46	29	29	20	8	−2	55	0.3	8	2	J
F	86	71	49	32	30	22	9	0	53	0.7	18	5	F
M	93	77	54	33	34	25	12	1	48	1.1	28	5	M
A	97	82	60	39	36	28	16	4	50	1.6	41	8	A
M	98	84	65	51	37	29	18	11	57	5.0	127	12	M
J	95	84	67	56	35	29	19	13	64	5.2	132	15	J
J	95	83	67	59	35-	28	19	15	69	7.7	196	18	J
A	98	83	67	56	37	28	19	13	70	7.8	198	20	A
S	93	82	64	50	34	28	18	10	66	3.8	97	12	S
O	90	76	59	40	32	24	15	4	67	2.0	51	10	O
N	89	71	53	34	32	22	12	1	67	2.2	56	7	N
D	82	68	46	26	28	20	8	−3	56	0.6	15	2	D

TIBET

Tibet is a region of high plateaux and encircling mountains situated in the south centre of China. Its southern boundary includes the highest peaks of the Himalayan mountains, such as Everest. Most of the region is above 12,000 ft (3700 m) and some extensive areas rise above 16,000 ft (4900 m). Winters are severe with frequent light snow and hard frost. Considering the altitude, summer temperatures are surprisingly warm in the daytime, but there is a very sharp drop of temperature at night. Most of the precipitation is rain during the summer, when moist air is drawn into Tibet by the Asian monsoon winds.

In the west and north of Tibet some winter precipitation in the form of snow occurs; but the permanent snowline is surprisingly high at about 20,000 ft (6600 m). Apart from the low temperatures, strong winds, which accentuate wind chill, are the worst feature of the climate. The table for **Lhasa** shows conditions in the valleys and lower southeastern part of Tibet. For much of the year the air is very clear and sunshine is abundant.

SINKIANG AND THE WESTERN INTERIOR

This remote and sparsely populated region of Central Asia is almost entirely desert. It has a continental type of climate with cold winters and hot summers. The very sparse precipitation is well distributed around the year with a winter maximum in some places; this is brought by weak depressions moving in from the west. Humidity is low throughout the year and the climate is generally healthy; the principal hazards are very low temperatures accompanied by strong winds in winter and occasional very high temperatures in summer. Climate varies locally depending on altitude; there are some high mountains on the border with the USSR and Tibet but extensive areas of interior lowland. The table for **Kashgar** illustrates conditions in the west of Sinkiang at medium levels.

Lhasa (Tibet) 12,090 ft (3685 m) 29°40′ N 91°07′ E 7 years — CHINA

	Temperature °F				Temperature °C				Relative humidity	Precipitation			
	Highest recorded	Average daily		Lowest recorded	Highest recorded	Average daily		Lowest recorded	0830 hours	Average monthly		Average no. days with 0.1 in + (2.5 mm +)	
		max.	min.			max.	min.		%	in	mm		
J	61	44	14	3	16	7	−10	−16	71	0	0	0	J
F	72	48	20	5	22	9	−7	−15	71	0.5	13	0.4	F
M	69	53	28	14	21	12	−2	−10	72	0.3	8	1	M
A	76	60	33	18	24	16	1	−8	67	0.2	5	0.4	A
M	79	67	41	27	26	19	5	−3	59	1.0	25	3	M
J	89	75	49	36	32	24	9	2	64	2.5	64	8	J
J	84	74	49	35	29	23	9	2	71	4.8	122	13	J
A	81	72	48	37	27	22	9	3	72	3.5	89	10	A
S	78	70	45	32	26	21	7	0	71	2.6	66	7	S
O	74	62	34	18	23	17	1	8	64	0.5	13	2	O
N	69	55	23	10	21	13	−5	−12	71	0.1	3	0.1	N
D	61	48	16	5	16	9	−9	−15	71	0	0	0	D

Kashgar 4296 ft (1309 m) 39°24′ N 76°07′ E 10 years — CHINA

	Temperature °F				Temperature °C				Relative humidity	Precipitation			
	Highest recorded	Average daily		Lowest recorded	Highest recorded	Average daily		Lowest recorded	0800 hours	Average monthly		Average no. days with 0.1 in + (2.5 mm +)	
		max.	min.			max.	min.		%	in	mm		
J	51	33	12	−7	11	1	−11	−22	76	0.6	15	1	J
F	62	43	19	−4	17	6	−7	−20	71	0.1	3	0.5	F
M	78	56	35	8	26	13	2	−13	57	0.5	13	1	M
A	93	71	48	27	34	22	9	−3	47	0.2	5	1	A
M	97	81	58	39	36	27	14	4	46	0.3	8	1	M
J	102	89	64	42	39	32	18	6	44	0.2	5	1	J
J	106	92	68	53	41	33	20	12	49	0.4	10	1	J
A	101	90	66	54	38	32	19	12	54	0.3	8	2	A
S	98	83	57	39	37	28	14	4	55	0.1	3	1	S
O	89	71	43	29	32	22	6	−2	57	0.1	3	0.1	O
N	70	54	29	1	21	12	−2	−17	67	0.2	5	1	N
D	62	38	17	−15	17	3	−8	−26	79	0.3	8	0.4	D

INNER MONGOLIA

Situated to the north and east of Sinkiang, this is a region of mountain ranges and extensive semi-desert lowlands. It adjoins central Siberia (see p. 440) and Mongolia (see p. 264). It has an extreme continental type of climate with very cold winters and warm summers. The sparse precipitation is well distributed around the year. The summers are somewhat cooler than Sinkiang but winters are even colder, resembling those of Manchuria and north China. The ground is snow-covered for 100–150 days a year. See the table for **Urumchi** and the description of Mongolia on p. 264.

Strong winds in winter and spring often raise great clouds of dust which are blown eastwards into north China. This is one of the more unpleasant features of the climate. The severe winters make warm clothing very necessary and wind chill may increase the feeling of cold. Sunshine amounts vary from five to six hours a day in winter to about nine in summer.

HONG KONG

Hong Kong is a British Crown Colony, consisting of one major island, a number of smaller inhabited islands, and a portion of the Chinese mainland. Its total area is only 391 square miles (1013 sq. km). Situated in 22° N, it is just within the tropics and has a similar monsoon climate to that of south China described on p. 222. Rainfall is particularly heavy from early May until late September, but some rain occurs in all months. Although occasional cold spells, lasting a few days, occur in winter, snow and frost are virtually unknown and the period from October to March is generally warm and dry.

Humidity is high during the rather hot, wet summer and the weather is often very sultry and oppressive. Particularly between July and September, typhoons, moving northwards from the South China Sea, bring heavy rain and very violent winds which can cause damage to property and loss of life. Although mainly dry, the months from February to April are rather cloudy and sunshine then averages only three or four hours a day, as compared with an average of six to eight hours a day during the months July to December.

	Temperature °F			Temperature °C			Relative humidity	Precipitation		
	Highest recorded	Average daily	Lowest recorded	Highest recorded	Average daily	Lowest recorded		Average monthly		Average no. days with 0.004 in + (0.1 mm +)
		max.	min.			max.	min.			in	mm	
J	33	13	−7	−30	1	−11	−22	−34	—	0.6	15	17	J
F	34	17	−3	−25	1	−8	−19	−31	—	0.3	8	14	F
M	66	31	12	−11	19	−1	−11	−24	—	0.5	13	14	M
A	82	60	36	14	28	16	2	−10	—	1.5	38	9	A
M	90	72	47	15	32	22	8	−10	—	1.1	28	5	M
J	103	78	54	33	39	26	12	1	—	1.5	38	11	J
J	103	82	58	49	39	28	14	9	—	0.7	18	5	J
A	112	80	56	42	44	27	13	6	—	1.0	25	4	A
S	93	69	47	35	34	21	8	2	—	0.6	15	4	S
O	79	50	31	5	26	10	−1	−15	—	1.7	43	10	O
N	60	30	13	−27	16	−1	−11	−33	—	1.6	41	14	N
D	37	17	8	−25	3	−8	−13	−32	—	0.4	10	18	D

	Temperature °F			Temperature °C			Relative humidity		Precipitation		
	Highest recorded	Average daily	Lowest recorded	Highest recorded	Average daily	Lowest recorded	0630 hours	1230 hours	Average monthly		Average no. days with 0.04 in + (1 mm +)
		max.	min.			max.	min.	%	%	in	mm	
J	79	64	56	32	26	18	13	0	77	66	1.3	33	4	J
F	79	63	55	38	26	17	13	3	82	73	1.8	46	5	F
M	83	67	60	45	28	19	16	7	84	74	2.9	74	7	M
A	89	75	67	52	32	24	19	11	87	77	5.4	137	8	A
M	91	82	74	60	33	28	23	16	87	78	11.5	292	13	M
J	94	85	78	67	34	29	26	19	86	77	15.5	394	18	J
J	94	87	78	72	34	31	26	22	87	77	15.0	381	17	J
A	97	87	78	72	36	31	26	22	87	77	14.2	367	15	A
S	94	85	77	65	34	29	25	18	83	72	10.1	257	12	S
O	94	81	73	57	34	27	23	13	75	63	4.5	114	6	O
N	86	74	65	44	30	23	18	7	73	60	1.7	43	2	N
D	82	68	59	41	28	20	15	5	74	63	1.2	31	3	D

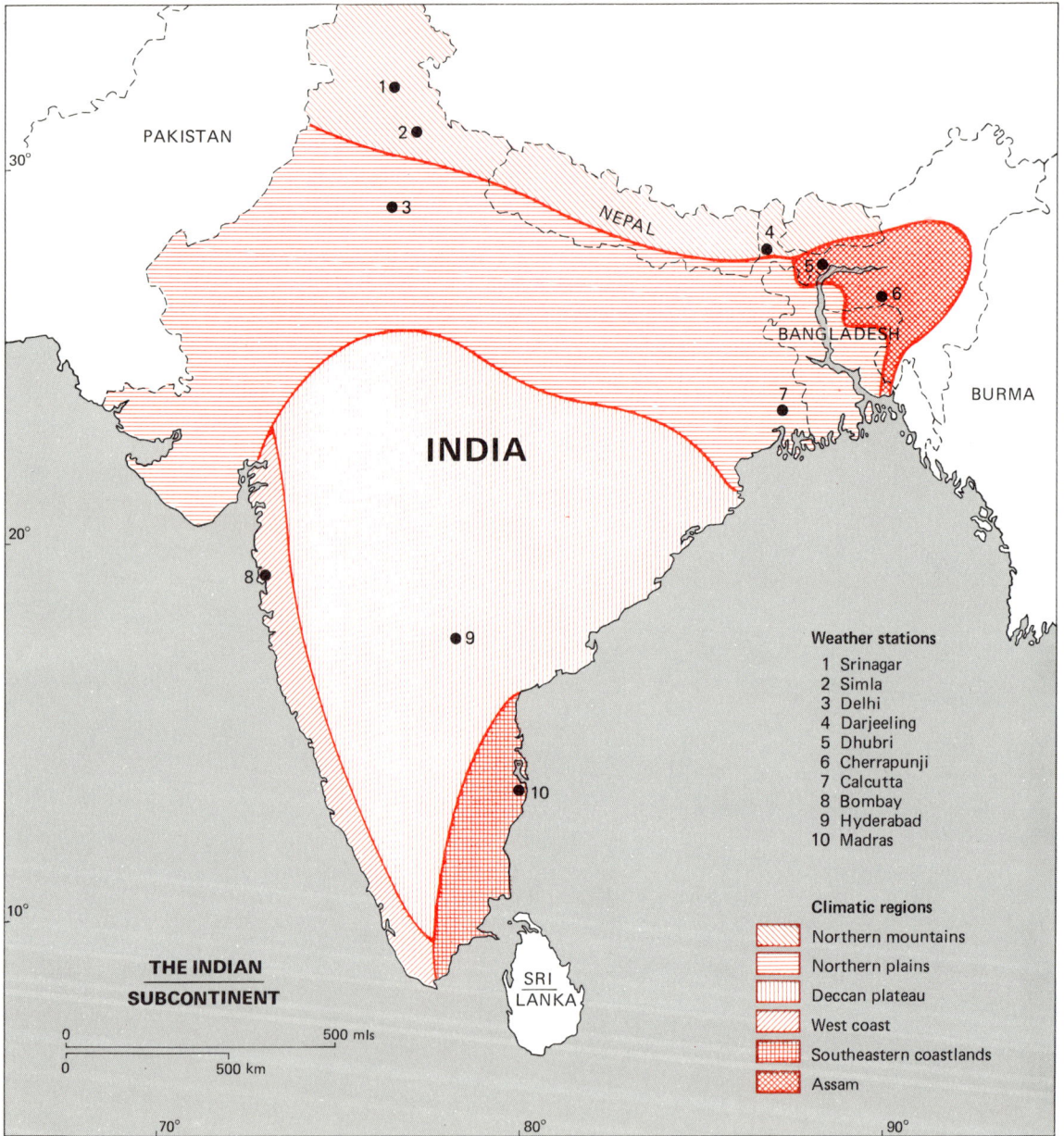

THE INDIAN SUBCONTINENT

INDIA

PAKISTAN

NEPAL

BANGLADESH

BURMA

SRI LANKA

30°
20°
10°

70°
80°
90°

1 ●
2 ●
● 3
4
5
● 6
7 ●
8 ●
● 9
● 10

Weather stations

1 Srinagar
2 Simla
3 Delhi
4 Darjeeling
5 Dhubri
6 Cherrapunji
7 Calcutta
8 Bombay
9 Hyderabad
10 Madras

Climatic regions

Northern mountains
Northern plains
Deccan plateau
West coast
Southeastern coastlands
Assam

0 ————————— 500 mls
0 ————————— 500 km

India is a large country, nearly half the size of the United States. It extends from 8° to 33° N, and includes vast plains like the Ganges valley and high mountains like the Himalayas – the highest in the world.

The wide variety in the terrain means a wide variety of climatic conditions. These range from permanent snowfields to tropical coastlands; from areas of virtual desert in the northwest plains to fertile, intensively cultivated rice fields in the northeast.

The climate of India is dominated by the great wind system known as the Asiatic monsoon. This is completely unlike the prevailing wind system that operates in many countries, i.e., a wind that prevails from the same direction throughout the year. The monsoon reverses direction at certain times of the year. For some months it will blow steadily from the southwest; for other months, from the northeast.

From June to October the country is influenced by the moist, rain-bearing monsoon from the southwest.

On some mountain ranges, facing the sea, rainfall can be very heavy indeed. The coolest, driest time over most of the country is from December to February when light northerly winds bring clear skies and little rain. From March to May the climate becomes hotter and hotter and the drought continues. The rains only come when the wind turns again to the southwest.

On average, the arrival of the rains – the 'burst of the monsoon' as it is called – comes to the south of India during late May or early June. It will reach the north about six weeks later. Some years, the rains will be torrential. Other years they may be light or locally variable; in this case, the monsoon will be said to have 'failed'. Results for food crops can, of course, be disastrous.

India can be conveniently divided into six climatic regions: the northern mountains, the northern plains, the Deccan peninsula, the west coast, the southeast coastlands, and Assam or the extreme northeast.

THE NORTHERN MOUNTAINS

This region includes the Himalayas and their foot-hills. Here some rain can occur all the year round. In winter light rain or snow is brought by disturbances travelling from the west. The main rainy season, however, is from July to October during the southwest monsoon. Winters are pleasant and cool at lower levels but it can get quite hot before the 'burst' of the monsoon. At intermediate levels, from 6000 to 8000 ft (1800 to 2450 m), the summer climate is very pleasant and cool. Kashmir (see table for **Srinagar**) and hill stations such as **Simla** and **Darjeeling** are popular refuges from the heat of the plains.

INDIA   Darjeeling 7431 ft (2265 m) 27°03′ N 88°16′ E 25 years

	Temperature °F			Temperature °C				Relative humidity		Precipitation			
	Highest recorded	Average daily		Lowest recorded	Highest recorded	Average daily		Lowest recorded	0800 hours	1630 hours	Average monthly		Average no. days with 0.1 in + (2.5 mm +)	
		max.	min.			max.	min.		%	%	in	mm		
J	61	47	35	27	16	8	2	−3	82	84	0.5	13	1	J
F	62	48	36	28	17	9	2	−2	84	80	1.1	28	3	F
M	74	57	42	31	23	14	6	−1	75	70	1.7	43	4	M
A	75	62	49	34	24	17	9	1	81	75	4.1	104	7	A
M	77	64	53	42	25	18	12	6	90	85	8.5	216	14	M
J	76	65	56	47	24	18	13	8	95	91	23.2	589	21	J
J	77	66	58	48	25	19	14	9	97	92	31.4	798	26	J
A	77	65	57	51	25	18	14	11	96	93	25.1	638	24	A
S	77	64	55	50	25	18	13	10	94	92	17.6	447	17	S
O	74	61	50	40	23	16	10	4	89	85	5.1	130	5	O
N	67	54	42	36	19	12	6	2	79	79	0.9	23	1	N
D	62	49	37	30	17	9	3	−1	78	78	0.3	8	1	D

Simla 7224 ft (2202 m) 31°06′ N 77°10′ E 30 years INDIA

	Temperature °F				Temperature °C				Relative humidity		Precipitation			
	Highest recorded	Average daily		Lowest recorded	Highest recorded	Average daily		Lowest recorded	0800 hours	1630 hours	Average monthly		Average no. days with 0.1 in + (2.5 mm +)	
		max.	min.			max.	min.		%	%	in	mm		
J	63	47	36	15	17	8	2	−9	49	59	2.4	61	4	J
F	67	48	37	18	19	9	3	−8	49	61	2.7	69	5	F
M	75	57	44	22	24	14	7	−6	38	43	2.4	61	5	M
A	83	65	52	32	28	18	11	0	36	35	2.1	53	4	A
M	86	72	58	40	30	22	14	4	40	35	2.6	66	5	M
J	87	73	61	46	31	23	16	8	60	59	6.9	175	10	J
J	82	69	60	50	28	21	16	10	88	87	16.7	424	20	J
A	78	67	59	52	26	19	15	11	91	91	17.1	434	19	A
S	76	67	57	41	24	19	14	5	75	77	6.3	160	9	S
O	75	63	51	39	24	17	11	4	47	52	1.3	33	2	O
N	67	57	45	32	19	14	7	0	36	44	0.5	13	1	N
D	68	51	40	21	20	11	4	−6	38	55	1.1	28	2	D

Srinagar (Kashmir) 5205 ft (1587 m) 34°05′ N 74°50′ E 30 years INDIA

	Temperature °F				Temperature °C				Relative humidity		Precipitation			
	Highest recorded	Average daily		Lowest recorded	Highest recorded	Average daily		Lowest recorded	0800 hours	1630 hours	Average monthly		Average no. days with 0.1 in + (2.5 mm +)	
		max.	min.			max.	min.		%	%	in	mm		
J	56	41	28	8	13	5	−2	−13	90	76	2.9	74	6	J
F	69	45	30	6	21	7	−1	−14	88	68	2.8	71	6	F
M	78	57	38	23	26	14	3	−5	84	57	3.6	91	7	M
A	88	66	45	33	31	19	7	1	79	52	3.7	94	8	A
M	96	76	52	37	36	24	11	3	71	43	2.4	61	5	M
J	99	85	58	45	37	29	14	7	67	40	1.4	36	3	J
J	99	88	65	52	37	31	18	11	73	46	2.3	58	5	J
A	97	87	64	51	36	31	18	11	78	49	2.4	61	5	A
S	95	82	54	40	35	28	12	4	76	43	1.5	38	3	S
O	93	72	41	29	34	22	5	−2	78	48	1.2	31	3	O
N	74	60	31	18	23	16	−1	−8	82	51	0.4	10	1	N
D	63	48	28	13	17	9	−2	−11	88	63	1.3	33	3	D

THE NORTHERN PLAINS

Extending from the Punjab to the Ganges delta, this low-lying region is everywhere hot and generally dry from March until June. Some scattered thunderstorms and squalls can occur at this time, particularly in the east around **Calcutta**. With the arrival of the main rains in July temperatures drop a little but the humidity may cause conditions to be sticky and unpleasant at night. Rainfall decreases from east to west and in the extreme west in Rajasthan the country verges on desert. In the winter season, from December to February, the weather is usually sunny and dry with occasional chilly nights and mornings. Some light rain may occur in the west at this time.

The table for **Delhi** is representative of the central plains, and that for **Jacobabad** in Pakistan (see p. 270) of the Ragasthan desert.

	Temperature °F			Temperature °C			Relative humidity		Precipitation			
	Highest recorded	Average daily	Lowest recorded	Highest recorded	Average daily	Lowest recorded	0800 hours	1730 hours	Average monthly		Average no. days with 0.1 in + (2.5 mm +)	
		max.	min.			max.	min.		%	%	in	mm	
J	89	80	55	44	32	27	13	7	85	52	0.4	10	0.8	J
F	98	84	59	46	37	29	15	8	82	45	1.2	31	2	F
M	104	93	69	50	40	34	21	10	79	46	1.4	36	2	M
A	107	97	75	61	42	36	24	16	76	56	1.7	43	3	A
M	108	96	77	65	42	36	25	18	77	62	5.5	140	7	M
J	111	92	79	70	44	33	26	21	82	75	11.7	297	13	J
J	98	89	79	73	37	32	26	23	86	80	12.8	325	18	J
A	96	89	78	74	36	32	26	23	88	82	12.9	328	18	A
S	97	90	78	72	36	32	26	22	86	81	9.9	252	13	S
O	96	89	74	63	36	32	24	17	85	72	4.5	114	6	O
N	92	84	64	51	33	29	18	11	79	63	0.8	20	1	N
D	87	79	55	45	31	26	13	7	80	55	0.2	5	0.3	D

	Temperature °F			Temperature °C			Relative humidity		Precipitation			
	Highest recorded	Average daily	Lowest recorded	Highest recorded	Average daily	Lowest recorded	0800 hours	1630 hours	Average monthly		Average no. days with 0.1 in + (25 mm +)	
		max.	min.			max.	min.		%	%	in	mm	
J	84	70	44	31	29	21	7	−1	72	41	0.9	23	2	J
F	89	75	49	32	32	24	9	0	67	35	0.7	18	2	F
M	103	87	58	45	39	31	14	7	49	23	0.5	13	1	M
A	114	97	68	53	46	36	20	12	35	19	0.3	8	1	A
M	115	105	79	65	46	41	26	18	35	20	0.5	13	2	M
J	115	102	83	66	46	39	28	19	53	36	2.9	74	4	J
J	113	96	81	71	45	36	27	22	75	59	7.1	180	8	J
A	104	93	79	72	40	34	26	22	80	64	6.8	173	8	A
S	105	93	75	64	41	34	24	18	72	51	4.6	117	4	S
O	103	93	65	51	39	34	18	11	56	32	0.4	10	1	O
N	93	84	52	41	34	29	11	5	51	31	0.1	3	0.2	N
D	83	73	46	34	28	23	8	1	69	42	0.4	10	1	D

THE DECCAN PENINSULA

The interior of the centre and south is a low plateau with a different climate from that of the coastlands. The three main seasonal divisions of the year apply equally well here, but rainfall is generally moderate compared with the coastlands and, in the northwest, rather low. On occasions, during the hot season, temperatures can approach those of the northern plains. Altitude is the main control on temperature, but towards the south even the cool season is typically tropical in temperature when warm sunny days are moderated by dry heat and pleasant cool evenings (see the table for **Hyderabad**).

THE WEST COAST

This consists of a narrow coastal plain backed by a steep mountain barrier, the Western Ghats. Rainfall is abundant and heavy during the southwest monsoon season. The heat can be very oppressive because of the humidity throughout the year, particularly in the hot season. Some hill stations in the Western Ghats have a pleasant climate during the hot season, but are very cloudy and wet during the monsoon. Towards the south some rain can occur at any time of the year and the monsoon arrives earlier.

The table for **Bombay** is representative of conditions at sea level.

Hyderabad 1778 ft (541 m) 17°26′ N 78°27′ E 30 years　　　　　　　　　**INDIA**

	Temperature °F			Temperature °C			Relative humidity		Precipitation			
	Highest recorded	Average daily	Lowest recorded	Highest recorded	Average daily	Lowest recorded	0800 hours	1630 hours	Average monthly		Average no. days with 0.1 in + (2.5 mm +)	
		max.	min.			max.	min.		%	%	in	mm	
J	95	84	60	47	35	29	16	8	73	41	0.3	8	0.5	J
F	99	89	64	52	37	32	18	11	64	34	0.4	10	1	F
M	106	97	70	60	41	36	21	16	54	27	0.5	13	1	M
A	110	101	76	61	43	38	24	16	53	34	1.2	31	2	A
M	112	104	80	67	44	40	27	19	52	35	1.1	28	2	M
J	111	95	76	64	44	35	24	18	70	55	4.4	112	7	J
J	99	87	73	67	37	31	23	19	81	65	6.0	152	11	J
A	97	87	73	67	36	31	23	19	80	68	5.3	135	10	A
S	97	87	72	64	36	31	22	18	81	70	6.5	165	9	S
O	97	88	69	57	36	31	21	14	72	53	2.5	64	4	O
N	92	84	63	46	33	29	17	8	71	45	1.1	28	2	N
D	92	83	59	46	33	28	15	8	73	41	0.3	8	0.4	D

Bombay 37 ft (11 m) 18°54′ N 72°49′ E 60 years　　　　　　　　　**INDIA**

	Temperature °F			Temperature °C			Relative humidity		Precipitation			
	Highest recorded	Average daily	Lowest recorded	Highest recorded	Average daily	Lowest recorded	0800 hours	1600 hours	Average monthly		Average no. days with 0.1 in + (2.5 mm +)	
		max.	min.			max.	min.		%	%	in	mm	
J	94	83	67	53	34	28	19	12	70	61	0.1	2.5	0.2	J
F	97	83	67	53	36	28	19	12	71	62	0.1	2.5	0.2	F
M	101	86	72	62	38	30	22	17	73	65	0.1	2.5	0.1	M
A	100	89	76	68	38	32	24	20	75	67	0	0	0.1	A
M	96	91	80	73	36	33	27	23	74	68	0.7	18	1	M
J	99	89	79	70	37	32	26	21	79	77	19.1	485	14	J
J	96	85	77	72	36	29	25	22	83	83	24.3	617	21	J
A	90	85	76	72	32	29	24	22	83	81	13.4	340	19	A
S	95	85	76	71	35	29	24	22	85	78	10.4	264	13	S
O	97	89	76	70	36	32	24	21	81	71	2.5	64	3	O
N	96	89	73	64	36	32	23	18	73	64	0.5	13	1	N
D	94	87	69	55	34	31	21	13	70	62	0.1	2.5	0.1	D

THE SOUTHEAST COASTLANDS

Here the main rains do not occur until the period October to December, and are often associated with tropical storms or cyclones developing in the Bay of Bengal. Because of the lack of cloud, the period of the southwest monsoon from June to September can be very unpleasant since temperature and humidity are high.

The east coast north of Banda has its main rainy season at the time of the southwest monsoon, but this area is occasionally affected by very heavy rain and strong winds caused by tropical cyclones between July to November (see the table for **Madras**).

INDIA
Madras 51 ft (16 m) 13°04′ N 80°15′ E 60 years

		Temperature °F				Temperature °C			Relative humidity		Precipitation			
	Highest recorded	Average daily		Lowest recorded	Highest recorded	Average daily		Lowest recorded	0800 hours	1700 hours	Average monthly		Average no. days with 0.1 in + (2.5 mm +)	
		max.	min.			max.	min.		%	%	in	mm		
J	91	85	67	57	33	29	19	14	87	67	1.4	36	2	J
F	98	88	68	59	37	31	20	15	83	66	0.4	10	0.7	F
M	102	91	72	62	39	33	22	17	80	67	0.3	8	0.4	M
A	109	95	78	68	43	35	26	20	74	72	0.6	15	0.9	A
M	113	101	82	70	45	38	28	21	63	67	1.0	25	1	M
J	110	100	81	69	43	38	27	21	59	61	1.9	48	4	J
J	106	96	79	71	41	36	26	22	65	62	3.6	91	7	J
A	104	95	78	69	40	35	26	21	71	66	4.6	117	8	A
S	102	94	77	69	39	34	25	21	75	70	4.7	119	7	S
O	102	90	75	62	39	32	24	17	83	75	12.0	305	11	O
N	94	85	72	59	34	29	22	15	86	75	14.0	356	11	N
D	91	84	69	57	33	29	21	14	87	72	5.5	140	5	D

This area is almost detached from the rest of India by Bangladesh. It is a region of plains and mountainous tracts. Its climate is similar to that of the northern plains and Himalayas, depending on altitude. Here some significant rainfall can occur in the period March to May but the main rainy season from June to October is, in places, very wet indeed and **Cherrapunji** at an altitude of 4300 ft (1300 m) has the distinction of being one of the three wettest places in the world with an annual rainfall averaging 425 in (10,800 mm)!

The table for **Dhubri** is representative of the lowlands.

Cherrapunji 4309 ft (1313 m) 25°15′ N 91°44′ E 35 years   **INDIA**

	Temperature °F			Temperature °C			Relative humidity		Precipitation			
	Highest recorded	Average daily		Lowest recorded	Highest recorded	Average daily		Lowest recorded	0830 hours	1730 hours	Average monthly		Average no. days with 0.1 in + (2.5 mm +)
		max.	min.			max.	min.		%	%	in	mm	
J	80	60	46	34	27	16	8	1	66	72	0.7	18	1	J
F	84	62	49	33	29	17	9	1	63	70	2.1	53	3	F
M	87	69	55	33	31	21	13	1	61	62	7.3	185	7	M
A	83	71	59	39	28	22	15	4	77	69	26.2	666	16	A
M	82	72	61	38	28	22	16	3	82	84	50.4	1280	22	M
J	82	72	64	53	28	22	18	12	91	90	106.1	2695	25	J
J	83	72	65	53	28	22	18	12	93	92	96.3	2446	27	J
A	83	73	65	56	28	23	18	13	92	91	70.1	1781	26	A
S	84	73	65	55	29	23	18	13	87	87	43.3	1100	19	S
O	85	72	61	51	29	22	16	11	76	84	19.4	493	9	O
N	80	67	54	44	27	19	12	7	64	80	2.7	69	2	N
D	74	62	48	39	23	17	9	4	63	79	0.5	13	0.7	D

	Temperature °F			Temperature °C				Relative humidity		Precipitation			
	Highest recorded	Average daily		Lowest recorded	Highest recorded	Average daily		Lowest recorded	0800 hours	1730 hours	Average monthly		Average no. days with 0.1 in + (2.5 mm +)	
		max.	min.			max.	min.		%	%	in	mm		
J	81	74	53	43	27	23	12	6	90	59	0.3	8	1	J
F	90	78	56	37	32	26	13	3	84	54	0.7	18	1	F
M	101	86	63	50	38	30	17	10	75	41	1.8	46	3	M
A	103	87	70	54	39	31	21	12	79	49	5.1	130	8	A
M	103	86	73	63	39	30	23	17	86	75	14.7	373	15	M
J	96	86	76	69	36	30	24	21	91	83	23.8	605	18	J
J	95	86	78	73	35	30	26	23	91	83	17.1	434	16	J
A	94	86	79	72	34	30	26	22	90	83	13.5	343	15	A
S	95	85	77	69	35	29	25	21	91	83	14.5	368	13	S
O	92	85	73	62	33	29	23	17	88	75	4.6	117	5	O
N	88	80	64	53	31	27	18	12	86	71	0.3	8	1	N
D	80	74	55	46	27	23	13	8	89	67	0.1	3	0	D

Indonesia is about half the size of India, consisting of a large number of islands between 5° N and 10° S of the equator and extending over 45° of longitude. The largest islands from west to east are Sumatra, Java, Borneo and Celebes but there are over 3000 smaller islands, of which Bali and the Moluccas are best known. Indonesia also includes the western portion (West Irian) of the large island of New Guinea (Papua). The climate of both eastern and western New Guinea are described on p. 309.

Most of the islands are very mountainous with numerous volcanic peaks and other mountain ranges exceeding 10,000 ft (3000 m). There are consequently many sharp local differences of climate within Indonesia; not only are temperatures much lower in the hills but the amount and season of maximum rainfall varies with the different exposure of the islands to the two main seasonal wind systems. The whole archipelago is alternately dominated by the north monsoon, blowing from China and the north Pacific between November and March, and the south monsoon blowing from the Indian Ocean and the Australian continent between May and September. For a few weeks around April and October the winds are light and variable in direction; this is the period of transition when the Doldrum belt, or inter-tropical convergence, moves north or south across the islands.

Apart from the reduced temperatures on the higher mountains, the weather and climate of Indonesia are typical of equatorial regions. Rainfall is almost everywhere heavy and well distributed around the year. Most places receive between 60 and 160 in (1500 and 4000 mm) of rain a year. Many places have two wetter periods during the passage of the Doldrum belt; but south-facing coasts and islands south of the equator tend to be wetter during the period of the south monsoon and north-facing coasts and the northern islands are wetter during the period of the north monsoon. Compare the climatic tables for **Jakarta** on the north coast of Java with those for **Amboina** in the Moluccas and **Balikpapan** on the southeast coast of Borneo. The table for **Makassar** represents conditions in the south of the Celebes.

Much of the rainfall is heavy and accompanied by thunder. Some parts of Indonesia have more thunderstorms than anywhere else in the world. In spite of the heavy rainfall sunshine hours are abundant in Indonesia. During the wetter months sunshine averages four to five hours a day and this rises to eight or nine hours a day during drier periods. **Jakarta**, one of the drier places in the country, receives three times as much rain as London but it falls on fewer days per year and for only half the number of hours.

Temperatures remain high throughout the year and there is very little difference from month to month. There are only two types of weather in Indonesia: fine and sunny or cloudy and wet. Only the extreme southern islands, such as Timor, are occasionally affected by strong winds associated with tropical cyclones; but local wind squalls may occur during thunderstorms. On the coast the daily range of temperature is small but this increases inland and in the hills. The cooler nights inland and the daytime sea breezes and strong monsoon winds afford the chief relief from the heat and humidity on the coast.

The weather may often feel muggy and oppressive to the visitor but heat stress is not severe. Dampness and humidity are the worst features of the climate and this may trouble the old or those not in good health.

INDONESIA — Amboina (Moluccas) 14 ft (4 m) 3°42′ S 128°10′ E 18 years

	Temperature °F				Temperature °C				Relative humidity		Precipitation			
	Highest recorded	Average daily		Lowest recorded	Highest recorded	Average daily		Lowest recorded	0600 hours	1400 hours	Average monthly		Average no. days with 0.004 in + (0.1 mm +)	
		max.	min.			max.	min.		%	%	in	mm		
J	96	88	76	72	36	31	24	22	89	66	5.0	127	13	J
F	96	88	76	73	36	31	24	23	89	64	4.7	119	13	F
M	95	88	76	72	35	31	24	22	90	67	5.3	135	15	M
A	93	86	76	71	34	30	24	22	92	72	11.0	279	19	A
M	90	84	75	70	32	29	24	21	92	74	20.3	516	22	M
J	87	82	74	69	31	28	23	21	91	76	25.1	638	24	J
J	86	81	74	68	30	27	23	20	90	76	23.7	602	23	J
A	87	81	74	67	31	27	23	19	89	75	15.8	401	20	A
S	88	83	74	66	31	28	23	19	91	71	9.5	241	15	S
O	91	85	74	66	33	29	23	19	91	68	6.1	155	13	O
N	94	88	75	70	34	31	24	21	92	66	4.5	114	11	N
D	96	88	76	68	36	31	24	20	91	64	5.2	132	13	D

INDONESIA — Balikpapan (Borneo) 23 ft (7 m) 1°17′ S 116°51′ E 6 years

	Temperature °F				Temperature °C				Relative humidity		Precipitation			
	Highest recorded	Average daily		Lowest recorded	Highest recorded	Average daily		Lowest recorded	0800 hours	1400 hours	Average monthly		Average no. days with 0.02 in + (0.5 mm +)	
		max.	min.			max.	min.		%	%	in	mm		
J	92	85	73	70	33	29	23	21	89	74	7.9	201	14	J
F	92	86	73	71	33	30	23	22	89	72	6.9	175	13	F
M	92	86	73	70	33	30	23	21	90	72	9.1	231	15	M
A	90	85	73	70	32	29	23	21	89	74	8.2	208	13	A
M	91	85	74	71	33	29	23	22	89	76	9.1	231	13	M
J	90	84	74	60	32	29	23	16	89	75	7.6	193	12	J
J	85	83	73	68	29	28	23	20	89	75	7.1	180	11	J
A	86	84	74	69	30	29	23	21	87	72	6.4	163	11	A
S	88	84	74	67	31	29	23	19	84	70	5.5	140	9	S
O	91	85	74	69	33	29	23	21	84	71	5.2	132	9	O
N	92	85	73	70	33	29	23	21	87	73	6.6	168	12	N
D	92	85	73	70	33	29	23	21	87	70	8.1	206	15	D

Jakarta (Java) 26 ft (8 m) 6°11′ S 106°50′ E 80 years — INDONESIA

	Temperature °F			Temperature °C			Relative humidity		Precipitation		
Highest recorded	Average daily		Lowest recorded	Highest recorded	Average daily		Lowest recorded	0600 hours	1400 hours	Average monthly		Average no. days with 0.04 in + (1 mm +)
	max.	min.			max.	min.		%	%	in	mm	
J	93	84	74	69	34	29	23	21	95	75	11.8	300	18	J
F	92	84	74	69	33	29	23	21	95	75	11.8	300	17	F
M	92	86	74	69	33	30	23	21	94	73	8.3	211	15	M
A	94	87	75	69	34	31	24	21	94	71	5.8	147	11	A
M	93	87	75	70	34	31	24	21	94	69	4.5	114	9	M
J	93	87	74	67	34	31	23	19	93	67	3.8	97	7	J
J	92	87	73	67	33	31	23	19	92	64	2.5	64	5	J
A	94	87	73	67	34	31	23	19	90	61	1.7	43	4	A
S	96	88	74	66	36	31	23	19	90	62	2.6	66	5	S
O	98	87	74	69	37	31	23	21	90	64	4.4	112	8	O
N	96	86	74	68	36	30	23	20	92	68	5.6	142	12	N
D	93	85	74	67	34	29	23	19	92	71	8.0	203	14	D

Makassar (Celebes) 6 ft (2 m) 5°08′ S 119°28′ E 10 years — INDONESIA

	Temperature °F			Temperature °C			Relative humidity		Precipitation		
Highest recorded	Average daily		Lowest recorded	Highest recorded	Average daily		Lowest recorded	0600 hours	1400 hours	Average monthly		Average no. days with 0.02 in + (0.5 mm +)
	max.	min.			max.	min.		%	%	in	mm	
J	88	84	74	70	31	29	23	21	90	80	27.0	686	25	J
F	89	84	75	70	32	29	24	21	90	77	21.1	536	20	F
M	89	85	74	70	32	29	23	21	91	77	16.7	424	18	M
A	91	86	74	69	33	30	23	21	91	72	5.9	150	10	A
M	91	87	74	63	33	31	23	17	91	70	3.5	89	8	M
J	91	86	72	63	33	30	22	17	90	67	2.9	74	6	J
J	92	86	70	63	33	30	21	17	89	65	1.4	36	4	J
A	94	87	69	62	34	31	21	17	87	65	0.4	10	2	A
S	95	87	70	58	35	31	21	14	83	66	0.6	15	2	S
O	92	87	72	65	33	31	22	18	85	71	1.7	43	5	O
N	91	86	74	66	33	30	23	19	89	73	7.0	178	11	N
D	89	84	74	69	32	29	23	21	90	79	24.0	610	22	D

INDONESIA — Medan (Sumatra) 77 ft (24 m) 3°35′ N 98°41′ E 16 years

	Temperature °F			Temperature °C			Relative humidity		Precipitation		
	Highest recorded	Average daily	Lowest recorded	Highest recorded	Average daily	Lowest recorded	0600 hours	1200 hours	Average monthly		Average no. days with 0.02 in + (0.5 mm +)
		max.	min.			max.	min.		%	%	in	mm	
J	93	85	71	65	34	29	22	18	94	66	5.4	137	11	J
F	94	87	71	65	34	31	22	18	93	61	3.6	91	7	F
M	95	88	72	65	35	31	22	18	93	61	4.1	104	8	M
A	95	89	73	67	35	32	23	19	93	62	5.2	132	10	A
M	96	89	73	65	36	32	23	18	93	63	6.9	175	12	M
J	95	89	72	63	35	32	22	17	93	63	5.2	132	9	J
J	96	89	72	64	36	32	22	18	92	59	5.3	135	9	J
A	95	89	72	65	35	32	22	18	93	61	7.0	178	13	A
S	96	88	72	66	36	31	22	19	94	66	8.3	211	14	S
O	93	86	72	64	34	30	22	18	94	69	10.2	259	17	O
N	93	86	72	60	34	30	22	16	88	69	9.7	246	17	N
D	94	85	72	65	34	29	22	18	88	68	9.0	229	15	D

INDONESIA — Padang (Sumatra) 22 ft (7 m) 0°56′ S 100°22′ E 17 years

	Temperature °F			Temperature °C			Relative humidity		Precipitation		
	Highest recorded	Average daily	Lowest recorded	Highest recorded	Average daily	Lowest recorded	0600 hours	1200 hours	Average monthly		Average no. days with 0.02 in + (0.5 mm +)
		max.	min.			max.	min.		%	%	in	mm	
J	93	87	74	70	34	31	23	21	88	67	13.8	351	16	J
F	94	87	74	69	34	31	23	21	88	66	10.2	259	13	F
M	93	87	74	70	34	31	23	21	88	66	12.1	307	15	M
A	92	87	75	71	33	31	24	22	89	66	14.3	363	17	A
M	93	88	75	71	34	31	24	22	87	65	12.4	315	14	M
J	93	87	74	68	34	31	23	20	86	63	12.1	307	12	J
J	92	87	74	70	33	31	23	21	85	62	10.9	277	12	J
A	92	87	74	69	33	31	23	21	86	64	13.7	348	14	A
S	91	86	74	70	33	30	23	21	87	65	6.0	152	16	S
O	92	86	74	70	33	30	23	21	88	68	19.5	495	20	O
N	91	86	74	70	33	30	23	21	89	68	20.4	518	21	N
D	91	86	74	70	33	30	23	21	89	69	18.9	480	20	D

Iran is a large country three times the size of France. It is bordered by the central Asian region of the USSR and the Caspian Sea to the north, by Afghanistan and Pakistan on the east, the Persian (Arabian) Gulf on the south and by Iraq and Turkey on the west. Much of the interior consists of a high plateau between 3000 and 5000 ft (900 and 1500 m) above sea level. The Iranian plateau is surrounded on all sides by mountains: the Elburz ranges on the north and the Zagros on the west and south. In the higher parts these mountains rise to between 10,000 and 15,000 ft (3000 and 4600 m) so that winter snows feed many of the country's rivers.

Much of Iran has a very harsh climate with great extremes of heat and cold between summer and winter. Large portions of central, southern and eastern Iran consist of desert and steppe with annual precipitation below 12 in (300 mm). With the exception of the northern slopes of the Elburz Mountains and the Caspian coastlands, rainfall is confined to the winter and spring months. In the extreme north of the country some rainfall occurs all round the year. Summers are everywhere warm to hot with almost continuous sunshine. Winter weather is changeable with a mixture of mild, wet spells and some very cold weather with frost and snow when cold air blows from Siberia. Along the shore of the Persian Gulf and Arabian Sea winters are much milder as shown by the tables for **Abadan** and **Bushire**. The high temperatures experienced here in summer are similar to those in lowland Iraq and there is a danger of heat exhaustion and even heatstroke.

Temperatures in the interior plateau are considerably lower in winter but they are very high during the long sunny summer (see the tables for **Tehran** and **Isfahan**). In the southern coastlands the high humidity makes the temperatures even more unpleasant in summer. In the interior daytime humidities are usually quite low in summer and the most dangerous conditions arise when high temperatures are combined with occasional strong, dusty winds.

The small area of Iran along the Caspian coast has a very different climate from the rest of the country. Here precipitation is heaviest from late summer until midwinter and occurs around the year. This region is much wetter and cloudier than the interior and the annual precipitation ranges from 35 to 80 in (800 to 2000 mm). It is a fertile, well-forested region and contrasts in a startling way with the arid landscape of interior Iran where most cultivation is dependent upon irrigation from underground water resources and streams fed by rain and snow falling on the surrounding mountains.

Spring and autumn are quite short seasons in Iran between the heat of summer and the more changeable and often cold weather of winter. These seasons are the best time to visit Iran even if the weather may, on occasions, be a little uncertain with short lapses into either the cold of winter or the heat of summer.

	Temperature °F				Temperature °C				Relative humidity	Precipitation			
	Highest recorded	Average daily		Lowest recorded	Highest recorded	Average daily		Lowest recorded	0900 hours	Average monthly		Average no. days with 0.04 in + (1 mm +)	
		max.	min.			max.	min.		%	in	mm		
J	77	63	44	26	25	17	7	−3	77	1.5	38	6	J
F	83	68	49	27	28	20	9	−3	75	1.7	43	5	F
M	93	76	55	36	34	24	13	2	59	0.6	15	3	M
A	109	88	64	45	43	31	18	7	45	0.8	20	3	A
M	116	101	74	60	47	38	23	16	33	0.1	3	1	M
J	118	108	78	67	48	42	26	19	25	0	0	0	J
J	122	112	82	73	50	44	28	23	25	0	0	0	J
A	123	113	81	71	51	45	27	22	29	0	0	0	A
S	118	107	73	60	48	42	23	16	33	0	0	0	S
O	110	97	65	53	43	36	18	12	39	0.1	3	0.4	O
N	97	81	57	33	36	27	14	1	60	1.0	25	3	N
D	84	68	48	24	29	20	9	−4	75	1.8	46	4	D

	Temperature °F				Temperature °C				Relative humidity		Precipitation			
	Highest recorded	Average daily		Lowest recorded	Highest recorded	Average daily		Lowest recorded	0730 hours	1530 hours	Average monthly		Average no. days with 0.01 in + (0.25 mm +)	
		max.	min.			max.	min.		%	%	in	mm		
J	80	64	51	32	27	18	11	0	82	78	2.9	74	5	J
F	85	65	53	37	29	18	12	3	82	76	1.8	46	3	F
M	105	73	59	42	41	23	15	6	76	71	0.8	20	2	M
A	103	81	67	47	39	27	19	8	72	72	0.4	10	1	A
M	107	89	76	58	42	32	24	14	73	74	0	0	0	M
J	112	92	81	67	44	33	27	19	74	72	0	0	0	J
J	112	95	84	74	44	35	29	23	75	73	0	0	0	J
A	115	97	84	69	46	36	29	21	72	71	0	0	0	A
S	107	94	79	63	42	34	26	17	71	69	0	0	0	S
O	101	88	72	55	38	31	22	13	68	68	0.1	3	0.2	O
N	93	78	63	42	34	26	17	6	74	71	1.6	41	3	N
D	87	68	55	37	31	20	13	3	82	77	3.2	81	4	D

Isfahan 5817 ft (1773 m) 32°34′ N 51°44′ E 22 years — IRAN

	Temperature °F			Temperature °C				Relative humidity		Precipitation			
	Highest recorded	Average daily		Lowest recorded	Highest recorded	Average daily		Lowest recorded	0730 hours	1530 hours	Average monthly		Average no. days with 0.1 in + (2.5 mm +)	
		max.	min.			max.	min.		%	%	in	mm		
J	65	47	24	−3	18	8	−4	−19	74	53	0.6	15	3	J
F	74	53	29	7	23	12	−2	−14	68	40	0.4	10	3	F
M	82	61	37	12	28	16	3	−11	57	33	1.0	25	2	M
A	88	72	46	26	31	22	8	−3	55	25	0.6	15	2	A
M	96	83	54	37	36	28	12	3	50	27	0.2	5	1	M
J	110	92	62	48	43	33	17	9	42	18	0	0	0.1	J
J	107	98	67	48	42	37	19	9	41	15	0	0	0.2	J
A	108	96	64	53	42	36	18	12	42	15	0	0	0.1	A
S	100	90	56	42	38	32	13	6	44	19	0	0	0.1	S
O	92	77	46	30	33	25	8	−1	51	24	0.1	3	0.3	O
N	77	63	37	16	25	17	3	−9	64	35	0.6	15	2	N
D	73	52	29	9	23	11	−2	−13	72	45	0.8	20	1	D

Tehran 4002 ft (1220 m) 35°41′ N 51°25′ E 22 years — IRAN

	Temperature °F			Temperature °C				Relative humidity		Precipitation			
	Highest recorded	Average daily		Lowest recorded	Highest recorded	Average daily		Lowest recorded	0730 hours	1730 hours	Average monthly		Average no. days with 0.1 in + (2.5 mm +)	
		max.	min.			max.	min.		%	%	in	mm		
J	65	45	27	−5	18	7	−3	−21	77	75	1.8	46	4	J
F	67	50	32	4	19	10	0	−16	73	59	1.5	38	4	F
M	85	59	39	16	29	15	4	−9	61	39	1.8	46	5	M
A	91	71	49	28	33	22	9	−2	54	40	1.4	36	3	A
M	99	82	58	39	37	28	14	4	55	47	0.5	13	2	M
J	107	93	66	51	42	34	19	11	50	49	0.1	3	1	J
J	109	99	72	59	43	37	22	15	51	41	0.1	3	0.5	J
A	109	97	71	57	43	36	22	14	47	46	0.1	3	0.2	A
S	101	90	64	47	38	32	18	8	49	49	0.1	3	0.3	S
O	90	76	53	38	32	24	12	3	53	54	0.3	8	1	O
N	84	63	43	19	29	17	6	−7	63	66	0.8	20	3	N
D	68	51	33	10	20	11	1	−12	76	75	1.2	31	4	D

IRAQ

Iraq is an almost landlocked country lying between
Turkey on the north, Iran on the east, Saudi Arabia and
Kuwait on the south and Jordan and Syria on the west.
It has a very short coastline on the Persian (Arabian)
Gulf. Most of the country is flat and low-lying and
consists of the low plateau of the Syrian and Arabian
deserts to the west and, in central Iraq, the broad
valleys of the rivers Tigris and Euphrates (ancient
Mesopotamia). These rivers enter the Gulf in a combined stream, the Shatt al Arab, near Basra. The
northeast of Iraq (Kurdistan) is mountainous and the
climate is similar to that found in the mountains of
western Iran (see p. 243).

The western desert region and Mesopotamia have a
very harsh climate with a marked contrast between the
extremely hot, sunny and dry summers and a cooler
winter during which some rain falls. Iraq experiences
some of the highest temperatures anywhere in the
world. These scorching conditions are often
accompanied by a persistent dusty, northwesterly
wind, the shamal, which adds to the unpleasantness.
Heat exhaustion and even heatstroke are hazards.
There is no great difference in summer temperatures
from north to south, but temperatures are distinctly

lower and more pleasant at this time in the Kurdistan
mountains. Winters are very mild in the south, but
become cooler towards the north. Frost and snow
occasionally occur at low levels in the north and
snowfall may be heavy in Kurdistan.

Most of the country has a desert or steppe climate
with annual rainfall below 8 in (200 mm). Only in the
northern plains around Mosul and Kirkuk and in the
Kurdistan mountains is precipitation heavier. The
summer months from May to September are virtually
rainless and the heaviest precipitation comes between
December and March. Melting snow in spring in the
mountains of Turkey, Iran and Kurdistan causes the
rivers Tigris and Euphrates to flood in a spectacular
manner between March and May at a time when the
long, hot, dry summer in Iraq is beginning.

The climatic table for **Baghdad** is representative of
conditions around the year in most of lowland Iraq.
That for **Basra** shows the higher summer humidity in
the south where the summer heat is even more oppressive. Conditions in the northern plains are similar to
those illustrated by the climatic table for **Deir ez Zor** in
Syria (p. 286).

Baghdad 111 ft (34 m) 33°20′ N 44°24′ E 15 years

	Temperature °F			Temperature °C			Relative humidity		Precipitation		
	Highest recorded	Average daily	Lowest recorded	Highest recorded	Average daily	Lowest recorded	0600 hours	1500 hours	Average monthly		Average no. days with 0.04 in + (1 mm +)
		max.	min.			max.	min.		%	%	in	mm	
J	77	60	39	18	25	16	4	−8	84	51	0.9	23	4	J
F	86	64	42	23	30	18	6	−5	78	42	1.0	25	3	F
M	90	71	48	27	32	22	9	−3	73	36	1.1	28	4	M
A	104	85	57	37	40	29	14	3	64	34	0.5	13	3	A
M	112	97	67	51	44	36	19	11	47	19	0.1	3	1	M
J	119	105	73	58	48	41	23	14	34	13	0	0	0	J
J	121	110	76	62	49	43	24	17	32	12	0	0	0	J
A	120	110	76	64	49	43	24	18	33	13	0	0	0	A
S	116	104	70	51	47	40	21	11	38	15	0	0	0	S
O	107	92	61	39	42	33	16	4	49	22	0.1	3	1	O
N	94	77	51	29	34	25	11	−2	70	39	0.8	20	3	N
D	79	64	42	20	26	18	6	−7	84	52	1.0	25	5	D

Basra 8 ft (2.5 m) 30°34′ N 47°47′ E 10 years

	Temperature °F			Temperature °C			Relative humidity		Precipitation		
	Highest recorded	Average daily	Lowest recorded	Highest recorded	Average daily	Lowest recorded	0500 hours	1600 hours	Average monthly		Average no. days with 0.04 in + (1 mm +)
		max.	min.			max.	min.		%	%	in	mm	
J	81	64	45	24	27	18	7	−4	89	62	1.4	36	5	J
F	87	68	48	28	31	20	9	−2	87	55	1.1	28	4	F
M	95	75	55	36	35	24	13	2	81	49	1.2	31	3	M
A	105	85	63	47	41	29	17	8	76	43	1 2	31	3	A
M	114	95	76	48	46	35	24	9	65	40	0.2	5	0.7	M
J	115	100	81	69	46	38	27	21	60	41	0	0	0	J
J	123	104	81	72	51	40	27	22	58	35	0	0	0	J
A	120	105	78	68	49	41	26	20	56	32	0	0	0	A
S	116	102	72	58	47	39	22	14	62	32	0	0	0	S
O	114	94	64	45	46	34	18	7	67	36	0	0	0	O
N	98	80	57	38	37	27	14	3	83	52	1.4	36	2	N
D	85	69	48	29	29	21	9	−2	89	62	0.8	20	3	D

ISRAEL

Israel is a small country on the eastern shores of the Mediterranean with landborders with Lebanon and Syria on the north, Jordan on the east and Egypt on the south. About 60 per cent of the country's 10,000 square miles (25,000 sq. km) consists of the Negev, the southern desert. The Negev lies south of Beersheba and extends to **Eilat** on the Gulf of Aqaba.

The weather and climate of Israel are very similar to those described for Syria on p. 284. The main contrast of weather and climate within Israel is between that of the Negev and the northern part of the country. The northern part of Israel has a typical Mediterranean climate with abundant sunshine, mild, wet winters and long, hot, dry summers. Winter rainfall can be quite heavy but falls on a small number of days. On the coast the summer heat is at times rather oppressive and humid but is tempered by afternoon sea breezes. Winters here are mild, and frost and snow are very rare events (see the table for **Haifa**).

Inland in Galilee and in the occupied West Bank territory of Samaria and Judea the country is hilly, with heights ranging from 1650 to 3300 ft (500 to 1000 m). Rainfall is rather heavier here and snow may occasionally fall. Nights are chilly in winter and fresh and cool in summer. The summer heat in the hills is drier and less oppressive than on the coast (see table for **Jerusalem**).

In the southern desert or Negev, annual rainfall is low, decreasing from about 8 in (200 mm) in the north to as little as 2 in (50 mm) at **Eilat** on the Gulf of Aqaba. The scanty rainfall in the Negev comes as short but heavy local showers. These may occur at any time from September until April. Cloudy skies are rare here even in midwinter. Winter nights may be quite cold with frost and occasional snow or sleet. Except under khamsin conditions nights in the desert are rarely very hot and may feel pleasantly fresh after the dry heat of the day.

The most unpleasant weather in Israel, as in neighbouring countries, occurs when hot dry winds 'import' high temperatures from the Arabian desert. These khamsin winds go under the Hebrew name sharav in Israel. They are most frequent and most severe at the beginning and end of the hot, dry summer period.

Israel has a very sunny climate with an average of between six and seven hours sunshine a day in winter and twelve in summer. Israel is one of the few countries to have exploited its sunshine for solar heating of domestic hot water. A great many homes make use of rooftop solar heating panels for this purpose.

ISRAEL

Eilat 7 ft (2 m) 29°33′ N 34°57′ E 4 years

	Temperature °F				Temperature °C				Relative humidity		Precipitation		
	Highest recorded	Average daily		Lowest recorded	Highest recorded	Average daily		Lowest recorded	0830 hours	1430 hours	Average monthly		Average no. days with 0.04 in + (1 mm +)	
		max.	min.			max.	min.		%	%	in	mm		
J	81	70	50	37	27	21	10	3	60	39	0	0	1	J
F	87	73	52	37	31	23	11	3	62	40	0.3	8	1	F
M	93	79	57	47	34	26	14	8	56	38	0.3	8	2	M
A	105	87	64	51	41	31	18	11	46	30	0.2	5	1	A
M	112	96	62	60	44	36	17	16	41	28	0	0	0.1	M
J	112	101	75	69	44	38	24	21	38	20	0	0	0	J
J	116	103	79	72	47	39	26	22	36	13	0	0	0	J
A	114	104	79	74	46	40	26	23	40	24	0	0	0	A
S	110	99	77	70	43	37	25	21	52	27	0	0	0	S
O	103	92	70	60	39	33	21	16	55	34	0	0	0	O
N	98	82	61	46	37	28	16	8	56	38	0	0	1	N
D	88	74	53	41	31	23	12	5	58	42	0.3	8	1	D

Haifa 33 ft (10 m) 32°48′ N 34°59′ E 16 years — ISRAEL

	Temperature °F				Temperature °C				Relative humidity		Precipitation			
	Highest recorded	Average daily		Lowest recorded	Highest recorded	Average daily		Lowest recorded	0830 hours	1430 hours	Average monthly		Average no. days with 0.04 in + (1 mm +)	
		max.	min.			max.	min.		%	%	in	mm		
J	79	65	49	29	26	18	9	−2	66	56	6.9	175	13	J
F	87	67	50	27	31	19	10	−3	65	56	4.3	109	11	F
M	104	71	53	33	40	22	12	1	62	56	1.6	41	7	M
A	109	77	58	40	43	25	14	4	60	57	1.0	25	4	A
M	112	83	65	50	44	28	18	10	62	59	0.2	5	1	M
J	109	85	71	56	43	29	22	13	67	66	0	0	0	J
J	96	88	75	63	36	31	24	17	70	68	0	0	0	J
A	99	90	76	65	37	32	24	18	70	69	0	0	0	A
S	107	88	74	61	42	31	23	16	67	66	0.1	3	0.2	S
O	106	85	68	47	41	29	20	8	66	66	1.0	25	2	O
N	97	78	60	44	36	26	16	7	61	56	3.7	94	7	N
D	85	68	53	33	29	20	12	1	66	56	7.3	185	11	D

Jerusalem 1485 ft (557 m) 31°47′ N 35°13′ E 19 years — ISRAEL

	Temperature °F				Temperature °C				Relative humidity		Precipitation			
	Highest recorded	Average daily		Lowest recorded	Highest recorded	Average daily		Lowest recorded	0830 hours	1330 hours	Average monthly		Average no. days with 0.04 in + (1 mm +)	
		max.	min.			max.	min.		%	%	in	mm		
J	77	55	41	26	25	13	5	−3	77	66	5.2	132	9	J
F	80	56	42	27	27	13	6	−3	74	58	5.2	132	11	F
M	87	65	46	30	31	18	8	−1	61	57	2.5	64	3	M
A	102	73	50	36	39	23	10	2	56	42	1.1	28	3	A
M	103	81	57	42	39	27	14	6	47	33	0.1	3	0.6	M
J	107	85	60	47	42	29	16	8	48	32	0	0	0.1	J
J	100	87	63	50	38	31	17	10	52	35	0	0	0	J
A	103	87	64	52	39	31	18	11	58	36	0	0	0	A
S	103	85	62	50	39	29	17	10	61	36	0	0	0.1	S
O	97	81	59	47	36	27	15	8	60	36	0.5	13	1	O
N	88	70	53	39	31	21	12	4	65	50	2.8	71	4	N
D	79	59	45	27	26	15	7	−3	73	60	3.4	86	7	D

JAPAN

Japan comprises a group of islands between 45° and 32° N off the east coast of Asia. The total area of the country is about one and a half times that of Great Britain. From north to south the main islands are Hokkaido, Honshu (the largest island and sometimes called 'the mainland'), Shikoku and Kyushu. All the islands are hilly or even mountainous, particularly Honshu where the highest peaks such as Fujiyama rise to over 12,000 ft (3600 m). There are numerous other peaks rising over 6500 ft (2000 m), many of which are extinct or even active volcanoes. The higher mountains in Hokkaido and Honshu are snow-covered throughout the year and there are many opportunities for winter sports.

The climate of Japan around the year is much influenced by the great seasonal wind reversal of the Asian monsoon but there are important differences between Korea or north China and Japan. The relatively narrow Sea of Japan separates the mainland from Japan. The Japanese islands have a climate modified and moderated by the sea; winters are less cold than in the same latitude on the continent and precipitation is much heavier. Winter precipitation is particularly heavy on the west coasts of northern Honshu and in Hokkaido. Here snowfall is heavy as the cold, outblowing winter monsoon from Siberia and Manchuria is warmed and picks up moisture over the sea. In parts of this area winter precipitation is greater than that in summer. Elsewhere in Japan winter is a relatively drier season. Much of the cloud and precipitation is associated with depressions which develop where warm, humid Pacific air meets cold continental air along the North Pacific polar front. Winter weather is variable and changeable over the whole of Japan but particularly so in the north and west.

In summer and early autumn much of the heavy rain is brought by typhoons, or tropical cyclones, which move north from the South China Sea or the region east of the Philippines. In some parts of central and southern Japan there is a double rainfall maximum; one in early summer, the so-called Bai-U or plum rains, and a second in late summer or early autumn, brought by typhoons.

Winters in northern Japan, particularly in Hokkaido, are severe with heavy falls of snow. At sea level the climate is much like that of Newfoundland or northern New England (see the tables for **Hakodate** in southern Hokkaido and **Akita** in northern Honshu).

In the south of Honshu and in Kyushu and Shikoku the winters are mild and almost subtropical. This is particularly so around the coasts of the Inland Sea, the narrow stretch of water which separates these islands. Winter rainfall is light here and snow and frost very rare (see the tables for **Nagasaki** and **Ashizuri**).

In northern Japan the summers are short but quite warm and on the eastern coasts the summers are wetter than winter. In central and southern Japan the summers are very warm but excessively hot days are rare. Because the country is dominated by moist maritime air at this time with frequent cloud, the summer heat is often sultry and oppressive, particularly in Japan's great cities.

In the mountains temperatures are sufficiently reduced by altitude as to be quite pleasant in summer. Here on sunny days in spring and summer conditions can be quite delightful. Compare the climatic table for **Oiwake**, inland in the hills at 3300 ft (1006 m), with that for **Tokyo**, on the coast of central Honshu and representative of some of the major cities of Japan.

In most places in Japan the daily sunshine amounts are only moderate because of the humid atmosphere and abundant rain. They are lowest in Hokkaido and northern Honshu, where they average from two to three hours a day in winter to five or six hours a day in summer. Farther south there is more sunshine with an average of six to seven hours a day around the year. Summer sunshine is often less than that in spring which is a drier season. Spring is perhaps the most pleasant season in Japan; the weather is usually warm and sunny, but fresher and drier than in summer or autumn.

Akita 33 ft (10 m) 39°41′ N 140°06′ E 30 years — JAPAN

	Temperature °F				Temperature °C				Relative humidity		Precipitation			
	Highest recorded	Average daily		Lowest recorded	Highest recorded	Average daily		Lowest recorded	0630 hours	1430 hours	Average monthly		Average no. days with 0.04 in + (1 mm +)	
		max.	min.			max.	min.		%	%	in	mm		
J	57	35	23	−3	14	2	−5	−19	81	73	5.6	142	22	J
F	56	37	23	−12	13	3	−5	−24	82	71	4.1	104	20	F
M	70	42	28	−3	21	6	−2	−19	81	67	4.1	104	18	M
A	77	55	39	19	25	13	4	−7	84	63	4.3	109	12	A
M	86	64	47	29	30	18	8	−2	88	68	4.4	112	11	M
J	93	73	57	39	34	23	14	4	91	71	5.0	127	8	J
J	95	79	65	50	35	26	18	10	95	78	7.8	198	12	J
A	96	83	67	48	36	28	19	9	94	71	7.4	188	9	A
S	93	76	59	38	34	24	15	3	94	71	8.3	211	14	S
O	80	64	47	29	27	18	8	−2	90	65	7.4	188	15	O
N	74	52	37	24	23	11	3	−4	87	70	7.5	191	21	N
D	71	40	28	−2	22	4	−2	−19	80	72	7.0	178	21	D

Ashizuri 213 ft (65 m) 32°44′ N 133°01′ E 12 years — JAPAN

	Temperature °F				Temperature °C				Relative humidity		Precipitation			
	Highest recorded	Average daily		Lowest recorded	Highest recorded	Average daily		Lowest recorded	0600 hours	1400 hours	Average monthly		Average no. days with 0.04 in + (1 mm +)	
		max.	min.			max.	min.		%	%	in	mm		
J	69	53	40	24	21	12	4	−4	68	57	2.5	64	6	J
F	70	53	40	26	21	12	4	−3	69	57	5.6	142	7	F
M	73	59	45	30	23	15	7	−1	70	58	6.3	160	9	M
A	75	66	54	39	24	19	12	4	75	63	7.4	188	8	A
M	82	72	62	49	28	22	17	9	83	71	9.6	244	11	M
J	84	76	67	57	29	24	19	14	89	79	12.7	323	13	J
J	92	83	75	67	33	28	24	19	91	80	10.1	257	13	J
A	94	85	77	68	34	29	25	20	89	77	8.4	213	11	A
S	90	82	72	61	32	28	22	16	85	75	12.7	323	13	S
O	83	73	63	48	28	23	17	9	76	65	11.0	279	9	O
N	79	66	54	38	26	19	12	3	74	63	6.9	175	8	N
D	74	58	45	30	23	14	7	−1	71	61	4.2	107	7	D

	Temperature °F			Temperature °C				Relative humidity		Precipitation		
	Highest recorded	Average daily	Lowest recorded	Highest recorded	Average daily		Lowest recorded	0630 hours	1430 hours	Average monthly		Average no. days with 0.04 in + (1 mm +)
		max. min.			max.	min.		%	%	in	mm	
J	55	32 19	−7	13	0	−7	−22	81	71	2.6	66	13	J
F	51	34 19	−5	11	1	−7	−21	81	69	2.3	58	11	F
M	62	40 26	−2	17	4	−3	−19	80	67	2.6	66	11	M
A	71	51 35	19	22	11	2	−7	81	62	2.8	71	9	A
M	80	59 43	30	27	15	6	−1	85	67	3.3	84	9	M
J	82	65 51	36	28	18	11	2	90	76	3.5	89	9	J
J	90	73 61	43	32	23	16	6	93	79	5.4	137	10	J
A	92	78 64	48	33	26	18	9	93	76	5.1	130	9	A
S	88	72 56	35	31	22	13	2	90	69	7.0	178	13	S
O	80	62 44	25	27	17	7	−4	85	64	4.7	119	11	O
N	71	49 34	11	22	9	1	−12	79	62	4.1	104	13	N
D	61	37 24	−3	16	3	−4	−19	81	72	3.2	81	15	D

	Temperature °F			Temperature °C				Relative humidity		Precipitation		
	Highest recorded	Average daily	Lowest recorded	Highest recorded	Average daily		Lowest recorded	0530 hours	1330 hours	Average monthly		Average no. days with 0.04 in + (1 mm +)
		max. min.			max.	min.		%	%	in	mm	
J	70	49 36	22	21	9	2	−6	74	59	2.8	71	11	J
F	73	50 36	24	23	10	2	−4	75	60	3.3	84	9	F
M	76	57 41	26	24	14	5	−3	74	56	4.9	125	11	M
A	82	66 50	34	28	19	10	1	79	60	7.3	185	11	A
M	85	73 57	42	29	23	14	6	84	65	6.7	170	10	M
J	94	78 65	53	34	26	18	12	88	70	12.3	312	13	J
J	96	85 73	59	36	29	23	15	91	72	10.1	257	10	J
A	98	88 74	63	37	31	23	17	86	65	6.9	175	9	A
S	94	81 68	52	34	27	20	11	83	67	9.8	249	11	S
O	87	72 58	41	31	22	14	5	75	55	4.5	114	6	O
N	81	63 49	33	27	17	9	1	75	59	3.7	94	8	N
D	75	53 40	26	24	12	4	−3	76	63	3.2	81	10	D

Oiwake 3300 ft (1006 m) 36°20′ N 138°33′ E 10 years   JAPAN

| | Temperature °F | | | | Temperature °C | | | | Relative humidity | | Precipitation | | | |
| | Highest recorded | Average daily | | Lowest recorded | Highest recorded | Average daily | | Lowest recorded | 0600 hours | 1400 hours | Average monthly | | Average no. days with 0.04 in + (1 mm +) | |
		max.	min.			max.	min.		%	%	in	mm		
J	58	35	14	−5	14	2	−10	−21	88	49	1.0	25	5	J
F	59	35	14	−1	15	2	−10	−18	91	51	1.7	43	6	F
M	71	43	19	−2	22	6	−7	−19	89	50	2.4	61	7	M
A	80	55	31	13	27	13	−1	−11	90	54	3.3	84	10	A
M	83	65	37	21	28	18	3	−6	88	56	4.0	102	9	M
J	84	69	50	35	29	21	10	2	95	68	6.3	160	13	J
J	91	76	60	45	33	24	16	7	97	72	7.4	188	15	J
A	93	78	64	46	34	26	18	8	96	70	6.1	155	12	A
S	87	71	54	38	31	22	12	3	97	74	6.3	160	14	S
O	78	63	42	26	26	17	6	−3	97	67	5.8	147	10	O
N	70	52	30	19	21	11	−1	−7	92	61	2.2	56	6	N
D	69	41	21	2	21	5	−6	−17	91	59	1.5	38	6	D

Tokyo 19 ft (6 m) 35°41′ N 139°46′ E 60 years   JAPAN

| | Temperature °F | | | | Temperature °C | | | | Relative humidity | | Precipitation | | | |
| | Highest recorded | Average daily | | Lowest recorded | Highest recorded | Average daily | | Lowest recorded | 0630 hours | 1430 hours | Average monthly | | Average no. days with 0.04 in + (1 mm +) | |
		max.	min.			max.	min.		%	%	in	mm		
J	72	47	29	17	22	8	−2	−8	73	48	1.9	48	5	J
F	77	48	31	18	25	9	−1	−8	71	48	2.9	74	6	F
M	77	54	36	22	25	12	2	−6	75	53	4.2	107	10	M
A	85	63	46	30	29	17	8	−1	81	59	5.3	135	10	A
M	88	71	54	36	31	22	12	?	85	62	5.8	147	10	M
J	93	76	63	47	34	24	17	8	89	68	6.5	165	12	J
J	99	83	70	55	37	28	21	13	91	69	5.6	142	10	J
A	101	86	72	60	38	30	22	16	92	66	6.0	152	9	A
S	96	79	66	51	36	26	19	11	91	68	9.2	234	12	S
O	90	69	55	36	32	21	13	2	88	64	8.2	208	11	O
N	81	60	43	26	27	16	6	−3	83	58	3.8	97	7	N
D	74	52	33	20	23	11	1	−7	77	51	2.2	56	5	D

JORDAN

Jordan is a small, almost landlocked, country with an area of about 35,000 square miles (90,000 sq. km). It is bordered by Syria on the north, by Iraq and Saudi Arabia on the east and south and by Israel on the west. In the extreme south at Aqaba it has a short coastline on the Gulf of Aqaba branch of the Red Sea.

The general conditions of climate and weather around the year are similar to those described for Syria on p. 284. About 90 per cent of Jordan is desert with an annual rainfall below 8 in (200 mm) and falling as low as 1–2 in in places. This is part of the great desert of Arabia and Syria. Summers are uniformly hot and sunny, but on occasions the winter weather can be cold with occasional snow on the higher ground. The scanty rainfall occurs in winter and spring, usually as heavy showers.

The northwestern part of the country is hilly with some areas rising to over 3300 ft (1000 m). The altitude and proximity to the Mediterranean make this the wettest and most fertile part of Jordan. Here the annual rainfall varies from as much as 32 in (800 mm) in the higher parts to as little as 12 in (300 mm). The rain mostly falls between November and March (see the table for **Amman**).

On the western side of these mountains there is a long north-to-south valley, much of which is well below Mediterranean level. In this valley the river Jordan flows south to the Dead Sea, the lowest spot on the face of the earth. Here winters are very mild and summers particularly hot while the whole area has a very low rainfall. To the west of the Jordan valley are the hills of Samaria and Judea described for Israel (see the table for **Jerusalem** on p. 249). This area is often called the Occupied West Bank of Palestine; it was part of Jordan between 1949 and 1967, since when it has been occupied and administered by Israel.

Jordan is a very sunny country with average daily sunshine hours ranging from six to seven in winter and as much as twelve to thirteen in summer. Although summer temperatures are high in the desert the heat is usually moderated by low humidity and a stiff daytime breeze while the nights are cool and pleasant. The worst weather is that brought by hot, dry winds from Arabia (the khamsin). These are most likely to blow in early or late summer and last for a day or two at a time. Under these conditions heat stress may be felt.

KAMPUCHEA

Kampuchea, formerly called Cambodia, is a small country in Indo-China about the same size as England. It has a short southwest coastline on the Gulf of Siam. It has landborders with Thailand, Laos and Vietnam on the west, north and east respectively. The general features of the climate of the country are similar to those described for Vietnam on p. 291. There is a small, hilly region in the southwest and the slopes facing the Gulf of Siam have a heavy rainfall. Elsewhere the country is low-lying and rainfall is rather lower than in much of Vietnam.

The dry season from December to April is hot and sunshine averages about 8 hours a day. The main rainy season is much more cloudy; humidity is higher and the weather is then sultry and oppressive. Temperatures remain quite high in the lowlands throughout the year. There may be frequent heat stress as a result of the high temperatures and humidity during the rainy season but this is not usually severe.

Amman 2548 ft(777 m) 31°57′ N 35°57′ E 25 years   **JORDAN**

	Temperature °F			Temperature °C			Relative humidity		Precipitation		
	Highest recorded	Average daily	Lowest recorded	Highest recorded	Average daily	Lowest recorded	0830 hours	1430 hours	Average monthly		Average no. days with 0.04 in + (1 mm +)
		max.	min.			max.	min.		%	%	in	mm	
J	76	54	39	21	24	12	4	−6	80	56	2.7	69	8	J
F	85	56	40	23	29	13	4	−5	78	52	2.9	74	8	F
M	90	60	43	26	32	16	6	−3	57	44	1.2	31	4	M
A	103	73	49	34	39	23	9	1	53	34	0.6	15	3	A
M	105	83	57	41	41	28	14	5	39	28	0.2	5	0.8	M
J	109	87	61	46	43	31	16	8	40	28	0	0	0	J
J	104	89	65	56	40	32	18	13	41	30	0	0	0	J
A	109	90	65	55	43	32	18	13	45	30	0	0	0	A
S	103	88	62	52	39	31	17	11	53	31	0	0	0	S
O	99	81	57	44	37	27	14	7	53	31	0.2	5	1	O
N	91	70	50	35	33	21	10	2	66	40	1.3	33	4	N
D	77	59	42	25	25	15	6	−4	77	53	1.8	46	5	D

Phnom Penh 39 ft(12 m) 10°33′ N 104°55′ E period not known   **KAMPUCHEA**

	Temperature °F			Temperature °C			Relative humidity	Precipitation		
	Highest recorded	Average daily	Lowest recorded	Highest recorded	Average daily	Lowest recorded	All hours	Average monthly		Average no. days with 0.1 in + (2.5 mm +)
		max.	min.			max.	min.	%	in	mm	
J	96	87	70	57	35	31	21	14	71	0.3	7	1	J
F	98	90	72	59	37	32	22	15	71	0.4	10	1	F
M	102	92	74	66	39	34	23	19	70	1.6	40	3	M
A	105	94	76	68	41	35	24	20	73	3.0	77	6	A
M	100	92	76	69	38	34	24	21	81	5.3	134	14	M
J	101	91	76	70	38	33	24	21	81	6.0	155	15	J
J	98	89	75	68	37	32	24	20	83	6.7	171	16	J
A	97	89	76	72	36	32	25	22	83	6.3	160	16	A
S	96	88	76	72	36	31	25	22	85	8.8	224	19	S
O	93	87	76	70	34	30	24	21	83	10.1	257	17	O
N	93	86	74	64	34	30	23	18	79	5.0	127	9	N
D	95	86	71	58	35	30	22	14	74	1.8	45	4	D

KUWAIT

Kuwait is one of the largest of the smaller states of the Arabian peninsula. It has landborders with Iraq and Saudi Arabia and a coastline on the Arabian (Persian) Gulf. It is a low-lying desert country where the average annual rainfall is about 5 in (125 mm). Most rain falls between November and March and there are very few rainy days. Winter temperatures are mild and only occasionally does it feel cold, when northerly or northwesterly winds bring cold air from Iran or Iraq. Summers are uniformly hot and temperatures can rise very high when hot winds blow from the heart of Arabia.

On the coast temperatures are a little lower than inland but the heat is rendered even more uncomfortable by the high humidity. Another unpleasant feature of the weather is the occasional sandstorm when strong winds blow from the interior. As in other parts of Arabia there is some danger of heat exhaustion or even heatstroke during the hottest weather and visitors should take sensible precautions until they have become acclimatized. For more detail see the description for Saudi Arabia on p. 276.

KUWAIT

Kuwait 16 ft (5 m) 29°21′ N 48°00′ E 14 years

	Temperature °F				Temperature °C				Relative humidity		Precipitation		
	Highest recorded	Average daily		Lowest recorded	Highest recorded	Average daily		Lowest recorded	0530 hours	1430 hours	Average monthly		Average no. days with 0.1 in + (2.5 mm +)	
		max.	min.			max.	min.		%	%	in	mm		
J	82	61	49	33	28	16	9	1	77	61	0.9	23	2	J
F	78	65	51	36	26	18	11	2	68	61	0.9	23	2	F
M	90	72	59	40	32	22	15	4	72	61	1.1	28	2	M
A	103	83	68	54	39	28	20	12	67	55	0.2	5	0.9	A
M	109	94	77	60	43	34	25	16	67	55	0	0	0.3	M
J	119	98	82	72	48	37	28	22	62	49	0	0	0	J
J	118	103	86	78	48	39	30	26	45	41	0	0	0	J
A	115	104	86	68	46	40	30	20	50	46	0	0	0	A
S	117	100	81	67	47	38	27	19	52	51	0	0	0	S
O	105	91	73	57	41	33	23	14	64	60	0.1	3	0	O
N	100	77	62	43	38	25	17	6	66	59	0.6	15	1	N
D	79	65	53	36	26	18	12	2	76	65	1.1	28	3	D

Laos is a completely landlocked country of Indo-China, bordered by Burma and China on the north, Vietnam on the east, Kampuchea on the south and Thailand on the west. It is about as large as the United Kingdom and much of the country is rather hilly and mountainous.

The general features of the weather and climate of Laos are similar to those described for Vietnam on p. 291. It has a single rainy season with a maximum rainfall between May and September or October. The rest of the year is dry and rather sunny. Temperatures remain rather high the year round but in the northern

mountains occasional cooler days may come during the winter season of the north monsoon. As in northern Vietnam, cooler cloudier weather at this time is associated with outbreaks of colder continental air from China.

The humidity is significantly lower during the dry season and, in spite of the warmth, the weather is more comfortable and pleasant than during the rather muggy and sultry days of the main monsoon rains. See the tables for **Luang Prabang** and **Vientiane** which are representative of the lower parts of Laos.

Luang Prabang 942 ft (287 m) 19°53′ N 102°08′ E 28 years

		Temperature °F			Temperature °C			Relative humidity		Precipitation			
	Highest recorded	Average daily		Lowest recorded	Highest recorded	Average daily		Lowest recorded	1000 hours	1600 hours	Average monthly		Average no. days with 0.04 in +	
		max.	min.			max.	min.		%	%	in	mm	(1 mm +)	
J	103	82	56	33	39	28	13	1	80	59	0.6	15	2	J
F	102	89	58	46	39	32	14	8	75	49	0.7	18	2	F
M	106	93	63	50	41	34	17	10	68	48	1.2	31	4	M
A	113	96	69	57	45	36	21	14	67	49	4.3	109	8	A
M	111	95	73	63	44	35	23	17	67	57	6.4	163	13	M
J	104	93	74	57	40	34	23	14	71	71	6.1	155	12	J
J	102	90	74	67	39	32	23	19	71	71	9.1	231	17	J
A	104	90	74	57	40	32	23	14	80	76	11.8	300	19	A
S	100	91	73	51	38	33	23	11	73	70	6.5	165	12	S
O	101	89	69	55	38	32	21	13	72	69	3.1	79	7	O
N	97	85	64	43	36	29	18	6	73	67	1.2	31	3	N
D	91	81	59	40	33	27	15	4	79	62	0.5	13	1	D

	Temperature °F				Temperature °C				Relative humidity	Precipitation		
	Highest recorded	Average daily		Lowest recorded	Highest recorded	Average daily		Lowest recorded	All hours	Average monthly		Average no. days with 0.04 in + (1 mm +)
		max.	min.			max.	min.		%	in	mm	
J	95	83	57	39	35	28	14	4	77	0.2	5	1	J
F	98	86	63	46	37	30	17	8	75	0.6	15	2	F
M	104	91	67	54	40	33	19	12	71	1.5	38	4	M
A	103	93	73	63	39	34	23	17	74	3.9	99	7	A
M	102	90	73	69	39	32	23	21	82	10.5	267	15	M
J	96	89	75	70	36	32	24	21	85	11.9	302	17	J
J	94	87	75	70	34	31	24	21	87	10.5	267	18	J
A	98	88	75	70	37	31	24	21	86	11.5	292	18	A
S	95	87	75	70	35	31	24	21	86	11.9	302	16	S
O	94	87	70	55	34	31	21	13	82	4.3	109	7	O
N	94	85	65	51	34	29	18	11	79	0.6	15	1	N
D	92	83	60	41	33	28	16	5	78	0.1	3	1	D

This small mountainous country lies at the eastern end of the Mediterranean. It is bordered by Syria on the north and east and by Israel on the south. With an area of some 3400 square miles (8000 sq. km), it is about the size of Yorkshire or a little smaller than the state of Connecticut. The general weather and climatic conditions of Lebanon are similar to those described for Syria on p. 284. Temperature and precipitation, however, vary greatly from place to place because of the large differences of altitude. Snow lies on the higher mountains until mid-June and some small patches survive throughout the dry, sunny summer.

The country consists of two parallel mountain ranges, running from north to south: the Lebanon Mountains on the west and the Anti-Lebanon range with Mount Hermon on the east. These mountains rise to an average height of over 6000 ft (1800 m) but with summits exceeding 10,000 ft (3000 m). These ranges are separated by a narrow north to south valley, the Bekaa, which is everywhere above 3300 ft (1000 m). There is a very narrow plain along the Mediterranean coast.

Summers are warm to hot with a rather high humidity on the coast so that the nights may be muggy and a little unpleasant. The daytime heat is usually tempered by an afternoon sea breeze. Winters are very mild along the coast (see the table for **Beirut**). Winter rainfall can be heavy on the coast and it turns to snow

on the Lebanon Mountains.

Inland the Bekaa valley and the eastern mountains are much drier; but no part of Lebanon is a desert such as is found extensively in Syria and Jordan. Summers are delightfully sunny, fresh and cool in the mountains where there are numerous summer resorts. From the higher mountain resorts skiing is possible from late December until April or May. It is often said that, in winter and spring, one can ski in the morning and swim in the Mediterranean in the afternoon. Visitors may find the Mediterranean a little cool for swimming before May, however, and to do both in one day requires fairly rapid transit by car on mountain roads!

Conditions inland and in the Bekaa valley are represented by the table for **Ksara**. Winters are drier but cooler than on the coast, with frequent snow and frost.

On the coast and in the Lebanon Mountains the winter rain and snow may be very heavy, and disturbed weather brought by Mediterranean depressions may last for several days at a time. In between these unsettled spells of weather there are long periods when it is fine, mild and sunny. In early and late summer Lebanon is often affected, for a few days at a time, by the hot dry khamsin which blows out of Arabia. These winds bring the hottest days and conditions may then be distinctly unpleasant with danger of heat stress.

Beirut 111 ft (34 m) 33°54′ N 35°28′ E 62 years

	Temperature °F			Temperature °C			Relative humidity		Precipitation			
	Highest recorded	Average daily	Lowest recorded	Highest recorded	Average daily	Lowest recorded	0900 hours	1500 hours	Average monthly		Average no. days with 0.04 in + (1 mm +)	
		max.	min.			max.	min.		%	%	in	mm	
J	77	62	51	31	25	17	11	−1	72	70	7.5	191	15	J
F	87	63	51	30	31	17	11	−1	72	70	6.2	158	12	F
M	97	66	54	36	36	19	12	2	72	69	3.7	94	9	M
A	99	72	58	43	37	22	14	6	72	67	2.2	56	5	A
M	107	78	64	50	42	26	18	10	69	64	0.7	18	2	M
J	104	83	69	56	40	28	21	13	67	61	0.1	3	0.4	J
J	98	87	73	64	37	31	23	18	66	58	0	0	0	J
A	99	89	74	62	37	32	23	17	65	57	0	0	0	A
S	99	86	73	60	37	30	23	16	64	57	0.2	5	1	S
O	101	81	69	52	38	27	21	11	65	62	2.0	51	4	O
N	91	73	61	41	33	23	16	5	67	61	5.2	132	8	N
D	84	65	55	30	29	18	13	−1	70	69	7.3	185	12	D

	Temperature °F				Temperature °C				Relative humidity	Precipitation			
	Highest recorded	Average daily		Lowest recorded	Highest recorded	Average daily		Lowest recorded	All hours	Average monthly		Average no. days with 0.04 in + (1 mm +)	
		max.	min.			max.	min.		%	in	mm		
J	68	51	34	17	20	11	1	−8	78	4.8	122	15	J
F	71	53	37	19	22	12	3	−7	75	6.5	165	12	F
M	82	61	40	26	28	16	4	−3	62	1.9	48	10	M
A	91	69	46	31	33	21	8	−1	55	1.7	43	5	A
M	97	78	52	38	36	26	11	3	50	0.5	13	2	M
J	97	84	57	45	36	29	14	7	45	0	0	0.3	J
J	101	87	61	50	38	31	16	10	44	0	0	0	J
A	104	90	61	50	40	32	16	10	45	0	0	0.1	A
S	103	86	57	44	39	30	14	7	49	0	0	0.5	S
O	93	79	52	39	34	26	11	4	52	0.7	18	4	O
N	86	66	45	30	30	19	7	−1	65	2.7	69	7	N
D	70	55	38	20	21	13	3	−7	76	4.2	107	12	D

The Federation of Malaysia consists of three separate territories: Malaya, Sarawak and Sabah (formerly British North Borneo). Malaya is a narrow mountainous peninsula south of Thailand; Sarawak and Sabah occupy the northern portion of the large island of Borneo and have a landborder with Indonesia. In all three territories the highest mountains rise to over 6500 ft (2000 m).

Situated between 1° and 6° N the whole of Malaysia has an equatorial climate with high temperatures and wet months round the year. The principal differences of climate within the country are those arising from differences of altitude and the exposure of the coastal lowlands to the alternating southwest and northeast monsoon winds. The former blow from April to September and the latter from November to February. There is a brief period of light variable winds during the changeover in March and October. Coasts exposed to the northeast monsoon in Malaysia tend to be wetter than those exposed to the southwest monsoon. Rainfall is well distributed throughout the year and falls on as many as 150 to 200 days almost everywhere. In most places there is a definite double rainy season with the heaviest rains falling in the two periods March to May and September to November. The tables for **Kuching** and **Labuan** in Sarawak and Sabah show that here the period November to March, when the northeast mon-

soon is blowing, is the wettest period.

Temperatures vary little from month to month, humidity is high, and there is no large daily range of temperature so night-time temperatures are oppressive. Temperatures are distinctly lower in the hills where there are a number of resorts but, although there is little stress from temperature in the hills, the higher humidity, greater rain and less sunshine offset this benefit. The tables for **Kuala Lumpur**, which is situated inland at low level, and **Penang** on the west coast are representative of the lowland areas of Malaya. That for **Cameron Highlands** shows the cooler, wetter conditions in the mountains. The table for **Singapore** (see p. 279) is more representative of the east coast of Malaya.

The climate of Malaya is rather oppressive and humid for the unacclimatized visitor but severe heat stress is rare. The worst months are March, April and October when winds are light during the changeover from the southwest to northeast monsoons. During the afternoons conditions on the coast are relieved by sea breezes. Wind speed is the most important influence in Malaysia in mitigating the oppressive sultry heat. Daily hours of sunshine are inversely proportional to amount of rain. They average from four to five hours during the wettest months to eight or nine during the drier periods. As in many other parts of the equatorial regions much of the rain is heavy and accompanied by thunder.

Cameron Highlands 4750 ft (1448 m) 4°28′ N 101°23′ E 26 years **MALAYSIA**

	Temperature °F			Temperature °C			Relative humidity		Precipitation		
Highest recorded	Average daily		Lowest recorded	Highest recorded	Average daily		Lowest recorded	0700 hours	1300 hours	Average monthly		Average no. days with 0.01 in + (0.25 mm +)
	max.	min.			max.	min.		%	%	in	mm	
J	77	71	56	36	25	22	13	2	95	76	6.6	168	17	J
F	79	72	55	40	26	22	13	4	95	73	5.2	132	14	F
M	79	73	55	43	26	23	13	6	97	75	8.5	216	19	M
A	80	74	57	47	27	23	14	8	97	78	11.7	297	23	A
M	79	74	58	45	26	23	14	7	98	79	9.7	246	22	M
J	80	74	56	41	27	23	13	5	97	73	5.5	140	16	J
J	79	73	55	44	26	23	13	7	98	73	4.8	122	15	J
A	78	72	56	45	26	22	13	7	98	76	6.4	163	19	A
S	78	72	57	46	26	22	14	8	98	78	10.3	262	22	S
O	77	72	57	44	25	22	14	7	98	80	13.4	340	26	O
N	78	71	57	44	26	22	14	7	97	81	13.0	330	24	N
D	77	71	56	42	25	22	13	6	96	79	9.0	229	21	D

	Temperature °F			Temperature °C				Relative humidity		Precipitation			
	Highest recorded	Average daily		Lowest recorded	Highest recorded	Average daily		Lowest recorded	0700 hours	1300 hours	Average monthly		Average no. days with 0.01 in + (0.25 mm +)	
		max.	min.			max.	min.		%	%	in	mm		
J	96	90	72	64	36	32	22	18	97	60	6.2	158	14	J
F	98	92	72	68	37	33	22	20	97	60	7.9	201	14	F
M	98	92	73	68	37	33	23	20	97	58	10.2	259	17	M
A	96	91	74	70	36	33	23	21	97	63	11.5	292	20	A
M	97	91	73	69	36	33	23	21	97	66	8.8	224	16	M
J	96	91	72	68	36	33	22	20	96	63	5.1	130	13	J
J	96	90	73	67	36	32	23	19	95	63	3.9	99	12	J
A	96	90	73	68	36	32	23	20	96	62	6.4	163	14	A
S	95	90	73	68	35	32	23	20	96	64	8.6	218	17	S
O	95	89	73	69	35	32	23	21	96	65	9.8	249	20	O
N	95	89	73	69	35	32	23	21	97	66	10.2	259	20	N
D	95	89	72	66	35	32	22	19	97	61	7.5	191	18	D

	Temperature °F			Temperature °C				Relative humidity	Precipitation			
	Highest recorded	Average daily		Lowest recorded	Highest recorded	Average daily		Lowest recorded	1400 hours	Average monthly		Average no. days with 0.004 in + (0.1 mm +)	
		max.	min.			max.	min.		%	in	mm		
J	93	85	72	66	34	29	22	19	75	24.0	610	24	J
F	93	86	72	64	34	30	22	18	74	20.1	510	21	F
M	93	88	73	69	34	31	23	21	73	12.9	328	22	M
A	96	90	73	69	36	32	23	21	71	11.0	279	20	A
M	95	90	73	70	35	32	23	21	70	10.3	262	21	M
J	96	91	73	67	36	33	23	19	66	7.1	180	15	J
J	97	90	72	67	36	32	22	19	66	7.7	196	18	J
A	96	91	72	65	36	33	22	18	68	9.2	234	19	A
S	94	89	72	66	34	32	22	19	70	8.6	218	20	S
O	94	89	73	69	34	32	23	21	71	10.5	267	24	O
N	93	88	72	69	34	31	22	21	74	14.1	358	26	N
D	92	87	72	69	33	31	22	21	75	18.2	462	25	D

Labuan (Sabah) 58 ft (18 m) 5°17′ N 115°16′ E 20 years — MALAYSIA

	Temperature °F			Temperature °C			Relative humidity		Precipitation		
	Highest recorded	Average daily	Lowest recorded	Highest recorded	Average daily	Lowest recorded	0930 hours	1530 hours	Average monthly		Average no. days with 0.01 in + (0.25 mm +)
		max.	min.			max.	min.		%	%	in	mm	
J	92	86	76	68	33	30	24	20	85	81	4.4	112	9	J
F	92	86	76	68	33	30	24	20	86	81	4.6	117	11	F
M	93	87	76	63	34	31	24	17	85	80	5.9	150	10	M
A	95	89	76	60	35	32	24	16	85	78	11.7	297	15	A
M	96	89	76	59	36	32	24	15	85	79	13.6	345	19	M
J	94	88	76	60	34	31	24	16	85	78	13.8	351	16	J
J	93	88	77	68	34	31	25	20	85	78	12.5	318	15	J
A	94	88	76	68	34	31	24	20	82	76	11.7	297	17	A
S	92	87	76	64	33	31	24	18	83	77	16.4	417	18	S
O	94	87	76	63	34	31	24	17	83	78	18.3	465	21	O
N	93	87	76	69	34	31	24	21	83	78	16.5	419	21	N
D	93	86	76	69	34	30	24	21	84	79	11.2	285	19	D

Penang 17 ft (5 m) 5°25′ N 100°19′ E 48 years — MALAYSIA

	Temperature °F			Temperature °C			Relative humidity		Precipitation		
	Highest recorded	Average daily	Lowest recorded	Highest recorded	Average daily	Lowest recorded	0830 hours	1430 hours	Average monthly		Average no. days with 0.01 in + (0.25 mm +)
		max.	min.			max.	min.		%	%	in	mm	
J	98	90	73	66	37	32	23	19	75	68	3.7	94	8	J
F	97	91	73	66	36	33	23	19	74	64	3.1	79	7	F
M	98	92	74	67	37	33	23	19	75	64	5.6	142	11	M
A	98	91	75	67	37	33	24	19	79	66	7.4	188	14	A
M	96	90	74	67	36	32	23	19	78	66	10.7	272	16	M
J	97	90	74	68	36	32	23	20	77	67	7.7	196	12	J
J	95	90	74	69	35	32	23	21	77	67	7.5	191	12	J
A	96	89	73	69	36	32	23	21	78	67	11.6	295	15	A
S	98	88	73	68	37	31	23	20	80	69	15.8	401	18	S
O	94	89	73	67	34	32	23	19	81	70	16.9	429	21	O
N	95	88	73	65	35	31	23	18	79	71	11.9	302	19	N
D	95	89	73	67	35	32	23	19	76	68	5.8	147	11	D

MONGOLIA

The Mongolian People's Republic is a large but very sparsely populated country in the heart of Asia. It is bordered by the USSR on the north and by China on the south. With an area of 604,000 square miles (1,565,000 sq. km), it is almost three times the size of France yet it has a population of a little over a million. In the west and north there are mountains rising to over 10,000 ft (3000 m) but there are extensive areas of flat or undulating plains which are desert in the south and steppe grassland in the north and east.

Mongolia has an extreme continental type of climate similar to that of south-central Siberia or Manchuria. Winters are long and very cold. There is a swift transition in April to a short, warm summer and an equally rapid return to the winter cold in October. Rainfall is everywhere low; probably no more than 15–20 in (375–500 mm) a year in the mountains and as little as 5 in (125 mm) in the drier lowland parts. Winter is almost entirely dry, with occasional light snow, except in the western mountains where snow is heavier. The wetter parts receive almost all their precipitation between June and September when moist air is able to penetrate the interior under the influence of the Chinese summer monsoon.

The table for **Ulan Bator** shows conditions over much of the country, but southern Mongolia receives even less rain. Conditions during the short summer are quite pleasant, but during the long, cold winter very warm clothing is required and, when strong winds arise, wind chill can be very severe. On many days during the winter, however, winds are light, the sky is clear and there is abundant sunshine.

NEPAL

This small mountainous country lies on the southern side of the Himalayan Mountains between Tibet to the north and India to the south. It includes within, or along its northern border, some of the highest mountains in the world; Everest rises to 29,028 ft (8848 m). The country is only between 100 and 150 miles (160 and 240 km) wide from north to south and in this distance the altitude decreases from the high Himalayan peaks to the lowlands of the Terai in the plain region of northern India. There is thus in Nepal a range of climatic conditions from tropical forest or jungle to the permanent snowfields and glaciers of the Himalayas.

The weather and climate are controlled by the same general features as those described on p. 229 for India: the seasonal alternation of the monsoon winds. The main rainy season in Nepal is from late June to September. This is a period of warm to hot temperatures, much cloud and frequent heavy rain. At this time sunshine averages only two to three hours a day. During the rest of the year the weather is much more settled and pleasant. The days are mild or even warm, except on the higher mountains, and sunshine averages from six to nine hours a day.

The table for **Katmandu** illustrates conditions in the valleys and in the Himalayan foothill region where the majority of the population live. Rainfall in Nepal decreases from east to west so that the tables for **Darjeeling** (p. 230) and **Simla** (p. 231) in India are representative of the east and west of the country respectively. They also indicate better than the table for **Katmandu** the likely temperature conditions in the more highly populated regions of Nepal.

Apart from some danger of flooding during the heaviest rains, the climate of Nepal is rarely hazardous and for much of the year is very pleasant.

Ulan Bator 4347 ft (1325 m) 47°55′ N 106°50′ E 12 years — MONGOLIA

	Temperature °F				Temperature °C				Relative humidity		Precipitation			
	Highest recorded	Average daily		Lowest recorded	Highest recorded	Average daily		Lowest recorded	0700 hours	1300 hours	Average monthly		Average no. days with 0.04 in + (1 mm +)	
		max.	min.			max.	min.		%	%	in	mm		
J	21	−2	−26	−47	−6	−19	−32	−44	81	73	0	0	1	J
F	35	9	−21	−48	2	−13	−29	−44	78	66	0	0	1	F
M	64	25	−7	−39	18	−4	−22	−39	78	61	0.1	3	2	M
A	76	44	17	−11	24	7	−8	−24	64	42	0.2	5	2	A
M	86	55	29	10	30	13	−2	−12	64	40	0.4	10	4	M
J	97	69	44	24	36	21	7	−4	68	44	1.1	28	5	J
J	92	71	51	34	33	22	11	1	77	54	3.0	76	10	J
A	91	69	46	20	33	21	8	−7	76	49	2.0	51	8	A
S	83	58	35	13	28	14	2	−11	78	43	0.9	23	3	S
O	73	43	18	−16	23	6	−8	−27	77	48	0.2	5	2	O
N	52	22	−4	−32	11	−6	−20	−36	82	57	0.2	5	2	N
D	32	3	−19	−45	0	−16	−28	−43	88	75	0.1	3	1	D

Katmandu 4388 ft (1338 m) 27°42′ N 85°12′ E 9 years — NEPAL

	Temperature °F				Temperature °C				Relative humidity		Precipitation			
	Highest recorded	Average daily		Lowest recorded	Highest recorded	Average daily		Lowest recorded	0800 hours	1700 hours	Average monthly		Average no. days with 0.1 in + (2.5 mm +)	
		max.	min.			max.	min.		%	%	in	mm		
J	77	65	35	28	25	18	2	−2	89	70	0.6	15	1	J
F	77	67	39	31	25	19	4	−1	90	68	1.6	41	5	F
M	92	77	45	35	33	25	7	2	73	53	0.9	23	2	M
A	95	83	53	40	35	28	12	4	68	54	2.3	58	6	A
M	96	86	61	50	36	30	16	10	72	61	4.8	122	10	M
J	97	85	67	58	36	29	19	14	79	72	9.7	246	15	J
J	91	84	68	64	33	29	20	18	86	82	14.7	373	21	J
A	92	83	68	63	33	28	20	17	87	84	13.6	345	20	A
S	92	83	66	56	33	28	19	13	86	83	6.1	155	12	S
O	92	80	56	43	33	27	13	6	88	81	1.5	38	4	O
N	83	74	45	31	28	23	7	−1	90	78	0.3	8	1	N
D	76	67	37	29	24	19	3	−2	89	73	0.1	3	0.2	D

NORTH KOREA

The Democratic People's Republic of North Korea occupies the northern half of the Korean peninsula. It has a relatively long landborder, along the Yalu river, with the Chinese province of Manchuria. The north is a mountainous region with many areas rising between 6000 and 8000 ft (1800 and 2450 m).

The general features of the weather and climate of North Korea are described in more detail on p. 280 for South Korea. This account indicates in what ways the conditions in North Korea differ from those in the south.

The climate of North Korea is rather more continental and extreme than that of the south. This is because it has a long landborder and is more open to cold winds which blow from Manchuria and Siberia in winter. Conditions in winter can be very cold; rivers freeze up for between three and four months and ice forms along the coast, blocking harbours and impeding navigation. Snow falls on as many as thirty-seven days at **Pyongyang** and on many more days in the far north. In the north there may be as many as 200 days with frost a year. The summer months are generally warm but, in the far north, summers are not warm enough for rice to be grown.

The tables for **Wonsan** on the east coast, and **Pyongyang** in a lowland area near the west coast, show that there is no very great difference between temperatures and rainfall throughout the year from one side of the country to the other.

The most unpleasant feature of the weather and climate of North Korea is undoubtedly the extreme cold and frequent wind chill in winter. Warm clothing is necessary at this time.

Pyongyang 89 ft (27 m) 39°01′ N 125°49′ E 42 years **NORTH KOREA**

	Temperature °F			Temperature °C			Relative humidity	Precipitation		
	Highest recorded	Average daily	Lowest recorded	Highest recorded	Average daily	Lowest recorded	All hours	Average monthly		Average no. days with 0.04 in + (1 mm +)
		max.	min.			max.	min.		%	in	mm	
J	—	27	8	—	—	−3	−13	—	74	0.6	15	3	J
F	—	33	14	—	—	1	−10	—	70	0.4	11	3	F
M	—	44	26	—	—	7	−4	—	66	1.0	25	4	M
A	—	60	38	—	—	16	3	—	63	1.8	46	5	A
M	—	71	49	—	—	22	9	—	66	2.6	67	7	M
J	—	80	59	—	—	26	15	—	71	3.0	76	7	J
J	—	83	68	—	—	29	20	—	80	9.3	237	12	J
A	—	84	68	—	—	29	20	—	80	9.0	228	10	A
S	—	76	56	—	—	24	14	—	75	4.4	112	7	S
O	—	64	42	—	—	18	6	—	73	1.8	45	6	O
N	—	47	29	—	—	9	−2	—	73	1.6	41	7	N
D	—	32	15	—	—	0	−10	—	74	0.8	21	4	D

Wonsan 120 ft (37 m) 39°11′ N 127°26′ E 29 years **NORTH KOREA**

	Temperature °F			Temperature °C			Relative humidity		Precipitation		
	Highest recorded	Average daily	Lowest recorded	Highest recorded	Average daily	Lowest recorded	0530 hours	1330 hours	Average monthly		Average no. days with 0.04 in + (1 mm +)
		max.	min.			max.	min.		%	%	in	mm	
J	54	34	17	−7	12	1	−8	−22	57	42	1.2	31	5	J
F	58	36	20	−3	14	2	−7	−19	67	47	1.4	36	4	F
M	76	45	29	4	24	7	−2	−16	65	46	1.9	48	5	M
A	88	59	40	24	31	15	4	−4	72	49	2.8	71	6	A
M	99	69	50	34	37	21	10	1	72	50	3.5	89	7	M
J	101	75	59	45	38	24	15	7	84	62	4.9	124	9	J
J	103	80	67	53	39	27	19	12	89	72	10.8	274	14	J
A	100	81	68	52	38	27	20	11	92	73	12.5	318	13	A
S	94	74	58	39	34	23	14	4	88	65	7.0	178	9	S
O	87	65	47	29	31	18	8	−2	77	53	3.0	76	6	O
N	76	51	34	8	24	11	1	−13	67	50	2.6	66	5	N
D	64	38	23	−4	18	3	−5	−20	65	49	1.2	31	3	D

OMAN

This small Arab state occupies the northeastern corner of the Arabian peninsula. It has coastlines on the Gulf of Oman to the north and the Arabian Sea to the south. Inland it is bordered by the United Arab Emirates, Saudi Arabia and the People's Democratic Republic of Yemen.

The northern part of Oman consists of the Jebel Akhdar, a mountain range rising to just over 10,000 ft (3000 m). The annual rainfall on the higher parts of Jebel Akhdar probably exceeds 20 in (400 mm). In the rest of Oman the annual rainfall is below 5 in (125 mm) except in the hills of Dhofar in the extreme south. Along the south coast the cloudy rainy season is between June and September, but in the Jebel Akhdar and in the lowlands of the north rain may fall at any time of the year. Very occasionally a tropical cyclone in the Arabian Sea brings a spell of very wet, windy weather to the coast of Oman and this may cause damage through wind and flood.

Temperatures and humidity are high throughout the year on the coast and the period May to September is the hottest and most unpleasant season. Temperatures rise even higher inland towards the Rub al Khali, but here humidity is lower so that the high temperatures are more tolerable and the nights are cooler. Unless sensible precautions are taken there is a danger of heat exhaustion or even heatstroke during the hottest weather. Sunshine amounts are high throughout the year. See the table for **Muscat** and details for Saudi Arabia on p. 276.

OMAN — **Muscat** 15 ft (5 m) 23°37′ N 58°35′ E 24 years

	Temperature °F			Temperature °C			Relative humidity		Precipitation			
	Highest recorded	Average daily	Lowest recorded	Highest recorded	Average daily	Lowest recorded	0800 hours	1600 hours	Average monthly		Average no. days with 0.01 in + (0.25 mm +)	
		max.	min.			max.	min.		%	%	in	mm	
J	87	77	66	51	31	25	19	11	72	71	1.1	28	2	J
F	90	77	67	53	32	25	19	12	73	73	0.7	18	1	F
M	107	83	72	62	42	28	22	17	71	70	0.4	10	1	M
A	105	90	78	66	41	32	26	19	64	68	0.4	10	1	A
M	112	98	86	75	44	37	30	24	58	60	0	0	0	M
J	116	100	88	78	47	38	31	26	72	72	0.1	3	0	J
J	113	97	87	77	45	36	31	25	77	77	0	0	0	J
A	108	92	84	75	42	33	29	24	82	80	0	0	0	A
S	107	93	83	73	42	34	28	23	75	77	0	0	0	S
O	105	93	80	69	41	34	27	21	69	74	0.1	3	0	O
N	96	86	73	62	36	30	23	17	69	72	0.4	10	1	N
D	92	79	68	60	33	20	20	16	70	71	0.7	18	2	D

Pakistan is a large country, about one and a half times the size of France. It is situated in the northwestern part of the great Indian subcontinent. Its western border with Iran and Afghanistan is mountainous and its short northern border with China and its northeastern border with India in the Pamir and Karakoram ranges includes some of the higher Himalayan peaks. On the south and east it has a long border with the Punjab and Sind provinces of India; this is a region of low-lying plains, part of the great Indus valley.

Most of the country has a climate dominated by the influence of the great seasonal wind reversal called the Asiatic monsoon. (For a fuller description of this see p. 229 for India.) The year may be divided into three principal seasons. From mid-October until late February is the cool season when the weather is generally pleasant, sunny and quite warm by day but with chilly nights and occasional frost. The northern and western parts of the country receive some rain at this time, brought by depressions moving in from the west. Conditions in the higher mountains at this time are distinctly cold. The hottest season is from early March until late June. During this period midday temperatures in the south and centre of the country rise to very high levels. The heat is distinctly unpleasant in spite of the low humidity. Some occasional rain, usually of a showery, thundery type, may occur at this time. Such brief storms are often preceded or accompanied by dust storms. The rainy season over most of the country is from late June until early October. This is the season of the southwest monsoon and although temperatures are a little lower the higher humidity can cause discomfort.

Not all parts of Pakistan are equally wet during the rainy season. The desert region of the south and southeast receives little rain at this time and is sunny and hot; see the table for **Jacobabad** which has the reputation of being one of the hottest places in the world from April until September. **Karachi**, on the coast of the Arabian Sea, also gets little rain and, although cooler than inland, has a very unpleasant climate at this time because of the higher humidity. The mountainous regions of the north and west of the country receive much less rain during the period of the southwest monsoon and may be wetter during the cooler winter season; see the table for **Peshawar** which has a sequence of weather throughout the year more like that found in Iran to the west. It is in the eastern and central plains of the country that the full effect of the monsoon rains is felt. Here the climate throughout the year is more akin to that found in the northern plains of India (see the table for **Islamabad**).

Sunshine amounts are high around the year in most of Pakistan, ranging from six to seven hours a day in the cool season to ten to twelve during the hot season. There is an increase in cloudiness over most of the country during the wet season even though rainfall amounts may be small in some areas. For example, in July and August daily sunshine hours average only four or five at **Karachi** even though the rainfall is much less than in the north of the country.

Snowfall is heavy on the higher mountains in the north but reliable measurements of its actual depth are not available. The melting snow from these mountains, together with the heavy summer rainfall from the monsoon, feeds the five great rivers of the Punjab plains which unite to form the Indus. Were it not for the irrigation flow from these rivers much of the Punjab and Sind lowlands would be a more extensive desert than is, in fact, the case.

In the hottest parts of Pakistan there is a danger of heat exhaustion or even heatstroke during the hot season and visitors should allow themselves a few days to become acclimatized before engaging in strenuous exercise. The heat is often so great that, without air conditioning, indoor temperatures at night are very uncomfortable. (See map p. 228.)

	Temperature °F				Temperature °C				Relative humidity	Precipitation		
	Highest recorded	Average daily		Lowest recorded	Highest recorded	Average daily		Lowest recorded	1200 hours	Average monthly		Average no. days with 0.01 in + (2.5 mm +)
		max.	min.			max.	min.		%	in	mm	
J	75	61	36	25	24	16	2	−4	44	2.5	64	7	J
F	88	66	43	28	31	19	6	−2	46	2.5	64	6	F
M	97	75	50	34	36	24	10	1	37	3.2	81	7	M
A	111	88	59	45	44	31	15	7	26	1.7	42	6	A
M	115	99	70	54	46	37	21	12	19	0.9	23	4	M
J	118	104	77	57	48	40	25	14	23	2.2	55	7	J
J	115	97	77	63	46	36	25	17	45	9.2	233	13	J
A	108	93	75	57	42	34	24	14	54	10.2	258	10	A
S	102	93	70	54	39	34	21	12	44	3.3	85	5	S
O	100	90	59	45	38.	32.	15	7	29	0.8	21	2	O
N	90	82	48	30	32	28	9	−1	26	0.5	12	1	N
D	81	68	37	27	27	20	3	−3	39	0.9	23	3	D

	Temperature °F				Temperature °C				Relative humidity		Precipitation		
	Highest recorded	Average daily		Lowest recorded	Highest recorded	Average daily		Lowest recorded	0800 hours	1600 hours	Average monthly		Average no. days with 0.1 in + (2.5 mm +)
		max.	min.			max.	min.		%	%	in	mm	
J	83	73	44	32	28	23	7	0	65	34	0.2	5	0.7	J
F	98	77	49	30	37	25	9	−1	54	35	0.3	8	0.9	F
M	110	91	61	44	43	33	16	7	45	31	0.2	5	0.7	M
A	116	102	71	52	47	39	22	11	41	30	0.2	5	0.5	A
M	123	111	78	62	51	44	26	17	43	27	0.1	3	0.4	M
J	127	114	85	72	53	46	29	22	57	31	0.3	8	0.3	J
J	126	109	86	76	52	43	30	24	65	42	0.9	23	1	J
A	117	104	83	68	47	40	28	20	71	49	0.9	23	1	A
S	113	103	76	60	45	39	24	16	68	40	0.2	5	0.3	S
O	108	99	66	51	42	37	19	11	56	31	0	0	0.1	O
N	99	87	53	39	37	31	12	4	56	29	0	0	0.1	N
D	83	75	45	33	28	24	7	1	63	31	0.2	5	0.5	D

Karachi 13 ft (4 m) 24°48′ N 66°59′ E 43 years   **PAKISTAN**

	Temperature °F			Temperature °C			Relative humidity		Precipitation			
	Highest recorded	Average daily	Lowest recorded	Highest recorded	Average daily	Lowest recorded	0800 hours	1600 hours	Average monthly		Average no. days with 0.1 in + (2.5 mm +)	
		max.	min.			max.	min.		%	%	in	mm	
J	89	77	55	40	32	25	13	4	63	45	0.5	13	1	J
F	93	79	58	43	34	26	14	6	72	49	0.4	10	1	F
M	106	85	67	47	41	29	19	8	79	57	0.3	8	1	M
A	111	90	73	57	44	32	23	14	87	62	0.1	3	0.2	A
M	118	93	79	65	48	34	26	18	88	68	0.1	3	0.1	M
J	114	93	82	68	46	34	28	20	86	69	0.7	18	1	J
J	110	91	81	73	43	33	27	23	88	73	3.2	81	2	J
A	99	88	79	73	37	31	26	23	90	74	1.6	41	2	A
S	106	88	77	69	41	31	25	21	89	71	0.5	13	1	S
O	108	91	72	57	42	33	22	14	83	57	0	0	0.1	O
N	100	87	64	48	38	31	18	9	68	49	0.1	3	0.3	N
D	91	80	57	39	33	27	14	4	64	45	0.2	5	1	D

Peshawar 1161 ft (354 m) 34°01′ N 71°34′ E 30 years   **PAKISTAN**

	Temperature °F			Temperature °C			Relative humidity		Precipitation			
	Highest recorded	Average daily	Lowest recorded	Highest recorded	Average daily	Lowest recorded	0800 hours	1530 hours	Average monthly		Average no. days with 0.1 in + (2.5 mm +)	
		max.	min.			max.	min.		%	%	in	mm	
J	76	63	40	26	24	17	4	−3	73	45	1.4	36	3	J
F	86	66	43	31	30	19	6	−1	75	43	1.5	38	3	F
M	93	75	52	36	34	24	11	2	68	43	2.4	61	5	M
A	108	85	60	41	42	29	16	5	59	39	1.8	46	4	A
M	118	98	70	52	48	37	21	11	41	28	0.8	20	2	M
J	120	106	77	65	49	41	25	18	43	25	0.3	8	1	J
J	122	103	79	69	50	39	26	21	61	38	1.3	33	2	J
A	118	99	78	68	48	37	26	20	70	45	2.0	51	3	A
S	110	96	71	58	43	36	22	14	65	39	0.8	20	2	S
O	101	88	58	52	38	31	14	11	60	32	0.2	5	1	O
N	91	77	46	33	33	25	8	1	63	40	0.3	8	1	N
D	83	67	39	28	28	19	4	−2	73	42	0.7	18	2	D

PHILIPPINES

The Republic of the Philippines consists of an archipelago of over 7000 islands in the western Pacific situated between 4° and 21° N. The largest islands are, from north to south; Luzon, Samar, Leyte, Panay, Palawan and Mindanao. They support most of the population and the main cities. All the larger islands are mountainous and have very indented coastlines so that the country has a rugged and confused relief. There are many mountain ranges and isolated peaks rising to between 6000 and 10,000 ft (1800 and 3000 m). The area of the country is 116,000 square miles (300,000 sq. km), rather larger than Great Britain.

The southern islands have an almost equatorial climate with significant rain around the year (see the table for **Zamboanga** on Mindanao). The central and northern islands have a tropical monsoon type of climate, similar to that of Indo-China, with a single season of heavy rain. In most areas the wettest time is from July to October when the wind system of the western Pacific is affected by the monsoonal influence of the Asian continent. Winds are then southwesterly to southeasterly (see the tables for **Manila** in Luzon and **Iloilo** on Panay island).

Rainfall is particularly heavy in the period August to October when much of it comes from tropical cyclones, called typhoons, in the South China Sea. The severest of these typhoons produce very high wind speeds and torrential rain. Most of them develop east of the Philippines and move westwards into the South China Sea where they deepen and intensify. A number of typhoons affect some part of the Philippines each year and the most severe cause widespread damage and loss of life through flooding and landslides, as well as wind damage.

Annual rainfall is over 40 in (1000 mm) almost everywhere, and where warm, damp Pacific air is forced to rise over coastal mountains annual rainfall often exceeds 160–200 in (4000–5000 mm). Coasts facing northeast are exposed to the Pacific trade winds between November and March and these areas have their heaviest rainfall at this time (see table for **Surigao** on the eastern side of Mindanao island).

Temperatures remain fairly high throughout the year except in the mountains, but excessive heat is rare. The worst feature of the climate, apart from the occasional typhoon, is the high humidity and cloud during the rainy season; on many days the weather is muggy and oppressive. In the dry season the weather is more pleasant with much sunshine, up to seven or eight hours a day on average, with refreshing sea breezes on the coast.

There are a number of mountain resorts, such as Baguio, the summer capital, on Luzon island. Although temperatures may be much lower here, rain and cloud increase.

Iloilo 46 ft (14 m) 10°42′ N 122°34′ E 15 years   **PHILIPPINES**

	Temperature °F			Temperature °C			Relative humidity		Precipitation			
	Highest recorded	Average daily	Lowest recorded	Highest recorded	Average daily	Lowest recorded	0600 hours	1400 hours	Average monthly		Average no. days with 0.04 in + (1 mm +)	
		max.	min.			max.	min.		%	%	in	mm	
J	92	85	73	68	33	29	23	20	91	68	2.5	64	9	J
F	96	87	74	68	36	31	23	20	90	63	1.8	46	5	F
M	95	88	74	68	35	31	23	20	89	59	1.3	33	4	M
A	98	92	76	71	37	33	24	22	89	59	1.7	43	5	A
M	98	91	77	72	37	33	25	22	90	67	6.2	158	13	M
J	96	89	76	71	36	32	24	22	92	71	10.4	264	16	J
J	95	87	76	72	35	31	24	22	90	75	17.6	447	20	J
A	94	87	76	72	34	31	24	22	91	74	15.2	386	18	A
S	97	88	76	72	36	31	24	22	91	75	12.4	315	17	S
O	94	88	75	69	34	31	24	21	92	73	10.6	269	16	O
N	95	87	75	69	35	31	24	21	93	72	8.3	211	13	N
D	93	86	74	67	34	30	23	19	93	70	4.7	119	11	D

Manila 47 ft (14 m) 14°35′ N 120°59′ E 60 years   **PHILIPPINES**

	Temperature °F			Temperature °C			Relative humidity		Precipitation			
	Highest recorded	Average daily	Lowest recorded	Highest recorded	Average daily	Lowest recorded	0600 hours	1300 hours	Average monthly		Average no. days with 0.01 in + (0.25 mm +)	
		max.	min.			max.	min.		%	%	in	mm	
J	95	86	69	58	35	30	21	14	89	63	0.9	23	6	J
F	96	88	69	60	36	31	21	16	88	59	0.5	13	3	F
M	98	91	71	61	37	33	22	16	85	55	0.7	18	4	M
A	100	93	73	63	38	34	23	17	85	55	1.3	33	4	A
M	101	93	75	68	38	34	24	20	88	61	5.1	130	12	M
J	100	91	75	71	38	33	24	22	91	68	10.0	254	17	J
J	97	88	75	69	36	31	24	21	91	74	17.0	432	24	J
A	95	87	75	69	35	31	24	21	92	73	16.6	422	23	A
S	95	88	75	69	35	31	24	21	93	73	14.0	356	22	S
O	95	88	74	67	35	31	23	19	92	71	7.6	193	19	O
N	93	87	72	62	34	31	22	17	91	69	5.7	145	14	N
D	94	86	70	60	34	30	21	16	90	67	2.6	66	11	D

	Temperature °F			Temperature °C			Relative humidity		Precipitation		
	Highest recorded	Average daily	Lowest recorded	Highest recorded	Average daily	Lowest recorded	0630 hours	1430 hours	Average monthly		Average no. days with 0.04 in + (1 mm +)
		max.	min.			max.	min.		%	%	in	mm	
J	88	83	74	67	31	28	23	19	93	80	21.4	544	24	J
F	90	84	73	68	32	29	23	20	93	77	14.8	376	18	F
M	90	85	74	68	32	29	23	20	93	76	19.9	506	21	M
A	92	87	74	69	33	31	23	21	95	76	10.0	254	19	A
M	95	88	76	70	35	31	24	21	94	72	6.2	158	13	M
J	97	88	76	70	36	31	24	21	94	70	4.9	125	10	J
J	94	88	76	71	34	31	24	22	89	68	7.0	178	13	J
A	96	88	76	72	36	31	24	22	89	66	5.1	130	11	A
S	99	88	76	72	37	31	24	22	90	68	6.6	168	13	S
O	94	87	75	70	34	31	24	21	91	73	10.7	272	17	O
N	92	85	75	70	33	29	24	21	94	78	16.8	427	20	N
D	91	83	74	66	33	28	23	19	94	80	24.4	620	24	D

	Temperature °F			Temperature °C			Relative humidity		Precipitation		
	Highest recorded	Average daily	Lowest recorded	Highest recorded	Average daily	Lowest recorded	0600 hours	1400 hours	Average monthly		Average no. days with 0.04 in + (1 mm +)
		max.	min.			max.	min.		%	%	in	mm	
J	95	88	73	66	35	31	23	19	92	70	2.1	53	5	J
F	94	88	73	66	34	31	23	19	92	71	2.2	56	5	F
M	95	89	74	68	35	32	23	20	92	70	1.5	38	5	M
A	96	88	74	69	36	31	23	21	93	74	2.0	51	6	A
M	95	88	75	72	35	31	24	22	93	76	3.5	89	9	M
J	95	88	75	71	35	31	24	22	94	77	4.2	107	12	J
J	95	87	74	70	35	31	23	21	94	77	4.9	125	12	J
A	95	88	75	70	35	31	24	21	93	75	4.0	102	10	A
S	95	88	74	70	35	31	23	21	94	76	4.7	119	11	S
O	95	88	74	70	35	31	23	21	93	76	5.6	142	11	O
N	95	88	74	68	35	31	23	20	94	75	4.2	107	11	N
D	94	89	73	67	34	32	23	19	93	73	3.4	86	9	D

This small Arab country consists of a low-lying peninsula on the north coast of Saudi Arabia. It is surrounded by the waters of the Arabian (Persian) Gulf on three sides. It has a climate similar to that of Bahrain (p. 210) and the United Arab Emirates (p. 290). It is very hot and rainless from May until September with occasional showery rain during the rest of the year. Winter temperatures are mild to warm and the weather is then generally sunny and pleasant. In summer conditions are often unpleasantly hot with some danger of heat exhaustion or heatstroke. Conditions on the coast are made even more unpleasant by the high humidity which more than cancels the slightly lower temperatures. The climatic tables for **Bahrain** (p. 210) and **Sharjah**, United Arab Emirates (p. 290) are representative of conditions throughout the year in Qatar. For more detail about the weather and climate of Arabia see the description for Saudi Arabia on p. 276.

SAUDI ARABIA

Saudi Arabia comprises the greater part of the Arabian peninsula. It is a large country, most of which is desert. It is bordered on the north by Jordan and Iraq. In the east of Saudi Arabia there is a short coastline on the Arabian (Persian) Gulf but there are landborders with the small Gulf states of Kuwait, Qatar, the United Arab Emirates and Oman. There is a long landborder with Oman and with the People's Democratic Republic of Yemen on the south. In the southwest of the peninsula it borders the Yemen Arab Republic, to the north of which it has a long coastline on the Red Sea. The general features of the weather and climate of Arabia are described here and only briefer descriptions of the other states of the peninsula are given under the separate country headings.

Most of Arabia is desert with a low and unreliable rainfall. Where the rainfall is greater, this is a result of higher mountainous areas where the lower temperatures produce some relief from the fierce, dry summer heat. Most of the peninsula consists of a rolling plateau of low to medium elevation which slopes northeastwards from a higher mountainous rim on the west to a low plain on the shores of the Gulf.

In the southwest the mountains of the Asir province of Saudi Arabia and of the Yemen rise to between 8000 and 12,000 ft (2400 and 3600 m). In the northeast of the peninsula the Jebel Akhdar mountains of Oman rise to just over 10,000 ft (3000 m). Along the south coast of the peninsula there is a narrow coastal plain on the Arabian Sea. This is separated from the sandy desert of the Rub al Khali by ranges of hills in Hadhramaut and Dhofar. At the foot of the western mountains there is a narrow coastal plain fronting the Red Sea, behind which there is a steep rise inland so that the climate of the plain is hotter and more humid than that found inland.

Only in the higher areas, the mountains of Yemen and Oman, does the annual rainfall exceed 20 in (400 mm). Elsewhere it is low and unreliable; below 8 in (200 mm) and often less than 4 in (100 mm). North of **Jidda**, **Riyadh** and **Muscat** rainfall is almost confined to the period from November to April or May and is brought by weak disturbances coming from the Mediterranean or North Africa. In the southern part of Arabia and particularly in the mountains of Yemen and Oman some rain may fall in any month; along the south coast and in the Yemen mountains it falls mainly in the period May to October when it is associated with the southwest monsoon which dominates the Arabian Sea and India at this time.

Over much of Arabia, with the exception of the mountains, temperatures during the period May to September rise very high and this is one of the few areas of the world where temperatures above 120° F (48° C) are not unusual. Inland the daytime humidity falls quite low and there is usually a sharp drop of temperature at night. Although midday temperatures do not rise so high on the coast conditions here may be even more uncomfortable because of the high humidity; the nights are particularly unpleasant. This can be seen by comparing the tables for **Riyadh** and **Jidda** in Saudi Arabia with those for **Kuwait** (p. 256) and **Sharjah** in the United Arab Emirates (p. 290). These last two stations are on the Gulf coast while **Jidda** is on the Red Sea coast.

In the interior, and in the higher mountains in the northwest of Saudi Arabia, winter temperatures occasionally fall low enough for frost and snow to occur. Winter nights in the desert are distinctly chilly. Any strong wind is likely to raise dust and sand which can add to the unpleasant conditions, whether it is a cold winter blast or a burning dry wind in summer. Sunshine amounts are very large over most of Arabia, ranging from six to eight hours a day in winter to as much as twelve to thirteen in summer. In the mountains of Yemen and in the hills facing the Arabian Sea in Oman and Muscat the period from June to September is much cloudier than elsewhere in Arabia since the dominant southwest monsoon is very warm and moist; low clouds, drizzle and light rain are frequent.

Any visitor to the states of the Arabian peninsula should be prepared for very hot conditions between May and October. Both in the very hot, dry interior and on the muggy coasts of the Gulf and Red Sea there are occasions when heat exhaustion and heatstroke can be a threat, particularly to new arrivals and those who do not take sensible precautions.

Jidda 20 ft (6 m) 21°28′ N 39°10′ E 5 years   **SAUDI ARABIA**

	Temperature °F			Temperature °C			Relative humidity		Precipitation			
	Highest recorded	Average daily	Lowest recorded	Highest recorded	Average daily	Lowest recorded	0800 hours	1400 hours	Average monthly		Average no. days with 0.04 in + (1 mm +)	
		max.	min.			max.	min.		%	%	in	mm	
J	92	84	66	49	33	29	19	9	58	54	0.2	5	0.8	J
F	95	84	65	52	35	29	18	11	52	52	0	0	0.3	F
M	101	85	67	55	38	29	19	13	52	52	0	0	0.3	M
A	104	91	70	54	40	33	21	12	52	56	0	0	0.5	A
M	108	95	74	55	42	35	23	13	51	55	0	0	0	M
J	117	97	75	67	47	36	24	19	56	55	0	0	0	J
J	108	99	79	70	42	37	26	21	55	50	0	0	0	J
A	108	99	80	73	42	37	27	23	59	51	0	0	0	A
S	108	96	77	70	42	36	25	21	65	61	0	0	0	S
O	105	95	73	68	41	35	23	20	60	61	0	0	0	O
N	105	91	71	63	41	33	22	17	55	59	1.0	25	2	N
D	93	86	67	50	34	30	19	10	55	54	1.2	31	1	D

Riyadh 1938 ft (590 m) 24°39′ N 46°42′ E 3 years   **SAUDI ARABIA**

	Temperature °F			Temperature °C			Relative humidity		Precipitation			
	Highest recorded	Average daily	Lowest recorded	Highest recorded	Average daily	Lowest recorded	0500 hours	1600 hours	Average monthly		Average no. days with 0.04 in + (1 mm +)	
		max.	min.			max.	min.		%	%	in	mm	
J	86	70	46	19	30	21	8	−7	70	44	0.1	3	1	J
F	91	73	48	29	33	23	9	−2	63	37	0.8	20	1	F
M	101	82	56	33	38	28	13	1	65	36	0.9	23	3	M
A	104	89	64	36	40	32	18	2	64	34	1.0	25	4	A
M	110	100	72	59	43	38	22	15	51	31	0.4	10	1	M
J	113	107	77	67	45	42	25	19	47	31	0	0	0	J
J	113	107	78	67	45	42	26	19	33	19	0	0	0	J
A	112	107	75	62	44	42	24	17	35	19	0	0	0	A
S	111	102	72	63	44	39	22	17	42	24	0	0	0	S
O	101	94	61	50	38	34	16	10	47	25	0	0	0	O
N	94	84	55	35	34	29	13	2	60	33	0	0	0	N
D	87	70	49	32	31	21	9	0	75	52	0	0	0	D

SIKKIM

This tiny mountain state lies in the Himalayan foothills immediately east of Nepal. It is bordered by China, Nepal, Bhutan and India. It has a range of climate which varies with altitude as described on p. 264 for Nepal.

The table for **Darjeeling** in India (p. 230) is representative of conditions in the lower regions of the state.

This tiny state consists of Singapore island with a total area of 224 square miles (581 sq. km) at the southern tip of the Malayan peninsula. Until 1965 it formed part of the Federation of Malaysia, but since then it has been an independent state of the British Commonwealth. It has a climate similar in all respects to that described on p. 261 for Malaysia. It is hot, wet and distinctly humid throughout the year. The most unpleasant months are March and September when winds are light.

Singapore 33 ft (10 m) 1°18′ N 103°50′ E 39 years

	Temperature °F			Temperature °C			Relative humidity		Precipitation			
	Highest recorded	Average daily		Lowest recorded	Highest recorded	Average daily		Lowest recorded	0900 hours	1500 hours	Average monthly		Average no. days with 0.01 in +
		max.	min.			max.	min.		%	%	in	mm	(0.25 mm +)
J	93	86	73	68	34	30	23	20	82	78	9.9	252	17	J
F	94	88	73	66	34	31	23	19	77	71	6.8	173	11	F
M	94	88	75	67	34	31	24	19	76	70	7.6	193	14	M
A	95	88	75	70	35	31	24	21	77	74	7.4	188	15	A
M	97	89	75	70	36	32	24	21	79	73	6.8	173	15	M
J	95	88	75	70	35	31	24	21	79	73	6.8	173	13	J
J	93	88	75	70	34	31	24	21	79	72	6.7	170	13	J
A	93	87	75	69	34	31	24	21	78	72	7.7	196	14	A
S	93	87	75	69	34	31	24	21	79	72	7.0	178	14	S
O	93	87	74	69	34	31	23	21	78	72	8.2	208	16	O
N	92	87	74	69	33	31	23	21	79	75	10.0	254	18	N
D	93	87	74	69	34	31	23	21	82	78	10.1	257	19	D

SOUTH KOREA

South Korea occupies the southern half of the Korean peninsula between the Yellow Sea and the Sea of Japan. In area the country is a little smaller than England. It has a border with the People's Republic of North Korea approximately along the 38° parallel of latitude. Much of the country is hilly or even mountainous; in the east there are many hills rising above 3000 ft (915 m) but the largest areas of lowland are in the west.

The general features of the weather and climate of the Korean peninsula are described here. Where conditions are different in North Korea they are mentioned on p. 266.

Situated on the eastern side of the great land mass of Eurasia, Korea has a rather extreme continental climate considering that it is surrounded by water on three sides. The winters are very cold. Nowhere else in the world, in a similar latitude, are winters so cold with such frequent frost and snow. Summers are warm and, at times, hot. Most of the annual rainfall occurs between June and September. Some precipitation occurs in all months but, from November until early April, this is often snow. Snow falls on an average of twenty-eight days a year at **Seoul** and on about ten days in the far south.

The transition from the cold, dry winter to the warm, wet summer occurs rather quickly between April and early May, and there is a similar rather abrupt return to winter conditions in late October and early November. Over most of the country summer temperatures are high enough for rice to be grown extensively.

Korea is one of the most northerly countries to be affected by the great seasonal wind reversal called the Asiatic monsoon. In winter the winds are predominantly from the west and north, bringing very cold but dry air from north China and Siberia. In summer the winds are mainly from the east and south, bringing warm, moist air from the Pacific Ocean. The weather can be somewhat variable from day to day at all seasons since the country is affected by frontal systems and depressions moving from the west. These bring rain or snow and occasional thaws in winter. In summer these disturbances are associated with the spells of heaviest rainfall. About once a year a typhoon moves up from the South China Sea and brings very heavy rain and strong winds at any time between June and September.

A surprising feature of the Korean winter is the large amount of sunshine, averaging as much as six to seven hours a day. Even when temperatures remain below freezing all day the sun may shine from a clear blue sky while the cold is intensified by the strong wind. Hours of sunshine are rather less during the wetter period in summer. The strong wind-chill factor intensifies the cold so that warm winter clothing is essential. Otherwise the climate is not particularly uncomfortable and is generally healthy. Humidity is higher in the summer so that some days may feel distinctly muggy and uncomfortable.

Temperatures decrease from south to north, particularly in winter, so that South Korea is rather warmer than the north around the year. The tables for **Seoul** near the border with North Korea, and for **Pusan** in the south of the country, show the warmer conditions farther south.

Pusan 41 ft (13 m) 35°06′ N 129°01′ E 29 years

| | Temperature °F | | | Temperature °C | | | Relative humidity | | Precipitation | | |
| | Highest recorded | Average daily | Lowest recorded | Highest recorded | Average daily | Lowest recorded | 0530 hours | 1330 hours | Average monthly | | Average no. days with 0.04 in + (1 mm +) |
		max.	min.			max.	min.		%	%	in	mm	
J	65	43	29	7	18	6	−2	−14	57	41	1.7	43	5	J
F	64	45	31	11	18	7	−1	−12	61	45	1.4	36	3	F
M	69	53	37	19	21	12	3	−7	65	50	2.7	69	7	M
A	78	62	47	29	26	17	8	−2	73	59	5.5	140	8	A
M	84	69	55	42	29	21	13	6	75	59	5.2	132	7	M
J	92	75	62	49	33	24	17	9	82	71	7.9	201	10	J
J	94	81	71	57	34	27	22	14	90	76	11.6	295	10	J
A	96	85	73	60	36	29	23	16	87	71	5.1	130	8	A
S	90	78	65	49	32	26	18	9	82	64	6.8	173	8	S
O	80	70	54	36	27	21	12	2	73	54	2.9	74	5	O
N	75	59	43	26	24	15	6	−3	69	52	1.6	41	4	N
D	67	48	33	10	19	9	1	−12	65	49	1.2	31	3	D

Seoul 285 ft (87 m) 37°34′ N 126°58′ E 22 years

SOUTH KOREA

| | Temperature °F | | | Temperature °C | | | Relative humidity | | Precipitation | | |
| | Highest recorded | Average daily | Lowest recorded | Highest recorded | Average daily | Lowest recorded | 0530 hours | 1330 hours | Average monthly | | Average no. days with 0.04 in + (1 mm +) |
		max.	min.			max.	min.		%	%	in	mm	
J	54	32	15	−8	12	0	−9	−22	78	51	1.2	31	8	J
F	61	37	20	−3	16	3	−7	−19	77	47	0.8	20	6	F
M	72	47	29	5	22	8	−2	−15	77	46	1.5	38	7	M
A	83	62	41	25	28	17	5	−4	83	46	3.0	76	8	A
M	90	72	51	36	32	22	11	2	87	51	3.2	81	10	M
J	98	80	61	49	37	27	16	9	87	54	5.1	130	10	J
J	98	84	70	55	37	29	21	13	91	67	14.8	376	16	J
A	99	87	71	58	37	31	22	14	90	62	10.5	267	13	A
S	91	78	59	38	33	26	15	3	89	55	4.7	119	9	S
O	86	67	45	25	30	19	7	−4	88	48	1.6	41	7	O
N	74	51	32	11	23	11	0	−12	83	52	1.8	46	9	N
D	58	37	20	−12	14	3	−7	−24	79	52	1.0	25	9	D

SRI LANKA

Sri Lanka, often still called Ceylon, is a large island in the Indian Ocean immediately south of India. It consists of extensive lowland regions around the coast and a large mountainous interior where the highest peaks rise to over 8000 ft (2400 m). Situated between 6° and 10° N, it has a typical tropical climate which is somewhat modified by the seasonal wind reversal of the Asiatic monsoon (see p. 229 for India).

At lower levels temperatures remain high throughout the year and the high humidity and warm nights may feel uncomfortable to the visitor who has not yet become acclimatized. On the coast, however, the heat is modified by afternoon sea breezes so that it is rarely dangerous. In the interior highlands temperatures are significantly reduced by altitude with the result that the climate is delightful for most of the year; rarely too hot by day and rarely so chilly as to be uncomfortable at night; frost is a very rare occurrence here.

Most of the country has an abundant or moderate rainfall which is well distributed throughout the year. The southwestern coast and mountain slopes are the wettest regions and here rainfall is greatest during the two periods April to June and October to November.

The northeastern side of the island, particularly the lowlands, is much drier with little rain between February and September. The main rainy season here is between October and January when the northeast monsoon blows onshore. This area is often called the 'dry zone' but the term is a relative one. The southwest monsoon brings rather more rain to the southwestern side of the island between May and September but its arrival does not mark the same abrupt transition between a hot, dry season and a warm, wet season such as occurs in much of the Indian subcontinent.

Daily sunshine amounts vary from six to eight hours over much of the country, being least during the rainiest seasons when cloudy disturbed weather may last for spells of two to three days. In many parts of the country much rainfall comes in afternoon showers accompanied by thunder.

The tables for **Colombo** and **Trincomalee** are representative of the lowlands of the southwest and northeast respectively. That for **Nuwara Eliya** shows the cooler conditions experienced in the higher parts of the interior.

SRI LANKA — Colombo 24 ft (7 m) 6°54′ N 79°52′ E 25 years

		Temperature °F			Temperature °C				Relative humidity		Precipitation			
	Highest recorded	Average daily		Lowest recorded	Highest recorded	Average daily		Lowest recorded	0930 hours	1530 hours	Average monthly		Average no. days with 0.04 in + (1 mm +)	
		max.	min.			max.	min.		%	%	in	mm		
J	94	86	72	59	34	30	22	15	73	67	3.5	89	7	J
F	96	87	72	61	36	31	22	16	71	66	2.7	69	6	F
M	96	88	74	64	36	31	23	18	71	66	5.8	147	8	M
A	92	88	76	70	33	31	24	21	74	70	9.1	231	14	A
M	91	87	78	69	33	31	26	21	78	76	14.6	371	19	M
J	89	85	77	72	32	29	25	22	80	78	8.8	224	18	J
J	88	85	77	71	31	29	25	22	79	77	5.3	135	12	J
A	88	85	77	71	31	29	25	22	78	76	4.3	109	11	A
S	89	85	77	71	32	29	25	22	76	75	6.3	160	13	S
O	89	85	75	69	32	29	24	21	77	76	13.7	348	19	O
N	90	85	73	66	32	29	23	19	77	75	12.4	315	16	N
D	91	85	72	63	33	29	22	17	74	69	5.8	147	10	D

Nuwara Eliya 6168 ft (1880 m) 6°58′ N 80°46′ E 9 years   **SRI LANKA**

	Temperature °F				Temperature °C			Relative humidity		Precipitation		
	Highest recorded	Average daily		Lowest recorded	Highest recorded	Average daily		Lowest recorded	0800 hours	1700 hours	Average monthly		Average no. days with 0.1 in + (2.5 mm +)
		max.	min.			max.	min.		%	%	in	mm	
J	76	67	47	27	24	19	8	−3	89	69	6.7	170	13	J
F	75	70	44	29	24	21	7	−2	87	68	1.7	43	6	F
M	75	71	46	32	24	22	8	0	84	66	4.3	109	11	M
A	76	71	49	38	24	22	9	3	89	79	4.7	119	15	A
M	78	70	53	33	26	21	12	1	88	79	6.9	175	18	M
J	75	66	55	45	24	19	13	7	89	86	10.9	277	25	J
J	76	65	55	45	24	18	13	7	89	83	11.8	300	25	J
A	74	67	54	44	23	19	12	7	89	83	7.7	196	22	A
S	75	67	53	41	24	19	12	5	88	84	8.9	226	20	S
O	75	68	52	41	24	20	11	5	89	85	10.6	269	22	O
N	74	68	51	33	23	20	11	1	89	83	9.5	241	22	N
D	74	68	48	30	23	20	9	−1	91	80	8.0	203	17	D

Trincomalee 24 ft (7 m) 8°35′ N 81°15′ E 25 years   **SRI LANKA**

	Temperature °F				Temperature °C			Relative humidity		Precipitation		
	Highest recorded	Average daily		Lowest recorded	Highest recorded	Average daily		Lowest recorded	0930 hours	1530 hours	Average monthly		Average no. days with 0.04 in + (1 mm +)
		max.	min.			max.	min.		%	%	in	mm	
J	92	80	75	65	33	27	24	18	79	78	6.8	173	10	J
F	96	82	76	66	36	28	24	19	72	70	2.6	66	4	F
M	101	85	76	67	38	29	24	19	72	70	1.9	48	4	M
A	102	89	78	67	39	32	26	19	69	68	2.3	58	5	A
M	104	92	79	67	40	33	26	19	67	61	2.7	69	5	M
J	103	92	79	71	39	33	26	22	65	54	1.1	28	2	J
J	101	92	78	70	38	33	26	21	65	53	2.0	51	3	J
A	102	92	77	69	39	33	25	21	65	56	4.2	107	6	A
S	102	92	77	70	39	33	25	21	65	61	4.2	107	6	S
O	102	88	76	69	39	31	24	21	72	69	8.7	221	13	O
N	97	84	75	67	36	29	24	19	80	78	14.1	358	17	N
D	91	81	75	66	33	27	24	19	80	79	14.3	363	16	D

SYRIA

The climate and weather of Syria are very similar to those in the three other countries of the eastern Mediterranean – frequently known as the Levant States: Lebanon, Israel and Jordan. The general features of the climate of all four countries and the factors governing the climate are described here; briefer descriptions of the other three countries are given under the country headings.

These countries all have a climate and sequence of weather throughout the year that is transitional between the Mediterranean and the Arabian desert. The summers, lasting from April or early May until September or early October, are sunny, hot and dry with very little change of weather from day to day. During the rest of the year there is greater variability from day to day as Mediterranean depressions bring cloudy, rainy weather and also occasional cold spells in the midwinter period during which frost and snow may occur even at low levels. These cold spells are rare and less severe along the Mediterranean coast. Inland, and in the mountains, the cold spells may be severe with frequent snow.

The probability of disturbed weather with cloud and rain is greatest in the months December to February which is the main rainy season. Even during the midwinter period, however, the weather is often sunny and dry for long periods. There is some variation from year to year in the start and end of the hot, dry settled weather of summer so that some heavy downpours of rain may occur at the beginning and end of summer. These brief wet spells are the 'former' and 'latter' rains referred to in the Bible (Deut. 11:14). Apart from the gradual increase of temperature from March to May and the similar decrease from September to November there is no marked spring and autumn as occurs in countries farther north. The main seasonal contrast is the beginning and end of the settled weather of summer.

One of the most notable, and certainly the most unpleasant or even dangerous, features of the weather of these countries is brief spells of hot winds blowing from the east and southeast. These winds 'import' very hot and dusty air from Arabia and, on occasion, temperatures may rise as high as 110°–120° F (43°–49° C). Such spells of weather are named khamsin in Arabic or sirocco in Italian. They are most frequent at the beginning and end of the summer season and are rare in midsummer. In extreme cases there is a danger of heat stress or even heatstroke unless elementary precautions are taken (see p. 15).

Syria is the largest of the Levant countries and, because of its size and east-to-west extent, shows the greatest contrast between the milder, wetter Mediterranean conditions on the coast and the desert conditions of the interior. About 60 per cent of Syria lying east of **Aleppo** and **Damascus** has a desert or semi-desert climate with an annual rainfall below 8 in (200 mm). This is the hottest region in summer and it is often quite cold in winter with occasional snow and frequent frost (see the table for **Deir ez Zor**). Rainfall, although infrequent, may be quite heavy and very local causing some spectacular desert floods.

To the north and west of this desert region there is a band of steppe country where some unirrigated cultivation can be carried out. This belt, often called the Fertile Crescent, includes the large cities of **Aleppo** and **Damascus**. Here annual rainfall is between 8 and 20 in (200 and 500 mm). Temperatures throughout the year are very similar to those found in the Syrian desert.

Between this inland steppe region and the Mediterranean there are a series of mountain ranges and hills where rainfall is much greater and there is also a good deal of snow. Except for Mount Hermon in the southwest, which has a climate similar to that of the Lebanon Mountains (see p. 259), these western hills and mountains are not quite as wet or snowy as in Lebanon. There are a number of small mountain resorts which are popular as a relief from the summer heat of the interior and the larger cities.

Along the Mediterranean coast there is a narrow plain where conditions are very similar to those found along the coast of Lebanon (see the table for **Beirut** on p. 259). Summers are warm and humid and winters are very mild with spells of cloud and heavy rain, alternating with fine sunny weather. Syria has a very sunny climate with an average of six to seven hours of sunshine a day in winter and as much as twelve to thirteen in summer.

Aleppo 1280 ft (390 m) 36°14′ N 37°08′ E 8 years — SYRIA

	Temperature °F			Temperature °C			Relative humidity	Precipitation		
	Highest recorded	Average daily	Lowest recorded	Highest recorded	Average daily	Lowest recorded		Average monthly		Average no. days with 0.04 in + (1 mm +)
		max.	min.			max.	min.			in	mm	
J	63	50	34	9	17	10	1	−13	—	3.5	89	11	J
F	69	56	37	14	21	13	3	−10	—	2.5	64	10	F
M	87	64	39	19	31	18	4	−7	—	1.5	38	7	M
A	93	75	48	28	34	24	9	−2	—	1.1	28	4	A
M	105	85	56	32	41	29	13	0	—	0.3	8	2	M
J	117	94	63	48	47	34	17	9	—	0.1	3	0.4	J
J	115	97	69	60	46	36	21	16	—	0	0	0	J
A	110	97	69	59	43	36	21	15	—	0	0	0.2	A
S	106	92	61	44	41	33	16	7	—	0	0	0.1	S
O	99	81	54	41	37	27	12	5	—	1.0	25	4	O
N	86	67	45	27	30	19	7	−3	—	2.2	56	8	N
D	65	54	38	18	18	12	3	−8	—	3.3	84	10	D

Damascus 2362 ft (720 m) 33°30′ N 36°20′ E 9 years — SYRIA

	Temperature °F			Temperature °C			Relative humidity		Precipitation		
	Highest recorded	Average daily	Lowest recorded	Highest recorded	Average daily	Lowest recorded	0830 hours	1430 hours	Average monthly		Average no. days with 0.04 in + (1 mm +)
		max.	min.			max.	min.	%	%	in	mm	
J	69	53	36	21	21	12	2	−6	81	57	1.7	43	7	J
F	86	57	39	23	30	14	4	−5	78	53	1.7	43	6	F
M	83	65	42	28	28	18	6	−2	62	42	0.3	8	2	M
A	95	75	49	33	35	24	9	−1	50	32	0.5	13	3	A
M	101	84	55	44	38	29	13	7	44	26	0.1	3	1	M
J	102	91	61	48	39	33	16	9	45	22	0	0	0.1	J
J	108	96	64	55	42	36	18	13	43	19	0	0	0	J
A	113	99	64	55	45	37	18	13	47	21	0	0	0	A
S	102	91	60	50	39	33	16	10	48	24	0.7	18	2	S
O	93	81	54	42	34	27	12	6	54	31	0.4	10	2	O
N	86	67	47	28	30	19	8	−2	73	46	1.6	41	5	N
D	69	56	40	23	21	13	4	−5	81	59	1.6	41	5	D

	Temperature °F			Temperature °C				Relative humidity	Precipitation		
	Highest recorded	Average daily	Lowest recorded	Highest recorded	Average daily		Lowest recorded	All hours	Average monthly		Average no. days with 0.04 in + (1 mm +)
		max.	min.			max.	min.		%	in	mm	
J	72	53	35	16	22	12	2	−9	80	1.6	41	6	J
F	72	58	38	18	22	14	3	−8	73	0.8	20	5	F
M	91	70	42	24	33	21	6	−4	65	0.3	8	3	M
A	103	80	52	37	39	27	11	3	61	0.8	20	4	A
M	105	92	61	46	41	33	16	8	45	0.1	3	0.7	M
J	111	99	70	45	44	37	21	7	36	0	0	0.1	J
J	114	105	78	67	46	41	26	19	29	0	0	0	J
A	113	104	76	68	45	40	24	20	38	0	0	0	A
S	111	97	68	48	44	36	20	9	39	0	0	0	S
O	97	86	56	43	36	30	13	6	48	0.2	5	2	O
N	90	72	46	25	32	22	8	−4	51	1.5	38	5	N
D	68	58	37	17	20	14	3	−8	60	0.9	23	4	D

TAIWAN

Taiwan, sometimes called by its old name Formosa, is an independent state not recognized as such by the government of mainland China. It consists of an island rather larger than Wales or the state of Vermont, situated between 22° and 25° N and lying about 100 miles (160 km) off the coast of China. It is mountainous and rugged with the highest peak rising to over 13,000 ft (4000 m).

The whole island shares in the tropical monsoon type of climate experienced on the southern Chinese mainland. Rainfall is almost everywhere over 80 in (2000 mm) a year at low levels and much more in the mountains. More rain falls in the period May to September than in the rest of the year. Some of the heaviest falls of rain from July to September are brought by the typhoons of the South China Sea. As they move northwards towards Japan they bring strong

winds and heavy rain to the whole island. In winter disturbed weather with cloud and rain affects the north and east coasts rather more than the south. This can be seen by comparing the table for **Taipei**, in the north, with that for **Hengch'un** in the extreme south. **Taipei** not only has more rain in winter but on many more days.

The summer heat is made more oppressive by high humidity so that at low levels some days can be distinctly unpleasant. The winter and spring weather of Taiwan, however, can be very pleasant. The north of the island has a cooler winter than the south. The climate is quite sunny for much of the year with sunshine hours averaging from six hours a day in winter to seven or eight in summer. These amounts are much reduced in the cloudy wetter hills.

Hengch'un 77 ft (24 m) 22°00′ N 120°45′ E 30 years   **TAIWAN**

	Temperature °F			Temperature °C			Relative humidity		Precipitation		
	Highest recorded	Average daily		Lowest recorded	Highest recorded	Average daily		Lowest recorded	0600 hours	1400 hours	Average monthly		Average no. days with 0.04 in + (1 mm +)
		max.	min.			max.	min.		%	%	in	mm	
J	87	75	64	50	31	24	18	10	78	62	0.9	23	4	J
F	88	76	63	50	31	24	17	10	80	60	1.1	28	4	F
M	92	80	67	53	33	27	19	12	79	60	0.9	23	3	M
A	93	84	71	59	34	29	22	15	84	61	2.0	51	3	A
M	95	87	74	63	35	31	23	17	87	67	7.4	188	10	M
J	95	87	76	65	35	31	24	18	91	74	14.4	366	14	J
J	94	88	77	71	34	31	25	22	93	75	17.3	439	18	J
A	92	87	76	67	33	31	24	19	93	76	21.4	544	17	A
S	93	87	75	66	34	31	24	19	89	71	11.1	282	13	S
O	93	84	73	61	34	29	23	16	76	64	6.2	158	5	O
N	89	80	70	55	32	27	21	13	75	61	1.4	36	5	N
D	88	76	66	49	31	24	19	9	76	61	0.7	18	3	D

Taipei 30 ft (9 m) 25°02′ N 121°31′ E 37 years   **TAIWAN**

	Temperature °F			Temperature °C			Relative humidity		Precipitation		
	Highest recorded	Average daily		Lowest recorded	Highest recorded	Average daily		Lowest recorded	0600 hours	1400 hours	Average monthly		Average no. days with 0.04 in + (1 mm +)
		max.	min.			max.	min.		%	%	in	mm	
J	86	66	54	37	30	19	12	3	91	71	3.4	86	9	J
F	88	65	53	32	31	18	12	0	92	75	5.3	135	13	F
M	91	70	57	35	33	21	14	2	90	69	7.0	178	12	M
A	95	77	63	46	35	25	17	8	92	71	6.7	170	14	A
M	98	83	69	50	37	28	21	10	92	68	9.1	231	12	M
J	99	89	73	60	37	32	23	16	93	68	11.4	290	13	J
J	101	92	76	67	38	33	24	19	91	62	9.1	231	10	J
A	100	91	75	66	38	33	24	19	91	64	12.0	305	12	A
S	97	88	73	56	36	31	23	13	92	66	9.6	244	10	S
O	95	81	67	51	35	27	19	11	90	65	4.8	122	9	O
N	92	75	62	34	33	24	17	1	90	65	2.6	66	7	N
D	88	69	57	35	31	21	14	2	90	69	2.8	71	8	D

THAILAND

Thailand, previously known as Siam, in southeast Asia, is about the same size as France. It is bordered by Burma on the north and west and by Laos and Cambodia on the east. It has a coastline on the Gulf of Siam which is part of the Pacific Ocean. The south of the country consists of the narrow Kra Isthmus dividing the Pacific from the Indian Ocean and joining the Malayan peninsula to the mainland of southeast Asia. Situated between 6° and 20° N, the country has an equatorial climate in the extreme south while the centre and north have a tropical monsoon climate similar to that of Burma. The north is hilly and even mountainous with land rising over 3300 ft (1000 m) but most of the centre and east of Thailand is low-lying with only gentle hills and slopes.

Most of Thailand has abundant, but not excessive, rainfall and this is largely confined to the months from May to October. During this season the weather is dominated by the southwest monsoon blowing from the Indian Ocean and bringing warm, humid air and much cloud. The months from November to April are much drier with rain only falling on a few days a month. This is the period of the northeast monsoon when the wind is blowing overland from China or Indo-China and the air is consequently much drier. In the Kra Isthmus these winds bring more rain since they are more likely to have their origin in the Pacific Ocean or to have blown across the Gulf of Siam. More rain falls in the south at this time but the extreme north is virtually dry for two or three months.

In the centre and south of the country there is no great variation in temperature from month to month but in the north the period of the northeast monsoon is definitely cooler. This may be seen by comparing the table for **Chiengmai** in the northern hills with that for **Bangkok** in the south–centre of the country. In most of Thailand the hottest months are April and May before the cloudier, rainy weather brought by the southwest monsoon. Sunshine amounts are everywhere lowest during the months June to September when they average four to five hours a day. During the rest of the year they average nine to ten hours.

The weather of the wet season is oppressive over most of Thailand because of the combination of high temperature and humidity. During the sunnier months of the dry season conditions are fresher and there is usually more wind. Although severe heat stress is rare in Thailand, visitors will find the weather of the wet season rather uncomfortable.

Bangkok 7 ft (2 m) 13°45′ N 100°28′ E 37 years   **THAILAND**

		Temperature °F			Temperature °C				Relative humidity		Precipitation			
	Highest recorded	Average daily		Lowest recorded	Highest recorded	Average daily		Lowest recorded	0630 hours	1230 hours	Average monthly		Average no. days with 0.04 in + (1 mm +)	
		max.	min.			max.	min.		%	%	in	mm		
J	100	89	68	55	38	32	20	13	91	53	0.3	8	1	J
F	106	91	72	56	41	33	22	13	92	55	0.8	20	1	F
M	104	93	75	62	40	34	24	17	92	56	1.4	36	3	M
A	106	95	77	67	41	35	25	19	90	58	2.3	58	3	A
M	106	93	77	71	41	34	25	22	91	64	7.8	198	9	M
J	100	91	76	70	38	33	24	21	90	67	6.3	160	10	J
J	101	90	76	71	38	32	24	22	91	66	6.3	160	13	J
A	99	90	76	72	37	32	24	22	92	66	6.9	175	13	A
S	98	89	76	69	37	32	24	21	94	70	12.0	305	15	S
O	100	88	75	64	38	31	24	18	93	70	8.1	206	14	O
N	99	87	72	56	37	31	22	13	92	65	2.6	66	5	N
D	100	87	68	52	38	31	20	11	91	56	0.2	5	1	D

Chiengmai 1030 ft (314 m) 18°47′ N 98°59′ E 13 years   **THAILAND**

		Temperature °F			Temperature °C				Relative humidity		Precipitation			
	Highest recorded	Average daily		Lowest recorded	Highest recorded	Average daily		Lowest recorded	0630 hours	1230 hours	Average monthly		Average no. days with 0.04 in + (1 mm +)	
		max.	min.			max.	min.		%	%	in	mm		
J	97	84	56	43	36	29	13	6	96	52	0	0	0.5	J
F	97	89	58	49	36	32	14	9	93	44	0.4	10	1	F
M	102	94	63	55	39	34	17	13	88	40	0.3	8	2	M
A	105	97	71	59	41	36	22	15	88	49	1.4	36	5	A
M	106	94	73	67	41	34	23	19	90	60	4.8	122	12	M
J	100	90	74	69	38	32	23	21	92	67	4.4	112	15	J
J	99	88	74	66	37	31	23	19	94	69	8.4	213	21	J
A	99	88	74	70	37	31	23	21	95	73	7.6	193	20	A
S	96	88	73	65	36	31	23	18	96	72	9.8	249	17	S
O	96	87	70	60	36	31	21	16	96	69	3.7	94	8	O
N	99	86	66	54	37	30	19	12	96	63	1.2	31	4	N
D	97	83	59	43	36	28	15	6	96	57	0.5	13	2	D

UNITED ARAB EMIRATES

This territory consists of a union of seven small Arab sheikhdoms formerly under British protection and, at that time, called the Trucial Oman. They lie on the southern shore of the Arabian (Persian) Gulf between Qatar on the west and Oman on the east. They have a land boundary with Saudi Arabia on the northern fringes of the Rub al Khali. Most of the country is flat and consists of a sand or rocky desert. Annual rainfall is very low and mostly occurs between November and March. Temperatures are very high between May and September and warm to mild for the rest of the year. Winters are warmer than in Kuwait or the interior of Saudi Arabia.

Summer conditions are most unpleasant on the coast where humidity is high. Both inland and on the coast there is some danger of heat exhaustion and heatstroke during the hottest weather. The table for **Sharjah** is representative of conditions on the coast. For more detail about the weather and climate of Arabia see the description for Saudi Arabia on p. 276.

UNITED ARAB EMIRATES

Sharjah 18 ft (5.5 m) 25°20′ N 55°24′ E 11 years

	Temperature °F			Temperature °C			Relative humidity		Precipitation			
	Highest recorded	Average daily	Lowest recorded	Highest recorded	Average daily	Lowest recorded	0730 hours	1530 hours	Average monthly		Average no. days with 0.1 in + (2.5 mm +)	
		max.	min.			max.	min.		%	%	in	mm	
J	85	74	54	37	29	23	12	3	81	61	0.9	23	2	J
F	91	75	57	46	33	24	14	8	81	63	0.9	23	2	F
M	104	80	60	46	40	27	16	8	74	61	0.4	10	1	M
A	103	86	65	53	39	30	18	12	66	63	0.2	5	0.3	A
M	109	93	72	61	43	34	22	16	61	63	0	0	0	M
J	112	97	77	67	44	36	25	19	64	65	0	0	0	J
J	117	100	82	73	47	38	28	23	64	64	0	0	0	J
A	118	103	82	73	48	39	28	23	66	64	0	0	0	A
S	113	99	77	69	45	37	25	21	73	64	0	0	0	S
O	104	92	71	64	40	33	22	18	77	62	0	0	0	O
N	97	87	64	54	36	31	18	12	78	59	0.4	10	0.2	N
D	88	78	58	47	31	26	14	8	82	62	1.4	36	2	D

290

Vietnam is a country of southeast Asia rather larger than Britain and about half the size of the state of Texas. Extending between 9° and 23° N, it lies entirely within the tropics. It has a long coastline on the Gulf of Tonkin and the South China Sea. On the landward side it borders China in the north and Laos and Kampuchea in the west. Like other countries of the region, it has a tropical monsoon type of climate dominated by south to southeasterly winds from May until September and northerly to northeasterly winds between October and April. There is a twice yearly period of variable winds at the time of transition from the north to south monsoon.

There are considerable areas of high land rising to over 8000 ft (2450 m), particularly in the northwest and in the central highlands facing the South China Sea. In the north around **Hanoi** and in the south around **Ho Chi Minh City** (formerly Saigon) there are extensive low-lying regions in the Red river delta and the Mekong delta respectively. These two lowlands contain a large proportion of the population and the productive rice-growing areas.

The general features of the climate of Vietnam also apply to the two adjoining countries, Laos and Kampuchea; all three countries are often grouped together under the name Indo-China. Over most of Indo-China there is a single rainy season at the time of the south monsoon between May and September. During the rest of the year rainfall is infrequent and light. Annual rainfall is almost everywhere above 40 in (1000 mm) and it rises to between 80 and 100 in (2000 and 2500 mm) on the hills, particularly those facing the sea.

On the coast and in those parts of the central highlands which face northeast the season of maximum rainfall is between September and January (see the table for **Tourane**). This area often receives heavy rain from typhoons, or severe tropical storms, which develop in the western Pacific at this time of year. This is also a time of much cloud and frequent drizzle (called locally the crachin). In the north of Vietnam there are more cloudy days with occasional light rain during the period of the northeast monsoon. The south of the country is more likely to be dry and sunny at this time. Compare the tables for **Hanoi** and **Ho Chi Minh City**.

In the southern and central parts of Indo-China temperatures remain high around the year, but in the north there is a definite cooler season as the north monsoon brings colder air from central China from time to time. Frost and occasional snow only occur on the highest mountains in the north for a few days a year. In the south of Vietnam, and in Kampuchea and Laos, the lowlands are sheltered from any such outbreaks of colder northerly air and the dry season is warm to hot with much sunshine.

The weather of Vietnam, Laos and Kampuchea is rather sultry and oppressive during the rainy season and the humidity is high at this time. On the coast and in the hills the frequent cloud and high humidity combine with lack of sunshine to make this time of the year rather unpleasant in spite of the reduction of temperatures with height.

	Temperature °F				Temperature °C			Relative humidity		Precipitation			
	Highest recorded	Average daily		Lowest recorded	Highest recorded	Average daily		Lowest recorded	1000 hours	1600 hours	Average monthly		Average no. days with 0.04 in + (1 mm +)	
		max.	min.			max.	min.		%	%	in	mm		
J	92	68	56	42	33	20	13	6	78	68	0.7	18	7	J
F	94	69	58	43	34	21	14	6	82	70	1.1	28	13	F
M	98	74	63	53	37	23	17	12	83	76	1.5	38	15	M
A	103	82	69	50	39	28	20	10	83	75	3.2	81	14	A
M	109	90	74	60	43	32	23	16	77	69	7.7	196	15	M
J	104	92	78	69	40	33	26	21	78	71	9.4	239	14	J
J	104	91	78	71	40	33	26	22	79	72	12.7	323	15	J
A	101	90	78	70	38	32	26	21	82	75	13.5	343	16	A
S	99	88	76	63	37	31	24	17	79	73	10.0	254	14	S
O	96	84	71	57	36	29	22	14	75	69	3.9	99	9	O
N	97	78	64	44	36	26	18	7	74	68	1.7	43	7	N
D	98	72	59	44	37	22	15	7	75	67	0.8	20	7	D

	Temperature °F				Temperature °C			Relative humidity		Precipitation			
	Highest recorded	Average daily		Lowest recorded	Highest recorded	Average daily		Lowest recorded	1000 hours	1600 hours	Average monthly		Average no. days with 0.04 in + (1 mm +)	
		max.	min.			max.	min.		%	%	in	mm		
J	98	89	70	57	37	32	21	14	69	61	0.6	15	2	J
F	102	91	71	61	39	33	22	16	66	56	0.1	3	1	F
M	103	93	74	64	39	34	23	18	63	58	0.5	13	2	M
A	104	95	76	68	40	35	24	20	63	60	1.7	43	4	A
M	102	92	76	70	39	33	24	21	71	71	8.7	221	16	M
J	100	89	75	69	38	32	24	21	77	78	13.0	330	21	J
J	94	88	75	67	34	31	24	19	79	80	12.4	315	23	J
A	95	88	75	68	35	31	24	20	77	78	10.6	269	21	A
S	96	88	74	69	36	31	23	21	78	80	13.2	335	21	S
O	94	88	74	68	34	31	23	20	77	80	10.6	269	20	O
N	95	87	73	64	35	31	23	18	74	75	4.5	114	11	N
D	97	87	71	57	36	31	22	14	72	68	2.2	56	7	D

	Temperature °F				Temperature °C			Relative humidity	Precipitation				
	Highest recorded	Average daily		Lowest recorded	Highest recorded	Average daily		Lowest recorded	All hours	Average monthly		Average no. days with 0.04 in + (1 mm +)	
		max.	min.			max.	min.		%	in	mm		
J	87	75	66	52	31	24	19	11	86	4.0	102	15	J
F	98	78	68	58	37	26	20	14	86	1.2	31	7	F
M	97	81	69	60	36	27	21	15	86	0.5	12	4	M
A	104	86	73	64	40	30	23	18	85	0.7	18	4	A
M	102	91	76	71	39	33	24	22	81	1.9	47	8	M
J	104	94	77	73	40	34	25	23	77	1.7	42	7	J
J	100	92	77	71	38	34	25	22	78	3.9	99	11	J
A	102	93	76	71	39	34	25	21	77	4.6	117	12	A
S	97	88	75	70	37	31	24	21	84	17.6	447	17	S
O	92	83	73	63	34	28	23	17	85	20.1	530	21	O
N	88	80	71	59	31	27	22	15	86	8.7	221	21	N
D	87	77	68	56	31	25	20	13	86	8.2	209	20	D

YEMEN ARAB REPUBLIC

This small, mountainous, and previously isolated country occupies the southwestern portion of the Arabian peninsula. It has a narrow coastal plain on the Red Sea but the land rises steeply to a mountainous interior over 12,000 ft (3600 m) above sea level. It is bordered by Saudi Arabia on the north and by the People's Democratic Republic of Yemen on the south.

It is an exceptional part of Arabia since the mountains receive moderate to abundant rainfall between March and September so that coffee and a wide variety of crops are grown. In the higher regions temperatures are much lower than elsewhere in Arabia. Here the climate is quite pleasant with mild winters and warm, moist but generally sunny summers. No reliable climatic data is available for the higher part of the country and the description above is based on travellers' accounts. In the lowland along the Red Sea coast the weather is hot and humid for most of the year and similar to that on the Red Sea coast of Saudi Arabia. Conditions here are represented by the tables for **Kamaran Island** and **Jidda** in Saudi Arabia (p. 277). In this lowland the rainfall is rather low, averaging about 4 in (100 mm) a year and may occur in both winter and summer.

YEMEN, PEOPLE'S DEMOCRATIC REPUBLIC

This country at the extreme south of the Arabian peninsula consists of the former British colony of Aden and the Arab sheikhdoms of the former Aden Protectorate. It has a long coastline on the Arabian Sea and landborders with the Yemen Arab Republic, Saudi Arabia and Oman. The interior includes a small portion of the great sand desert of the Rub al Khali which is mainly in Saudi Arabia (see p. 276). Between this desert and the coast there are ranges of hills within which runs a broad valley, the Wadi Hadhramaut. This area receives rather more rainfall and is settled and more densely populated.

Climatic conditions along the coast are represented by the table for **Khormaksar**, the airport of Aden. Here rainfall is low throughout the year and most of the coastal plain is desert. Temperatures and humidity are high throughout the year and the period from June to September is the most uncomfortable time when midday temperatures regularly rise to near 100° F (38° C) with a high humidity. Daily sea breezes help to mitigate the heat on the coast. Inland in the hills both temperatures and humidity are a little lower. Here, rainfall is a little more and mostly falls between May and September.

Kamaran Island 20 ft (6 m) 15°20′ N 42°37′ E 26 years **YEMEN ARAB REPUBLIC**

	Temperature °F			Temperature °C			Relative humidity		Precipitation			
	Highest recorded	Average daily	Lowest recorded	Highest recorded	Average daily	Lowest recorded	0900 hours	1500 hours	Average monthly		Average no. days with 0.04 in + (1 mm +)	
		max.	min.			max.	min.		%	%	in	mm	
J	88	82	74	66	31	28	23	19	79	69	0.2	5	0.6	J
F	89	83	74	67	32	28	23	19	77	65	0.2	5	0.9	F
M	94	86	77	70	34	30	25	21	75	65	0.1	3	0.6	M
A	98	89	79	73	37	32	26	23	74	61	0.1	3	0.3	A
M	102	95	82	74	39	35	28	23	70	56	0.1	3	0.2	M
J	104	97	84	75	40	36	29	24	67	55	0	0	0.1	J
J	105	98	85	72	41	37	29	22	63	52	0.5	13	2	J
A	103	97	85	72	39	36	29	22	67	55	0.7	18	1	A
S	104	97	84	74	40	36	29	23	71	58	0.1	3	0.5	S
O	102	93	82	73	39	34	28	23	67	57	0.1	3	0.5	O
N	94	87	78	68	34	31	26	20	74	63	0.4	10	0.8	N
D	90	83	75	68	32	28	24	20	77	68	0.9	23	2	D

Khormaksar 22 ft (7 m) 12°50′ N 45°01′ E 6 years **YEMEN, PEOPLE'S DEMOCRATIC REPUBLIC**

	Temperature °F			Temperature °C			Relative humidity		Precipitation			
	Highest recorded	Average daily	Lowest recorded	Highest recorded	Average daily	Lowest recorded	0300 hours	1500 hours	Average monthly		Average no. days with 0.04 in + (1 mm +)	
		max.	min.			max.	min.		%	%	in	mm	
J	86	82	72	61	30	28	22	16	78	63	0.2	5	1	J
F	87	83	73	63	31	28	23	17	79	65	0	0	0.5	F
M	95	86	76	67	35	30	24	19	82	66	0.2	5	0.3	M
A	99	89	77	68	37	32	25	20	83	66	0	0	0	A
M	103	93	81	75	39	34	27	24	83	66	0	0	0	M
J	106	98	84	79	41	37	29	26	76	51	0	0	0	J
J	104	97	83	73	40	36	28	23	76	49	0.2	5	1	J
A	101	96	82	74	38	36	28	23	78	50	0.1	3	0.7	A
S	101	96	83	77	38	36	28	25	78	56	0	0	0.2	S
O	100	91	76	66	38	33	24	19	77	58	0	0	0.2	O
N	91	86	73	65	33	30	23	18	77	61	0	0	0.2	N
D	87	83	73	62	31	28	23	17	76	62	0.2	5	2	D

Australasia

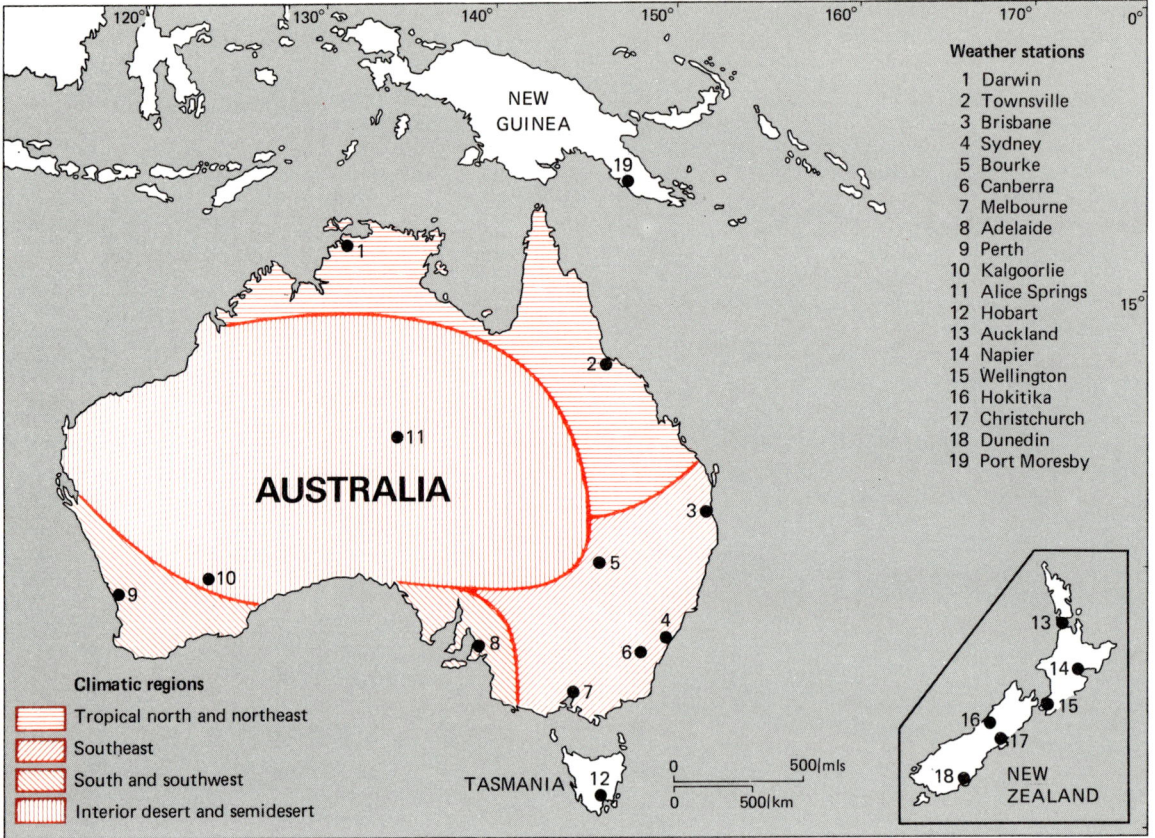

120° 130° 140° 150° 160° 170° 0°

NEW
GUINEA

15°

Weather stations

1 Darwin
2 Townsville
3 Brisbane
4 Sydney
5 Bourke
6 Canberra
7 Melbourne
8 Adelaide
9 Perth
10 Kalgoorlie
11 Alice Springs
12 Hobart
13 Auckland
14 Napier
15 Wellington
16 Hokitika
17 Christchurch
18 Dunedin
19 Port Moresby

AUSTRALIA

TASMANIA

Climatic regions

Tropical north and northeast
Southeast
South and southwest
Interior desert and semidesert

0   500|mls
0   500|km

13
14
15
16
17
18

NEW
ZEALAND

The Commonwealth of Australia consists of a large island continent lying between 11° and 39° S and the large offshore island of Tasmania between 41° and 44° S. The country is only a little smaller than the United States but in its sparse population it may be compared with Canada. Most of Australia's population lives in the climatically more favoured eastern, southern and southwestern coastal areas. Between half and two thirds of the country is desert or scrubland with a low and unreliable rainfall and this region is almost uninhabited. Nearly half Australia lies within the tropics.

The greater part of Australia consists of flat or gently undulating plains between 500 and 2000 ft (150 and 600 m) above sea level. The east coast is backed by an almost continuous range of hills or mountains which are highest on the border between New South Wales and Victoria in the south. Here the Snowy Mountains include the highest peak in Australia at 7300 ft (2225 m). This is the only part of the country to experience significant snowfall and even here it does not lie throughout the year. For much of the year the east coast is exposed to the persistent and regular southeast trade winds blowing off the Pacific and this is the wettest part of the country. To the west of these eastern highlands rainfall decreases towards the interior which is desert.

Central Australia is situated in the latitude of the persistent subtropical anticyclonic belt and this is another reason for its dryness. In this respect it resembles the Sahara and Kalahari deserts of Africa, but it is not quite so rainless as the Sahara.

The wetter districts of Australia form a crescent around the 'dry heart' of the country. In the north and northeast, where temperatures are tropical, rainfall follows the sun and there is a very clear maximum fall at the time of high sun between November and April. At this season winds on the north coast are from the northwest: the Australian monsoon, the counterpart of the outblowing Asiatic winter monsoon. These winds have become hot and humid as they cross the equatorial seas around Indonesia and the Philippines.

The east and southeast coasts of Australia get rain at all seasons with rather more in the summer. The south and southwest coasts in South and Western Australia are affected by westerly cyclonic disturbances during the cooler winter season and have their maximum rainfall at this time. The desert region reaches the coast between 18° and 30° S on the west coast and between 125° and 135° E on the south coast so that the wetter coastal fringe of the country is not continuous.

Much of Australia is warm or hot around the year and even along the cooler southern coasts the winters are mild rather than cold. Only Tasmania, which is in the same latitude as New Zealand, has a temperate climate comparable with that of Britain or northwest Europe. Very high temperatures occasionally occur almost anywhere in Australia when winds blow out from the interior and 'import' the high temperatures and low humidities of the interior desert to the coastal regions. Only Tasmania escapes such extremes of heat; it also has abundant rain around the year. The combination of prolonged heat-waves and drought is one of the main climatic hazards of much of Australia and is the main cause of the bush fires which may rage for days.

Tropical cyclones, similar to the typhoons of the North Pacific and South China Sea, occur two or three times each year in the seas to the northeast and northwest of Australia. The northern part of the Queensland coast and the north and west coasts from **Darwin** southwards are affected by the torrential rain and sometimes by the very high winds near the storm centre. On the northwest coast of Australia these storms go by the distinctive and expressive Australian name of 'Willy Willies'.

Because much of the country is fairly low and flat, contrasts of weather and climate are gradual and there are few sharp local changes. For a more detailed description the country can be divided into four climatic regions, in addition to Tasmania which is more temperate in climate: the tropical region of the north and northeast, southeastern Australia, southern and western Australia, and the desert and semi-arid regions of central Australia. These climatic regions rarely coincide with state boundaries. Only Victoria and Tasmania, the two smallest states, do not include part of the dry interior.

THE TROPICAL REGION OF THE NORTH AND NORTHEAST

This region consists of the coastlands of Queensland, the Northern Territory and Western Australia and the inland districts which have more than 20 in (500 mm) annual rainfall. On the east coast its southern limit is rather to the north of **Brisbane** but, as the table for **Brisbane** shows, winter temperatures here are very close to those normally regarded as constituting a tropical climate. **Brisbane** differs from places farther north in that it gets some rain in all months, as distinct from **Townsville** and **Darwin** which are more typically tropical in having a virtual drought during the low sun period. This region is typically tropical in having a combination of heat, rainfall and high humidity during the summer or high sun period of November to March. At this time the weather can be distinctly sultry and oppressive. The higher temperatures and lower humidities experienced inland towards the dry interior are more bearable than the sticky heat of the coast.

Like most of Australia, this region has a very sunny climate with daily sunshine hours averaging six to seven hours during the wetter cloudier months and eight to ten during the dry months. Annual sunshine hours are similar to those found in California or the European Mediterranean lands.

AUSTRALIA Brisbane (Queensland) 137 ft (42 m) 27°28' N 153°02' E 53 years

	Temperature °F				Temperature °C				Relative humidity		Precipitation			
	Highest recorded	Average daily		Lowest recorded	Highest recorded	Average daily		Lowest recorded	0900 hours	1500 hours	Average monthly		Average no. days with 0.01 in + (0.25 mm +)	
		max.	min.			max.	min.		%	%	in	mm		
J	110	85	69	59	43	29	21	15	66	59	6.4	163	13	J
F	106	85	68	58	41	29	20	14	69	60	6.3	160	14	F
M	99	82	66	52	37	28	19	11	72	60	5.7	145	15	M
A	95	79	61	44	35	26	16	7	71	56	3.7	94	12	A
M	90	74	56	41	32	23	13	5	73	55	2.8	71	10	M
J	89	69	51	37	32	21	11	3	73	54	2.6	66	8	J
J	83	68	49	36	28	20	9	2	72	51	2.2	56	8	J
A	88	71	50	37	31	22	10	3	69	49	1.9	48	7	A
S	95	76	55	41	35	24	13	5	64	51	1.9	48	8	S
O	101	80	60	43	38	27	16	6	60	53	2.5	64	9	O
N	106	82	64	48	41	28	18	9	60	57	3.7	94	10	N
D	106	85	67	56	41	29	19	13	62	56	5.0	127	12	D

Darwin (Northern Territory) 97 ft (30 m) 12°28′ S 130°51′ E 58 years   AUSTRALIA

	Temperature °F			Temperature °C			Relative humidity		Precipitation		
	Highest recorded	Average daily	Lowest recorded	Highest recorded	Average daily	Lowest recorded	0800 hours	1400 hours	Average monthly		Average no. days with 0.01 in + (0.25 mm +)
		max.	min.			max.	min.		%	%	in	mm	
J	100	90	77	68	38	32	25	20	78	71	15.2	386	20	J
F	101	90	77	69	38	32	25	21	79	72	12.3	312	18	F
M	102	91	77	68	39	33	25	20	78	67	10.0	254	17	M
A	104	92	76	66	40	33	24	19	69	54	3.8	97	6	A
M	102	91	73	60	39	33	23	16	63	47	0.6	15	1	M
J	99	88	69	56	37	31	21	13	61	47	0.1	3	1	J
J	98	87	67	56	37	31	19	13	59	44	0	0	0	J
A	98	89	70	58	37	32	21	14	63	45	0.1	3	0	A
S	102	91	74	63	39	33	23	17	65	49	0.5	13	2	S
O	105	93	77	69	41	34	25	21	65	52	2.0	51	5	O
N	103	94	78	69	39	34	26	21	68	58	4.7	119	10	N
D	102	92	78	69	39	33	26	21	73	65	9.4	239	15	D

Townsville (Queensland) 48 ft (15 m) 19°14′ S 146°51′ E 31 years   AUSTRALIA

	Temperature °F			Temperature °C			Relative humidity		Precipitation		
	Highest recorded	Average daily	Lowest recorded	Highest recorded	Average daily	Lowest recorded	0900 hours	1500 hours	Average monthly		Average no. days with 0.01 in + (0.25 mm +)
		max.	min.			max.	min.		%	%	in	mm	
J	104	87	76	66	40	31	24	19	73	70	10.9	277	15	J
F	110	87	75	65	43	31	24	18	73	68	11.2	285	12	F
M	95	86	73	61	35	30	23	16	71	68	7.2	183	10	M
A	97	84	70	54	36	29	21	12	66	62	3.3	84	6	A
M	90	81	65	48	32	27	18	9	65	60	1.3	33	5	M
J	87	77	61	41	31	25	16	5	66	60	1.4	36	4	J
J	85	75	59	42	29	24	15	6	64	58	0.6	15	3	J
A	89	77	61	45	32	25	16	7	63	59	0.5	13	3	A
S	94	80	66	52	34	27	19	11	63	61	0.7	18	2	S
O	94	83	71	53	34	28	22	12	64	64	1.3	33	4	O
N	101	85	74	63	38	29	23	17	65	66	1.9	48	5	N
D	101	87	76	65	38	31	24	18	70	69	5.4	137	12	D

SOUTHEASTERN AUSTRALIA

This region consists of the state of Victoria and the greater part of New South Wales, but excludes the drier western and northwestern part of this state. This part of Australia has attracted the most extensive colonization by Europeans since the first settlement near **Sydney** in the late eighteenth century. It has a climate that is best described as warm-temperate with no real cold season, warm to hot summers and rain well distributed throughout the year. The weather can be changeable at all times of the year and summers are liable to prolonged heat-waves and droughts. The hazard of drought is much greater inland as the average rainfall decreases; prolonged drought and unreliable rainfall have been persistent themes in the settlement history of Australia.

Cold spells are brief and never severe on the coast, as the tables for **Sydney** and **Melbourne** show. Tempera-

tures can drop much lower inland (see the tables for **Canberra** and **Bourke**). The temperatures for **Canberra** also illustrate the effect of a moderate altitude in lowering the winter minimum temperatures. The low annual rainfall at **Bourke** illustrates the transition to the semi-arid conditions of the interior. It should be noted that the extreme maximum temperatures at **Bourke** are higher than those recorded in the tropical regions of the north and that both **Sydney** and **Melbourne** occasionally record temperatures well above 100° F (38° C). Latitude here begins to affect the number of sunshine hours. Summer sunshine averages eight to nine hours a day in summer but only five to six in winter. At **Melbourne**, which gets more cloud and disturbed weather despite a lower rainfall, sunshine hours a day in winter are only three to four as against seven to eight in summer.

AUSTRALIA   Bourke (New South Wales) 361 ft (110 m) 30°05′ S 145°58′ E 63 years

	Temperature °F			Temperature °C			Relative humidity		Precipitation			
	Highest recorded	Average daily	Lowest recorded	Highest recorded	Average daily	Lowest recorded	0830 hours	1430 hours	Average monthly		Average no. days with 0.01 in + (0.25 mm +)	
		max.	min.			max.	min.		%	%	in	mm	
J	125	99	70	48	52	37	21	9	42	23	1.4	36	3	J
F	120	97	69	49	49	36	21	9	48	26	1.5	38	3	F
M	117	91	64	35	47	33	18	2	52	29	1.1	28	3	M
A	107	82	55	35	42	28	13	2	57	35	1.1	28	3	A
M	95	73	47	27	35	23	8	−3	67	44	1.0	25	4	M
J	86	65	42	25	30	18	6	−4	76	51	1.1	28	4	J
J	84	65	40	26	29	18	4	−3	74	48	0.9	23	5	J
A	94	70	43	27	34	21	6	−3	64	38	0.8	20	3	A
S	100	77	49	29	38	25	9	−2	53	30	0.8	20	3	S
O	112	85	56	35	44	29	13	2	45	26	0.9	23	4	O
N	115	93	63	38	46	34	17	3	43	25	1.2	31	4	N
D	121	97	67	41	49	36	19	5	42	25	1.4	36	5	D

Canberra (Australian Capital Territory) 1837 ft (560 m) 35°20′ S 149°15′ E 23 years AUSTRALIA

	Temperature °F			Temperature °C			Relative humidity		Precipitation		
	Highest recorded	Average daily	Lowest recorded	Highest recorded	Average daily	Lowest recorded	0900 hours	1500 hours	Average monthly		Average no. days with 0.01 in + (0.25 mm +)
		max.	min.			max.	min.		%	%	in	mm	
J	109	82	55	38	43	28	13	3	56	35	1.9	48	7	J
F	103	82	55	33	39	28	13	1	61	39	1.7	43	7	F
M	99	76	51	31	37	24	11	−1	69	42	2.2	56	7	M
A	91	67	44	27	33	19	7	−3	75	51	1.6	41	7	A
M	73	60	37	19	23	16	3	−7	82	57	1.8	46	7	M
J	66	53	34	18	19	12	1	−8	85	64	2.1	53	9	J
J	65	52	33	14	18	11	1	−10	85	63	1.8	46	10	J
A	73	55	35	18	23	13	2	−8	81	59	2.2	56	11	A
S	83	61	38	24	28	16	3	−4	72	50	1.6	41	9	S
O	94	68	43	27	34	20	6	−3	64	45	2.2	56	11	O
N	98	75	48	28	37	24	9	−2	59	41	1.9	48	8	N
D	103	80	53	32	39	27	12	0	56	36	2.0	51	8	D

Melbourne (Victoria) 115 ft (35 m) 37°49′ S 144°58′ E 88 years AUSTRALIA

	Temperature °F			Temperature °C			Relative humidity		Precipitation		
	Highest recorded	Average daily	Lowest recorded	Highest recorded	Average daily	Lowest recorded	0830 hours	1430 hours	Average monthly		Average no. days with 0.01 in + (0.25 mm +)
		max.	min.			max.	min.		%	%	in	mm	
J	114	78	57	42	46	26	14	6	58	48	1.9	48	9	J
F	110	78	57	40	43	26	14	4	62	50	1.8	46	8	F
M	107	75	55	37	42	24	13	3	64	51	2.2	56	9	M
A	95	68	51	35	35	20	11	2	72	56	2.3	58	13	A
M	84	62	47	30	29	17	8	−1	79	62	2.1	53	14	M
J	72	57	44	28	22	14	7	−2	83	67	2.1	53	16	J
J	69	56	42	27	21	13	6	−3	82	65	1.9	48	17	J
A	77	59	43	28	25	15	6	−2	76	60	1.9	48	17	A
S	89	63	46	31	32	17	8	−1	68	55	2.3	58	15	S
O	98	67	48	32	37	19	9	0	61	52	2.6	66	14	O
N	106	71	51	37	41	22	11	3	60	52	2.3	58	13	N
D	111	75	54	40	44	24	12	4	59	51	2.3	58	11	D

	Temperature °F			Temperature °C			Relative humidity		Precipitation		
	Highest recorded	Average daily	Lowest recorded	Highest recorded	Average daily	Lowest recorded	0900 hours	1500 hours	Average monthly		Average no. days with 0.01 in + (0.25 mm +)
		max.	min.			max.	min.		%	%	in	mm	
J	114	78	65	51	46	26	18	11	68	64	3.5	89	14	J
F	108	78	65	49	42	26	18	9	71	65	4.0	102	13	F
M	103	76	63	49	39	24	17	9	73	65	5.0	127	14	M
A	91	71	58	45	33	22	14	7	76	64	5.3	135	14	A
M	86	66	52	40	30	19	11	4	77	63	5.0	127	13	M
J	80	61	48	36	27	16	9	2	77	62	4.6	117	12	J
J	78	60	46	36	26	16	8	2	76	60	4.6	117	12	J
A	82	63	48	37	28	17	9	3	72	56	3.0	76	11	A
S	92	67	51	41	33	19	11	5	67	55	2.9	74	12	S
O	99	71	56	42	37	22	13	6	65	57	2.8	71	12	O
N	103	74	60	46	39	23	16	8	65	60	2.9	74	12	N
D	107	77	63	48	42	25	17	9	66	62	2.9	74	13	D

SOUTHERN AND WESTERN AUSTRALIA

This region consists of two small districts separated by the desert coast along the Great Australian Bight where the annual rainfall is below 10 in (250 mm). The area around Spencer Gulf in South Australia, parts of western Victoria and the southwestern part of Western Australia are distinctive in having a Mediterranean type of climate. Rainfall is moderate and mainly falls in the winter. Summers are warm to hot with an almost complete drought. The winter season gets much changeable weather, associated with cyclonic disturbances in the westerly wind belt which affects the south of Australia during this season.

The tables for **Perth** and **Adelaide** are representative of the wetter parts of these two districts. The mildness of the winter is illustrated by the fact that at neither place has the temperature ever fallen below freezing point. The winter maximum of rainfall is very clearly marked at both places, but **Perth** gets a much heavier rainfall than **Adelaide**. The extent of this wet winter climate is rather greater in Western Australia than it is in South Australia where the transition to desert inland is quite rapid. During the hot, dry summer, temperatures can occasionally rise very high: over 110° F (43° C). In summer these areas average between nine and ten hours of sunshine a day as compared with five to six in winter.

Adelaide (South Australia) 140 ft (43 m) 34°56′ S 138°35′ E 86 years — AUSTRALIA

	Temperature °F			Temperature °C			Relative humidity		Precipitation		
	Highest recorded	Average daily	Lowest recorded	Highest recorded	Average daily	Lowest recorded	0830 hours	1430 hours	Average monthly		Average no. days with 0.01 in + (0.25 mm +)
		max.	min.		max.	min.		%	%	in	mm	
J	118	86	61	45	48	30	16	7	38	31	0.8	20	5	J
F	114	86	62	45	46	30	17	7	41	32	0.7	18	5	F
M	111	81	59	44	44	27	15	7	46	36	1.0	25	5	M
A	99	73	55	40	37	23	13	4	55	45	1.8	46	10	A
M	89	66	50	37	32	19	10	3	67	56	2.7	69	13	M
J	76	61	47	33	24	16	8	1	76	65	3.0	76	15	J
J	74	59	45	32	23	15	7	0	76	63	2.6	66	16	J
A	85	62	46	32	29	17	8	0	69	57	2.6	66	16	A
S	91	66	48	33	33	19	9	1	60	52	2.1	53	13	S
O	103	73	51	36	39	23	11	2	51	42	1.7	43	10	O
N	113	79	55	41	45	26	13	5	43	36	1.1	28	8	N
D	115	83	59	43	46	28	15	6	39	32	1.0	25	6	D

Perth (Western Australia) 197 ft (60 m) 31°57′ S 115°51′ E 44 years — AUSTRALIA

	Temperature °F			Temperature °C			Relative humidity		Precipitation		
	Highest recorded	Average daily	Lowest recorded	Highest recorded	Average daily	Lowest recorded	0830 hours	1430 hours	Average monthly		Average no. days with 0.01 in + (0.25 mm +)
		max.	min.		max.	min.		%	%	in	mm	
J	110	85	63	49	43	29	17	9	51	44	0.3	8	3	J
F	112	85	63	48	44	29	17	9	53	43	0.4	10	3	F
M	106	81	61	46	41	27	16	8	58	45	0.8	20	5	M
A	100	76	57	39	38	24	14	4	61	49	1.7	43	8	A
M	90	69	53	34	32	21	12	1	72	58	5.1	130	15	M
J	82	64	50	35	28	18	10	2	76	63	7.1	180	17	J
J	76	63	48	34	24	17	9	1	76	63	6.7	170	19	J
A	82	64	48	35	28	18	9	2	73	61	5.7	145	19	A
S	91	67	50	39	33	19	10	4	67	58	3.4	86	15	S
O	95	70	53	40	35	21	12	4	60	55	2.2	56	12	O
N	105	76	57	42	41	24	14	6	54	49	0.8	20	7	N
D	108	81	61	48	42	27	16	9	50	47	0.5	13	5	D

THE DESERT AND SEMI-ARID REGIONS OF CENTRAL AUSTRALIA

This is the most extensive climatic region of Australia and includes parts of each mainland state with the exception of Victoria. In the north it can be roughly defined by the 20 in (500 mm) annual rainfall limit and in the south by the 12 in (300 mm) annual rainfall line. Rainfall is everywhere scanty and unreliable. The cool season rainfall of the south is much more effective than the hot season rainfall of the tropical north of Australia. Compare the table for **Alice Springs**, which is almost in the centre of the continent, and that for **Kalgoorlie** which is on the desert margin of Western Australia.

Like most continental interiors there is a considerable daily and seasonal change of temperature. Both **Alice Springs** and **Kalgoorlie** have experienced temperatures below freezing and at **Alice Springs**, which is almost within the tropics, they have fallen below freezing point in several winter months. These desert areas are the sunniest part of Australia. Daily sunshine hours average nine to ten around the year. The high temperatures are to some extent mitigated by low humidity. Occasional dust storms during strong winds are a minor climatic hazard.

Alice Springs (Northern Territory) 1901 ft (579 m) 23°38′ S 133°58′ E 18 years   AUSTRALIA

| | Temperature °F | | | Temperature °C | | | Relative humidity | | Precipitation | | |
| | Highest recorded | Average daily | Lowest recorded | Highest recorded | Average daily | Lowest recorded | 0800 hours | 1430 hours | Average monthly | | Average no. days with 0.01 in + (0.25 mm +) |
		max.	min.			max.	min.		%	%	in	mm	
J	111	97	70	51	44	36	21	11	31	23	1.7	43	4	J
F	109	95	69	48	43	35	21	9	34	24	1.3	33	3	F
M	110	90	63	45	43	32	17	7	36	25	1.1	28	3	M
A	99	81	54	36	37	27	12	2	40	28	0.4	10	2	A
M	96	73	46	29	36	23	8	−2	47	32	0.6	15	2	M
J	86	67	41	22	30	19	5	−6	54	35	0.5	13	2	J
J	86	67	39	19	30	19	4	−7	49	31	0.3	8	1	J
A	96	73	43	25	36	23	6	−4	39	25	0.3	8	2	A
S	100	81	49	31	38	27	9	−1	31	22	0.3	8	1	S
O	106	88	58	39	41	31	14	4	27	21	0.7	18	3	O
N	108	93	64	42	42	34	18	6	27	21	1.2	31	4	N
D	111	96	68	50	44	36	20	10	29	22	1.5	38	4	D

Kalgoorlie (Western Australia) 1247 ft (370 m) 30°45′ S 121°30′ E 30 years   AUSTRALIA

| | Temperature °F | | | Temperature °C | | | Relative humidity | | Precipitation | | |
| | Highest recorded | Average daily | Lowest recorded | Highest recorded | Average daily | Lowest recorded | 0900 hours | 1500 hours | Average monthly | | Average no. days with 0.01 in + (0.25 mm +) |
		max.	min.			max.	min.		%	%	in	mm	
J	114	93	64	47	46	34	18	8	44	25	0.4	10	3	J
F	115	92	64	48	46	33	18	9	49	30	0.8	20	2	F
M	107	86	61	43	42	30	16	6	53	22	0.9	23	4	M
A	102	78	55	37	39	26	13	3	58	38	0.9	23	4	A
M	92	69	49	35	33	21	9	2	65	46	1.2	31	5	M
J	82	63	45	31	28	17	7	−1	74	52	1.2	31	6	J
J	81	62	43	30	27	17	6	−1	73	45	0.9	23	7	J
A	87	65	44	29	31	18	7	−2	64	42	0.9	23	6	A
S	96	73	48	32	36	23	9	0	53	33	0.5	13	3	S
O	103	78	52	33	39	26	11	1	46	28	0.7	18	4	O
N	111	87	58	38	44	31	14	3	42	25	0.6	15	3	N
D	113	92	62	46	45	33	17	8	42	25	0.7	18	2	D

TASMANIA

This rugged island, a little smaller than Scotland, is mountainous so there are quite big differences in weather and climate between the coastal regions and the interior. The highest mountains rise to over 5000 ft (1500 m) and, on the west, are fully exposed to the stormy westerly winds which bring heavy rainfall, over 100 in (2500 mm) a year in places. The eastern lowlands, represented by the table for **Hobart**, have a much lower rainfall of between 20 and 30 in (500 and 750 mm) a year. The weather is changeable and often disturbed around the year.

Tasmania's climate is strongly influenced by the relative warmth of the southern ocean so that winters are mild at sea level and summers rarely excessively hot. Its climate and weather throughout the year are rather similar to that of northwest Europe, particularly Brittany or northwest Spain. Daily sunshine hours range from four to five in winter to seven or eight in summer, sunnier than much of northwest Europe. The occasional high temperatures in summer (over 100° F or 38° C) occur when very warm air is drawn southwards from the central region of Australia. Although snow is often heavy in winter on the mountains it does not lie throughout the summer.

AUSTRALIA — Hobart (Tasmania) 177 ft (54 m) 42°53′ S 147°20′ E 70 years

	Temperature °F			Temperature °C			Relative humidity		Precipitation			
	Highest recorded	Average daily	Lowest recorded	Highest recorded	Average daily	Lowest recorded	0900 hours	1500 hours	Average monthly		Average no. days with 0.01 in + (0.25 mm +)	
		max. / min.			max. / min.		%	%	in	mm		
J	105	71 / 53	40	41	22 / 12	4	58	53	1.9	48	13	J
F	104	71 / 53	39	40	22 / 12	4	62	56	1.5	38	10	F
M	99	68 / 51	35	37	20 / 11	2	66	56	1.8	46	13	M
A	87	63 / 48	33	31	17 / 9	1	72	61	1.9	48	14	A
M	78	58 / 44	29	26	14 / 7	−2	77	63	1.8	46	14	M
J	69	53 / 41	29	21	12 / 5	−2	79	70	2.2	56	16	J
J	66	52 / 40	28	19	11 / 4	−2	80	69	2.1	53	17	J
A	72	55 / 41	30	22	13 / 5	−1	75	61	1.9	48	18	A
S	82	59 / 43	30	28	15 / 6	−1	67	58	2.1	53	17	S
O	92	63 / 46	32	33	17 / 8	0	63	56	2.3	58	18	O
N	98	66 / 48	35	37	19 / 9	2	59	54	2.4	61	16	N
D	105	69 / 51	38	41	21 / 11	3	58	54	2.1	53	14	D

The island of New Guinea is three times the size of Great Britain and lies to the north of the Australian continent between the equator and 12° S. The western half of the island is part of Indonesia and the eastern half (Papua) is administered by Australia. The island has a single range of high mountains running from east to west with the highest peak rising to 16,400 ft (5000 m). There is an extensive swampy lowland in the south.

The weather and climate of New Guinea are tropical, similar to that described in greater detail on p. 239 for Indonesia. Because of the great range of altitude, and the different exposures of the north and south coasts to the seasonally alternating north and south monsoons, there are great variations in the amount of rainfall and the time of heaviest fall from place to place. Temperatures at low levels are high throughout the year with little variation from month to month. The table for **Port Moresby**, on the south coast, is representative of the temperature and humidity around the year at low

levels. **Port Moresby**, however, with an annual rainfall of 45 in (1125 mm), is one of the driest places on the island. Most places have between 80 and 120 in (2000 and 3000 mm) of rain a year and in the mountains this may rise as high as 200 in (5000 mm). The highest mountain in western New Guinea carries a permanent snowfield although it is almost on the equator.

Much of the rain comes in heavy downpours, accompanied by thunder, during afternoon and evening storms; but longer periods of rain occur during the wettest months. The weather in the lowlands is sultry and humid but at higher levels the lower temperature makes for much more pleasant conditions. Much of the island is still very inaccessible and some parts are still little known or explored.

The weather and climate of the neighbouring islands of New Britain, New Ireland and the small islands of the Bismarck Archipelago, between 2° and 6° S, are similar to that of the main island of New Guinea.

Port Moresby 126 ft (38 m) 9°29′ S 147°09′ E 19 years

| | Temperature °F | | | Temperature °C | | | Relative humidity | | Precipitation | | |
| | Highest recorded | Average daily | Lowest recorded | Highest recorded | Average daily | Lowest recorded | 0900 hours | 1500 hours | Average monthly | | Average no. days with 0.1 in + (2.5 mm +) |
		max.	min.			max.	min.		%	%	in	mm	
J	98	89	76	69	37	32	24	21	72	69	7.0	178	8	J
F	96	87	76	69	36	31	24	21	73	72	7.6	193	7	F
M	96	88	76	70	36	31	24	21	74	73	6.7	170	9	M
A	96	87	75	65	36	31	24	18	75	74	4.2	107	5	A
M	94	86	75	70	34	30	24	21	77	77	2.5	64	2	M
J	91	84	74	64	33	29	23	18	78	77	1.3	33	3	J
J	90	83	73	66	32	28	23	19	78	78	1.1	28	2	J
A	90	82	73	66	32	28	23	19	77	77	0.7	18	2	A
S	94	84	74	66	34	29	23	19	78	77	1.0	25	2	S
O	94	86	75	68	34	30	24	20	75	76	1.4	36	2	O
N	96	88	76	69	36	31	24	21	73	73	1.9	48	3	N
D	97	90	76	70	36	32	24	21	72	69	4.4	112	6	D

NEW ZEALAND

New Zealand consists of two main islands – North and South Island – together with some small offshore islands. It is situated between 34° and 47° S in the South Pacific and has an area a little larger than Great Britain. Situated 1200 miles (1900 km) from the nearest large land-mass, in the belt of disturbed westerly winds, it has a very equable maritime climate more like that of western Britain than that of Portugal with which it can be compared in latitude. (See map p. 298.)

Weather in New Zealand is very changeable throughout the year and all months are moderately wet. Fine sunny spells of weather can occur at any time of the year, however, and the country has more sunshine than might be expected in such a variable climate. Daily sunshine hours average from four to five in winter to six or seven in summer in most parts of New Zealand. The north of the country and the east coasts are rather more sunny than the extreme south and the wetter west coast of South Island.

Both North and South Islands are hilly and mountainous. The west coast of South Island is backed by the high New Zealand Alps with Mt Cook, the highest peak, rising to over 12,000 ft (3700 m). There are several volcanic peaks in North Island rising above 8000 ft (2400 m). These higher mountains carry snow throughout the year. In the New Zealand Alps there are extensive snowfields and glaciers as precipitation on the western side of South Island is heavy: as much as 80–100 in (2000–2500 mm) and over 200 in (5000 mm) in the mountains.

Snow can occur almost anywhere at sea level in New Zealand but it is very rare in the extreme north of North Island. Here the climate is almost subtropical with very mild winters and warm, rather humid, summers. The table for **Auckland** is representative of this, the warmest part of the country. The tables for **Wellington** and **Napier** show that temperatures are only a little lower elsewhere in North Island where frost is very rare on the coast but can be quite frequent inland.

The tables for **Christchurch**, **Dunedin** and **Hokitika** in South Island show that temperatures are a little lower here throughout the year. Extremes of heat and cold, however, are very rare in New Zealand thanks to the dominant influence of the ocean. **Hokitika** on the west coast is much wetter in all months than **Christchurch** or **Dunedin**. The table for **Christchurch** is representative of the Canterbury Plains, the driest part of the country, but inland winter temperatures are rather lower and frost more frequent. The lowlands to the east of the New Zealand Alps are often affected by a warm, very dry wind which suddenly raises the temperature for a few hours or a day or so. This is a föhn-type wind and occurs when strong westerly winds crossing the mountains are warmed as the air descends on the lee side. The wind melts snow in winter but can dessicate crops in summer.

New Zealand as a whole has a very healthy and pleasant climate with few weather hazards. The combination of weather, altitude and scenery provide excellent opportunities for a range of sports and outdoor activities.

Auckland (North Island) 85 ft (26 m) 36°47′ S 174°39′ E 36 years   NEW ZEALAND

	Temperature °F			Temperature °C			Relative humidity		Precipitation		
	Highest recorded	Average daily	Lowest recorded	Highest recorded	Average daily	Lowest recorded	0900 hours	1500 hours	Average monthly		Average no. days with 0.01 in + (0.25 mm +)
		max.	min.			max.	min.		%	%	in	mm	
J	90	73	60	45	32	23	16	7	71	62	3.1	79	10	J
F	90	73	60	47	32	23	16	8	72	61	3.7	94	10	F
M	86	71	59	42	30	22	15	6	74	65	3.2	81	11	M
A	81	67	56	39	27	19	13	4	78	69	3.8	97	14	A
M	73	62	51	36	23	17	11	2	80	70	5.0	127	19	M
J	70	58	48	35	21	14	9	2	83	73	5.4	137	19	J
J	67	56	46	33	19	13	8	1	84	74	5.7	145	21	J
A	67	58	46	34	19	14	8	1	80	70	4.6	117	19	A
S	71	60	49	34	22	16	9	1	76	68	4.0	102	17	S
O	75	63	52	36	24	17	11	2	74	66	4.0	102	16	O
N	81	66	54	41	27	19	12	5	71	64	3.5	89	15	N
D	89	70	57	43	32	21	14	6	70	64	3.1	79	12	D

Christchurch (South Island) 32 ft (10 m) 43°32′ S 172°37′ E 52 years   NEW ZEALAND

	Temperature °F			Temperature °C			Relative humidity		Precipitation		
	Highest recorded	Average daily	Lowest recorded	Highest recorded	Average daily	Lowest recorded	0900 hours	1430 hours	Average monthly		Average no. days with 0.01 in + (0.25 mm +)
		max.	min.			max.	min.		%	%	in	mm	
J	96	70	53	34	35	21	12	1	65	59	2.2	56	10	J
F	94	69	53	35	34	21	12	2	71	60	1.7	43	8	F
M	90	66	50	30	32	19	10	−1	75	69	1.9	48	9	M
A	82	62	45	26	28	17	7	−3	82	71	1.9	48	10	A
M	78	56	40	21	26	13	4	−6	85	69	2.6	66	12	M
J	69	51	36	22	21	11	2	6	87	72	2.6	66	13	J
J	70	50	35	23	21	10	2	−5	87	76	2.7	69	13	J
A	70	52	36	23	21	11	2	−5	81	66	1.9	48	11	A
S	81	57	40	23	27	14	4	−5	72	69	1.8	46	10	S
O	88	62	44	26	31	17	7	−3	63	60	1.7	43	10	O
N	90	66	47	31	32	19	8	−1	64	64	1.9	48	10	N
D	92	69	51	33	33	21	11	1	67	60	2.2	56	10	D

	Temperature °F				Temperature °C				Relative humidity		Precipitation			
	Highest recorded	Average daily		Lowest recorded	Highest recorded	Average daily		Lowest recorded	0900 hours	1500 hours	Average monthly		Average no. days with 0.01 in + (0.25 mm +)	
		max.	min.			max.	min.		%	%	in	mm		
J	94	66	50	36	34	19	10	2	69	68	3.4	86	14	J
F	90	66	50	37	32	19	10	3	71	68	2.8	71	11	F
M	85	63	48	34	29	17	9	1	74	70	3.0	76	13	M
A	85	59	45	31	29	15	7	−1	77	71	2.8	71	13	A
M	72	53	41	29	22	12	5	−2	76	76	3.2	81	14	M
J	68	49	39	24	20	9	4	−4	77	76	3.2	81	13	J
J	66	48	37	23	19	9	3	−5	77	74	3.1	79	13	J
A	70	51	38	25	21	11	3	−4	73	73	3.0	76	13	A
S	77	55	41	29	25	13	5	−2	71	70	2.7	69	14	S
O	83	59	42	30	28	15	6	−1	67	69	3.0	76	14	O
N	85	62	45	32	29	17	7	0	68	69	3.2	81	14	N
D	88	65	48	35	31	18	9	2	73	71	3.5	89	15	D

	Temperature °F				Temperature °C				Relative humidity	Precipitation			
	Highest recorded	Average daily		Lowest recorded	Highest recorded	Average daily		Lowest recorded	0900 hours	Average monthly		Average no. days with 0.01 in + (0.25 mm +)	
		max.	min.			max.	min.		%	in	mm		
J	79	66	53	35	26	19	12	2	80	10.3	262	14	J
F	84	67	53	37	29	19	12	3	80	7.5	191	12	F
M	84	65	51	35	29	18	11	2	83	9.4	239	14	M
A	74	61	47	31	23	16	8	−1	87	9.3	236	15	A
M	72	57	42	28	22	14	6	−2	87	9.6	244	15	M
J	64	53	38	26	18	12	3	−3	88	9.1	231	15	J
J	65	53	37	25	18	12	3	−4	86	8.6	218	16	J
A	67	54	38	26	19	12	3	−3	84	9.4	239	16	A
S	68	56	42	27	20	13	6	−3	80	8.9	226	17	S
O	74	59	46	30	23	15	8	−1	78	11.5	292	19	O
N	74	61	48	32	23	16	9	0	78	10.5	267	18	N
D	79	64	51	33	26	18	11	1	80	10.3	262	16	D

Napier (North Island) 5 ft (2 m) 39°29′ S 176°55′ E 34 years — NEW ZEALAND

	Temperature °F				Temperature °C				Relative humidity		Precipitation			
	Highest recorded	Average daily		Lowest recorded	Highest recorded	Average daily		Lowest recorded	0930 hours	1530 hours	Average monthly		Average no. days with 0.01 in + (0.25 mm +)	
		max.	min.			max.	min.		%	%	in	mm		
J	94	75	57	41	34	24	14	5	63	60	2.9	74	8	J
F	94	74	57	38	34	23	14	3	71	60	3.0	76	8	F
M	89	71	55	39	32	22	13	4	77	69	2.9	74	8	M
A	84	67	50	31	29	19	10	−1	80	68	3.0	76	8	A
M	77	62	47	31	25	17	8	−1	81	68	3.5	89	10	M
J	81	57	41	29	27	14	5	−2	80	68	3.4	86	11	J
J	71	56	41	27	22	13	5	−3	83	70	4.0	102	12	J
A	71	58	42	27	22	14	6	−3	77	69	3.3	84	12	A
S	80	62	45	31	27	17	7	−1	73	68	2.2	56	10	S
O	81	66	49	31	27	19	9	−1	68	63	2.2	56	9	O
N	89	69	51	35	32	21	11	2	67	61	2.4	61	9	N
D	93	73	55	38	34	23	13	3	65	61	2.3	58	8	D

Wellington (North Island) 415 ft (127 m) 41°16′ S 174°46′ E 65 years — NEW ZEALAND

	Temperature °F				Temperature °C				Relative humidity		Precipitation			
	Highest recorded	Average daily		Lowest recorded	Highest recorded	Average daily		Lowest recorded	0900 hours	1500 hours	Average monthly		Average no. days with 0.01 in + (0.25 mm +)	
		max.	min.			max.	min.		%	%	in	mm		
J	85	69	56	39	29	21	13	4	73	67	3.2	81	10	J
F	88	69	56	41	31	21	13	5	75	71	3.2	81	9	F
M	81	67	54	39	27	19	12	4	76	69	3.2	81	11	M
A	74	63	51	36	23	17	11	2	79	76	3.8	97	13	A
M	71	58	47	32	22	14	8	0	80	77	4.6	117	16	M
J	69	55	44	30	21	13	7	−1	81	78	4.6	117	17	J
J	66	53	42	29	19	12	6	−2	81	76	5.4	137	18	J
A	66	54	43	29	19	12	6	−2	80	74	4.6	117	17	A
S	69	57	46	31	21	14	8	−1	76	75	3.8	97	15	S
O	75	60	48	34	24	16	9	1	75	74	4.0	102	14	O
N	81	63	50	36	27	17	10	2	76	69	3.5	89	13	N
D	83	67	54	38	28	19	12	3	74	69	3.5	89	12	D

Caribbean Islands

Situated between 10° and 26° N, and therefore almost entirely within the tropics, all the West Indian islands have a distinctly oceanic variety of tropical climate. Because of the similarity of weather and climate over this whole area, the Caribbean Islands are described together. Short notes only appear under the separate headings for each political unit or group of small islands.

The islands form a large arc extending eastwards from the Yucatan peninsula of Mexico and the Florida peninsula of the United States. The larger islands are, from west to east: Cuba, Jamaica, Hispaniola (divided into the two separate political units of Haiti and the Dominican Republic) and Puerto Rico. To the north of these larger islands lies a group of small scattered islands: the Bahamas and the Turks and Caicos Islands. East of Puerto Rico the chain of islands curves south-wards as the Lesser Antilles to terminate in Trinidad which is close to the coast of Venezuela. The Lesser Antilles are often divided into the Leeward Islands group in the north and the Windward Islands group in the south.

Despite the large area over which these islands are scattered there is a strong similarity of weather and climate everywhere. The waters of the Atlantic Ocean and the Caribbean Sea are warm at all times of the year, being influenced by ocean currents from equatorial latitudes which unite to form the Gulf Stream to the north of the Caribbean. The area lies for the whole year under the influence of the northeast trade winds, or the North Atlantic anticyclone which lies farthest south in the winter period.

Almost everywhere the wettest months are from May to October and the winter period is relatively, but by no means completely, dry. The area experiences no great extremes of temperature; winters are warm and sunny and summers are hot, but without excessively high temperatures so that heat stress is rarely felt. Almost nowhere in the Caribbean have maximum temperatures above 100° F (38° C) been experienced and only in Cuba and the northern islands of the Bahamas do winter temperatures occasionally fall much below 60° F (15° C). This equability of temperature is a consequence of the strong influence of the warm sea. Waves of cold air from North America in winter and spring affect only western Cuba and the northern Bahamas for a few days and the air arriving in the islands may be as much as 10°–15° F (5°–8° C) warmer than when it left the coast of the mainland.

Most of the larger and many of the smaller islands are mountainous and this gives rise to numerous local differences of weather and climate. Apart from the fall of temperature with altitude, there is often a big increase of rainfall on the mountains; and the northern and eastern slopes and coasts of the islands are usually considerably wetter than the southern and western sides which are sheltered from the persistent northeast trade winds. Unfortunately most of the climatic data available for the West Indian islands is from places at or near sea level, but a good example of the increase of rainfall with altitude can be seen by comparing the table for **Camp Jacob** on the island of Guadeloupe with that for **Plymouth** on the nearby island of Montserrat – both in the Leeward Islands. **Camp Jacob**, at an altitude of 1750 ft (530 m), has more than twice the annual rainfall of **Plymouth**. It is known that annual rainfall on the highest mountains in Cuba and Jamaica is two or three times that of the places at sea level for which tables are given in this book. In these wetter mountain areas cloud is more frequent than at sea level at all times of the year.

The Caribbean Islands have developed an important tourist trade and one reason for this is the large number of hours of sunshine around the year. Daily sunshine hours average from seven to nine, with more hours in the driest months. The winter months are the driest and sunniest and, at this time, the slightly lower temperatures are made more pleasant by frequent sea breezes and lower humidity. Even in the warmest months the combination of temperature and humidity is rarely very uncomfortable if moderated by a strong breeze.

The tables show that some places have a large number of days with rain; as many as one in two or one in three. This should not be taken to imply that it rains all day; on many days cloud builds up in the afternoon to give short thundery showers in the late afternoon and evening. Prolonged spells of rain are rare and are usually associated with hurricanes or tropical storms which are the worst features of the weather and climate of the Caribbean.

Hurricanes occur between June and November and are most frequent in the months of August and September. During the worst of these storms between 10 and 20 in (250 and 500 mm) of rain may fall over a period of two or three days and the very violent winds may cause damage. Individual islands may go several years without experiencing a severe hurricane and, on the larger islands, their worst effects may be confined to only one area. Over the area as a whole, however, some two to three hurricanes may occur each year. They develop east of the Caribbean and move westwards before curving north and east close to the North American mainland. A significant proportion of the rainfall in the months August to October may be caused by hurricanes since places which escape the centre of the storm with its damaging winds may be affected by the cloud and heavy rainfall on the fringe. Tropical storms which do not develop to full hurricane intensity may bring a period of two or three days of cloud and rain.

The Bahamas and the neighbouring Turks and Caicos Islands are the most northerly group of Caribbean Islands. They extend from 21° to 27° N in a southeast to northwest direction and stand between the open waters of the Atlantic and the enclosed Caribbean Sea. There are about a dozen large islands and numerous small islands or coral reefs called 'cays'. Most of the islands are low-lying and their annual rainfall is rather lower than that of some other islands in the West Indies.

The climatic table for **Nassau** on New Providence Island in the north of the group shows that winter temperatures here are occasionally rather low when cold air blows out of the North American continent in winter or spring. Otherwise average temperatures are similar to the rest of the Caribbean Islands. Such cold waves do not affect the island of **Grand Turk** in the extreme southeast of the group (see the table for **Grand Turk**).

Grand Turk 11 ft (3 m) 21°29′ N 71°07′ W 10 years   **THE BAHAMAS**

	Temperature °F			Temperature °C			Relative humidity	Precipitation		
	Highest recorded	Average daily	Lowest recorded	Highest recorded	Average daily	Lowest recorded		Average monthly		Average no. days with 0.01 in + (0.25 mm +)
		max.	min.			max.	min.			in	mm
J	86	81	70	60	30	27	21	16	—	2.2	56	13	J
F	88	81	70	61	31	27	21	16	—	1.4	36	8	F
M	90	82	71	63	32	28	22	17	—	1.1	28	8	M
A	91	84	73	67	33	29	23	19	—	1.5	38	6	A
M	93	86	75	66	34	30	24	19	—	2.6	66	8	M
J	96	87	77	68	36	31	25	20	—	1.6	41	9	J
J	91	88	77	70	33	31	25	21	—	1.7	43	10	J
A	94	89	78	71	34	32	26	22	—	2.0	51	12	A
S	95	88	77	66	35	31	25	19	—	3.2	81	11	S
O	93	87	76	70	34	31	24	21	—	4.0	102	13	O
N	91	84	73	65	33	29	23	18	—	4.5	114	14	N
D	89	82	71	66	32	28	22	19	—	2.7	69	13	D

	Temperature °F				Temperature °C				Relative humidity		Precipitation			
	Highest recorded	Average daily		Lowest recorded	Highest recorded	Average daily		Lowest recorded	0700 hours	1300 hours	Average monthly		Average no. days with 0.04 in + (1 mm +)	
		max.	min.			max.	min.		%	%	in	mm		
J	85	77	65	41	29	25	18	5	84	64	1.4	36	6	J
F	86	77	64	43	30	25	18	6	82	62	1.5	38	5	F
M	88	79	66	46	31	26	19	8	81	64	1.4	36	5	M
A	91	81	69	53	33	27	21	12	79	65	2.5	64	6	A
M	92	84	71	53	33	29	22	12	79	65	4.6	117	9	M
J	94	87	74	62	34	31	23	17	81	68	6.4	163	12	J
J	94	88	75	67	34	31	24	19	80	69	5.8	147	14	J
A	94	89	76	67	34	32	24	19	82	70	5.3	135	14	A
S	92	88	75	65	33	31	24	18	84	73	6.9	175	15	S
O	92	85	73	54	33	29	23	12	83	71	6.5	165	13	O
N	89	81	70	49	32	27	21	9	83	68	2.8	71	9	N
D	86	79	67	45	30	26	19	7	84	66	1.3	33	6	D

Cuba is the largest of the islands of the Caribbean. It is about as large as the state of Pennsylvania and a little smaller than England. It extends for a distance of almost 700 miles (1100 km) from west to east but has an average width of only about 75 miles (110 km). Although there are mountains rising to between 3000 and 6000 ft (900 and 1800 m) much of the island is low-lying.

The table for **Havana** is representative of the low-lying parts on the north of the island. Rainfall on the north coast is rather more than in the south and the hills may receive over 100 in (2500 mm) a year. The driest region of the island is in the southeast around Guàntánámo where rain is as low as 20 in (500 mm) a year. Western Cuba is occasionally affected in winter and spring by waves of cold air from the interior of North America which cause temperatures to drop below 50° F (10° C) for a day or two. Such low temperatures are most unusual for the Caribbean Islands.

Havana 80 ft (24 m) 23°08′ N 82°21′ W 25 years

	Temperature °F			Temperature °C			Relative humidity		Precipitation		
	Highest recorded	Average daily		Lowest recorded	Highest recorded	Average daily		Lowest recorded	0530 hours	1130 hours	Average monthly		Average no. days with 0.04 in + (1 mm +)
		max.	min.			max.	min.		%	%	in	mm	
J	89	79	65	50	32	26	18	10	85	64	2.8	71	6	J
F	91	79	65	50	33	26	18	10	85	61	1.8	46	4	F
M	91	81	67	53	33	27	19	12	84	58	1.8	46	4	M
A	94	84	69	55	34	29	21	13	83	58	2.3	58	4	A
M	94	86	72	59	34	30	22	15	85	62	4.7	119	7	M
J	96	88	74	66	36	31	23	19	87	65	6.5	165	10	J
J	93	89	75	66	34	32	24	19	87	62	4.9	125	9	J
A	95	89	75	68	35	32	24	20	88	64	5.3	135	10	A
S	94	88	75	67	34	31	24	19	89	66	5.9	150	11	S
O	94	85	73	63	34	29	23	17	87	68	6.8	173	11	O
N	91	81	69	55	33	27	21	13	85	65	3.1	79	7	N
D	89	79	67	51	32	26	19	11	84	64	2.3	58	6	D

THE DOMINICAN REPUBLIC

The Dominican Republic occupies the eastern two thirds of the large Caribbean island of Hispaniola and has a land border with Haiti on the west. The country has an area of nearly 19,000 square miles (49,000 sq. km), twice as large as the state of Vermont or Wales. It is the most mountainous of the Caribbean Islands with the highest peaks rising to over 10,000 ft (3000 m), but there are also considerable areas of lowland.

Apart from the mountains, which are cooler and wetter, the weather and climate are represented by the table for **Ciudad Trujillo** (Santo Domingo) on the south coast. The north coast is almost twice as wet throughout the year and has rather more rain in the winter season than is usual in the Caribbean.

HAITI

The Republic of Haiti occupies the western third of the large Caribbean island of Hispaniola; it has a land-border with the Dominican Republic. With an area of 10,700 square miles (28,000 sq. km) it is a little larger than Wales or the state of Maryland and lies east of Cuba and Jamaica in the central Caribbean.

The country is mountainous and there are many local variations in rainfall depending on relief and aspect; the north coast is wetter than the south. The table for **Port au Prince** is representative of the temperature and rainfall in the lower districts of the island. Afternoon humidity is rather lower than is usual on the coast in the Caribbean. This may be caused by a föhn effect as the moist northeast trade winds are drawn across the mountains in the interior.

Ciudad Trujillo 57 ft (17 m) 18°29′ N 69°54′ W 25 years   **THE DOMINICAN REPUBLIC**

	Temperature °F			Temperature °C			Relative humidity		Precipitation		
	Highest recorded	Average daily	Lowest recorded	Highest recorded	Average daily	Lowest recorded	0900 hours	1500 hours	Average monthly		Average no. days with 0.04 in + (1 mm +)
		max.	min.			max.	min.		%	%	in	mm	
J	92	84	66	59	33	29	19	15	91	64	2.4	61	7	J
F	93	85	66	60	34	29	19	16	88	58	1.4	36	6	F
M	94	84	67	60	34	29	19	16	90	60	1.9	48	5	M
A	95	85	69	62	35	29	21	17	90	62	3.9	99	7	A
M	94	86	71	65	34	30	22	18	89	65	6.8	173	11	M
J	96	87	72	67	36	31	22	19	90	66	6.2	158	12	J
J	98	88	72	68	37	31	22	20	90	66	6.4	163	11	J
A	98	88	73	64	37	31	23	18	90	66	6.3	160	11	A
S	98	88	72	68	37	31	22	20	91	66	7.3	185	11	S
O	95	87	72	66	35	31	22	19	92	66	6.0	152	11	O
N	97	86	70	61	36	30	21	16	92	66	4.8	122	10	N
D	95	85	67	62	35	29	19	17	91	66	2.4	61	8	D

Port au Prince 121 ft (37 m) 18°33′ N 72°20′ W 42 years   **HAITI**

	Temperature °F			Temperature °C			Relative humidity		Precipitation		
	Highest recorded	Average daily	Lowest recorded	Highest recorded	Average daily	Lowest recorded	0700 hours	1300 hours	Average monthly		Average no. days with 0.04 in + (1 mm +)
		max.	min.			max.	min.		%	%	in	mm	
J	93	87	68	62	34	31	20	17	71	44	1.3	33	3	J
F	95	88	68	61	35	31	20	16	71	44	2.3	58	5	F
M	98	89	69	60	37	32	21	16	70	45	3.4	86	7	M
A	98	89	71	61	37	32	22	16	71	49	6.3	160	11	A
M	99	90	72	66	37	32	22	19	75	54	9.1	231	13	M
J	99	92	73	66	37	33	23	19	71	50	4.0	102	8	J
J	101	94	74	67	38	34	23	19	68	43	2.9	74	7	J
A	101	93	73	68	38	34	23	20	72	49	5.7	145	11	A
S	99	91	73	67	37	33	23	19	76	54	6.9	175	12	S
O	98	90	72	66	37	32	22	19	79	56	6.7	170	12	O
N	96	88	71	64	36	31	22	18	77	54	3.4	86	7	N
D	93	87	69	60	34	31	21	16	73	48	1.3	33	3	D

JAMAICA

Jamaica is one of the larger of the West Indian islands. It is situated west of Haiti and south of Cuba and has an area of 4400 square miles (11,500 sq. km), about the size of the state of Connecticut.

It is one of the more mountainous islands of the Caribbean with the highest peaks of the Blue Mountains reaching over 7500 ft (2300 m). The northern slopes of these mountains may have up to 200 in (5000 mm) of rain a year as compared with about 30 in (750 mm) on the drier, sheltered south coast (see the table for **Kingston**). In spite of the low annual rainfall, the south coast has experienced as much as 10 in (250 mm) or more in twenty-four hours during the passage of a hurricane.

JAMAICA   **Kingston** 110 ft (34 m) 17°58′ N 76°48′ W 33 years

	Temperature °F				Temperature °C			Relative humidity		Precipitation			
	Highest recorded	Average daily		Lowest recorded	Highest recorded	Average daily		Lowest recorded	0700 hours	1500 hours	Average monthly		Average no. days with 0.04 in + (1 mm +)	
		max.	min.			max.	min.		%	%	in	mm		
J	93	86	67	57	34	30	19	14	84	61	0.9	23	3	J
F	92	86	67	59	33	30	19	15	84	62	0.6	15	3	F
M	93	86	68	58	34	30	20	14	81	62	0.9	23	2	M
A	93	87	70	63	34	31	21	17	79	66	1.2	31	3	A
M	94	87	72	66	34	31	22	19	77	68	4.0	102	4	M
J	95	89	74	68	35	32	23	20	78	68	3.5	89	5	J
J	96	90	73	66	36	32	23	19	77	65	3.5	89	4	J
A	97	90	73	68	36	32	23	20	82	70	3.6	91	7	A
S	96	89	73	68	36	32	23	20	85	70	3.9	99	6	S
O	96	88	73	65	36	31	23	18	88	73	7.1	180	9	O
N	96	87	71	62	36	31	22	17	87	68	2.9	74	5	N
D	96	87	69	57	36	31	21	14	85	62	1.4	36	4	D

These islands are the northerly islands of the Lesser Antilles. Their climate and weather are also appropriate to the Virgin Islands and other smaller islands lying between 15° N and the eastern end of Puerto Rico.

Temperature and humidity around the year in the Leeward Islands are very similar to those described in general for the Caribbean, as is the amount and distribution of sunshine. The tables for **Roseau** in Dominica and **Plymouth** in Montserrat show that, near sea level and on the low-lying islands, the annual rainfall is about 50–80 in (1250–2000 mm) well distributed throughout the year, with a wetter season from July to November. The table for **Camp Jacob** on the island of Guadeloupe, at an altitude of 1750 ft (530 m), shows that rainfall increases on the more mountainous islands and on the windward slopes exposed to the constant and moist northeast trade winds.

All these islands lie in the track of violent tropical hurricanes which are most likely to develop between August and October. The severest of these storms may only strike a particular island every few years but the appreciable rainfall they, and less violent disturbances, bring to a wider area accounts for the heavier rainfall during these months.

Camp Jacob (Guadeloupe) 1750 ft (533 m) 16°01′ N 61°42′ W 10 years   **THE LEEWARD ISLANDS**

	Temperature °F			Temperature °C			Relative humidity		Precipitation			
	Highest recorded	Average daily		Lowest recorded	Highest recorded	Average daily		Lowest recorded	0700 hours	1700 hours	Average monthly		Average no. days with 0.04 in + (1 mm +)
		max.	min.			max.	min.		%	%	in	mm	
J	86	77	64	56	30	25	18	13	83	80	9.2	234	23	J
F	88	76	63	54	31	24	17	12	82	77	6.1	155	18	F
M	85	77	63	56	29	25	17	13	82	75	8.1	206	20	M
A	85	79	65	58	29	26	18	14	82	76	7.3	185	20	A
M	87	80	67	60	31	27	19	16	85	77	11.5	292	23	M
J	86	80	69	57	30	27	21	14	83	76	14.1	358	25	J
J	86	81	68	57	30	27	20	14	83	76	17.6	447	27	J
A	88	82	69	57	31	28	21	14	82	75	15.3	389	26	A
S	89	82	69	63	32	28	21	17	84	78	16.4	417	23	S
O	92	81	68	59	33	27	20	15	84	81	12.4	315	24	O
N	91	80	67	60	33	27	19	16	84	79	12.3	312	22	N
D	88	78	65	58	31	26	18	14	85	81	10.1	257	23	D

THE LEEWARD ISLANDS — Plymouth (Montserrat) 130 ft (40 m) 16°43′ N 62°13′ W 14 years

	Temperature °F			Temperature °C			Relative humidity		Precipitation			
	Highest recorded	Average daily	Lowest recorded	Highest recorded	Average daily	Lowest recorded	0900 hours	1500 hours	Average monthly		Average no. days with 0.04 in + (1 mm +)	
		max.	min.			max.	min.		%	%	in	mm	
J	89	82	70	62	32	28	21	17	69	65	4.8	122	12	J
F	91	83	70	62	33	33	21	17	66	61	3.4	86	9	F
M	93	85	70	62	34	29	21	17	65	59	4.4	112	9	M
A	94	86	72	63	34	30	22	17	62	59	3.5	89	8	A
M	96	88	74	67	36	31	23	19	63	60	3.8	97	10	M
J	98	88	75	66	37	31	24	19	65	63	4.4	112	13	J
J	98	87	75	70	37	31	24	21	66	64	6.1	155	14	J
A	98	88	75	69	37	31	24	21	68	66	7.2	183	16	A
S	97	89	74	67	36	32	23	19	68	66	6.6	168	13	S
O	94	87	74	67	34	31	23	19	69	66	7.7	196	14	O
N	98	85	73	59	37	29	23	15	70	68	7.1	180	16	N
D	92	83	72	64	33	28	22	18	70	67	5.5	140	13	D

THE LEEWARD ISLANDS — Roseau (Dominica) 60 ft (18 m) 15°18′ N 61°23′ W 17 years

	Temperature °F			Temperature °C			Relative humidity		Precipitation			
	Highest recorded	Average daily	Lowest recorded	Highest recorded	Average daily	Lowest recorded	0900 hours	1500 hours	Average monthly		Average no. days with 0.04 in + (1 mm +)	
		max.	min.			max.	min.		%	%	in	mm	
J	91	84	68	60	33	29	20	16	76	65	5.2	132	16	J
F	93	85	67	61	34	29	19	16	73	62	2.9	74	10	F
M	96	87	68	61	36	31	20	16	70	59	2.9	74	13	M
A	97	88	69	63	36	31	21	17	66	61	2.4	61	10	A
M	97	90	71	64	36	32	22	18	67	61	3.8	97	11	M
J	96	90	73	68	36	32	23	20	69	65	7.7	196	15	J
J	95	89	72	65	35	32	22	18	75	69	10.8	274	22	J
A	95	89	73	67	35	32	23	19	76	69	10.3	262	22	A
S	95	90	73	65	35	32	23	18	74	67	8.9	226	16	S
O	98	89	72	65	37	32	22	18	75	70	7.8	198	16	O
N	95	87	71	64	35	31	22	18	78	70	8.8	224	18	N
D	93	86	69	62	34	30	21	17	77	67	6.4	163	16	D

The Netherlands Antilles consist of two distinct groups which are, politically, an integral part of the Netherlands. Close to the coast of Venezuela in 12° to 13° N, the three islands of Curaçao, Aruba and Bonaire have a total land area of about 360 square miles (940 sq. km). Another group of three very small islands with an area of 26 square miles (68 sq. km) lies east of Puerto Rico in 18° N.

The larger southern islands have a rather dry climate for this latitude and the climatic conditions throughout the year are represented by the table for **Willemstad** on the island of Curaçao. The islands share this relative aridity with the narrow coastal strip of northern Venezuela described on p. 203. Temperature and humidity in both groups of islands are typical of the Caribbean area. The northern group of tiny islands has similar weather throughout the year to that described for the Leeward Islands on p. 323.

Willemstad (Curaçao) 75 ft (23 m) 12°06′ N 68°56′ W 24 years **THE NETHERLANDS ANTILLES**

	Temperature °F			Temperature °C			Relative humidity		Precipitation		
	Highest recorded	Average daily	Lowest recorded	Highest recorded	Average daily	Lowest recorded	0830 hours	1430 hours	Average monthly		Average no. days with 0.04 in + (1 mm +)
		max.	min.			max.	min.	%	%	in	mm	
J	87	83	75	68	31	28	24	20	77	69	2.1	53	14	J
F	91	84	74	66	33	29	23	19	78	68	1.0	25	8	F
M	90	84	74	63	32	29	23	17	76	66	0.8	20	7	M
A	91	86	76	68	33	30	24	20	76	67	1.1	28	4	A
M	96	86	77	70	36	30	25	21	76	68	0.8	20	4	M
J	94	87	78	71	34	31	26	22	76	68	1.0	25	7	J
J	94	87	77	72	34	31	25	22	77	68	1.5	38	9	J
A	95	88	78	71	35	31	26	22	77	67	1.2	31	8	A
S	96	89	78	71	36	32	26	22	77	67	1.1	28	6	S
O	94	88	78	70	34	31	26	21	77	70	4.2	107	9	O
N	92	86	76	68	33	30	24	20	79	72	4.4	112	15	N
D	91	84	75	69	33	29	24	21	78	71	3.9	99	16	D

PUERTO RICO

Puerto Rico is the most easterly of the large islands in the central Caribbean and is situated midway between Hispaniola and the Leeward Islands. It has an area of about 3400 square miles (8800 sq. km). It is a mountainous island with the highest land rising to over 4000 ft (1200 m) so the centre and north coast of the island, exposed to the northeast trade winds, are rather wetter throughout the year than the sheltered south coast.

The table for **San Juan**, which is on the north coast, shows that here, as on the north coast of the Dominican Republic, the annual rainfall is well spread over the year and there is no dry season. This is rather unusual for the Caribbean and is a local effect of the moist trade winds being forced to rise over the mountains close to the coast.

TRINIDAD

Trinidad, and the neighbouring small island of Tobago, are the most southerly islands of the Lesser Antilles. At two points Trinidad is only a few miles from the coast of Venezuela and its climate is very similar to that of the northeast coast of that country. The table for **St Clair** shows that rainfall is well distributed throughout the year with a definite wetter season in the period June to November. Temperatures are a little higher in Trinidad than in the Caribbean Islands farther north. Trinidad is too far south to be affected by violent tropical storms in the form of hurricanes, which pass to the north of the island.

San Juan 82 ft (25 m) 18°29′ N 60°07′ W 48 years **PUERTO RICO**

	Temperature °F			Temperature °C				Relative humidity		Precipitation			
	Highest recorded	Average daily		Lowest recorded	Highest recorded	Average daily		Lowest recorded	0900 hours	1200 hours	Average monthly		Average no. days with 0.01 in + (0.25 mm +)	
		max.	min.			max.	min.		%	%	in	mm		
J	88	80	70	63	31	27	21	17	81	75	4.3	109	20	J
F	91	80	70	62	33	27	21	17	79	74	2.7	69	15	F
M	91	81	70	63	33	27	21	17	76	74	2.9	74	15	M
A	93	82	72	65	34	28	22	18	75	75	4.1	104	14	A
M	94	84	74	66	34	29	23	19	76	75	5.9	150	16	M
J	93	85	75	66	34	29	24	19	76	77	5.4	137	17	J
J	92	85	75	70	33	29	24	21	77	78	5.7	145	19	J
A	93	85	76	68	34	29	24	20	77	77	6.3	160	20	A
S	94	86	75	69	34	30	24	21	78	77	6.2	158	18	S
O	94	85	75	68	34	29	24	20	79	76	5.6	142	18	O
N	93	84	73	66	34	29	23	19	80	76	6.3	160	19	N
D	90	81	72	62	32	27	22	17	81	77	5.4	137	21	D

St Clair 67 ft (20 m) 10°40′ N 61°31′ W 49 years **TRINIDAD**

	Temperature °F			Temperature °C				Relative humidity		Precipitation			
	Highest recorded	Average daily		Lowest recorded	Highest recorded	Average daily		Lowest recorded	0700 hours	1500 hours	Average monthly		Average no. days with 0.01 in + (0.25 mm +)	
		max.	min.			max.	min.		%	%	in	mm		
J	95	87	69	57	35	31	21	14	89	68	2.7	69	14	J
F	96	88	68	57	36	31	20	14	87	65	1.6	41	10	F
M	98	89	68	54	37	32	20	12	85	63	1.8	46	9	M
A	98	90	69	55	37	32	21	13	83	61	2.1	53	9	A
M	99	90	71	59	37	32	22	15	84	63	3.7	94	12	M
J	99	89	71	60	37	32	22	16	87	69	7.6	193	19	J
J	98	88	71	52	37	31	22	11	88	71	8.6	218	22	J
A	99	88	71	61	37	31	22	16	87	73	9.7	246	23	A
S	101	89	71	58	38	32	22	14	87	73	7.6	193	19	S
O	96	89	71	61	36	32	22	16	87	74	6.7	170	18	O
N	96	89	71	60	36	32	22	16	89	76	7.2	183	18	N
D	97	88	69	60	36	31	21	16	89	71	4.9	125	17	D

THE WINDWARD ISLANDS

The Windward Islands are the southern islands of the Lesser Antilles. These islands lie between 15° N and the coast of the South American continent; they do not include Trinidad and Tobago for which there is a separate note and table on pp. 326–7. The largest islands of this group are Barbados, Martinique, St Lucia, Grenada and St Vincent.

Although small these larger islands are hilly or mountainous and this tends to increase the rainfall above what might occur on one of the small, flat islands in this group. As the tables show, Barbados is less wet around the year than Martinique and St Lucia, both of which have higher mountains. All months receive appreciable rain but the heaviest rain is more likely to occur from July to November. This is the hurricane season and, although the most violent of these tropical storms may only strike a particular island every few years, less severe ones cause appreciable rainfall over quite a wide area. Temperature, humidity and sunshine throughout the year are typical of the Caribbean area. The climatic tables for Barbados, Martinique and St Lucia reflect conditions on the west coasts of the islands which are more sheltered from the prevailing winds.

THE WINDWARD ISLANDS   Bridgetown (Barbados) 181 ft (55 m) 13°08′ N 59°36′ W 35 years

	Temperature °F			Temperature °C				Relative humidity		Precipitation			
	Highest recorded	Average daily		Lowest recorded	Highest recorded	Average daily		Lowest recorded	0800 hours	1700 hours	Average monthly		Average no. days with 0.04 in + (1 mm +)	
		max.	min.			max.	min.		%	%	in	mm		
J	87	83	70	61	31	28	21	16	75	71	2.6	66	13	J
F	87	83	69	61	31	28	21	16	72	66	1.1	28	8	F
M	89	85	70	62	32	29	21	17	69	64	1.3	33	8	M
A	89	86	72	64	32	30	22	18	67	65	1.4	36	7	A
M	91	87	73	66	33	31	23	19	69	67	2.3	58	9	M
J	90	87	74	67	32	31	23	19	72	70	4.4	112	14	J
J	90	86	74	68	32	30	23	20	75	71	5.8	147	18	J
A	95	87	74	69	35	31	23	21	76	72	5.8	147	16	A
S	91	87	74	67	33	31	23	19	76	73	6.7	170	15	S
O	92	86	73	67	33	30	23	19	78	76	7.0	178	15	O
N	89	85	73	66	32	29	23	19	79	78	8.1	206	16	N
D	88	83	71	64	31	28	22	18	77	73	3.8	97	14	D

	Temperature °F			Temperature °C			Relative humidity		Precipitation		
	Highest recorded	Average daily	Lowest recorded	Highest recorded	Average daily	Lowest recorded	0600 hours	1600 hours	Average monthly		Average no. days with 0.01 in + (0.25 mm +)
		max.	min.			max.	min.		%	%	in	mm	
J	90	83	69	59	32	28	21	15	90	77	4.7	119	19	J
F	91	84	69	60	33	29	21	16	88	73	4.3	109	15	F
M	91	85	69	56	33	29	21	13	88	72	2.9	74	15	M
A	94	86	71	63	34	30	22	17	88	71	3.9	99	13	A
M	93	87	73	66	34	31	23	19	88	74	4.7	119	18	M
J	92	86	74	66	33	30	23	19	89	77	7.4	188	21	J
J	90	86	74	68	32	30	23	20	90	78	9.4	239	22	J
A	94	87	74	66	34	31	23	19	91	78	10.3	262	22	A
S	96	88	74	68	36	31	23	20	91	79	9.3	236	29	S
O	94	87	73	65	34	31	23	18	92	80	9.7	246	19	O
N	92	86	72	64	33	30	22	18	92	81	7.9	201	20	N
D	89	84	71	61	32	29	22	16	91	79	5.9	150	19	D

	Temperature °F			Temperature °C			Relative humidity		Precipitation		
	Highest recorded	Average daily	Lowest recorded	Highest recorded	Average daily	Lowest recorded	0700 hours	1200 hours	Average monthly		Average no. days with 0.04 in + (1 mm +)
		max.	min.			max.	min.		%	%	in	mm	
J	87	82	69	57	31	28	21	14	90	70	5.3	135	18	J
F	89	83	69	59	32	28	21	15	90	68	3.6	91	13	F
M	90	84	69	59	32	29	21	15	88	65	3.8	97	13	M
A	95	87	71	63	35	31	22	17	87	64	3.4	86	10	A
M	97	88	73	67	36	31	23	19	87	65	5.9	150	16	M
J	97	88	74	67	36	31	23	19	86	69	8.6	218	21	J
J	95	87	74	69	35	31	23	21	89	71	9.3	236	23	J
A	94	88	74	68	34	31	23	20	90	69	10.6	269	22	A
S	94	88	73	68	34	31	23	20	91	70	9.9	252	21	S
O	91	87	72	66	33	31	22	19	93	69	9.3	236	19	O
N	90	85	71	65	32	29	22	18	92	75	9.1	231	20	N
D	89	83	70	61	32	28	21	16	92	71	7.8	198	19	D

Europe

ALBANIA

Albania is a small, mountainous country about the same size as Wales or the state of Maryland. It has a coastline on the Mediterranean and its land frontier with Yugoslavia and Greece traverses some of the wildest mountain scenery in Europe. The climate on the coast is typically Mediterranean with mild, wet winters and warm, sunny and rather dry summers. Inland conditions vary depending on altitude but the higher areas above 5000 ft (1500 m) are rather cold and frequently snowy in winter; here cold conditions with lying snow may linger into spring. For a Mediterranean country the precipitation is rather heavy; coastlands are quite wet in winter and mountain areas are among the wetter parts of Europe.

Midsummer months are generally sunny but the fine weather can be interrupted by occasional thundery downpours. It is rarely excessively hot on the coast and, although often rather humid, the daily sea breezes make conditions quite pleasant. Winter conditions on the coast are generally mild but occasional cold winds from the north and east may bring an unwelcome chill for a few days when the mountains inland are covered with snow. When a warm humid wind – the sirocco – blows from the southwest or south, conditions may feel oppressive. This is particularly the case in autumn when Mediterranean sea temperatures are at their highest. The sirocco then often precedes wet weather and a return to cooler temperatures. For conditions on the coast see the table for **Vlórë**.

Inland and in the mountains the annual sequence of weather is similar to that on the coast but the summers are cooler and less humid (see the table for **Tiranë**). During the stormier conditions of autumn and winter, rain may be heavy and cold and snow severe. Everywhere summer and early autumn are the most settled months. Sunshine amounts are quite high, averaging over eleven hours a day in July and four hours a day in January.

Tiranë 292 ft (89 m) 41°20′ N 19°47′ E 10 years | | | | | | | | | | | | | **ALBANIA**

	Temperature °F			Temperature °C			Relative humidity		Precipitation			
	Highest recorded	Average daily		Lowest recorded	Highest recorded	Average daily		Lowest recorded	0730 hours	1430 hours	Average monthly		Average no. days with 0.004 in + (0.1 mm +)
		max.	min.			max.	min.		%	%	in	mm	
J	65	53	36	18	19	12	2	−8	83	58	5.3	135	13	J
F	71	54	36	18	22	12	2	−8	83	54	6.0	152	13	F
M	78	59	41	25	26	15	5	−4	83	53	5.0	128	14	M
A	82	65	47	31	28	18	8	−1	83	54	4.6	117	13	A
M	91	74	53	37	33	23	12	3	83	56	4.8	122	12	M
J	99	82	60	42	37	28	16	6	74	49	3.4	86	7	J
J	101	87	63	51	38	31	17	11	72	42	1.3	32	5	J
A	105	89	62	51	40	31	17	10	75	39	1.3	32	4	A
S	95	81	58	42	35	27	14	5	82	45	2.4	60	6	S
O	87	73	50	35	31	23	10	1	85	59	4.1	105	9	O
N	78	63	47	27	25	17	8	−3	86	63	8.3	211	16	N
D	72	56	40	20	22	14	5	−7	83	63	6.8	173	16	D

Vlórë 10 ft (3 m) 40°28′ N 19°29′ E 10 years | | | | | | | | | | | | | **ALBANIA**

	Temperature °F			Temperature °C			Relative humidity		Precipitation			
	Highest recorded	Average daily		Lowest recorded	Highest recorded	Average daily		Lowest recorded	0730 hours	1430 hours	Average monthly		Average no. days with 0.004 in + (0.1 mm +)
		max.	min.			max.	min.		%	%	in	mm	
J	72	56	42	23	22	13	6	−5	69	56	4.7	120	13	J
F	76	56	42	23	24	14	6	−5	68	54	4.2	106	12	F
M	81	60	46	26	27	16	8	−3	72	57	3.6	92	14	M
A	84	66	51	33	29	19	10	0	70	55	3.1	79	11	A
M	96	74	57	43	36	23	14	6	71	56	2.1	54	9	M
J	97	81	63	51	36	27	17	11	67	51	1.1	28	6	J
J	102	85	66	56	39	30	19	13	65	48	0.4	9	3	J
A	101	87	66	57	39	30	19	14	65	46	1.0	26	3	A
S	92	81	61	49	34	27	16	10	70	50	1.3	32	5	S
O	89	74	57	42	32	23	14	6	70	54	4.6	116	10	O
N	82	66	53	34	28	19	11	1	72	62	7.6	192	17	N
D	76	59	46	25	25	15	8	−4	69	60	5.6	141	17	D

ANDORRA

This tiny independent principality is high in the eastern Pyrenees on the border between France and Spain. Lying on the southern or Spanish side of the crest line, it is rather sheltered and therefore drier than much of the French Pyrenees. The whole country lies above 2750 ft (840 m). Winters are cold but rather dry and sunny. The midsummer months are slightly drier than spring and autumn and, with the cool temperatures, summer is a pleasant season.

The table for **Les Escaldes** is representative of the valleys in this small state. Temperatures are lower in the higher mountainous area. (See map p. 352.)

ANDORRA   **Les Escaldes (Las Escaldas)** 3545 ft (1080 m) 42°30′ N 1°31′ E 9 years

	Temperature °F			Temperature °C			Relative humidity	Precipitation		
	Highest recorded	Average daily	Lowest recorded	Highest recorded	Average daily	Lowest recorded		Average monthly		Average no. days with 0.004 in + (0.1 mm +)
		max.	min.			max.	min.			in	mm	
J	59	43	30	9	15	6	−1	−13	—	1.3	34	4	J
F	63	45	30	0	17	7	−1	−18	—	1.5	37	6	F
M	68	54	35	16	20	12	2	−9	—	1.8	46	6	M
A	77	58	39	25	25	14	4	−4	—	2.5	63	10	A
M	84	62	43	32	29	17	6	0	—	4.1	105	15	M
J	97	73	39	36	36	23	10	2	—	2.7	69	9	J
J	95	79	54	41	35	26	12	5	—	2.6	65	8	J
A	91	76	53	39	33	24	12	4	—	3.9	98	10	A
S	88	71	49	36	31	22	10	2	—	3.2	81	9	S
O	81	60	42	23	27	16	6	−5	—	2.9	73	8	O
N	68	51	35	23	20	10	2	−5	—	2.7	68	6	N
D	55	42	31	12	13	6	−1	−11	—	2.7	69	7	D

Austria is one of the most mountainous countries in Europe. Most of the west, centre and south of the country is made up of the eastern Alps which extend uninterrupted from Switzerland and Italy. In Austria the higher peaks rise to over 12,000 ft (3700 m) and are snow-covered throughout the year. The Alps are dissected by deep valleys, however, so that very different climatic and weather conditions occur over quite short distances. The most extensive lowland in Austria is found in the north and east along the Danube valley from Linz to **Vienna** and east of **Vienna** where, along the Hungarian border, the land becomes almost flat. The southeast of the country lies south of the main Alpine ranges and here in the lower valleys and around the lakes the summers may, at times, experience almost Mediterranean warmth and dryness.

The sequence of weather around the year does not vary very much from one part of the country to another. The weather can be changeable at all times of the year. Everywhere the summer months are the wettest but summer rainfall is more likely to be heavy and thundery and therefore of shorter duration. Winters are rather cold everywhere and during prolonged cold spells temperatures may be lowest in the valleys and lowlands. The coldest conditions in winter usually occur with east to northeast winds bringing very low temperatures from eastern Europe and Russia. The character of summer or winter may differ from year to year. On average, sunshine amounts are greater than in northwest Europe but lower than in Mediterranean countries. They range from nine to ten hours a day in July to between two to three in January.

Austria can be divided into three broad climatic regions: the Alps, the Danube valley and the Vienna basin, and the southeast including Styria and Carinthia.

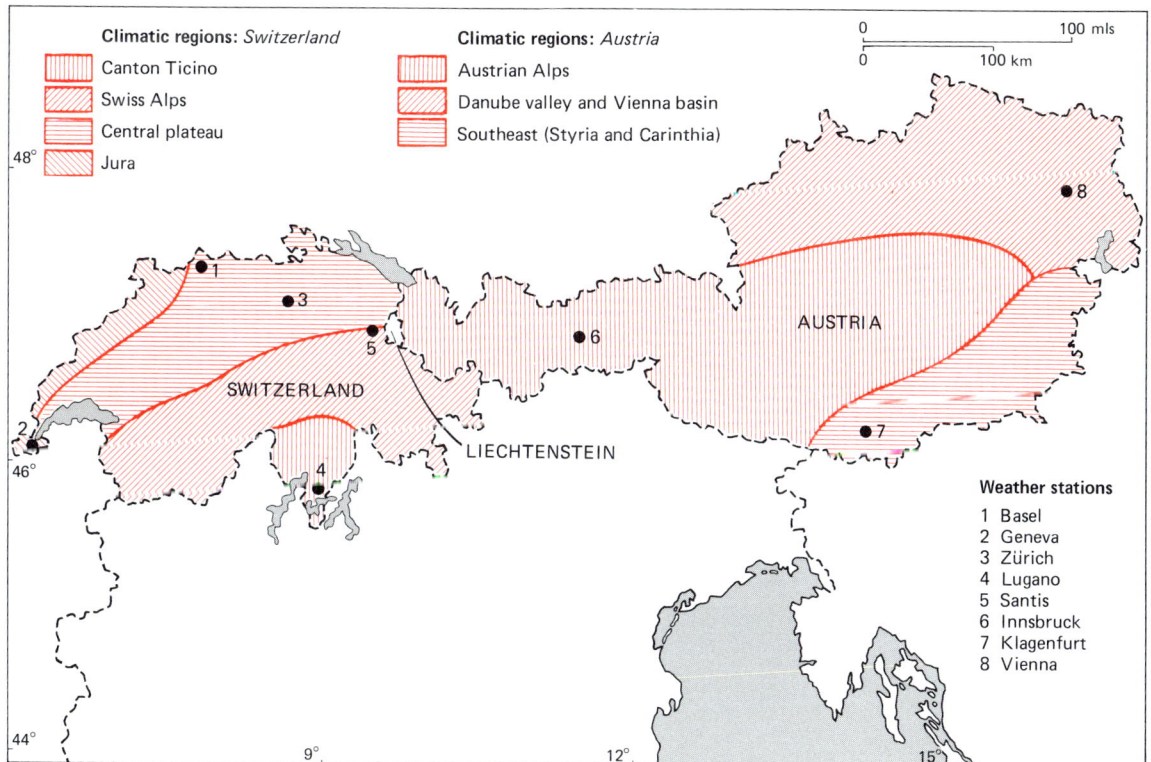

Climatic regions: *Switzerland*
- Canton Ticino
- Swiss Alps
- Central plateau
- Jura

Climatic regions: *Austria*
- Austrian Alps
- Danube valley and Vienna basin
- Southeast (Styria and Carinthia)

Weather stations
1 Basel
2 Geneva
3 Zürich
4 Lugano
5 Santis
6 Innsbruck
7 Klagenfurt
8 Vienna

THE ALPS

In winter the higher Alpine winter sports resorts are much sunnier than the valleys where conditions are often cloudy and foggy with low temperatures persisting for several days. Although temperatures may be lower on the mountains it may feel warmer in calm and sunny conditions. The reverse is the case in summer when the mountains may become cloudy during the hotter part of the day and the valleys stay sunny.

Certain Alpine valleys, particularly those running from south to north, experience a very warm, dry wind – the föhn. This may blow from twenty to forty days a year. The föhn is most frequent in autumn and spring when it can melt snow with prodigious speed. It is then dangerous for it can trigger off avalanches on the mountain slopes. The air may become so dry during the föhn that there is a serious fire risk to wooden buildings. The source of the warm air is to the south of the Alps but it is warmed and dried as it crosses the mountains and descends on the northern side. For details of climate and weather in this area see the table for **Innsbruck**.

THE DANUBE VALLEY AND THE VIENNA BASIN

This is the driest part of the country. Winter snowfall is rarely deep but the snow may last for some weeks during cold winters. In general, conditions here are very similar to those in southern Germany throughout the year (see the table for **Vienna**).

Innsbruck 1910 ft (582 m) 47°16′ N 11°24′ E 30 years   **AUSTRIA**

	Temperature °F				Temperature °C				Relative humidity		Precipitation			
	Highest recorded	Average daily		Lowest recorded	Highest recorded	Average daily		Lowest recorded	0700 hours	1400 hours	Average monthly		Average no. days with 0.004 in + (0.1 mm +)	
		max.	min.				max.	min.		%	%	in	mm		
J	65	34	20	−16	19	1	−7	−27	86	67	2.1	54	13	J
F	64	40	24	−16	18	4	−5	−27	85	58	1.9	49	13	F
M	77	51	0	2	25	11	0	−17	83	46	1.6	41	11	M
A	83	60	39	23	29	16	4	−5	82	43	2.1	52	14	A
M	91	68	46	28	33	20	8	−2	81	43	2.9	73	15	M
J	97	74	52	34	36	24	11	1	84	48	4.3	110	19	J
J	98	77	55	40	37	25	13	4	86	52	5.3	134	19	J
A	94	75	54	38	35	24	12	3	88	52	4.3	108	17	A
S	87	69	49	30	31	21	10	−1	90	53	3.2	81	14	S
O	76	58	40	24	25	15	5	−5	90	55	2.6	67	12	O
N	73	46	0	5	23	8	0	−15	88	65	2.1	53	12	N
D	64	36	24	−13	18	2	−4	−25	87	70	1.8	46	13	D

Vienna 666 ft (203 m) 48°15′ N 16°22′ E 30 years   **AUSTRIA**

	Temperature °F				Temperature °C				Relative humidity		Precipitation			
	Highest recorded	Average daily		Lowest recorded	Highest recorded	Average daily		Lowest recorded	0700 hours	1400 hours	Average monthly		Average no. days with 0.004 in + (0.1 mm +)	
		max.	min.				max.	min.		%	%	in	mm		
J	56	34	25	7	13	1	−4	−22	81	72	1.5	39	15	J
F	65	38	28	9	19	3	−3	−23	80	66	1.7	44	14	F
M	75	47	30	12	24	8	−1	−11	78	57	1.7	44	13	M
A	81	58	42	26	27	15	6	−3	72	49	1.8	45	13	A
M	91	67	50	32	33	19	10	0	74	52	2.8	70	13	M
J	97	73	56	39	36	23	14	4	74	55	2.6	67	14	J
J	101	76	60	48	38	25	15	9	74	54	3.3	84	13	J
A	94	75	59	46	34	24	15	8	78	54	2.8	72	13	A
S	89	68	53	32	32	20	11	0	83	56	1.7	42	10	S
O	82	56	44	26	28	14	7	−3	86	64	2.2	56	13	O
N	67	45	37	16	20	7	3	−9	84	74	2.1	52	14	N
D	62	37	30	5	17	3	−1	−15	84	76	1.8	45	15	D

THE SOUTHEAST (STYRIA AND CARINTHIA)

In some of the sheltered valleys in this part of Austria the summers are notably warmer and sunnier than north of the Alps. During settled weather the almost uninterrupted sunshine appears to bring a touch of the Mediterranean to the area, but heavy thunderstorms and more unsettled weather are rarely absent for long. Although spring may be a little earlier here, the winters can be as cold and severe as farther north (see the table for **Klagenfurt**).

AUSTRIA   **Klagenfurt** 1470 ft (448 m) 46°39′ N 14°20′ E 30 years

	Temperature °F				Temperature °C				Relative humidity		Precipitation		
	Highest recorded	Average daily		Lowest recorded	Highest recorded	Average daily		Lowest recorded	0700 hours	1400 hours	Average monthly		Average no. days with 0.004 in + (0.1 mm +)	
		max.	min.			max.	min.		%	%	in	mm		
J	53	30	17	−17	12	−1	−9	−27	92	77	1.6	41	9	J
F	61	38	20	−15	16	3	−7	−26	91	65	1.8	45	8	F
M	72	49	28	−2	22	9	−2	−19	90	52	1.5	39	8	M
A	82	59	37	19	28	15	3	−7	89	49	2.8	71	11	A
M	87	67	45	24	31	20	7	−5	88	53	3.5	88	14	M
J	94	73	52	35	35	23	11	2	87	53	4.9	125	15	J
J	99	77	55	39	37	25	13	4	89	54	4.9	125	14	J
A	94	76	54	38	34	24	12	3	93	56	4.1	104	13	A
S	90	69	49	30	32	20	10	−1	95	59	3.3	83	10	S
O	74	56	40	18	24	14	5	−8	96	67	3.5	89	13	O
N	64	42	32	11	18	6	0	−12	95	77	3.0	75	12	N
D	59	33	24	−9	15	1	−4	−23	94	83	2.1	52	10	D

Belgium is a small country about the same size as the Netherlands which borders it on the north. It has a short coastline on the North Sea and is bordered on the west by France and on the east by West Germany and Luxembourg. The general character of the climate is similar to that of the Netherlands with considerable variation from day to day and from one year to another.

The northern part of the country is low-lying and similar to the adjoining Netherlands. The climate of this area is well represented by the table for **Ostend** and is similar to that of the Netherlands.

The central part of the country is of moderate elevation and consists of gently rolling countryside. Here the climate is a little colder in winter and warmer in summer than along the coast. It is also rather wetter in summer and thunderstorms are more frequent (see the table for **Brussels**). The north and centre of the country contain the most productive agricultural districts and the largest towns.

The southern third of the country is rather sparsely populated. This is the Ardennes region which consists of forested hills with an average elevation of 1000–1600 ft (300–500 m). Here the winters are distinctly colder and, in an average year, snow may lie for as many as fifty days in the higher parts as compared with an average of ten days in the north of the country. Winters here are also wetter than farther north and hill fog occurs frequently. Summer in the Ardennes is only a little cooler than in the north and not very much wetter. The table for **Virton** is representative of conditions in the valleys and lower parts of the Ardennes.

Except during severe winter weather in the Ardennes, the weather and climate of Belgium are rarely unpleasant or uncomfortable. Average daily sunshine amounts range from about two hours a day in January to between seven and eight hours in June.

Brussels 328 ft (100 m) 50°48′ N 4°21′ E 10 years   **BELGIUM**

	Temperature °F			Temperature °C			Relative humidity		Precipitation		
	Highest recorded	Average daily	Lowest recorded	Highest recorded	Average daily	Lowest recorded	0630 hours	1230 hours	Average monthly		Average no. days with 0.004 in +
		max.	min.			max.	min.		%	%	in	mm	(0.1 mm +)

	Highest recorded	max.	min.	Lowest recorded	Highest recorded	max.	min.	Lowest recorded	0630 %	1230 %	in	mm	days	
J	56	40	30	2	13	4	−1	−17	92	86	2.6	66	21	J
F	68	44	32	12	20	7	0	−11	92	81	2.4	61	17	F
M	72	51	36	20	22	10	2	−7	91	74	2.1	53	17	M
A	76	58	41	29	24	14	5	−2	91	71	2.4	60	18	A
M	84	65	46	29	29	18	8	−2	90	65	2.2	55	16	M
J	91	72	52	34	33	22	11	1	87	65	3.0	76	15	J
J	98	73	54	41	37	23	12	5	91	68	3.7	95	17	J
A	93	72	54	42	34	22	12	6	93	69	3.2	80	18	A
S	88	69	51	38	31	21	11	3	94	69	2.5	63	13	S
O	79	60	45	28	26	15	7	−2	93	77	3.3	83	17	O
N	66	48	38	20	19	9	3	−7	93	85	3.0	75	20	N
D	59	42	32	10	15	6	0	−12	92	86	3.5	88	19	D

Ostend 33 ft (10 m) 51°14′ N 2°55′ E 10 years

	Temperature °F				Temperature °C				Relative humidity		Precipitation			
	Highest recorded	Average daily		Lowest recorded	Highest recorded	Average daily		Lowest recorded	0600 hours	1200 hours	Average monthly		Average no. days with 0.004 in + (0.1 mm +)	
		max.	min.			max.	min.		%	%	in	mm		
J	56	41	33	9	13	5	1	−13	91	90	1.6	41	13	J
F	63	44	35	14	17	6	2	−10	92	86	1.5	38	12	F
M	66	48	37	22	19	9	3	−6	91	82	1.2	31	11	M
A	73	53	42	29	23	11	6	−1	91	80	1.5	38	12	A
M	83	59	49	38	28	15	10	3	89	78	1.3	34	11	M
J	90	65	53	42	32	18	12	6	89	79	1.5	38	10	J
J	90	67	56	46	32	20	13	8	90	80	2.4	62	12	J
A	88	68	56	49	31	20	13	10	91	80	2.3	58	13	A
S	84	66	53	41	29	19	12	5	92	80	2.2	56	10	S
O	77	59	47	35	25	15	9	1	93	83	2.7	68	13	O
N	63	50	40	22	17	10	5	−5	93	89	2.9	74	15	N
D	57	43	36	17	14	6	2	−9	94	91	2.4	60	16	D

BELGIUM

Virton 794 ft (242 m) 49°33′ N 5°34′ E 10 years

	Temperature °F				Temperature °C				Relative humidity		Precipitation			
	Highest recorded	Average daily		Lowest recorded	Highest recorded	Average daily		Lowest recorded	0630 hours	1230 hours	Average monthly		Average no. days with 0.004 in + (0.1 mm +)	
		max.	min.			max.	min.		%	%	in	mm		
J	55	38	28	0	13	3	−2	−18	96	89	3.0	75	18	J
F	65	43	30	3	19	6	−1	−16	95	84	2.8	72	17	F
M	72	49	32	10	22	10	0	−12	95	72	2.4	61	16	M
A	78	57	38	25	26	14	3	−4	90	63	2.6	66	17	A
M	83	64	42	25	28	18	6	−4	89	61	2.4	61	16	M
J	91	71	49	32	33	22	10	0	87	62	2.4	62	14	J
J	97	72	51	36	36	22	11	2	90	64	2.9	74	14	J
A	90	72	51	37	32	22	11	3	93	68	3.5	88	17	A
S	88	68	47	32	31	20	8	0	95	69	2.9	74	15	S
O	76	58	40	25	25	15	5	−4	95	77	2.6	67	16	O
N	64	46	36	16	18	8	2	−9	94	85	3.4	85	19	N
D	58	40	30	9	15	4	−1	−13	96	90	4.1	103	18	D

Bulgaria is in southeast Europe where the climate is transitional between that of the Mediterranean and that of the plains of southern Russia. It has a coastline on the Black Sea and on the north the Danube forms the boundary with Rumania. The western and southern borders with Yugoslavia and Greece respectively pass through mountainous country rising to between 6000 and 9000 ft (1800 and 2750 m).

The largest areas of lowland are along the coast and in the valley of the river Maritsa in the centre of the country. Here the summers are warm and occasionally rather hot while the winters are fairly cold (see the tables for **Varna** and **Plovdiv**). Rainfall is moderate and well distributed throughout the year with a slight summer maximum. On the coast (**Varna**) the winters are slightly warmer but even here spells of bitterly cold weather can occur when winds blow from the northeast carrying cold air from Russia. During such cold spells the Danube and other rivers may freeze over. Hot spells in summer are associated with winds from both the northeast and the southeast.

During settled spells of weather in summer, conditions on the Black Sea coast may resemble those around the Mediterranean and this area has developed some summer tourist resorts. Such fine, hot spells, however, may be interrupted by thunderstorms with hail and heavy rain. The total number of wet days is not large throughout the whole country but snow is frequent in winter and even occasionally in spring.

In the higher parts of the country (see the table for **Sofia**) winters are colder and the summers pleasant and fresh. Snow may lie until June on the highest mountains. There are opportunities for winter sports in the mountains.

Although the climate is generally temperate and pleasant, its variability throughout the year means that it may at times be uncomfortably cold in winter and rather warm and sultry in summer. Spring can be a very changeable season with rapid alternations between warm and cold days. Daily hours of sunshine range from about two in January to as much as ten in midsummer.

Plovdiv 525 ft (160 m) 42°29′ N 24°45′ E 9 years   **BULGARIA**

	Temperature °F			Temperature °C			Relative humidity		Precipitation		
	Highest recorded	Average daily	Lowest recorded	Highest recorded	Average daily	Lowest recorded	0630 hours	1330 hours	Average monthly		Average no. days with 0.008 in + (0.2 mm +)
		max.	min.			max.	min.		%	%	in	mm	
J	60	40	26	−9	16	5	−3	−23	91	76	1.5	39	8	J
F	73	45	28	−13	23	7	−2	−25	88	67	1.3	33	8	F
M	77	54	34	1	25	12	1	−18	88	60	1.5	37	8	M
A	87	65	43	25	31	18	5	−4	83	53	1.4	36	9	A
M	89	74	50	32	32	23	10	0	81	53	2.0	51	11	M
J	97	82	57	43	36	28	14	6	76	50	2.6	65	9	J
J	104	87	61	47	40	31	16	8	73	45	1.5	37	8	J
A	101	86	59	47	38	30	15	8	76	46	1.1	28	6	A
S	94	78	52	32	35	26	11	0	85	48	1.3	32	5	S
O	91	69	46	28	33	21	8	−3	91	59	1.6	41	9	O
N	74	54	37	18	23	12	3	−8	92	69	1.9	49	8	N
D	66	43	29	1	19	6	−2	−17	90	76	1.7	44	10	D

BULGARIA

Sofia 1805 ft (550 m) 42°42′ N 23°20′ E 9 years

| | Temperature °F | | | | Temperature °C | | | | Relative humidity | | Precipitation | | | |
| | Highest recorded | Average daily | | Lowest recorded | Highest recorded | Average daily | | Lowest recorded | 0630 hours | 1330 hours | Average monthly | | Average no. days with 0.008 in + (0.2 mm +) | |
		max.	min.			max.	min.		%	%	in	mm		
J	61	35	25	−6	16	2	−4	−21	88	78	1.4	36	9	J
F	63	39	27	−2	17	4	−3	−19	85	69	1.1	28	10	F
M	75	50	33	5	24	10	1	−15	82	56	1.6	41	10	M
A	83	60	42	23	28	16	5	−5	77	50	2.4	61	12	A
M	85	69	50	32	29	21	10	0	75	52	3.4	87	13	M
J	90	76	56	40	32	24	14	4	72	51	2.9	73	12	J
J	98	81	60	44	37	27	16	7	71	46	2.7	68	10	J
A	93	79	59	46	34	26	15	8	75	46	2.5	64	9	A
S	93	70	52	29	34	22	11	−2	82	51	1.6	41	7	S
O	86	63	46	28	30	17	8	−2	86	59	2.6	65	11	O
N	76	48	37	20	24	9	3	−7	90	72	1.9	48	10	N
D	62	38	28	3	17	4	−2	−16	87	77	1.9	49	12	D

BULGARIA

Varna 115 ft (35 m) 43°12′ N 27°55′ E 9 years

| | Temperature °F | | | | Temperature °C | | | | Relative humidity | | Precipitation | | | |
| | Highest recorded | Average daily | | Lowest recorded | Highest recorded | Average daily | | Lowest recorded | 0700 hours | 1400 hours | Average monthly | | Average no. days with 0.008 in + (0.2 mm +) | |
		max.	min.			max.	min.		%	%	in	mm		
J	69	42	30	4	20	6	−1	−16	89	80	1.1	28	8	J
F	71	43	30	9	21	6	−1	−13	86	75	1.2	30	9	F
M	75	51	36	17	24	11	2	−8	86	70	1.0	26	7	M
A	85	60	44	28	30	16	7	−2	83	68	1.5	37	8	A
M	93	71	53	36	34	22	12	2	83	69	1.0	26	8	M
J	96	79	61	48	35	26	16	9	78	67	2.5	64	9	J
J	102	86	65	50	39	30	19	10	75	61	1.8	45	6	J
A	98	85	64	52	36	29	18	11	79	60	1.5	37	6	A
S	93	78	58	37	34	26	14	3	83	62	1.1	27	5	S
O	90	69	52	34	32	21	11	1	88	68	2.3	58	8	O
N	76	55	43	22	24	13	6	−6	87	72	1.4	35	9	N
D	70	45	34	8	21	7	1	−14	88	79	2.5	63	11	D

Cyprus is the largest island in the eastern Mediterranean. It has a typical Mediterranean climate but its proximity to the land-mass of southwest Asia causes it to be one of the hottest parts of the Mediterranean in midsummer. This applies particularly to the central plain and the coastal regions. The island is mountainous and the two main mountain masses, the Kyrenia range in the north and the Troödos mountains rising to over 6000 ft (nearly 2000 m), have a cooler and wetter climate which supports excellent pine forests.

Summers are hot or warm, depending on altitude, and almost completely rainless from late May to mid-September. During this period the weather is constant from day to day and almost completely cloudless. The rest of the year is more changeable with the heaviest rainfall and greatest chance of disturbed weather in the midwinter months. Temperatures in winter are generally mild except in the mountains where, above 3300 ft (1000 m), snow becomes frequent and on the summit of Troödos it may lie for four to five months. During this time skiing is possible. Disturbed winter weather rarely lasts for more than a few days. During spring and autumn settled weather may last for two or three weeks with brief interruptions of stormy wet weather.

Conditions around the coast are represented by the table for **Kyrenia**. In summer the high daytime temperatures on the coast are tempered by cooling sea breezes but the nights may feel rather warm and sultry. The table for **Nicosia** is representative of conditions at low levels inland where daytime temperatures are very high in midsummer. The evenings and nights, however, feel cooler than on the coast. In the higher parts of the mountains summer conditions feel delightfully cool and fresh after the heat of the lowlands. There are numerous hill resorts for tourists.

Cyprus is a very sunny island even in winter. The average number of daily hours of sunshine ranges from six in midwinter to twelve or thirteen in midsummer. For those who find high temperatures unpleasant, the best time to visit Cyprus is in the spring when the weather is generally sunny and warm and the island is colourful with flowering plants. In late summer and autumn the island appears scorched and dry after the long summer drought. Although hardy northerners may be tempted to swim on a sunny day in winter they will find the sea around Cyprus to be rather chilly from December until early May.

Kyrenia 66 ft (20 m) 35°20′ N 33°19′ E 26 years

	Temperature °F			Temperature °C			Relative humidity		Precipitation		
	Highest recorded	Average daily	Lowest recorded	Highest recorded	Average daily	Lowest recorded	0800 hours	1400 hours	Average monthly		Average no. days with 0.008 in + (0.2 mm +)
		max. | min.			max. | min.		%	%	in | mm		
J	76	62 | 48	25	24	16 | 9	−4	75	70	4.6 | 117		13 | J
F	73	62 | 48	31	23	17 | 9	−1	74	67	3.1 | 79		10 | F
M	81	65 | 49	35	27	19 | 10	2	70	67	2.4 | 60		7 | M
A	87	71 | 53	37	31	22 | 12	3	70	68	0.8 | 20		4 | A
M	97	78 | 60	43	36	26 | 16	6	68	68	0.5 | 13		2 | M
J	106	86 | 67	52	41	30 | 20	11	68	65	0.1 | 2		0 | J
J	105	91 | 72	55	41	33 | 22	13	64	62	0 | 0		0 | J
A	107	92 | 73	57	42	33 | 23	14	65	60	0 | 0		0 | A
S	103	87 | 69	56	39	31 | 21	13	65	60	0.2 | 5		1 | S
O	97	81 | 63	51	36	27 | 17	11	67	62	1.5 | 37		3 | O
N	90	73 | 58	40	32	23 | 14	4	73	66	2.7 | 68		7 | N
D	75	65 | 52	34	24	18 | 11	1	75	69	5.2 | 133		11 | D

	Temperature °F			Temperature °C				Relative humidity		Precipitation		
	Highest recorded	Average daily		Lowest recorded	Highest recorded	Average daily		Lowest recorded	0800 hours	1400 hours	Average monthly		Average no. days with 0.008 in +
		max.	min.			max.	min.		%	%	in	mm	(0.2 mm +)
J	71	59	42	26	22	15	5	−3	83	66	3.0	76	14	J
F	79	61	42	22	26	16	5	−6	80	61	1.8	45	10	F
M	86	66	44	29	30	19	7	−2	73	55	1.4	36	8	M
A	95	75	50	34	35	24	10	1	64	46	0.7	18	4	A
M	109	85	58	45	43	29	14	7	55	41	0.9	22	3	M
J	111	92	65	51	44	34	18	11	52	37	0.4	9	1	J
J	111	98	70	59	44	37	21	15	51	34	0	1	0	J
A	112	98	69	58	44	37	21	14	57	35	0.1	2	0	A
S	107	92	65	53	42	33	18	12	60	38	0.4	10	1	S
O	105	83	58	42	41	28	14	6	65	45	1.0	25	4	O
N	91	72	51	30	33	22	10	−1	75	53	1.3	33	6	N
D	75	63	45	27	24	17	7	−3	82	63	2.7	68	11	D

CZECHOSLOVAKIA

Czechoslovakia is an entirely landlocked country in the middle of Europe. Its climate is transitional between the milder, wetter conditions of Atlantic Europe and the more extreme conditions (severe winters and warm summers) found in Russia. Extending for about 480 miles (800 km) from west to east, the eastern region of the country (Slovakia) is more mountainous and has a more extreme climate than the west (Bohemia). Much of the country is hilly, rising to over 3300 ft (1000 m) and the higher mountains rise to over 5000 ft (1500 m). Some of the largest local differences of climate within the country are a result of these differences of altitude.

Apart from such differences as arise from the above factors there is no great variability in weather and climate from one part of the country to another. This can be seen by comparing the tables for **Prague** in Bohemia, **Brno** in Moravia and **Kosice** in Slovakia. Weather is everywhere rather changeable throughout the year. The longest spells of settled weather occur during calm spells in winter. Conditions are then cold with much fog in low-lying areas. In winter snow may lie from between forty and 100 days, depending on altitude. The most unpleasant winter conditions occur when cold easterly winds bring very low temperatures. Precipitation in winter is rather low and spring and summer are the wettest seasons. Disturbed rainy weather lasting a few days is often brought by disturbances which originate over the northern Mediterranean at this time. Summers are moderately warm but extreme heat is rare. Hot spells usually end with thunderstorms and these often break out in the afternoons of otherwise fine, sunny days.

The table for **Prague** is representative of conditions in the western part of the country and that for **Kosice** is typical of conditions in the east. Conditions in central Czechoslovakia are illustrated by the table for **Brno**. These tables show only small differences from west to east and all three places are at similar altitudes.

The number of days with rain is rather lower than in western Europe and the average number of hours of sunshine is rather greater. In midsummer sunshine averages about eight hours a day.

Brno 732 ft (223 m) 49°12′ N 16°34′ E 14 years   **CZECHOSLOVAKIA**

	Temperature °F			Temperature °C			Relative humidity		Precipitation		
	Highest recorded	Average daily	Lowest recorded	Highest recorded	Average daily	Lowest recorded	0700 hours	1400 hours	Average monthly		Average no. days with 0.004 in + (0.1 mm +)
		max.	min.			max.	min.		%	%	in	mm	
J	58	34	24	−4	14	1	−5	−20	88	77	1.2	30	12	J
F	60	37	24	−12	16	3	−5	−25	88	69	1.3	32	11	F
M	73	47	30	6	23	8	−1	−14	87	58	0.9	22	8	M
A	81	59	39	21	27	15	4	−6	82	49	1.4	36	12	A
M	89	68	47	27	32	20	9	−3	77	49	1.9	49	11	M
J	96	74	53	37	35	23	12	3	77	52	2.6	67	13	J
J	98	77	57	40	37	25	14	5	81	52	3.2	81	14	J
A	97	76	55	41	36	25	13	5	85	53	2.9	73	13	A
S	90	70	49	32	32	21	9	0	90	55	1.7	42	10	S
O	79	58	40	19	26	14	4	−7	91	63	1.4	36	10	O
N	64	45	35	13	18	7	2	−10	91	77	1.5	38	12	N
D	57	38	30	−1	14	3	−1	−19	91	82	1.6	40	14	D

CZECHOSLOVAKIA — Kosice 761 ft (232 m) 48°42′ N 21°16′ E 15 years

	Temperature °F				Temperature °C				Relative humidity		Precipitation			
	Highest recorded	Average daily		Lowest recorded	Highest recorded	Average daily		Lowest recorded	0730 hours	1430 hours	Average monthly		Average no. days with 0.004 in + (0.1 mm +)	
		max.	min.			max.	min.		%	%	in	mm		
J	51	33	19	−16	10	0	−7	−27	87	78	1.2	30	13	J
F	55	35	22	−12	13	2	−6	−24	86	72	1.2	30	13	F
M	70	47	29	1	21	8	−2	−17	83	59	1.0	26	10	M
A	84	60	38	20	29	15	3	−7	77	51	1.5	38	11	A
M	87	69	47	27	31	21	8	−3	74	51	2.2	57	13	M
J	92	74	53	36	34	24	12	2	75	55	3.3	84	14	J
J	95	78	56	40	35	26	13	4	77	53	3.3	84	13	J
A	103	78	55	37	39	25	13	3	80	53	3.2	80	13	A
S	91	71	47	30	33	21	9	−1	86	53	1.9	47	9	S
O	81	58	38	12	27	14	3	−11	89	61	1.6	41	10	O
N	63	45	33	7	17	7	0	−14	90	76	1.9	49	13	N
D	58	37	27	−1	15	3	−3	−18	90	82	1.5	39	15	D

CZECHOSLOVAKIA — Prague 860 ft (262 m) 50°04′ N 14°26′ E 23 years

	Temperature °F				Temperature °C				Relative humidity		Precipitation			
	Highest recorded	Average daily		Lowest recorded	Highest recorded	Average daily		Lowest recorded	0700 hours	1400 hours	Average monthly		Average no. days with 0.004 in + (0.1 mm +)	
		max.	min.			max.	min.		%	%	in	mm		
J	55	49	7	−9	13	10	−13	−23	84	73	0.7	18	13	J
F	64	53	10	−18	18	11	−12	−28	83	67	0.7	18	11	F
M	71	64	18	6	22	18	−8	−14	82	55	0.7	18	10	M
A	84	73	29	21	29	23	−2	−6	77	47	1.1	27	11	A
M	90	82	36	29	32	28	2	−2	75	45	1.9	48	13	M
J	98	88	44	41	36	31	7	5	74	46	2.1	54	12	J
J	100	91	49	43	38	33	9	6	77	49	2.7	68	13	J
A	97	89	47	41	36	32	8	5	81	48	2.1	55	12	A
S	92	84	38	32	33	29	4	0	84	51	1.2	31	10	S
O	79	71	29	21	26	22	−2	−6	87	60	1.3	33	13	O
N	63	57	24	14	18	14	−5	−10	87	73	0.8	20	12	N
D	56	50	14	−6	13	10	−10	−21	87	78	0.8	21	13	D

Denmark consists of the peninsula of Jutland and a group of islands at the entrance to the Baltic Sea between Sweden and Germany. Its cool maritime climate is rather similar to that of Britain or the state of Washington. Because of its small size and low elevation – no part of Denmark is higher than 600 ft (180 m) – weather and climate do not vary much throughout the country.

Spells of cold weather occur in most winters when the waters of the Baltic freeze in whole or in part. In some winters such spells may be prolonged. If this happens the waters of the Sound between Zeeland and south Sweden may freeze. The average duration of winter snow cover is about thirty days but in some winters there may be little snow.

Conditions in summer are variable from year to year and from day to day. Although spells of warm settled weather may last for a few weeks in some years, it rarely becomes unpleasantly hot. Precipitation occurs all the year round but summer and autumn are the wettest seasons. The west coast (see the table for **Fanø**) is a little wetter than the east (see the table for **Copenhagen**).

When Atlantic storms cross the country or move into the North Sea, quite severe gales may affect Denmark and the west coast has the reputation of being particularly exposed and windswept. Such gales may occur at all times of the year but are less frequent and less severe in summer. Denmark has a generally pleasant climate the year round and, apart from the occasional cold winter, rarely suffers extremes of weather. Daily sunshine hours range from between one and two in winter to about eight in summer.

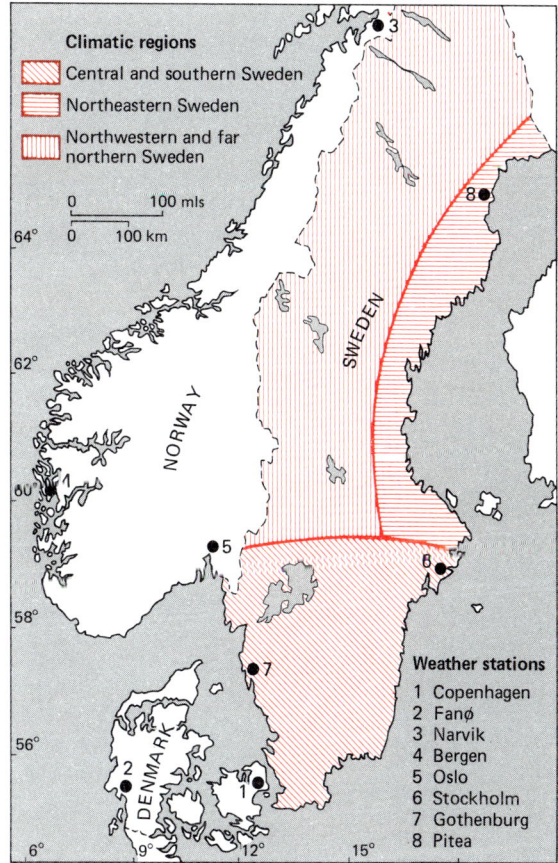

Copenhagen 33 ft (9 m) 55°41′ N 12°33′ E 30 years

	Temperature °F				Temperature °C				Relative humidity		Precipitation			
	Highest recorded	Average daily		Lowest recorded	Highest recorded	Average daily		Lowest recorded	0800 hours	1400 hours	Average monthly		Average no. days with 0.004 in + (0.1 mm +)	
		max.	min.			max.	min.		%	%	in	mm		
J	50	36	28	−12	10	2	−2	−24	88	85	1.9	49	17	J
F	57	36	28	−3	14	2	−3	−20	86	83	1.5	39	13	F
M	65	41	31	0	19	5	−1	−18	85	78	1.3	32	12	M
A	70	51	38	16	22	10	3	−9	79	68	1.5	38	13	A
M	82	61	46	29	28	16	8	−2	70	59	1.7	43	11	M
J	91	67	52	37	33	19	11	3	70	60	1.9	47	13	J
J	87	71	57	46	31	22	14	8	74	62	2.8	71	14	J
A	87	70	56	42	31	21	14	6	78	64	2.6	66	14	A
S	80	64	51	34	27	18	11	1	83	69	2.4	62	15	S
O	68	54	44	25	20	12	7	−4	86	76	2.3	59	16	O
N	58	45	38	20	14	7	3	−7	88	83	1.9	48	16	N
D	54	40	34	12	12	4	1	−11	89	87	1.9	49	17	D

Fanø 10 ft (3 m) 55°27′ N 8°24′ E 30 years

	Temperature °F				Temperature °C				Relative humidity		Precipitation			
	Highest recorded	Average daily		Lowest recorded	Highest recorded	Average daily		Lowest recorded	0730 hours	1330 hours	Average monthly		Average no. days with 0.004 in + (0.1 mm +)	
		max.	min.			max.	min.		%	%	in	mm		
J	49	37	29	−8	10	3	−2	−22	90	89	2.4	60	17	J
F	49	37	28	−6	10	3	−2	−21	89	88	1.8	45	13	F
M	64	42	31	0	18	6	−1	−18	89	83	1.5	38	12	M
A	77	51	37	23	25	10	3	−5	86	75	1.5	39	12	A
M	86	60	45	29	30	16	7	−2	80	67	1.7	43	11	M
J	91	66	51	35	33	19	11	1	78	66	1.7	43	12	J
J	95	70	56	41	35	21	13	5	81	69	2.9	74	14	J
A	91	69	56	38	33	21	13	4	83	69	3.4	85	15	A
S	84	64	51	34	29	18	11	1	86	73	3.5	88	16	S
O	69	55	44	21	21	13	7	−6	89	80	3.2	82	17	O
N	57	46	38	20	14	8	3	−7	91	88	2.7	68	19	N
D	58	41	33	8	15	5	1	−13	92	91	2.5	64	19	D

This small group of islands is situated in the stormiest part of the North Atlantic midway between Scotland and Iceland. They are a former dependancy of Denmark but are now self-governing.

Under the influence of the warm ocean current of the Gulf Stream the climate is very mild for the latitude. Winters in the Faeroes are warmer than those in Denmark, 6° of latitude to the south. The islands are cloudy, wet and windy throughout the year for they lie in the path of the majority of Atlantic depressions. They are never very cold for long in winter and the summers are cool and sunless. Daily sunshine in the summer months averages only about four hours.

Hoyvik 66 ft (20 m) 62°02′ N 6°45′ W 27 years

	Temperature °F			Temperature °C			Relative humidity		Precipitation		
	Highest recorded	Average daily		Lowest recorded	Highest recorded	Average daily		Lowest recorded	0830 hours	1430 hours	Average monthly		Average no. days with 0.004 in + (0.1 mm +)
		max.	min.			max.	min.		%	%	in	mm	
J	59	43	35	14	15	6	2	−10	81	82	5.9	149	25	J
F	53	42	34	13	12	6	1	−10	82	82	5.4	136	22	F
M	55	44	36	17	13	7	2	−9	82	81	4.5	114	23	M
A	56	46	37	20	13	8	3	−7	81	80	4.2	106	22	A
M	66	49	41	24	19	10	5	−5	82	82	2.6	67	16	M
J	66	53	45	33	19	12	7	1	83	83	2.9	74	16	J
J	72	56	48	36	22	13	9	2	86	84	3.1	79	18	J
A	71	56	49	38	22	14	9	3	87	84	3.8	96	20	A
S	65	54	46	32	18	12	8	0	85	84	5.2	132	21	S
O	62	50	42	24	17	10	5	−4	83	82	6.2	157	24	O
N	58	47	39	23	15	8	4	−5	83	84	6.1	156	24	N
D	54	45	37	14	12	7	3	−10	82	83	6.6	167	26	D

FINLAND

Finland extends between 60° and 70° N. Consequently, it has a severe winter climate resembling that of Alaska or the Yukon. By contrast the summers can be surprisingly warm, particularly in the south of the country. In the north, beyond the Arctic Circle, the long duration of sunshine in midsummer compensates, to some extent, for the northerly latitude.

The south and centre of the country is low-lying. It is a land of pine forests and innumerable lakes of varying sizes. The north, or Finnish Lapland, is higher, but only along the northwestern border with Norway do hills rise above 3000 ft (900 m). Off the southwest coast there are innumerable tiny islands and this is the mildest part of the country in winter for the more open waters of the Baltic do not freeze so often as the Gulfs of Bothnia and Finland.

In the south and centre of the country the summers are as warm as those of Denmark and south Sweden (see the tables for **Helsinki** on the coast and **Tampere** inland). The winters are long and cold with snow lying for an average of between ninety and 120 days. Summer precipitation is nowhere very heavy and in winter it is mostly snow.

In the north of the country the snow cover lasts from mid-October until late April or mid-May. Here, in the brief Arctic summer, daytime temperatures may rise almost as high as in the south and sunshine may average as much as nine to ten hours a day (see the table for **Inari**). The weather is changeable from day to day at all seasons, however, for Finland is influenced to some extent by weather disturbances originating over the Atlantic. The longest spells of settled weather are most frequent in winter.

Warm clothing is essential in the winter months and in severe weather there is a danger of frostbite, particularly in Arctic Finland, if suitable clothing is not worn. One irritant, an indirect result of the summer climate, is the swarms of mosquitos and gnats which appear during the warm weather. These are particularly troublesome in the north of the country.

FINLAND · Helsinki 151 ft (46 m) 60°12′ N 24°55′ E 30 years

	Temperature °F			Temperature °C				Relative humidity		Precipitation			
	Highest recorded	Average daily		Lowest recorded	Highest recorded	Average daily		Lowest recorded	0730 hours	1330 hours	Average monthly		Average no. days with 0.004 in + (0.1 mm +)	
		max.	min.			max.	min.		%	%	in	mm		
J	44	26	17	−28	7	−3	−9	−33	89	87	2.2	56	20	J
F	53	25	15	−22	12	−4	−10	−30	89	82	1.7	42	18	F
M	59	32	20	−15	15	0	−7	−26	86	70	1.4	36	14	M
A	69	44	30	8	21	6	−1	−14	81	66	1.7	44	13	A
M	79	56	40	22	26	14	4	−6	70	58	1.6	41	12	M
J	88	66	49	32	31	19	9	0	72	59	2.0	51	13	J
J	92	71	55	42	33	22	13	5	76	63	2.7	68	14	J
A	86	68	53	38	30	20	12	4	83	67	2.8	72	15	A
S	76	59	46	25	24	15	8	−4	89	72	2.8	71	15	S
O	64	47	37	14	18	8	3	−10	91	79	2.9	73	18	O
N	51	37	30	3	11	3	−1	−16	90	86	2.7	68	19	N
D	49	31	23	−18	9	−1	−5	−28	90	89	2.6	66	20	D

	Temperature °F				Temperature °C				Relative humidity	Precipitation			
	Highest recorded	Average daily		Lowest recorded	Highest recorded	Average daily		Lowest recorded		Average monthly		Average no. days with 0.004 in + (0.1 mm +)	
		max.	min.			max.	min.			in	mm		
J	38	17	−1	−43	4	−9	−18	−41	—	0.9	22	14	J
F	42	16	2	−43	6	−9	−17	−42	—	0.8	19	13	F
M	46	26	7	−37	8	−3	−14	−38	—	0.6	15	10	M
A	56	35	17	−19	13	2	−9	−29	—	0.8	20	9	A
M	75	47	31	11	24	8	0	−12	—	1.1	29	13	M
J	82	57	42	28	28	14	6	−2	—	2.1	54	16	J
J	88	63	48	35	31	17	9	2	—	2.1	53	15	J
A	79	59	45	32	26	15	7	0	—	2.6	66	16	A
S	75	47	38	22	24	9	3	−6	—	1.7	44	15	S
O	56	34	26	−1	14	1	−3	−18	—	1.1	28	13	O
N	44	24	13	−32	7	−4	−10	−36	—	1.0	25	13	N
D	36	18	0	−40	2	−8	−18	−40	—	1.2	30	15	D

	Temperature °F				Temperature °C				Relative humidity		Precipitation			
	Highest recorded	Average daily		Lowest recorded	Highest recorded	Average daily		Lowest recorded	0730 hours	1330 hours	Average monthly		Average no. days with 0.004 in + (0.1 mm +)	
		max.	min.			max.	min.		%	%	in	mm		
J	45	24	12	−33	7	−5	−11	−36	87	86	1.5	38	17	J
F	48	24	12	−33	9	−4	−11	−36	86	81	1.2	30	14	F
M	54	31	16	−23	12	0	−9	−31	86	69	1.0	25	11	M
A	71	45	28	−7	22	7	−2	−22	83	63	1.4	35	12	A
M	83	58	38	19	28	14	3	−7	74	54	1.7	42	11	M
J	88	67	48	28	31	19	9	−2	73	56	1.9	48	12	J
J	91	72	54	34	33	22	12	1	78	59	3.0	76	14	J
A	89	69	51	31	32	20	11	−1	86	63	3.0	75	14	A
S	80	57	44	22	27	14	7	−6	90	69	2.2	57	15	S
O	63	45	35	7	17	7	2	−14	90	79	2.2	57	16	O
N	51	35	28	−7	10	2	−2	−22	90	87	1.9	49	18	N
D	48	29	20	−27	9	−2	−6	−32	89	88	1.6	41	18	D

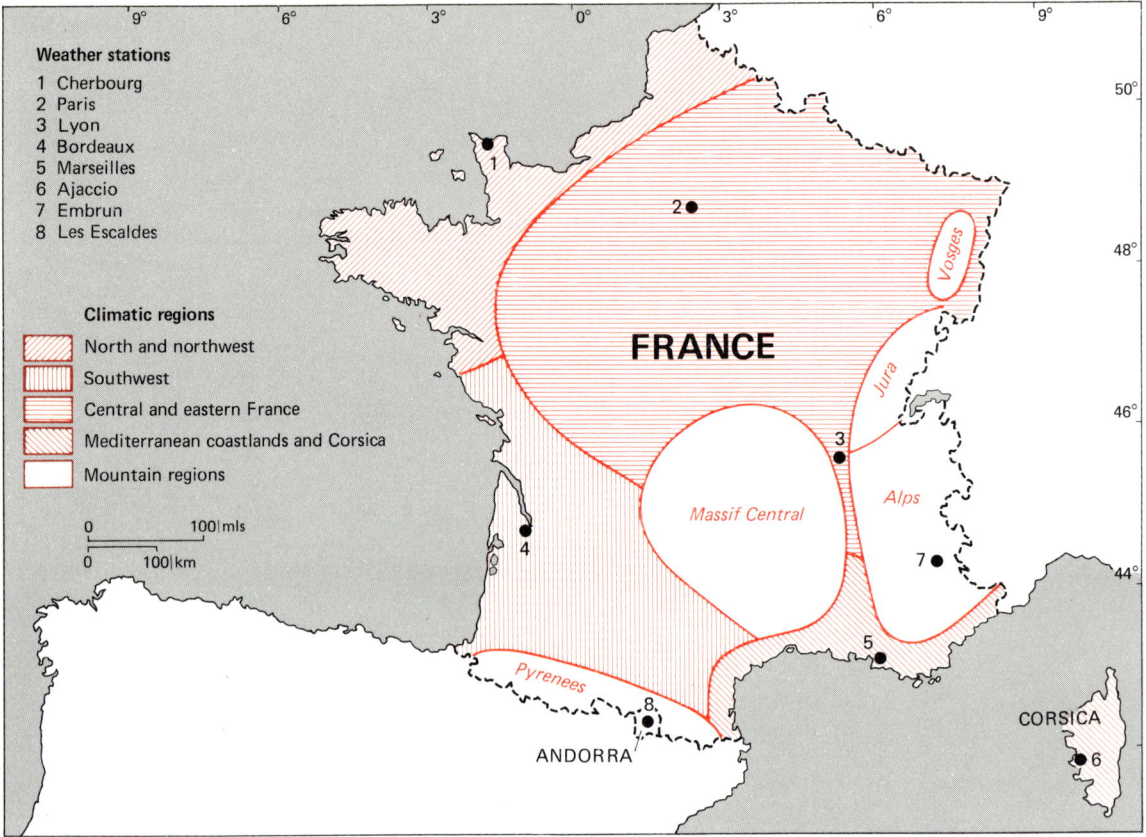

Weather stations

1 Cherbourg
2 Paris
3 Lyon
4 Bordeaux
5 Marseilles
6 Ajaccio
7 Embrun
8 Les Escaldes

Climatic regions

North and northwest
Southwest
Central and eastern France
Mediterranean coastlands and Corsica
Mountain regions

100 mls
100 km

FRANCE

Vosges

Jura

Alps

Massif Central

Pyrenees

ANDORRA

CORSICA

France is a large country, two and a half times as big as Great Britain, extending for some 600 miles (1000 km) from north to south and from east to west. Although much of northern and western France is low-lying and rather flat, there are some high mountain regions in the south and east: part of the western Alps, the Pyrenees which form the border with Spain, and the Massif Central which rises to over 6000 ft (1800 m) in its southern and central parts. Consequently, there are considerable variations of climate within France.

Northern and northwestern France are most affected by the changeable weather brought in by Atlantic disturbances and its climate is rather similar to that of Britain. Southern France has a Mediterranean-type climate and is warmer than the north, particularly in summer. Central and eastern France, roughly east of a line through Dunkirk, **Paris** and **Lyon**, has a more continental climate which bears some resemblance to that found in West Germany and Switzerland. The high mountain areas have their own distinctive climates with heavier precipitation, much of it snow in winter; these areas are colder all the year round. Only along the Mediterranean coast and in the adjacent mountain regions is summer a generally settled, sunny and warm season. Everywhere else in France the weather can be changeable at all times of the year.

It is most convenient for purposes of description to divide France into five climatic regions and to describe briefly the weather found in each.

NORTHERN AND NORTHWESTERN FRANCE

This area comprises the coasts and adjacent inland areas from the Belgian border to the mouth of the River Loire (see the table for **Cherbourg**). This area has the most maritime climate in all France. Winters are generally mild and frost and snow are not too frequent, becoming less so in the west. Rain occurs at all times of the year. The summers are a little warmer than those found in southern Britain. Average daily hours of sunshine range from two in midwinter to between seven and eight in midsummer.

SOUTHWESTERN FRANCE

This is mainly a lowland region often called by its historic name of Aquitaine (see the table for **Bordeaux**). Here the summers are significantly warmer and sunnier than in the northwest of France. Winters are generally mild and cold spells do not last for long. Summers can be rather wet, particularly towards the Pyrenees and the Spanish border, but the rain tends to be heavy and of short duration. Summers have more sunshine and longer spells of settled weather than farther north.

	Temperature °F			Temperature °C			Relative humidity		Precipitation		
	Highest recorded	Average daily	Lowest recorded	Highest recorded	Average daily	Lowest recorded	0600 hours	1200 hours	Average monthly		Average no. days with 0.004 in + (0.1 mm +)
		max.	min.			max.	min.		%	%	in	mm
J	58	47	40	21	14	8	4	−6	83	79	4.3	109	19	J
F	65	47	39	14	18	8	4	−10	82	76	3.0	75	15	F
M	73	51	41	25	23	10	5	−4	83	74	2.4	62	13	M
A	75	54	45	31	24	12	7	0	83	73	1.9	49	12	A
M	86	59	49	38	30	15	9	4	85	73	1.6	41	11	M
J	89	64	54	43	31	18	12	6	86	74	1.5	39	10	J
J	89	67	57	46	32	19	14	8	86	74	2.2	55	12	J
A	91	67	57	48	33	20	14	9	88	75	2.8	71	12	A
S	87	65	56	43	30	19	13	6	86	74	3.1	79	15	S
O	78	60	51	38	26	15	10	3	84	73	3.9	99	16	O
N	66	53	46	31	19	12	8	−1	83	77	5.2	133	17	N
D	62	49	42	22	17	10	5	−6	84	79	4.7	119	19	D

	Temperature °F			Temperature °C			Relative humidity		Precipitation		
	Highest recorded	Average daily	Lowest recorded	Highest recorded	Average daily	Lowest recorded	0600 hours	1200 hours	Average monthly		Average no. days with 0.004 in + (0.1 mm +)
		max.	min.			max.	min.		%	%	in	mm
J	65	49	35	10	18	9	2	−12	93	80	3.5	90	16	J
F	72	51	36	5	22	11	2	−15	91	73	3.0	75	13	F
M	78	59	40	21	26	15	4	−6	91	64	2.5	63	13	M
A	88	63	43	23	31	17	6	−5	91	60	1.9	48	13	A
M	92	69	48	26	34	20	9	−3	91	60	2.4	61	14	M
J	101	75	54	37	38	24	12	3	91	62	2.6	65	11	J
J	101	78	57	41	39	25	14	5	91	61	2.2	56	11	J
A	99	78	56	42	37	26	14	6	93	60	2.8	70	12	A
S	97	74	54	29	36	23	12	−2	96	67	3.3	84	13	S
O	87	65	47	22	30	18	8	−5	96	71	3.3	83	14	O
N	75	55	40	21	24	13	5	−6	95	80	3.8	96	15	N
D	70	49	37	11	21	9	3	−12	94	83	4.3	109	17	D

CENTRAL AND EASTERN FRANCE
(EXCLUDING THE MOUNTAIN AREAS OF THE VOSGES, JURA AND ALPS)

This area is marked by rather colder winters with a greater chance of frost and snow than in the northwest. Summers also tend to be a little warmer. Rainfall is generally low and tends to fall in summer when it is often associated with thunderstorms. Winters become colder towards the east and they are not any warmer farther south. In winter occasional very cold spells can occur. There is a definite increase in summer warmth in the south and an increase in sunshine from an average of seven to nine hours a day. Compare the tables for **Paris** and **Lyon**.

Paris 246 ft (75 m) 48°49′ N 2°20′ E 30 years   **FRANCE**

	Temperature °F			Temperature °C			Relative humidity		Precipitation		
	Highest recorded	Average daily	Lowest recorded	Highest recorded	Average daily	Lowest recorded	0600 hours	1200 hours	Average monthly		Average no. days with 0.004 in + (0.1 mm +)
		max.	min.			max.	min.		%	%	in	mm	
J	58	43	34	10	15	6	1	−12	88	80	2.2	56	17	J
F	71	45	34	6	21	7	1	−15	87	73	1.8	46	14	F
M	78	54	39	24	26	12	4	−4	85	63	1.4	35	12	M
A	86	60	43	32	30	16	6	0	82	54	1.7	42	13	A
M	91	68	49	36	33	20	10	2	83	55	2.2	57	12	M
J	100	73	55	42	38	23	13	6	83	58	2.1	54	12	J
J	104	76	58	48	40	25	15	9	83	57	2.3	59	12	J
A	95	75	58	46	35	24	14	8	87	61	2.5	64	13	A
S	92	70	53	37	33	21	12	3	90	65	2.2	55	13	S
O	83	60	46	27	28	16	8	−3	91	71	2.0	50	13	O
N	69	50	40	23	21	10	5	−5	91	79	2.0	51	15	N
D	62	44	36	9	17	7	2	−13	90	82	2.0	50	16	D

Lyon 656 ft (200 m) 45°43′ N 4°57′ E 30 years   **FRANCE**

	Temperature °F			Temperature °C			Relative humidity		Precipitation		
	Highest recorded	Average daily	Lowest recorded	Highest recorded	Average daily	Lowest recorded	0630 hours	1230 hours	Average monthly		Average no. days with 0.004 in + (0.1 mm +)
		max.	min.			max.	min.		%	%	in	mm	
J	64	42	30	2	18	5	−1	−17	89	80	2.1	52	15	J
F	71	45	31	−7	22	7	0	−21	87	72	1.8	46	12	F
M	73	55	37	14	23	13	3	−10	87	60	2.1	53	11	M
A	86	61	42	24	30	16	6	−4	84	56	2.2	56	11	A
M	90	69	49	33	32	20	9	1	83	56	2.7	69	13	M
J	98	75	55	36	37	24	13	2	82	55	3.4	85	11	J
J	103	80	59	44	40	27	15	6	79	50	2.2	56	10	J
A	103	79	58	44	40	26	14	6	85	54	3.5	89	11	A
S	96	73	53	33	36	23	12	1	89	60	3.7	93	11	S
O	82	61	45	24	28	16	7	−5	92	69	3.0	77	12	O
N	73	50	38	18	23	10	4	−8	91	78	3.2	80	14	N
D	66	43	33	−3	19	6	0	−20	90	80	2.2	57	14	D

THE MEDITERRANEAN COASTLANDS AND THE ISLAND OF CORSICA

Apart from the island of Corsica represented by the table for **Ajaccio**, a Mediterranean climate is confined to the Rhône valley south of Valence and the coastlands of Languedoc and Provence at the foot of the Cevennes and southern Alps. Here summers are warm, or even hot, with a three-month period when rain rarely falls. When it does rain at this season it is heavy and often associated with thunder. Sunshine is abundant, as much as eleven to twelve hours a day in summer and five in midwinter. Winters are generally mild and sunny but this pleasant weather is often interrupted by very changeable cold and blustery weather brought by a northerly wind called the mistral. This blows with particular strength in the Rhône valley and around Marseille. The mistral can bring unseasonably cold weather for a few days in spring. The Côte d'Azur from Toulon to the Italian border, including the small independent principality of Monaco, is much less exposed to the cold blasts of the mistral and in Corsica the cold is moderated by the warm waters of the Mediterranean.

Corsica, which is particularly popular as a holiday resort because of its mild winters at sea level and hot sunny summers, is a mountainous island. In the interior altitudes exceed 6500 ft (2000 m) and here winter snowfall can be heavy and snow cover last well into spring.

Ajaccio (Corsica) 12 ft (4 m) 41°55′ N 8°48′ E 30 years   FRANCE

	Temperature °F			Temperature °C				Relative humidity		Precipitation			
	Highest recorded	Average daily		Lowest recorded	Highest recorded	Average daily		Lowest recorded	0630 hours	1230 hours	Average monthly		Average no. days with 0.004 in + (0.1 mm +)	
		max.	min.			max.	min.		%	%	in	mm		
J	69	55	38	23	21	13	3	−5	84	66	3.0	76	12	J
F	74	56	39	21	23	14	4	−6	85	67	2.6	65	10	F
M	79	60	41	25	26	16	5	−4	85	67	2.1	53	9	M
A	85	64	45	29	29	18	7	−2	85	66	1.9	48	9	A
M	91	70	50	37	33	21	10	3	83	69	2.0	50	8	M
J	99	77	56	45	37	25	14	7	78	65	0.8	21	4	J
J	98	81	60	49	37	27	16	9	75	65	0.4	10	1	J
A	101	82	60	48	39	28	16	9	78	64	0.6	16	2	A
S	97	78	58	46	36	26	15	8	83	64	2.0	50	6	S
O	88	71	52	36	31	22	11	2	84	63	3.5	88	10	O
N	79	63	45	28	26	18	7	−2	87	66	3.8	97	11	N
D	72	58	40	26	22	15	4	−4	85	66	3.9	98	13	D

Marseille 13 ft (4 m) 43°27′ N 5°13′ E 30 years   FRANCE

	Temperature °F			Temperature °C				Relative humidity		Precipitation			
	Highest recorded	Average daily		Lowest recorded	Highest recorded	Average daily		Lowest recorded	0630 hours	1230 hours	Average monthly		Average no. days with 0.004 in + (0.1 mm +)	
		max.	min.			max.	min.		%	%	in	mm		
J	65	50	35	13	18	10	2	−11	82	68	1.7	43	8	J
F	71	53	36	2	22	12	2	−17	81	60	1.3	32	6	F
M	75	59	41	14	24	15	5	−10	80	57	1.7	43	7	M
A	83	64	46	28	29	18	8	−2	79	54	1.7	42	7	A
M	89	71	52	32	31	22	11	0	78	54	1.8	46	8	M
J	99	79	58	42	37	26	15	5	72	50	0.9	24	4	J
J	102	84	63	46	39	29	17	8	69	45	0.4	11	2	J
A	99	83	63	47	37	28	17	9	75	49	1.3	34	5	A
S	94	77	58	34	34	25	15	1	81	54	2.4	60	6	S
O	84	68	51	30	29	20	10	−1	84	61	3.0	76	8	O
N	73	58	43	22	23	15	6	−5	85	66	2.7	69	9	N
D	68	52	37	13	20	11	3	−11	83	68	2.6	66	10	D

THE MOUNTAIN REGIONS

The principal mountain regions of France are the Vosges in Alsace and Lorraine, the Jura and Alps along the borders with Switzerland and Italy, the Pyrenees in the extreme south, and the higher parts of the Massif Central. These areas are the wettest and coldest regions of France and much of the winter precipitation is snow. Winter sports are best developed in the Alps and Pyrenees but can be pursued for a shorter period in the other mountain regions. The weather and climate of the French Alps and Jura is very similar to that found in the Swiss Alps (see p. 422). **Embrun** illustrates conditions at medium levels in the heart of the French Alps. In the Pyrenees precipitation tends to be greatest in winter and autumn but, in the Vosges, Jura and the northern Alps, summer and autumn are the wettest seasons. The southern Alps, Pyrenees and parts of the Massif Central have relatively fine and rather warm weather during the summer, considering their height, but this may be briefly interrupted by cloud, rain and thunder. The most unpleasant aspect of the summer weather in these mountain areas is the frequent and sudden onset of cloud towards midday which may obscure the peaks but leave the valleys clear. In winter, conditions are often reversed with the mountains rising into clear blue skies and the valleys enveloped in low cloud and fog. Severe frosts may occur in settled calm weather in all valley regions in winter.

FRANCE

Embrun 2858 ft (871 m) 44°34′ N 6°30′ E 30 years

		Temperature °F			Temperature °C			Relative humidity		Precipitation			
	Highest recorded	Average daily		Lowest recorded	Highest recorded	Average daily		Lowest recorded	0630 hours	1230 hours	Average monthly		Average no. days with 0.004 in + (0.1 mm +)	
		max.	min.			max.	min.		%	%	in	mm		
J	62	41	24	3	17	5	−5	−16	69	54	1.9	49	9	J
F	68	45	26	−2	20	7	−3	−19	69	49	1.7	43	8	F
M	74	53	33	11	24	12	0	−12	68	41	1.9	48	8	M
A	80	60	38	22	26	15	3	−5	72	39	2.0	51	9	A
M	85	67	45	28	29	19	7	−3	76	43	2.4	61	11	M
J	91	73	50	31	33	23	10	−1	78	45	2.4	62	10	J
J	93	79	54	38	34	26	12	3	75	40	1.9	48	7	J
A	93	77	53	39	34	25	12	4	77	42	2.6	65	8	A
S	89	71	49	32	31	22	10	0	80	49	2.8	70	8	S
O	74	61	42	22	23	16	5	−5	77	51	2.8	70	9	O
N	67	50	33	16	20	10	1	−9	75	54	2.7	68	10	N
D	59	42	26	6	15	6	−3	−15	71	57	2.6	65	10	D

East Germany or the German Democratic Republic lies in the North European Plain between West Germany and Poland. Its area of 41,000 square miles (106,000 sq. km) is about half that of West Germany. It has a coastline on the Baltic Sea in the north. Most of the country is low-lying and rather flat but in the south and southwest along the border with Czechoslovakia and West Germany it includes parts of the Harz Mountains, the Thuringian Forest and the Ore Mountains where some land rises to over 3000 ft (900 m).

In general terms the weather and climate of the country is similar to that of West Germany but, because of its more easterly position, the winters are colder and snow and frost occur more frequently. The weather can be changeable at all times of the year, but cold spells may be prolonged in some winters and spells of fine, dry weather in summer are not infrequent. The winter freezing of canals and rivers is more frequent than it is in West Germany.

The country can be divided into three climatic regions and these are an easterly extension of regions in West Germany: the Baltic coast and adjacent areas, the central region and Berlin, and the hill country of Saxony and Thuringia.

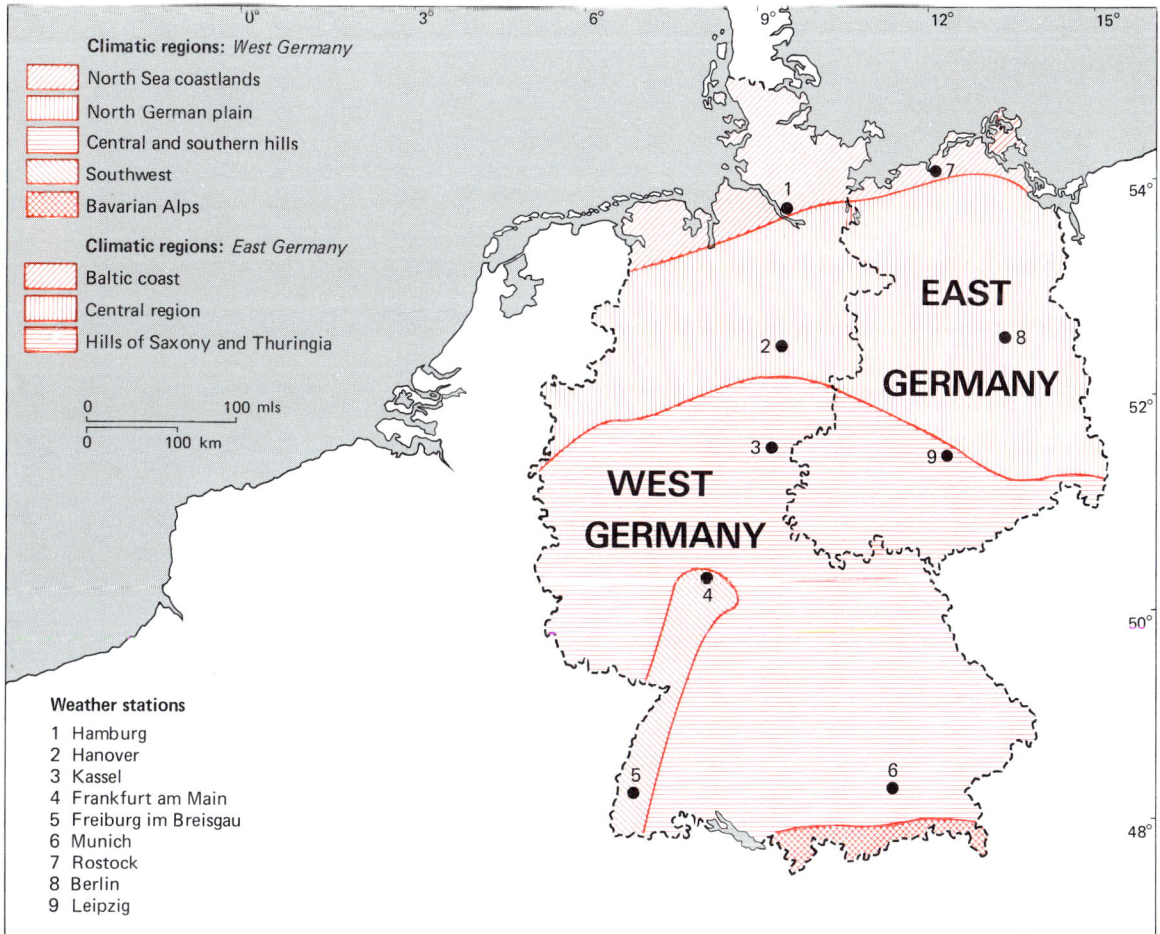

Climatic regions: *West Germany*

- North Sea coastlands
- North German plain
- Central and southern hills
- Southwest
- Bavarian Alps

Climatic regions: *East Germany*

- Baltic coast
- Central region
- Hills of Saxony and Thuringia

0   100 mls
0   100 km

Weather stations

1 Hamburg
2 Hanover
3 Kassel
4 Frankfurt am Main
5 Freiburg im Breisgau
6 Munich
7 Rostock
8 Berlin
9 Leipzig

EAST GERMANY

WEST GERMANY

THE BALTIC COAST AND ADJACENT AREAS

Here the winters are a little warmer and rather cloudier than farther inland. However, because the waters of the Baltic often freeze over in whole or in part during severe winters, the region is colder than the North Sea districts of West Germany (see the table for **Rostock**).

THE CENTRAL REGION AND BERLIN

This is part of the North German Plain and conditions are well represented by the table for **Berlin**. Rainfall over the year is quite low with a maximum in summer. Much of the summer rainfall is showery and accompanied with thunder. Winters are rather cold and on occasions quite severe, with canals and lakes freezing over. Summers have more sunshine than along the Baltic coast, with an average of eight hours a day in midsummer compared with two hours a day in mid-winter.

	Temperature °F			Temperature °C				Relative humidity		Precipitation			
	Highest recorded	Average daily		Lowest recorded	Highest recorded	Average daily		Lowest recorded	0700 hours	1400 hours	Average monthly		Average no. days with 0.004 in + (0.1 mm +)	
		max.	min.			max.	min.		%	%	in	mm		
J	52	36	28	−1	11	2	−2	−18	91	86	1.8	46	18	J
F	60	36	26	−3	15	2	−3	−20	91	84	1.4	36	16	F
M	69	44	31	1	21	7	−1	−18	90	72	1.2	30	12	M
A	79	52	37	24	26	11	3	−5	86	65	1.7	42	15	A
M	88	62	44	27	31	17	7	−3	80	60	1.9	48	12	M
J	92	68	51	36	33	20	10	2	79	61	2.4	60	12	J
J	92	72	55	43	34	22	13	6	83	63	3.1	79	15	J
A	89	71	55	42	32	21	13	5	88	65	2.8	71	14	A
S	84	64	49	33	29	18	9	1	90	66	2.7	69	13	S
O	72	54	43	24	22	12	6	−5	92	76	2.6	65	18	O
N	60	44	36	16	15	7	2	−9	93	86	1.5	39	15	N
D	57	38	30	2	14	3	−1	−16	93	88	1.8	45	17	D

	Temperature °F			Temperature °C				Relative humidity		Precipitation			
	Highest recorded	Average daily		Lowest recorded	Highest recorded	Average daily		Lowest recorded	0700 hours	1400 hours	Average monthly		Average no. days with 0.004 in + (0.1 mm +)	
		max.	min.			max.	min.		%	%	in	mm		
J	55	35	26	−6	13	2	−3	−21	89	82	1.8	46	17	J
F	62	37	26	−8	17	3	−3	−22	89	78	1.6	40	15	F
M	71	46	31	6	22	8	0	−14	88	67	1.3	33	12	M
A	86	56	39	21	30	13	4	−6	84	60	1.7	42	13	A
M	90	66	47	27	32	19	8	−3	80	57	1.9	49	12	M
J	95	72	53	38	35	22	12	3	80	58	2.6	65	13	J
J	99	75	57	42	37	24	14	5	84	61	2.9	73	14	J
A	98	74	56	43	37	23	13	6	88	61	2.7	69	14	A
S	93	68	50	34	34	20	10	1	92	65	1.9	48	12	S
O	77	56	42	24	25	13	6	−4	93	73	1.9	49	14	O
N	63	45	36	17	17	7	2	−9	92	83	1.8	46	16	N
D	59	38	29	0	15	3	−1	−18	91	86	1.7	43	15	D

THE HILL COUNTRY OF SAXONY AND THURINGIA

This area is in the southwest and south and has a climate similar to that of southwest West Germany (see p. 370). The table for **Leipzig** illustrates conditions in the lower part of this region. At higher altitudes winters are colder and snow may lie for some time. This is also the wettest area of East Germany.

EAST GERMANY **Leipzig** 463 ft (141 m) 51°19′ N 12°25′ E 27 years

		Temperature °F				Temperature °C			Relative humidity		Precipitation			
	Highest recorded	Average daily		Lowest recorded	Highest recorded	Average daily		Lowest recorded	0700 hours	1400 hours	Average monthly		Average no. days with 0.004 in + (0.1 mm +)	
		max.	min.			max.	min.		%	%	in	mm		
J	55	36	27	−10	13	2	−3	−24	86	78	1.6	41	17	J
F	62	38	26	−9	17	3	−3	−23	87	75	1.5	39	15	F
M	71	47	32	6	22	8	0	−15	86	66	1.5	38	14	M
A	85	57	40	22	29	14	4	−6	82	57	1.6	41	14	A
M	88	66	47	26	31	19	8	−3	80	55	2.1	52	13	M
J	98	72	51	40	36	22	12	5	79	56	2.7	69	13	J
J	100	75	57	45	38	24	14	7	82	58	3.3	83	15	J
A	100	74	56	42	38	24	13	6	85	57	2.4	62	13	A
S	94	68	50	34	35	20	10	1	89	61	1.7	42	13	S
O	81	57	42	23	27	14	6	−5	90	68	1.9	49	14	O
N	67	46	36	18	20	8	2	−8	89	78	1.6	41	15	N
D	62	39	30	−5	17	4	−1	−21	88	81	1.5	38	15	D

The Federal Republic of West Germany has an area of almost 96,000 square miles (249,000 sq. km). Its greatest extent is from north to south between Denmark and Switzerland. The north of the country is rather flat and low-lying, but central and southern Germany is mainly a hilly region. This increase in altitude southwards compensates for the effect of decreasing latitude, so in summer there is little difference in average temperature between the north and south. In winter there is some decrease in temperature from west to east, and the increasing altitude and proximity to the Alps means that southern Germany has colder and snowier winters than the north. On occasions, however, the winters can be quite cold in north Germany, particularly when spells of persistent easterly winds 'import' cold from Russia.

Like much of western Europe the weather can be very variable at all times of the year in West Germany and the character of winter or summer may vary from one year to another. Over much of the country summer is marginally the wettest season but on the higher hills and mountains autumn may be as wet or slightly wetter than summer.

For a more detailed description of weather and climate West Germany can be divided into five climatic regions: the North Sea coast and the Schleswig-Holstein area, the inland districts of north Germany, the hills of central and southern Germany, southwest Germany, and the Bavarian Alps. For West Berlin, see p. 363. (See map p. 361.)

THE NORTH SEA COAST AND THE SCHLESWIG-HOLSTEIN AREA

This is the mildest area of the country in winter and most open to the changeable, stormier conditions from the Atlantic. There is a tendency for autumn to be the wettest season. The Baltic coasts of Schleswig-Holstein are colder in winter than the North Sea coast. Rainfall is generally rather low. Average daily sunshine ranges from about two hours in winter to six or seven in midsummer. See the table for **Hamburg**.

INLAND DISTRICTS OF NORTH GERMANY

The weather in general is a little colder in winter and warmer in summer than near the coast. Summer temperatures increase slightly from west to east, but the winters tend to become colder eastwards. During severe spells of winter weather canals and even navigable rivers may freeze up. See the table for **Hanover**.

Hamburg 72 ft (22 m) 53°38′ N 10°00′ E 30 years **WEST GERMANY**

| | Temperature °F | | | Temperature °C | | | Relative humidity | | Precipitation | | | |
| | Highest recorded | Average daily | Lowest recorded | Highest recorded | Average daily | Lowest recorded | 0630 hours | 1330 hours | Average monthly | | Average no. days with 0.004 in + (0.1 mm +) | |
		max.	min.			max.	min.		%	%	in	mm		
J	57	36	28	−9	14	2	−2	−23	89	84	2.3	58	18	J
F	65	37	28	−20	19	3	−2	−29	89	80	1.9	48	16	F
M	70	44	31	6	21	7	−1	−14	88	68	1.5	39	13	M
A	81	55	38	19	27	13	3	−7	85	61	2.1	52	14	A
M	90	64	45	23	32	18	7	−5	81	57	2.2	56	14	M
J	94	69	51	34	35	21	11	1	81	59	2.5	63	14	J
J	95	73	55	38	35	22	13	3	85	63	3.3	83	17	J
A	96	72	54	37	36	22	12	3	89	63	3.2	81	16	A
S	90	66	49	30	32	19	10	−1	91	65	2.4	62	15	S
O	77	55	43	21	25	13	6	−6	92	74	2.3	59	17	O
N	63	45	37	18	17	7	3	−8	92	83	2.2	57	18	N
D	62	39	31	2	17	4	0	−16	91	86	2.2	57	18	D

Hanover 171 ft (52 m) 52°20′ N 9°43′ E 30 years **WEST GERMANY**

| | Temperature °F | | | Temperature °C | | | Relative humidity | | Precipitation | | | |
| | Highest recorded | Average daily | Lowest recorded | Highest recorded | Average daily | Lowest recorded | 0630 hours | 1330 hours | Average monthly | | Average no. days with 0.004 in + (0.1 mm +) | |
		max.	min.			max.	min.		%	%	in	mm		
J	57	37	28	−19	14	3	−3	−29	88	81	1.8	46	18	J
F	61	38	28	−12	16	4	−2	−24	89	77	1.7	44	17	F
M	72	46	32	2	22	8	0	−17	89	67	1.4	36	13	M
A	81	56	38	21	27	13	3	−6	86	59	1.9	47	15	A
M	91	64	45	27	33	18	7	−3	82	55	2.0	51	14	M
J	93	70	51	35	34	21	10	2	81	57	2.5	63	14	J
J	95	73	55	42	35	23	13	5	85	61	3.1	79	16	J
A	100	73	54	39	38	23	12	4	88	59	2.7	69	15	A
S	91	67	49	30	33	19	9	−1	91	64	2.1	52	14	S
O	79	56	42	18	26	13	6	−8	92	73	2.2	56	15	O
N	65	46	36	12	18	8	2	−11	91	81	2.1	54	17	N
D	59	39	31	−6	15	4	−1	−21	90	84	1.8	46	17	D

THE HILLS OF CENTRAL AND SOUTHERN GERMANY

Here there are many local variations of climate because of the differences of altitude. In the valleys the temperatures may be similar to those in the middle Rhine area (see the table for **Frankfurt am Main**) but at higher levels the table for **Munich** is more appropriate. The higher mountain regions such as the Harz, the Eifel and the Black Forest rise to over 3000 ft (900 m) and have frequent and often prolonged snow in winter. Summers are changeable with heavy thunderstorms. The summers are rather sunnier than those farther north and the number of wet days is not so great. See the tables for **Kassel** and **Munich**.

Kassel 650 ft (198 m) 51°20′ N 9°31′ E 28 years WEST GERMANY

	Temperature °F				Temperature °C				Relative humidity		Precipitation			
	Highest recorded	Average daily		Lowest recorded	Highest recorded	Average daily		Lowest recorded	0630 hours	1320 hours	Average monthly		Average no. days with 0.004 in + (0.1 mm +)	
		max.	min.			max.	min.		%	%	in	mm		
J	55	36	27	−15	13	2	−3	−26	87	81	1.9	48	17	J
F	61	38	27	−9	16	3	−3	−23	87	75	1.6	40	15	F
M	70	47	32	6	21	8	0	−15	87	64	1.3	34	13	M
A	82	55	39	23	28	13	4	−5	83	58	1.9	47	15	A
M	90	64	45	27	32	18	7	−3	82	55	2.3	59	13	M
J	91	70	51	27	33	21	11	−3	82	56	2.4	62	14	J
J	95	73	55	42	35	23	13	6	85	58	2.9	73	16	J
A	96	72	54	41	36	22	12	5	88	57	2.5	63	14	A
S	91	66	49	31	33	19	9	−1	91	62	2.1	52	13	S
O	74	55	42	24	24	13	5	−5	92	70	2.1	53	15	O
N	65	45	36	18	18	7	2	−8	89	79	2.0	51	16	N
D	60	38	30	−1	16	3	−1	−18	89	84	1.9	49	16	D

Munich 1719 ft (524 m) 48°08′ N 11°42′ E 29 years WEST GERMANY

	Temperature °F				Temperature °C				Relative humidity		Precipitation			
	Highest recorded	Average daily		Lowest recorded	Highest recorded	Average daily		Lowest recorded	0700 hours	1400 hours	Average monthly		Average no. days with 0.004 in + (0.1 mm +)	
		max.	min.			max.	min.		%	%	in	mm		
J	62	35	23	−20	16	1	−5	−29	87	77	2.3	59	16	J
F	68	38	23	−21	20	3	−5	−30	87	71	2.1	53	16	F
M	74	48	30	0	24	9	−1	−18	86	61	1.9	48	13	M
A	84	56	38	3	29	14	3	−16	82	55	2.4	62	15	A
M	87	64	45	22	31	18	7	−6	81	57	4.3	109	15	M
J	94	70	51	37	35	21	11	3	80	58	4.9	125	17	J
J	95	74	55	40	35	23	13	5	81	57	5.5	139	16	J
A	96	73	54	38	36	23	12	3	85	58	4.2	107	16	A
S	90	67	48	28	32	20	9	−3	89	61	3.4	85	13	S
O	82	56	40	21	28	13	4	−6	91	68	2.6	66	13	O
N	67	44	33	10	20	7	0	−12	92	78	2.2	57	15	N
D	60	36	26	−8	16	2	−4	−22	90	82	1.9	47	15	D

SOUTHWEST GERMANY

This is a small area from the Rhine gorge near Frankfurt to the Swiss border at Basel. Because it is low-lying and farther south it has the warmest springs and summers in Germany (see the table for **Frankfurt am Main** and **Freiburg im Breisgau**). It is a sunny area with as much as eight hours of sunshine a day. Winters are, however, quite cold because of proximity to the Alps and distance from oceanic influences.

THE BAVARIAN ALPS

This small, mountainous region extends along the Austrian border and contains the highest mountains in Germany. It is a popular area for winter sports and has some lake and summer resorts. It shares a typical Alpine type of climate with the Austrian Tyrol (see p. 336). Summers may be rather wet, but at lower levels there is much sunny weather. Winters are cold and snowy.

Frankfurt am Main 338 ft (103 m) 50°07′ N 8°39′ E 29 years   **WEST GERMANY**

	Temperature °F			Temperature °C			Relative humidity		Precipitation			
	Highest recorded	Average daily	Lowest recorded	Highest recorded	Average daily	Lowest recorded	0630 hours	1330 hours	Average monthly		Average no. days with 0.004 in + (0.1 mm +)	
		max.	min.			max.	min.		%	%	in	mm	
J	57	38	29	−11	14	3	−2	−24	86	77	2.3	58	17	J
F	65	41	30	−3	18	5	−1	−19	86	70	1.7	44	15	F
M	75	51	35	17	24	11	2	−8	84	57	1.5	38	12	M
A	87	60	42	26	31	16	6	−4	79	51	1.7	44	14	A
M	94	69	49	29	34	20	9	−2	78	50	2.2	55	14	M
J	101	74	55	39	38	23	13	4	78	52	2.9	73	14	J
J	101	77	58	46	38	25	15	8	81	53	2.8	70	14	J
A	100	76	57	44	38	24	14	7	85	54	3.0	76	14	A
S	94	69	52	33	34	21	11	1	89	60	2.2	57	13	S
O	78	58	44	25	26	14	7	−4	91	68	2.1	52	14	O
N	65	47	38	19	19	8	3	−7	89	77	2.2	55	16	N
D	56	39	32	0	14	4	0	−18	88	81	2.1	54	16	D

Freiburg im Breisgau 850 ft (259 m) 48°01′ N 7°50′ E 27 years   **WEST GERMANY**

	Temperature °F			Temperature °C			Relative humidity		Precipitation			
	Highest recorded	Average daily	Lowest recorded	Highest recorded	Average daily	Lowest recorded	0630 hours	1330 hours	Average monthly		Average no. days with 0.004 in + (0.1 mm +)	
		max.	min.			max.	min.		%	%	in	mm	
J	64	39	29	−9	18	4	−2	−23	85	78	2.4	61	17	J
F	70	41	28	−8	21	5	−2	−22	85	72	2.1	53	14	F
M	74	51	34	9	24	11	1	−13	83	60	2.1	52	13	M
A	85	59	41	21	29	15	5	−6	80	56	2.7	68	15	A
M	89	67	48	28	32	20	9	−2	81	57	3.1	79	14	M
J	97	72	53	38	36	22	12	3	81	60	4.6	117	15	J
J	101	76	57	40	39	24	14	5	80	58	4.2	106	15	J
A	99	75	56	38	37	24	13	3	84	59	3.9	100	14	A
S	93	69	51	32	34	21	11	0	88	63	3.9	98	14	S
O	81	58	43	23	27	14	6	−5	90	70	2.6	67	14	O
N	69	47	36	17	21	8	2	−9	88	76	2.7	69	15	N
D	61	40	31	−5	16	5	−1	−21	86	79	2.1	52	17	D

GIBRALTAR

Gibraltar is only 4 square miles (10 sq. km) and is a British Crown Colony situated at the extreme south of Spain commanding the narrow strait at the entrance to the Mediterranean. It consists of a rocky peninsula rising to over 1000 ft (300 m).

Gibraltar has a characteristic Mediterranean climate with a very dry summer. The winters are considerably wetter than much of southern Spain due to exposure to Atlantic storms. Winters are rather warmer and the summers not quite so hot as the adjoining regions of Spain. Because of the peculiar shape of the rocky mountain which obstructs the flow of easterly and westerly winds in the strait, the winds around Gibraltar are often particularly gusty. Both the airfield and the port can be affected by these turbulent winds on occasions.

GIBRALTAR — North Front 7 ft (2 m) 36°09′ N 5°21′ W 15 years

	Temperature °F				Temperature °C				Relative humidity		Precipitation			
	Highest recorded	Average daily		Lowest recorded	Highest recorded	Average daily		Lowest recorded	0830 hours	1430 hours	Average monthly		Average no. days with 0.04 in + (1 mm +)	
		max.	min.			max.	min.		%	%	in	mm		
J	74	60	50	37	23	16	10	3	81	70	6.0	152	10	J
F	75	62	51	33	24	17	11	1	79	67	3.9	98	7	F
M	81	65	54	38	27	18	12	3	78	66	4.2	106	10	M
A	82	68	56	45	28	20	13	7	74	64	2.3	59	6	A
M	87	73	60	47	31	23	15	8	72	62	1.0	25	4	M
J	91	78	64	57	33	25	18	14	73	62	0.2	4	1	J
J	101	83	68	58	38	28	20	14	72	60	0	1	0	J
A	99	83	69	57	37	29	21	14	73	60	0.1	3	1	A
S	92	79	67	57	33	26	19	14	76	65	0.9	23	2	S
O	92	73	62	50	33	23	17	10	78	69	2.2	55	5	O
N	84	66	57	46	29	19	14	8	81	72	4.5	114	7	N
D	75	62	53	36	24	17	11	2	80	70	5.0	127	10	D

The United Kingdom of Great Britain consists of England, Scotland, Wales and Northern Ireland. Situated off the northwest coast of Europe, these islands extend between 50° and 60° N. The climate of Britain is notoriously variable and changeable from day to day. Weather is generally cool to mild with frequent cloud and rain but occasional settled spells of weather occur at all seasons.

Visitors to Britain are often surprised by the long summer days which are a consequence of the northerly latitude; in the north of Scotland in midsummer the day is eighteen hours long and twilight lasts all night. Conversely, the winter days are short. The frequent changes of weather affect all parts of the country in very much the same way; there are no great differences from one part of the country to another.

While the south is usually a little warmer than the north and the west wetter than the east, the continual changes of British weather mean that, on occasions, these differences may be reversed. Extremes of weather are rare in Britain but they do occur. For example, in December 1981 and January 1982, parts of southern and central England experienced for a few days lower temperatures than central Europe or Moscow! During the long spells of hot sunny weather in the summers of 1975 and 1976 parts of Britain were drier and warmer than many places in the western Mediterranean.

The greatest extremes of weather and climate in Britain occur in the mountains of Scotland, Wales and northern England. Here at altitudes exceeding 2000 ft (600 m) conditions are wet and cloudy for much of the year with annual rainfall exceeding 60 in (1500 mm) and in places reaching as much as 200 in (5000 mm). These are among the wettest places in Europe. Winter conditions may be severe with very strong winds, driving rain or snow blizzards.

In spite of occasional heavy snowfalls on the Scottish mountains, conditions are not really good for skiing and there has been only a limited development of winter sports resorts. Because of the severe conditions which can arise very suddenly on mountains, walkers and climbers who go unprepared face the risk of exposure or even frostbite. Conditions may be vastly different from that suggested by the weather at lower levels.

Virtually all permanent settlement in Britain lies below 1000 ft (300 m) and at these levels weather conditions are usually much more congenial. As a general rule the western side of Britain is cloudier, wetter and milder in winter with cooler summers than in the east (see tables for **Oban**, **Belfast**, **Cardiff** and **Aberystwyth**). The eastern side of Britain is drier the year round with a tendency for summer rain to be heavier than that of winter. The east is a little colder in winter and warmer in summer (see the tables for **London**, **York** and **Edinburgh**). Much of central England (see the table for **Birmingham**) has very similar weather to that of the east and south of the country. The table for **Plymouth** shows that the southwest of England shares the greater summer warmth of southern England but experiences rather milder and wetter winters than the east of the country.

The average number of hours of sunshine is greatest in the south and southeast of England and least in the north and west. The west of Scotland and Wales and Northern Ireland have rather less sunshine than most of England. In Britain daily sunshine hours range from between one and two in midwinter to between five and seven in midsummer. Winter sunshine is much reduced in Britain because of frequent fogs and low cloud. This is a consequence of winds from the Atlantic and seas surrounding Britain which bring high humidity. For the same reason British mountains are particularly cloudy and wet.

The chief differences of weather and climate in Britain can be summed up by saying that Scotland is rarely much colder than England despite its more northerly latitude. Summers in Scotland, however, are usually shorter and rather cooler. Wales, western Scotland and Northern Ireland are wetter the year round than most of England. The northwest of England and the Lake District are, however, particularly wet and cloudy.

Snow may occur anywhere in Britain in winter or even spring but, except on the hills, it rarely lies for more than a few days. In some winters there may be very little snow, but every fifteen or twenty years it may lie for some weeks during a prolonged cold spell.

Visitors to Britain will rarely experience severe or unpleasant weather for long unless they venture on the hills. They should be prepared for rapid changes of weather at all seasons, however, and recognize that there is good reason for weather being a major talking point in Britain. Visitors to Northern Ireland should consult the description of weather for Ireland (Eire) (p. 385) which applies to the whole of the island.

Aberystwyth (Wales) 453 ft (138 m) 52°25′ N 4°03′ W 30 years

	Temperature °F			Temperature °C				Relative humidity	Precipitation		
	Highest recorded	Average daily		Lowest recorded	Highest recorded	Average daily		Lowest recorded		Average monthly		Average no. days with 0.01 in + (0.25 mm +)
		max.	min.			max.	min.			in	mm	
J	57	44	36	12	14	7	2	−11	—	3.8	97	21	J
F	59	44	35	16	15	7	2	−9	—	2.8	72	17	F
M	68	49	38	20	20	9	3	−7	—	2.4	60	16	M
A	73	52	41	27	23	11	5	−3	—	2.2	56	16	A
M	78	58	45	30	26	15	7	−1	—	2.6	65	16	M
J	87	62	50	39	31	17	10	4	—	3.0	76	16	J
J	88	64	54	43	31	18	12	6	—	3.9	99	19	J
A	85	65	54	41	29	18	12	5	—	3.7	93	18	A
S	78	62	51	36	26	16	11	2	—	4.3	108	19	S
O	77	56	46	28	25	13	8	−2	—	4.7	118	20	O
N	63	50	41	27	17	10	5	−3	—	4.4	111	20	N
D	59	47	38	22	15	8	4	−6	—	3.8	96	22	D

Belfast (Northern Ireland) 217 ft (67 m) 54°39′ N 6°13′ W 30 years

	Temperature °F			Temperature °C				Relative humidity		Precipitation		
	Highest recorded	Average daily		Lowest recorded	Highest recorded	Average daily		Lowest recorded	0830 hours	1430 hours	Average monthly		Average no. days with 0.01 in + (0.25 mm +)
		max.	min.			max.	min.		%	%	in	mm	
J	56	43	35	9	13	6	2	−13	92	87	3.2	80	20	J
F	57	44	35	11	14	7	2	−12	91	80	2.1	52	17	F
M	67	49	37	10	19	9	3	−12	88	74	2.0	50	16	M
A	69	53	39	24	21	12	4	−4	83	69	1.9	48	16	A
M	79	59	43	26	26	15	6	−3	79	66	2.1	52	15	M
J	83	64	49	31	28	18	9	−1	80	71	2.7	68	16	J
J	85	65	52	39	29	18	11	4	84	73	3.7	94	19	J
A	82	65	51	34	28	18	11	1	87	75	3.0	77	17	A
S	78	61	49	28	26	16	9	−2	89	78	3.2	80	18	S
O	70	55	44	24	21	13	7	−4	91	80	3.3	83	19	O
N	61	48	39	21	16	9	4	−6	92	85	2.8	72	19	N
D	58	44	37	13	14	7	3	−11	92	89	3.5	90	21	D

Birmingham (England) 535 ft (163 m) 52°29′ N 1°56′ W 30 years — GREAT BRITAIN

	Temperature °F			Temperature °C				Relative humidity		Precipitation			
	Highest recorded	Average daily	Lowest recorded	Highest recorded	Average daily		Lowest recorded	0900 hours	1500 hours	Average monthly		Average no. days with 0.01 in + (0.25 mm +)	
		max.	min.			max.	min.		%	%	in	mm		
J	56	42	35	11	13	5	2	−12	89	82	3.0	74	17	J
F	60	43	35	16	16	6	2	−9	89	76	2.1	54	15	F
M	69	48	37	19	21	9	3	−7	85	68	2.0	50	13	M
A	75	54	40	29	24	12	5	−2	75	58	2.1	53	13	A
M	85	60	45	30	29	16	7	−1	74	58	2.5	64	14	M
J	87	66	51	37	31	19	10	3	74	59	2.0	50	13	J
J	90	68	54	43	32	20	12	6	75	62	2.7	69	15	J
A	91	68	54	43	33	20	12	6	80	64	2.7	69	14	A
S	81	63	51	37	27	17	10	3	84	67	2.4	61	14	S
O	77	55	45	28	25	13	7	−2	88	73	2.7	69	15	O
N	67	48	40	24	19	9	5	−4	90	80	3.3	84	17	N
D	58	44	37	21	14	6	3	−6	90	84	2.6	67	18	D

Cardiff (Wales) 203 ft (62 m) 51°30′ N 3°10′ W 30 years — GREAT BRITAIN

	Temperature °F			Temperature °C				Relative humidity	Precipitation			
	Highest recorded	Average daily	Lowest recorded	Highest recorded	Average daily		Lowest recorded	0900 hours	Average monthly		Average no. days with 0.01 in + (0.25 mm +)	
		max.	min.			max.	min.		%	in	mm		
J	59	45	35	2	15	7	2	−17	89	4.3	108	18	J
F	61	45	35	15	16	7	2	−9	87	2.8	72	14	F
M	68	50	38	18	20	10	3	−8	82	2.5	63	13	M
A	75	56	41	27	24	13	5	−3	74	2.6	65	13	A
M	84	61	46	31	29	16	8	−1	74	3.0	76	13	M
J	87	68	51	39	31	19	11	4	73	2.5	63	13	J
J	88	69	54	44	31	20	12	7	76	3.5	89	14	J
A	91	69	55	43	33	21	13	6	78	3.8	97	15	A
S	83	64	51	35	28	18	11	2	81	3.9	99	16	S
O	77	58	46	26	25	14	8	−3	85	4.3	109	16	O
N	65	51	41	26	18	10	5	−3	88	4.7	116	17	N
D	59	46	37	19	15	8	3	−7	89	4.3	108	18	D

Edinburgh (Scotland) 440 ft (134 m) 55°55′ N 3°11′ W 30 years

	Temperature °F				Temperature °C			Relative humidity	Precipitation		
	Highest recorded	Average daily		Lowest recorded	Highest recorded	Average daily		Lowest recorded	0900 hours	Average monthly		Average no. days with 0.01 in + (0.25 mm +)
		max.	min.			max.	min.		%	in	mm	
J	57	42	34	17	14	6	1	−8	84	2.2	57	17	J
F	58	43	34	15	14	6	1	−9	83	1.5	39	15	F
M	68	46	36	21	20	8	2	−6	81	1.5	39	15	M
A	72	51	39	25	22	11	4	−4	75	1.5	39	14	A
M	76	56	43	31	24	14	6	−1	76	2.1	54	14	M
J	83	62	49	37	28	17	9	3	75	1.9	47	15	J
J	83	65	52	42	28	18	11	6	78	3.3	83	17	J
A	82	64	52	40	28	18	11	4	80	3.0	77	16	A
S	77	60	49	33	25	16	9	1	80	2.2	57	16	S
O	68	54	44	28	20	12	7	−2	82	2.6	65	17	O
N	67	48	39	24	19	9	4	−4	83	2.4	62	17	N
D	58	44	36	20	14	7	2	−7	84	2.2	57	18	D

GREAT BRITAIN London (England) 16 ft (5 m) 51°28′ N 0°19′ W 30 years

	Temperature °F				Temperature °C			Relative humidity		Precipitation		
	Highest recorded	Average daily		Lowest recorded	Highest recorded	Average daily		Lowest recorded	0900 hours	1500 hours	Average monthly		Average no. days with 0.01 in + (0.25 mm +)
		max.	min.			max.	min.		%	%	in	mm	
J	58	43	36	15	14	6	2	−10	86	77	2.1	54	15	J
F	61	44	36	15	16	7	2	−9	85	72	1.6	40	13	F
M	71	50	38	18	21	10	3	−8	81	64	1.5	37	11	M
A	78	56	42	28	26	13	6	−2	71	56	1.5	37	12	A
M	86	62	47	30	30	17	8	−1	70	57	1.8	46	12	M
J	91	69	53	41	33	20	12	5	70	58	1.8	45	11	J
J	93	71	56	45	34	22	14	7	71	59	2.2	57	12	J
A	92	71	56	43	33	21	13	6	76	62	2.3	59	11	A
S	86	65	52	37	30	19	11	3	80	65	1.9	49	13	S
O	78	58	46	26	26	14	8	−4	85	70	2.2	57	13	O
N	66	50	42	23	19	10	5	−5	85	78	2.5	64	15	N
D	59	45	38	19	15	7	4	−7	87	81	1.9	48	15	D

Oban (Scotland) 226 ft (69 m) 56°25′ N 5°30′ W 30 years — **GREAT BRITAIN**

| | Temperature °F | | | Temperature °C | | | | Relative humidity | Precipitation | | |
| | Highest recorded | Average daily | Lowest recorded | Highest recorded | Average daily | Lowest recorded | | | Average monthly | Average no. days with 0.01 in + (0.25 mm +) | |
		max.	min.			max.	min.	%	in	mm	
J	56	43	35	17	13	6	2	−8	—	5.8	146	20	J
F	55	44	35	20	13	7	1	−7	—	4.3	109	17	F
M	67	48	37	22	19	9	3	−6	—	3.3	83	15	M
A	69	52	40	29	21	11	4	−2	—	3.5	90	17	A
M	78	58	44	25	26	14	7	−4	—	2.8	72	16	M
J	84	61	49	37	29	16	9	3	—	3.4	87	16	J
J	85	63	51	41	29	17	11	5	—	4.7	120	20	J
A	81	63	51	38	27	17	11	3	—	4.6	116	19	A
S	75	60	49	33	24	15	9	1	—	5.6	141	19	S
O	72	54	44	23	22	12	7	−5	—	6.7	169	21	O
N	60	49	40	23	16	9	4	−5	—	5.8	146	20	N
D	58	45	37	21	14	7	3	−6	—	6.8	172	22	D

Plymouth (England) 89 ft (27 m) 50°21′ N 4°07′ W 30 years — **GREAT BRITAIN**

| | Temperature °F | | | Temperature °C | | | | Relative humidity | | Precipitation | | |
| | Highest recorded | Average daily | Lowest recorded | Highest recorded | Average daily | Lowest recorded | | 0830 hours | 1430 hours | Average monthly | Average no. days with 0.01 in + (0.25 mm +) | |
		max.	min.			max.	min.	%	%	in	mm	
J	57	47	39	16	14	8	4	−9	89	81	3.9	99	19	J
F	59	47	38	17	15	8	4	−8	88	78	2.9	74	15	F
M	67	50	40	23	19	10	5	−5	86	74	2.7	69	14	M
A	72	54	43	29	22	12	6	−2	78	69	2.1	53	12	A
M	79	59	47	31	26	15	8	−1	77	71	2.5	63	12	M
J	82	64	52	35	28	18	11	2	80	73	2.1	53	12	J
J	84	66	55	45	29	19	13	7	81	74	2.8	70	14	J
A	88	67	55	39	31	19	13	4	83	75	3.0	77	14	A
S	81	64	53	37	27	18	12	3	86	75	3.1	78	15	S
O	74	58	49	29	23	15	9	−2	88	77	3.6	91	16	O
N	63	52	44	25	17	11	7	−4	88	79	4.5	113	17	N
D	58	49	41	23	14	9	5	−5	89	82	4.3	110	18	D

377

	Temperature °F			Temperature °C			Relative humidity	Precipitation		
	Highest recorded	Average daily	Lowest recorded	Highest recorded	Average daily	Lowest recorded	0900 hours	Average monthly		Average no. days with 0.01 in + (0.25 mm +)
		max.	min.			max.	min.		%	in	mm	
J	59	43	33	7	15	6	1	−14	89	2.3	59	17	J
F	62	44	34	14	17	7	1	−10	87	1.8	46	15	F
M	70	49	36	9	21	10	2	−13	81	1.5	37	13	M
A	75	55	40	27	24	13	4	−3	73	1.6	41	13	A
M	85	61	44	30	29	16	7	−1	71	2.0	50	13	M
J	90	67	50	36	32	19	10	2	71	2.0	50	14	J
J	88	70	54	41	31	21	12	5	74	2.4	62	15	J
A	92	69	53	39	33	21	12	4	77	2.7	68	14	A
S	84	64	50	31	29	18	10	−1	80	2.2	55	14	S
O	78	57	44	24	26	14	7	−4	85	2.2	56	15	O
N	66	49	39	20	19	10	4	−7	88	2.6	65	17	N
D	60	45	36	18	16	7	2	−8	88	2.0	50	17	D

Greece is situated in the extreme southeast of Europe. It is a mountainous country with a very indented coastline and it includes numerous islands in the Aegean Sea, the Ionian Islands in the west, of which Corfu is the best known, and the large island of Crete which lies in the middle of the eastern Mediterranean.

As a result of this intermingling of mountain, island and sea there are many local differences in the weather and climate within the country but the general features of weather around the year are much the same.

In the north the climate bears some resemblance to that found in Bulgaria and southern Yugoslavia; elsewhere the influence of the Mediterranean is dominant. Summers are warm or even hot with almost no cloud or rain for three months. The wettest season is winter when the weather is generally mild at sea level although occasional spells of cold weather occur. Snow may fall almost anywhere in Greece in winter but it is rare in the islands and does not lie for long at sea level. Spring and autumn are short seasons of transition from winter rain to summer heat and sun, when the weather may be very changeable from day to day. For those who dislike heat April and May or September or October may be the most enjoyable seasons in Greece.

An outstanding feature of the Greek climate is the large amount of sunshine. This varies from four to five hours a day in midwinter to as much as twelve to fourteen hours a day in midsummer. These amounts may be rather reduced in the mountains and in the extreme north. Rain tends to be heavy when it occurs and rarely lasts for very long except in the mountains or along the wetter west coast.

Around the coasts and on the islands the summer heat is greatly tempered by strong to fresh daytime breezes. On a few occasions, however, when the air is calm the daytime heat can be oppressive inland or in a large town such as **Athens**. During the three summer months a persistent northerly wind, known as the etesian, blows in the Aegean and it may on occasions reach near gale force. It is strongest by day and drops to a near calm at night.

In the mountain regions of Greece, where many areas rise above 6500 ft (2000 m), the weather in winter and even into spring can be severe with frequent and heavy falls of snow and prolonged frost. Here summers are very pleasant since the days are sunny and often warm. The table for **Trikkala** illustrates conditions inland at moderate elevation and within the mountains.

Eastern Greece is the driest part of the country and the table for **Athens** is representative of much of eastern Greece at low levels. The table for **Salonika** shows that in northern Greece the winters are a little colder and the summers are not quite so rainless; summer thunderstorms occur here. Conditions in the Aegean Islands and Crete are illustrated by the table for **Náxos**; here the winters are the mildest in the country and the summer heat is tempered by sea breezes and the persistent etesian wind.

Visitors to Greece may find the sea rather too chilly for bathing in April or even early May despite the high air temperature on sunny days. On the other hand in October or even November the sea still retains much of its summer warmth.

Athens 351 ft (107 m) 37°58′ N 24°43′ E 30 years

	Temperature °F				Temperature °C				Relative humidity		Precipitation			
	Highest recorded	Average daily		Lowest recorded	Highest recorded	Average daily		Lowest recorded	0730 hours	1330 hours	Average monthly		Average no. days with 0.004 in + (0.1 mm +)	
		max.	min.			max.	min.		%	%	in	mm		
J	70	55	44	24	21	13	6	−4	77	62	2.4	62	16	J
F	73	57	44	22	23	14	7	−6	74	57	1.5	37	11	F
M	82	60	46	31	28	16	8	−1	71	54	1.5	37	11	M
A	90	68	52	32	32	20	11	0	65	48	1.0	23	9	A
M	97	77	61	43	36	25	16	6	60	47	1.0	23	8	M
J	107	86	68	57	42	30	20	14	50	39	0.6	14	4	J
J	108	92	73	61	42	33	23	16	47	34	0.2	6	2	J
A	109	92	73	60	43	33	23	16	48	34	0.3	7	3	A
S	101	84	67	53	38	29	19	12	58	42	0.6	15	4	S
O	98	75	60	45	37	24	15	7	70	52	2.0	51	8	O
N	82	66	53	30	28	19	12	−1	78	61	2.2	56	12	N
D	72	58	47	25	22	15	8	−4	78	63	2.8	71	15	D

GREECE

Náxos 10 ft (3 m) 37°06′ N 25°24′ E 10 years

	Temperature °F				Temperature °C				Relative humidity		Precipitation			
	Highest recorded	Average daily		Lowest recorded	Highest recorded	Average daily		Lowest recorded	0730 hours	1330 hours	Average monthly		Average no. days with 0.004 in + (0.1 mm +)	
		max.	min.			max.	min.		%	%	in	mm		
J	70	58	50	37	21	15	10	3	75	69	3.6	91	12	J
F	76	59	49	32	25	15	10	0	75	68	2.9	73	9	F
M	81	61	51	38	27	16	11	3	75	67	2.7	69	8	M
A	86	67	56	46	30	20	13	8	74	65	0.8	19	4	A
M	91	73	61	52	33	23	16	11	73	65	0.5	12	3	M
J	94	78	68	59	35	26	20	15	72	65	0.4	11	1	J
J	100	81	72	63	38	27	22	17	72	66	0.1	2	0	J
A	94	82	72	62	35	28	22	17	74	67	0	1	0	A
S	94	78	69	54	34	26	20	12	74	66	0.4	11	1	S
O	90	75	64	52	32	24	18	11	76	67	1.8	45	4	O
N	82	68	58	47	28	20	15	8	75	67	1.9	48	6	N
D	72	62	53	34	22	17	12	1	75	69	3.7	93	12	D

Salonika 82 ft (25 m) 40°37′ N 22°57′ E 27 years **GREECE**

	Temperature °F			Temperature °C			Relative humidity		Precipitation			
	Highest recorded	Average daily	Lowest recorded	Highest recorded	Average daily	Lowest recorded	0730 hours	1330 hours	Average monthly		Average no. days with 0.004 in + (0.1 mm +)	
		max.	min.			max.	min.		%	%	in	mm	
J	67	49	35	13	20	9	2	−10	85	71	1.7	44	11	J
F	76	53	37	16	24	12	3	−9	80	61	1.3	34	8	F
M	86	58	41	24	30	14	5	−5	79	61	1.5	38	9	M
A	86	67	49	30	30	20	10	−1	75	58	1.6	41	9	A
M	100	77	58	41	38	25	14	5	73	57	1.6	40	10	M
J	100	85	65	49	38	29	18	10	66	50	1.6	40	7	J
J	107	90	70	58	42	32	21	14	63	48	0.9	22	4	J
A	104	90	69	51	40	32	21	10	65	48	0.6	14	3	A
S	99	82	63	47	37	28	17	8	73	54	1.1	29	5	S
O	91	71	55	39	33	22	13	4	81	62	2.2	57	8	O
N	76	61	47	27	24	16	9	−3	85	70	2.2	55	11	N
D	70	53	39	19	21	11	4	−7	86	73	2.2	56	11	D

Trikkala 489 ft (149 m) 39°33′ N 21°46′ E 6 years **GREECE**

	Temperature °F			Temperature °C			Relative humidity		Precipitation			
	Highest recorded	Average daily	Lowest recorded	Highest recorded	Average daily	Lowest recorded	0730 hours	1330 hours	Average monthly		Average no. days with 0.004 in + (0.1 mm +)	
		max.	min.			max.	min.		%	%	in	mm	
J	68	48	33	11	20	9	0	−12	84	72	3.3	84	13	J
F	71	55	35	18	22	13	2	−8	80	60	2.7	69	11	F
M	79	61	40	28	26	16	4	−2	76	54	2.3	59	10	M
A	88	70	47	30	31	21	8	−1	73	51	3.2	80	9	A
M	94	78	54	39	35	25	12	4	70	48	2.4	61	9	M
J	105	87	61	49	41	31	16	10	61	40	2.0	51	7	J
J	110	94	67	50	44	35	19	10	53	34	0.8	19	4	J
A	107	93	66	53	42	34	19	12	56	33	0.5	12	3	A
S	104	86	60	47	40	30	15	8	67	42	1.1	27	5	S
O	98	76	54	36	37	25	12	2	77	53	3.2	80	9	O
N	78	62	45	29	26	17	7	−2	84	66	0.4	90	11	N
D	69	51	38	18	21	11	4	−8	87	75	4.9	125	17	D

HUNGARY

Hungary is a completely landlocked country in central Europe. Surrounded by the Alps and Carpathian mountains, it is cut off from the moderating influence of the Atlantic Ocean. Most of the country is low-lying and rather flat, consisting of the broad valleys of the rivers Danube and Tisza. Only small areas in the north and west, such as the Bakony Forest, rise above 2000 ft (600 m). There are no great differences of weather and climate within the country. The tables for **Budapest** and **Debrecen** show very similar features throughout the year.

Its inland situation gives Hungary a rather extreme type of climate compared with western Europe; there is a considerable difference between summer and winter. Spells of weather tend to persist for longer than in more oceanic climates. Summers or winters, however, may differ considerably from one year to another. Summer drought or wetness may persist for a whole season, while some winters may be particularly cold and snowy.

Spring and early summer are generally the wettest time of year but much of the rain comes in heavy thundery downpours; in early summer almost one day in three may have a thunderstorm. Daily hours of sunshine in summer are between nine to ten. Much of the time the summer weather is pleasantly warm or even hot.

Winters are in general cold and snow lies on the ground for between thirty and forty days on average – longer in severe winters. Fog is frequent during settled weather in winter. The Danube is often completely frozen over during severe cold spells and floating ice is usually a hazard to navigation from January to March. The severest and most unpleasant winter weather comes when bitterly cold, easterly winds blow from Russia.

The transition from winter to summer and vice versa often comes rather quickly so that spring and autumn are not the well-defined seasons of western Europe. There may be abrupt and unpleasant changes of temperature from day to day at these times.

Budapest 456 ft (139 m) 47°26′ N 19°11′ E 26 years **HUNGARY**

	Temperature °F			Temperature °C			Relative humidity		Precipitation			
	Highest recorded	Average daily	Lowest recorded	Highest recorded	Average daily	Lowest recorded	0730 hours	1430 hours	Average monthly		Average no. days with 0.004 in + (0.1 mm +)	
		max.	min.			max.	min.		%	%	in	mm	
J	57	34	25	−9	14	1	−4	−23	85	76	1.5	37	13	J
F	63	39	28	−4	17	4	−2	−20	83	68	1.7	44	12	F
M	74	50	35	15	23	10	2	−9	79	55	1.5	38	11	M
A	85	62	44	26	29	17	7	−3	72	48	1.8	45	11	A
M	91	71	52	34	33	22	11	1	72	49	2.8	72	13	M
J	103	78	58	39	39	26	15	4	72	49	2.7	69	13	J
J	101	82	62	43	38	28	16	6	71	47	2.2	56	10	J
A	102	81	60	47	39	27	16	8	74	47	1.9	47	9	A
S	95	74	53	36	35	23	12	2	79	49	1.3	33	7	S
O	90	61	44	24	32	16	7	−5	86	60	2.2	57	10	O
N	70	47	38	17	21	8	3	−8	88	76	2.8	70	14	N
D	58	39	30	8	15	4	−1	−13	87	81	1.8	46	13	D

Debrecen 364 ft (111 m) 47°30′ N 21°38′ E 28 years **HUNGARY**

	Temperature °F			Temperature °C			Relative humidity		Precipitation			
	Highest recorded	Average daily	Lowest recorded	Highest recorded	Average daily	Lowest recorded	0730 hours	1430 hours	Average monthly		Average no. days with 0.004 in + (0.1 mm +)	
		max.	min.			max.	min.		%	%	in	mm	
J	58	33	21	−18	14	0	−6	−28	89	78	1.3	34	13	J
F	64	38	25	−14	18	3	−4	−26	88	71	1.4	35	11	F
M	78	50	32	0	25	10	0	−18	85	59	1.2	30	11	M
A	87	62	41	21	31	16	5	−6	80	51	1.5	37	11	A
M	91	71	50	28	33	22	10	−3	78	52	2.4	60	13	M
J	100	77	56	38	38	25	13	4	78	53	3.2	80	13	J
J	101	81	59	42	38	27	15	6	78	50	2.2	56	11	J
A	103	80	57	41	39	27	14	5	82	50	2.5	64	10	A
S	98	73	50	29	36	23	10	−2	87	50	1.6	40	8	S
O	88	61	41	16	31	16	5	−9	90	59	1.9	49	10	O
N	71	47	36	11	22	9	2	−12	91	75	2.1	53	12	N
D	63	38	28	−3	17	3	−2	−20	91	80	1.5	39	13	D

ICELAND

Iceland is an island in the stormiest region of the North Atlantic between Norway and Greenland. Two features control its weather and climate: it lies in the track most frequented by depressions throughout the year; it also lies in the path of the current of warm oceanic water called the Gulf Stream. Consequently, the weather is disturbed and changeable throughout the year but the temperatures at sea level are surprisingly mild during the winter for the latitude. The Arctic Circle just touches the north coast of the island.

Inland Iceland is mountainous, with several volcanic peaks rising above 5000 ft (1500 m). These higher areas are covered with snow throughout the year and there are extensive ice fields at higher levels. Although very cold air from the Arctic occasionally affects the island in winter and spring and drifting ice may block inlets on the north coast, the main port and capital, **Reykjavik**, is ice free throughout the year. The summers are generally cool and cloudy with brief spells of fine, pleasant weather. Much of the winter precipitation is snow and autumn and winter are the wettest seasons.

ICELAND   **Reykjavik** 59 ft (18 m) 64°08′ N 21°56′ W 30 years

		Temperature °F				Temperature °C			Relative humidity		Precipitation			
	Highest recorded	Average daily		Lowest recorded	Highest recorded	Average daily		Lowest recorded	0830 hours	1430 hours	Average monthly		Average no. days with 0.004 in + (0.1 mm +)	
		max.	min.			max.	min.		%	%	in	mm		
J	50	35	28	1	10	2	−2	−17	81	79	3.5	89	20	J
F	50	37	28	8	10	3	−2	−14	78	75	2.5	64	17	F
M	58	39	30	6	14	4	−1	−14	78	72	2.4	62	18	M
A	59	43	33	9	15	6	1	−13	80	73	2.2	56	18	A
M	69	50	39	19	21	10	4	−7	75	67	1.7	42	16	M
J	69	54	45	32	21	12	7	0	78	72	1.7	42	15	J
J	74	57	48	35	23	14	9	1	81	72	2.0	50	15	J
A	70	56	47	32	21	14	8	0	81	71	2.2	56	16	A
S	68	52	43	26	20	11	6	−4	82	73	2.6	67	19	S
O	60	45	38	14	16	7	3	−10	83	78	3.7	94	21	O
N	53	39	32	11	12	4	0	−12	80	80	3.1	78	18	N
D	53	36	29	2	11	2	−2	−17	81	80	3.1	79	20	D

The Republic of Ireland, often called Eire, is the largest portion of the island lying to the west of Britain. It shares with the rest of the British Isles a mild, changeable climate with very rare extremes of heat or cold. Ireland is even more influenced by the warm waters of the North Atlantic than England and, consequently, its climate is a little wetter the year round, milder in winter and cooler and cloudier in summer. This mild, rainy climate is particularly favourable to the growth of grass and moss and for this reason Ireland has been called the Emerald Isle.

The driest parts of the country are the east and south (see the tables for **Dublin** and **Cork**). The east and the interior (see the table for **Mullingar**) have slightly warmer summers and cooler winters. The west coast is more influenced by the Atlantic and is both wetter and cloudier with particularly mild winters (see the table for **Valentia**). Differences of weather and climate, however, are relatively small throughout the country. Snow is very rare along the west and south coasts but occurs on a few days a year in the east and on the mountains. Although there are numerous mountain ranges in Ireland, few of these exceed 2600 ft (800 m) and even at these heights snow does not lie for long.

In the wetter west of the country rain is frequent but on many days it is very light and in the form of drizzle. The sunniest parts of the country are the east and south coasts with sunshine hours averaging from two a day in winter to six in midsummer. Over most of Ireland spring is the driest time of the year and May is the sunniest month. Except in the extreme east around **Dublin** autumn and winter are the wettest seasons. Occasional severe weather in winter takes two forms: storms and gales which particularly affect the west; and rare spells with frost and snow when cold easterly or northerly winds bring severe weather to the whole British Isles.

For Northern Ireland, see the table for **Belfast**, p. 374.)

IRELAND Cork 49 ft (15 m) 51°54′ N 8°29′ W 30 years

| | Temperature °F | | | Temperature °C | | | | Relative humidity | Precipitation | | |
| | Highest recorded | Average daily | Lowest recorded | Highest recorded | Average daily | | Lowest recorded | 0930 hours | Average monthly | | Average no. days with 0.04 in + (1 mm +) |
		max.	min.			max.	min.		%	in	mm	
J	58	47	36	15	14	9	2	−9	89	4.7	119	15	J
F	59	48	37	20	15	9	3	−7	88	3.1	79	11	F
M	64	52	39	23	18	11	4	−5	87	3.7	94	12	M
A	72	56	42	28	22	13	5	−2	81	2.2	57	11	A
M	79	61	45	30	26	16	7	−1	78	2.8	71	11	M
J	84	66	51	37	29	19	10	3	79	2.2	57	10	J
J	82	68	54	41	28	20	12	5	80	2.8	70	11	J
A	85	68	53	37	29	20	12	3	83	2.8	71	11	A
S	79	64	50	34	26	18	10	1	86	3.7	94	12	S
O	70	58	45	23	21	14	7	−5	90	3.9	99	12	O
N	64	52	40	21	18	11	4	−6	90	4.6	116	14	N
D	60	49	38	19	16	9	3	−7	89	4.8	122	16	D

IRELAND Dublin 154 ft (47 m) 53°22′ N 6°21′ W 30 years

| | Temperature °F | | | Temperature °C | | | | Relative humidity | Precipitation | | |
| | Highest recorded | Average daily | Lowest recorded | Highest recorded | Average daily | | Lowest recorded | 0930 hours | Average monthly | | Average no. days with 0.04 in + (1 mm +) |
		max.	min.			max.	min.		%	in	mm	
J	58	46	34	10	14	8	1	−12	88	2.6	67	13	J
F	62	47	35	14	17	8	2	−10	86	2.2	55	10	F
M	69	51	37	15	21	10	3	−9	82	2.0	51	10	M
A	72	55	39	23	22	13	4	−5	76	1.8	45	11	A
M	77	60	43	22	25	15	6	−6	75	2.4	60	10	M
J	84	65	48	33	29	18	9	1	76	2.2	57	11	J
J	86	67	52	38	30	20	11	3	78	2.8	70	13	J
A	81	67	51	36	27	19	11	2	80	2.9	74	12	A
S	78	63	48	30	25	17	9	−1	83	2.8	72	12	S
O	76	57	43	24	24	14	6	−4	85	2.8	70	11	O
N	65	51	39	20	18	10	4	−7	88	2.6	67	12	N
D	63	47	37	15	17	8	3	−9	88	2.9	74	14	D

Mullingar 354 ft (108 m) 53°31′ N 7°21′ W 17 years   IRELAND

	Temperature °F			Temperature °C			Relative humidity		Precipitation			
	Highest recorded	Average daily	Lowest recorded	Highest recorded	Average daily	Lowest recorded	0930 hours	1430 hours	Average monthly		Average no. days with 0.04 in + (1 mm +)	
		max.	min.			max.	min.		%	%	in	mm	
J	56	44	34	16	13	7	1	−9	93	85	3.5	88	14	J
F	58	45	34	10	15	7	1	−12	92	79	2.5	63	12	F
M	69	50	37	15	21	10	3	−9	89	72	2.3	59	11	M
A	71	55	39	26	22	13	4	−3	82	68	2.2	55	12	A
M	78	60	43	30	26	16	6	−1	78	66	2.4	61	11	M
J	86	64	48	35	30	18	9	2	80	69	3.0	75	12	J
J	83	66	51	40	29	19	11	5	84	73	3.5	89	14	J
A	85	67	51	39	30	19	10	4	87	73	3.4	87	13	A
S	78	62	48	32	26	17	9	0	90	75	3.9	99	15	S
O	73	56	44	27	23	13	6	−3	92	78	3.7	94	13	O
N	63	49	39	24	17	10	4	−5	94	84	3.4	86	14	N
D	58	46	36	16	14	8	2	−9	94	88	4.4	111	18	D

Valentia 30 ft (9 m) 51°56′ N 10°15′ W 30 years   IRELAND

	Temperature °F			Temperature °C			Relative humidity		Precipitation			
	Highest recorded	Average daily	Lowest recorded	Highest recorded	Average daily	Lowest recorded	0930 hours	1430 hours	Average monthly		Average no. days with 0.04 in + (1 mm +)	
		max.	min.			max.	min.		%	%	in	mm	
J	57	49	40	19	14	9	5	−7	84	79	6.5	165	20	J
F	62	49	40	22	17	9	4	−5	83	76	4.2	107	15	F
M	68	52	42	26	20	11	5	−3	81	73	4.1	103	14	M
A	75	55	43	29	24	13	6	−2	77	71	3.0	75	13	A
M	79	59	47	32	26	15	8	0	76	72	3.4	86	13	M
J	81	62	51	36	27	17	11	2	80	77	3.2	81	13	J
J	85	64	54	43	30	18	12	6	83	79	4.2	107	15	J
A	86	65	55	40	30	18	13	4	84	78	3.7	95	15	A
S	80	62	52	35	27	17	11	2	84	78	4.8	122	16	S
O	74	58	48	28	24	14	9	−2	85	78	5.5	140	17	O
N	65	53	44	28	18	12	7	−2	84	79	5.9	151	18	N
D	60	50	42	23	16	10	6	−5	84	81	6.6	168	21	D

ITALY

Italy can be divided into three distinct geographical regions: the southern side of the Alps where Italy borders France, Switzerland, Austria and Yugoslavia; the great plain of the Po valley from Turin to **Venice**; and the long and mountainous peninsula of central and southern Italy together with the large islands of Sardinia and Sicily. Each of these regions has a distinctive and different type of weather and climate.

Occasionally all parts of Italy experience very high temperatures in summer and even autumn when the sirocco blows. This is a warm, humid wind, originating over North Africa, which acquires its humidity over the Mediterranean. A spell of sirocco weather in autumn often ends with very heavy rain accompanied by thunder. Sea temperatures around Italy are usually sufficiently warm to make bathing pleasant from mid-May until October, but the water can be surprisingly cold on warm sunny days in spring.

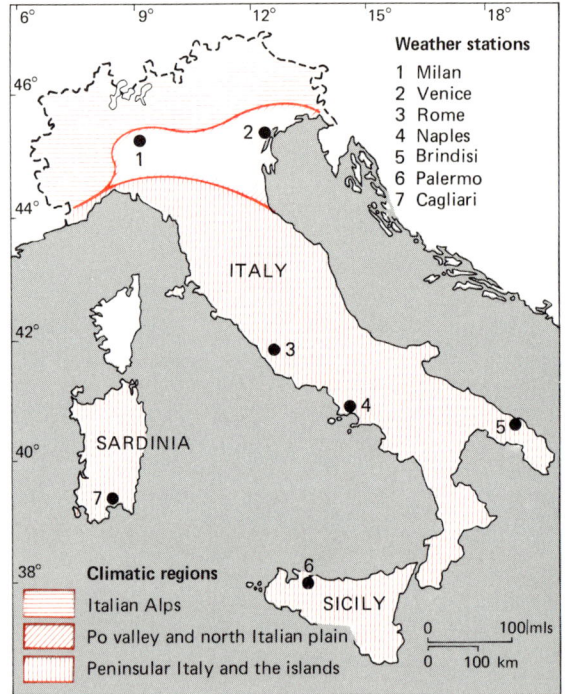

Weather stations
1 Milan
2 Venice
3 Rome
4 Naples
5 Brindisi
6 Palermo
7 Cagliari

Climatic regions
Italian Alps
Po valley and north Italian plain
Peninsular Italy and the islands

0   100 mls
0   100 km

ALPINE ITALY

In the Italian Alps, where the higher mountains rise above 10,000 ft (3000 m), the climate is similar to that of the Swiss and Austrian Alps (pp. 422 and 336). Precipitation on the Italian side, however, is rather heavier. The lower slopes and valleys of the Italian Alps are also a little warmer both in summer and winter. Summer tends to be the rainiest season and thunder storms are frequent in spring, summer and autumn. The mildest winters and warmest and sunniest summers are found in the region of lakes Maggiore, Como and Garda. Here sunshine averages from three to four hours a day in winter and up to nine hours in summer. A föhn wind sometimes blows from the north and raises temperatures and lowers humidity.

This is a remarkable flat and low-lying region of dense population and great agricultural productivity. It extends from Turin to **Venice** and almost as far as the port of Trieste. It has a distinctive climate with rain well distributed around the year. The summers are as hot and almost as sunny as those in southern Italy. Winters are surprisingly cold for about three months. Fog, frost and snow are quite frequent and this area is colder than **Paris** or **London** in midwinter.

Summer and autumn rainfall is often in the form of thunderstorms but the rain falls on a small number of days. Hours of sunshine range from an average of two to three a day in winter to nine in summer. The small area around Trieste is, in winter, sometimes affected by strong and gusty winds, the bora, which bring very cold air from central Europe (see the tables for **Milan** and **Venice**).

Milan 397 ft (121 m) 45°28′ N 9°11′ E 16 years   **ITALY**

	Temperature °F			Temperature °C			Relative humidity		Precipitation		
	Highest recorded	Average daily	Lowest recorded	Highest recorded	Average daily	Lowest recorded	0630 hours	1230 hours	Average monthly		Average no. days with 0.04 in + (1 mm +)
		max.	min.		max.	min.		%	%	in	mm	
J	60	40	32	14	15	5	0	−10	90	82	1.6	44	6	J
F	68	46	35	13	20	8	2	−11	87	73	2.4	60	7	F
M	72	56	43	28	22	13	6	−2	88	65	3.0	77	7	M
A	84	65	49	33	29	18	10	0	86	57	3.7	94	8	A
M	92	74	57	42	33	23	14	6	86	59	3.0	76	8	M
J	96	80	63	49	35	27	17	9	84	56	4.7	118	9	J
J	101	84	67	51	38	29	20	10	85	61	2.5	64	6	J
A	97	82	66	54	36	28	19	12	89	58	3.6	91	7	A
S	91	75	61	45	33	24	16	7	91	63	2.7	69	5	S
O	79	63	52	35	26	17	11	1	94	73	4.9	125	8	O
N	69	51	43	29	21	10	6	−1	92	80	4.8	122	10	N
D	64	43	35	19	18	6	2	−7	94	89	3.0	77	7	D

	Temperature °F			Temperature °C			Relative humidity		Precipitation		
	Highest recorded	Average daily	Lowest recorded	Highest recorded	Average daily	Lowest recorded	0700 hours	1300 hours	Average monthly		Average no. days with 0.04 in + (1 mm +)
		max.	min.		max.	min.		%	%	in	mm	
J	57	42	33	18	14	6	1	−8	86	76	1.5	37	6	J
F	64	46	35	15	18	8	2	−9	80	76	1.9	48	6	F
M	72	53	41	24	22	12	5	−5	86	68	2.4	61	7	M
A	81	62	49	35	27	17	10	2	86	67	3.1	78	9	A
M	91	70	56	41	33	21	14	5	85	69	2.6	65	8	M
J	91	76	63	47	33	25	17	8	83	65	2.7	69	8	J
J	94	81	66	53	34	27	19	12	82	64	2.1	52	7	J
A	93	80	65	55	34	27	18	13	84	63	2.7	69	7	A
S	87	75	61	49	31	24	16	9	87	64	2.3	59	5	S
O	80	65	53	38	27	19	11	3	88	68	3.0	77	7	O
N	69	53	44	28	21	12	7	−2	88	75	3.7	94	9	N
D	59	46	37	24	15	8	3	−4	88	79	2.4	61	8	D

PENINSULAR ITALY AND THE ISLANDS

The long Italian peninsula, from Genoa and Rimini in the north to Reggio di Calabria and Brindisi in the south, has a mountainous interior where the Appennines rise to over 6000 ft (1800 m). The climate of the coastlands is thus very different from that of the interior, particularly in winter. The higher areas are cold, wet and often snowy. The coastal regions, where most of the large towns are located, have a typical Mediterranean climate with mild winters and hot and generally dry summers. The length and intensity of the summer dry season increases southwards (compare the tables for **Rome**, **Naples** and **Brindisi**). There is no great difference in the temperatures at sea level from north to south. The east coast of the peninsula is not so wet as the west coast. The east coast north of Pescara is occasionally affected by the cold bora winds in winter and spring, but the wind is less strong here than around Trieste.

The whole of peninsular Italy and the large islands of Sicily and Sardinia have very changeable weather in autumn, winter and spring in marked contrast to the settled sunny weather of summer. Disturbed weather can continue into late May and commence any time after early September. Throughout the winter, however, cloudy rainy days alternate with spells of mild, sunny weather.

The least number of rainy days and the highest number of hours of sunshine occur in the extreme south of the mainland and in Sicily and Sardinia. Here sunshine averages from four to five hours a day in winter and up to ten or eleven hours in summer. The heat of summer is usually moderated on the coast by daytime sea breezes, but the nights can occasionally be warm and even humid (see the tables for **Palermo** and **Cagliari**).

Brindisi 84 ft (28 m) 40°38′ N 17°56′ E 16 years — ITALY

	Temperature °F			Temperature °C			Relative humidity		Precipitation			
	Highest recorded	Average daily	Lowest recorded	Highest recorded	Average daily	Lowest recorded	0700 hours	1300 hours	Average monthly		Average no. days with 0.04 in + (1 mm +)	
		max.	min.			max.	min.		%	%	in	mm	
J	66	54	43	28	19	12	6	−2	82	73	3.0	77	11	J
F	72	56	44	29	22	13	7	−2	81	68	2.2	57	7	F
M	72	58	47	25	22	15	8	−4	82	67	2.3	59	8	M
A	81	65	51	37	27	18	11	3	81	67	1.9	47	7	A
M	92	72	58	43	34	22	14	6	80	67	1.5	39	5	M
J	100	79	65	54	38	26	18	12	75	65	1.0	25	3	J
J	103	84	70	53	39	29	21	12	75	64	0.6	14	1	J
A	104	84	70	59	40	29	21	15	75	62	1.2	30	2	A
S	93	79	65	49	34	26	18	10	80	66	1.5	38	4	S
O	85	71	59	44	30	22	15	7	83	70	3.1	79	6	O
N	78	64	53	38	26	18	11	3	83	72	3.8	96	10	N
D	76	58	47	30	24	14	8	−1	84	73	3.3	83	9	D

Cagliari (Sardinia) 23 ft (7 m) 39°12′ N 9°05′ E 16 years — ITALY

	Temperature °F			Temperature °C			Relative humidity		Precipitation			
	Highest recorded	Average daily	Lowest recorded	Highest recorded	Average daily	Lowest recorded	0630 hours	1230 hours	Average monthly		Average no. days with 0.04 in + (1 mm +)	
		max.	min.			max.	min.		%	%	in	mm	
J	70	58	44	28	21	14	7	−2	87	73	2.0	50	8	J
F	70	58	45	30	21	15	7	−1	87	69	2.0	50	7	F
M	76	62	47	33	25	17	9	1	88	66	1.8	45	7	M
A	83	66	51	40	28	19	11	4	86	65	1.2	31	5	A
M	95	74	57	44	35	23	14	7	85	65	1.0	26	4	M
J	99	81	64	50	37	27	18	10	82	58	0.5	13	1	J
J	104	87	69	58	40	30	21	14	81	58	0	1	0	J
A	100	86	69	60	38	30	21	15	82	61	0.4	10	1	A
S	95	81	66	53	35	27	19	12	86	61	1.3	32	3	S
O	84	74	59	46	29	23	15	8	89	64	2.1	54	6	O
N	79	66	52	40	26	19	11	4	87	67	2.8	72	9	N
D	76	60	48	30	24	16	9	−1	87	73	2.6	67	9	D

	Temperature °F			Temperature °C			Relative humidity		Precipitation			
	Highest recorded	Average daily	Lowest recorded	Highest recorded	Average daily	Lowest recorded	0700 hours	1300 hours	Average monthly		Average no. days with 0.04 in + (1 mm +)	
		max.	min.			max.	min.		%	%	in	mm	
J	69	53	40	24	20	12	4	−4	77	68	4.6	116	11	J
F	69	55	41	25	20	13	5	−4	78	67	3.4	85	10	F
M	77	59	44	25	25	15	6	−4	77	62	2.9	73	9	M
A	80	65	48	34	27	18	9	1	79	61	2.4	62	8	A
M	90	72	54	37	32	22	12	3	85	63	1.7	44	7	M
J	95	79	61	45	35	26	16	7	75	58	1.2	31	4	J
J	96	84	65	52	36	29	18	11	73	53	0.8	19	2	J
A	99	84	65	55	37	29	18	13	74	53	1.3	32	3	A
S	93	79	61	46	34	26	16	8	78	59	2.5	64	5	S
O	84	71	54	38	29	22	12	3	79	63	4.2	107	9	O
N	79	63	48	29	26	17	9	−2	81	68	5.8	147	11	N
D	67	56	44	24	20	14	6	−4	80	70	5.3	135	12	D

ITALY   **Palermo (Sicily)** 102 ft (31 m) 38°06′ N 13°19′ E 16 years

	Temperature °F			Temperature °C			Relative humidity		Precipitation			
	Highest recorded	Average daily	Lowest recorded	Highest recorded	Average daily	Lowest recorded	0700 hours	1300 hours	Average monthly		Average no. days with 0.04 in + (1 mm +)	
		max.	min.			max.	min.		%	%	in	mm	
J	87	60	46	33	30	16	8	0	76	67	2.8	71	12	J
F	80	62	47	32	27	16	8	0	72	63	1.7	43	8	F
M	85	63	48	34	30	17	9	1	72	60	2.0	50	8	M
A	93	68	52	38	34	20	11	4	70	60	1.9	49	6	A
M	97	74	58	46	36	24	14	8	71	58	0.8	19	3	M
J	103	81	64	52	40	27	18	11	68	54	0.4	9	2	J
J	106	85	69	56	41	30	21	14	64	52	0.1	2	0	J
A	107	86	70	61	42	30	21	16	64	52	0.7	18	2	A
S	106	83	66	52	41	28	19	11	66	53	1.6	41	4	S
O	95	77	60	49	35	25	16	9	72	61	3.0	77	8	O
N	89	71	54	40	32	21	12	5	74	64	2.8	71	8	N
D	78	64	49	36	26	18	10	2	74	65	2.4	62	10	D

	Temperature °F			Temperature °C				Relative humidity		Precipitation		
	Highest recorded	Average daily		Lowest recorded	Highest recorded	Average daily		Lowest recorded	0700 hours	1300 hours	Average monthly		Average no. days with 0.04 in + (1 mm +)
		max.	min.			max.	min.		%	%	in	mm	
J	66	52	40	24	19	11	5	−5	85	68	2.8	71	8	J
F	68	55	42	21	20	13	5	−6	86	64	2.4	62	9	F
M	74	59	45	28	23	15	7	−2	83	56	2.2	57	8	M
A	78	66	50	35	26	19	10	1	83	54	2.0	51	6	A
M	89	74	56	38	31	23	13	3	77	54	1.8	46	5	M
J	98	82	63	50	36	28	17	10	74	48	1.5	37	4	J
J	98	87	67	54	36	30	20	12	70	42	0.6	15	1	J
A	104	86	67	53	40	30	20	12	73	43	0.8	21	2	A
S	92	79	62	51	33	26	17	11	83	50	2.5	63	5	S
O	84	71	55	39	29	22	13	4	86	59	3.9	99	8	O
N	74	61	49	30	23	16	9	−1	87	66	5.9	129	11	N
D	65	55	44	27	19	13	6	−3	85	70	3.7	93	10	D

LIECHTENSTEIN

Situated in the central Alps between Switzerland and Austria, this small independent principality has an area of about 62 square miles (158 sq. km). It contains part of the upper Rhine valley and mountains rising to 8500 ft (2600 m). It has a similar climate to that described on pp. 422 and 336 for the Swiss and Austrian Alps (see the tables for **Innsbruck** and **Zürich**).

LUXEMBOURG

Luxembourg is only about as large as an average British or American county. It has had a customs union with Belgium and the Netherlands since 1948. The north of the country consists of part of the forested Ardennes hills and has a similar climate to the neighbouring area of Belgium (see the description on p. 339 and the table for **Virton** p. 340).

Southern Luxembourg borders France on the south-west and West Germany on the east. It is the most populous area and contains the capital of the same name. In the extreme southeast is part of the sheltered Moselle valley where summers and autumns are warm enough for vines to be cultivated for wine-making.

The south of the country is drier and sunnier than the north. On occasions winters can be quite severe with snow cover lasting for some weeks. Its inland position and the shelter of the Ardennes exclude the milder influence of the sea which is more evident in the Netherlands and north Belgium.

MALTA

The Maltese islands of Malta and Gozo lie in the central Mediterranean midway between Sicily and North Africa. The total area is small, only 122 square miles (316 sq. km), and is low-lying and flat. The weather and climate are strongly influenced by the sea and have a very characteristic Mediterranean flavour, similar to that found in southern Italy or southern Greece.

Winters are mild with only rare occurrences of cold weather brought by north and northeast winds from central Europe. Summers are warm, dry and very sunny. Daytime temperatures in summer are usually mitigated by cooling sea breezes, but in spring and autumn a very hot wind from Africa occasionally brings unpleasantly high temperatures. This is the sirocco, which also affects Italy and Greece; in Malta the air is usually rather drier because of the short sea track from the African coast. Annual rainfall in Malta is rather low and the length of the dry season in summer is longer than in southern Italy. Malta has a very sunny climate with an average of five to six hours of sunshine a day in midwinter and over twelve hours a day in summer.

Luxembourg 1083 ft (330 m) 49°37′ N 6°03′ E 12 years — LUXEMBOURG

| | Temperature °F | | | Temperature °C | | | | Relative humidity | | Precipitation | | | |
	Highest recorded	Average daily	Lowest recorded	Highest recorded	Average daily	Lowest recorded	0630 hours	1230 hours	Average monthly		Average no. days with 0.004 in + (0.1 mm +)	
		max.	min.			max.	min.		%	%	in	mm		
J	52	37	29	5	11	3	−1	−15	92	86	2.4	61	20	J
F	63	40	31	−3	17	4	−1	−20	91	78	2.6	65	16	F
M	73	49	35	13	23	10	1	−11	88	64	1.7	42	14	M
A	85	57	40	25	29	14	4	−4	85	58	1.9	47	13	A
M	86	65	46	29	30	18	8	−2	87	59	2.5	64	15	M
J	92	70	52	39	34	21	11	4	88	61	2.5	64	14	J
J	98	73	55	42	37	23	13	5	89	61	2.4	60	14	J
A	92	71	54	40	33	22	12	4	91	63	3.3	84	15	A
S	91	66	50	34	33	19	10	1	93	67	2.8	72	16	S
O	72	56	43	24	22	13	6	−5	95	76	2.1	53	15	O
N	63	44	37	19	17	7	3	−7	93	86	2.6	67	19	N
D	57	39	33	8	14	4	0	−14	95	91	3.2	81	20	D

Valletta 230 ft (70 m) 35°54′ N 14°31′ E 17 years — MALTA

| | Temperature °F | | | Temperature °C | | | | Relative humidity | | Precipitation | | | |
	Highest recorded	Average daily	Lowest recorded	Highest recorded	Average daily	Lowest recorded	0800 hours	1400 hours	Average monthly		Average no. days with 0.04 in + (1 mm +)	
		max.	min.			max.	min.		%	%	in	mm		
J	73	58	50	41	23	14	10	5	76	67	3.5	90	12	J
F	76	59	51	41	24	15	10	5	76	66	2.4	60	8	F
M	79	61	52	41	26	16	11	5	78	65	1.5	39	5	M
A	82	65	56	45	28	18	13	7	78	64	0.6	15	2	A
M	94	71	61	53	34	22	16	12	75	63	0.5	12	2	M
J	103	79	67	57	39	26	19	14	72	60	0.1	2	0	J
J	103	84	72	64	39	29	22	18	71	59	0	0	0	J
A	104	85	73	62	40	29	23	17	76	62	0.3	8	1	A
S	98	81	71	61	37	27	22	16	76	64	1.1	29	3	S
O	91	75	66	61	33	24	19	16	77	65	2.5	63	6	O
N	79	67	60	49	26	20	16	9	78	67	3.6	91	9	N
D	72	61	54	42	22	16	12	6	77	68	4.3	110	13	D

MONACO

The tiny independent principality of Monaco, consisting almost entirely of the town of **Monte Carlo**, is situated on the Mediterranean coast of France. It is in the heart of the popular seaside resort area of the Côte d'Azur and enjoys a Mediterranean type of climate which is described on p. 358 for Mediterranean France. The area of Monaco is less than 1 square mile.

MONACO

Monte Carlo 180 ft (55 m) 43°43′ N 7°25′ E 30 years

	Temperature °F				Temperature °C				Relative humidity		Precipitation		
	Highest recorded	Average daily		Lowest recorded	Highest recorded	Average daily		Lowest recorded	0630 hours	1330 hours	Average monthly		Average no. days with 0.004 in + (0.1 mm +)
		max.	min.			max.	min.		%	%	in	mm	
J	70	54	47	32	21	12	8	0	67	67	2.4	61	5	J
F	66	55	47	30	19	13	8	−1	70	69	2.3	58	5	F
M	68	57	50	34	20	14	10	1	74	73	2.8	71	7	M
A	77	61	54	39	25	16	12	4	77	72	2.6	65	5	A
M	84	66	59	46	29	19	15	8	78	75	2.5	64	5	M
J	93	73	66	54	34	23	19	12	79	75	1.3	33	4	J
J	91	78	71	57	33	26	22	14	78	71	0.8	21	1	J
A	93	78	71	57	34	26	22	14	76	72	0.9	22	2	A
S	87	74	67	52	31	24	20	11	77	71	2.6	66	4	S
O	80	68	61	45	27	20	16	7	73	71	4.5	113	7	O
N	72	61	54	41	22	16	12	5	72	72	4.8	123	7	N
D	68	56	49	33	20	14	10	1	71	72	3.9	99	6	D

The Netherlands, often known as Holland, is a small country with a long coastline on the North Sea. The greater part of the country is low-lying and does not rise more than 100 ft (30 m) above sea level. Substantial portions of the provinces of north and south Holland, the offshore islands in the mouth of the Scheldt, and the West Frisian Islands are near, or below, sea level. These areas have been reclaimed from the sea over the centuries. A small area in the southern province of Limburg rises above 1000 ft (300 m). Proximity to the sea, low elevation and the presence of numerous sluggish rivers and canals impose a uniformity on the climate of the country so there are very small differences from place to place.

The coastal regions have the mildest climate throughout the year (see the table for **Vlissingen**) and the lowest rainfall. In summer the slightly higher midday temperatures are more likely to produce thunderstorms accompanied by heavy showers. Climatic conditions inland are best shown by the table for **De Bilt** near Utrecht which is representative of the densely populated area between Rotterdam and Amsterdam.

As in most countries in northwest Europe, the weather in the Netherlands can be very changeable from day to day at all times of the year and the character of each season may vary from one year to another. In winter spells of cold weather, lasting from one week to two months or more, rivers and canals may freeze. In mild winters this may not occur at all. In summer, fine, hot weather may last for some weeks on occasions but the weather may also be cool and unsettled. Rainfall is well distributed over the year but tends to fall on fewer days in summer and to be heavier. Average daily sunshine amounts range from about two hours in January to between seven and eight hours in June.

Gales are quite frequent on the coast, particularly in autumn and winter. The flat countryside makes the Netherlands a rather windy place at all times of the year. In the past this aspect of the weather was fully utilized by the Dutch who built numerous windmills to pump water from the low-lying land reclaimed from the sea and the rivers. On rare occasions in the past severe northerly gales have whipped up storm waves and a tidal surge in the North Sea sufficiently high to batter and breach the coastal dikes. This last flood occurred in January 1953 with disastrous consequences, inundating land below sea level and causing great loss of life.

Except during prolonged cold spells in winter the weather in the Netherlands is rarely unpleasant or uncomfortable. When it does freeze many people indulge in the traditional Dutch winter sport of skating on the numerous canals.

De Bilt 10 ft (3 m) 52°06′ N 5°11′ E 30 years

	Temperature °F			Temperature °C			Relative humidity		Precipitation			
	Highest recorded	Average daily	Lowest recorded	Highest recorded	Average daily	Lowest recorded	0730 hours	1330 hours	Average monthly		Average no. days with 0.004 in + (0.1 mm +)	
		max.	min.			max.	min.		%	%	in	mm	
J	55	40	31	−13	13	4	−1	−25	90	82	2.7	68	22	J
F	63	42	31	−7	17	5	−1	−22	90	76	2.1	53	19	F
M	71	49	34	11	21	10	1	−12	86	65	1.7	44	16	M
A	79	56	40	24	26	13	4	−4	79	61	1.9	49	16	A
M	90	64	46	27	32	18	8	−3	75	59	2.1	52	14	M
J	98	70	51	33	37	21	11	1	75	59	2.3	58	14	J
J	93	72	55	40	34	22	13	4	79	64	3.0	77	17	J
A	94	71	55	39	35	22	13	4	82	65	3.4	87	18	A
S	94	67	50	32	34	19	10	0	86	67	2.8	72	19	S
O	78	57	44	18	26	14	7	−8	90	72	2.8	72	20	O
N	64	48	38	18	18	9	3	−8	92	81	2.8	70	21	N
D	58	42	33	4	14	5	1	−15	91	85	2.5	64	21	D

	Temperature °F			Temperature °C				Relative humidity		Precipitation			
	Highest recorded	Average daily		Lowest recorded	Highest recorded	Average daily		Lowest recorded	0700 hours	1300 hours	Average monthly		Average no. days with 0.004 in +	
		max.	min.			max.	min.		%	%	in	mm	(0.1 mm +)	
J	55	41	34	6	13	5	1	−15	89	82	2.4	62	20	J
F	62	41	33	−3	17	5	1	−20	87	80	1.8	45	17	F
M	69	47	37	21	20	9	3	−6	87	72	1.6	40	16	M
A	79	53	42	28	26	12	5	−2	81	67	1.6	41	15	A
M	85	61	48	34	30	16	9	1	78	65	1.7	42	13	M
J	91	66	54	40	33	19	12	4	78	66	2.0	50	12	J
J	93	69	57	43	34	21	14	6	81	68	2.8	71	15	J
A	92	70	58	45	33	21	14	7	82	68	2.6	65	15	A
S	91	66	55	40	33	19	13	5	84	69	2.9	73	16	S
O	79	57	48	27	26	14	9	−3	87	74	2.8	70	19	O
N	63	49	41	23	17	9	5	−5	89	82	2.8	72	20	N
D	58	43	36	8	15	6	2	−14	89	85	2.3	58	20	D

NORWAY

Norway extends for about 1100 miles from south to north between 58° and 71° N and has an area of 125,000 square miles (324,000 sq. km). The northern part of the country within the Arctic Circle has continuous daylight at midsummer and Arctic twilight all day in winter. Norway has a long and very indented coastline on the North Sea and Atlantic Ocean with many steep-sided inlets or fiords. There are innumerable small islands offshore. Much of the interior is high mountain and plateau, rising over 5000 ft (1500 m). Except in the south around **Oslo**, the country is narrow from east to west. There is a long landborder with Sweden and, in the far north in Lapland, with Finland and the USSR. The largest area of lowland is around **Oslo** and this is the driest and warmest part of the country in summer.

The interior highlands have an Arctic type of climate in winter with snow, strong winds and severe frosts, but during fine spells in summer the daytime temperatures can rise quite high with long hours of sunshine. The weather and climate are similar to that of northern Sweden (see p. 418 and map p. 347).

By contrast the coastal areas have comparatively mild conditions in winter because the warm Atlantic water of the Gulf Stream reaches to the extreme north of Norway. This keeps the sea from freezing and maintains open harbours throughout the year. On occasions in winter strong cold winds blow down into the fiords from the snow-covered highlands.

The climate and weather of Norway are very much influenced by Atlantic weather disturbances so that the weather is changeable throughout the year. Gales, rain and cloud are the dominant features of this coast and rainfall is frequent and heavy (see the table for **Bergen**). Towards the north, rainfall decreases but falls frequently and snow is common at sea level in winter (see the table for **Narvik**). In the more extensive areas of lowland in the south the winters are colder with more frequent frost than on the Atlantic coast, but summers are warmer and drier (see the table for **Oslo**).

The **Spitzbergen** (Svalbard) archipelago of Norwegian territory is situated in the Arctic Ocean between 77° and 80° N. It has a severe Arctic type of climate. Winters are very cold and in the short summer snow scarcely melts at sea level. In the mountainous interior there are glaciers and permanent snowfields. The north coasts of the islands are permanently enclosed in pack ice. The islands have long been inhabited, formerly by whalers but now as a meteorological station. Coal mines are jointly worked by Norway and the USSR. Winter conditions are severe and Arctic clothing is essential for survival outdoors. Similar conditions apply in winter in northern and central Norway at higher levels.

	Temperature °F			Temperature °C				Relative humidity		Precipitation			
	Highest recorded	Average daily		Lowest recorded	Highest recorded	Average daily		Lowest recorded	0630 hours	1230 hours	Average monthly		Average no. days with 0.004 in + (0.1 mm +)	
		max.	min.			max.	min.		%	%	in	mm		
J	56	38	31	8	13	3	−1	−14	80	77	5.6	143	20	J
F	52	38	30	12	11	3	−1	−11	80	74	5.6	142	17	F
M	68	43	33	14	20	6	0	−10	79	67	4.3	109	16	M
A	72	49	37	22	22	9	3	−6	80	68	5.5	139	19	A
M	81	58	44	28	27	14	7	−2	78	64	3.3	83	15	M
J	89	61	49	33	32	16	10	1	83	71	5.0	126	17	J
J	87	66	54	41	31	19	12	5	86	73	5.6	142	20	J
A	85	65	54	40	30	19	12	4	87	73	6.6	168	20	A
S	79	59	49	34	26	15	10	1	87	74	9.0	228	21	S
O	67	52	43	26	20	11	6	−3	85	76	9.3	235	23	O
N	60	46	38	22	15	8	3	−6	81	77	8.3	211	21	N
D	62	41	34	17	16	5	1	−8	81	79	8.0	204	22	D

	Temperature °F			Temperature °C				Relative humidity		Precipitation			
	Highest recorded	Average daily		Lowest recorded	Highest recorded	Average daily		Lowest recorded	0730 hours	1300 hours	Average monthly		Average no. days with 0.004 in + (0.1 mm +)	
		max.	min.			max.	min.		%	%	in	mm		
J	48	29	19	−4	9	−2	−7	−20	75	74	2.2	55	15	J
F	48	29	19	−2	9	−2	−7	−19	75	72	1.9	47	15	F
M	51	34	22	0	11	1	−5	−18	76	68	2.4	61	17	M
A	62	41	29	10	16	5	−2	−13	70	62	1.8	45	15	A
M	75	49	37	20	24	9	3	−7	75	65	1.7	44	17	M
J	83	56	45	31	29	14	7	−1	78	69	2.6	65	17	J
J	86	65	51	39	30	18	11	4	81	71	2.3	58	16	J
A	81	62	49	36	27	16	10	2	87	75	3.3	84	19	A
S	73	53	43	26	23	12	6	−3	85	71	3.8	97	20	S
O	60	43	35	16	16	6	2	−9	78	73	3.4	86	20	O
N	55	37	28	8	13	3	−2	−13	75	74	2.3	59	15	N
D	52	31	24	−2	11	−1	−5	−19	72	73	2.2	57	16	D

	Temperature °F			Temperature °C				Relative humidity		Precipitation		
	Highest recorded	Average daily	Lowest recorded	Highest recorded	Average daily		Lowest recorded	0630 hours	1230 hours	Average monthly		Average no. days with 0.004 in + (0.1 mm +)
		max.	min.			max.	min.		%	%	in	mm	
J	51	28	19	−15	11	−2	−7	−26	86	82	1.9	49	15	J
F	57	30	19	−12	14	−1	−7	−24	84	74	1.4	35	12	F
M	60	39	25	−4	16	4	−4	−20	80	64	1.0	26	9	M
A	71	50	34	5	22	10	1	−15	75	57	1.7	43	11	A
M	83	61	43	27	28	16	6	−3	68	52	1.7	44	10	M
J	93	68	50	35	34	20	10	2	69	55	2.8	70	13	J
J	91	72	55	39	33	22	13	4	74	59	3.2	82	15	J
A	88	70	53	39	31	21	12	4	79	61	3.7	95	14	A
S	78	60	46	26	26	16	8	−4	85	66	3.2	81	14	S
O	68	48	38	18	20	9	3	−8	88	72	2.9	74	14	O
N	55	38	31	4	13	3	−1	−16	88	83	2.7	68	16	N
D	51	32	25	−5	11	0	−4	−21	87	85	2.5	63	17	D

	Temperature °F			Temperature °C				Relative humidity		Precipitation		
	Highest recorded	Average daily	Lowest recorded	Highest recorded	Average daily		Lowest recorded	0700 hours	1300 hours	Average monthly		Average no. days with 0.004 in + (0.1 mm +)
		max.	min.			max.	min.		%	%	in	mm	
J	41	19	9	−24	5	−7	−13	−31	83	82	1.0	26	13	J
F	40	19	7	−24	4	−7	−14	−31	82	82	1.0	25	12	F
M	39	16	6	−27	4	−9	−15	−33	83	83	0.9	24	12	M
A	42	22	11	−22	6	−5	−12	−30	82	80	0.6	15	10	A
M	56	31	24	−2	13	−1	−5	−19	82	80	0.8	20	10	M
J	55	39	33	21	13	4	1	−6	85	84	0.8	19	9	J
J	60	45	39	30	16	7	4	−1	89	87	1.0	25	11	J
A	55	43	38	28	13	6	3	−2	88	85	1.6	40	14	A
S	54	37	32	16	12	3	0	−9	84	82	1.4	36	14	S
O	47	31	23	3	8	−1	−5	−16	81	81	1.5	39	13	O
N	43	27	17	−16	6	−3	−8	−27	82	82	1.5	37	14	N
D	42	22	13	−17	6	−6	−10	−27	82	82	1.2	31	14	D

Poland lies in eastern Europe between East Germany and the USSR. It has a long border with Czechoslovakia in the south and a coastline on the Baltic Sea in the north. Most of the country consists of a low-lying rolling plain below 1000 ft (300 m) but in the south it includes part of the Sudeten Mountains in the west and the higher Carpathian Mountains which rise over 6000 ft (1800 m) towards the east.

Most of Poland has a very similar climate and the same sequence of weather throughout the year. Winter cold increases towards the east and in the southern mountains while the coastlands of the Baltic Sea have slightly milder winters and cooler summers (see the table for **Gdynia**). Precipitation is well distributed around the year with a summer maximum of rain, often heavy and accompanied by thunder. Much of the winter precipitation is snow. Snow covers the ground for an average of forty days each winter in the north and west and for as much as sixty to seventy days in the south and east. Snow lies for up to 100 days a year in the Carpathians and winter sports are possible here. Over most of Poland total annual precipitation is quite low, between 20 and 25 in (500 and 625 mm).

Summer temperatures do not differ very much over the country. It rarely gets excessively hot but fine, sunny spells of weather and occasional droughts occur. Winters are distinctly cold and the length of really cold spells varies considerably from year to year. The worst winter weather occurs when strong easterly winds blow and on these occasions the winter cold is similar to that found in Russia. When an anticyclone becomes settled over eastern Europe in winter the cold may be prolonged but it is more bearable as there is little wind chill in the calm air and the weather may be alternately foggy or sunny.

The tables for **Poznan** and **Warsaw** illustrate conditions over much of Poland. Those for **Cracow** and **Przemysl** are representative of the colder south and east of the country.

Like much of western and central Europe, the weather can be changeable at all times of the year, but winters are more likely to have prolonged spells of one type of weather. Daily sunshine hours average from one to two hours in midwinter to as much as six to seven hours in summer.

Cracow 686 ft (209 m) 50°04′ N 19°58′ E 14 years

	Temperature °F			Temperature °C				Relative humidity		Precipitation			
	Highest recorded	Average daily		Lowest recorded	Highest recorded	Average daily		Lowest recorded	0730 hours	1330 hours	Average monthly		Average no. days with 0.004 in + (0.1 mm +)	
		max.	min.			max.	min.		%	%	in	mm		
J	52	32	22	−10	11	0	−5	−23	88	81	1.1	28	16	J
F	60	34	22	−16	16	1	−5	−27	87	78	1.1	28	15	F
M	70	45	30	5	21	7	−1	−15	88	71	1.4	35	12	M
A	83	55	38	21	29	13	3	−6	85	60	1.8	46	15	A
M	91	67	48	29	33	20	9	−2	80	56	1.8	46	12	M
J	93	72	54	37	34	22	12	3	81	60	3.7	94	15	J
J	95	76	58	47	35	24	15	9	83	61	4.4	111	16	J
A	94	73	56	43	34	23	14	6	87	63	3.6	91	15	A
S	86	66	49	31	30	19	10	−1	91	66	2.4	62	12	S
O	80	56	42	24	27	14	5	−4	92	71	1.9	49	14	O
N	70	44	33	11	21	6	1	−12	93	82	1.5	37	15	N
D	62	37	28	−1	17	3	−2	−18	90	85	1.4	36	16	D

	Temperature °F				Temperature °C				Relative humidity		Precipitation			
	Highest recorded	Average daily		Lowest recorded	Highest recorded	Average daily		Lowest recorded	0700 hours	1300 hours	Average monthly		Average no. days with 0.004 in + (0.1 mm +)	
		max.	min.			max.	min.		%	%	in	mm		
J	52	35	27	−3	11	1	−3	−20	86	82	1.3	33	15	J
F	56	35	25	−11	14	1	−4	−24	86	80	1.2	31	15	F
M	65	40	30	9	18	4	−1	−13	86	76	1.1	27	12	M
A	75	48	36	20	24	9	2	−7	83	71	1.4	36	13	A
M	88	59	45	28	31	15	7	−2	78	69	1.7	42	11	M
J	91	66	52	36	33	19	11	2	77	67	2.8	71	11	J
J	96	70	58	46	36	21	14	8	81	70	3.3	84	13	J
A	93	70	57	45	34	21	14	7	83	69	3.0	75	12	A
S	85	64	51	35	29	18	11	2	85	69	2.3	59	14	S
O	74	55	44	26	24	13	7	−4	86	72	2.4	61	15	O
N	60	44	36	13	16	7	2	−10	87	80	1.1	29	11	N
D	54	38	31	4	12	3	−1	−16	88	84	1.8	46	16	D

	Temperature °F				Temperature °C				Relative humidity		Precipitation			
	Highest recorded	Average daily		Lowest recorded	Highest recorded	Average daily		Lowest recorded	0700 hours	1300 hours	Average monthly		Average no. days with 0.004 in + (0.1 mm +)	
		max.	min.			max.	min.		%	%	in	mm		
J	52	33	24	−9	11	1	−5	−23	89	83	0.9	24	15	J
F	57	34	22	−18	14	1	−5	−28	89	79	1.1	29	14	F
M	70	44	30	5	21	7	−1	−15	88	70	1.0	26	11	M
A	83	54	37	21	29	12	3	−6	85	60	1.6	41	14	A
M	89	67	47	28	32	20	8	−2	78	52	1.9	47	11	M
J	96	72	52	33	35	23	11	1	77	54	2.1	54	11	J
J	101	76	57	39	38	24	14	4	83	59	3.2	82	16	J
A	94	73	55	41	35	23	13	5	87	60	2.6	66	13	A
S	90	67	48	29	32	19	9	−2	91	61	1.8	45	11	S
O	77	56	41	21	25	13	5	−6	93	72	1.5	38	14	O
N	63	43	33	12	17	6	1	−11	93	83	0.9	23	12	N
D	55	37	28	−9	13	3	−2	−23	91	87	1.5	39	17	D

Przemysl 659 ft (201 m) 49°47′ N 22°48′ E 11 years   **POLAND**

	Temperature °F			Temperature °C				Relative humidity		Precipitation			
	Highest recorded	Average daily		Lowest recorded	Highest recorded	Average daily		Lowest recorded	0730 hours	1330 hours	Average monthly		Average no. days with 0.004 in + (0.1 mm +)	
		max.	min.			max.	min.		%	%	in	mm		
J	57	32	20	−15	14	0	−7	−26	83	74	1.1	27	14	J
F	59	34	21	−16	15	1	−6	−27	82	71	0.9	24	14	F
M	75	43	29	−13	24	6	−2	−25	83	64	1.0	25	10	M
A	87	55	37	12	31	13	3	−11	83	59	1.7	43	13	A
M	88	67	46	28	31	19	8	−2	79	55	2.2	57	12	M
J	92	73	53	35	34	23	12	2	82	60	3.5	88	13	J
J	98	75	57	43	37	24	14	6	84	63	4.1	105	15	J
A	91	73	55	38	33	23	13	3	88	63	3.7	93	14	A
S	88	67	48	31	31	19	9	0	90	63	2.3	58	12	S
O	86	57	40	20	30	14	5	−7	89	67	2.0	50	12	O
N	67	43	33	3	20	6	1	−16	90	78	1.7	43	13	N
D	61	38	28	2	16	3	−2	−17	86	78	1.7	43	16	D

Warsaw 361 ft (110 m) 52°13′ N 21°03′ E 14 years   **POLAND**

	Temperature °F			Temperature °C				Relative humidity		Precipitation			
	Highest recorded	Average daily		Lowest recorded	Highest recorded	Average daily		Lowest recorded	0700 hours	1330 hours	Average monthly		Average no. days with 0.04 in + (0.1 mm +)	
		max.	min.			max.	min.		%	%	in	mm		
J	51	32	22	−20	11	0	−6	−29	90	84	1.1	27	15	J
F	56	32	21	−16	13	0	−6	−27	89	80	1.3	32	14	F
M	65	42	28	6	18	6	−2	−14	90	70	1.1	27	11	M
A	80	53	37	22	27	12	3	−6	85	61	1.5	37	13	A
M	92	67	48	27	34	20	9	−3	80	56	1.8	46	11	M
J	93	73	54	38	34	23	12	3	82	59	2.7	69	13	J
J	95	75	58	45	35	24	15	7	86	63	3.8	96	16	J
A	92	73	56	44	33	23	14	7	90	63	2.6	65	13	A
S	88	66	49	34	31	19	10	1	92	64	1.7	43	12	S
O	78	55	41	17	26	13	5	−9	93	73	1.5	38	12	O
N	63	42	33	10	17	6	1	−12	93	83	1.2	31	12	N
D	55	35	28	−14	13	2	−3	−26	92	87	1.7	44	16	D

PORTUGAL

Portugal is a small country about the same size as Scotland. It has a coastline on the Atlantic Ocean and a land frontier with Spain. Together with Ireland, it occupies the most westerly position in Europe and its weather and climate are much influenced by the Atlantic. Its southerly latitude gives it a Mediterranean type of climate, similar to that of the state of California, but one where the summer heat is tempered by the Atlantic influence.

On the coast the winters are particularly mild. The north and the central interior of Portugal include mountain and plateaux rising in places over 6000 ft (1800 m); here the summers are much cooler and winters may be quite cold (see the table for **Braganza**, situated at medium height in the extreme north).

Winter is the wet season everywhere in Portugal but autumn rain can sometimes be heavy in the north as the fine weather of summer breaks. The length and severity of the summer drought increases from north to south.

This can be seen by comparing the monthly rainfall and number of wet days at **Oporto**, **Lisbon** and **Faro** in the climatic tables. Summer sunshine and temperature and winter mildness also increase southwards. The south-facing coast of the Algarve region is the sunniest, driest and warmest part of the country but the summer heat rarely reaches the unpleasant levels sometimes found in southeastern Spain. Another favourable aspect of this region for tourists is the higher sea temperatures as compared with those on the west-facing coasts farther north where seas are more likely to be rough.

Snow is very rare at sea level in Portugal but it becomes more frequent inland and on the higher areas of the north. Winter rainfall is rather heavy north of **Lisbon** and the weather in the far north is often wet and stormy. Most parts of Portugal are sunny. Daily hours of sunshine average from four to five in winter and ten to eleven in summer in the north. These figures rise to six in winter and twelve in summer in the far south.

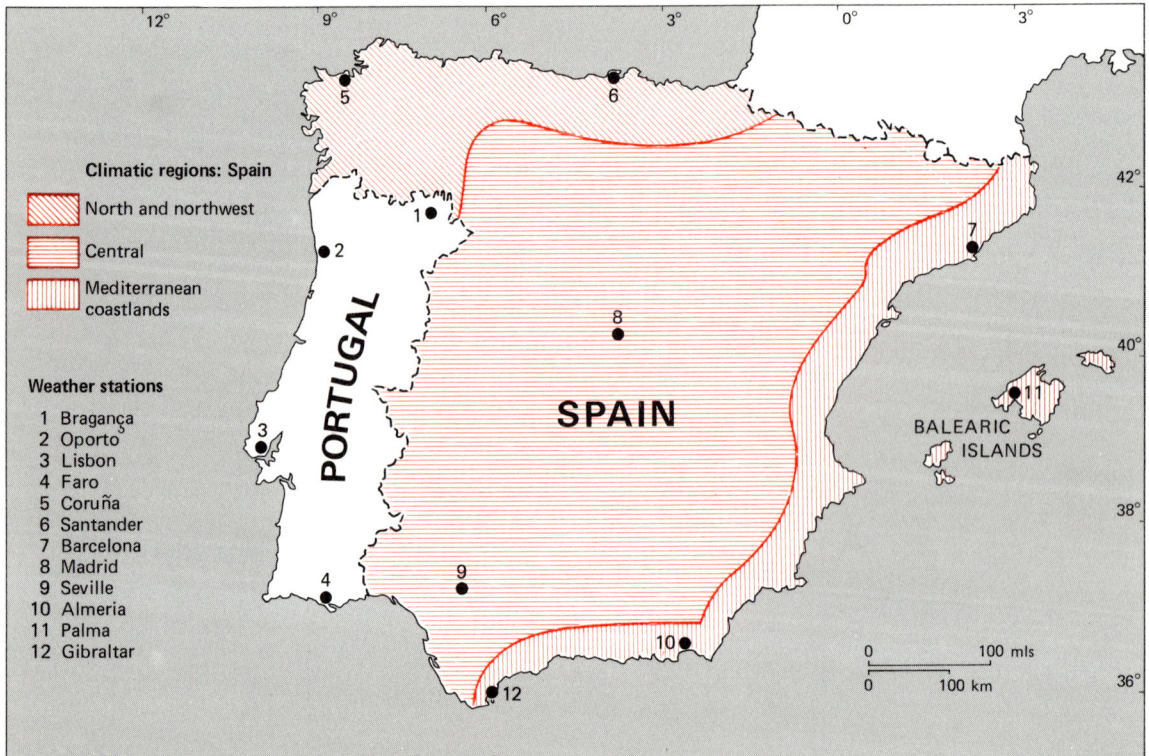

Climatic regions: Spain
- North and northwest
- Central
- Mediterranean coastlands

Weather stations
1 Bragança
2 Oporto
3 Lisbon
4 Faro
5 Coruña
6 Santander
7 Barcelona
8 Madrid
9 Seville
10 Almeria
11 Palma
12 Gibraltar

Braganza 2362 ft (720 m) 41°49′ N 6°46′ W 30 years PORTUGAL

	Temperature °F			Temperature °C				Relative humidity		Precipitation			
	Highest recorded	Average daily	Lowest recorded	Highest recorded	Average daily		Lowest recorded	0530 hours	1130 hours	Average monthly		Average no. days with 0.004 in + (0.1 mm +)	
		max.	min.			max.	min.		%	%	in	mm		
J	64	46	32	10	18	8	0	−12	90	80	5.9	149	15	J
F	71	51	33	12	21	11	1	−11	88	73	4.1	104	12	F
M	77	55	38	19	25	13	3	−7	86	68	5.2	133	15	M
A	83	60	40	24	29	16	5	−4	83	59	2.9	73	10	A
M	88	65	45	28	31	19	7	−2	83	59	2.7	69	11	M
J	98	75	51	33	36	24	11	1	80	53	1.7	42	7	J
J	103	82	55	37	40	28	13	3	76	47	0.6	15	3	J
A	101	83	55	33	38	28	13	1	77	47	0.6	16	4	A
S	96	74	50	30	36	24	10	−1	82	55	1.5	39	7	S
O	83	64	44	25	29	18	7	−4	87	66	3.1	79	10	O
N	72	53	38	20	22	12	3	−6	90	74	4.3	110	14	N
D	62	46	33	14	17	8	1	−10	90	81	5.7	144	17	D

Faro 118 ft (36 m) 37°01′ N 7°55′ W 30 years PORTUGAL

	Temperature °F			Temperature °C				Relative humidity		Precipitation			
	Highest recorded	Average daily	Lowest recorded	Highest recorded	Average daily		Lowest recorded	0830 hours	1430 hours	Average monthly		Average no. days with 0.004 in + (0.1 mm +)	
		max.	min.			max.	min.		%	%	in	mm		
J	75	60	48	31	24	15	9	−1	79	72	2.8	70	9	J
F	73	61	49	31	23	16	10	−1	76	70	2.1	52	7	F
M	79	64	52	36	26	18	11	2	76	72	2.8	72	10	M
A	89	67	55	41	32	20	13	5	69	67	1.2	31	6	A
M	91	71	58	45	33	22	14	7	68	67	0.8	21	4	M
J	95	77	64	50	35	25	18	10	66	65	0.2	5	1	J
J	106	83	67	54	41	28	20	12	63	62	0	1	0	J
A	99	83	68	46	37	28	20	8	63	63	0	1	0	A
S	94	78	65	50	34	26	19	10	67	66	0.7	17	2	S
O	89	72	60	46	32	22	16	8	70	68	2.0	51	6	O
N	83	66	55	41	28	19	13	5	75	70	2.6	65	8	N
D	71	61	50	34	22	16	10	1	77	70	2.6	67	9	D

PORTUGAL

Lisbon 253 ft (77 m) 38°43′ N 9°09′ W 30 years

	Temperature °F				Temperature °C				Relative humidity		Precipitation			
	Highest recorded	Average daily		Lowest recorded	Highest recorded	Average daily		Lowest recorded	0830 hours	1430 hours	Average monthly		Average no. days with 0.004 in + (0.1 mm +)	
		max.	min.			max.	min.		%	%	in	mm		
J	69	57	46	31	21	14	8	−1	85	71	4.3	111	15	J
F	78	59	47	29	25	15	8	−1	80	64	3.0	76	12	F
M	81	63	50	37	27	17	10	3	78	64	4.2	109	14	M
A	88	67	53	40	31	20	12	4	69	56	2.1	54	10	A
M	94	71	55	44	34	21	13	6	68	57	1.7	44	10	M
J	100	77	60	50	38	25	15	10	65	54	0.6	16	5	J
J	104	81	63	54	40	27	17	12	62	48	0.1	3	2	J
A	105	82	63	56	40	28	17	13	64	49	0.2	4	2	A
S	96	79	62	51	36	26	17	10	70	54	1.3	33	6	S
O	96	72	58	44	35	22	14	7	75	59	2.4	62	9	O
N	80	63	52	39	27	17	11	4	81	68	3.7	93	13	N
D	70	58	47	32	21	15	9	0	84	72	4.1	103	15	D

PORTUGAL

Oporto 312 ft (95 m) 41°08′ N 8°36′ W 30 years

	Temperature °F				Temperature °C				Relative humidity		Precipitation			
	Highest recorded	Average daily		Lowest recorded	Highest recorded	Average daily		Lowest recorded	0830 hours	1430 hours	Average monthly		Average no. days with 0.004 in + (0.1 mm +)	
		max.	min.			max.	min.		%	%	in	mm		
J	71	56	40	25	22	13	5	−4	87	69	6.3	159	18	J
F	84	58	41	25	29	14	5	−4	84	65	4.4	112	15	F
M	83	61	46	29	29	16	8	−2	81	65	5.8	147	17	M
A	89	65	48	33	32	18	9	1	76	61	3.4	86	13	A
M	92	67	51	38	33	20	11	4	74	65	3.4	87	13	M
J	98	73	56	44	37	23	13	7	74	64	1.6	41	7	J
J	104	76	58	48	40	25	15	9	73	60	0.8	20	5	J
A	103	77	58	48	39	25	15	9	76	60	1.0	26	6	A
S	99	75	56	42	37	24	14	6	80	63	2.0	51	10	S
O	94	69	51	35	34	21	11	2	82	64	4.1	105	15	O
N	78	62	46	30	26	17	8	−1	85	68	5.8	148	18	N
D	71	57	42	25	22	14	5	−4	86	70	6.6	168	18	D

Rumania is an almost landlocked country in southeastern Europe. It has a short coastline on the Black Sea south of the mouth of the river Danube. Its southern border is with Bulgaria. It is bordered on the west by Yugoslavia and Hungary and it has a long northern border with the Ukrainian Republic of the USSR. The east and south of the country are low-lying and rather flat; the centre and west include the Carpathian Mountains and their foothills, with ridges and peaks rising over 6000 ft (1800 m).

Rumania has a climate of the continental type, rather like that of the steppes of the southern USSR with cold, snowy winters and warm summers. Precipitation is normally rather low except in the higher parts of the Carpathians. Spring and summer are the wettest seasons when thunderstorms are most frequent. Winter precipitation is mostly snow. Snow lies from thirty to fifty days at low levels and up to 100 days a year in the mountains. The mildest area in winter is along the coast of the Black Sea (see the table for **Constanta**). Inland the Danube and other rivers usually freeze in winter. The change from winter conditions to those of summer is often rather abrupt and spring is a short but changeable season in Rumania. Late summer and autumn are often rather dry.

The weather can be changeable at all times of the year and there are considerable variations from one year to another. In dry summers the plains in the north and east can suffer from drought as hot, dry winds blow out of the Russian steppes. On the other hand, in winter the most severe weather occurs when cold winds from the same region sweep the country. Winter is the time of heaviest rainfall. Summers in Rumania are generally warm and sunny with an average of between nine to ten hours of sunshine a day. Winter sunshine is rather low, averaging only two to three hours a day.

Away from the Black Sea coast there are no great differences in climate from one part of the country to another, apart from the cooler and wetter summers in the Carpathians. During cold spells in winter frost may be as severe in the plains as in the mountains. The climatic tables for **Bucharest** and **Arad** represent conditions east and west of the Carpathians respectively.

Arad 381 ft (116 m) 46°10′ N 21°19′ E 28 years   **RUMANIA**

	Temperature °F			Temperature °C			Relative humidity	Precipitation		
	Highest recorded	Average daily	Lowest recorded	Highest recorded	Average daily	Lowest recorded	All hours	Average monthly		Average no. days with 0.004 in + (0.1 mm +)
		max.	min.			max.	min.		%	in	mm	
J	61	35	22	−17	16	2	−5	−27	84	1.4	36	11	J
F	63	40	26	−22	17	5	−4	−30	80	1.3	34	11	F
M	78	52	33	6	26	11	1	−14	68	1.4	35	11	M
A	91	63	42	22	33	17	5	−5	62	1.8	46	10	A
M	94	72	50	29	34	22	10	−2	63	2.5	64	12	M
J	100	78	56	36	38	26	13	2	63	2.7	68	11	J
J	103	83	58	44	40	28	15	7	59	2.1	54	9	J
A	105	82	58	41	40	28	14	5	60	1.7	43	8	A
S	103	76	52	29	40	24	11	−2	62	1.6	41	7	S
O	90	63	43	18	32	17	6	−8	72	1.7	44	9	O
N	73	50	37	13	23	10	3	−11	81	2.1	52	12	N
D	65	41	29	−9	18	5	−2	−23	84	1.6	41	12	D

	Temperature °F			Temperature °C				Relative humidity	Precipitation		
	Highest recorded	Average daily		Lowest recorded	Highest recorded	Average daily		Lowest recorded	All hours	Average monthly		Average no. days with 0.004 in + (0.1 mm +)
		max.	min.			max.	min.		%	in	mm	
J	60	34	19	−26	16	1	−7	−32	87	1.8	46	11	J
F	68	38	23	−15	20	4	−5	−26	84	1.0	26	9	F
M	84	50	30	−2	29	10	−1	−19	73	1.1	28	9	M
A	89	64	41	25	32	18	5	−4	63	2.3	59	11	A
M	98	74	51	31	37	23	10	0	63	3.0	77	13	M
J	99	81	57	40	37	27	14	5	62	4.8	121	12	J
J	102	86	60	46	39	30	16	8	58	2.1	53	10	J
A	106	85	59	44	41	30	15	7	59	1.8	45	7	A
S	101	78	52	33	39	25	11	0	63	1.8	45	5	S
O	95	65	43	21	35	18	6	−6	73	1.1	29	7	O
N	74	49	35	6	24	10	2	−14	85	1.4	36	12	N
D	65	39	26	−9	18	4	−3	−23	89	1.1	27	10	D

	Temperature °F			Temperature °C				Relative humidity	Precipitation		
	Highest recorded	Average daily		Lowest recorded	Highest recorded	Average daily		Lowest recorded	All hours	Average monthly		Average no. days with 0.004 in + (0.1 mm +)
		max.	min.			max.	min.		%	in	mm	
J	62	37	25	−10	17	3	−4	−23	89	1.1	29	10	J
F	67	40	28	0	20	4	−3	−18	87	0.9	23	8	F
M	87	46	33	9	31	8	1	−13	83	0.8	21	7	M
A	85	56	42	23	30	13	6	−5	82	1.1	28	7	A
M	94	66	52	35	34	19	11	2	81	1.4	35	8	M
J	97	75	60	42	36	24	16	6	78	1.6	41	8	J
J	94	81	64	47	35	27	18	8	73	1.4	35	5	J
A	94	80	63	46	35	27	17	8	75	1.2	31	4	A
S	90	73	57	31	32	23	14	−1	79	0.9	24	4	S
O	85	63	49	25	29	17	9	−4	84	1.5	38	6	O
N	76	51	40	13	24	11	4	−11	89	1.6	40	10	N
D	69	43	31	3	21	6	−1	−16	90	1.3	34	9	D

This small, independent republic lies in the Appennine Mountains at an altitude of 2500 ft (750 m) inland from the Adriatic town of Rimini. It has a modified Mediterranean type of climate as described on p. 390 for peninsular Italy. The area of San Marino is about 38 square miles (98 sq. km).

SPAIN

Spain is a country almost as large as France. Together with Portugal, with which it has a long landborder on the west, it forms a large peninsula south of the Pyrenees with the Atlantic Ocean on its western and northern side and the Mediterranean Sea on the south and east. The large size of the peninsula and the different climatic influences of the Atlantic and Mediterranean result in a variety of climates within Spain. It is a mistake to think of the whole country as having a typical Mediterranean climate such as is found in the tourist areas along the east and south coasts and in the Balearic Islands.

In the north the Pyrenees and Cantabrian Mountains rise to between 6000 ft and 10,000 ft (1800 and 3000 m). Much of interior Spain is a plateau with an average height of between 1500 and 3000 ft (450 and 900 m), crossed by a number of mountain ranges (sierras). In the south of the country (Andalusia) the valley of the Quadalquivir forms a wide lowland to the south of which lies the high Sierra Nevada which dominates the narrow Mediterranean coastlands. These large differences of altitude and the contrast between coast and interior give Spain a range of climatic and weather conditions. Although most of the country is hot and sunny in summer there are great differences of temperature in winter; the coastlands are mild but the interior is frequently cold and snowy. Skiing can be enjoyed on the nearest mountain ranges to most of the large towns of the country.

Spain can be divided into three climatic regions: the north and northwest, central Spain, and the Mediterranean coastlines of the east and south including the Balearic Islands. (See map p. 404.)

NORTH AND NORTHWESTERN SPAIN

This is the part of the country most influenced by depressions travelling in from the Atlantic, particularly in autumn and winter. It is the rainiest and cloudiest part of Spain. Although summers are cooler, cloudier and wetter than elsewhere in the country there is still a considerable amount of warm, sunny weather. Rainfall decreases from west to east in the Pyrenees but is quite high on the seaward slopes of the Cantabrians and in the extreme northwest (Galicia). Daily hours of sunshine average from three in winter to seven or eight in summer. See the tables for **Coruña** (in Galicia) and **Santander**.

Coruña 190 ft (58 m) 43°22′ N 8°25′ W 27 years **SPAIN**

	Temperature °F			Temperature °C			Relative humidity		Precipitation			
	Highest recorded	Average daily	Lowest recorded	Highest recorded	Average daily	Lowest recorded	0630 hours	1230 hours	Average monthly		Average no. days with 0.004 in + (0.1 mm +)	
		max.	min.			max.	min.		%	%	in	mm	
J	69	55	45	28	20	13	7	−2	81	74	4.7	118	19	J
F	81	55	44	27	27	13	7	−3	82	71	3.2	80	15	F
M	80	59	47	34	27	15	8	1	82	70	3.6	92	16	M
A	85	61	48	36	30	16	9	2	81	69	2.6	67	12	A
M	83	64	51	38	29	18	11	3	83	71	2.1	54	12	M
J	87	68	55	45	31	20	13	7	83	73	1.8	45	9	J
J	92	71	58	50	34	22	15	10	84	71	1.1	28	8	J
A	92	73	59	49	34	23	15	9	86	70	1.8	46	9	A
S	87	71	57	44	31	22	14	7	87	72	2.4	61	11	S
O	88	66	53	40	31	19	12	5	85	72	3.4	87	14	O
N	77	60	49	34	25	15	9	1	84	74	4.9	124	17	N
D	68	56	46	30	20	13	8	−1	84	77	5.3	135	19	D

Santander 217 ft (66 m) 43°28′ N 3°49′ W 27 years **SPAIN**

	Temperature °F			Temperature °C			Relative humidity		Precipitation			
	Highest recorded	Average daily	Lowest recorded	Highest recorded	Average daily	Lowest recorded	0630 hours	1230 hours	Average monthly		Average no. days with 0.004 in + (0.1 mm +)	
		max.	min.			max.	min.		%	%	in	mm	
J	70	53	44	28	21	12	7	−2	78	72	4.7	119	16	J
F	79	54	44	25	26	12	7	−4	80	71	3.5	88	14	F
M	86	58	47	24	30	14	8	−4	79	69	3.1	78	13	M
A	92	60	49	36	33	15	10	2	82	72	3.3	83	13	A
M	88	62	53	38	31	17	11	4	85	75	3.5	89	14	M
J	93	68	58	46	34	20	14	8	86	76	2.5	63	13	J
J	94	71	61	52	35	22	16	11	85	75	2.1	54	11	J
A	104	72	62	53	40	22	16	12	87	75	3.3	84	14	A
S	93	70	59	37	34	21	15	3	86	74	4.5	114	14	S
O	85	65	54	41	30	18	12	5	84	72	5.2	133	14	O
N	74	59	49	35	24	15	10	2	80	72	4.9	125	15	N
D	71	55	46	32	21	13	8	0	79	72	6.3	159	18	D

Rainfall is generally rather low over most of the interior although winter snowfall may be quite heavy and lie for a long time on the mountains. In late summer much of the country has a burnt and barren appearance after the long summer drought. The old French saying, 'Africa begins at the Pyrenees', has some truth in it if it is taken to refer to the heat and dry appearance of much of the countryside in summer. Summers are generally hot, particularly in the Quadalquivir valley in the south, where some of the highest temperatures in Europe are recorded. Spring and early summer tend to be the wettest season in many places but the rainfall is light and not very effective as it often falls in short, heavy showers. Winters have frequent cold spells with biting winds blowing off the snow-covered sierras. Dust and hot winds are the most unpleasant features of the summer weather but the low humidity makes the heat more bearable than in some of the coastal regions. The length of the dry summer season increases from north to south. Sunshine amounts are quite high throughout the year, ranging from an average of five hours a day in winter to as much as twelve hours in midsummer.

The table for **Madrid** is representative of the conditions in the higher parts of interior Spain, while that for **Seville**, in the Quadalquivir valley, is typical of the lower and hotter parts of Andalusia.

	Temperature °F			Temperature °C			Relative humidity		Precipitation			
	Highest recorded	Average daily	Lowest recorded	Highest recorded	Average daily	Lowest recorded	0700 hours	1300 hours	Average monthly		Average no. days with 0.004 in + (0.1 mm +)	
		max.	min.			max.	min.		%	%	in	mm	
J	64	47	35	14	18	9	2	−10	86	71	1.5	39	8	J
F	72	52	36	16	22	11	2	−9	83	62	1.3	34	7	F
M	78	59	41	26	26	15	5	−4	80	56	1.7	43	10	M
A	85	65	45	31	29	18	7	−1	74	49	1.9	48	9	A
M	92	70	50	33	33	21	10	1	72	49	1.9	47	10	M
J	98	80	58	44	37	27	15	6	66	41	1.0	27	5	J
J	102	87	63	47	39	31	17	8	58	33	0.4	11	2	J
A	100	85	63	45	38	30	17	7	62	35	0.6	15	3	A
S	96	77	57	40	36	25	14	4	72	46	1.3	32	6	S
O	83	65	49	31	28	19	10	0	81	58	2.1	53	8	O
N	72	55	42	27	22	13	5	−3	84	65	1.9	47	9	N
D	61	48	36	18	16	9	2	−8	86	70	1.9	48	10	D

	Temperature °F			Temperature °C			Relative humidity		Precipitation			
	Highest recorded	Average daily	Lowest recorded	Highest recorded	Average daily	Lowest recorded	0630 hours	1230 hours	Average monthly		Average no. days with 0.004 in + (0.1 mm +)	
		max.	min.			max.	min.		%	%	in	mm	
J	76	59	42	27	24	15	6	−3	87	75	2.6	66	8	J
F	80	63	44	26	27	17	7	−3	85	69	2.4	61	6	F
M	90	69	48	34	32	20	9	1	84	67	3.5	90	9	M
A	97	74	52	36	36	24	11	2	80	61	2.2	57	7	A
M	108	80	56	37	42	27	13	3	77	57	1.6	41	6	M
J	110	90	63	41	44	32	17	5	73	48	0.3	8	1	J
J	114	98	67	52	46	36	20	11	67	43	0	1	0	J
A	120	97	68	54	49	36	20	12	70	45	0.2	5	0	A
S	105	90	64	49	41	32	18	9	73	53	0.8	19	2	S
O	102	78	57	39	39	26	14	4	82	65	2.8	70	6	O
N	89	68	50	32	32	20	10	0	86	72	2.6	67	7	N
D	75	60	44	27	24	16	7	−3	88	73	3.1	79	8	D

MEDITERRANEAN SPAIN – THE EAST AND SOUTH COASTLANDS AND BALEARICS

This area includes the internationally famous tourist resorts – the Costa Brava in the north and the Costa del Sol in the south. Sunshine amounts are high: from six hours a day in winter to twelve in midsummer. Winters are mild and much warmer than inland. While the summers are hot and at times humid the afternoon heat is usually tempered by sea breezes. In the south conditions can occasionally become rather unpleasant when a hot, dry wind (the leveche) blows from North Africa. In much of the region, rain is very rare during the months June to August but north of Valencia the coast is liable to occasional heavy downpours of thundery rain in summer. Around **Barcelona** and farther north autumn tends to be wetter than winter; here the total rainfall is greater than in the south, some parts of which are dry even in winter. In the drier regions there are considerable differences in the amount of rainfall from year to year. See the tables for **Barcelona**, which is representative of the northern coastal regions, and **Almeria**, which is typical of the drier regions in the south. See also the table and description for **Gibraltar** on p. 372.

The Balearic Islands, which include Majorca, Menorca and Ibiza, are situated between 100 and 150 miles (170 and 250 km) to the east of Spain and are popular as a winter and summer resort for North Europeans. They have a climate similar to that of southeastern Spain (see the table for **Palma**, Majorca).

SPAIN   **Almeria** 20 ft (6 m) 36°50′ N 2°28′ W 27 years

	Temperature °F			Temperature °C			Relative humidity		Precipitation		
	Highest recorded	Average daily	Lowest recorded	Highest recorded	Average daily	Lowest recorded	0700 hours	1300 hours	Average monthly		Average no. days with 0.004 in + (0.1 mm +)
		max.	min.		max.	min.		%	%	in	mm	
J	73	60	46	35	23	16	8	2	78	70	1.2	31	6	J
F	78	61	47	32	26	16	9	0	78	70	0.8	21	4	F
M	80	64	51	37	27	18	11	3	78	68	0.8	21	5	M
A	85	68	55	42	30	20	13	5	78	67	1.1	28	5	A
M	95	72	59	47	35	22	15	8	77	67	0.7	18	3	M
J	97	78	65	55	36	26	18	13	77	67	0.2	4	1	J
J	100	83	70	58	38	29	21	15	77	67	0	0	0	J
A	99	84	71	60	37	29	22	16	79	68	0.2	6	1	A
S	97	81	68	50	36	27	20	10	79	68	0.6	16	3	S
O	89	73	60	46	32	23	16	8	79	68	1.0	25	5	O
N	80	67	54	40	27	19	12	5	79	70	1.1	27	4	N
D	78	62	49	37	25	17	9	3	77	70	1.4	36	5	D

Barcelona 305 ft (93 m) 41°24′ N 2°09′ E 27 years **SPAIN**

	Temperature °F			Temperature °C			Relative humidity		Precipitation		
	Highest recorded	Average daily	Lowest recorded	Highest recorded	Average daily	Lowest recorded	0700 hours	1300 hours	Average monthly		Average no. days with 0.004 in + (0.1 mm +)
		max.	min.			max.	min.		%	%	in	mm	
J	73	55	43	28	23	13	6	−2	74	61	1.2	31	5	J
F	71	57	45	20	21	14	7	−7	71	58	1.5	39	5	F
M	76	60	48	33	24	16	9	1	75	60	1.9	48	8	M
A	82	65	52	39	28	18	11	4	73	59	1.7	43	9	A
M	90	71	57	41	32	21	14	5	72	59	2.1	54	8	M
J	94	78	65	52	35	25	18	11	68	59	1.5	37	6	J
J	96	82	69	58	35	28	21	14	70	59	1.1	27	4	J
A	97	82	69	56	36	28	21	13	75	63	1.9	49	6	A
S	89	77	66	51	32	25	19	10	79	66	3.0	76	7	S
O	82	69	58	41	28	21	15	5	77	64	3.4	86	9	O
N	76	62	51	37	25	16	11	3	75	64	2.1	52	6	N
D	70	56	46	28	21	13	8	−3	72	62	1.8	45	6	D

Palma (Majorca) 33 ft (10 m) 39°33′ N 2°39′ E 27 years **SPAIN**

	Temperature °F			Temperature °C			Relative humidity		Precipitation		
	Highest recorded	Average daily	Lowest recorded	Highest recorded	Average daily	Lowest recorded	0700 hours	1300 hours	Average monthly		Average no. days with 0.004 in + (0.1 mm +)
		max.	min.			max.	min.		%	%	in	mm	
J	71	57	43	27	22	14	6	−3	83	72	1.5	39	8	J
F	73	59	44	25	23	15	6	−4	82	70	1.3	34	6	F
M	74	62	46	30	24	17	8	−1	81	69	2.0	51	8	M
A	79	66	51	33	26	19	10	1	77	66	1.3	32	6	A
M	88	71	55	40	31	22	13	5	77	67	1.1	29	5	M
J	98	79	62	47	37	26	17	8	70	65	0.7	17	3	J
J	101	84	67	54	39	29	20	12	70	65	0.1	3	1	J
A	99	84	68	52	37	29	20	11	75	65	1.0	25	3	A
S	94	80	65	40	35	27	18	4	79	69	2.2	55	5	S
O	88	73	57	34	31	23	14	1	83	71	3.0	77	9	O
N	78	65	50	33	26	18	10	1	83	72	1.9	47	8	N
D	74	59	46	31	24	15	8	−1	82	72	1.6	40	9	D

SWEDEN

Two important influences on the climate of Sweden are its northern latitude, between 55° and 69° N, and the shelter from milder and wetter Atlantic winds provided by the high mountains and plateaux along the country's western border with Norway. Most of Sweden has a typical continental climate with a moderate to large range of temperature between summer and winter. The one exception to this is the southwest of the country from **Gothenburg** to Malmö where winter temperatures are modified by an open ocean which rarely freezes. The enclosed waters of the Baltic Sea often freeze, in whole or in part, in winter; therefore the east coast of Sweden is much colder, particularly towards the north where the waters of the Gulf of Bothnia freeze each winter.

The high latitude means that much of the country has very long hours of daylight in summer and very short days in winter. North of the Arctic Circle at 66° N this amounts to twenty-four hours of sun and twenty-four hours of Arctic twilight in midsummer and midwinter respectively.

Precipitation is relatively low except on the higher mountains and is rather greater in summer than winter. North of Stockholm much of the winter precipitation is snow.

Winters become progressively longer and colder towards the north of the country. The average number of days with a mean temperature below freezing point increases from seventy-one at Malmö to 120 at **Stockholm** and 184 at Haparanda near the Arctic Circle.

Temperatures are surprisingly similar in midsummer over much of the country. The long summer days help to raise temperatures in the north so that on fine days temperatures may be as high here as in the south. Because of the generally changeable nature of the Swedish summer weather, however, the visitor should not expect to find fine weather every day. A wet, cool spell in summer in northern Sweden can be rather miserable.

The country can be divided broadly into three climatic regions: central and southern Sweden, the northeast or the low-lying shores of the Gulf of Bothnia, and the northwest or far north. (See map p. 347.)

CENTRAL AND SOUTHERN SWEDEN

This region lies approximately south of a line from **Oslo** in Norway to Uppsala on the east coast of Sweden. The area is mostly low-lying and contains some large lakes.

Winters are less severe than farther north and the climate permits a varied agriculture (see the tables for **Gothenburg** and **Stockholm**).

Gothenburg 135 ft (41 m) 57°42′ N 11°58′ E 30 years　　　　SWEDEN

	Temperature °F				Temperature °C			Relative humidity		Precipitation			
	Highest recorded	Average daily		Lowest recorded	Highest recorded	Average daily		Lowest recorded	0700 hours	1300 hours	Average monthly		Average no. days with 0.004 in + (0.1 mm +)	
		max.	min.			max.	min.		%	%	in	mm		
J	46	34	26	−15	8	1	−3	−26	85	81	2.0	51	15	J
F	48	34	25	−4	9	1	−4	−20	85	76	1.3	34	12	F
M	63	39	29	−3	17	4	−2	−19	83	67	1.1	29	10	M
A	68	49	37	12	22	9	3	−11	77	59	1.5	39	12	A
M	83	60	45	29	28	16	7	−2	70	54	1.3	34	10	M
J	90	66	53	37	32	19	12	3	73	58	2.1	54	12	J
J	90	70	57	46	32	21	14	8	77	62	3.4	86	14	J
A	86	68	56	41	30	20	13	5	81	63	3.3	84	14	A
S	77	61	50	32	25	16	10	0	84	67	3.0	75	16	S
O	68	51	43	21	20	11	6	−6	84	72	2.6	65	15	O
N	55	43	37	18	13	6	3	−8	85	80	2.4	62	16	N
D	52	38	32	4	11	4	0	−16	86	83	2.2	57	17	D

Stockholm 144 ft (44 m) 59°21′ N 18°04′ E 30 years　　　　SWEDEN

	Temperature °F				Temperature °C			Relative humidity		Precipitation			
	Highest recorded	Average daily		Lowest recorded	Highest recorded	Average daily		Lowest recorded	0700 hours	1300 hours	Average monthly		Average no. days with 0.004 in + (0.1 mm +)	
		max.	min.			max.	min.		%	%	in	mm		
J	49	30	23	−19	10	−1	−5	−28	85	83	1.7	43	16	J
F	53	30	22	−13	12	−1	−5	−25	83	77	1.2	30	14	F
M	59	37	26	−8	15	3	−4	−22	82	68	1.0	25	10	M
A	68	47	34	11	20	8	1	−12	76	60	1.2	31	11	A
M	82	58	43	26	28	14	6	−3	66	53	1.3	34	11	M
J	90	67	51	34	32	19	11	1	68	55	1.8	45	13	J
J	94	71	57	46	35	22	14	8	74	59	2.4	61	13	J
A	88	68	56	41	31	20	13	5	81	64	3.0	76	14	A
S	78	60	49	32	26	15	9	0	87	69	2.4	60	14	S
O	63	49	41	20	17	9	5	−7	88	76	1.9	48	15	O
N	54	40	34	12	12	5	1	−11	89	85	2.1	53	16	N
D	54	35	29	3	12	2	−2	−16	88	86	1.9	48	17	D

THE NORTHEAST OR THE LOW-LYING SHORES OF THE GULF OF BOTHNIA

Although the winters are severe and become longer and colder farther north, the summers are surprisingly warm for the latitude, particularly during settled weather. Precipitation is low, but snow cover is prolonged in winter (see the table for **Pitea**).

THE NORTHWEST AND FAR NORTH

This is mostly a plateau of moderate to high elevation. Temperatures are largely controlled by altitude and at the higher levels snow cover persists throughout the year. In sheltered valleys precipitation may be much less than on the surrounding hills. Here, during fine weather, winter temperatures sink very low while summer temperatures may rise surprisingly high. The greater part of the area, however, has a severe winter climate with short, changeable summers.

	Temperature °F				Temperature °C				Relative humidity		Precipitation			
	Highest recorded	Average daily		Lowest recorded	Highest recorded	Average daily		Lowest recorded	0730 hours	1330 hours	Average monthly		Average no. days with 0.004 in + (0.1 mm +)	
		max.	min.			max.	min.		%	%	in	mm		
J	46	21	8	−36	8	−6	−13	−38	82	82	1.5	37	13	J
F	47	22	6	−34	9	−6	−14	−37	82	79	1.0	25	13	F
M	53	31	12	−24	12	−1	−11	−31	80	71	0.9	23	9	M
A	64	40	25	−9	18	5	−4	−23	77	66	1.1	28	10	A
M	77	53	35	18	25	11	2	−8	65	56	1.2	30	8	M
J	90	62	46	30	32	17	8	−1	66	57	1.9	47	11	J
J	95	69	53	38	35	21	12	3	70	61	2.0	50	12	J
A	83	65	50	30	28	19	10	−1	78	65	2.7	68	12	A
S	75	55	42	20	24	13	5	−7	83	69	2.7	69	12	S
O	68	42	31	−3	20	6	0	−20	86	77	1.9	48	12	O
N	52	32	22	−17	11	0	−6	−27	87	86	1.9	48	14	N
D	46	26	14	−24	8	3	−10	−31	84	83	1.7	44	15	D

SWITZERLAND

This small, mountainous, landlocked country has a wide variety of climatic conditions because of the great range of altitude. The higher peaks of the Alps rise to over 12,000 ft (3600 m) and are snow-covered throughout the year. At lower levels in the Alpine valleys and on the central Swiss plateau summers can be quite warm, but this is the wettest period of the year in Switzerland. Much of the summer rainfall is heavy and often accompanied by severe thunderstorms.

Like other parts of west–central Europe, Switzerland is open to climatic influences from the Atlantic and from eastern Europe and the weather at all times of the year is changeable. The most settled weather occurs when the country is influenced by an anticyclone. In summer this brings warm, sunny weather, but in winter this may bring either cold, sunny weather or easterly winds with cloudy skies. Midwinter, rather than midsummer, is more likely to be a time of settled weather.

The country can be divided into four climatic regions: Canton Ticino or the extreme south, the Alps, the central or Swiss plateau, and the Jura Mountains. (See map p. 335.)

This small area around lakes Maggiore and Lugano is the warmest part of the country in summer and at low levels the winters are relatively mild. It lies south of the main Alpine ranges and is, from time to time, influenced by warmer Mediterranean air. The summers are rather similar to those of the adjoining north Italian plain but are distinctly wet with the rain occurring in heavy downpours. In settled weather it can be quite hot and sunny here. At low levels prolonged frost is rare in winter (see the table for **Lugano**).

Lugano 906 ft (276 m) 46°00′ N 8°58′ E 30 years   **SWITZERLAND**

	Temperature °F				Temperature °C				Relative humidity		Precipitation		
	Highest recorded	Average daily		Lowest recorded	Highest recorded	Average daily		Lowest recorded	0700 hours	1300 hours	Average monthly		Average no. days with 0.01 in + (0.25 mm +)
		max.	min.			max.	min.		%	%	in	mm	
J	76	43	29	13	25	6	−2	−11	76	56	2.5	63	7	J
F	76	48	31	13	25	9	−1	−11	74	52	2.6	67	7	F
M	81	56	37	20	27	13	3	−7	76	50	3.9	99	9	M
A	89	63	44	28	31	17	7	−2	74	50	5.8	148	11	A
M	91	69	50	33	33	21	10	1	77	53	8.5	215	15	M
J	97	77	57	40	36	25	14	4	74	50	7.8	198	13	J
J	100	81	60	46	38	27	16	8	74	48	7.3	185	11	J
A	98	80	60	47	36	27	15	9	78	51	7.7	196	12	A
S	90	74	55	36	32	23	13	2	82	54	6.3	159	10	S
O	83	62	47	28	28	16	8	−2	85	57	6.8	173	10	O
N	73	51	38	25	23	11	3	−4	82	59	5.8	147	10	N
D	71	44	31	15	21	7	0	−9	79	59	3.7	95	9	D

THE ALPS

The Alpine ranges cover half the country and extend from **Geneva** to the Austrian border. There are great differences between the climate of the valleys and the higher mountains. In winter the valleys are frequently cloudy and foggy with persistent frost. By contrast, during settled weather, the mountains are relatively sunny and daytime temperatures may feel quite warm. In winter the climate of the winter sports resorts is thus more pleasant than that found in the valleys or on the Swiss plateau. In summer, conditions may be quite the reverse: the mountains shrouded in cloud by day and the valleys basking in warm, clear weather.

In fine weather a number of local winds occur in the Alps. In the larger valleys there is a tendency for daytime breezes to blow up the valley and for a reverse down-valley wind to occur at night. Near glaciers this night-time wind can be very cold. A more widespread wind known as the föhn can affect large areas of the Alps under certain meteorological conditions. It is a warm wind, bringing air of very low relative humidity. Although it can blow in valleys on the southern side of the Alps, it is more severe on the northern side and blows particularly where valleys trend from south to north. It is most noticeable in late winter and spring and can melt snow very quickly. At higher levels it can trigger dangerous avalanches, and at lower levels the very dry air and strong wind increases the fire risk in wooden buildings. With the onset of a föhn wind temperature may rise as much as 27°–36° F (15°–20° C) within an hour. Such conditions may last for two or three days (see the table for **Santis**).

THE CENTRAL OR SWISS PLATEAU

This is the lowest part of the country and extends from Lake Geneva to Lake Konstanz. All the large towns of Switzerland and the majority of the population are situated here. Winters are generally cold with much persistent cloud and fog. Conditions in winter are rather similar to those in the deeper Alpine valleys. Freezing conditions may last for several weeks during severe winters and snow is frequent even during milder and more changeable winters. Summers are generally warm but rather wet (see the table for **Zürich**).

		Temperature °F			Temperature °C				Relative humidity		Precipitation			
	Highest recorded	Average daily		Lowest recorded	Highest recorded	Average daily		Lowest recorded	0700 hours	1300 hours	Average monthly		Average no. days with 0.01 in + (0.25 mm +)	
		max.	min.			max.	min.		%	%	in	mm		
J	38	20	13	−15	3	−7	−11	−26	76	74	8.0	202	16	J
F	42	20	13	−23	6	−7	−11	−30	76	74	7.1	180	15	F
M	45	24	16	−11	7	−4	−9	−24	75	73	6.5	164	14	M
A	53	29	20	−3	12	−2	−6	−19	79	78	6.5	166	16	A
M	64	37	28	4	18	3	−2	−15	76	77	7.8	197	16	M
J	63	43	34	17	17	6	1	−8	77	80	9.8	249	19	J
J	69	47	37	23	21	8	3	−5	79	79	11.9	302	18	J
A	65	47	38	22	19	8	3	−5	78	78	10.9	278	18	A
S	61	43	34	9	16	6	1	−13	77	75	8.2	209	15	S
O	55	35	27	2	13	2	−3	−17	74	72	7.2	183	13	O
N	47	27	20	−2	8	−3	−7	−19	75	72	7.5	190	13	N
D	43	22	15	−11	6	−6	−10	−24	75	71	6.7	169	15	D

		Temperature °F			Temperature °C				Relative humidity		Precipitation			
	Highest recorded	Average daily		Lowest recorded	Highest recorded	Average daily		Lowest recorded	0700 hours	1300 hours	Average monthly		Average no. days with 0.01 in + (0.25 mm +)	
		max.	min.			max.	min.		%	%	in	mm		
J	62	36	26	2	17	2	−3	−17	88	74	2.9	74	14	J
F	66	41	28	−10	19	5	−2	−23	88	65	2.7	69	13	F
M	71	51	34	12	22	10	1	−11	86	55	2.5	64	12	M
A	87	59	40	22	30	15	4	−6	81	51	3.0	76	13	A
M	92	67	47	29	33	19	8	−2	80	52	4.0	101	14	M
J	97	73	53	38	36	23	12	4	80	52	5.1	129	15	J
J	100	76	56	44	38	25	14	7	81	52	5.4	136	14	J
A	97	75	56	41	36	24	13	5	85	53	4.9	124	14	A
S	89	69	51	32	32	20	11	0	90	57	4.0	102	12	S
O	80	57	43	25	27	14	6	−4	92	64	3.0	77	12	O
N	67	45	35	17	20	7	2	−9	90	73	2.9	73	12	N
D	60	37	29	9	15	3	−2	−13	89	76	2.5	64	13	D

THE JURA MOUNTAINS

This small, narrow part of Switzerland extends from Basel to **Geneva** along the French border. The Jura rise to less than half the altitude of the Alps, but the valleys are narrow and the ridges steep. This area is rather wetter than the Swiss plateau and in winter the mountains carry snow for long periods. In some enclosed valleys winter temperatures can sometimes sink very low as cold air drains into the valley bottom. Summers are similar to those on the Swiss plateau but rather more cloudy and wet.

SWITZERLAND

Geneva 1329 ft (405 m) 46°12′ N 6°09′ E 30 years

	Temperature °F			Temperature °C				Relative humidity		Precipitation			
	Highest recorded	Average daily	Lowest recorded	Highest recorded	Average daily	Lowest recorded		0700 hours	1300 hours	Average monthly		Average no. days with 0.01 in + (0.25 mm +)	
		max.	min.			max.	min.		%	%	in	mm		
J	60	38	29	10	16	4	−2	−13	87	78	2.5	63	11	J
F	67	42	30	−1	20	6	−1	−18	86	71	2.2	56	9	F
M	72	51	36	13	22	10	2	−10	84	62	2.2	55	9	M
A	81	59	42	26	27	15	5	−3	79	56	2.0	51	9	A
M	89	66	49	29	32	19	9	−2	79	58	2.7	68	11	M
J	96	73	55	40	36	23	13	4	78	58	3.5	89	11	J
J	98	77	58	43	36	25	15	6	77	56	2.5	64	9	J
A	97	76	58	41	36	24	14	5	82	59	3.7	94	11	A
S	90	69	53	36	32	21	12	2	87	65	3.9	99	10	S
O	77	58	44	27	25	14	7	−3	89	71	2.8	72	10	O
N	65	47	37	19	19	8	3	−7	88	76	3.3	83	11	N
D	59	40	31	8	15	4	0	−13	88	79	2.3	59	10	D

Turkey extends for 1000 miles (1600 km) from west to east. A small part of the country, Turkish Thrace, west of the Bosphorus, is geographically in Europe; it borders Greece and Bulgaria on the west and has a similar climate (see the table for **Istanbul**). The rest of the country, Anatolia or Asia Minor, is strictly in Asia but by Turkey's membership of the Council of Europe she is now regarded as a European country.

Anatolia consists of a high plateau which becomes more mountainous towards the east where the country borders the USSR and Iran. It is enclosed by the Pontic ranges in the north and the Taurus and Anti-Taurus in the south. These mountains and isolated volcanic peaks such as Mt Ararat in eastern Turkey rise to well over 10,000 ft (3000 m) and may carry snow throughout the year.

There are thus considerable differences of climate within Turkey. The narrow coastlands and mountain slopes facing the Black Sea on the north, the Aegean on the west and the Mediterranean on the south have wetter and milder winters than the interior. The interior plateau has low rainfall and cold or very cold winters. Towards the east the winter cold is similar to that found in parts of the USSR. Except at higher levels, summers in the interior are warm or even hot with occasional thunderstorms. Winter precipitation here is mostly snow and towards the east this may lie on the ground for between three and four months (compare winter temperatures for **Ankara** and **Kars**).

The coastal regions have much milder winters and here snow is rare. Turkish Thrace, around **Istanbul** and the Black Sea coast, is a little colder in winter than the west and south coasts (see the table for **Samsun**). The Black Sea coast has some rain all the year round and east of **Samsun** this becomes heavy in summer and autumn. Summers are here warm and humid and the weather is often changeable and cloudy. South of **Istanbul** the Aegean and Mediterranean coasts have a typical Mediterranean climate with increasingly dry, hot summers (see the table for **Izmir**). Here midwinter is the rainy season when most of the disturbed weather occurs.

The hottest and driest area of Turkey in summer is the low-lying plain at the foot of the Taurus Mountains along the border with Syria. Here conditions become typical of the Middle East. The region is a semi-arid steppe with only winter rain.

Except for the eastern part of the Black Sea coastlands, most of Turkey has a very sunny climate even in winter. Average daily sunshine amounts range from three to four hours in midwinter to as much as twelve to thirteen hours in summer. Although summer temperatures are rather high, the heat is tempered by the low humidity inland and the sea breezes along the coast. Occasionally the nights may be sticky and humid on the Aegean and Mediterranean coasts. The worst feature of the climate is the severe cold experienced in the interior in winter, and occasionally in early spring.

Ankara 2825 ft (862 m) 39°57′ N 32°53′ E 26 years

	Temperature °F			Temperature °C			Relative humidity		Precipitation			
	Highest recorded	Average daily	Lowest recorded	Highest recorded	Average daily	Lowest recorded	0700 hours	1400 hours	Average monthly		Average no. days with 0.04 in + (1 mm +)	
		max.	min.			max.	min.		%	%	in	mm	
J	59	39	24	−13	15	4	−4	−25	85	70	1.3	33	8	J
F	64	42	26	−12	18	6	−3	−24	84	67	1.2	31	8	F
M	80	51	31	3	27	11	−1	−16	81	52	1.3	33	7	M
A	89	63	40	20	32	17	4	−7	72	40	1.3	33	7	A
M	94	73	49	31	34	23	9	−1	68	38	1.9	48	7	M
J	98	78	53	35	37	26	12	2	64	34	1.0	25	5	J
J	100	86	59	44	38	30	15	7	57	28	0.5	13	2	J
A	100	87	59	40	38	31	15	4	54	25	0.4	10	1	A
S	96	78	52	29	36	26	11	−2	62	31	0.7	18	3	S
O	89	69	44	27	32	21	7	−3	72	37	0.9	23	5	O
N	78	57	37	0	26	14	3	−18	82	52	1.2	31	6	N
D	63	43	29	−13	17	6	−2	−25	86	71	1.9	48	9	D

TURKEY

Istanbul 374 ft (114 m) 41°06′ N 29°03′ E 25 years

	Temperature °F				Temperature °C				Relative humidity		Precipitation			
	Highest recorded	Average daily		Lowest recorded	Highest recorded	Average daily		Lowest recorded	0700 hours	1400 hours	Average monthly		Average no. days with 0.004 in + (0.1 mm +)	
		max.	min.			max.	min.		%	%	in	mm		
J	66	46	37	18	19	8	3	−8	82	75	4.0	109	18	J
F	71	47	36	18	22	9	2	−8	82	72	3.6	92	14	F
M	82	51	38	21	28	11	3	−6	81	67	2.8	72	14	M
A	85	60	45	31	30	16	7	−1	81	62	1.8	46	9	A
M	94	69	53	38	35	21	12	3	82	61	1.5	38	8	M
J	99	77	60	47	37	25	16	8	79	58	1.3	34	6	J
J	100	82	65	49	38	28	18	9	79	56	1.3	34	4	J
A	105	82	66	53	41	28	19	11	79	55	1.2	30	4	A
S	100	76	61	43	38	24	16	6	81	59	2.3	58	7	S
O	91	68	55	35	33	20	13	1	83	64	3.2	81	11	O
N	80	59	48	25	27	15	9	−4	82	71	4.0	103	14	N
D	73	51	41	16	23	11	5	−9	82	74	4.7	119	18	D

TURKEY

Izmir 92 ft (28 m) 38°27′ N 27°15′ E 39 years

	Temperature °F				Temperature °C				Relative humidity		Precipitation			
	Highest recorded	Average daily		Lowest recorded	Highest recorded	Average daily		Lowest recorded	0700 hours	1400 hours	Average monthly		Average no. days with 0.04 in + (1 mm +)	
		max.	min.			max.	min.		%	%	in	mm		
J	73	55	39	12	23	13	4	−11	75	62	4.4	112	10	J
F	73	57	40	12	23	14	4	−11	75	51	3.3	84	8	F
M	84	63	43	19	29	17	6	−7	72	52	3.0	76	7	M
A	91	70	49	30	33	21	9	−1	69	48	1.7	43	5	A
M	106	79	56	37	41	26	13	3	65	45	1.3	33	4	M
J	105	87	63	50	41	31	17	10	56	40	0.6	15	2	J
J	108	92	69	52	42	33	21	11	53	31	0.2	5	0	J
A	107	92	69	53	42	33	21	12	57	37	0.2	5	1	A
S	103	85	62	42	39	29	17	6	64	42	0.8	20	2	S
O	98	76	55	31	37	24	13	−1	71	49	2.1	53	4	O
N	89	67	49	19	32	19	9	−7	77	58	3.3	84	6	N
D	79	58	42	20	26	14	6	−7	77	64	4.8	122	10	D

Kars 5741 ft (1751 m) 40°36′ N 43°05′ E 18 years TURKEY

	Temperature °F				Temperature °C				Relative humidity	Precipitation			
	Highest recorded	Average daily		Lowest recorded	Highest recorded	Average daily		Lowest recorded	All hours	Average monthly		Average no. days with 0.04 in + (1 mm +)	
		max.	min.			max.	min.		%	in	mm		
J	41	21	−1	−32	5	−6	−18	−36	65	1.1	28	7	J
F	44	25	3	−35	7	−4	−16	−37	68	1.1	28	7	F
M	66	34	12	−29	19	1	−11	−34	71	1.1	28	8	M
A	75	50	28	−9	24	10	−2	−23	70	1.7	43	9	A
M	80	63	38	19	27	17	3	−7	69	3.4	86	15	M
J	85	70	43	30	29	21	6	−1	67	2.9	74	12	J
J	94	77	49	33	34	25	9	1	63	2.1	53	8	J
A	94	79	49	33	34	26	9	1	60	2.1	53	7	A
S	90	71	40	24	32	22	4	−4	61	1.2	31	5	S
O	77	59	32	1	25	15	0	−17	69	1.6	41	7	O
N	70	44	23	−12	21	7	−5	−24	72	1.2	31	6	N
D	52	29	9	−31	11	−2	−13	−35	71	1.0	25	7	D

Samsun 131 ft (40 m) 41°17′ N 36°19′ E 24 years TURKEY

	Temperature °F				Temperature °C				Relative humidity	Precipitation			
	Highest recorded	Average daily		Lowest recorded	Highest recorded	Average daily		Lowest recorded	All hours	Average monthly		Average no. days with 0.04 in + (1 mm +)	
		max.	min.			max.	min.		%	in	mm		
J	72	50	38	20	22	10	3	−7	69	2.9	74	10	J
F	77	51	38	20	25	11	3	−7	72	2.6	66	10	F
M	90	54	40	20	32	12	4	−7	75	2.7	69	11	M
A	94	59	45	28	34	15	7	−2	77	2.3	58	9	A
M	99	67	53	36	37	19	12	2	79	1.8	46	8	M
J	95	74	60	46	35	23	16	8	75	1.5	38	6	J
J	103	79	65	51	39	26	18	11	73	1.5	38	4	J
A	102	80	65	49	39	27	18	9	72	1.3	33	4	A
S	94	75	61	44	34	24	16	7	74	2.4	61	6	S
O	95	69	56	38	35	21	13	3	75	3.2	81	7	O
N	90	62	49	27	32	17	9	−3	72	3.5	89	8	N
D	76	55	43	23	24	13	6	−5	68	3.4	86	9	D

THE UNION OF SOVIET SOCIALIST REPUBLICS

The Soviet Union, or USSR, is a vast country, about three times the size of the United States and occupying one sixth of the land area of the world. It comprises the greater part of eastern Europe and the whole northern portion of Asia. The traditional geographical division between European Russia and Siberia is the Ural mountains which extend from north to south in about 60° E.

The whole of the northern part of the USSR is within the Arctic Circle while the several Soviet republics in Transcaucasia and central Asia are between 35° and 40° N. (For the sake of convenience the whole of the USSR is included in the European section of this book.)

Within the Soviet Union the range of climates varies from extremely cold Arctic conditions to deserts and subtropical regions where tea and rice can be cultivated. The dominant feature of the Russian climate, however, is the extreme cold of winter which affects all but a few small regions in the south of the country. This harsh Russian winter has helped to defeat invaders such as Napoleon and Hitler and it affects almost all aspects of Soviet life. Adaptation to the Russian winter is a necessary but difficult process. Anyone proposing to visit the Soviet Union between late October and April should study the temperatures in the following tables

and take appropriate clothing! Only Antarctica, the Greenland icecap, northern and central Canada and Alaska experience such prolonged cold, snow and frost as are found in much of the USSR in winter.

Surprisingly, over much of the country, temperatures in midsummer are quite warm, even in the short summers of northern and eastern Siberia. There is a very rapid rise of temperature in spring, the season of the thaw (the *rasputitsa*), and an equally rapid fall of temperature in the autumn. Over most of the country, in effect, there are but two seasons, winter and summer. This is a characteristic feature of what climatologists call a continental climate, some of the best examples of which can be found in the Soviet Union.

There are two principal reasons for the cold of the Russian winter and its continental climate: the great size of the land-mass of Europe and Asia which means that the Soviet Union is isolated from the moderating influence of warm ocean waters; and the high latitude of much of the country with a northern coastline on the Arctic Ocean that is frozen for the greater part of the year.

Two consequences of the Russian winter are important economically. Except in the extreme south of

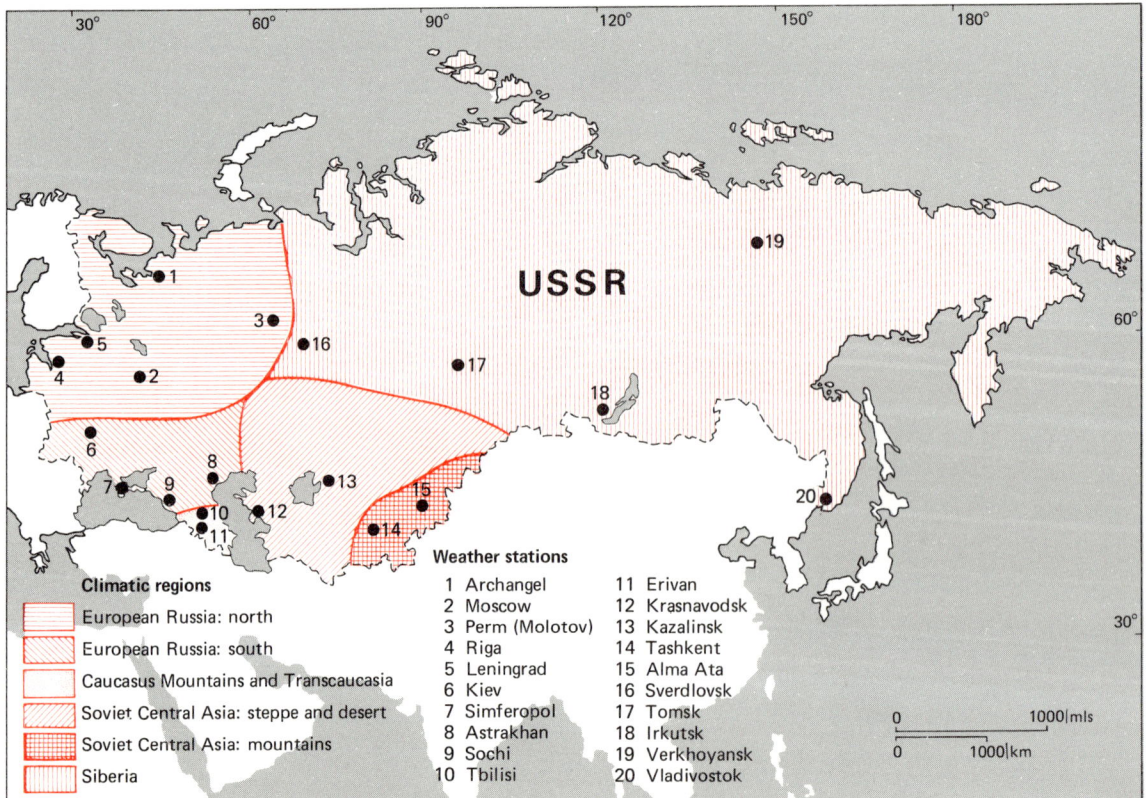

Climatic regions

- European Russia: north
- European Russia: south
- Caucasus Mountains and Transcaucasia
- Soviet Central Asia: steppe and desert
- Soviet Central Asia: mountains
- Siberia

Weather stations

1	Archangel	11	Erivan
2	Moscow	12	Krasnavodsk
3	Perm (Molotov)	13	Kazalinsk
4	Riga	14	Tashkent
5	Leningrad	15	Alma Ata
6	Kiev	16	Sverdlovsk
7	Simferopol	17	Tomsk
8	Astrakhan	18	Irkutsk
9	Sochi	19	Verkhoyansk
10	Tbilisi	20	Vladivostok

European Russia, the rivers freeze over for prolonged periods in winter and inland water transport comes to a halt. Road transport is also difficult and therefore the railways and air services are particularly important in the Soviet Union. The length of the season when rivers are completely frozen varies from about seventy days in the west of the country to as much as 250 days in northern and eastern Siberia. It is a good general rule in the Soviet Union that the severity of the winter increases eastwards. The only harbours which are normally ice free throughout the year are those on the Black Sea coast in the south and around Murmansk, adjoining Arctic Norway, where the influence of the warm Gulf Stream from the Atlantic raises sea temperatures. A shipping route from the Atlantic to the Pacific oceans along the Arctic coast of the Soviet Union is kept open for a brief period in summer with the aid of powerful icebreakers.

So intense is the cold in winter that about 45 per cent of the area of the Soviet Union, in northern and eastern Siberia, has a phenomenon called permafrost where the subsoil remains frozen all the year although the topsoil may thaw out in the summer. This raises special problems in building construction and for the laying of pipelines, as well as making cultivation difficult.

Apart from the mountainous areas along parts of the southern borders of the Soviet Union, precipitation over most of the country is rather low. There are large areas where there is insufficient rain for successful agriculture and in some of the major grain-producing regions of the southern steppes of the USSR summer droughts may reduce yields drastically in some years. Over most of the country the wettest season is spring and early summer and the rainfall is of the showery, thundery type. Winter snowfall, although frequent, is rarely very heavy and in some parts of the country strong winds often sweep the ground bare of snow.

For a more detailed description of weather and climate the country is divided into a number of climatic regions which, as far as possible, coincide with the constituent Soviet republics which make up the USSR.

EUROPEAN RUSSIA: THE NORTH AND CENTRE

This region comprises the Estonian, Latvian, Lithuanian, Byelorussian Republics and part of the Russian Soviet Federal Socialist Republic. It extends from the western borders of the USSR to the Ural mountains and from the shores of the Barents and Kara Seas in the north to the border with the Ukraine in the south. Most of the region is below 1000 ft (300 m) and is level or rolling country. This part of the Soviet Union has the most variable weather both in summer and winter as it is more open to the influence of weather disturbances coming from northwest Europe. The mildest areas in winter are along the Baltic coast (see the table for **Riga**). Even here, winters are cold as the Baltic often freezes. **Leningrad**, at the head of the Gulf of Finland, is colder in winter as the water here freezes for much longer. The summers at **Riga** and **Leningrad** are a little cooler than farther east.

The increasing severity of the winter eastwards and northwards is illustrated by a comparison of the tables for **Moscow**, **Perm** (near the Urals) and **Archangel** (close to the Arctic Circle). Summers become warmer eastwards and southwards. This whole region has a summer maximum of precipitation but along and near the Baltic autumn is wetter than spring. In the whole of this region winter sunshine is low, averaging about one hour a day. Summer sunshine, however, averages from eight to ten hours a day. In the northern part of the region the increasing length of daylight is an important influence on both warmth and sunshine.

USSR **Archangel** 43 ft (13 m) 64°35′ N 40°30′ E 8 years

		Temperature °F				Temperature °C			Relative humidity		Precipitation			
	Highest recorded	Average daily		Lowest recorded	Highest recorded	Average daily		Lowest recorded	0830 hours	1430 hours	Average monthly		Average no. days with 0.004 in + (0.1 mm +)	
		max.	min.			max.	min.		%	%	in	mm		
J	38	10	−5	−39	3	−12	−20	−40	82	81	1.2	31	21	J
F	36	13	0	−42	2	−10	−18	−41	81	75	0.8	19	17	F
M	48	25	8	−30	9	−4	−13	−35	83	70	1.0	25	18	M
A	61	41	24	−7	16	5	−4	−22	74	60	1.1	29	12	A
M	79	53	35	15	26	12	2	−10	65	55	1.7	42	11	M
J	83	63	44	26	28	17	6	−3	63	53	2.1	52	14	J
J	88	68	50	33	31	20	10	0	71	58	2.4	62	15	J
A	88	65	49	25	31	19	10	−4	80	65	2.2	56	16	A
S	79	53	41	18	26	12	5	−8	87	73	2.5	63	18	S
O	57	40	31	−4	14	4	−1	−20	88	83	2.5	63	22	O
N	48	29	20	−34	9	−2	−7	−37	90	88	1.9	47	22	N
D	40	18	6	−41	4	−8	−15	−40	83	83	1.6	41	24	D

Leningrad 13 ft (4 m) 59°58′ N 30°18′ E 8 years USSR

	Temperature °F				Temperature °C				Relative humidity		Precipitation			
	Highest recorded	Average daily		Lowest recorded	Highest recorded	Average daily		Lowest recorded	0800 hours	1400 hours	Average monthly		Average no. days with 0.004 in + (0.1 mm +)	
		max.	min.			max.	min.		%	%	in	mm		
J	38	19	8	−25	3	−7	−13	−32	86	84	1.4	35	21	J
F	38	22	11	−27	3	−5	−12	−33	81	73	1.2	30	17	F
M	54	32	18	−16	12	0	−8	−26	85	70	1.2	31	14	M
A	68	46	33	8	20	8	0	−13	79	65	1.4	36	12	A
M	81	59	42	24	27	15	6	−4	69	57	1.8	45	13	M
J	85	68	51	35	29	20	11	2	68	53	2.0	50	12	J
J	91	70	55	41	33	21	13	5	75	61	2.8	72	13	J
A	88	69	55	34	31	20	13	1	79	61	3.1	78	14	A
S	84	60	47	29	29	15	9	−2	86	68	2.5	64	17	S
O	65	48	39	17	18	9	4	−8	88	78	3.0	76	18	O
N	54	35	28	−1	12	2	−2	−18	89	85	1.8	46	18	N
D	41	26	18	−10	5	−3	−8	−23	88	86	1.6	40	22	D

Moscow 512 ft (156 m) 55°45′ N 37°34′ E 8 years USSR

	Temperature °F				Temperature °C				Relative humidity		Precipitation			
	Highest recorded	Average daily		Lowest recorded	Highest recorded	Average daily		Lowest recorded	0830 hours	1430 hours	Average monthly		Average no. days with 0.004 in + (0.1 mm +)	
		max.	min.			max.	min.		%	%	in	mm		
J	36	15	3	−25	2	−9	−16	−32	82	77	1.5	39	18	J
F	37	22	8	−25	3	−6	−14	−32	82	66	1.5	38	15	F
M	61	32	18	−18	16	0	−8	−28	82	64	1.4	36	15	M
A	76	50	34	−14	25	10	1	−26	73	54	1.5	37	13	A
M	86	66	46	28	30	19	8	−2	58	43	2.1	53	13	M
J	87	70	51	34	30	21	11	1	62	47	2.3	58	12	J
J	89	73	55	41	32	23	13	5	68	54	3.5	88	15	J
A	88	72	53	37	31	22	12	3	74	55	2.8	71	14	A
S	83	61	45	28	28	16	7	−2	78	59	2.3	58	13	S
O	74	48	37	5	24	9	3	−15	81	67	1.8	45	15	O
N	53	35	26	−7	12	2	−3	−22	87	79	1.9	47	15	N
D	41	24	15	−17	5	−5	−10	−27	85	83	2.1	54	23	D

	Temperature °F			Temperature °C				Relative humidity		Precipitation			
	Highest recorded	Average daily	Lowest recorded	Highest recorded	Average daily		Lowest recorded	1000 hours	1600 hours	Average monthly		Average no. days with 0.004 in + (0.1 mm +)	
		max.	min.			max.	min.		%	%	in	mm		
J	34	9	−5	−47	1	−13	−20	−44	79	76	1.6	40	21	J
F	40	15	0	−41	5	−9	−18	−41	79	69	1.1	28	15	F
M	50	28	12	−30	10	−2	−11	−34	77	61	1.1	29	16	M
A	77	47	30	−7	25	9	−1	−22	61	50	1.0	26	10	A
M	85	62	42	13	29	17	5	−10	58	49	2.4	62	14	M
J	94	68	48	27	35	20	9	−3	60	53	2.9	73	16	J
J	94	75	55	38	35	24	13	3	71	61	3.5	89	14	J
A	86	68	50	32	30	20	10	0	69	57	2.6	67	13	A
S	80	57	42	25	27	14	6	−4	73	61	2.1	52	15	S
O	63	40	30	−3	17	4	−1	−20	79	72	2.4	60	21	O
N	49	28	18	−21	10	−2	−8	−29	83	80	2.0	51	20	N
D	40	16	3	−41	4	−9	−16	−41	79	77	1.7	43	19	D

	Temperature °F			Temperature °C				Relative humidity		Precipitation			
	Highest recorded	Average daily	Lowest recorded	Highest recorded	Average daily		Lowest recorded	0730 hours	1330 hours	Average monthly		Average no. days with 0.004 in + (0.1 mm +)	
		max.	min.			max.	min.		%	%	in	mm		
J	39	25	14	−19	4	−4	−10	−28	83	79	1.2	31	19	J
F	40	27	15	−19	5	−3	−10	−28	83	74	1.1	29	18	F
M	69	35	20	−9	21	2	−7	−23	85	69	1.1	27	16	M
A	75	50	34	12	24	10	1	−11	81	61	1.3	33	13	A
M	83	61	42	23	29	16	6	−5	77	59	1.7	44	13	M
J	90	69	49	30	32	21	9	−1	69	53	1.8	45	11	J
J	91	71	52	39	33	22	11	4	76	55	2.1	53	12	J
A	89	70	52	32	32	21	11	0	81	59	2.8	70	16	A
S	85	63	47	30	29	17	8	−1	84	64	2.5	64	17	S
O	74	52	40	19	23	11	4	−7	88	75	2.4	62	19	O
N	63	39	30	3	17	4	−1	−16	87	78	2.4	62	19	N
D	45	29	20	−17	7	−2	−7	−27	88	84	1.9	47	21	D

This area covers the Ukrainian and Moldavian Republics but excludes the Caucasus region. Although the winters are still cold here and spells of extremely cold weather occur when easterly winds blow from Siberia, the winter is shorter and the spring thaw comes earlier (see the table for **Kiev**). Towards the southeast, in the steppe region north of the Caucasus and west of the Caspian Sea, the climate becomes distinctly drier. **Astrakhan** (see table), where the Volga river enters the Caspian Sea, has almost a desert climate. This steppe is rather windswept and hot, dry winds in summer (the sukhovey) raise temperatures and bring very low humidity which harms crops. The opposite of this hot wind is the buran, a bitterly cold wind often associated with blizzards in winter.

Two small areas in the south are particularly favoured with mild winters: the south coast of the Crimean peninsula (see the table for **Simferopol**) and the eastern shores of the Black Sea (see the table for **Sochi**). These areas are sometimes called the Russian Riviera and are popular summer holiday resorts. Although the summer climate here is sunny, with ten or more hours of sunshine a day, rain falls all the year round and on the east coast of the Black Sea is particularly heavy.

Astrakhan 59 ft (18 m) 46°16′ N 48°02′ E 8 years **USSR**

	Temperature °F			Temperature °C			Relative humidity		Precipitation		
	Highest recorded	Average daily	Lowest recorded	Highest recorded	Average daily	Lowest recorded	0900 hours	1500 hours	Average monthly		Average no. days with 0.004 in + (0.1 mm +)
		max.	min.			max.	min.		%	%	in	mm	
J	55	28	15	−21	13	−2	−9	−29	87	75	0.6	16	11	J
F	58	31	15	−20	14	−1	−9	−29	84	68	0.4	11	8	F
M	65	43	27	−7	18	6	−3	−22	79	56	0.5	14	9	M
A	84	62	40	22	29	17	4	−6	52	35	0.5	14	5	A
M	93	78	53	33	34	25	12	0	45	31	0.6	16	5	M
J	100	83	61	43	38	29	16	6	51	37	0.8	19	6	J
J	102	88	65	52	39	31	18	11	48	35	0.4	10	4	J
A	102	86	62	43	39	30	17	6	51	37	1.0	25	5	A
S	92	75	53	33	33	24	11	1	60	40	0.9	22	5	S
O	79	60	40	16	26	16	5	−9	72	50	0.6	16	6	O
N	67	46	32	11	20	8	0	−12	85	69	0.6	16	9	N
D	51	34	23	−11	11	1	−5	−24	88	78	0.7	17	11	D

Kiev 587 ft (179 m) 50°24′ N 30°27′ E 8 years

		Temperature °F			Temperature °C				Relative humidity		Precipitation			
	Highest recorded	Average daily		Lowest recorded	Highest recorded	Average daily		Lowest recorded	0800 hours	1400 hours	Average monthly		Average no. days with 0.004 in + (0.1 mm +)	
		max.	min.			max.	min.		%	%	in	mm		
J	46	24	14	−13	8	−4	−10	−25	87	81	2.3	58	18	J
F	49	28	17	−8	9	−2	−8	−22	87	75	2.3	59	18	F
M	72	37	25	−13	22	3	−4	−25	86	69	2.0	51	16	M
A	81	56	41	21	27	14	5	−6	77	56	1.8	45	11	A
M	86	69	51	31	30	21	11	−1	69	50	1.9	49	13	M
J	93	75	56	39	34	24	14	4	71	51	2.2	55	11	J
J	94	77	59	48	34	25	15	9	73	53	3.6	91	13	J
A	94	76	58	38	35	24	14	3	78	55	3.6	91	12	A
S	85	68	50	35	30	20	10	2	80	54	1.2	30	8	S
O	79	56	42	23	26	13	6	−5	87	65	1.3	33	10	O
N	65	42	32	1	18	6	0	−17	92	82	2.2	56	15	N
D	51	30	22	−12	11	−1	−6	−24	89	84	2.3	59	19	D

USSR

Simferopol 673 ft (205 m) 45°01′ N 33°59′ E 8 years

		Temperature °F			Temperature °C				Relative humidity		Precipitation			
	Highest recorded	Average daily		Lowest recorded	Highest recorded	Average daily		Lowest recorded	0830 hours	1430 hours	Average monthly		Average no. days with 0.004 in + (0.1 mm +)	
		max.	min.			max.	min.		%	%	in	mm		
J	63	37	24	−3	17	3	−5	−20	87	79	1.8	46	15	J
F	69	40	26	−5	21	5	−3	−21	84	73	1.5	37	15	F
M	82	47	31	8	28	9	−1	−14	79	61	1.6	40	12	M
A	88	60	41	15	31	16	5	−9	67	49	1.1	28	9	A
M	89	71	50	34	32	22	10	1	62	47	1.5	38	9	M
J	94	78	57	44	34	25	14	7	64	47	1.4	35	9	J
J	94	82	60	50	35	28	16	10	63	45	2.5	64	8	J
A	98	82	60	39	37	28	15	4	64	42	1.5	39	6	A
S	97	74	53	38	36	23	12	3	70	46	1.4	36	7	S
O	85	63	44	23	30	17	7	−5	79	52	0.9	24	6	O
N	80	54	40	14	26	12	4	−10	86	71	1.7	43	13	N
D	70	44	32	1	21	7	0	−18	87	81	2.1	52	16	D

		Temperature °F				Temperature °C			Relative humidity		Precipitation		
	Highest recorded	Average daily		Lowest recorded	Highest recorded	Average daily		Lowest recorded	0830 hours	1430 hours	Average monthly		Average no. days with 0.004 in + (0.1 mm +)
		max.	min.			max.	min.		%	%	in	mm	
J	68	51	38	8	20	10	3	−13	71	68	7.9	201	17	J
F	69	51	39	10	21	10	4	−12	69	65	5.0	126	14	F
M	76	55	42	26	25	13	5	−3	73	68	5.1	130	15	M
A	84	61	48	28	29	16	9	−2	74	69	4.6	116	14	A
M	88	69	55	42	31	21	13	6	75	68	3.7	93	12	M
J	92	75	61	47	33	24	16	8	73	68	4.0	101	10	J
J	96	80	66	55	35	26	19	13	74	69	2.4	60	.7	J
A	96	80	66	56	35	27	19	13	72	68	4.0	101	9	A
S	90	76	62	48	32	25	16	9	69	63	4.2	106	9	S
O	84	68	53	26	29	20	12	−3	71	64	3.6	91	9	O
N	79	62	49	31	26	17	10	−1	69	63	5.6	143	12	N
D	73	56	43	19	23	13	6	−7	71	66	7.2	183	15	D

THE CAUCASUS MOUNTAINS AND TRANSCAUCASIA

This region comprises the three republics of Georgia, Armenia and Azerbaijan. Here the climate is almost tropical in summer and the winters are warmer than in the regions north of the Caucasus. Cold spells, however, do occur and low temperatures are frequent in winter, both on the high mountains and in the deep, enclosed valleys. The greater part of the region is mountainous but between the Caucasus mountains and the mountains of Armenia and Azerbaijan there are some wide valleys; there are also lowlands along the shores of the Caspian and Black Sea. Here conditions are milder in winter and quite hot in summer. The tables for **Tbilisi** and **Erivan** illustrate the range of conditions found here at different altitudes. The western part of this region is rather wet the year round, but the Caspian coast and some interior valleys are much drier.

	Temperature °F			Temperature °C				Relative humidity		Precipitation			
	Highest recorded	Average daily		Lowest recorded	Highest recorded	Average daily		Lowest recorded	0700 hours	1300 hours	Average monthly		Average no. days with 0.004 in + (0.1 mm +)	
		max.	min.			max.	min.		%	%	in	mm		
J	53	29	15	−16	12	−2	−9	−27	89	69	0.9	23	9	J
F	61	34	18	−13	16	1	−8	−25	87	64	1.0	25	8	F
M	80	50	30	0	27	10	−1	−18	81	56	1.1	28	7	M
A	84	66	42	26	29	19	6	−3	70	46	1.9	48	11	A
M	91	76	50	37	33	24	10	3	74	52	2.1	53	12	M
J	97	87	57	43	36	31	14	6	65	39	0.9	23	6	J
J	104	93	63	48	40	34	17	9	62	36	0.6	15	4	J
A	102	92	64	50	39	33	18	10	66	36	0.3	8	2	A
S	93	83	55	35	34	28	13	2	71	39	0.5	13	3	S
O	81	69	45	29	27	21	7	−2	84	47	0.9	23	5	O
N	68	50	34	11	20	10	1	−12	89	64	1.2	31	7	N
D	61	38	26	3	16	3	−3	−16	91	75	1.1	28	8	D

	Temperature °F			Temperature °C				Relative humidity		Precipitation			
	Highest recorded	Average daily		Lowest recorded	Highest recorded	Average daily		Lowest recorded	0900 hours	1500 hours	Average monthly		Average no. days with 0.004 in + (0.1 mm +)	
		max.	min.			max.	min.		%	%	in	mm		
J	67	45	30	9	20	7	−1	−13	79	60	0.7	17	6	J
F	72	47	31	5	22	9	0	−15	75	53	0.6	15	7	F
M	76	56	38	21	24	13	3	−6	69	50	1.1	27	8	M
A	84	63	46	25	29	17	8	−4	66	49	2.4	61	13	A
M	90	75	54	36	32	24	12	3	61	47	3.0	75	12	M
J	95	82	61	42	35	28	16	6	57	42	2.1	54	11	J
J	103	87	67	54	40	31	19	12	57	40	1.8	46	8	J
A	99	86	65	57	37	30	19	14	60	42	1.8	46	9	A
S	96	78	59	41	36	26	15	5	66	49	1.8	45	8	S
O	85	68	49	28	29	20	10	−2	71	53	1.2	30	7	O
N	73	57	41	25	23	14	5	−4	78	60	1.1	27	7	N
D	72	48	34	13	22	9	1	−11	80	65	0.8	19	7	D

This region – the steppe and desert of the Kazakh, Uzbek and Turkmen Republics – is the driest part of the Soviet Union and includes extensive deserts as well as semi-arid steppes. The summers are warm to hot but the heat is made more bearable by the low humidity. The winters are cold but generally dry and sunny over most of the region. **Krasnovodsk** on the Caspian shores (see the table) is unusually mild in winter compared with the rest of the region (see also the table for **Kazalinsk**). This is a result of the moderating influence of the Caspian Sea which never freezes.

Kazalinsk 207 ft (63 m) 45°46′ N 62°06′ E 10 years　　　　　　　　　　　　　　　　　　　　　　**USSR**

	Temperature °F			Temperature °C				Relative humidity		Precipitation			
	Highest recorded	Average daily		Lowest recorded	Highest recorded	Average daily		Lowest recorded	0700 hours	1300 hours	Average monthly		Average no. days with 0.004 in +	
		max.	min.			max.	min.		%	%	in	mm	(0.1 mm +)	
J	41	16	5	−27	5	−9	−15	−33	88	80	0.4	10	7	J
F	51	21	5	−26	11	−6	−15	−32	88	75	0.4	10	5	F
M	73	35	17	−22	23	2	−8	−30	88	68	0.5	13	4	M
A	87	58	27	11	31	14	−3	−12	74	48	0.5	13	4	A
M	102	76	52	27	39	24	11	−3	59	37	0.6	15	4	M
J	108	86	61	45	42	30	16	7	58	37	0.2	5	2	J
J	106	90	65	50	41	32	18	10	59	34	0.2	5	2	J
A	106	85	61	47	41	29	16	8	63	37	0.3	8	2	A
S	98	74	49	36	37	23	9	2	70	41	0.3	8	2	S
O	85	57	35	13	29	14	2	−11	79	48	0.4	10	3	O
N	67	37	23	13	19	3	−5	−11	90	72	0.5	13	5	N
D	53	24	15	−23	12	−4	−9	−31	91	80	0.6	15	6	D

	Temperature °F			Temperature °C				Relative humidity		Precipitation			
	Highest recorded	Average daily		Lowest recorded	Highest recorded	Average daily		Lowest recorded	0700 hours	1300 hours	Average monthly		Average no. days with 0.004 in + (0.1 mm +)	
		max.	min.			max.	min.		%	%	in	mm		
J	61	38	32	1	16	3	0	−17	77	69	0.5	13	5	J
F	66	42	35	8	19	6	2	−13	75	66	0.5	13	4	F
M	79	51	40	14	26	11	4	−10	73	62	0.7	18	6	M
A	83	61	49	29	28	16	9	−2	70	56	0.9	23	5	A
M	96	75	61	46	36	24	16	8	60	48	0.4	10	3	M
J	104	84	70	50	40	29	21	10	58	45	0.4	10	1	J
J	108	90	76	53	42	32	24	12	55	42	0.2	5	1	J
A	103	89	75	57	39	32	24	14	52	41	0.2	5	1	A
S	98	80	66	45	37	27	19	7	56	45	0.2	5	1	S
O	85	67	55	33	29	19	13	1	61	51	0.4	10	2	O
N	75	54	44	8	24	12	7	−13	69	60	0.5	13	4	N
D	65	46	38	8	18	8	3	−13	76	68	0.5	13	6	D

THE MOUNTAINS OF SOVIET CENTRAL ASIA

The Kirghiz and Tadzhik Republics and part of eastern Kazakhstan is a mountainous region on the borders of Afghanistan and China. It includes the highest peaks within the Soviet Union, some of which rise to over 20,000 ft (6000 m). These mountains carry snow the year round. However, because of the distance from the sea and the shelter of the Pamir and Himalayan ranges to the south and southeast, it is a rather dry region considering its height. Winters are cold but spring comes earlier than farther north. The tables for **Alma Ata** and **Tashkent** illustrate conditions in the valleys of this region.

Alma Ata 2543 ft (775 m) 43°16′ N 76°53′ E 19 years   USSR

	Temperature °F			Temperature °C			Relative humidity		Precipitation		
Highest recorded	Average daily		Lowest recorded	Highest recorded	Average daily		Lowest recorded	0700 hours	1300 hours	Average monthly		Average no. days with 0.004 in + (0.1 mm +)
	max.	min.			max.	min.		%	%	in	mm	
J	53	23	7	−30	12	−5	−14	−34	87	72	1.3	33	9	J
F	57	26	9	−25	14	−3	−13	−32	86	69	0.9	23	6	F
M	76	39	22	−18	24	4	−6	−28	85	66	2.2	56	10	M
A	84	56	38	13	29	13	3	−11	72	53	4.0	102	12	A
M	96	68	50	31	36	20	10	−1	66	49	3.7	94	11	M
J	100	76	57	39	38	24	14	4	66	48	2.6	66	10	J
J	100	81	60	45	38	27	16	7	65	43	1.4	36	9	J
A	98	80	57	39	37	27	14	4	66	39	1.2	31	6	A
S	94	71	47	27	34	22	8	−3	72	39	1.0	25	4	S
O	85	55	35	2	29	13	2	−17	80	49	2.0	51	7	O
N	74	39	23	−17	23	4	−5	−27	85	67	1.9	48	8	N
D	59	29	15	−25	15	−2	−9	−32	86	72	1.3	33	7	D

Tashkent 1569 ft (478 m) 41°20′ N 69°18′ E 19 years   USSR

	Temperature °F			Temperature °C			Relative humidity		Precipitation		
Highest recorded	Average daily		Lowest recorded	Highest recorded	Average daily		Lowest recorded	0700 hours	1300 hours	Average monthly		Average no. days with 0.004 in + (0.1 mm +)
	max.	min.			max.	min.		%	%	in	mm	
J	66	37	21	−19	19	3	−6	−28	82	63	2.1	53	10	J
F	76	44	27	−14	24	7	−3	−26	78	58	1.1	28	8	F
M	86	53	37	−3	30	12	3	−19	77	55	2.6	66	12	M
A	91	65	47	23	33	18	8	−5	72	52	2.3	58	10	A
M	103	78	56	33	39	26	13	1	66	42	1.4	36	7	M
J	106	87	62	43	41	31	17	6	59	34	0.5	13	4	J
J	106	92	64	48	41	33	18	9	63	33	0.2	5	1	J
A	102	89	60	46	39	32	16	8	61	32	0.1	3	1	A
S	96	80	52	33	36	27	11	1	66	34	0.1	3	1	S
O	95	65	41	21	35	18	5	−6	76	43	1.2	31	5	O
N	81	53	35	−7	27	12	2	−22	79	55	1.5	38	7	N
D	72	44	29	−12	22	7	−2	−24	79	62	1.6	41	9	D

SIBERIA

This region extends from the Urals to the Pacific Ocean in the east, and from the Arctic Ocean to the southern borders of the USSR with China and Mongolia, east of the central Asian region. Western Siberia is mostly low-lying and generally flat. Towards the east and north-east, however, the country becomes more mountainous with deeper valleys. It is still a remote and sparsely populated region north of the band of settlement along the Trans-Siberian railway. There are few significant differences of weather and climate within this vast territory.

Winters are everywhere very cold and prolonged, but the short summers can be quite warm and pleasant by day once the winter snow has melted. Summers become shorter northwards but even as far north as **Verkhoy-ansk** (see the table) the brief summer has some very warm days. **Verkhoyansk** has the reputation of being one of the coldest spots on earth and of having the largest difference between summer and winter tempera-tures. The tables for **Sverdlovsk**, **Tomsk** and **Irkutsk**, places all in approximately the same latitude in central Siberia, show the similarity of temperatures from west to east. The winter precipitation is quite light and all of it falls as snow. Summer is everywhere the wettest season.

The table for **Vladivostock** illustrates the rather different climate and weather experienced in a narrow strip along the coast of the Pacific. Winters are still cold and harbours freeze. This is because the dominant winter wind is from the west or northwest and brings very cold Siberian air to the coast. In summer there is a reversal of wind direction as the east Asian summer monsoon brings warm moist winds off the Pacific so the coastal regions are comparatively wet at this time.

USSR Irkutsk 1532 ft (467 m) 52°16′ N 104°19′ E 10 years

	Temperature °F				Temperature °C				Relative humidity		Precipitation			
	Highest recorded	Average daily		Lowest recorded	Highest recorded	Average daily		Lowest recorded	0700 hours	1300 hours	Average monthly		Average no. days with 0.04 in + (1 mm +)	
		max.	min.			max.	min.		%	%	in	mm		
J	36	3	−15	−58	2	−16	−26	−50	84	75	0.5	13	3	J
F	41	10	−13	−47	5	−12	−25	−44	85	63	0.4	10	3	F
M	58	25	2	−34	14	−4	−17	−37	85	53	0.3	8	2	M
A	85	42	20	−24	29	6	−7	−31	75	43	0.6	15	4	A
M	88	56	33	6	31	13	1	14	67	40	1.3	33	8	M
J	95	68	44	24	35	20	7	4	73	47	2.2	56	7	J
J	98	70	50	33	37	21	10	1	83	56	3.1	79	9	J
A	92	68	48	27	33	20	9	−3	87	59	2.8	71	11	A
S	84	57	35	14	29	14	2	−10	89	54	1.7	43	8	S
O	73	41	21	−23	23	5	−6	−31	88	56	0.7	18	6	O
N	56	20	2	−39	13	−7	−17	−39	89	71	0.6	15	4	N
D	37	4	−12	−51	3	−16	−24	−46	88	85	0.6	15	4	D

	Temperature °F				Temperature °C				Relative humidity		Precipitation			
	Highest recorded	Average daily		Lowest recorded	Highest recorded	Average daily		Lowest recorded	0700 hours	1300 hours	Average monthly		Average no. days with 0.004 in + (0.1 mm +)	
		max.	min.			max.	min.		%	%	in	mm		
J	40	6	−5	−45	4	−14	−21	−43	84	79	0.5	13	12	J
F	38	14	1	−44	3	−10	−17	−42	85	72	0.4	10	8	F
M	58	25	10	−35	14	−4	−12	−37	86	63	0.5	13	8	M
A	73	42	26	−5	23	6	−3	−21	77	49	0.7	18	7	A
M	88	57	39	17	31	14	4	−8	70	47	1.9	48	13	M
J	90	65	49	28	32	18	9	−2	74	51	2.7	69	14	J
J	94	70	54	37	34	21	12	3	79	55	2.6	66	14	J
A	89	65	50	30	32	18	10	−1	85	59	2.7	69	15	A
S	86	54	41	18	30	12	5	−8	87	61	1.6	41	14	S
O	69	37	28	−6	21	3	−2	−21	86	69	1.2	31	13	O
N	50	20	11	−39	10	−7	−12	−39	86	78	1.1	28	14	N
D	39	10	0	−45	4	−12	−18	−43	86	82	0.8	20	14	D

	Temperature °F				Temperature °C				Relative humidity		Precipitation			
	Highest recorded	Average daily		Lowest recorded	Highest recorded	Average daily		Lowest recorded	0700 hours	1300 hours	Average monthly		Average no. days with 0.004 in + (0.1 mm +)	
		max.	min.			max.	min.		%	%	in	mm		
J	36	0	−12	−58	2	−18	−24	−50	82	78	1.1	28	20	J
F	40	8	−7	−52	4	−13	−22	−47	83	70	0.7	18	14	F
M	49	22	2	−44	9	−6	−17	−42	83	61	0.8	20	13	M
A	76	38	20	−17	24	3	−7	−27	79	55	0.9	23	11	A
M	84	54	37	1	29	12	3	−17	70	50	1.6	41	14	M
J	95	67	48	28	35	19	9	−2	76	55	2.7	69	15	J
J	96	73	54	35	36	23	12	2	83	58	2.6	66	13	J
A	89	68	50	29	32	20	10	−2	88	62	2.6	66	15	A
S	83	57	40	21	28	14	4	−6	89	61	1.6	41	13	S
O	72	37	27	−20	22	3	−3	−29	87	70	2.0	51	18	O
N	47	15	6	−53	8	−9	−14	−47	85	77	1.8	46	20	N
D	37	4	−7	−57	3	−16	−22	−49	84	81	1.5	38	22	D

	Temperature °F			Temperature °C			Relative humidity		Precipitation			
	Highest recorded	Average daily	Lowest recorded	Highest recorded	Average daily	Lowest recorded	0700 hours	1300 hours	Average monthly		Average no. days with 0.004 in + (0.1 mm +)	
		max.	min.			max.	min.		%	%	in	mm	
J	2	−54	−63	−89	−17	−48	−53	−67	70	70	0.2	5	8	J
F	14	−41	−56	−90	−10	−41	−49	−68	71	69	0.2	5	7	F
M	38	−13	−39	−77	3	−25	−39	−60	74	60	0.1	3	4	M
A	52	19	−10	−66	11	−7	−23	−54	74	50	0.2	5	4	A
M	79	42	23	−19	26	6	−5	−28	63	47	0.3	8	5	M
J	94	60	48	19	34	16	9	−7	62	45	0.9	23	7	J
J	98	66	47	29	37	19	8	−2	72	49	1.1	28	8	J
A	92	58	40	18	33	14	4	−8	79	54	1.0	25	8	A
S	77	43	27	2	25	6	−3	−17	87	61	0.5	13	7	S
O	55	12	−3	−48	13	−11	−19	−44	84	70	0.3	8	7	O
N	34	−31	−40	−70	1	−35	−40	−57	79	78	0.3	8	8	N
D	13	−52	−56	−84	−11	−47	−49	−64	75	75	0.2	5	8	D

	Temperature °F			Temperature °C			Relative humidity		Precipitation			
	Highest recorded	Average daily	Lowest recorded	Highest recorded	Average daily	Lowest recorded	0700 hours	1300 hours	Average monthly		Average no. days with 0.04 in + (1 mm +)	
		max.	min.			max.	min.		%	%	in	mm	
J	37	13	0	−22	3	−11	−18	−30	71	58	0.3	8	2	J
F	46	22	6	−20	8	−6	−14	−29	72	55	0.4	10	2	F
M	56	33	19	−7	13	1	−7	−22	75	56	0.7	18	4	M
A	66	46	34	17	19	8	1	−8	80	59	1.2	31	5	A
M	74	55	43	31	23	13	6	−1	83	65	2.1	53	8	M
J	88	63	52	39	31	17	11	4	90	76	2.9	74	10	J
J	92	71	60	47	33	22	16	8	91	79	3.3	84	10	J
A	90	75	64	50	32	24	18	10	90	74	4.7	119	9	A
S	84	68	55	39	29	20	13	4	85	64	4.3	109	7	S
O	73	55	41	17	23	13	5	−8	76	53	1.9	48	5	O
N	63	36	24	0	17	2	−4	−18	71	55	1.2	31	4	N
D	51	20	8	−15	11	−7	−13	−26	71	56	0.6	15	3	D

Yugoslavia has a varied geography and climate. The area best known and visited by tourists, the Dalmatian coast, is scenically attractive and consists of a mountain-backed coastal strip with numerous offshore islands in the Adriatic Sea. The climate here is Mediterranean with mild winters and hot, sunny summers (see the table for **Dubrovnik**). Sunshine averages about four hours a day in winter to as much as twelve in summer. The summers are not rainless for the fine weather is interrupted by occasional heavy thunderstorms. The frequency of these storms increases from south to north.

The one unpleasant feature of the winter climate is the bora, a strong and gusty north or northeast wind, which brings cold air from central Europe down to the coast for a few days at a time. Autumn and winter rainfall on the coast is quite heavy and the Dinaric Alps, south of **Dubrovnik**, are one of the wettest areas in Europe in winter. The rain does not fall on an excessively large number of days, however.

Inland, across the western ranges of the Dinaric Alps, Yugoslavia is a country of moderately high mountains, averaging from 4000 to 6000 ft (1200 to 1800 m). The height decreases eastwards, and along the border with Hungary and Rumania the country is low-lying and forms part of the Danube valley and Hungarian plain. In the extreme north Yugoslavia includes a small part of the eastern Alps. Here the weather and climate are similar to that found in southern Austria (see p. 338 and the table for **Ljubljana**). In the south of the country in Macedonia and Montenegro the weather and climate show traces of Mediterranean influence and conditions are similar to those found in northern Greece and Albania.

Despite these considerable differences of relief, there is a broad similarity in the weather and climate over much of the interior of Yugoslavia. Winters are rather cold with frequent snow which lies for long periods in the mountains. Summers are warm, becoming quite hot in the south. Although summer is the wettest season, there is much fine weather and abundant sunshine. The tables for **Belgrade** and **Skopje** are typical of conditions inland. They illustrate the rather warmer summers in the south and the tendency for summers to be drier here. The similarity of winter conditions from north to south is shown by a comparison of the monthly temperatures for **Ljubljana** and **Skopje**. Daily hours of sunshine over most of interior Yugoslavia range from two to three in winter to nine or ten in summer.

Belgrade 433 ft (132 m) 44°48′ N 20°28′ E 30 years

	Temperature °F			Temperature °C				Relative humidity		Precipitation		
	Highest recorded	Average daily		Lowest recorded	Highest recorded	Average daily		Lowest recorded	0730 hours	1430 hours	Average monthly		Average no. days with 0.004 in + (0.1 mm +)
		max.	min.			max.	min.		%	%	in	mm	
J	68	37	26	−12	20	3	−3	−25	85	75	1.9	47	14	J
F	70	42	29	−5	21	5	−2	−21	83	67	1.8	46	13	F
M	86	52	36	8	30	11	2	−14	77	56	1.8	46	12	M
A	87	64	45	21	31	18	7	−6	72	49	2.1	54	13	A
M	94	73	54	29	34	23	12	−1	73	51	2.9	74	14	M
J	98	79	59	43	37	26	15	6	74	51	3.8	96	13	J
J	103	83	62	47	39	28	17	8	71	47	2.4	61	9	J
A	103	83	62	46	39	28	17	8	73	46	2.2	55	9	A
S	107	76	56	35	42	24	13	2	76	47	2.0	50	8	S
O	94	64	47	20	35	18	8	−7	82	58	2.2	55	11	O
N	74	51	39	17	23	11	4	−8	85	71	2.4	61	14	N
D	70	42	32	−3	21	5	0	−19	85	76	2.2	55	14	D

YUGOSLAVIA — Dubrovnik 161 ft (49 m) 42°39′ N 18°06′ E 19 years

	Temperature °F				Temperature °C				Relative humidity		Precipitation			
	Highest recorded	Average daily		Lowest recorded	Highest recorded	Average daily		Lowest recorded	0700 hours	1400 hours	Average monthly		Average no. days with 0.004 in + (0.1 mm +)	
		max.	min.			max.	min.		%	%	in	mm		
J	66	53	42	19	19	12	6	−7	63	59	5.5	139	13	J
F	69	55	43	24	21	13	6	−5	65	63	4.9	125	13	F
M	73	58	47	29	23	14	8	−2	64	63	4.1	104	11	M
A	80	63	52	37	26	17	11	3	67	66	4.1	104	10	A
M	84	70	58	44	29	21	14	6	69	69	3.0	75	10	M
J	93	78	65	52	34	25	18	11	64	66	1.9	48	6	J
J	99	83	69	58	37	29	21	15	67	61	1.0	26	4	J
A	98	82	69	52	37	28	21	11	57	61	1.5	38	3	A
S	94	77	64	49	34	25	18	9	63	63	4.0	101	7	S
O	82	69	57	42	28	21	14	6	64	63	6.4	162	11	O
N	76	62	51	27	24	17	10	−3	67	65	7.8	198	16	N
D	67	56	46	26	19	14	8	−4	67	65	7.0	178	15	D

YUGOSLAVIA — Ljubljana 981 ft (299 m) 46°04′ N 14°31′ E 17 years

	Temperature °F				Temperature °C				Relative humidity		Precipitation			
	Highest recorded	Average daily		Lowest recorded	Highest recorded	Average daily		Lowest recorded	0700 hours	1400 hours	Average monthly		Average no. days with 0.004 in + (0.1 mm +)	
		max.	min.			max.	min.		%	%	in	mm		
J	57	36	25	−16	14	2	−4	−27	91	81	3.5	88	13	J
F	66	41	25	−18	19	5	−4	−28	90	70	3.5	89	11	F
M	73	50	32	4	23	10	0	−16	88	60	3.0	76	11	M
A	85	60	40	22	30	15	4	−5	87	56	3.9	98	13	A
M	88	68	48	27	31	20	9	−3	88	56	4.8	121	16	M
J	100	75	54	39	38	24	12	4	87	56	5.2	133	16	J
J	102	80	57	45	39	27	14	7	89	54	4.5	113	12	J
A	95	78	57	40	35	26	14	4	93	55	5.0	127	12	A
S	88	71	51	35	31	22	11	1	95	62	5.6	142	10	S
O	80	59	43	28	27	15	6	−2	95	70	5.9	151	14	O
N	68	47	36	13	20	8	2	−11	93	80	5.2	131	15	N
D	60	39	30	6	16	4	−1	−15	93	86	4.5	114	15	D

	Temperature °F				Temperature °C				Relative humidity		Precipitation			
	Highest recorded	Average daily		Lowest recorded	Highest recorded	Average daily		Lowest recorded	0730 hours	1430 hours	Average monthly		Average no. days with 0.004 in + (0.1 mm +)	
		max.	min.			max.	min.		%	%	in	mm		
J	67	40	27	−6	20	5	−3	−21	91	76	1.5	39	11	J
F	75	47	28	−8	24	8	−3	−22	90	65	1.3	32	8	F
M	94	53	33	−2	34	12	1	−19	88	58	1.5	37	9	M
A	85	67	42	26	30	19	5	−3	81	48	1.5	38	8	A
M	96	74	50	29	36	23	10	−2	80	52	2.1	54	12	M
J	102	82	56	42	39	28	13	6	75	47	1.9	47	8	J
J	105	87	59	44	41	31	15	7	70	42	1.1	29	7	J
A	105	88	58	40	41	31	14	4	72	39	1.1	28	4	A
S	98	79	52	33	37	26	11	1	84	46	1.4	35	7	S
O	92	65	43	25	34	19	6	−4	93	59	2.4	61	9	O
N	70	53	37	12	21	12	3	−11	94	72	2.2	55	12	N
D	70	45	30	1	21	7	−1	−17	94	76	2.1	53	9	D

Oceanic Islands

ASCENSION ISLAND

Ascension Island is situated in latitude 8° S in the middle of the South Atlantic. It is remote and has no regular commercial air or steamer service. The climate is tropical although the island has a low annual rainfall for a tropical island.

Ascension amounts to a mere 34 square miles (88 sq. km) and consists of a single mountain rising to 2870 ft (875 m). Temperatures are warm to hot around the year. The ocean moderates the heat, however, and this dry, sunny and warm climate is healthy and pleasant around the year.

THE AZORES

The Azores consist of a group of ten main islands situated about 800 miles (1300 km) west of Portugal. The islands are an integral part of Portugal, having been discovered and settled by the Portuguese in the fifteenth century. The land area of the Azores is rather less than that of the state of Rhode Island. All the islands are hilly or mountainous, with peaks rising to between 2000 and 7500 ft (600 and 2300 m).

The Azores have a very mild climate throughout the year with no great extremes of temperature. Summer days are warm but never really hot and in winter cold weather with frost and snow is unknown at sea level.

Winter weather can be stormy and changeable when deep Atlantic depressions track across or near the islands. Summer is generally a more settled season but occasional storms and wet weather can occur.

Sunshine amounts are only moderate for the latitude and range from an average of three to four hours a day in winter to seven to eight in summer. Rainfall is well distributed around the year but is heavier and more frequent in winter.

The table for **Angra do Heroismo** is representative of conditions at or near sea level.

Georgetown 55 ft (17 m) 7°56′ S 14°25′ W 29 years   **ASCENSION ISLAND**

	Temperature °F			Temperature °C			Relative humidity		Precipitation			
	Highest recorded	Average daily	Lowest recorded	Highest recorded	Average daily	Lowest recorded	0800 hours	2000 hours	Average monthly		Average no. days with 0.04 in + (1 mm +)	
		max.	min.			max.	min.		%	%	in	mm	
J	89	85	73	67	32	29	23	19	68	73	0.2	5	2	J
F	91	87	74	67	33	31	23	19	67	70	0.4	10	2	F
M	94	88	75	67	34	31	24	19	67	71	0.7	18	3	M
A	95	88	75	67	35	31	24	19	67	72	1.1	28	4	A
M	92	87	74	67	33	31	23	19	66	69	0.5	13	3	M
J	90	85	73	65	32	29	23	18	65	70	0.5	13	3	J
J	89	84	72	67	32	29	22	19	65	70	0.5	13	3	J
A	88	83	71	65	31	28	22	18	66	69	0.4	10	3	A
S	88	82	71	66	31	28	22	19	67	71	0.3	8	2	S
O	88	83	71	65	31	28	22	18	66	71	0.3	8	3	O
N	88	83	71	66	31	28	22	19	66	71	0.2	5	1	N
D	89	84	72	67	32	29	22	19	67	71	0.1	3	1	D

Angra do Heroismo 296 ft (90 m) 38°39′ N 27°14′ W 20 years   **THE AZORES**

	Temperature °F			Temperature °C			Relative humidity		Precipitation			
	Highest recorded	Average daily	Lowest recorded	Highest recorded	Average daily	Lowest recorded	1000 hours	1600 hours	Average monthly		Average no. days with 0.004 in + (0.1 mm +)	
		max.	min.			max.	min.		%	%	in	mm	
J	66	61	53	39	19	16	12	4	79	80	5.6	143	21	J
F	66	60	53	39	19	16	12	4	79	80	5.2	131	19	F
M	67	60	53	40	20	16	12	4	78	79	5.9	150	21	M
A	70	62	54	43	21	17	12	6	76	77	3.0	77	14	A
M	75	65	56	47	24	18	14	8	76	76	2.8	70	14	M
J	77	70	61	52	25	21	16	11	77	77	1.9	49	11	J
J	82	74	64	54	28	23	18	12	74	74	1.7	43	9	J
A	83	76	66	59	28	24	19	15	73	73	1.7	44	11	A
S	82	74	64	57	28	23	18	14	74	75	3.9	98	13	S
O	76	69	61	50	25	21	16	10	75	77	5.0	126	18	O
N	73	65	58	46	23	18	14	8	75	78	5.6	143	19	N
D	69	62	55	41	21	17	13	5	78	80	4.4	112	18	D

BERMUDA

The island of Bermuda, an area of only 20 square miles (52 sq. km), lies in the North Atlantic in latitude 32° N at a distance of 700 miles (1125 km) from New York. It has a subtropical climate much influenced by the warmth of the North Atlantic waters, for it is fully in the path of the warm Gulf Stream. Summers are warm to hot and the winters mild with occasional warm, sunny days.

An abundant rainfall is well distributed throughout the year but falls on fewer days than in drier places in North America or Britain. Bermuda has a sunny climate with daily sunshine hours ranging from five to six in winter to nine or ten in summer and is a popular tourist spot for visitors from North America. The main island, and a series of smaller ones which are all part of a coral reef, are low-lying, with no land higher than 250 ft (75 m). The table for **Hamilton** is representative of the island.

Bermuda is occasionally affected by hurricanes which have moved north from the Caribbean, but these violent tropical storms are usually in the decaying stage by the time they reach this latitude.

CANARY ISLANDS

The Canaries form an archipelago of seven main islands, situated in about latitude 28° N, some 60 miles (100 km) off the coast of North Africa. They are rugged volcanic islands with the highest peak, on the island of Tenerife, rising to 12,200 ft (3700 m). This high mountain is snow-capped around the year, in marked contrast to the mild temperatures experienced at or near sea level in winter. The waters of the Atlantic Ocean are here rather cool because of the cold Canaries current; thus, summer temperatures rarely rise very high, while the winters are mild.

The warmest days in summer occur when hot, dry air is drawn out from the Sahara desert and reaches as far as the islands. This air may sometimes be dust-laden with fine particles blown from the desert. This air, however, reaches the islands with a raised relative humidity and lower temperatures after its passage across the cool ocean water. The weather may be disturbed for a few days at a time in winter under the influence of an Atlantic depression but such stormy and wet periods are not frequent. Some fog and cloud may occur in the summer months which are usually dry and sunny with no very hot days. The northern shores of the islands, being more exposed to the predominant northeast trade winds, are rather wetter than the sheltered southern coasts. Daily sunshine hours range from an average of six in winter to as many as eleven in the summer months.

Administratively the islands are an integral part of Spain, having been occupied by Spain in the fifteenth century. The table for **Las Palmas** is representative of conditions at or near sea level.

Hamilton 151 ft (46 m) 32°17′ N 64°46′ W 57 years   **BERMUDA**

		Temperature °F				Temperature °C			Relative humidity		Precipitation			
	Highest recorded	Average daily		Lowest recorded	Highest recorded	Average daily		Lowest recorded	0730 hours	1430 hours	Average monthly		Average no. days with 0.04 in + (1 mm +)	
		max.	min.			max.	min.		%	%	in	mm		
J	81	68	58	41	27	20	14	5	78	70	4.4	112	14	J
F	81	68	57	40	27	20	14	4	76	69	4.7	119	13	F
M	84	68	57	41	29	20	14	5	77	69	4.8	122	12	M
A	87	71	59	42	31	22	15	6	78	70	4.1	104	9	A
M	88	76	64	49	31	24	18	9	81	75	4.6	117	9	M
J	92	81	69	58	33	27	21	14	82	74	4.4	112	9	J
J	98	85	73	62	37	29	23	17	81	73	4.5	114	10	J
A	99	86	74	62	37	30	23	17	79	69	5.4	137	13	A
S	98	84	72	59	37	29	22	15	81	73	5.2	132	10	S
O	92	79	69	53	33	26	21	12	79	72	5.8	147	12	O
N	87	74	63	49	31	23	17	9	76	70	5.0	127	13	N
D	81	70	60	45	27	21	16	7	77	70	4.7	119	15	D

Las Palmas 20 ft (6 m) 28°11′ N 15°28′ W 45 years   **CANARY ISLANDS**

		Temperature °F				Temperature °C			Relative humidity		Precipitation			
	Highest recorded	Average daily		Lowest recorded	Highest recorded	Average daily		Lowest recorded	0800 hours	1500 hours	Average monthly		Average no. days with 0.004 in + (0.1 mm +)	
		max.	min.			max.	min.		%	%	in	mm		
J	86	70	58	46	30	21	14	8	72	71	1.4	36	8	J
F	84	71	58	47	29	22	14	8	74	72	0.9	23	5	F
M	86	71	59	47	30	22	15	8	73	72	0.9	23	5	M
A	91	71	61	50	33	22	16	10	73	72	0.5	13	3	A
M	88	73	62	54	31	23	17	12	72	72	0.2	5	1	M
J	89	75	65	58	32	24	18	14	73	74	0	0	0.9	J
J	95	77	67	60	35	25	19	16	77	76	0	0	0.8	J
A	99	79	70	62	37	26	21	17	75	76	0	0	0.8	A
S	96	79	69	59	36	26	21	15	75	75	0.2	56	1	S
O	95	79	67	56	35	26	19	13	75	74	1.1	28	5	O
N	88	76	64	52	31	24	18	11	74	74	2.1	53	7	N
D	85	72	60	47	29	22	16	8	73	73	1.6	41	8	D

CAPE VERDE ISLANDS

The Cape Verdes consist of a group of ten main islands and a number of smaller islets with a total land area of 1560 square miles (4040 sq. km). They are situated between 14° to 16° N about 300 miles (480 km) off the west coast of Africa. The islands are volcanic and hilly. They have a rather low and unreliable rainfall, being at the northern limit of the tropical rain belt. Most of the rain falls between August and October. The rainfall is very low at sea level but increases in the hills.

The temperature is typically tropical with no cool season, although there is a small range of temperature around the year; the coolest months are December to March. The combination of moderately high temperature and a high humidity can be unpleasant except when this is tempered by the daily sea breeze. Daily hours of sunshine average from seven to ten and are highest in the months February to June. There is rather more cloud during the rainier months.

FALKLAND ISLANDS

The Falklands consist of two main islands with a number of smaller islands, most of which are uninhabited. They are situated between 51° and 52° S, some 400 miles from the coast of South America. The total land area of the islands is about half as large as Wales, or the size of the state of Connecticut. The islands have a number of hills or low mountains, rising to between 1500 and 2000 ft (450 and 600 m), but much of the area is low-lying.

The weather and climate of the Falklands are similar to those of the Hebrides or Shetland Islands, but with a longer and slightly more severe winter. The Falklands are situated in the very stormy latitudes of the southern westerly winds or 'Roaring Forties' and gales are very frequent, particularly during the winter months. The weather is very changeable throughout the year with much cloud and rain but the total annual rainfall is not large.

The number of days with rain is similar to that in Britain and the number of days with snow is rather greater than that in the Shetland Islands. Sleet and snow are frequent in the winter months but the snow does not lie very deep or very long since the weather is so frequently changing. The summers are cool and during the brief, fine, settled spells temperatures never rise very high.

The average number of hours of sunshine a day ranges from two to three in winter to about six in summer.

The table for **Stanley** is representative of conditions at or near sea level.

Porto da Praia 112 ft (35 m) 14°54′ N 23°31′ W 25 years   **CAPE VERDE ISLANDS**

	Temperature °F				Temperature °C				Relative humidity		Precipitation			
	Highest recorded	Average daily		Lowest recorded	Highest recorded	Average daily		Lowest recorded	0930 hours	1530 hours	Average monthly		Average no. days with 0.04 in + (1 mm +)	
		max.	min.			max.	min.		%	%	in	mm		
J	86	77	68	63	30	25	20	17	63	59	0.1	3	0.9	J
F	87	77	67	56	31	25	19	13	59	57	0	0	0.3	F
M	91	78	68	62	33	26	20	17	58	55	0	0	0.1	M
A	93	79	69	64	34	26	21	18	58	54	0	0	0	A
M	92	81	70	65	33	27	21	18	59	55	0	0	0	M
J	93	82	72	67	34	28	22	19	62	59	0	0	0	J
J	91	83	75	66	33	28	24	19	68	66	0.2	5	0.5	J
A	90	84	76	72	32	29	24	22	73	71	3.8	97	8	A
S	94	84	77	72	34	29	25	22	74	73	4.5	114	7	S
O	91	85	76	72	33	29	24	22	69	65	1.2	31	3	O
N	90	82	74	68	32	28	23	20	64	63	0.3	8	0.9	N
D	87	79	71	64	31	26	22	18	63	62	0.1	3	0.5	D

Stanley 6 ft (2 m) 51°42′ S 57°51′ W 25 years   **FALKLAND ISLANDS**

	Temperature °F				Temperature °C				Relative humidity	Precipitation			
	Highest recorded	Average daily		Lowest recorded	Highest recorded	Average daily		Lowest recorded	0900 hours	Average monthly		Average no. days with 0.04 in + (1 mm +)	
		max.	min.			max.	min.		%	in	mm		
J	76	56	42	30	24	13	6	−1	78	2.8	71	17	J
F	74	55	41	30	23	13	5	−1	79	2.3	58	12	F
M	70	53	40	27	21	12	4	−3	82	2.5	64	15	M
A	63	49	37	21	17	9	3	−6	86	2.6	66	14	A
M	58	44	34	20	14	7	1	−7	88	2.6	66	15	M
J	51	41	31	12	11	5	−1	−11	89	2.1	53	13	J
J	50	40	31	16	10	4	−1	−9	89	2.0	51	13	J
A	52	41	31	12	11	5	−1	−11	87	2.0	51	13	A
S	59	45	33	13	15	7	1	−11	84	1.5	38	12	S
O	64	48	35	22	18	9	2	−6	80	1.6	41	11	O
N	71	52	37	26	22	11	3	−3	75	2.0	51	12	N
D	71	54	39	29	22	12	4	−2	77	2.8	71	15	D

GALAPAGOS ISLANDS

This island group lies almost on the equator about 650 miles (1050 km) west of the coast of Ecuador. There are some fifteen larger, and hundreds of smaller, islands with a total area of about 3000 square miles (7770 sq. km). They are famous for their unusual flora and fauna and are now a nature reserve.

The islands have an unusual climate in view of their proximity to the equator; rainfall is low and temperatures are lower than would be expected. There are no extremes of heat or cold. This is a consequence of their location in the Pacific Ocean where the cooler waters of the Humboldt current have a marked effect on the weather (see pp. 181 and 198 for Chile and Peru respectively). Although there is more rain on the larger islands which are hilly, as the table for **Seymour Island** shows, rainfall is low at sea level and comes in the period January to April. Light drizzle and even fog, however, are not uncommon at other times of the year.

GRAHAM LAND

The continent of Antarctica is twice the size of the United States and is the largest area in the world with a permanent ice cap. Glaciers covered with snow extend to the coast which is fringed by large areas of pack and drift ice. Only the highest mountains in the interior project through this vast thickness of ice.

The table for **Stonington Island**, just within the Antarctic Circle off the peninsula of Graham Land, illustrates temperature conditions on the fringes of the continent. Inland conditions are even harsher and they are made more severe by the altitude of much of the interior and the frequent strong winds above gale force. The centre of the continent at the South Pole is over 9200 ft (2800 m). Virtually all precipitation in Antarctica is snow and this is frequently whipped up from the surface in fierce blizzards. The weather is changeable throughout the year. During the long Antarctic winter conditions outdoors often reach or exceed the limits of human tolerance through the combination of low temperature and wind. This results in excessive wind chill and frostbite unless appropriate clothing is worn or shelter sought when conditions get too bad.

During calm, sunny days in summer, particularly on the coast, temperatures rise above freezing point and with no wind the temperatures may feel quite warm.

Seymour Island 36 ft (11 m) 0°28′ S 90°18′ W 3 years   **GALAPAGOS ISLANDS**

	Temperature °F			Temperature °C			Relative humidity	Precipitation			
	Highest recorded	Average daily	Lowest recorded	Highest recorded	Average daily	Lowest recorded		Average monthly		Average no. days with trace or more	
		max.	min.			max.	min.			in	mm	
J	90	86	72	66	32	30	22	19	—	0.8	20	8	J
F	90	86	75	70	32	30	24	21	—	1.4	36	9	F
M	93	88	75	70	34	31	24	21	—	1.1	28	6	M
A	90	87	75	71	32	31	24	22	—	0.7	18	6	A
M	89	86	73	69	32	30	23	21	—	0	0	4	M
J	87	83	71	68	31	28	22	20	—	0	0	4	J
J	88	81	69	67	31	27	21	19	—	0	0	9	J
A	87	81	67	60	31	27	19	16	—	0	0	8	A
S	86	80	66	59	30	27	19	15	—	0	0	7	S
O	86	81	67	58	30	27	19	14	—	0	0	2	O
N	86	81	68	62	30	27	20	17	—	0	0	4	N
D	88	83	70	61	31	28	21	16	—	0	0	6	D

Stonington Island 28 ft (9 m) 68°11′ S 67°01′ W 3 years   **GRAHAM LAND**

	Temperature °F			Temperature °C			Relative humidity		Precipitation		
	Highest recorded	Average daily	Lowest recorded	Highest recorded	Average daily	Lowest recorded	0730 hours	1330 hours	Average monthly		Average no. days with 0.04 in + (1 mm +)	
		max.	min.			max.	min.	%	%	in	mm	
J	43	37	27	11	6	3	−3	−12	74	71	0.4	10	3	J
F	45	34	25	12	7	1	−4	−11	72	68	0.6	15	4	F
M	46	28	18	−31	8	−2	−8	−35	86	83	1.0	25	7	M
A	44	24	14	−16	7	−4	−10	−27	79	77	1.0	25	7	A
M	39	21	7	−33	4	−6	−14	−36	84	85	1.7	43	9	M
J	44	17	2	−35	7	−8	−17	−37	81	82	1.1	28	6	J
J	40	18	3	−32	4	−8	−16	−36	85	85	1.3	33	7	J
A	40	16	−2	−35	4	−9	−19	−37	85	84	1.0	25	7	A
S	41	17	3	−39	5	−8	−16	−39	79	80	1.6	41	7	S
O	42	24	9	−20	6	−4	−13	−29	80	79	1.7	43	8	O
N	47	27	16	−4	8	−3	−9	−20	75	73	0.9	23	5	N
D	44	36	26	9	7	2	−3	−13	69	67	0.2	5	1	D

HAWAIIAN ISLANDS

These islands are a state of the USA.

They are situated between 18° and 22° N in the central Pacific, almost midway between North America and Japan. In area the islands are rather smaller than Wales or the state of Massachusetts; about 6400 square miles (16,400 sq. km). There are eight main islands and they are all hilly and mountainous and consist of both extinct and active volcanoes. On the islands of Hawaii and Maui these peaks exceed 10,000 ft (3000 m) in height.

The islands have a tropical oceanic climate with temperatures much moderated both by altitude and by regular sea breezes at lower levels. As the tables show, there is no great difference in average daily temperatures around the year and, although warm or even hot, the combination of temperature and humidity is rarely unpleasant. There are some remarkable differences in annual rainfall between the southwest coasts, which are relatively dry (see the table for **Honolulu**), and the northeastern coasts exposed to the trade winds (see the table for **Pepeekeo**) which receive much heavier rainfall in all months. In the drier parts of the islands the wettest season is the time of low sun between October and March, which is rather unusual in the tropics.

Some mountain slopes on the island of Hawaii are amongst the wettest regions of the world, with an annual rainfall exceeding 400 in (10,000 mm). The difference in the amount of cloud between the wetter and drier areas causes the average daily sunshine hours to vary between seven and ten hours throughout the year at **Honolulu** to a mere four to five hours at the wetter places. The islands are occasionally affected by tropical cyclones during the period May to November, which otherwise is the drier time of year. Such severe storms, however, are less frequent here than in the Caribbean or the South China Sea and west Pacific.

	Temperature °F				Temperature °C				Relative humidity		Precipitation			
	Highest recorded	Average daily		Lowest recorded	Highest recorded	Average daily		Lowest recorded	0800 hours	1200 hours	Average monthly		Average no. days with 0.01 in + (0.25 mm +)	
		max.	min.			max.	min.		%	%	in	mm		
J	84	76	69	54	29	24	21	12	75	66	4.1	104	14	J
F	84	76	67	52	29	24	19	11	75	67	2.6	66	11	F
M	84	77	67	53	29	25	19	12	73	65	3.1	79	13	M
A	86	78	68	59	30	26	20	15	69	64	1.9	48	12	A
M	87	80	70	60	31	27	21	16	69	64	1.0	25	11	M
J	88	81	72	63	31	27	22	17	69	63	0.7	18	12	J
J	88	82	73	63	31	28	23	17	70	63	0.9	23	14	J
A	88	83	74	63	31	28	23	17	71	64	1.1	28	13	A
S	88	83	74	63	31	28	23	17	71	65	1.4	36	13	S
O	90	82	72	63	32	28	22	17	73	66	1.9	48	13	O
N	86	80	70	59	30	27	21	15	74	67	2.5	64	13	N
D	85	78	69	55	29	26	21	13	75	68	4.1	104	15	D

Pepeekeo 100 ft (31 m) 19°51′ N 155°03′ W 34 years   **HAWAIIAN ISLANDS**

	Temperature °F				Temperature °C				Relative humidity	Precipitation			
	Highest recorded	Average daily		Lowest recorded	Highest recorded	Average daily		Lowest recorded		Average monthly		Average no. days with 0.01 in + (0.25 mm +)	
		max.	min.			max.	min.			in	mm		
J	87	78	64	56	31	26	18	13	—	12.3	312	20	J
F	87	78	63	56	31	26	17	13	—	9.2	234	16	F
M	89	78	64	56	32	26	18	13	—	14.4	366	22	M
A	86	78	65	57	30	26	18	14	—	11.4	290	24	A
M	88	80	66	59	31	27	19	15	—	8.5	216	22	M
J	86	81	67	58	30	27	19	14	—	6.7	170	22	J
J	88	82	68	61	31	28	20	16	—	9.6	244	25	J
A	88	82	68	61	31	28	20	16	—	10.8	274	26	A
S	88	82	68	59	31	28	20	15	—	10.6	269	24	S
O	89	82	68	60	32	28	20	16	—	10.0	254	23	O
N	89	81	66	58	32	27	19	14	—	12.2	310	22	N
D	90	79	65	57	32	26	18	14	—	12.1	307	22	D

MADEIRA

The Madeira group of islands consists of the two inhabited islands of Madeira and Porto Santo and several small uninhabited islands. The total land area is small: 305 square miles (790 sq. km). Administratively the islands are an integral part of Portugal, having been occupied and settled by the Portuguese in the fifteenth century.

The main island of Madeira is volcanic and mountainous, with its highest peaks rising to over 6000 ft (1800 m). Its mild winters and generally warm, sunny summers have made it a popular holiday resort. The islands are situated about 450 miles (725 km) west of the coast of Morocco.

The climate of Madeira is similar to that found around the Mediterranean or in coastal California but the ocean waters moderate the temperature so that the island never suffers extremes of heat or cold. The winter months are quite wet, particularly at higher levels, and stormy and cloudy conditions may last for a few days at a time. There are also spells of fine, settled weather in winter with mild to cool temperatures. There is little cloudy weather from May until September but occasional light rain may fall and fog can occur. In general the island has a sunny climate with an average of five to six hours' sunshine a day in winter and as much as seven to eight in summer. Days can be cloudy and cool as late as April at sea level and for much longer in the mountains.

The table for **Funchal** is representative of conditions at sea level.

MALDIVE ISLANDS (INCLUDING THE LACCADIVES AND CHAGOS ARCHIPELAGO)

These islands extend in a long chain some 1200 miles (1900 km) from north to south in the Arabian Sea and Indian Ocean between 12° N and 6° S. There are over 7000 islands, many of them merely low-lying coral reefs; only about 200 islands are inhabited.

The Maldives have a tropical climate with abundant rainfall and moderately high temperatures around the year. The table for **Minnicoy,** is representative of the northern islands. The islands near or south of the equator have rain more evenly distributed throughout the year or a maximum fall in the period November to March. Daily hours of sunshine average three to four in the wetter months and as much as eight to nine in the drier season. The northern islands are very occasionally affected by violent storms as tropical cyclones develop in the Arabian Sea between August and November. These bring very strong winds and torrential rain.

Funchal 82 ft (25 m) 32°38′ N 16°55′ W 30 years   **MADEIRA**

	Temperature °F			Temperature °C			Relative humidity		Precipitation			
	Highest recorded	Average daily	Lowest recorded	Highest recorded	Average daily	Lowest recorded	0900 hours	1500 hours	Average monthly		Average no. days with 0.04 in + (1 mm +)	
		max.	min.		max.	min.		%	%	in	mm		
J	79	66	56	42	26	19	13	6	66	66	2.5	64	6	J
F	82	65	56	40	28	18	13	4	65	65	2.9	74	6	F
M	82	66	56	44	28	19	13	7	66	67	3.1	79	7	M
A	84	67	58	44	29	19	14	7	64	65	1.3	33	4	A
M	88	69	60	48	31	21	16	9	65	65	0.7	18	2	M
J	96	72	63	48	36	22	17	9	68	68	0.2	5	0.9	J
J	98	75	66	55	37	24	19	13	67	67	0	0	0.2	J
A	103	76	67	52	39	24	19	11	67	67	0	0	0.4	A
S	95	76	67	55	35	24	19	13	65	67	1.0	25	3	S
O	92	74	65	47	33	23	18	8	64	66	3.0	76	7	O
N	87	71	61	45	31	22	16	7	64	65	3.5	89	6	N
D	80	67	58	41	27	19	14	5	67	67	3.3	84	7	D

Minnicoy 9 ft (3 m) 8°18′ N 73°00′ E 20 years   **MALDIVE ISLANDS**

	Temperature °F			Temperature °C			Relative humidity		Precipitation			
	Highest recorded	Average daily	Lowest recorded	Highest recorded	Average daily	Lowest recorded	0800 hours	1700 hours	Average monthly		Average no. days with 0.1 in + (2.5 mm +)	
		max.	min.		max.	min.		%	%	in	mm		
J	90	85	73	63	32	29	23	17	74	73	1.8	46	3	J
F	90	85	75	63	32	29	24	17	74	75	0.7	18	1	F
M	92	86	77	71	33	30	25	22	72	74	0.9	23	1	M
A	98	87	80	72	37	31	27	22	72	74	2.3	58	3	A
M	98	88	79	71	37	31	26	22	76	77	7.0	178	9	M
J	93	86	77	72	34	30	25	22	81	81	11.6	295	17	J
J	90	85	76	69	32	29	24	21	79	82	8.9	226	14	J
A	90	85	77	70	32	29	25	21	79	79	7.8	198	12	A
S	90	85	77	72	32	29	25	22	79	79	6.3	160	10	S
O	92	85	76	70	33	29	24	21	77	78	7.3	185	11	O
N	91	85	74	68	33	29	23	20	78	79	5.5	140	8	N
D	90	85	74	69	32	29	23	21	74	80	3.4	86	4	D

MAURITIUS

This small but densely populated island consists of a series of volcanic hills rising to a height of between 2000 and 2600 ft (600 and 800 m) with a fringing coastal plain. It is situated in latitude 20° S in the Indian Ocean about 500 miles (800 km) east of Madagascar.

Mauritius has a tropical oceanic climate with moderately high temperatures and humidity throughout the year. Temperatures never rise to such high levels as to be really uncomfortable or dangerous, although on occasions the nights may be rather sticky and oppressive. Rain occurs in all months but the wettest period is from December to April. During these months tropical cyclones occasionally strike the island or pass near enough to give very heavy rainfall and violent damaging winds.

The table for **Port Louis** illustrates conditions at lower levels on the island. The south and southeast coasts, being exposed to the dominant southeast trade winds, receive almost twice as much rain as **Port Louis** and rainfall is also heavier on the higher ground inland. Outside the main rainy season the weather is generally sunny and pleasant with slightly lower temperatures and a strong sea breeze.

RÉUNION

This small island is situated in latitude 21° S in the Indian Ocean. It lies 120 miles west-southwest of Mauritius and has a very similar sequence of weather around the year (see the table for Mauritius on p. 461). The island consists of a high volcanic mountain rising to 10,000 ft (3000 m) and rainfall is very heavy on the south and southeast slopes exposed to the trade winds. Like Mauritius, it is occasionally affected by tropical cyclones between December and April. Formerly a French colony, Réunion is now an overseas department of France.

ST HELENA

St Helena is a remote island in the South Atlantic. It is situated in latitude 15° S and is 1200 miles (1930 km) from the coast of southern Africa. It has an area of 47 square miles (122 sq. km) and is rather mountainous, with a single peak rising to 2700 ft (820 m).

St Helena has a tropical climate with no great extremes of temperature. **Jamestown** on the north coast has a very low annual rainfall but this coast is sheltered from the southeast trade winds which bring a much heavier fall to the south coast and to the higher ground; as much as 30–40 in (750–1000 mm). No sunshine records are available for the island but on the north coast the weather is warm, sunny and dry for much of the year. The climate of the island is rarely unpleasant or hazardous, although Napoleon, when exiled there from 1815 until his death in 1821, found much to complain about in its climate and dampness.

Port Louis 181 ft (55 m) 20°06′ S 57°32′ E 40 years   **MAURITIUS**

	Temperature °F			Temperature °C			Relative humidity		Precipitation			
	Highest recorded	Average daily	Lowest recorded	Highest recorded	Average daily	Lowest recorded	0700 hours	1300 hours	Average monthly		Average no. days with 0.1 in + (2.5 mm +)	
		max.	min.			max.	min.		%	%	in	mm	
J	95	86	73	63	35	30	23	17	86	67	8.5	216	12	J
F	91	85	73	64	33	29	23	18	88	71	7.8	198	11	F
M	90	84	72	63	32	29	22	17	90	72	8.7	221	11	M
A	88	82	70	58	31	28	21	14	89	71	5.0	127	9	A
M	85	79	66	55	29	26	19	13	88	68	3.8	97	7	M
J	83	76	63	51	28	24	17	11	87	65	2.6	66	6	J
J	80	75	62	51	27	24	17	11	85	64	2.3	58	6	J
A	80	75	62	50	27	24	17	10	85	61	2.5	64	6	A
S	83	77	63	51	28	25	17	11	83	58	1.4	36	4	S
O	88	80	64	55	31	27	18	13	80	57	1.6	41	4	O
N	91	83	67	57	33	28	19	14	77	56	1.8	46	4	N
D	95	85	71	62	35	29	22	17	81	61	4.6	117	7	D

Jamestown 40 ft (12 m) 15°55′ S 5°43′ W 7 years   **ST HELENA**

	Temperature °F			Temperature °C			Relative humidity		Precipitation			
	Highest recorded	Average daily	Lowest recorded	Highest recorded	Average daily	Lowest recorded	0930 hours	1530 hours	Average monthly		Average no. days with 0.04 in + (1 mm +)	
		max.	min.			max.	min.		%	%	in	mm	
J	89	80	69	63	32	27	21	17	63	62	0.3	8	4	J
F	90	81	70	66	32	27	21	19	65	64	0.4	10	4	F
M	92	82	71	66	33	28	22	19	64	61	0.8	20	5	M
A	93	81	70	63	34	27	21	17	65	62	0.4	10	3	A
M	83	76	67	61	28	24	19	16	72	70	0.7	18	4	M
J	81	74	65	61	27	23	18	16	72	69	0.7	18	6	J
J	79	72	63	58	26	22	17	14	74	71	0.3	8	8	J
A	78	72	63	59	26	22	17	15	76	74	0.4	10	3	A
S	78	72	63	58	26	22	17	14	75	69	0.2	5	2	S
O	78	73	64	60	26	23	18	16	72	70	0.1	3	0.7	O
N	80	74	65	62	27	23	18	17	72	69	0	0	0	N
D	82	76	66	60	28	24	19	16	65	64	0.1	3	1	D

SÃO TOMÉ AND PRÍNCIPE

These two islands lie almost on the equator in the Gulf of Guinea about 170 miles (274 km) from the African coast. Their land area is only 370 square miles (960 sq. km).

The islands have an equatorial type of climate with high temperatures and humidity throughout the year.

Rainfall is moderately heavy and the climate is rather cloudy, muggy and oppressive. The driest months are from June to September and rainfall outside these months is often heavy. The number of sunshine hours is rather low, ranging from four to six hours a day on average.

SEYCHELLES

The Seychelles consist of over ninety small islands with a total land area similar to that of the Virgin Islands in the Caribbean. They are situated between 4° and 5° S in the Indian Ocean. Most of the islands are low-lying but the largest island, Mahé, has hills rising to 3000 ft (900 m). The islands are about 800 miles (1300 km) from the coast of East Africa. They have a tropical climate and have recently become well-known as a tourist resort.

The table for **Port Victoria** is representative of temperature and humidity throughout the year. The amount of rainfall round the year varies with altitude and is rather higher on the southern sides of the islands which are exposed to the dominant southeast trade winds. Rainfall is everywhere moderate to heavy and the wettest months are November to March. The Seychelles are rarely if ever affected by tropical cyclones. The combination of moderately high temperature and high humidity is tempered by regular daytime sea breezes. The nights may feel muggy and oppressive, particularly to the visitor who is not yet acclimatized, but the climate is neither hazardous nor unpleasant.

São Tomé 16 ft (5 m) 0°20′ N 6°43′ E 10 years — SÃO TOMÉ AND PRÍNCIPE

	Temperature °F			Temperature °C				Relative humidity		Precipitation			
	Highest recorded	Average daily		Lowest recorded	Highest recorded	Average daily		Lowest recorded	0930 hours	1530 hours	Average monthly		Average no. days with 0.04 in + (1 mm +)	
		max.	min.			max.	min.		%	%	in	mm		
J	90	86	73	68	32	30	23	20	83	78	3.2	81	6	J
F	91	86	73	68	33	30	23	20	82	78	4.2	107	8	F
M	91	87	73	68	33	31	23	20	80	76	5.9	150	9	M
A	91	86	73	68	33	30	23	20	81	77	5.0	127	10	A
M	90	85	73	65	32	29	23	18	80	79	5.3	135	8	M
J	88	83	71	61	31	28	22	16	77	74	1.1	28	2	J
J	87	82	69	59	31	28	21	15	74	70	0	0	0	J
A	87	82	69	56	31	28	21	13	73	70	0	0	0.3	A
S	89	84	70	62	32	29	21	17	76	74	0.9	23	3	S
O	89	84	71	66	32	29	22	19	79	79	4.3	109	9	O
N	89	84	71	65	32	29	22	18	81	79	4.6	117	9	N
D	89	84	72	67	32	29	22	19	81	79	3.5	89	7	D

Port Victoria 15 ft (5 m) 4°37′ S 55°27′ E 60 years — SEYCHELLES

	Temperature °F			Temperature °C				Relative humidity		Precipitation			
	Highest recorded	Average daily		Lowest recorded	Highest recorded	Average daily		Lowest recorded	0930 hours	1530 hours	Average monthly		Average no. days with 0.1 in + (2.5 mm +)	
		max.	min.			max.	min.		%	%	in	mm		
J	88	83	76	69	31	28	24	21	79	78	15.2	386	15	J
F	89	84	77	71	32	29	25	22	77	76	10.5	267	10	F
M	90	85	77	69	32	29	25	21	75	74	9.2	234	11	M
A	92	86	77	71	33	30	25	22	74	74	7.2	183	10	A
M	91	85	77	69	33	29	25	21	75	74	6.7	170	9	M
J	89	83	77	67	32	28	25	19	77	75	4.0	102	9	J
J	86	81	75	67	30	27	24	19	77	76	3.3	84	8	J
A	87	81	75	68	31	27	24	20	76	75	2.7	69	7	A
S	88	82	76	68	31	28	24	20	76	75	5.1	130	8	S
O	89	83	75	68	32	28	24	20	76	75	6.1	155	9	O
N	89	84	75	68	32	29	24	20	75	74	9.1	231	12	N
D	91	83	75	69	33	28	24	21	78	78	13.4	340	15	D

ISLANDS IN THE WESTERN PACIFIC NORTH OF THE EQUATOR

These four main groups of islands – Caroline, Gilbert, Marianas and Marshall – extend over a very large area of the western Pacific between the equator and about latitude 20° N and between the Philippines and longitude 180° E or W. Many of the smaller islands are low coral reefs or atolls; the larger islands are mountainous and consist of the peaks of submerged mountains rising out of the ocean.

Climatically they all experience very similar conditions of temperature and humidity throughout the year. They have a typical tropical oceanic climate with moderately high temperatures and humidity which vary very little from month to month. The daily range of temperature is also quite small – about 10° F (4°–5° C). All have abundant or moderately heavy rainfall with a wetter season from June to November. Islands near the equator have rainfall more evenly spread throughout the year. The actual amount of rainfall on each island depends on both the altitude of the land and on exposure to the dominant winds: the northeast trade winds in the low sun period and the southeast monsoon in the high sun period.

Islands more than 5° N of the equator are liable to experience tropical cyclones (the typhoons of the South China Sea) with their heavy rainfall and very strong winds which can do considerable damage. The main season for such storms is from July to November. The worst of such storms may only affect one particular island every two or three years, but the much larger area of heavy rain associated with a cyclone contributes to the heavier rainfall of these months.

All the islands have moderately large amounts of sunshine, averaging between six and eight hours a day in spite of a large number of days on which some rain falls. Much of the rainfall is in the form of short, heavy showers but days with continuous rain are more frequent in the wetter months. Although the combination of temperature and humidity is often rather muggy and oppressive, particularly at night, the daytime temperatures are usually moderated and feel more comfortable because of the brisk winds, both daytime sea breezes and the predominant and regular trade winds.

The tables for **Saipan** in the Marianas and for **Ujelang** in the Marshalls illustrate conditions in this large area of the western Pacific. That for **Nauru**, in the Gilbert Islands, is more typical of islands on or near the equator; here rainfall is more evenly distributed throughout the year and tropical cyclones are never experienced.

Nauru 87 ft (27 m) 0°32′ S 167°03′ E 15 years　　　　　　　　　　　　**GILBERT ISLANDS**

	Temperature °F			Temperature °C				Relative humidity		Precipitation			
Highest recorded	Average daily		Lowest recorded	Highest recorded	Average daily		Lowest recorded	0900 hours	1400 hours	Average monthly		Average no. days with 0.1 in + (2.5 mm +)	
	max.	min.			max.	min.		%	%	in	mm		
J	94	88	74	68	34	31	23	20	75	74	12.4	315	15	J
F	93	88	75	66	34	31	24	19	75	73	8.1	206	11	F
M	94	89	75	69	34	32	24	21	74	73	7.1	180	9	M
A	94	90	75	69	34	32	24	21	72	71	3.7	94	6	A
M	95	90	75	68	35	32	24	20	71	70	2.1	53	5	M
J	94	90	74	66	34	32	23	19	71	70	3.9	99	8	J
J	94	89	74	69	34	32	23	21	72	71	6.1	155	11	J
A	94	89	74	66	34	32	23	19	70	69	7.6	193	10	A
S	95	90	75	66	35	32	24	19	69	68	4.8	122	6	S
O	94	90	74	63	34	32	23	17	68	68	3.9	99	5	O
N	95	90	74	67	35	32	23	19	70	69	6.0	152	7	N
D	94	89	74	67	34	32	23	19	73	71	9.4	239	13	D

Saipan 676 ft (206 m) 15°14′ N 145°46′ E 8 years　　　　　　　　　　　　**MARIANAS ISLANDS**

	Temperature °F			Temperature °C				Relative humidity		Precipitation			
Highest recorded	Average daily		Lowest recorded	Highest recorded	Average daily		Lowest recorded	0600 hours	1400 hours	Average monthly		Average no. days with 0.01 in + (0.25 mm +)	
	max.	min.			max.	min.		%	%	in	mm		
J	85	81	72	67	29	27	22	19	85	73	2.7	69	12	J
F	85	81	72	69	29	27	22	21	84	70	3.6	91	11	F
M	86	82	73	68	30	28	23	20	87	71	3.8	97	13	M
A	87	83	74	69	31	28	23	21	87	69	2.8	71	14	A
M	87	84	74	69	31	29	23	21	89	72	3.7	94	13	M
J	87	84	75	70	31	29	24	21	88	71	5.1	130	17	J
J	88	83	74	69	31	28	23	21	91	78	10.0	254	23	J
A	87	84	75	69	31	29	24	21	91	77	13.1	333	23	A
S	89	83	74	70	32	28	23	21	91	79	13.3	338	22	S
O	87	83	75	70	31	28	24	21	91	79	11.4	290	22	O
N	85	83	75	71	29	28	24	22	89	78	7.4	188	19	N
D	85	82	74	70	29	28	23	21	86	75	5.4	137	19	D

	Temperature °F			Temperature °C				Relative humidity		Precipitation			
	Highest recorded	Average daily		Lowest recorded	Highest recorded	Average daily		Lowest recorded	0700 hours	1400 hours	Average monthly		Average no. days with 0.01 in + (0.25 mm +)	
		max.	min.			max.	min.		%	%	in	mm		
J	90	84	77	72	32	29	25	22	81	77	2.1	53	13	J
F	91	85	77	72	33	29	25	22	82	76	1.8	46	13	F
M	91	86	77	73	33	30	25	23	82	76	2.6	66	12	M
A	91	86	77	73	33	30	25	23	84	78	5.3	135	17	A
M	90	87	78	73	32	31	26	23	85	79	6.6	168	19	M
J	90	87	78	73	32	31	26	23	85	79	7.1	180	21	J
J	93	88	77	72	34	31	25	22	86	79	8.4	213	23	J
A	94	88	77	71	34	31	25	22	87	78	8.5	216	22	A
S	93	88	77	73	34	31	25	23	87	80	10.3	262	24	S
O	95	88	77	73	35	31	25	23	87	80	10.4	264	23	O
N	92	87	78	73	33	31	26	23	86	80	9.6	244	22	N
D	90	86	78	72	32	30	26	22	82	78	4.9	125	19	D

There are many islands in this part of the Pacific, east of Australia and north of New Zealand, which go under the collective terms of Melanesia, Polynesia or South Sea Islands. The area involved lies between the equator and the Tropic of Capricorn and between 145° E and 170° W. Many of the islands are tiny and are merely low atolls or portions of large coral reefs; some of the larger islands are mountainous and carry a considerable population: Fiji, New Hebrides, New Caledonia, Tonga, Samoa and the Solomon Islands.

These islands share the features of a tropical oceanic climate as described in more detail for islands in the western Pacific north of the equator (see p. 464). The Melanesian and Polynesian islands, however, being south of the equator, have their season of maximum rainfall between November and April; on some islands there is no great difference between the amount of rain from month to month. Tropical cyclones are less frequent in the South Pacific than in the western Pacific and South China Sea and islands within 5° of the equator never experience these violent and damaging storms.

On some of the larger and mountainous islands, such as New Caledonia, Tonga, Fiji and Samoa, rainfall varies with altitude and with the exposure of the coast to the dominant southeast trade winds. This can be illustrated by comparing the much lower rainfall at **Noumea** in New Caledonia with that at **Suva** in Fiji or **Apia** in Samoa. The number of wet days, however, varies much less from island to island.

Except in the wettest places, where cloud is more frequent, all the islands have moderately large amounts of sunshine, averaging from six to eight hours a day. Much of the rainfall comes in short heavy showers, often after a sunny morning, but longer periods of heavy rain lasting a day or so occur in the wetter months.

The tables for islands in this area of the Pacific show that the principal difference in the weather and climate is the amount of rainfall per month. Temperature and humidity are very similar from one island to another. The climate may generally be described as pleasant and healthy, although the combination of high temperature and humidity can be a little oppressive when not tempered by sea breezes or a brisk wind.

Apia 7 ft (2 m) 13°48′ S 171°46′ W 19 years   **SAMOA AND TONGA**

		Temperature °F			Temperature °C			Relative humidity		Precipitation			
	Highest recorded	Average daily		Lowest recorded	Highest recorded	Average daily		Lowest recorded	0830 hours	1430 hours	Average monthly		Average no. days with 0.04 in + (1 mm +)	
		max.	min.			max.	min.		%	%	in	mm		
J	91	86	75	69	33	30	24	21	82	79	17.9	455	22	J
F	92	85	76	70	33	29	24	21	81	78	15.2	386	19	F
M	91	86	74	70	33	30	23	21	81	78	14.1	358	19	M
A	91	86	75	69	33	30	24	21	79	76	10.0	254	14	A
M	90	85	74	67	32	29	23	19	78	76	6.3	160	12	M
J	90	85	74	67	32	29	23	19	77	73	5.1	130	7	J
J	91	85	74	63	33	29	23	17	77	75	3.2	81	9	J
A	90	84	75	65	32	29	24	18	76	73	3.5	89	9	A
S	90	84	74	65	32	29	23	18	75	75	5.2	132	11	S
O	93	85	75	66	34	29	24	19	77	76	6.7	170	14	O
N	92	86	74	69	33	30	23	21	78	75	10.5	267	16	N
D	91	85	74	70	33	29	23	21	79	77	14.6	371	19	D

SOLOMON ISLANDS

Kieta 240 ft (73 m) 6°10′ S 155°36′ E 9 years

	Temperature °F				Temperature °C				Relative humidity		Precipitation			
	Highest recorded	Average daily		Lowest recorded	Highest recorded	Average daily		Lowest recorded	0800 hours	1400 hours	Average monthly		Average no. days with 0.1 in + (2.5 mm +)	
		max.	min.			max.	min.		%	%	in	mm		
J	95	88	76	64	35	31	24	18	78	79	10.5	267	15	J
F	95	88	75	66	35	31	24	19	77	76	10.7	272	14	F
M	96	88	76	70	36	31	24	21	78	78	11.2	285	12	M
A	94	87	76	71	34	31	24	22	80	80	11.7	297	14	A
M	94	87	75	65	34	31	24	18	80	79	9.3	236	14	M
J	92	86	75	69	33	30	24	21	82	81	9.0	229	13	J
J	93	85	74	70	34	29	23	21	80	80	10.9	277	13	J
A	92	85	74	70	33	29	23	21	80	80	9.4	239	14	A
S	92	87	74	69	33	31	23	21	79	79	8.0	203	13	S
O	94	88	75	69	34	31	24	21	75	77	9.8	249	14	O
N	96	88	75	68	36	31	24	20	76	79	9.6	244	12	N
D	94	89	75	66	34	32	24	19	75	76	9.4	239	14	D

NEW CALEDONIA

Noumea 30 ft (9 m) 22°16′ S 166°27′ E 22 years

	Temperature °F				Temperature °C				Relative humidity		Precipitation			
	Highest recorded	Average daily		Lowest recorded	Highest recorded	Average daily		Lowest recorded	0900 hours	1500 hours	Average monthly		Average no. days with 0.01 in + (0.25 mm +)	
		max.	min.			max.	min.		%	%	in	mm		
J	97	86	72	64	36	30	22	18	72	70	3.7	94	10	J
F	99	85	73	64	37	29	23	18	75	72	5.1	130	12	F
M	95	85	72	63	35	29	22	17	76	73	5.7	145	16	M
A	96	83	70	61	36	28	21	16	77	74	5.2	132	13	A
M	91	79	66	56	33	26	19	13	75	71	4.4	112	15	M
J	89	77	64	55	32	25	18	13	76	70	3.7	94	13	J
J	87	76	62	52	31	24	17	11	76	69	3.6	91	13	J
A	85	76	61	54	29	24	16	12	72	68	2.6	66	12	A
S	90	78	63	55	32	26	17	13	70	67	2.5	64	8	S
O	93	80	65	56	34	27	18	13	68	66	2.0	51	7	O
N	94	83	68	60	34	28	20	16	69	67	2.4	61	7	N
D	98	86	70	63	37	30	21	17	70	68	2.6	66	6	D

Suva 20 ft (6 m) 18°08′ S 178°26′ E 43 years   **FIJI**

	Temperature °F			Temperature °C			Relative humidity		Precipitation			
	Highest recorded	Average daily	Lowest recorded	Highest recorded	Average daily	Lowest recorded	0800 hours	1400 hours	Average monthly		Average no. days with 0.04 in + (1 mm +)	
		max.	min.			max.	min.		%	%	in	mm	
J	95	86	74	67	35	29	23	19	78	74	11.4	290	18	J
F	97	86	74	67	36	29	23	19	80	76	10.7	272	18	F
M	98	86	74	66	37	29	23	19	81	76	14.5	368	21	M
A	94	84	73	61	34	29	23	16	81	77	12.2	310	19	A
M	93	82	71	61	34	28	22	16	82	79	10.1	257	16	M
J	90	80	69	58	32	27	21	14	81	74	6.7	170	13	J
J	90	79	68	55	32	26	20	13	80	73	4.9	125	14	J
A	90	79	68	57	32	26	20	14	80	74	8.3	211	15	A
S	90	80	69	57	32	27	21	14	78	73	7.7	196	16	S
O	93	81	70	57	34	27	21	14	76	73	8.3	211	15	O
N	93	83	71	55	34	28	22	13	76	74	9.8	249	15	N
D	97	85	73	62	36	29	23	17	77	74	12.5	318	18	D

Tana 125 ft (38 m) 19°30′ S 169°20′ E 8 years   **NEW HEBRIDES**

	Temperature °F			Temperature °C			Relative humidity		Precipitation			
	Highest recorded	Average daily	Lowest recorded	Highest recorded	Average daily	Lowest recorded	0900 hours	2100 hours	Average monthly		Average no. days with 0.1 in + (2.5 mm +)	
		max.	min.			max.	min.		%	%	in	mm	
J	89	83	73	66	32	28	23	19	80	87	10.1	257	12	J
F	90	84	74	66	32	29	23	19	83	88	10.7	272	12	F
M	94	84	73	65	34	29	23	18	82	87	11.1	282	11	M
A	88	81	72	60	31	27	22	16	82	85	13.3	338	13	A
M	85	79	70	59	29	26	21	15	77	82	9.6	244	9	M
J	86	77	67	57	30	25	19	14	78	83	5.0	127	9	J
J	86	76	67	57	30	24	19	14	78	83	6.2	158	9	J
A	85	76	65	54	29	24	18	12	72	80	4.9	125	5	A
S	85	76	67	55	29	24	19	13	77	81	3.9	99	7	S
O	84	78	68	55	29	26	20	13	77	82	5.4	137	8	O
N	86	80	70	61	30	27	21	16	76	83	6.5	165	7	N
D	88	82	72	62	31	28	22	17	79	86	7.9	201	10	D

ISLANDS IN THE SOUTH PACIFIC

These groups of numerous small islands – Cook Islands, Society Islands, Marquesas Islands, Tuamotu Islands and Austral Islands – lie between 10° and 25° S and 120° and 160° W in the south-central Pacific. Tahiti, which is mountainous, is the largest and best known of these islands, but many are merely flat coral reefs and atolls.

The weather and climate are typical of a tropical oceanic environment as described in more detail for islands in the western Pacific north of the equator (see p. 464). Rainfall is moderate to heavy and occurs in all months but with a wetter period between November and March or April. Tropical storms of the cyclone or typhoon type are less frequent here than in the western Pacific but do occur occasionally. Weather can be quite variable from day to day. Periods of continuous rain lasting a day or more are not unusual, but much rain comes in heavy afternoon or evening downpours after an otherwise fine, sunny day. The climate is generally healthy and pleasant; the moderately high temperature and humidity are tempered by brisk daytime winds, either as afternoon sea breezes or as predominant southeast trade winds.

The tables for **Papeetee** on Tahiti and **Makatea** in the Tuamotu group of islands are representative of this large oceanic area.

	Temperature °F			Temperature °C			Relative humidity		Precipitation		
	Highest recorded	Average daily	Lowest recorded	Highest recorded	Average daily	Lowest recorded	0600 hours	1800 hours	Average monthly		Average no. days with 0.01 in + (0.25 mm +)
		max. min.			max. min.		%	%	in	mm	
J	94	89 75	69	34	32 24	21	87	80	6.7	170	16	J
F	94	88 74	68	34	31 23	20	88	83	8.8	234	18	F
M	93	89 74	68	34	32 23	20	89	82	6.1	155	17	M
A	93	87 74	67	34	31 23	19	89	85	7.1	180	17	A
M	91	86 73	64	33	30 23	18	85	82	3.6	91	14	M
J	90	85 72	60	32	29 22	16	85	82	4.8	122	10	J
J	89	84 71	62	32	29 22	17	84	80	3.2	81	10	J
A	89	84 71	62	32	29 22	17	84	80	4.3	109	16	A
S	90	85 71	64	32	29 22	18	82	80	3.7	94	13	S
O	93	86 73	66	34	30 23	19	82	80	3.3	84	10	O
N	95	88 74	66	35	31 23	19	84	81	5.1	130	17	N
D	94	89 74	68	34	32 23	20	87	82	5.5	140	17	D

	Temperature °F			Temperature °C			Relative humidity		Precipitation		
	Highest recorded	Average daily	Lowest recorded	Highest recorded	Average daily	Lowest recorded	0800 hours	1600 hours	Average monthly		Average no. days with 0.1 in + (2.5 mm +)
		max. min.			max. min.		%	%	in	mm	
J	95	89 72	67	35	32 22	19	82	77	9.9	252	16	J
F	92	89 72	67	33	32 22	19	82	77	9.6	244	16	F
M	92	89 72	67	33	32 22	19	84	78	16.9	429	17	M
A	92	89 72	67	33	32 22	19	85	78	5.6	142	10	A
M	91	87 70	65	33	31 21	18	84	78	4.0	102	10	M
J	90	86 69	61	32	30 21	16	85	79	3.0	76	8	J
J	89	86 68	61	32	30 20	16	83	77	2.1	53	5	J
A	86	86 68	61	30	30 20	16	83	78	1.7	43	6	A
S	87	86 69	62	31	30 21	17	81	76	2.1	53	6	S
O	89	87 70	62	32	31 21	17	79	76	3.5	89	9	O
N	90	88 71	64	32	31 22	18	80	77	5.9	150	13	N
D	91	88 72	66	33	31 22	19	81	78	9.8	249	14	D

Index